INFORMATION SYSTEMS - THE NEXT GENERATION

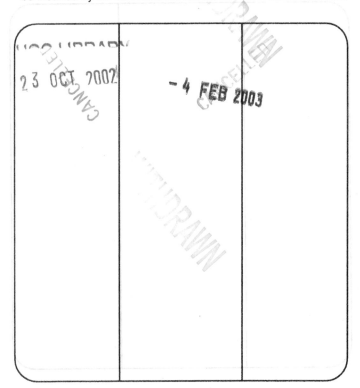

INFORMATION SYSTEMS - THE NEXT GENERATION

Proceedings of the 4th UKAIS Conference
University of York
7-9 April 1999

Laurence Brooks and Chris Kimble
Editors

Published by McGRAW-HILL Publishing Company
Shoppenhangers Road, Maidenhead, Berkshire, SL6 2QL, England
Tel 01628 502500; Fax 01628 770224

British Library Cataloguing in Publication Data
The CIP data of this title is available from the British Library

Library of Congress Cataloging-in-Publication Data
The CIP data of this title is available from the Library of Congress, Washington DC, USA

ISBN   0 07 709558 8

Printed and bound in Great Britain at the Basingstoke Press (75) Ltd, Basingstoke

TABLE OF CONTENTS

PREFACE

This book contains the papers presented at the fourth annual conference of the **UK Academy for Information Systems** (UKAIS) which took place at the University of York, between the 7th and 9th April 1999. The theme of this fourth conference is 'Information Systems - The Next Generation'. The sequence of papers in the book reflects the thematic clustering of the papers in the conference.

The UKAIS arose from a concern about the way IS teaching and research was funded, and the lack of recognition of information systems as a distinct academic discipline. The UKAIS was established in 1994 to remedy this situation. UKAIS is a charity, whose aims are to promote a better understanding of information systems within the United Kingdom and to improve the practice of information systems teaching and research. Previous to the formation of the UKAIS, UK many academics in information systems felt isolated in departments of computer science, business schools and elsewhere. The Academy has provided a forum to meet with other teachers and researchers in information systems.

To achieve our aims, we need to be an effective combination of a 'learned society' and 'pressure group'. By continually improving the quality and relevance of our teaching and through innovative and rigorous research we can contribute to both academic development and excellence in IS practice in the UK. However, we must also be influential in obtaining better understanding of the uniqueness of our subject by the higher education funding councils, the research funding councils, professional bodies, HM government and UK business. In order to achieve these aims, we meet with research funding bodies, educational institutions, representatives of government and practitioners on a regular basis. Most recently, we have made representations to the DTI regarding the Dearing Report and HEFCE regarding the research assessment exercise. In the last 4 years we have achieved recognition that IS is not being dealt with successfully by such bodies and we have been invited to suggest ways of improving the situation. There is now recognition of the IS skills shortage. This is all a first step. In the next 2-3 years, it will be critical for the Academy to argue further its case for change.

IS teaching and research are supported by the UKAIS through its annual conference, PhD consortia, workshops, regional group meetings and the quarterly newsletter. Members also get good discounts on the major UK information systems journals. The UKAIS definition of IS and proposed syllabus for courses in IS are being widely adopted. We now have seven regional groups (Central Scotland, East Midlands, London, Northern, Northern Scotland, Wales & West and Wessex) each having regular programmes of events. The 1999 annual PhD consortium (there have been five previously held under the auspices of the Academy) will take place at the University of Central England in Birmingham on July 6th – 8th.

As well as the papers in the book, the conference itself has additional activities, such as plenary talks given by eminent academics and practitioners as well as panel sessions (not forgetting good food and wine). Any event like this involves a lot of hard work and enthusiasm. The conference was organised by David Allen, Laurence Brooks, Donal Flynn, Chris Kimble and David Wainwright. At least two referees assessed each submitted paper and 71 papers were accepted from almost 100 submissions. Ray Hackney, from the National Board of the Academy, together with David Allen, Laurence Brooks, Donal Flynn, Chris Kimble and David Wainwright, from the Northern Regional Group, acted as the programme committee.

Further acknowledgements are well deserved. Four speakers from outside the Academy gave their time: Peter Checkland, Andrew Kakabadse, Mike Jackson and Philip Swann (from Marks and Spencer). We also wish to express our gratitude to Alfred Waller at publisher's McGraw-Hill who has been particularly helpful to the UKAIS in supporting this project. We gratefully acknowledge the contributions of the National Railway Museum for the conference dinner, The University of York campus for the use of their facilities and the general support of the Department of Computer Science at the University of York. Finally, we thank Jane White for her excellent administrative support.

David Avison, Laurence Brooks, Tom Gough, Ray Hackney, Chris Kimble,
Philip Powell, Steve Smithson, Frank Stowell and John Ward

CHAPTER 1

IS INFORMATION SYSTEMS A SCIENCE?

Deepak Khazanchi and Bjørn Erik Munkvold
Northern Kentucky University, Agder College, Norway.

Abstract

The Information Systems (IS) discipline is apparently undergoing an identity crisis. This article briefly outlines some of the challenges that we face as a discipline and argues that notwithstanding underlying philosophical differences, it can be concluded that IS is a "scientific discipline." This conclusion is reached through an assessment of the debate surrounding the issue of whether IS should be a discipline and an analysis of the IS discipline using some key characteristics of "science."

1   INTRODUCTION

Information Systems is a relatively young discipline and since its origin there has been a question of whether IS can be regarded as a distinct discipline, or whether it is merely to be seen as a subset of the various reference disciplines from which the field has borrowed, e.g. computer science and organizational science (Benbasat and Weber, 1996). In an editorial in the journal, *Information Systems Research*, King (1993) rhetorically asserts *'what is the information systems field?'* He then goes on to answer the question thus: *'... information systems is probably not even a field, but rather an intellectual convocation that arose from the confluence of interests among individuals from many fields...'* (p. 293). Different aspects of these questions have been recurring throughout the development of the information systems (IS) field. Various conference panels and workshops have been conducted that debate these fundamental issues (Benbasat and Weber, 1996). Introna and Whitley (1997) surmise that the IS discipline is undergoing a Kuhnian crisis. This assessment may not be altogether accurate. Any discipline whose members do not continuously question its fundamental concepts, models and philosophy through introspection is likely to rapidly make it invalid and obsolete. This is especially true of Information Systems where "information technology" is a key enabling vehicle.

This ongoing and at times fragmented discussion is clearly indicative of the interest in understanding the nature and philosophical underpinnings of Information Systems. The IFIP WG8.2 has been very active in providing a forum for different viewpoints in this deliberation (see e.g., Falkenberg et. al., 1995) about the essential nature of the IS "field."

The 1984 IFIP WG 8.2 colloquium title astutely summed up this problem under the theme "IS research - a doubtful science?" This title was chosen to *'call into question the notion of research in information systems being a science, in the same sense as research in the physical or natural sciences, and to ask whether the scientific research methodology is the only relevant methodology for information systems research or indeed whether it is an appropriate one at all'* (Mumford et al., 1985, p. 3). Several contributors to this colloquium addressed the current status of scientism in information systems research, arguing that the emulation of scientific methods from the natural sciences in IS research actually represents an anomaly of this research (e.g., Galliers, 1985; Klein and Lyytinen, 1985).

The rest of the paper proceeds as follows. First the issue of whether IS should be viewed as a discipline is briefly addressed. Next, the nature of science is outlined. The fundamental characteristics of science are used to frame the discussion about the nature of the IS discipline. Thus, in the ensuing discussion, we attempt to elaborate on the following questions: What is the conceptual domain of the "information systems" discipline? What kinds of phenomena are included in the study of Information Systems? (Or, What is the scope of IS?) These questions go to the crux of understanding whether Information Systems is (or should be regarded as) a scientific discipline.

2   SHOULD IS BE VIEWED AS A DISCIPLINE?

This question is even more relevant today than ever before. Discussing and addressing it is a means for overcoming this identity crisis that exists within our academic community. Also, to truly begin an argument about the "scientific" nature of Information Systems this question needs to be addressed up front. The term discipline literally means a *'field of study'* (Mariam-Webster Online Dictionary, 1998). The subject matter of Information Systems, though diverse, does constitute a discipline according to this definition. Academicians (both IS and non-IS) often criticize IS by calling it an "applied discipline." But clearly the presumption in such a statement is that it is, at a minimum, a discipline. Notwithstanding the naysayers, IS has been clearly accepted as a mainstream academic and university discipline with IS programs existing in a large number of institutions and businesses colleges. Furthermore, from an academic perspective some evidence is accumulating to support this contention. Using citation analysis and the foundational disciplines of computer science, management science and organization science as a basis, Culnan and Swanson (1986) and Culnan (1987) analyzed IS articles published during 1980-85. They surmise from this analysis that IS '... *is emerging as a distinct field of study with its own cumulative tradition'* (p. 34).

Some authors opine that IS cannot be viewed as a discipline because it has no "intellectual core"--it borrows from many "referent" disciplines (King, 1993). This rationale is insidious in that if explicitly applied it could very well rule out most natural sciences. Take the example of Physics; it has been greatly influenced by related disciplines such as Mathematics, Electronics Engineering, Computer Science, and even Information Systems! *The relationship of physics to its bordering disciplines is a reciprocal one... Much of contemporary research in physics depends on the high-speed computer. It allows the theoretician to perform computations that are too lengthy or complicated to be done with paper and pencil. Also, it allows experimentalists to incorporate the computer into their apparatus, so that the results of measurements can be provided nearly instantaneously on-line as summarized data while an experiment is in progress.'* (Britannica Online, 1998). In this context, some authors also contend that although reliance on reference disciplines adds to the potential diversity of the IS field, rigorous research should focus on expanding our thinking beyond reference disciplines and even impact the subject matter of reference disciplines (Benbasat and Weber, 1996; Robey, 1996).

Borrowing from Hunt's (1992) discussion of the essential nature of the marketing field, it can be similarly asserted that Information Systems is an applied discipline, a university discipline, a professional discipline, and has responsibilities to society, students, practice and the academy itself. IS as a vocation has and will clearly provide a means for individuals to rise up in the socioeconomic ladder with a prosperous career. This description of IS is not incommensurate with the pragmatic nature of most business disciplines today.

Clearly the question whether IS should be considered a science is intricately linked with the question of it being viewed as a discipline. The above discussion gives us a starting point for understanding the "essence" and place of IS as a scientific discipline in the context of business education and practice.

3 THE NATURE OF SCIENCE

The ultimate goal of social science or any other scientific endeavor is to provide a *'cumulative body of verifiable knowledge'* that allows us to *'explain, predict,* and *understand'* the specific phenomena that interest us (Frankfort-Nachmias and Nachmias, 1996, p. 8). This is also true of the Information Systems field. Based on a version of the natural science model (Burrell and Morgan, 1979), Hunt (1983, p. 17-18) maintains that a science as contrasted with other disciplines has some key distinguishing characteristics:

- Any science must have a distinct subject matter, a set of phenomena which serves as a focal point for investigation;
- A science has some means of describing and classifying its subject matter;
- Every science presupposes the existence of underlying uniformities or regularities among the phenomena that comprise its subject matter. The discovery of these underlying uniformities yields empirical regularities, law-like generalizations, laws, principles, and theories.
- A science utilizes the "method of science" to investigate its subject matter.

As positivism has been the dominant perspective in IS research (Orlikowski and Baroudi, 1991), most IS research would fit under the above guidelines. However, we do recognize that an increasing number of scholars are questioning the use of the 'scientific method' in IS research, arguing that the principles of natural sciences cannot be transferred to the realm of social science involving human actors (Galliers, 1985; Klein and Lyytinen, 1985). As a result, there is growing interest in alternative research paradigms such as interpretivism (Walsham, 1993) and action research (Lau, 1997).

Although underlying philosophical differences may lead one to interpret the characteristics of science described above differently, these fundamental attributes provide a good starting point for discussing the nature of the IS discipline. Hence, we will base the ensuing discussion on this description of science. The reason for this is that the natural science model continues to have a major influence on IS research. Second, the goal of this paper is to address the issue of whether IS can be viewed as a science regardless of philosophical perspective. In doing so, we accept the fallibility of this approach and in the words of Rand (1998) argue that *'social science is a science... even if our subjects lie to us, even if they refuse to answer questions and even if they change their minds after they answer the question and even if they intentionally misunderstand what we are trying to get at.'* Third, clearly much of the argument about the term "science" is a rhetorical one. Our definition and characterization of science underscores this notion while arguing for rationality and the insistence that all claimants of advancement of knowledge in the IS field must be called upon to systematically and clearly explain their findings.

3.1   A Caveat: On Our Philosophical and Paradigmatic Orientations

The authors of this paper represent different perspectives, one is a declared scientific realist in the tradition of Hunt (1990) and the other is an interpretivist in the tradition of Walsham (1993). Thus, this paper also represents an example of how it is possible to reconcile different perspectives regarding the question of whether Information Systems is a discipline and a scientific endeavor.

4   THE NATURE OF INFORMATION SYSTEMS

4.1   Information Systems Phenomena

> *'Any science must have a distinct subject matter, a set of phenomena, which serves as a focal point for investigation'.*

One way to understand the essence of IS and the nature of IS-related phenomena (as contrasted with non-IS phenomena) is to analyze some of the definitions attributed to this phrase. A very basic definition of the term IS is based on the meaning of the terms "information" and "system." Information has been defined as "meaningfully processed data," where "meaningful" implies relevance to a consumer (user) of information and "data" implies raw symbols or facts. A system is a collection of interrelated components that work together for a common purpose. Hence, an Information System is a collection of interrelated components (hardware, software, procedures, people, databases) that work together to *'collect (or retrieve), process, store, and distribute information to support decision-making and control an organization'* (Laudon and Laudon, 1994, p. 8). Thus, information technology is the enabling mechanism for the activity of gathering and processing data, producing information outputs, and disseminating information to users. Although IT and IS have been used equivalently, especially by practitioners, we consider IT to be a subset of IS. In an attempt to incorporate the diversity of the IS phenomenon while limiting the scope of the field, Ein-Dor and Segev (1993, p. 167) define IS as "any computerized system with a user or operator interface, provided the computer is not physically embedded."

Contrasting disciplines that are closely allied because of the use of technology as one key component, Avgerou and Cornford (1995, p. 132) argue that *'while computer science is about how computers work (as hardware and software), and software engineering is about building technical systems (ensembles of hardware and software) that meet given specifications,* **information systems** *is about understanding what is or might be done with these technical systems, and the effects they have in the human/organizational/social world'* (emphasis added).

Another way to understand the nature and scope of IS is to consider the impact of reference disciplines. Some authors have argued that IS at a minimum has a support base of three foundational fields: computer science, management science, and organizational science (e.g., Culnan, 1986). Others (Benbasat and Weber, 1996; Swanson and Ramiller, 1993) have also identified economics and cognitive science as additional foundational disciplines from which IS research has continued to borrow. An obvious problem in the IS field is the rapid development of technology and its applications. This contributes to frequent shifts in focus as a result of new areas of deployment, for example electronic commerce and knowledge management. In fact it could be argued that this is one example where reference disciplines such as marketing and organizational science have been directly impacted by the conceptual development in the IS field--especially in the areas of E-commerce, knowledge management and data warehousing/mining.

Apparently, the main difference (if any) between various descriptions of IS relates to an attempt by authors and organizations to limit the scope or bound the field. In other words, although there is some agreement on what subject matter should be clearly excluded from IS, many authors seem to disagree about the topics that should be included within its purview. Notwithstanding these differences, every IS researcher or practitioner would agree that there exist some common elements in all descriptions of Information Systems. Further, even though the study of IS phenomena may be impacted by concepts and theories from numerous referent disciplines, the 'information system' with its implicit enabling mechanism, 'information technology', is always the central subject matter of interest. To the extent that *an information system enabled by information technology within an organizational context* is the focal point of the information systems field, it seems to fulfill this requirement for 'science.'

4.2   Describing and Classifying the IS field

'A science has some means of describing and classifying its subject matter'.

Beyond defining the notion of IS, several attempts have also been made to classify the subject matter, phenomena, and research streams in the information systems field. Gosain and Lee (1997), Swanson and Ramiller (1993), Ein-Dor and Segev (1993), and Culnan (1986) have all attempted to either systematically describe the range of IS phenomena being investigated or categorize the various research approaches adopted by investigators in the IS field. As evidenced by the findings reported by these and other authors, the scope and domain of Information Systems is quite encompassing in its reach and consequently includes a variegated assortment of topics in its subject matter.

Gosain and Lee (1997) examined differences in IS research and practice by examining nearly 3,000 articles published over a five year period in four IS journals and five magazines. They found support for the "rapid shifting" of themes in IS research. They subdivided the themes of IS research into four quadrants based on the degree of importance placed by practitioner magazine and academic IS journals on specific topics. They identify IOS, User training & support, expert systems/NLP, and reengineering as four areas of common interest. The other three quadrants include topical areas such as HCI, Managerial decision making, IS strategy in one category, Database and data management, organization issues, CSCW in another, and IT impact, marketing, IT applications in the last quadrant. Similarly, Swanson and Ramiller (1993) analyzed the flow of manuscripts (397 of them) into one journal, *Information Systems Research*, and identified eight research themes with each theme having its own set of categories. The eight major thematic areas include CSCW, DSS/KBS, Systems Projects, Evaluation and Control, Users, Economics and Strategy, Introduction and Impact, and IS research. A broader analysis based in foundational reference disciplines was conducted by Culnan (1987) and reported in a series of articles. She studied the intellectual development of MIS through a co-citation analysis of literature between 1980 and 1985. Her key finding is that the intellectual structure of the IS field can be clustered around five latent factors: foundations, micro (individual) approaches to MIS design and use, MIS management, Macro (Organizational) approaches to MIS design and use, and MIS curriculum.

In contrast to the above classifications of the IS field, Ein-Dor and Segev (1993) focus on the information system phenomenon itself. They identify seventeen major types of information systems and argue that these can be categorized into two major rather fragmented paths of development: the *applied artificial intelligence path* and the *human interface path*. According to the authors, this taxonomy of IS can be used to anticipate the evolution of new systems and consequently of issues that can be addressed through further research.

Figure 1 illustrates a synthesis of the topical areas that constitute the IS field along with the primary and secondary reference disciplines that have had a major impact in its development. Based on the writings described in the previous paragraphs and the categories reported by Swanson and Ramiller (1993), this figure depicts one classification of the scope and domain of the IS field.

Primary reference disciplines

Computer science   Management science   Organization science

Cognitive science   Economics

Information Systems

Computer-Supported Cooperative Work	**Information and Interface**	**Decision Support and Knowledge-based systems**	**Economics and strategy**
Asynchronous and synchronous collaboration	Information economics	DSS	IS economics
Workflow	Information and mangerial decision making	Expert systems	IS, strategic management, and business outcomes
GSS	HCI	Knowledge aquisition	IOS
		Knowledge management	Electronic commerce
		Data warehousing	
Systems projects	**Evaluation and control**	**Users**	**Introduction and Impact**
System development process	IS performance evaluation	IS-user relationships	IS implementation
System project estimation	Data management	User perceptions and attitudes	IT diffusion
User involvement	Computer resource allocation	User information evaluation and satisfaction	Organizational outcomes
Requirements analysis and modeling	IS security and control		**IS research**
Data modeling and database design	IS ethics	End user computing	IS typologies
Software maintenance	IS personnel		Research perspectives and methodologies

Secondary reference disciplines

Sociology   Information science   Linguistics

Anthropology   Ergonomics   Systems science

Figure 1: Classifying information systems and reference disciplines

Although this chart represents a useful typology there is no need to prematurely circumscribe the subject matter that can be included in the information systems field. Kaplan (1964, p. 70) uses the phrase "premature closure" to describe the same notion. Implicit in this statement is the fact that rational people can potentially disagree about the number and labels of categories or the topics included in each category.

As evidenced from the previous discussion, it is potentially feasible to describe and classify the subject matter and research approaches in information systems in different ways. Although these typologies for the IS field will not be completely satisfactory to all people, they do provide a useful analytical basis for understanding the nature and scope of IS phenomena being investigated. In conclusion, it can be asserted that the scope of the IS field is indisputably broad and somewhat ambiguous. But, tolerating ambiguity engenders 'creativity in science' and may not be a bad thing for an evolving discipline like ours (Kaplan 1964, p. 71). As is the case with every other science, to the extent that the Information Systems discipline does seek to describe and classify its subject matter (maybe not very well as yet) it would seem to fulfil this requirement.

4.3   Underlying uniformities in IS phenomena?

'Every science presupposes the existence of underlying uniformities or regularities among the phenomena that comprise its subject matter. The discovery of these underlying uniformities yields empirical regularities, law-like generalizations, laws, principles, and theories'.

By addressing this criterion, we enter the 'minefield' of diverging philosophical perspectives in IS research. Indeed, this criterion has also caused the largest controversy in our own discussion. The presupposition of the existence of "underlying uniformities or regularities among the phenomena under study" in general has been and still is a question for debate. The two major strands in this debate have been positivism and interpretivism (Orlikowski and Robey, 1991; Walsham, 1995b). Being rooted in the natural sciences, the positivist perspective is based on the ontological assumption that there exists an objective social reality that can be studied independently of the action of the human actors in this reality. The epistemological assumption following from this is that there exist unidirectional cause-effect relationships that can be identified and tested through the use of hypothetic-deductive logic and analysis. As the criterion discussed here also is based on the natural science model, it is easy to see how research conducted in the positivist perspective falls in line with this form of scientific inquiry.

In contrast, the interpretive perspective is based upon the ontological assumption that reality and our knowledge thereof are social constructions, incapable of being studied independent of the social actors that construct and make sense of this reality. Instead of seeking unidirectional cause-effect relationships, the focus according to this perspective is to understand the actors' view of their social world. Thus, the discovery of "empirical regularities" and "law-like generalizations" becomes problematic when viewed from this perspective. In the interpretive perspective, Walsham (1995a) presents four different types of generalization: the development of concepts, the generation of theory, the drawing of specific implications, and the contribution of rich insight. According to this perspective, generalizations should be viewed as tendencies rather than predictions, i.e. as *'explanations of particular phenomena derived from empirical interpretive research in specific IS settings, which may be valuable in the future in other organizations and contexts'* (ibid. p. 79).

While acknowledging the importance of this debate, in practice we feel that this often can be reduced to a matter of rhetoric. There is a tendency to present the perspectives in 'black and white', so that the description of positivism as applied by interpretivists often do not correspond to the actual views of the researchers in this paradigm and vice versa. In debating these issues, the proponents of the different perspectives in practice often can be found to be more open to each other's arguments than one may believe by looking at the debate in the literature. For example, many positivists today will acknowledge the contextual embeddedness of their research. In general, there also seems to be a trend towards mutual acknowledgment of these two perspectives (see for example, Benbasat and Weber, 1996; Robey, 1996; Orlikowski and Baroudi, 1991). For example, it has been reported that there are an increasing number of interpretivist studies being published in major IS journals (Walsham, 1995b).

It is also important to note here that the positivist and intepretivist perspectives actually comprise several varying perspectives that should be seen as constituting a continuum rather than a dichotomy. The many research perspectives applied by leading scholars in social science (Morgan, 1983) may also serve as examples of the many possible combinations of ontological, epistemological and methodological assumptions and considerations that are possible for IS research. Further, the different perspectives are also to be regarded as dynamic concepts, that are being developed and refined as part of the scientific discourse. As an illustration, Hirschheim (1985) traces the development of IS epistemology through positivism, anti-positivism, neo-positivism and post-positivism.

Related to the question of interest in this paper, we feel that it is most important to focus on the common ground rather than conflicting issues. From both perspectives, the ultimate goal of IS research (or any other for that matter) is to produce some form of knowledge that has relevance outside the context of the original research setting. The difference lies in the claims made about the status of this knowledge, i.e. law-like generalization vs. tendencies (Walsham, 1993). Also, not many IS researchers would likely deny the fact that clearly *some* progress has been made towards studying and identifying regularities in IS phenomena and *some* uniformities have been found. For example, the modified Technology Acceptance Model (TAM) is such a research achievement in point (Davis et. al., 1989). Rather than reducing the argument to the issue of whether "the" scientific method is appropriate for IS, the discipline can benefit by applying scientific principles to devise and revise our methods of investigation and validating findings, and engender the advancement of knowledge beyond its application to a very specific context. Thus notwithstanding differences in philosophical perspectives, one can conclude that the general aim of theory development and knowledge accumulation in IS research is a key argument favoring the status of IS as a science.

4.4   IS Research Methodology

'*A science utilizes the "method of science" to investigate its subject matter*'. Frankfort-Nachmias and Nachmias (1996, p. 23) state that '*the methodology of the scientific approach serves the purpose of providing rules of communications, rules for logical and valid reasoning, and rules for intersubjectivity (the ability to share knowledge). Social science is not united by subject matter but rather by their research methodology.*' In true scientific spirit, these 'rules' '*are constantly being improved as scientists look for new means for observation, measurement, inference, and generalization*' (ibid. p. 13). Even though conditions under which a study is done may change and '*newer circumstances may emerge*' (Galliers, 1985), the benefit of the scientific method lies in its *logic of justification*--a common set of procedures on which a science and its investigators accept or discard hypotheses or criticize new knowledge claims of peers.

Methodology has been an area of discourse in the IS field for many years. During the1984 IFIP WG 8.2 colloquium, the question of which methods should be applied in information systems research was one of the key issues. More recently, the question of methodological pluralism has also been addressed as part of the general debate of diversity in information systems research (Benbasat and Weber, 1996; Robey, 1996). In brief, the two strands in this debate consist of those who see diversity as a threat to the further development of the IS field, resulting in a lack of common focus and lack of accumulation of knowledge; On the other hand, there are those who argue that diversity both regarding issues and methods actually should be seen as a means for further advancing the field.

Regarding the relative status of the different methodological approaches, there also seems to be a tendency towards reconciliation. For example, there have been several attempts to combine the different philosophical perspectives (e.g. Lee, 1991). Today, methodological diversity is greater than ever before, as illustrated by the 1997 IFIP WG 8.2 conference (Lee, Liebenau and DeGross, 1997). The quality and diversity of IS research has increased with the development of the IS field while the requirements for methodological rigor and versatility have sharpened both for quantitative and qualitative research studies (Benbasat and Weber, 1996).

Methodological pluralism coupled with constructive but skeptical criticism of knowledge claims is a sound goal for the IS field. The main point relative to this criterion is that the application of different research methods in information systems research today is not incongruent with the fundamental goal of science: to add to the state of knowledge and understanding of IS by studying IS phenomena with a set of accepted criterion for conducting and communicating findings ("methodology") while assuring their validity.

5   SUMMARY AND CONCLUDING REMARKS

In this paper we have addressed the question of (a) whether information systems (IS) should be viewed as a discipline and (b) whether IS should be viewed as a science. This has been done through an examination of criteria applied to the natural sciences. From this we have concluded that IS is a science, i.e. a scientific discipline in contrast to purportedly non-scientific fields. It is worth noting that the very fact that this question is being raised and discussed is evidence of the scientific nature of IS research. Understanding the fallibility of our models and theories while continuing reflection and introspection is an essential practice for any science. However, there are some limitations embedded in the criteria chosen to analyze the scientific nature of IS in this paper. An interesting question for further inquiry is whether these criteria are "relevant" and "complete." That is, are there additional or alternative criteria that are better suited to the IS field?

Ultimately, the question of whether Information Systems can be termed a science clearly depends on whether we agree that the IS field does include a systematic body of organized knowledge based upon investigation of discernible phenomenon that are studied using diverse scientific methods akin to other social science disciplines. Additionally, if one believes that applying the term science requires replicability across researchers and subjects, it may still be possible to argue in favor of calling IS a science, although the term may be less appropriately applied under certain philosophical orientations. Much has been made by some authors of the fact that IS derives its models and theories from other reference disciplines. We have argued that this is not very different from the natural sciences such as Physics and Chemistry that clearly interbreed and are very much influenced by other reference disciplines such as Mathematics and Computer Science.

Finally, as a "thought experiment" let us consider what could happen if we concluded otherwise, that is, IS is not a scientific discipline and this also becomes the generally accepted view. What would have been lost cannot be expressed in serious terms except to assert that the IS community would have lost their common identity and ground for existence. We would argue that this would lead to a reductionist view of the role of information systems in organizations and society, as the focus would be shifted entirely to how the technology could support existing practices and business processes. We would be foregoing proactive research such as advocating how IS can and should be used to leverage performance and competitiveness in organizations, enhancing individual performance and well-being or producing positive societal effects. The development and use of information systems would become more restricted by the existing frames of the referent disciplines, rather than being able to impact these disciplines further and truly "interbreed" (Kaplan, 1964, p. 31).

References

Britannica Online (1998) 'The Physical Sciences: Physics: RELATIONS BETWEEN PHYSICS AND OTHER DISCIPLINES AND SOCIETY: Influence of related disciplines on physics'. On-line at http://www.eb.com:180/cgi-bin/g?DocF=macro/5005/5/42.html [Accessed 19th October].

Avgerou, C. and Cornford, T. (1995) 'Limitations of information systems theory and practice: a case for pluralism', in Falkenberg et. al. (1995), pp. 130-143

Benbasat, I. and Weber, R. (1996) 'Research Commentary: Rethinking "Diversity".' Information Systems Research, Vol. 7, No. 4, pp. 389-399.

Burrell, G. and Morgan, G. (1979) Sociological Paradigms and Organizational Analysis. Ashgate Publishing Company, Aldershot.

Culnan, M. and Swanson, E.B. (1986) 'Research in Management Information Systems, 1980-1984: Points of Work and Reference', MIS Quarterly, Vol. 10, No. 3, pp. 289-301.

Culnan, M. (1987) 'Mapping the Intellectual Structure of MIS, 1980-85: A Co-Citation Analysis', MIS Quarterly, Vol. 11, No. 3, pp. 340-353.

Davis, F.D., Bagozzi, R.P., and Warshaw, P.R. (1989) 'User Acceptance of Computer Technology: A Comparison of Two Theoretical Models', Management Science, Vol. 35, No. 8, pp. 982-1003.

Ein-Dor, P. and Segev, E. (1993) 'A Classification of Information Systems: Analysis and Interpretation', Information Systems Research, Vol. 4, No. 2, pp. 166-204.

Falkenberg E.D., Hesse, W. and Olivé, A. (Editors, 1995) Information Systems Concepts: Towards a consolidation of views. Chapman & Hall, London, UK.

Frankfort-Nachmias, C. and Nachmias, D. (1998) Research Methods in the Social Sciences (Fifth edition). St. Martin's Press, Inc., USA.

Galliers, R.D. (1985) 'In Search of a Paradigm for Information Systems Research', in Mumford, E. et al. (1985) Research Methods in Information Systems. North Holland, Amsterdam, pp. 281-297.

Gosain, S. and Lee, Z. (1997) 'Topics of Interest in IS: Comparing Academic Journals with the Practitioner Press', Proceedings of the International Conference on Information Systems, Atlanta, Georgia, pp. 263-284.

Hirschheim, R.A. (1985) 'Information Systems Epistemology: A Historical Perspective', in Mumford, E. et al. (1985) Research Methods in Information Systems. North Holland, Amsterdam, pp. 13-36.

Additional references can be obtained from the authors.

CHAPTER 2

STRUCTURALIST INFORMATICS: CHALLENGING POSITIVISM IN INFORMATION SYSTEMS

Matthew Chalmers
Glasgow University

Abstract

It is often assumed that the information representations used in interactive information systems are grounded firmly and objectively in mathematics. This positivist view is at odds, however, with contemporary mathematics and philosophy of science, which sees subjective, social, and situated symbol systems — semiology — at the base of all human information use. We describe some of the reasons behind the paradigm shifts away from positivism in mathematics and linguistics, relate them to the information access approaches of information retrieval, collaborative filtering and the path model, and so argue that a similar paradigm shift away from 'folk informatics' is not only needed, but has begun.

1   INTRODUCTION

The 50th anniversary of the publication of Vannevar Bush's *As We May Think* (Bush, 1945) occurred recently. Perhaps the most seminal document in the history of information systems research, *As We May Think* is often held as foundational to hypermedia, the World Wide Web, and information retrieval (IR). Interestingly, Bush does not put forward that the collection of links used in connecting hypermedia objects is a solution in itself. A 'sea of links' merely replicates the problem of having a sea of records, tuples or documents. Bush proposed that human activity in the form of 'trails' or 'paths' was the solution i.e. particular human–selected sequences of links associating information objects, and not the vast set of possible associations that hypermedia, databases and libraries provide. Note also that such a path does not directly involve content. It relies on human interpretation of content, but the meaning or value of an object is primarily given by the chosen context of a path. A link between two objects thus only has meaning within the context of a particular path of a particular person. The hypermedia and retrieval systems that declare an origin in Bush's work generally do not work with the phenomena of context and person as Bush proposed: context and person are not part of their underlying model of knowledge. Re-reading *As We May Think* and seeing this disparity between underlying models suggests we should look more closely at information systems' models of knowledge and interpretation.

Two complementary schools of thought exist with regard to the basic underlying assumptions and philosophies that guide our research in information systems. One can place theories and design practices based in objectivity and mathematics at one end of a spectrum, and those emphasising subjectivity and language at the other. In this paper we will focus on theory and practice of systems for accessing large bodies of information, and our examples from such schools will be information access approaches such as IR and collaborative filtering (CF). Within the context of this paper we will therefore treat 'information access' (and indeed 'informatics') effectively as representatives or synonyms for 'information systems.'

The first school of thought sees itself as part of traditional computer science, rooted in formal models and taxonomies that encompass the individual variations of users and that are often derived from experimentation and observation in controlled conditions. IR, based on content analysis of documents, fits this paradigm. Complementary views are held by those who hold the social and the semiological as primary, and consider that formal, mathematical models are insufficient to model the complexity of human activity and ultimately of limited utility in guiding system design and development. Collaborative filtering (Goldberg, 1992), sometimes known as recommender systems (Resnick, 1997), is an example here. In this paper we take a stance firmly towards the subjective and linguistic end of the spectrum, arguing that, even though theories and systems based on objective formalisations are extremely useful in particular situations, they are essentially inadequate to model and support the full complexity of human use of information. We suggest that this is due to traditional computer science having roots in reductionist, positivist models of knowledge and interpretation. As discussed in more detail later in this paper, we suggest that CF and its extensions such as the path model are examples of a nascent paradigm for information access systems that breaks away from these traditional roots.

In more general terms, we take the view that use of computer–based information is no different from any other human use of information. It is just another aspect of significant human action i.e. activity that both involves the use of symbols over time, and can be taken as symbolic. In other words, we treat informatics as an instance of semiology, as ultimately more akin to linguistics than our field's traditional ideal or exemplar, mathematics. We aim to make more visible some of the assumptions and models that underlie interactive information systems. We are often unaware of the models of knowledge and information that we build on, what they afford and what they inhibit, where they work well and where badly, how they work in isolation and in combination. Here we aim to make clearer some of those buried layers — the 'archaeology' (in the sense of Foucault (1972)) of information systems' foundations.

2   POSITIVISM AS INFORMATICS' TRADITIONAL PARADIGM

The opposing schools of thought mentioned above are exemplified by a recent exchange in the pages of SIGCHI Bulletin, discussing appropriate metaphors for navigation and organisation of files on the desktop. The most recent contribution at the time of writing was (Nardi, 1997). At issue was the importance of location-based searching over logical retrieval. In response to Nardi and Barreau, Fertig, Freeman and Gelernter put forward what might be considered a traditional computer science viewpoint, suggesting that better indexing tools would allow users to gain the benefits of storing large amounts of information. Nardi and Barreau suggested that such improvements would be valuable but would not address what they consider to be the paramount information management problem, the volume and heterogeneity of ephemeral information.

At the core of Nardi and Barreau's objections is a concern that "the alternatives offered by many developers of personal information management systems seem to view documents in the work space as a collection that can be easily characterized, ordered and retrieved based upon common characteristics, or based upon full text retrieval. These approaches ignore the complexity and variety of information in personal electronic environments. [...] Schemes that automatically characterize information may not provide enough flexibility to consider the richness of these environments, and schemes that allow characterization for visual retrieval may not easily accommodate all of the desired dimensions."

The same issues arise in the World Wide Web, where the scale, complexity and heterogeneity of information representation is increasingly problematic. As Tim Berners-Lee pointed out with regard to search engines for World Wide Web data (Berners-Lee, 1997), "they are notorious in their ineffectiveness. [...] A Web indexer has to read a page of hypertext and try to deduce the sorts of questions for which the page might provide the answer." Images, numerical data, audio, programs and applets: the variety of information is increasing along with the volume. Attempts are being made by various researchers to solve these problems, usually by adding some form of metadata. Due to the scale and distribution of ownership of information, most metadata has to be created manually by its owners, for example by page authors or site managers adding textual captions or tags. An example metadata scheme for Web data is PICS (Resnick, 1996).

If metadata, however, is not formally controlled to ensure consistent use, it becomes data: open to be written, read and interpreted as each person sees fit. The same problems of which metadata to choose (or trust) arise e.g. if a large commercial corporation sets up its own rating sites, how would you interpret its ratings of its own products' sites? When there is a large volume of metadata one will need to classify, index and search it, requiring 'metametadata' that may itself eventually become voluminous and problematic. In other words, with uncontrolled metadata we only defer the problem of matching available information to users' interests and activities — and when metadata open to individuals' use slips down to be just more data, the problem reappears.

Nardi and Barreau are amongst those in HCI who are critical of modelling the mind (and hence the user) as an algorithmic processor — an approach that was until recently considered the firmest foundation upon which to build interactive information systems. Typical research involved short–term controlled experiments in a laboratory–like setting, with experimental subjects introduced to new tools and techniques to be used in isolation from the other tools familiar from their everyday work, and away from their colleagues and workplace. Modern HCI theory criticises this approach as excessively reductionist, as demanding so much control over experimental conditions that 'inconvenient' phenomena essential and central to everyday work are excluded: the interleaving of tools both in and out of the computer, application to a set of familiar work topics and goals, and the setting within a community of use. By not taking into account the complexity and situatedness of human activity, it is difficult to offer the hoped–for practical benefits to systems designers.

Work such as Activity Theory (Nardi, 1996) takes a more realistic view of the subjectivity, dynamics and social context of individuals' action, broadening consideration from just the actor and the tool being designed to the other tools used, the intended outcome (at various levels of abstraction), and the community within which activity takes place. Activity theory has, however, been better for analysis and criticism than for driving system design, which we suggest is related to its greater concentration on activities than on artifacts i.e. on work's goals and actions rather than on the information and tools that represent and mediate work. Here we shift the balance toward the artifact, and towards system design, by emphasising how we represent, categorise and interpret information.

We see the need for a more radical break away from informatics' traditional belief in its ability to represent the world in logical and objective terms. We see this belief as naive, firstly because within formal informatics, the weakness of such a reductionist view has been demonstrated. Wegner recently published a formal proof that interactive computing is an inherently more powerful computational paradigm than purely algorithmic computing (Wegner, 1997). The main point for us here is Wegner's formal demonstration of the irreducibility of interaction to algorithms. We can gain greater expressiveness and analytic power with interaction-based approaches but only if we abandon our fields' traditional belief in algorithmic formalisability of information use.

Secondly, a reductionist stance does not reflect the contemporary state of mathematics. Wegner echoes this century's history of mathematics (and indeed physics) where the dream of reducing the world to a 'clean' and purely objective mathematical model was shown to be an illusion. In the next section, we see what we can learn from mathematics' reconsideration of its own foundations

3   FROM MATHEMATICS TO LANGUAGE

Underlying interactive information systems are abstract data representations that formalise the content and behaviour of some aspect of our world. We use such abstractions in order to input, store, index, manipulate and present our information. We use mathematically–based formal representational systems — algebraic structures, structures of order and topological structures — to represent the properties and relations between real world objects.

Since we use such mathematical schemes as foundations for building information representations, we should understand mathematics' foundations. Prior to the 20th century, mathematics had hoped for convincing proof that it was founded firmly in formal, objective absolutes, based purely on a logical process of naming things in the real world. This positivist paradigm was common to many intellectual fields, but was weakened by enduring problems such as the inability to ground Euclidean geometry in more than perceived self–evidence (in particular, the axiom of parallels), by Cantor's demonstration that the set of all sets is indeterminable, i.e. the 'metaset' of all sets is a set, which keeps slipping down from metadata to data.

Hilbert led the formalist attempt to shake off such contradictions and inconsistencies by rendering mathematics genuinely independent of perception of the 'real' world, asserting (as quoted in (Karatani, 1995)) that "the solid foundation of mathematics is in the consistency of its formal system: mathematics does not have to be 'true' as long as it is 'consistent,' and as long as this is the case, there is no need for further foundation." Even having discarded the claim to truth, however, claims to consistency were attacked from two directions. One blow was from within, in the form of Gödel's incompleteness theorem. This, in a self-referential manner related to that of Cantor, set up a paradox wherein meta-mathematics, understood as a class, gets mixed into the formal system as a member of that class. The other blow was from without, from Wittgenstein, who overturned the notion that mathematics' formal system can be solidly deduced from axioms. Proof is a language game (Wittgenstein, 1958), involving our invention of rules, systems and notations whose truth, as with all our natural language, is determined by our own social use rather than from axiomatic deduction. Gödel demonstrates the problem of consistency in the structures we use for information representation, while Wittgenstein replaces the axiomatic basis of their truth with semiological, socially constructed meanings.

A question one might then raise is: what is semiology based on? The contemporary view in this field is that we cannot dig further: there is 'no exit from language.' When we interact with a formalised or abstract representation of natural language or behaviour, we use it in our world of human interpretation and activity, and we necessarily involve natural language. We may try to step up to a metalevel by means of formalism and abstraction but inevitably we slip back down again. Within a controlled environment such as the computer, formal, self–consistent and finitely defined representational systems can operate, but in human–computer interaction the informal, subjective and infinite reassert themselves.

What can we take from contemporary semiology that will offer practical help in our informatics theory–building and information system design? We propose to draw from the paradigm that became dominant only a few decades before Gödel and Wittgenstein revolutionised mathematics' core, that has often been identified or equated with Wittgenstein's 'language game,' and that indirectly motivated mathematics' paradigm shift: structuralism (de Saussure, 1959). Here we aim to point out some of its key features that echo earlier discussion but that we later use in discussing information retrieval and collaborative filtering. A more extended discussion and comparison of these and other information access approaches is the subject of a forthcoming paper, (Chalmers, 1999).

Structuralism unified linguistics and semiology, and displaced positivism in linguistics. A word was held to be a symbol, and no longer seen as being part of a historically traceable process of absolutely and logically naming a thing in the real world.

Saussure's view was that naming was a relative or differential process. The elements of a language, at any given time, form a structure where any element only has meaning because of its relations and differences with other elements, and not by a one–to–one relationship of naming a unique, absolute, ideal thing in the world. While we may use a word to signify a thing in the world, we do not refer to one absolute and abstract thing that each other language also has exactly one word for. Our meaning is derived from our use of the word's similarities and differences to the other words of our language. A word means what we use it to mean, or, to quote Wittgenstein, "the meaning of a word is its use in the language."

In Saussure's theory of natural language, the medium can be anything, including speech, written text and physical motion of the body e.g. sign language and dance. We can choose to use anything and any combination of media to communicate: stone and steel in sculpture and architecture, paint and ink in printing and graphic design, and so forth. Symbol associations span the media used for expression: the picture of a pipe, the word 'pipe,' and the wooden pipe are interlinked. It is interpretive choice or reaction that creates significance, and so any action in any medium can be taken as significant, and hence as a symbol. Language, therefore, is the dynamic pattern of individuals' time–ordered symbolic activity in all media: subjective, situated and social.

4   REPRESENTATION IN INFORMATION SYSTEMS

Now we can see a fundamental limitation in the relatively common view that ignores information objects' use in human activity and objects' interrelatedness, treating each object in isolation and, as is generally the case in IR, restricting consideration to the content of each object (e.g. the words and images inside a document). To assume that the symbols contained inside an object faithfully and fully describe its meaning, irrespective of perception and use, is a positivist approach.

That perception of a structure or representation is bound up with the perception of use became familiar to many within information systems, especially HCI, via the ecological theory of perception popularised by authors such as Don Norman, but originally developed by J.J. Gibson (1979). Gibson stresses the complementarity of perceiver and environment. The values and meanings of things in the environment arise from the perception of what those things provide or offer as potential actions on the part of the perceiver — in Gibson's terms, their affordances — and not by universally naming and categorising absolute or objective properties. He emphasises the way that a theory of meaning must avoid "the philosophical muddle of assuming fixed classes of objects, each defined by its common features and then given a name. As Ludwig Wittgenstein knew, you cannot specify the necessary and sufficient features of the class of things to which a name is given. [...] You do not have to classify and label things in order to perceive what they afford." We start to see how contemporary philosophy has already influenced modern HCI theory.

Within HCI, Lucy Suchman (1987) has been instrumental in establishing the importance of situated action: how particular concrete circumstances have a strong influence on behaviour, and how strict plans are often merely resources for more flexible, dynamic, contingent action i.e. more like maps than scripts (Schmidt, 1997). Like Gibson, she generalises over objects in interfaces and objects in the physical world, treating them as elements of sign systems, as linguistic expressions. "The significance of a linguistic expression on some actual occasion, on the other hand, lies in its relationship to circumstances that are presupposed or indicated by, but not actually captured in, the expression itself. Language takes its significance from the embedding world, even while it transforms the world into something that can be thought of and talked about" (Suchman, 1997:58). We need to look beyond the content of the expression or object, towards the co–dependence and co–evolution of human behaviour and information structure, and the influence of context and situation of use usually unrepresented in our information systems. In Suchman we again see the influence of contemporary discourse on language and representation.

The most direct influence of contemporary philosophy on information access may be that of Heidegger's philosophical hermeneutics and Searle's speech act theory on the workflow model. In *Understanding Computers and Cognition*, Winograd and Flores (1986) took account of the situated use of information in work but, as (Chalmers, 1999) discusses in more detail, they then imposed a reductionist and objectified categorisation of user activity that made workflow an information access method that is famously inflexible and disempowering of the individual. Contrarily, workflow may be well suited to organisations which need strict control for safety, efficiency and legal reasons e.g. in performing complex medical trials and processing insurance claims.

In contrast with Gibson and Suchman, and indeed Winograd and Flores, traditional content-based approaches operate only on the subset of symbols and attributes that are conveniently accessible and contextually independent e.g. no matter who has a textual document and what activity they are involved in, the same set of words are accessible inside the document. Of course, this specificity affords a great strength: techniques such as indexing of contained words allow quick and automatic searching of large volumes of data, but we rely on the assumption that the context of use and interpretation of the person involved is not significant.

This assumption is true when one wishes to find all documents that contain the word 'pipe,' but false if one wishes to identify the documents that one individual person would consider to be about pipes, or would be useful to that person in learning how to make a pipe. Tasks such as the latter two seem irredeemably fuzzy and difficult to traditional IR but perfectly natural to us in our daily lives. Specification of information need generally requires the user to define what they want in terms of content and in a formal query language. For the former objective task IR works well, but for tasks involving subjectivity the information representation excludes the requisite phenomena of context and person, and interaction — querying — is notoriously difficult.

It is in this area that collaborative filtering is strong. CF deals with similarities in profiles of choice and use of information, and handles tasks such as "name a movie that I'll enjoy" with ease. Recommendations of useful or interesting information objects are specific to the person involved, but independent of their particular current activity or work context. Formalising why one liked or disliked an object is avoided or reduced, for example by selecting from a five point rating scale from 'very good' to 'very bad,' and so one can react according to one's informal understanding. Even simpler is Amazon.com's book recommender (www.amazon.com) where each book purchase serves as a positive rating and is added to the purchaser's profile.

Similarity of two profiles is considered high if they have similar ratings for the same objects. Given a person's profile, a small set of 'neighbours' is determined, being the most similar profiles. The system presents to a user a small number of objects that were rated highly in neighbours but that he or she has not yet rated. Sometimes one can explicitly choose the subset of people from whom profiles should be drawn, allowing use of one's knowledge of colleagues' and friends' expertise.

CF also cuts across boundaries between apparently heterogeneous data. Books, movies, music, people: CF operates on the names or identifiers of objects and not (necessarily) the content. It circumvents IR's intransigent difficulty with comparing symbols in different media e.g. in measuring the similarity of a word and an image.

CF systems need 'bootstrapping.' Objects that have not been rated can not be recommended, so CF relies on external sources, such as other information access tools, to introduce new objects to at least one user, so that their use or choice can be added to their profile. This is not a great weakness, however, as we of course use many tools (including IR tools) in our everyday work, each of which can offer use and selection information. CF is therefore explicitly dependent on other sources of information, in direct contrast to the independent (or isolated) operation assumed by IR.

Another characteristic of CF is that it does not offer contextually–specific recommendations. It does not take account of the temporal order of activity. A profile generally records what a person liked or used, but nothing of the time of use and the other symbols used around that time i.e. the context of use. Recommendations are therefore based on all of a person's history, and not their current task or activity. The path model extended CF by adding time to the information representation, in order to gain this contextual specificity (Chalmers, 1998). Paths, echoing *As We May Think*, are timestamped logs of symbol use over time e.g. logs of URL accesses in a web browser. The path model defines the context of a symbol's use by an individual as the other symbols used by that person within a selected window of time: user–selected, in current implementations. Information is presented to the user by taking the recently–used symbols in their path, finding the most similar windows of activity in the past of their chosen set of individuals, and finding symbols that were frequently used thereafter in the windows but were not used recently by the user.

In summary, CF and the path model break away from positivist approaches to information access such as IR because symbols are defined relatively, by similarities and differences in individuals' use, and not by appeal to objective classification. Heterogeneity of content types is unproblematic. They are based on very few *a priori* categories, instead relying on ephemeral, subjective and adaptive categorisation. Formalisation of information need by the user is avoided or minimised. These features form our basis for the claim that they are practical examples of a complementary paradigm to IR, and early examples of a structuralist or even poststructuralist informatics.

5   CONCLUSION

The implementation work in CF and paths has progressed so far with relatively little theoretical discourse to underpin it. In this paper we aim to help redress this imbalance, and to aid in future development, by making more explicit some of the representational issues and assumptions that informatics shares with other semiological fields. Our field has not taken full account of the way that information representation schemes have affordances: they are tools or objects built on characteristic strengths and weaknesses relative to our uses, interests and abilities. Such characteristics in themselves are neither good nor bad. It is lack of awareness of them and of their consequences that causes us problems. We should understand what assumptions our information representations are built on, and hence what they afford and what they inhibit, and so move beyond naive 'folk informatics'.

To achieve this understanding, and to broaden and strengthen our field's foundations, we must abandon reductionist, positivist theories of informatics and rebuild on a base of contemporary philosophy and semiology. This requires a paradigm shift, a Kuhnian revolution within our science. Informatics is younger than fields such as mathematics and linguistics, but sadly seems not to have learnt from them. It is less mature and relatively isolated in having a positivist theoretical infrastructure underlying its everyday practice — despite the contributions of a number of writers and researchers. As with any other symbol and tool, our field is most usefully understood as just one of many, interwoven with others involved in human language and meaning.

References

Berners-Lee, T. (1997) "World-Wide Computer", Comm. ACM, 40(2):57-58.

Bush, V. (1996) 'As We May Think', Atlantic Monthly, July 1945. Reprinted in ACM Interactions 3(2):37-46.

Chalmers, M., Rodden, K. & Brodbeck, D. (1998) 'The Order of Things: Activity-Centred Information Access', Proc. WWW7, 359–367.

Chalmers, M. (1999) 'Comparing Information Access Approaches', to appear in J.ASIS.

Foucault, M. (1972) The Archaeology of Knowledge, trans. A.M. Sheridan Smith, Routledge.

Gibson, J.J. (1979) The Ecological Approach to Visual Perception, Lawrence Erlbaum.

Goldberg, D. et al. (1992) 'Using collaborative filtering to weave an information tapestry', Comm. ACM 35(12):61-70, December 1992.

Karatani, K. (1995) Architecture as Metaphor: Language, Number, Money, MIT Press.

Nardi B. (ed.) (1996) Context & Consciousness: Activity Theory and Human-Computer Interaction, MIT Press.

Nardi, B. & Barreau, D. (1997) ''Finding and Reminding' Revisited: Appropriate Metaphors for File Organization at the Desktop', SIGCHI Bulletin, 29(1):76-78.

Resnick, P. & Miller, J. (1996) 'PICS: Internet Access Controls without Censorship', Comm. ACM, 39(10):87-93.

Resnick, P. & Varian, H. (eds.) (1997) Special Issue of Comm. ACM on Recommender Systems, 40(3).

de Saussure, F. (1959) Course in General Linguistics, trans. Wade Baskin, McGraw-Hill.

Schmidt, K. (1997) 'Of Maps and Scripts: The Status of Formal Constructs in Cooperative Work', Proc. ACM Group 97, 138–147.

Suchman, L. (1987) Plans and Situated Actions: The Problem of Human Machine Communication, Cambridge University Press.

Wegner, P. (1997) 'Why Interaction is More Powerful than Algorithms', Comm. ACM, 40(5):80-91.

Winograd, T. & Flores, F. (1986) Understanding Computers and Cognition, Addison Wesley.

CHAPTER 3

PARALLELS AND DIFFERENCES BETWEEN NATURAL AND ARTIFICIAL SYSTEMS

Mike Hobbs and Nigel Dalgliesh
University of Kent at Canterbury

Abstract

The modern armoury of sophisticated specification languages, design tools, Object Oriented techniques and components gives the current information systems professional unprecedented power to act. However, the increasing scope of the role of information systems continues to pose difficult problems. This paper discusses the parallels and differences between artificial and natural complex systems. The fundamental differences between seemingly similar activities suggests that the naive application of biologically inspired techniques of development are unlikely to be useful in the current context of information systems design.

1   INTRODUCTION

A perennial problem for developers of information systems is how to handle the increase in complexity caused by the increasing capability of information technologies. At one level stand-alone systems are being integrated into enterprise networks, which are in turn part of yet wider inter-organisational networks. At another level desktop and hand held computing are being joined by increasingly complex embedded systems. At all levels increasing communication between systems adds exponentially to the possible connections and interactions. These changes have implications for the analysis, design, implementation and operation of the information systems. New methodologies and techniques supply the tools and technology needed to support these systems but do little to help us control the increase in complexity.

The expansion of the role of information systems has created an artificial environment where entities exist, interact, and show many of the characteristics found in natural systems of the real world. Although natural systems do not explicitly process information, they do provide high levels of organisation at many levels, co-ordinate the use of resources, grow and adapt to changes in their environment. These are all desirable properties and tempt parallels to be drawn between natural and artificial information systems. However, there are significant differences that raise questions as to whether we would really want to apply principles from nature. In addition, an inclination for natural models should not justify their use without a full appreciation of the forces at work.

In this paper we outline some of the trends in information systems development that are leading towards similarities to natural complex systems. We go on to look at how complex systems are developed and sustained in nature and explore the parallels between natural and artificial complex systems. Finally, we discuss the differences between the two approaches and provide pointers to what needs to be borne in mind when looking for inspiration from the natural world.

2   THE PROBLEMS FACING INFORMATION SYSTEMS

One of the more significant developments in recent years is the use of object-oriented techniques and methodologies. These represent a fundamental shift in the way that information systems are designed and operated. The monolithic, isolated, hierarchical information system is giving way to collections of largely independent communicating objects. An important motivation for this approach is the need for businesses to be able to change and adapt to changing market circumstances. Facilitating change is becoming one of the main activities of management at operational, tactical and strategic levels. This has driven the requirement for flexible information systems to support that change.

A survey by (Johnson 95) still shows low success rates even with the latest tools and object oriented methodologies. This might be explained by the relative lack of experience in these techniques but there is little evidence that software productivity is radically improving. In the past much of the success of the more rigid development methodologies arose from the close match between a systematic structured approach to design and the typical highly structured environment for the information system. The diversity of modern system requirements means that this is no longer feasible. The range of activities and complexity of the systems has grown with the increasing capacity of the information systems.

The result of these developments is a scenario where information systems are increasingly made up of autonomous interacting components that are assembled according to an overarching design (Mowbray 97). The use of objects, or components, is an enormously powerful idea and is the cornerstone of a flexible, distributed approach to computing. Swapping components, or changing the rules that govern their use, can accommodate change. Complexity is managed by decreasing coupling between components and increasing cohesion within them. In a well ordered logical world this would seem to be an approach that can continue to manage increasing complexity by using more sophisticated components, or better design techniques. In principle we would hope that there are no limits to the scope of our information systems but there might be practical limits that restrict our ability to develop and control reliable software.

3   COMPLEXITY IN NATURE

The original purpose of many scientific disciplines was to explain phenomena of the natural world but for many centuries the successes of the formal reductionist approach, as applied by Descartes, have focused attention away from their initial inspiration. However, there is now a much greater appreciation of the principles that give rise to the complexity and order found in natural systems. Inspiration from nature and biology has been applied to some aspects of information processing systems. Evolutionary algorithms (Mitchell 98) take their inspiration from natural evolution and neural networks were supposed to mimic some aspects of the function of the brain (Rummelhart 89).

One of the single most remarkable features of the natural world is how complicated systems arise from simple components. There are many physical phenomena that exhibit this ability, from snowflakes to hurricanes, complicated patterns abound in nature. Plants and animals are the most interesting examples that exhibit self-organising adaptive behaviour at many levels. The key to these systems is emergence; simple small-scale interactions produce large-scale order and complex patterns of behaviour (Holland 89).

In the computing field cellular automata demonstrate how simple rules can exhibit complex behaviour. Originally devised by John von Neumann in the 1940's some of the ideas were developed by (Langton 89) and others in the late 1980's in the developing field of Artificial Life. This is an interdisciplinary field that studies complex self-organising systems. One of the fundamental questions of this area is how complex structures can develop and become self-sustaining. As with the physical phenomenon it became apparent that there was no central control mechanism telling the system how to behave.

4   PARALLELS BETWEEN ARTIFICIAL AND NATURAL COMPLEX SYSTEMS

Most business activities have traditionally fitted well with a rigorous or formal approach. The specification of clear goals and the engineering techniques to achieve them have been successful. However, the increasing capacity and scope of information systems means that they can be applied to areas that were once considered outside the IT department. Information systems are not being restricted by their expense, or limited capacity, but by questions of the appropriateness of fit. In the past it was possible to persuade the users change their behaviour to fit the requirements of the information system. It is now necessary to develop the information system to support the activities of the users and the wider organisational goals. For a long time the soft systems approach has understood the limits of the engineering paradigm to capture all the relevant aspects of an organisation. Checkland and Holwell (Chekland 98) advocate the holistic systems approach that acknowledges the co-operative nature of individuals within organisations. The background for this approach is a social and anthropological analysis that differs from the fundamental physical and biological systems that are the concern of this paper.

4.1   Design choices

One of the consequences of a more complex role for the information system is a need to define the boundaries of the engineering based modelling techniques we use. However, the focus on boundaries is perhaps a poor way of expressing the problem. For example, an organisation and its activities can be analysed into a set of business rules and the relations between those rules formally specified. The Business Objects Component Architecture (BOCA) provides a way of implementing these rules and the RM-ODP (ISO 96) model can be used to formally specify interactions between the business objects. This technology allows systems to be built from distributed autonomous entities that provide services to the system but remain independent. It is tempting to draw parallels between independent entities in these systems and truly independent entities in the real world. The real problem here are the limits to what can be represented by the business rules. Some of the most important actions of an organisation will lie outside what can be specified. Things like individual personalities and the culture of an organisation cannot be captured in a formal model. The gross behaviour of an organisation originates from many tiny interrelations between individuals and systems. Just like a Brownian motion experiment, we can't see the atoms of the gas but we know they have to be there because we can observe their effect on the much larger smoke particles. When we decide what to model and what to ignore we are making judgements about the level of detail and scale. In information systems we hope that small details are unimportant to the large-scale operation of the system. This is fundamentally at variance with real world phenomena where tiny features are able to propagate through non-linear dynamical systems to create large scale effects, as described and popularised by (Gleick 87).

4.2   Organisations as natural systems

There are three arguments as to why organisations could be considered in the same terms as biological systems. Firstly, their behaviour is ultimately derived from the collective behaviour of people who are complex biological systems. Secondly, they fit the bill in their own right, as they are adaptive self-organising systems that show emergent behaviour. This is a vital consideration — without non-deterministic dynamic behaviour the organisation would not be able to develop or adapt its actions. Finally, economic cycles and the activities of many industries follow the same kind of patterns that are seen in emergent evolving biological systems. At a suitable level of abstraction collections of businesses appear to behave in similar ways as collections of animals.

5   CAN WE USE NATURALLY INSPIRED APPROACHES?

Unfortunately, research into cellular automata has shown that it is very difficult to make the link between the underlying rules of interaction and the behaviour that the system exhibits (Hanson and Crutchfield 97). Even in very restricted systems such as Conway's game of life (Berlekamp *et. al.* 82) it is hard to predict the outcome of even small changes in the basic rules. Nature is good at developing complex behaviour but not a specific type of behaviour. Unlike artificial systems this behaviour is not directed and has no purpose other than its own expression. In this section we explore three different areas of natural complex systems, firstly we consider the much misused term evolution, then the inherent differences between physical matter and computer models, and finally we touch on issues of emergence.

5.1   Evolution or progression

The term evolution is often used to describe the human controlled process of a step by step progression. This is what using an evolutionary software paradigm typically means. However, the complex biological systems we see around us are not the product of a simple deterministic step by step optimisation process. Biological evolution does not *progress*, or *optimise*, as there is no concept of an independent measure of *better*. Evolving organisms relate to their environment and their fellow organisms not an external measure of utility. We can measure the progress that a human artefact has made from crude prototype to refined production model. However, in biological evolution the rules are part of the system; the ecosystem evolves with the creatures so there is no external judge of quality.

The one characteristic of mature, stable evolutionary systems is that they develop towards greater complexity of the whole ecology. Every time a creature adapts to utilise an ecological niche it provides a new opportunities for other creatures to co-evolve (Bedau 97). This is almost the opposite of a managed system where additional complexity reduces the ability of the system as a whole to function. Simplicity is key to efficiency in these systems so that control overheads are minimised.

Many organisational factors contribute to make an incremental approach to software development attractive. The system can be implemented one component at a time and maintained by changing components. Since the system is undergoing constant change, it is possible to continually re-engineer different aspects of the system to mirror changes in the organisation. However, there are two dangers with this approach. Firstly, the organisation may lose the ability to make radical changes when needed; an example of the refactoring problem (Fowler 97). Biological evolution is full of examples of dead-ends where the organism has been unable to change sufficiently to adapt to new conditions. Secondly, the sum of a number of small, independent changes may contribute to a larger behaviour change. As with the control problems of cellular automata mentioned above, unexpected interactions may cause changes to the emergent behaviour of the whole system.

5.2   Emergent properties of physical systems

Another problem with using natural inspiration is that the entire control structure of natural events is the inverse of the way in which artificial systems are currently produced. The complex interacting patterns we observe in nature are the result of bottom up emergent properties not top down control. One effect of this is that simulations of physical systems tend to require massive computing power. For example, modelling the trajectories of gas molecules requires complicated calculations on each element. However, nature has no need to *apply* a model to control the molecules, their behaviour is the system; they don't obey the laws of physics so much as instantiate them. There are no problems of scale for natural systems. Macroscopic physical laws are emergent from the inherent properties of matter; they describe the world but cannot be likened to the explicit control structures found in computer models.

An interesting example of a combination of evolution, self adaptation and the use of the inherent properties of physical systems is given by the experiments on a Field Programmable Gate Array (FPGA) by (Hirst 97). This device can be re-configured by software so that there is a feedback loop between the software controlling the processing and the physical processes that support it. A genetic algorithm was set the task of designing a simple filter for differentiating between a 10MHz signal and a 100MHz signal. The result was a circuit that relied on the analogue properties of the digital chip, which used a third of the components of a digital design and was much faster. The only drawbacks were that the behaviour was temperature dependent and the mechanisms used by the chip were unknown. This example demonstrates the power of the feedback loop in a dynamic self-sustaining system. It also suggests that to utilise emergent properties we have to give up explicit control. Changing from a predictable transparent mechanism to a self-regulating, non-linear box of tricks is unlikely to be appreciated in many business organisations or mission critical systems.

5.3   Designing with emergence

There are artificial systems that take advantage of the inherent properties of materials. Designers, architects and engineers all have to take account of the materials they are using when they create their designs. The strength bearing qualities of a girder can be determined and, within limits, relied on not to alter. Real objects are the ultimate object oriented component with a completely fixed way of interacting with the world. Unfortunately, this does not mean that the move to objects and components will make devising a software system as straightforward as building a house. The software world lacks are the all-pervasive laws of physics and chemistry that guide the interactions of the physical world for free. We are not geared up to take advantage of emergent properties at any level of system development.

Currently our design methodologies largely ignore the presence of emergent behaviour. We try and eliminate feedback loops where possible. This may have important implications to the development of autonomous communicating processes that will interact in unforeseen ways. This is particularly noticeable in the field of economics where the inadequacy of traditional formal systems have led to the development of non-linear, dynamic system models to explain the observed behaviour of industrial economies. (Ormerod 98) likens the economy to a living organism rather than a machine.

There are some areas where emergent behaviour is positively encouraged. Managers on the look out for 'synergy' between organisations are expressing the hope that the combined is greater than the sum of the parts. The Internet shows that a paradigm of unrestricted growth within a well-defined environment can be successful. The physical laws that have to be obeyed are supplied by TCP/IP protocols and there is no central control mechanism that dictates how the system operates. It will be interesting to see if the Internet will be a fruitful environment for other kinds of emergent behaviour.

6   CONCLUSIONS

Large software projects represent some of the most complex centrally planned systems ever created and yet these are insignificant compared with naturally evolved systems. There is a temptation to look towards nature for principles that can be used to guide the development and control of our information systems. Although there are many useful principles that can be borrowed it is important to recognise the essential differences between the artificial and the real domain. When comparing natural and artificial systems it seems that digital information systems are uniquely cut off from the expression of their underlying physical manifestation. However, this is also a necessary and desirable feature that allows software to run on different machines. Similarly, there are many reasons why we would not want our safety critical software to evolve new and surprising functionality. If natural systems are to be the inspiration for better software design methodologies there has to be a greater appreciation of the fundamental principles.

Information systems that are large enough to be useful tend to be difficult to build because they are inherently complicated. Nature shows that vastly complex systems can be built from very simple components. Unfortunately, the way in which these complex systems are developed is totally alien to current management and software engineering principles. There is a danger that natural and biological models may be inappropriately used to justify system development techniques. The opposite danger is that the inherent properties of components may be ignored in areas where artificial systems most resemble their natural counterparts.

A key area for further research is to identify how models of natural systems can be used to inform aspects of software engineering.

References

M.A Bedau, M.A., Snyder, E., Brown, C.T., and Packard, N.H, A Comparison of

Evolutionary Activity in Artificial Evolving Systems and the Biosphere, European conference on Artificial Life, Eds. Husbands, P. and Harvey, I., pp 125-133, MIT Press 1997.

Berlekamp, E., Conway, J., and Guy, R., Winning ways for your mathematical plays, Academic Press, 1982.

Checkland, P., Holwell, S., Information, systems and information systems, Wiley, 1998.

Fowler, M. UML Distilled, pp 30- 31, Addison Wesley, 1997.

Gleick, J., Chaos, Penguin, 1987.

Hanson, J.E., Crutchfield, J.P., Computational mechanics of cellular automata: An example, Physica D, pp 169-189, 1997.

Hirst, T., Evolutionary Signal Processing: A Preliminary Report, Fourth European conference on Artificial Life Eds Husbands, P., and Harvey, I., pp 425-431, MIT Press 1997.

Holland, J., Emergence from Chaos to Order, Helix Books 1998.

International Standard Organization, Reference Model for Open Distributed Processing International Standard 10746-1, ITU Recommendation X.901, 1996.

Langton, C.G., Life at the Edge of Chaos, Artificial Life II, A Proceedings Volume in the Santa Fe Institute Studies in the Sciences of Complexity, Eds Langton C.G., Taylor, C., Farmer, J.D., Rasmussen,S. Addison-Wesley, 1992.

Mitchell, M., An Introduction to Genetic Algorithms , MIT Press 1998.

Mowbray, T.J, and Malveau, R.C., CORBA Design Patterns, New York John Wiley & Sons Inc., 1997.

Ormerod, P., Butterfly Economics, Faber and Faber, 1998.

Rumelhart, D.E., and McClelland, J.E., (eds) Parallel Distributed Processing: Explorations in the Microstructure of Cognition, Vol1, Foundations. MIT press 1986.

CHAPTER 4

THE PROCESS PERSPECTIVE.

Dan Diaper and Gada Kadoda
Bournemouth University

Abstract

The concept of a process is defined by a process logic and this is contrasted with a characterisation of "traditional, Western approaches" as being based on declarative logic. A process perspective and a derived process model are presented and their application to Information System related research and development are briefly illustrated.

1   INTRODUCTION

This paper is about Information Systems, as much as it is about HCI, Software Engineering, Computing, IT, CSCW, BPR and all the other areas of endeavour that consider systems that involve people and computers interacting. This generality arises because this paper presents a perspective.

By definition, a perspective, or viewpoint, is something subjective (see Diaper, 1989a); it is possessed by someone or shared by a group of people, and somehow allows them to understand the universe in a particular way. Perspective, and its near synonyms such as view or framework, are terms that people use in disciplines like those listed above, apparently without any greater misunderstanding than is common with natural language communication.

Perspectives are difficult to define or describe adequately. For example, although using the term "framework", Morton and Bekerian (1986) contrast this with a model or theory: "Models or theories are expressed within a framework, although this is not always apparent and is rarely made explicit. ... The important feature of a framework is that it is not falsifiable. ... Within any interesting framework one can formulate theories or express models. It is these, and not the framework itself, that can be falsified." (p44)

While Morton and Bekerian's framework concerns cognitive models of human long term memory, it is one of the few, published attempts to describe a novel framework. This paper uses their framework structure to describe the process perspective. If there is any difference between frameworks and perspectives, then it is that the latter are more general, have a greater scope of application, and therefore, are even harder to describe.

Morton and Bekerian's structure consists of an "outline", a set of "kernel assumptions" and a set of "derived concepts".

While this paper concentrates on analysing a process perspective, in practical applications to Information Systems it will be one more to add to the several, non-process ones already available. Furthermore, different perspectives may be used at different levels of problem and solution specification; Diaper (1984) argues that solutions to problems must be at the same level as the problems' level of specification.

Dr. Karmen Guevara's plenary presentation at the HCI'93 conference, titled "Escaping from Boxes", highlighted the need for people to change their perspectives to meet the continuing changes in business practices and IT. The overall consensus of delegates seemed to be that Karmen was absolutely correct about the problem. There was no such agreement, however, as to where people should escape to, i.e. what were the alternative perspectives to "traditional models of Western thought"?

Winograd (1975), in the context of knowledge elicitation for expert/knowledge based systems, makes the distinction between "declarative knowledge", i.e., knowing what, from "procedural knowledge", i.e. knowing how. The traditional example of the latter is bicycle riding, which can only be learned by experience. Most social skills are of this type and much of the recent work in CSCW and groupware has illustrated how difficult it is to capture and describe, never mind engineer (e.g. Hutchison, 1994), the social, interpersonal aspects of group working.

A further problem is that declarative representational methods tend to be static. A process perspective naturally should be good at describing change and hence good at describing dynamic system properties.

A common view is that, generally, "Western thought" and, also, Indo-European derived languages such as English, are inherently declarative (e.g. Winograd, 1975). As a consequence, Bainbridge (1979; 1986) and Diaper (1989b) have argued that systematic distortions arise in representing knowledge when the representational system does not match the type of knowledge to be described. One importance of this, for this paper, is that before presenting a process perspective, it is necessary to at least show that there is a possible process logic for representing the perspective.

2   LOGIC

Descriptions of declarative and process logic, independent of any particular mathematical or logical notation, are contrasted below.

2.1   Declarative Logic
The essence of any declarative representation is that it describes objects, events, behaviours and so forth. To take one example, in task analysis nearly all methods at some, usually early, stage represent the world in terms of actions and objects, although the precise definition of what is an action or object varies across methods. These task

analytic representations are declarative because even the actions, while categorised separately, are merely described in the same way as objects. In task analysis, what is modelled is the changed state of the world as the task progresses, i.e. a sequence of declarative states. What declarative representational systems are good at representing is states; what they are poor at representing is the process of the transformation of states.

Without invoking any particular mathematical or logical notation, the simplest expressions possible all tend to have the form: $x \rightarrow y$.

Central to understanding the above expression is the assumption that, if one knows two out of three terms, then one can deduce the third. This is particularly convenient for a declarative logic because the term it is poorly suited to describe, the process operator "$\rightarrow$", need only be implicitly specified.

Of fundamental importance to computer science is that Set Theory is inherently declarative, and therefore many other computing representational systems such a graph theory, Z schema and VDM, state transition diagrams, etc., are also declarative. Set Theory can specify the relationship between two states, but it has no means of representing the process that transformed elements in one state into another. To offer an analogy, Set Theory and its derivatives represent states of the world like frames on a cinema film. What is missing is a cinema projector.

2.2   The Process Logic

Given that in the expression "$x \rightarrow y$" a declarative logic explicitly specifies the states x and y, then a process logic must specify the process itself, the $\rightarrow$, and the input state x. It has to be x and not y because we can make a "kernel assumption" that processes are unidirectional (Section 3, KA4). The basis of this assumption is simplicity in that any bidirectional process can always be represented as two unidirectional ones. This also accords with much experience, for example, that reverse engineering is not the same as "normal" engineering, or, in logic, that induction is not deduction done backwards.

The process logic thus has the form:

$$x \rightarrow ?$$

The output state ? is not specified in the process logic. The input state x is a state description and hence should be modelled declaratively, although the representational form will be constrained because it will need to be compatible with the description of the process.

"Western thought" already has some methods that are suitable for describing processes. It is common in mathematics, for example, for an output set to have elements that are unknown, e.g. the value of π, the next prime number, and so forth. While controversial (e.g. Lehman, 1991), in Osterweil's (1987) process programming approach the program is itself a process representation. At present, however, there still remains a problem with finding a suitable, general representational format for describing processes; ideally, one that is independent of time.

3   THE PROCESS PERSPECTIVE

It is theoretically possible to induce more than one process perspective from the process logic described above. This paper's process perspective will be described using Morton and Bekerian's scheme of kernal assumptions and derrived concepts. They say of these: "the kernel assumptions (KAs) are the irreducible minimum independent set of postulates. If any one of them were changed the framework would have different properties. The derived concepts (DCs) are theoretically interesting consequences of the kernel assumptions." (p48)

3.1.1   The Process Perspective's Kernel Assumptions
KA1. <u>A process must be able to accept a declarative input state.</u>
A process must have an input and, in theory, this state must be specifiable. In practice, specifications are incomplete and the process logic and process perspective will not stop the continuing need for requirements and systems analysis of extant systems. The role of "Acquisition Processes" is discussed below in the Derived General Process Model (the 80 Model).
KA2. <u>A process must be able to produce a declarative output state.</u>
There is simply no point in modelling a process that never has an output. While a process must be capable of an output, there is no necessity for it to be specified.
KA3. <u>The process must be described.</u>
While a formal process logic would require a logically complete description, in practical applications the process perspective merely requires that processes are described as well as possible: this requirement being no different from how declarative input and output states are described, as well as possible, e.g. as requirements, specifications, goals, targets, etc.

It could be argued that KA3 should more properly be a derived concept, from KA1 and KA2. The rationale for treating it as a kernel assumption is that such a derivation relies on logical arguments outside the process logic.
KA4. <u>Processes are unidirectional.</u>
This has already been discussed (Section 2.2) and, like KA3, it is presented as a kernel assumption because whatever "simplicity" argument is employed is also outside the process logic's current ambit. As with reducing bidirectionality to two unidirectional processes, one-to-many and many-to-one relationships between input and output states can be represented by several unidirectional processes.
KA5. <u>Processes take time.</u>
This property, and its ordinal equivalent, sequence, is not explored within this paper.

3.1.2   The Process Perspective's Derived Concepts
DC1. <u>There is no necessary relationship between input and output states, except that a process has operated on the input state to produce the output.</u>

This arises directly from the unidirectionality of processes (KA4) because if one has only the declarative input and output states then one cannot absolutely prove the nature of the process that operated. This is a version of Popper's falsification argument: it is possible to demonstrate that a particular process could not generate a specific output from a specific input, but it is impossible to prove that one, and only one, process is responsible for any specific input-output data.

DC2. A process will be constrained by its input.
Processes have scope in that, in the extreme case, inappropriate types of input will produce no output from the process. In practice, where some output is produced, it implies that the process logic is as susceptible to Garbage In-Garbage Out problems as other approaches.

DC3. The Derived General Process Model (The 80 Model).
Morton and Bekerian's scheme, while tidy, achieves this at times by forcing a separation between what appears to be closely related concepts. In part this is due to the informality underlying Morton and Bekerian's scheme. They admit that Derived Concepts are: "implications and consequences which are of theoretical interest. ... It will be apparent that they do not have the same logical status with respect to KAs." (p52)

The suspicion must be that the Derived Concepts are actually partial expressions of one or more, implicit, relatively high level models or theories. In the interests of brevity and clarity, one such model will be made explicit, rather than artificially separating a cluster of related Derived Concepts. There is no claim made as to the completeness of the Derived Concepts and alternative models to the Derived General Process Model, called the "80 Model" ("A.T.E." sounds like "eighty" and stands for: Acquisition, Transformation and Evaluation) presented below, are possible.

The 80 Model is intended to be intermediate, between the process logic and the process perspective. There is considerable scope for confusion about what is meant by "level" in this context. To make an analogy with physical, classical reductionism (see Diaper, 1984), if the process logic were an atomic level description, then the 80 Model would be a molecular description and the process perspective would be our mesoscopic, experiential world.

The 80 Model first assumes that processes will be applied iteratively (KA5). Second, it must be possible for output states to be evaluated in some way that does not require a pre-specified, declarative specification of the output state (see KA2). One alternative to the 80 Model is to make the process logic more complex by adding an evaluation function. This alternative is not proposed because it leads to increasingly complex expressions as other functions are also added to the process logic. Instead, the 80 Model specifies three classes of process, all of which have the same x → ? form.

The 80 Model's three process classes are:
Acquisition processes
Transformation processes
Evaluation processes

Acquisition processes are so named after Long's (1989) terminology and are thus concerned with abstracting from the real world, or from an existing model, a representation of it which is its output to a transformation process. Transformation processes are the "core" processes that, implicitly, much of the preceding part of this paper has been about. Evaluation processes evaluate the output of a transformation process. Evaluation criteria without reference to pre-specified goal states are possible with iteration as comparison can be made with previously generated states. Even without using comparisons, it is possible to have processes that evaluate an output state alone.

The 80 Model's three classes of process can be assembled in different ways to suit different applications, styles and so forth. To give one example, often when sophisticated output evaluations are undertaken, the evaluation process will use particular acquisition and transformation processes itself and these may not be the same as those used to generate the transformation process' output that is being evaluated. Similarly, the output of an evaluation process can itself be evaluated. To relate this example to Information System applications, many end user performance evaluation methods are only employed late in the design cycle and are not used for requirements analysis or systems analysis and design; in many cases this is an appropriate strategy.

3.2   The Process Perspective: A Outline

The 80 Model always provides a good starting point for applying the process perspective to a problem. The acquisition process' output will be the current model of the problem. The transformation processes are where the process perspective focuses a novel amount of effort compared to other approaches: on a equal effort scenario, the additional, process orientated effort will be at the expense of specifying output states, goals etc. What makes applications of this paper's process perspective different from other approaches is that each of the three types of process in the 80 Model all have the general property of not specifying their output and can be represented by the process logic $x \rightarrow ?$.

In practice it is very easy to tell if one is applying the process perspective or not; simply ask the question "Do I know what the outcome will be?" When using a pure process logic the only correct answer to this is "No." and if only a process logic is used to model a problem at all levels then this leads to the abandonment of all goals. While the first author has wrestled over several years with the concept that goals are completely unnecessary and undesirable, this is evidently not a comfortable concept for others and reliably meets with resistance when the author has presented it publicly. In practical applications for Information Systems, the process perspective will currently be more useful, and acceptable, when used on some parts of a problem rather than universally.

4   APPLYING THE PROCESS PESPECTIVE

The generality of the process perspective is huge because it was always intended to provide an alternative to "Western thought" which would: (a) be able to deal with, most of, the phenomena that the "Western thought" approach deals with well; and (b) more elegantly accommodate phenomena that are otherwise "difficult". The latter may be supported theoretically on the grounds that declarative systems are known to be poor at representing processes. The former, (a), requires an empirical approach to determine the extent of useful overlap between declarative and process approaches, i.e., what "most of" means. Ultimately, in engineering, usefulness is a necessary condition of success and this, of course, also can only determined empirically.

There already exists a recognised process approach in software quality assurance and maintenance. Sommerville (1996), for example, states "An underlying assumption of quality management is that the quality of the development process directly affects the quality of delivered products." (p615). The point about the process perspective here is that the concentration is on the method of production or maintenance and it is widely known, for example, that after some maintenance cycles, whatever metrics are used will indicate that, the latest version is worse than the previous one. The expectation, the belief or goal, is that over many cycles there will be an overall improvement. This belief is at a more general level than the maintenance processes that are applied to the current system and thus, at the level of application, the process perspective supports a model without a specified output state, in effect, goals are unspecified at this level.

Three approaches have been taken to investigating the capability of the process perspective to provide a useful alternative to a declarative approach. These are: (i) to reinterpret existing work; (ii) to apply it, informally, to existing, current work and problems; and (iii) to develop new methods. These three approaches have not been independent of the development of the process logic and perspective described in this paper. Limits on space in this paper preclude all but a brief discussion of the first of these, however, informal applications of the process perspective appear to have been successful, or at least non-disastrous, in areas such as cognitive modelling, management and planning. A new Process Analysis Method (PAM) is being developed to replace task analysis and related requirements analysis methods. Unlike existing methods, the PAM will have a process logic orientated notation, based on an object oriented paradigm, to support its use of the process perspective. Another application area being investigated is that of personal information systems, replacing declarative structures such as file directories with search processes that constructs temporary directories as the user requires. This initial work is intended to be the basis for a process approach to accessing poorly structured database systems and to anarchic ones, such as the World Wide Web.

Selecting existing Information Systems related work for re-expression by the process perspective is bound to be opportunistic, in part, and, for hopefully obvious reasons, the first author has started by using his own HCI and software engineering research. Of course, examples of applying the process perspective at different levels of engineering detail would obviously be desirable. Re-evaluating previously published work demonstrates that at least some of it can be represented by the process perspective. Indeed, no matter how wonderful any new proposals are, if they require most of the previous decades of work in the various Information System related disciplines to be discarded, then they are almost certainly not practical, i.e. we mustn't throw out the adolescent with the bath water.

To start with a high level application of the process perspective, all methods can easily be re-described within a process perspective.

Using task analysis in requirements and design as an example type of method, like software quality assurance, task analysis is based on the belief that a better system will result than if the task analysis is not carried out. In practice it is not possible to adequately test this belief. Further evidence that task analysis is better accommodated by the process perspective is that much of the task analysis literature itself concentrates on describing, and teaching by worked examples, methods, i.e. the process of doing the analysis.

A similar argument can be applied to other methods such as the structured ones (e.g. JSD, SSADM), formal ones (Z schema, VDM), and to approaches to requirements analysis including user modelling, ethnography, and so forth. Finally and like other methods, the iterative approaches to software development such as rapid prototyping, exploratory programming, etc. can be re-described from a process perspective, provided that the prototype is evaluated with respect to its current and previous states and not to a previously declared, process independent, output specification.

So, a task analyst, for example, does not know what the outcome of a task analysis will be and so concentrates effort on applying a method of task analysis. This is obvious when stated explicitly since if the results of the task analysis were known there would be no need to carry out the method. On the other hand, this view of task analysis, and of methods in general, was not obvious to the author for many of the years he worked in this field and his new understanding of task analysis directly resulted from the process perspective described in this paper. Furthermore, being able to state the obvious, but perhaps in a slightly different way, might be just the sort of desirable result we might expect from adopting a new, general perspective.

System simulations, which include prototypes (see Life et al., 1990), are another method such as those characterised above. The process perspective clarified the author's rationale for investigating, via high fidelity Wizard of Oz simulations, full natural language processing interfaces for expert systems. The rationale was to discover how little natural language processing was required. This can be contrasted with linguistic and other approaches that assume that human-machine communication should be based on human-human dialogue, i.e. their declared goal for a natural language processing machine is for it to be indistinguishable from a person.

Reinterpreting this work at a level lower than the methodological, the Wizard's Apprentice (Diaper, 1989c) was a proposal for an intelligent interface design tool that simulated the natural language analyst, not the dialogue participants. As such it models the process of dialogue analysis and the architecture of the developing intelligent interface is as simple and as flexible as possible so as to minimise constraints on its development, i.e. the content and the structure of the output is undefined. This process orientated, Wizard's Apprentice approach is being used to develop the new Process Analysis Method.

At an even lower level of analysis, this work analysed the grammar of the dialogues collected using a process perspective (Diaper and Shelton, 1989). User "utterances" were simply classified as traditional parts of speech and then a process was designed, which in theory could be automated with little or no artificial intelligence, that looked for left to right patterns of speech parts. The approach was surprisingly successful with greater than 90% of all user inputs being described by the resulting grammar; good enough, the authors claim, for engineering.

This natural language research can thus be described by the process perspective at three levels: the methodological, as a simulation; and at two levels of analytical detail, dialogue and syntax. These last two illustrate what we might hope for from a new perspective. The reinterpretation of the work in process perspective terms makes it clearer, even to the author, what the work was about. This research undoubtedly had an implicit process perspective, but if it had been explicit then the author would have been saved much angst, soul searching, etc. about why he was concentrating so much effort developing methods rather than things.

5   CONCLUSION

This paper has tried to establish that there is at least one plausible understanding of what might be meant by a process perspective. It was not clear to the author for many years that there was any real substance behind the term "process" and its various synonyms. The process logic, at a minimum, demonstrates that there is at least one definition of process that is different from declarative representation systems. The examples from the author's work demonstrate that a process perspective can be applied, even retrospectively, to reinterpret previous work from the new perspective. Whether it can be usefully applied by other people is less sure.

Perhaps the way to teach the process perspective is to start by teaching goal abandonment on the grounds that if people can cope with this then everything else about the processes perspective will naturally follow. The disadvantage of this teaching approach is that people are unlikely to be receptive to it unless they are already convinced that there will be major benefits to their losing one of the keystones of "Western thought", that of goals. This paper attempts to provide one basis for convincing people that they may gain from the pain of escaping from their existing boxes.

Acknowledgements

Our thanks to our Bournemouth University colleagues Prof. Martin Shepperd and Dr. Liguang Chen and to Jonathan Earthy of Lloyds Register who commented, at short notice, on a draft of this paper. Also to Bournemouth University and its School of Design, Engineering and Computing for supporting this work.

References

Bainbridge, L. (1979) 'Verbal Reports as Evidence of the Process Operator's Knowledge.' International Journal of Man-Machine Studies, 11, 431-436.

Bainbridge, L. (1986) 'Asking Questions and Accessing Knowledge.' Future Computing Systems, 1, 2, 143-150.

Diaper, D. (1984) 'An Approach to IKBS Development Based on a Review of "Conceptual Structures: Information Processing in Mind and Machine" by J. F. Sowa' Behaviour and Information Technology, 3, 3, 249-255.

Diaper, D. (1989a) 'Task Observation for Human-Computer Interaction.' in Diaper, D. (Ed.) 'Task Analysis for Human-Computer Interaction.', 210-237. Ellis Horwood.

Diaper, D. (1989b) 'Designing Expert Systems: From Dan to Beersheba.' in Diaper, D. (Ed.) 'Knowledge Elicitation: Principles, Techniques and Applications.', 15-46. Ellis Horwood.

Diaper, D. (1989c) 'The Wizard's Apprentice: A Program to Help Analyse Natural Language Dialogues.' in Sutcliffe, A. and Macaulay, L. (Eds.) 'People and Computers V.', 231-244. Cambridge University Press.

Diaper, D. and Shelton, T. (1989) 'Dialogues with the Tin Man: Computing a Natural Language Grammar for Expert System Naive Users.' in Peckham, J. (Ed.) 'Recent Developments and Applications of Natural Language Processing.', 98-116. Kogan Page.

Hutchison, A. (1994) 'CSCW as an Opportunity for Business Process Reengineering.' IFIP Transactions A (Computer Science and Technology), 29, 411-420.

Lehman, M.M. (1991) 'Software Engineering: The Software Process and their Support.' Software Engineering, 6, 5, 243-258.

Life, A., Narborough-Hall, C. and Hamilton, W., (Eds.) (1990) 'Simulation and the User Interface.' Taylor and Francis.

Long, J. (1989) 'Cognitive Ergonomics and Human-Computer Interaction: An Introduction.' in Long, J. and Whitefield, A. (Eds.) 'Cognitive Ergonomics and Human-Computer Interaction.', 4-34. Cambridge University Press.

Morton, J. and Bekerian, D. (1986) 'Three Ways of Looking at Memory.' in Sharkey, N.E. (Ed.) 'Advances in Cognitive Science 1.', 43-71. Ellis Horwood.

Osterweil, L.J. (1987) 'Software Processes are Software Too.' 9th. International Software Engineering Conference. IEEE Computer Society Press.

Sommerville, I. (1996) 'Software Engineering.'(Fifth Edition). Addison Wesley.

CHAPTER 5

INFORMATION SYSTEMS RESEARCH: THE NEED FOR A CRITICAL PERSPECTIVE

Stephen K Probert
Cranfield University

Abstract

It is argued that the changing nature of the role of information systems (IS) in contemporary organisations limits the effectiveness of most extant IS research methods for the purpose of developing an understanding of IS development and enhancement in such organisations. Therefore, some relevant epistemological and ontological notions, which could underpin an IS research method for critically understanding (and eventually improving) IS development and enhancement projects, are discussed. Much of the argument is based on the work of the Frankfurt School philosopher, Adorno (1903-1969).

1 THE CHANGING ROLE OF INFORMATION SYSTEMS

Today, much of the IS research agenda is now management-driven; the research problems having been re-cast as being concerned with "information management", rather than being concerned with primarily technical concerns (Earl, 1989). However, the management-driven research agenda has not been content "to rest on its laurels". Business Process Re-engineering (BPR) and, very recently, the problem of managing the knowledge worker (usually cast in terms of *organisational learning* and/or *knowledge management*) have become significant concerns (Currie, 1995). Both topics have spawned specialist journals; indeed the journal *Business Change and Re-engineering* was recently re-named *Knowledge and Process Management*! Of course it can properly be argued that organisations pass through various "stages of growth" (Galliers and Sutherland, 1991), and so not all organisations will be embracing approaches to *knowledge management* etc. Therefore, it must be admitted that the majority of organisations to which this work appertains are those which are relatively sophisticated users of IS/IT.

Looking back, over the past twenty or thirty years the shift of emphasis from technological issues to management issues, might (rather crudely) be explained by an *economic* relationship between *price* and *performance*. If the processing-power-per-dollar/pound continues to fall rapidly then changes to the "IS agenda" can be anticipated. The changes that have occurred in the IS agenda could be emphasised by the nature of the (managerial) questions that have been and will be asked, i.e.:

- e.g. 1970 'What can we do with computers in our organisation?'
- e.g. 1985 'How can we better integrate the various information systems in use in our organisation?'
- e.g. 2000 'What might people want to use information to do in our organisation (and how should people be helped to achieve these aims by appropriate IS)?'

The first sort of question needed a technological sort of answer - an example answer might be "payroll". However, it is widespread knowledge that - despite the technical attractions of payroll systems - such systems are "socially sensitive", i.e. they have to work correctly every week (or month)! But for as long as the question asked was 'What can we do with computers in our organisation?' the answers would always be related to those things that appeared to be the most tractable, "*The cultural focus of much of the implementation of the 1970s and 1980s was on installing the answer, finding the quick solution, finding the quick 'technological fix'. The focus was on the technical capabilities of the machine and its promise ...*" (Winfield, 1991, p. 19).

The second sort of question needed a managerial sort of answer (often based more on "business need" than on technical possibility) - such answers are probably the dominant sorts of answers today, although there is a developing trend for these answers to take a more strategic view of the *possibilities for exploiting* integrated systems. This indicates a shift from the second sort of question to the third - although the strategic questions are essentially still management questions. What makes the third sort of question different from the first two sorts is that it presupposes that the employees themselves have a vision of what the organisation is trying to achieve, and that they share the value-system embodied in that vision; that is it implies the need for a shift from *management* to *leadership* (see e.g. Handy, 1989, pp. 105-108). Much of the early BPR literature stressed such elements:

> *The fundamental error that most companies commit when they look at technology is to view it through the lens of their existing processes. They ask, "How can we use these new technological capabilities to enhance or streamline or improve what we are already doing?" Instead, they should be asking, "How can we use technology to allow us to do things that we are not already doing?" Reengineering, unlike automation, is about innovation. It is about exploiting the latest capabilities of technology to achieve entirely new goals. (Hammer and Champy, 1994, p. 85)*

The "information technology (IT) = possible solution" formula has increasingly given way to an "IT = possible opportunity" formula, *"The increasing tendency for organisations to privilege innovation over efficiency ... places a particular stress upon the human qualities of flexibility and creativity which even the 'impersonal machinery' ... of IT hardware cannot yet provide."* (Scarbrough and Corbett, 1992, p. 19).

Indeed, in order to achieve genuine business benefits, a more holistic approach (than was previously the case) is now seen as vital:

> *... [W]here IT has been involved in radical business change or transformation of business operations, technology has rarely been the only, or ultimately the most important, factor at work... Conversely when one hears IT projects described by IT directors as vehicles for organizational change, as forcing cultural change, or as taking the business into the 21st century, they are often descriptions of projects in trouble where technology has been the driver. (Earl, 1994, pp. 78-79)*

The end result of the shift in emphasis concerning the role of IT (from "solution" to "enabler") has two important implications for IS. Firstly, the role of people as *utilisers* (rather than *users*) of information systems is enhanced; secondly, it becomes more difficult to set a clear boundary between people and the systems with which they interact. Scarbrough and Corbett express these phenomena thus, *"... [T]echnology and organization are not ontologically separate categories, but rather mirror reflections of a mutual interchange of knowledge, meanings and political interests."* (Scarbrough and Corbett, 1992, p. 157). However, this creates a number of problems which are not adequately dealt with effectively by current IS research concepts; these problems - mostly philosophical in nature - will now be discussed.

2   THE EPISTEMOLOGY AND ONTOLOGY UNDERPINNING MOST INFORMATION SYSTEMS DEVELOPMENT METHODS

Although these concepts are important for researchers, it is not appropriate to explore all the various ways in which these concepts are treated in IS texts here, but it can be stated that it is generally the case that most contemporary approaches to developing information systems assume that some *practitioners* are going to "do most of the job" (even on a facilitative model). This straight-away implies a *subject-centred epistemology* and - correspondingly - a *"problematic" ontology* - basically along the lines of the Cartesian model of scientific enquiry. Williams (1978) provides a thorough explanation of the Cartesian project, but in straightforward terms, the analyst starts from a position of subjective ignorance and has to use his/her wits to discover what is the case in a complex and often confusing social (and technical) situation, *"Analysts work with their wits plus paper and pencil. That's about it."* (DeMarco, 1979, p. 12). Notwithstanding the introduction of CASE tools, this statement remains fairly typical of most statements about the situation that IS practitioners face today.

Now, although such accounts might seem *prima facie* to be realistic descriptions of the actual situation, the underlying epistemological assumptions embodied in such accounts are necessarily of a *subject-centred epistemology*. Fortunately, various other accounts of epistemology exist; some of these are subjective in orientation, whilst others are both objective but unsympathetic to logical positivism (e.g. Popper, 1979). Therefore the "standard epistemological model" usually employed in IS texts is not "definitely the case" (in philosophical terms). Furthermore, many of the "versions" of epistemology that accept that a subjective model of enquiry is the most appropriate (e.g. Quine and Ullian, 1978, Haack, 1995) are not discussed by most IS academics at all. However, the subject-centred model is, most probably, appropriate to questions of the first two types (discussed earlier), but is not so useful to the third type, essentially because the subject-centred model is, in a key sense, a *researcher-based* model. *Infusing the utilisers of information systems with a vision* is not normally considered to be a research activity, and is arguably not a very well-understood issue *per se*.

It seems likely that understanding the process of infusing people with a vision will be an important issue for successful IS practice in the near future (if it is not already), and that "the vision thing" will play a key role in determining the outcomes of IS developments in organisations. If so, a new approach - new to many IS researchers at any rate - to understanding the relationship between epistemology and ontology will be needed. It is possible that the relationship that will most usefully be considered is a dialectical one; especially if *IS developments are considered to be, in part, causally responsible for the actual nature (structure, processes, etc.) of contemporary organisations.* (I consider that it is churlish to deny this premise, although others would no doubt disagree.)

In some recent accounts of the process of requirements determination it is certainly evident that the *practitioner-as-enquiring-subject* model is outmoded; as an example - consider prototyping, "*We found that determining the requirements ... was often done in non-traditional ways... [P]rototyping, appropriately applied, is an effective technique for refining specifications by promoting mutual learning on the part of users and information systems staff. At some point this mutual learning can bring the "user" and the "developer" so close that these terms distinguish prior roles rather than current activities.*" (Ives and Vitale, 1996, p. 113). Westrup (1997) goes further in arguing that *users* and *developers* (i.e. practitioners) were always *constituted* in the first place, "*Users are not users until they are involved in development in some form. Requirements techniques organize so as to create users that will enable representation of the organization qua social... developers are also constituted in this process.*" (Westrup, 1997, pp. 187-188). This is a theme which we will return to shortly; for now it can be concluded that the terms 'user' and 'developer' have become somewhat outmoded, and that research approaches (and for that matter IS methods) which consider the practitioner to be an enquiring subject will be too limited to explain IS development and enhancement in contemporary organisations.

Moreover, all the homilies about the virtues of "interpretivism" (e.g. Stowell, 1993) tend to ignore recent - and arguably important - developments in philosophy which castigate the value of "subjective immediacy" (i.e. that which the analyst "immediately" perceives to be the case). This (critical) tradition can, in fact, be traced back to the 1930s (see Adorno, 1973a, 1982), although this tradition is now more generally associated with Foucault (e.g. 1982) and other "postmodern" philosophers. The study of IS has been impoverished by the over-simplification of some of these key issues, and changes in the "IS agenda" clearly necessitate a re-think of some core IS research concepts.

3   TOWARDS A NEW PARADIGM FOR IS RESEARCH

This section will go some way towards outlining the epistemological and ontological notions that could be utilised in IS research, if such research is to be relevant to gaining an understanding of how to successfully develop and enhance information systems in contemporary organisations. In the discussions that follow, a central *practical* issue in IS development is considered, and this has, as its corollary, an important *philosophical* issue (of course, there may be other aspects of philosophy relevant to this practical issue). The practical issue can be characterised as being concerned with how the practitioners acquire *knowledge* of the existing systems and of the users' information requirements. This issue is correlated by philosophers' concerns with *epistemology* and its relationship with *ontology*. Reflective considerations on these concerns may be used to inform proposals for a new approach to understanding what is needed to conduct research in IS. One critical philosopher who developed potentially useful ideas about the relationship between epistemology and ontology was Adorno (1903-1969). There is now a large body of IS literature concerned with the Habermasian tradition in critical social theory (Ngwenyama, *et al.*, 1997), but relatively little has been based on Adorno's work. Unfortunately, there is not space here for a discussion of the relative merits of these approaches.

Adorno's work enables a sort of "unified theory" of technology, culture, and administration to be put to work on investigating IS problems – one which does not identify science with technology. Such features are relevant to IS research in that, in many aspects of IS research, it is not possible to isolate the social and technical components of the area under investigation. In any case, it is somewhat reductionistic to attempt to separate the area of investigation into two component parts (social and technical) in a definite manner. Adorno was a key member of the Frankfurt School, and although it is difficult to summarise Adorno's ideas on the technology/culture dimension easily, essentially Adorno thought that culture (generally) has, regrettably, become a matter which is administered, and that technology has made this possible. The relevance for IS research is that such a view would generate a new, possibly more appropriate (but inevitably more complex), theory of the role that technology plays in shaping the culture of organisations (and vice versa). As Scarbrough and Corbett note:

> *... [T]he relationship between technology and organization is neither one of 'impacts' [of IT] nor of 'choice' [made by managers] per se. Rather, technology and organization are closely intertwined through flows of knowledge and ideas which transcend the individual organization but which find expression in, and are reinforced by, political interests and agendas at the organizational level. (Scarbrough and Corbett, 1992, p. 157)*

If Scarbrough and Corbett are even approximately right, then it would seem *prima facie* that simplistic distinctions between "hard" and "soft" systems approaches to achieving IS will not provide adequate forms of conceptualisation for IS developments *and* user-utilisation of the information made available as a result of IS - two notions which themselves may be much more intertwined than is often acknowledged (see e.g. Fitzgerald, 1990, Paul, 1995). As Gardner (*et al*) argue, the need now is for "tailorable" systems to be put in place; in such systems the concepts of 'developer' and 'user' (and 'technology' and 'organisation') are increasingly blurred:

> *A computer system is tailorable if it provides a user with control over its operation. This means a user should be able to regulate or operate the system, thus providing ultimate power to direct or manipulate a system's behaviour... A control is understood to be a device or interface widget that enables a user to regulate or operate a system and provides the user with the power to direct or determine its state. (Gardner, et al, 1995, p. 187)*

So, IS development should not be conceived as a once-and-for-all activity, but - rather - as an on-going, user-definable (and user-achievable) process. Such considerations from the world of IS practice have important implications for research into IS also. A "binary opposition" view of the distinction between "positivism" and "interpretivism" is surely inappropriate when the "objects" in the research area contain such "intertwinings" between technical and social aspects; the *tailorability* of an integrated system is surely an *emergent property* of the possibilities (and the constraints) created by definite technical "configurations", and the actual social arrangements, pertaining in the situation.

However, although it would be possible to develop a more integrated theory of the social and technical aspects of information systems based on Adorno's *oeuvre*, it should not be thought that Adorno's ideas can be straightforwardly employed to develop research methods appropriate to improving our understanding of IS development and enhancement; numerous dangers would lie in store for a researcher taking such a simplistic approach as, "*The nature and extent of Adorno's claim to attention must always be contingent on the degree to which his work can illuminate contemporary developments in culture, polity and society... an assessment must identify core themes in Adorno's analysis which continue to merit attention and to warrant further development.*" (Crook, 1994, p. 18). It should be noted that other researchers' works are relevant to the work outlined herein. Some important "new" researchers have emerged embodying (various degrees of) the "Adornean" tradition, e.g. Sloterdijk (1987) has written about the cynical condition (which in some ways links the concerns of Foucault to those of Adorno). As it is not appropriate to attempt to provide full details of Adorno's key ideas here (see Jay, 1984 for a useful summary), merely the essence of Adorno's epistemic considerations will be outlined below.

Adorno considers that there is a legitimate separation between the *subjects* (who carry out research) and the *objects* in the study, but generally this distinction is not made in an appropriate manner:

> *The separation of subject and object is both real and illusory. True, because in the cognitive realm it serves to express the real separation, the dichotomy of the human condition, a coercive development. False, because the resulting separation must not be hypostatised, not magically transformed into an invariant. (Adorno, 1978, pp. 498-499)*

Adorno considers that "the subject" makes possible the idea of critique - of a critical interpretation of reality. But the concept of 'the subject' is an intellectual construction - an abstraction - *derived* from (and not *prior to*) actual, real, living individuals, i.e., *"It is evident that the abstract concept of the transcendental subject - its thought forms, their unity, and the original productivity of consciousness - presupposes what it promises to bring about: actual, live individuals."* (Adorno, 1978, p. 500).

It should be noted that this is a Nietzschean argument (e.g. Nietzsche, 1956, pp. 178-180), and this debt is acknowledged by Adorno (1982). Although we can treat the subject as real (or "standing in for" real, live individuals), in Adorno's view the subject does not "make the world up" (this is often termed 'constructivism' - Adorno uses the term 'constitute' instead of *construct*) so, *"While our images of perceived reality may very well be Gestalten [Weltanschaunngen - in SSM jargon], the world in which we live is not; it is constituted differently than out of mere images of perception."* (Adorno, 1977, p. 126). However, Adorno does not argue for a return to "vulgar objectivism", because this would deny the possibility of a critical interpretation of the objective circumstances. The objective world is real enough, but what we see is always *mediated* by concepts (although we may not be aware of this all of the time) so, *"What must be eliminated is the illusion that ... the totality of consciousness, is the world, and not the self-contemplation of knowledge. The last thing the critique of epistemology ... is supposed to do is proclaim unmediated objectivism."* (Adorno, 1982, p. 27).

In the earlier quotation (above) concerning "perceived reality", what Adorno means by 'constituted differently' is that the world is, to a large extent, determined by economic realities, which he sometimes refers to using the term 'exchange':

> *The living human individual, as he is forced to act in the role for which he has been marked internally as well, is the homo oeconomicus incarnate, closer to the transcendental subject than to the living individual for which he immediately cannot but take himself... What shows up in the doctrine of the transcendental subject is the priority of the relations - abstractly*

rational ones, detached from the human individuals and their relationships -
that have their model in exchange. If the exchange form is the standard
social structure, its rationality constitutes people; what they are for
themselves, what they seem to be for themselves, is secondary. (Adorno,
1978, p. 501)

For Adorno (as for IS professionals) the world of economic activity is very real as,
"Somebody pays for what analysts and designers deliver. New systems have to be
justified by the benefits that they deliver. It is easy to use terms like "the users" and "user
management" ... and forget that they are subtitles for "the customer"." (Yeates, et al,
1994, p. 2). In fact, the IS practitioner should be seen not purely as some sort of
enquiring transcendental subject, but as an economically-constituted actuality. Adorno
argued that critique is only possible if some status is given to the subject who can
become critically aware of these sort of circumstances. Therefore Adorno preserves a
critical role for the subject, "To use the strength of the subject to break through the
fallacy of constitutive subjectivity ... Stringently to transcend the official separation of
pure philosophy and the substantive or formally scientific realm ..." (Adorno, 1973b).

At the very least, the economic activities which generate systems development
projects have a key determining role on the practitioners' foci of attention in IS projects;
systems analysts do not generate knowledge purely in the interest of advancing science.
What is needed are techniques for analysing the complex relationships that appertain
between the subjects conducting the IS work, and the objects in the study. Here, 'objects'
should be understood as meaning all the various items that need to be analysed in the
organisation; the term is not used here in the sense that it is used by the advocates of
"object orientation".

4   CONCLUSION

Research on IS should be able to link the cultural aspects of organisations (theoretically)
with the real economic pressures felt by the managers of those organisations. This is
because we are all (often) totally immersed in organisational situations, nevertheless we
are all sometimes able to see problems with the actually existing set of arrangements. We
may well be able to generate innovative solutions to those problems, if the organisational
culture (and the technical infrastructure) allows us to - and if the technical personnel can
enable us to. Therefore, whilst technical considerations remain essentially important to
success in IS practice, understanding the vague and yet undeniable tensions between the
social and economic aspects of organisations is clearly crucial to developing an
understanding of the necessary conditions for successful IS practice to be achieved; this
need has been recognised for nearly ten years now e.g., "*[A]lthough IT may enable the*
technical infrastructure to connect people and information together more effectively in
the networked firm, to realise the benefits we are looking for we need also to have - or to
develop - a favourable cultural setting for innovation and change."(Rockart and Short,

1991, p. 215)

However, most IS research methods seem to be currently mired in an "either/or" mentality (either investigate the social or the technical aspects of an IS). By generating a philosophically robust technique for developing critical analyses of current IS practices, some greater clarity and precision can be brought to our understanding of those practices. Further research is needed *both* on the development of an appropriate method for researching IS issues, *and* on substantive questions concerned with how to successfully go about developing, tailoring and enhancing information systems, such that the on-going socio-technical processes (concerned with making the right information available to the right people at the right time etc.) can be constantly improved.

References

Adorno, T. W. (1973) The Jargon of Authenticity. Routledge and Kegan Paul, London.

Adorno, T. W. (1973b) Negative Dialectics. Routledge, London.

Adorno, T. W. (1977) 'The Actuality of Philosophy', Telos, Vol. 31, pp.120-133.

Adorno, T. W. (1978) 'Subject and Object' in: The Essential Frankfurt School Reader, A. Arato and E. Gebhardt, eds., Blackwell, Oxford.

Adorno, T. W. (1982) Against Epistemology: A Metacritique. Blackwell, Oxford.

Crook, S. (1994) 'Introduction: Adorno and Authoritarian Irrationalism' in: *The Stars Down to Earth and Other Essays on the Irrational in Culture,* T. W. Adorno, Routledge, London.

Currie, W. (1995) Management Strategy for I.T.: An International Perspective. Pitman, London.

DeMarco, T. (1979) Structured Analysis and System Specification. Yourdon Press, Englewood Cliffs.

Earl, M. J. (1989) Management Strategies for Information Technology. Prentice Hall International, Hemel Hempstead.

Earl, M. J. (1994) 'Putting Information Technology in its Place: A Polemic for the Nineties' in: Strategic Information Management: Challenges and Strategies in Managing Information Systems, R. D. Galliers and S. H. Baker, eds., Butterworth-Heinemann, Oxford.

Fitzgerald, G. (1990) 'Achieving Flexible Information Systems: The Case for Improved Analysis. Journal of Information Technology, Vol. 5, pp. 5-11.

Foucault, M. (1982) 'The Subject and Power' Afterword in: Michel Foucault: Beyond Structuralism and Hermeneutics. H. L. Dreyfus and P. Rabinov, Harvester, Brighton.

Galliers, R. D. and Sutherland, A. R. (1994) 'Information Systems Management and Strategy Formulation: Applying and Extending the 'Stages of Growth' Concept' in: Strategic Information Management. R. D. Galliers and B. S. H. Baker, eds., Butterworth-Heinemann, Oxford.

Gardner, L. A., Paul, R. J. and Patel, N. (1995) 'Moving Beyond the Fixed Point Theorem with Tailorable Information Systems' in: Proceedings of the 3rd European

Conference on Information Systems, Athens/Greece, June 1-3 1995, G. Doukidis, B. Galliers, T. Jelassi, H. Krcmar and F. Land, eds.

Haack, S. (1995) Evidence and Inquiry. Blackwell, Oxford.

Hammer, M. and Champy, J. (1994) Reengineering the Corporation. Nicholas Brealey, London.

Handy, C. (1989) The Age of Unreason (2nd ed.). Arrow, London.

Ives, B. and Vitale, M. (1996) 'Strategic Information Systems: Some Organization Design Considerations' in: Information Management: the Organizational Dimension, M. J. Earl, ed., Oxford University Press, New York.

Jay, M. (1984) Adorno. Fontana, London.

Ngwenyama, O., Davis, G., Lyytinen, K., Truex, D. and Cule, P. (1997) 'Panel – Assessing Critical Social Theory Research in Information Systems' in: Information Systems and Qualitative Research, A. S. Lee, J. Liebenau, and J. I. DeGross, eds., Chapman and Hall, London.

Nietzsche, F. (1956) The Birth of Tragedy and the Genealogy of Morals. Doubleday, New York.

Paul, R. J. (1995) 'An O.R. View of Information Systems Development' Operational Research Tutorial Papers 1995. Operational Research Society, Birmingham.

Popper, K. R. Objective Knowledge (2nd ed.). Oxford University Press, Oxford.

Quine, W. V. and Ullian, J. S. (1978) The Web of Belief (2nd ed.). Random House, New York.

Rockart, J. F. and Short, J. E. (991) 'The Networking Organization and the Management of Interdependence' in: The Corporation of the 1990s: Information Technology and Organizational Transformation. M. S. Scott-Morton, ed., Oxford University Press, New York.

Scarbrough, H. and Corbett, J. M. (1992) Technology and Organization. Routledge, London.

Sloterdijk, P. (1987) Critique of Cynical Reason. Verso, London.

Stowell, F. (1993) 'Hermeneutics and Organisational Inquiry', Systemist, Vol. 15, No. 2, pp. 87-103.

Winfield, I. (1991) Organisations and Information Technology. Blackwell Scientific, Oxford.

Westrup, C. (1997) 'Constituting Users in Requirements Techniques' in: Information Systems and Qualitative Research, A. S. Lee, J. Liebenau, and J. I. DeGross, eds., Chapman and Hall, London.

Williams, B. (1978) Descartes: The Project of Pure Enquiry. Penguin, Harmondsworth.

CHAPTER 6

MANAGERS AND INFORMATION; AGENCY AND STRUCTURE

Alistair Mutch
The Nottingham Trent University

Abstract

Argues that for a satisfactory understanding of the relationship between managers and information, we need an adequate theory of the agency/structure divide. This is developed via a critique of Introna's use of Heidegger. It is argued that this prevents the generation of a satisfactory account of structural factors. An outline of an alternative approach is presented, based on a realist approach.

1   INTRODUCTION

In 1996 Clive Holtham, referring to debates in philosophy, argued that, "It is a tragedy that we are not having this same emotionally charged discussion about data, information, knowledge and wisdom in a business context because the longer we fail to do so, the longer we expend time, energy and investment in ways which due to our clouded thinking will not yield us, our business, or our societies real benefit." (Holtham, 1996: 46-7). The recent book by Lucas Introna, Management, Information and Power, has the potential to reopen this debate but, it will be argued, falls short in some key areas (Introna, 1997). This argument is developed from the perspective of an attempt to marry thinking from information management with perspectives drawn from the labour process tradition. This argument is in its turn girded by arguments drawn from the 'classical' tradition of Western Marxism and critical realism. In doing so it is necessary to recognise that attempts such as this are influenced by the practical constraints of attempting to synthesise voluminous literatures in each area. What follows on Heidegger, for example, is entirely based on secondary accounts and because of this may involve misreadings and misunderstandings. This risk is taken, however, in the cause of advancing the debate.

The paper starts with a brief outline of Introna's book, with a particular focus on the argument about the nature of management. It will be argued that, whilst in many features attractive and valuable, it does not adequately specify the structural dimensions of management. This will be demonstrated through a detailed analysis of Introna's account of the origins of management. The argument will be that there is the danger of replacing one myth, that of the rational decision maker, with another, that of the unconstrained manager. This weakness is related to the question of theory and to arguments about human intentionally. Whilst the critique of instrumental rationality is recognised as well made, this is argued not to exhaust the issue of reflexive human action. Based on the possibility of such action the outline of an alternative approach is suggested, one which starts from the dialectic of man and nature, drawing upon work on consciousness and language. It is argued that the possibility of pre-linguistic understanding suggests that there is a need to focus on the embodied character of human thought and action. This suggests a number of constraints on managers and their use of information. The paper concludes with some musings on the implications of this discussion for a potential rapprochement between ideas derived from systems development and organizational theory.

2   ATTACKING THE WRONG MYTH?

Management, Information and Power is an ambitious attempt to develop a perspective about the way in which managers use information which has consequences for the ways in which information technology is deployed. Starting from the perspective of one who was increasingly frustrated by his attempts to provide managers with information systems, Introna deploys a range of thinkers to find answers as to why these attempts were so unsuccessful. In doing so, he mounts a challenge to what he takes to be the dominant functionalist, rationalist paradigm in IS thinking, one which in turn rests on an assumption of managers as rational decision makers. This challenge is heavily based on a reading of Heidegger's notions of being-in the world, which is used to develop a picture of *"the manager that is always already in-the-world. The manager that cannot escape the messiness, the ambiguity, the play of force, in a world that cannot be unentangled."* (Introna, 1997, ix). This account has resonances of the demolition job done on strong artificial intelligence by Winograd and Flores when they talk, following Heidegger, of *"cognition as praxis - as concerned acting in the world. ... our condition of throwness - the condition of understanding in which our actions find some resonance or effectiveness in the world."* (Winograd and Flores, 1986: 33). This is a convincing account, but the attempts to bring in other perspectives (and there are many of them, drawn from Foucault, Wittgenstein, Habermas, Giddens and others) are less convincing. However, the focus of this paper is not on every area of the book, but on the main thrust of the critique developed.

The case developed against *"the archetypal, but mythical, modern manager, the perfect, rational and purposive being who is the expert of technology"* (Introna, 1997: 22) is a sound one, but are we to some extent tilting at windmills here? By this I mean that when we turn to conventional, mainstream accounts in management studies we find very little to support this picture of the manager. Of course, we can always find caricatures in some of the more pedestrian texts, but it is suggested that serious work has long rejected this image of the manager. Even (especially?) in the more managerialist literature one finds an appropriation of a 'post-modern' sensibility, concerned with the ambiguity and complexity of organizational life. This concern with subjectivity extends to the more critical reaches of management studies with, for example, Willmott calling for *"a more adequate appreciation of the nature and significance of managers' ambivalent positioning - as objects ('targets') as well as subjects ('agents') of forms of capitalist control"* (Willmott, 1997: 1354). The consequence of this ambivalence may be concerns which have ' contradictory consequences for the fulfilment of the so-called functions of capital' (Willmott, 1997:1353). These concerns can manifest themselves in claims which tend to suggest powers for managers which seem implausible. Alvesson and Willmott, for example, analysing the way in managers reacted to a particularly aggressive new Managing Director, argue that a clearer perspective on their part could:

> *"have reduced their anxiety and, as a consequence, enabled them to deal more effectively with their new boss ... they could have resolved individually and collectively to work towards the development of more democratic structures of corporate governance so that those occupying managerial positions (e.g. managing directors) become more accountable to fellow employees - a shift that, logically, requires managers to seek out, challenge and change diverse anti-democratic industrial structures and practices, including their own dealings with each other and their subordinates, Such a shift, it is worth stressing, would involve not only procedural changes in the structure of corporate governance but substantive, embodied changes in how managers make sense of their responsibilities and undertake their work"* (Alvesson and Willmott, 1996: 16).

This is a frankly untenable position, but only if one can conceive of the broader structures in which these managers operate. These structures, both within and outside the organisation, place constraints on the full range of actions which are feasible. The danger of the drift to subjectivity is that it fails to give due weight to these structures, both in the ways in which they form the sorts of actions which are perceived as possible and in the way in which they constrain the actions which are decided upon. There is a tendency in the literature on the managerial use of information to privilege the actions of knowledgeable agents, above all in an analysis which foregrounds the importance of managerial politics, at the expense of a considered treatment of the constraints which currently available methods of systems development might impose. This in turn is based on a resolutely anti-realist perspective. For example, Bloomfield and Vurdubakis can argue that:

> *all forms of administrative, political and managerial intervention are not reactions to reality 'as such' but to a reality socially and discursively*

constructed within documents. What one might call a 'textual reality'
(Bloomfield and Vurdubakis, 1997: 87).

The implications of such statements are quite substantial, for they can give rise to a form of analysis which stays at the level of the text and which fails to relate the texts that are generated to the nature of the world in which they are produced. In order to explore such relationships we need theoretical perspectives which provide an adequate account between agency and structure, an account which Introna, for all his suggestive insights, cannot supply. In the next section we examine why this might be so as a precursor to outlining an alternative approach.

3   MANAGEMENT AND THEORY

The problems with Introna's account can be seen in the passages which cover the origins of management. Introna starts from a notion of management as manus, *"the hand that is present, ready, actively involved"* (Introna, 1997: 85). The embodiment of this in artisan, craft production "was broken by the rapid development of technology"(86). Accounts by historians, however, would suggest that it was the social organisation of production, rather than the development of technology, that was the really significant step in the development of modern capitalism (Marglin, 1976). It was this socialisation of production that brought into being the circumstances in which the ideas of Taylorism could be developed. Taylorism, or scientific management, was a set of ideas about the organisation of work which stressed the separation of conception and execution and the importance of the professional manager. Introna argues that *"in some sense Taylor is the Descartes of management thought"* (88). Now, whilst the development of ideas is a crucial and interesting part of history, one would want to see this as only a small part of the origins of Taylorism. An alternative account would stress its origins in the fierce class conflict which characterised *fin de siecle* America (Littler, 1982). Modern management was born out of conflict, not out of technology or ideas. This conflict was not confined to a classical labour-versus capital struggle, but can in many ways be seen as a struggle for legitimacy *within* management. This should remind us that 'management' is not a homogeneous category analysis, but one that has its own fault lines (Armstrong, 1989). There are thus struggles between various parts of management - accountants, marketeers, engineers, IS developers - as to which fraction best represents the supposed interests of the owners of capital for whom these managers operate as agents. There are, then a number of tensions within management which need to be set in context of their central relationship to capital.

The importance of perspectives such as these is seen when set against some accounts of the changes which information technology might bring to management. For example a recent account argues that *"In our view, as the middle-manager concept becomes redefined the information needed to manage particular activities with respect to organizational processes and purpose will become democratically constructed and widely shared."* (Crowe, Beeby and Gammack, 209). Assessing such claims, it is argued, demands the construction of a theoretical account which links the activities of persons to their circumstances. Such an account might well suggest that there are powerful structural constraints which will significantly limit the extent of any such 'democratic construction'. However, whilst the Heideggerian perspective can help us enormously with the activities managers undertake, it is antithetical to the construction of the other part of the coupling, that which deals with the structures in which these activities take place. In the words of Callinicos, do these ideas:

> *rule out the possibility of social theory? In other words, does it deny that the explanation of social events can (or indeed must) invoke the structural properties of social systems ... Does it imply that all the investigator can do is to characterize the self-understanding of agents, indeed of necessity relying on the very conceptual vocabulary they themselves use to articulate this self-understanding...? (Callinicos, 1987: 99)*

The answer to these questions hinges on the notion of intentionality. For Introna, following Heidegger, *"the manager does not think about the world and then formulate objectives (intentions) to direct action in that world"* (Introna, 1997, 30). In part, these is derived from an argument against the notions of intentionality expressed in such areas as classical economics and the structural functionalist perspective which dominates much mainstream IS work. These traditions posit fully rational actors, whose rationality consists of the objective identification and maximisation of self interest. Such a theory has, of course, been challenged from many directions and one impact of the spread of IT enabled phenomena such as electronic commerce has been to bring this critique into the heart of economics itself (Mansell and Silverstone, 1997). However, we do not have to jettison the whole notions of actors who, within constraints, attempt to act in a reflexive fashion and who, in some sense, intend to carry out particular actions (regardless of whether those actions will in fact bring about the results which they intended). Callinicos develops a theory based on the notions of agents as strong evaluators, motivated by particular wants, which in turn is based on Davidson's Principle of Humanity. This involves a view of a common embodied human nature which rests at the base of our ability to communicate, starting *"from human sayings and doings in an objective world."* (Callinicos, 1987: 110). This enables us to construct theories rooted in this common nature which enable us to get outside the immediate understanding of the participants. In Davidson's words:

> *there is a ground level on which speakers share views, but also that what they share is a largely correct picture of a common world. The ultimate source of both objectivity and communication is the triangle that, by relating speaker, interpreter, and the world, determines the contents of thought and speech. Given this source, there is no room for a relativized concept of truth (in Callinicos, 1995: 82)*

This allows us the possibility of the construction of a theory which locates actors' activities in the broader circumstances in which they occur without reducing one to another. We need such a theory to help us answer a number of questions which are raised, but not dealt with, by Introna's account. These hinge on not only the structural impacts outlined above, but also the issue of managerial interpretation of information. Introna argues for interpretation as a creative act, but recognises that we *"talk of a 'good' or a 'better' interpretation"* in the creative arts (Introna, 1997: 60). What makes one manager's interpretation "better" than another? What sort of constraints and pressures bear upon managers to influence their interpretations? It is suggested that unless we have a theory which allows for both the impact of broader structures *and* the embodied nature of human existence then we will not be able to approach these questions. In Margaret Archer's words:

> on the one hand, 'social psychology' can tell us nothing about individual characteristics such as perception, consciousness and cognition nor about the psychology of personal proclivities and antipathies. Although it may add a great deal about their exercise and even modification in social settings, these autonomous individual properties have to be granted before we can talk of their exercise or modification, and, as features emergent from the biological stratum, they themselves constrain (and enable) what can be socially expressed and modified." (Archer, 1995: 104-5)

What we turn to now is an outline of some components of such a theory. To recap, such a theory starts from the premise of human intentionality, grounded in the relationship between people and nature. It use this relationship to look at the implications of our embodied nature and the limits these place on a purely linguistic theory of understanding. This of necessity involves the construction of an argument based on a wide range of what might appear very disparate literature.

4   CONSTRAINTS ON INFORMATION

We start with Marx's discussion of the labour process, which has at its core a dialectical relationship between people and nature:

> Labour is, in the first place, a process in which both man and Nature participate, and in which man of his own accord starts, regulates, and controls the material re-actions between himself and Nature. He opposes himself to Nature as one of her own forces, setting in motion arms and legs, head and hands, the natural forces of his body, in order to appropriate Nature's productions in a form adapted to his own wants. By thus acting on the external world and changing it, he at the same time changes his own nature. (Marx, 1998: 257)

This approach has three main implications. One is that people are at once a part of nature but at the same time differentiated from it. What causes this differentiation is the presence of intentionality. As Marx puts it in a famous passage:

> *We pre-suppose labour in a form that stamps it as exclusively human. A spider conducts operations that resemble those of a weaver, and a bee puts to shame many an architect in the construction of her cells. But what distinguishes the worst architect from the best of bees is this, that the architect raises his structure in imagination before he erects it in reality. At the end of every labour-process, we get a result that already existed in the imagination of the labourer at its commencement* (Marx, 1998: 257).

This process in turn acquires a social character as people co-operate in order to achieve shared purposes. In this lies the roots of language. The development of our understanding and its mediation through language lies at the heart of the arguments of those who conclude that we *only* understand through language (Bloomfield and Vurdubakis, 1997). Whilst this is undoubtedly the case for much of our understanding, it is possible to argue on one level that this is why we develop all sorts of techniques for scrutinising evidence and subjecting this to analysis. However, at a deeper level, studies of child development would suggest that there are levels of pre-linguistic understanding, understanding deriving from direct operations on nature. Egan, for example, draws upon Vygotsky to argue for 'somatic' understanding, understanding which a child acquires at an early stage of development and which continues to influence and interact with subsequent stages of development. Archer also uses work on conceptual formation before language acquisition to argue against what she sees as an over-socialised conception of the individual (Archer, 1995). The implication is that *"We are human beings before we are languaged human beings. ...Beneath the layers of socialization we are each of us a unique individual consciousness"* (Egan, 1997: 167). This is, of course, a view diametrically opposed to those presented by anti-humanists such as Foucault, with their 'de-centring' of the self, but it seems to accord better with the current scientific work being done. Finally, this understanding points to our embodied nature. There is no Cartesian separation of mind and body, a point which has important implications in its turn for our understanding of language (Damasio, 1995). This is that our use of language is based on metaphors based on our embodied nature and our living in the world. Dualisms such as 'inside/outside' and 'front/back' only make sense in this context (Lakoff and Johnson, 1980). What this suggests is that the range of interpretations is constrained by this common nature, an argument against the infinite play of readings advocated by some post-modernists. To summarise this part of the argument: humans are intentional actors engaged in a dialectical relationship with nature. As part of this relationship they develop a range of ways of knowing. Central to this, but not exhaustive of it, is linguistic understanding, which is an essentially social activity. However, the existence of other forms of understanding points to this social development being a relationship between individual selves. Further, the social understandings built up through language will in turn be based on the embodied nature of human experience.

In Edelman's words, "science-free phenomenology and grammatical exercises, whatever their value, place too narrow a set of limits on the philosophical exercise." (Edelman, 1992: 164). An examination of current work in the areas of consciousness and memory would suggest that there are some biological limitations to thought processes (Searle, 1997). However, they would also suggest that, there are emergent powers of systems, such as memory, which emerge from but are not reducible to more basic strata (Rose, 1993). In turn, these emergent powers at the level of human activity can be modified by the exercise of human intentionality, with a clear example being the transition from orality to literacy. In Ong's words "... these technologies of the word do not merely store what we know. They style what we know in ways which made it quite inaccessible and indeed unthinkable in an oral culture." (Ong, 1982: 155). This grasp of historical transitions is absent, Ong argues, from much of the work of 'textualists' such as Derrida and Foucault. The central concern of the approach championed by Margaret Archer, based on critical realism, is to embody such an historical dimension at the heart of social analysis, coupled with an emphasis on levels of existence, emergent powers and a dialectical relationship between these levels. Such an analysis can attend to the impacts of individual human limitations, the structures which such individuals build and the social interaction through which they build them, without reducing one to the other. What this brief account suggests is that we need an approach which includes the 'throwness' of the manager but which also enables us to look at the dialectic between the embodied nature of the individual manager, with all the limitations of individual psychology, and the structure in those managers find themselves (Mutch, 1998). This can help us find answers to two questions: what impact will information have on the function which managers perform and, within this and given these changes, what implications does information have for the way in managers carry out their activities?

5   CONCLUSION

The focus of this discussion has been on the issues raised by an attempt to marry insights from information systems and organizational theories. Such attempts suggest the need to tackle some more fundamental issues. What implications does this discussion have for future research in the area? This conclusion puts forward some tentative suggestions. One might be that, in the area of systems development, the notion of human involvement has to go beyond attention to the interface and to user participation. It has to grapple with the essentially political nature of the process and to set this in a context which recognises the work done by organisational and social theorists. However, in turn, those working in the organizational arena have to recognise the constraints imposed by systems development, to appreciate that to accept that technology imposes degrees of freedom is not to fall into the trap of technological determinism. In a sense, we have to extend the insight provided by Watson, when he argues that:

> *The challenge facing us is one of ... finding a way of accounting for the fact that managers indeed rarely exhibit the rational, analytical, planning and coordinating and commanding type of behaviour implied by 'classical' (and still popular) definitions of management whilst recognising at the same time that, for an organisation to survive and flourish in its environment, there has to be steering, coordinating, shaping and directing. (Watson, 1994: 37)*

To fulfil these latter tasks modern organisations depend upon IT enabled systems which take a whole variety of forms. These systems have to be designed and developed and this requirement poses real problems for organisational actors. The choices they take are not only conditioned by the context in which they find themselves (which may include a restriction of freedom to act because of previous design decisions by, for example, the developers of packaged software) but also in their turn condition future uses of those systems. Whilst there is choice in the process, the challenge for organisational theorists is to recognise the degree to which this is circumscribed. To facilitate this process there needs to be more contact between the two groups, a call which might reflect current thinking in organizational practice. That is, we are constantly being encouraged to produce graduates who are capable of moving easily between the worlds of IS and business; we also need academics who can achieve the same feat!

Such calls are, of course, bedevilled by issues of language and different ways of viewing the world. That is why debate on such ways of knowing is so important. The contemporary debates on 'knowledge management' offer one opportunity for such a debate to occur. If we return to Holtham's comment with which this paper opened, we can recognise that the issues he raises are now no longer obscure issues of academic debate, but have entrered the organisational mainstream. Now, that entry into the mainstream is often couched in a superficial fashion, but this is why we need more attempts to apply social and philosophical thinking to IS. This paper has argued for a perspective based on the ideas of critical realism as being a useful way of knowing in this area. It is an approach which is starting to have some impact, but which clearly needs further development (Reed, 1997; Samarajiva, 1997). In particular, the suggestion by Archer(1995) that the appropriate deployment of the approach is in the construction of 'analytical narratives' demands that concrete situations be explored. For this particular author, such explorations are in the areas of managerial information use, but there are other areas which might yield fruit. Finally, the debate on ways of knowing has to escape the boundaries of a narrow research community and inform the learning process. If students are to have to deal with a much more fluid, ambiguous world, then they need to recognise the debate which goes on about ways of knowing that world. Of course, this is easier said than done. The pressures of various stakeholders means that space in the curriculum is at a premium and accessible texts which raise these issues are scarce. However, what this might prompt is a debate about the purpose of higher education. If this seen as above all to be about stimulating and developing ways of knowing, as appears to be the thrust of Egan's (1997) challenging argument, then we need to return to the question of how best to bring alive the vital questions that IS raises about the way in which our organisations work.

References

Alvesson M. and Willmott, H., (1996) *Making Sense of Management. A Critical Introduction* Sage, London

Archer M., (1995) *Realist social theory the morphogenetic approach* Cambridge University Press, Cambridge

Armstrong P., (1989) ' Management, Labour Process and Agency ' Work, Employment & Society Vol 3, No 3, pp.307-322

Bloomfield B., Coombs R., Knights D. and Littler D., (1997) *Information Technology and Organizations*, Oxford University Press, Oxford

Bloomfield B. and Vurdubakis T., (1997) 'Paper Traces: Inscribing Organizations and Information Technology', in Bloomfield et al(eds) *Information Technology and Organizations,* pp. 85-111

Callinicos A., (1987) *Making History* Polity, Cambridge

Callinicos A., (1995) *Theories and Narratives* Polity, Cambridge

Crowe M., Beeby, R., and Gammack, J., (1997) *Constructing systems and information a process view* McGraw-Hill, Maidenhead

Damasio A. R., (1995) *Descartes' Error. Emotion, Reason and the Human Brain* Picador, London

Egan K., (1997) *The educated mind: how cognitive tools shape our understanding* University of Chicago, Chicago

Holtham C., (1996) ' Resolving the imbalance between information and technology ' in Best, D (ed) *The fouth resource information and its management,* Gower, Aldershot, pp. 41-58

Introna L. D., (1997) *Management, Information and Power* Macmillan, London

Lakoff G., and Johnson, M., (1980) *Metaphors we live by* University of Chicago Press,Chicago

Littler C. R., (1982) *The Development of the Labour Process in Capitalist Societies* Gower, Aldershot

Mansell R. and Silverstone R., (1997) *Communication by Design. The Politics of Information and Communication Technologies*, Oxford University Press: Oxford

Marglin S. A., (1976) ' What do bosses do? The origins and function of Hierarchy in Capitalist Production ' in Gorz(ed) *The Divsion of Labour*, Harvester, Hassocks, pp. 13-54

Marx K.,(1998) *Capital* Vol 1 ElecBook, London

Mutch A., (1998) ' Information, a Critical Realist Approach ' in *Proceedings of the 2nd Information Seeking in Context Conference* Taylor Graham, London

Ong W. J., (1982) *Orality and Literacy. The Technologizing of the Word* Methuen, London

Reed, M (1997) 'In Praise of Duality and Dualism: Rethinking Agency and Structure in Organizational Analysis', Organizational Studies, Vol 18 No 1, pp. 21-42

Rose S., (1993) *The Making of Memory. From molecules to mind* Bantam, London

Samarajiva R., (1997)   'Surveillance by Design: Public Networks and the Control of Consumption', in Mansell and Silverstone (eds) (1997) *Communication by Design*, pp. 129-156

Watson T., (1994) *In Search of Management. Culture Chaos and Control in Managerial Work* Routledge, London

Willmott H. C., (1998) ' Rethinking Management and Managerial Work Capitalism, Control and Subjectivity ' Human Relations Vol 50 No 11, pp. 1329-1359

Winograd T. and Flores, F. (1986) *Understanding Computers and Cognition. A New Foundation for Design* Addison-Wesley, Reading

CHAPTER 7

INFORMATION SYSTEMS RESEARCH: THE CASE FOR METHODOLOGICAL PLURALISM AND ABDUCTIVE REASONING

Michael Lloyd-Williams and Janet Collins
University of Wales Institute Cardiff

Abstract

Information systems, being a young and emerging discipline, may be viewed as being in a pre-paradigmatic state, or in a state of pre-development. This paper argues that given this situation, researchers within the information systems field should not be tied to a particular methodology or school of thought, but should be flexible in their approach and consider the possibilities offered by methodological pluralism and abductive reasoning when involved in research design activities. The paper concludes with a call for further investigation into how to conduct research within the field of information systems in order that we develop our ways of thinking, rather than remaining restricted in our approach.

1   INTRODUCTION

The current state of the 'discipline' of information systems (IS) has been widely documented in recent years. Among the numerous works discussing this issue are of those of Avison (1997a) and Cornford & Smithson (1996). In such texts, information systems is viewed as being a young, emerging, and indeed dynamic field of study, with contributions from numerous foundation disciplines including computer science, organization theory, business management, sociology, and psychology.

According to Barrow & Thomson (1997), this assortment of contributing disciplines is necessary to be able to comprehend and resolve the wide range of issues that may be encountered within the field of information systems. However, this richness of subject matter brings with it a particular problem - that of which approach to adopt when conducting information systems research. This dilemma is not a recent development, but according to Mingers (1997), has been the focus of concern for some time. The debate remains on-going, being fuelled recently by works including those of Mingers (1997), Allen & Ellis (1997), Barrow & Thomson (1997), and Warren et al (1997). However, there is currently little evidence to indicate that this activity - although valuable - is resulting in a consensus as to which are the most appropriate research techniques. Indeed, Avison (1997a) implies that the current lack of consensus may be viewed as being a *positive* aspect by arguing that those active in the field should not restrict the potential of the discipline by agreeing a limited set of research approaches.

This paper presents the argument that the emerging field of information systems should in fact be considered to be in a pre-paradigmatic state. It discusses some of the current issues facing information systems research, and argues that under such circumstances, researchers within the information systems field should not be tied to a particular methodology or school of thought, but be flexible in their approach. The paper concludes by arguing that researchers should consider the possibilities offered by methodological pluralism and abductive reasoning when involved in research design activities.

2 INFORMATION SYSTEMS AS A PRE-PARADIGMATIC DISCIPLINE

According to Kuhn's (1970, 1977) widely accepted notion of a disciplinary paradigm, a paradigm describes the *"entire constellation of beliefs, values, techniques, and so on"* shared by the discipline (Kuhn, 1970, p.175). Such paradigms may be viewed as being *well developed* or in a stage of *pre-development*. Bulick (1982) argues that a paradigmatic discipline is characterised by coherence of content, i.e., where a consensus exists regarding subject matter. A lack of such coherence (according to Bulick) is evidence of a discipline being in *a pre-paradigmatic* state. However, Bulick continues to argue that even a discipline which does exhibit a degree of consensus may *"share much of its subject content with other disciplines"* (Bulick, 1982, p. 3).

Adam & Fitzgerald (1996) maintain that the field of information systems is characterised by a lack of intellectual focus. Galliers et al (1997) cite the work of Dickson et al (1980) in describing the identity crisis and definitional uncertainty of the field. These claims are further supported by Warren et al (1997), who assert that information systems lacks definition in terms of its academic territory.

Given that the existence of a paradigm in its true sense is dependent upon a the existence of a consensus, then it must be accepted that information systems, being a young and emerging discipline, should be viewed as being in Bulick's (1982) pre-paradigmatic state, or indeed in Kuhn's (1970) state of pre-development. This is not to say that the field of information systems is not completely without coherence or consensus, but that this consensus is still developing.

3   INFORMATION SYSTEMS RESEARCH

Information systems research has been previously dominated by positivist approaches (Orlikowski & Baroudi, 1991; Kaplan & Douchon, 1988). However, in recent years, more naturalistic forms of enquiry have been employed by information systems researchers. Examples of such naturalistic approaches include interpretivism (Walsham, 1995), action research (Baskerville & Wood-Harper; 1998; Avison, 1997b), and case study research (Kaplan & Duchon, 1988). Rather than advocating the use of any single paradigm, Mingers (1997) advocates the combination of methodologies in a multi-paradigm research. Despite such necessary contributions to the on-going debate, Allen & Ellis (1997) cite Visala (1991) in describing the current theoretical position of information systems research as being one of fragmentation and unco-ordination. Allen & Ellis (1997) continue their criticism in arguing that cumulative traditions are rare, and that the field is divided into a number of schools and trends.

Moreover, the usefulness of the research performed using such approaches has been called into question. According to Warren et al (1997) and Senn (1998), there is often a mismatch between academic research and practitioner interests. Senn (1998) claims that much of information systems academic research is seen as untimely and mostly irrelevant on the part of information systems practitioners. This raises questions in relation to the validity of academic information systems research agendas. The apparent mismatch also suggests that the concept of what actually constitutes *good* research should be examined. Research may be respectable in terms of following expected procedures and adopting an appropriate philosophical stance, but may be of little practical use. Similarly, research may be of great practical use, but may not be credible in the eyes of certain purists. Much published research may also be criticised due to a lack of clarity in terms of stating philosophical assumptions. Many published articles appear to exhibit a level of confusion when discussing methodological aspects, whereas others do not even attempt to include a discussion of such issues.

Information systems research can therefore draw certain parallels with the current situation facing educational research. Both are inter-disciplinary fields, and both have academic and practitioner populations. Wilson (1998) compares educational research with research in the natural sciences, which allows predictions to be made that are well above the level of common sense. He argues that educational research exhibits no solid corpus of knowledge analogous to that of the natural sciences, and questions how many truths are provided by educational researchers that are demonstrably true, significantly above the level of common sense, and of direct practical value. Many of Wilson's (1998) arguments may also be applied to information systems research, which also lacks a consensual corpus of knowledge. We may also question how many truths are provided by information systems researchers that are demonstrably true, significantly above the level of common sense, and of direct practical value. This is not to claim that no such facts relating to information systems exist, but that they are limited in number. Wilson argues that the reason researchers experience difficulties within educational research is due to the fact that they are not clear about the field, the procedures, and the methodologies appropriate to it. We can thus draw further parallels with the field of information systems research, given the criticisms discussed previously in this paper, and - given the lack of a corpus of knowledge - may even go as far as to question whether we actually now *how* to carry out information systems research.

If we consider Wilson's (1998) views as being appropriate for the information systems research field, then his approach to facilitating progress should also be considered. Wilson encourages researchers to develop general qualities and abilities rather than religiously following predefined formats in the hope that results will eventually emerge. Moreover, in addition to a general knowledge of the *"various 'schools' or 'isms', researchers should be encouraged to think philosophically for themselves about their research topic, and the concepts and values embedded in it"* (Wilson, 1998, p. 163).

Information systems researchers should therefore not be tied to a particular methodology or school of thought, but should select the most appropriate research approach according to the prevailing circumstances. This argument may be linked directly to the concept of the researcher as *bricoleur*, as promoted by Denzin & Lincoln (1994). The concept is founded upon the view that the various methodologies available in the social sciences form a *bricolage*, and that the effective researcher should act as a bricoleur, combining available approaches as befitting a given situation. According to Denzin & Lincoln (1994), the bricoleur may not behave in a way expected or indeed accepted by the purists, however the approach is effective and gets the job done.

This view of adopting the most suitable approach for the job-in-hand rather than being constrained by a desire to adhere to a particular philosophical stance or research methodology appears to support the postmodern view that no methodology or paradigm should be viewed as being authoritative. However, we raise at this juncture a caveat to the effect that this paper is not proposing that we abandon all thoughts of rigour and adopt a less disciplined approach toward our research, but that the information systems researcher should develop an awareness of the suitable approaches for a given situation and utilise these approaches as appropriate. Given that the field of information systems is pre-paradigmatic, we should give significant thought to furthering our knowledge of *how* to conduct research within this rich and diverse subject-area, developing our *ways of thinking* rather than remaining limited in our approach.

4   THE CASE FOR METHODOLOGICAL PLURALISM AND ABDUCTIVE REASONING

Before further discussing the philosophical issues surrounding the potential for combining research methodologies and methods, it is appropriate to briefly address what is meant by research. There are many definitions of research in the extant literature, including Drew's (1980) "*systematic method of enquiry*", Stenhouse's (1981) "*systematic self-critical enquiry*", and Kerlinger's (1970) "*systematic and controlled empirical and critical investigation*". It is manifest that the consistent article in these (and indeed other) definitions is the notion that research is based upon a process of *systematic* and *controlled* enquiry. In other words, research should be sustained by a strategy, be disciplined, and be performed in a methodical fashion.

Prior to discussing the opportunities presented by methodological pluralism for research within the field of information systems, it should be made clear at this point that it is not the intention to preclude orthodox or quantitative research approaches from the discipline. Indeed, there is ample evidence both of the need for, and the use and practice of, quantitative approaches to performing information systems research. However, the scope of a quantitative approach may be extended to provide accounts of regularities and patterns (Bryman 1988) which can be used to assess, and even hypothesise, contextual and structural (qualitative) changes and diversities in the role of information systems within institutions. Apart from quantitative approaches, qualitative research can also be useful in helping us to understand the processual and evolving view of information systems and the information systems discipline.

An emerging information systems paradigm should not be dictated to by the separate existence of its inherent disciplines and methodologies; the latter should only serve to form the key perspectives and fundamental presuppositions which inform the research process and practice. For this to occur, experienced researchers and mentors should avoid being wedded to the search for one correct discipline and method, and systematically develop and apply a variety of complementing ontological and epistemological perspectives and assumptions in the method of enquiry (Atkinson 1995). Furthermore, it is possible that the information systems research community could generate many broad family resemblances between the contributing multidisciplinary paradigms, in terms of their collective assumptions, methods, and kind of data.

Allen & Ellis (1997) present powerful arguments for and against methodological pluralism in information systems. For the information systems discipline to progress towards a coherence of content it requires contexts of informed discussion, debate and intellectual imagination. Leininger (1995) urges researchers however to develop an in depth understanding of paradigms and their concomitant differences, and to endeavour to preserve the purpose and philosophy of each paradigm. She welcomes methodological pluralism with the proviso that the above understanding is nurtured and adhered to, whereby paradigms could well *complement* each other in the discovery of phenomena, theories and conceptual frameworks.

Peirce (1935) identified the abductive process as a progressive force contributing to scientific enquiry. Hoffman (1997) cites Peirce (1903) in defining abduction as "*the process of forming an explanatory hypothesis*". Using his original conception of pragmatism, Peirce viewed the process of enquiry as encompassing three components; deduction, induction and abduction. He argued for abductive reasoning and logic to contrast with the polar opposites of inductive and deductive logic. Willer & Webster (1970) outline the following stages within the abductive process which enable the reformulation of observable concepts to more abstract theoretical constructs:

- compile a list of observational assertions and concepts (continuously formulate, reject and reformulate concepts progressing towards theoretical constructs);
- organise or codify abstract statements and developed constructs and begin systematisation of theory;
- test developed constructs through inductive and deductive processes.

The processes of deduction and induction are used to draw inferences from the testing, confirming and where necessary modification of hypotheses by abductive reflection. Abductive inference requires a repeated interaction between existing ideas, former findings and observations, new observations, and new ideas. It requires researchers to posses an open-minded intellectual approach to embrace the dynamic, complex and multidisciplinary nature of information systems. Smith & Pitman (1997) discuss how the above approach, accompanied by deductive and inductive reflection, is considered relevant for conceptualising human nature as an evolutionary process which is driven by technology and culture. Hoffman (1998) illustrates that many of the discussions of the work of Peirce appear to exhibit a level of misunderstanding of the use of the pragmatist philosophy as a logic of enquiry. For example, abductive reasoning clearly forms a developmental role in theory formulation, as well as in the understanding of practical issues within information systems. Bartlett & Payne (1997) cite Corbin & Strauss (1990) in describing how the original grounded theory derives its theoretical underpinnings from pragmatism (abductive reasoning) and symbolic interactionism. The use of grounded theory to facilitate theory formulation has been previously advocated by Orlikowski (1993), as cited by Avison (1997a).

Furthermore, the essence of Peirce's definition of pragmatism can be interpreted as *complementing* nomothetic and ideographic research ideas and tools in a way which is *not* epistemologically confused as it is the logic of deduction which is applied to test theoretical constructs or find patterns in inductive and contextual data. Using the philosophy of pragmatism and abductive reasoning, Coffey & Atkinson (1996, p. 156) advocate the need for researchers to *"break free of the straight jackets of conventional logic"* of deduction and induction and not to be content to slot data into existing frameworks and ideas. They also argue for the need to avoid 'text book' methodological approaches and recommend greater discourse and communication between research in order to discover consistent and coherent sets of theoretical assumptions, perspectives or paradigms, with congruent methodological principles.

5   CONCLUSIONS

This paper has presented the argument that the emerging field of information systems should be considered to be in a pre-paradigmatic state, and that information systems researchers should not therefore be tied to any particular methodology or school of thought. Rather than focusing upon specific methodologies, we should accept that information systems is an inter-disciplinary field and exploit the various research approaches available as appropriate. This is not to suggest that we abandon the principle of rigour and adopt a less disciplined approach to our research, but that we adopt the most suitable approach for a given situation.

The paper concludes by arguing that under these circumstances, researchers should consider the possibilities offered by methodological pluralism and abductive reasoning when involved in research design activities. This stance suggests that we require further investigation into *how* to conduct research within the field of information systems in order to develop new *ways of thinking* rather than remaining limited in our approach. It is important therefore to map-out and clarify the changes which are occurring in the use, understanding and application of methodologies and methods within the information systems discipline. A potential starting point would require the information systems research community clearly identifying the philosophical assumptions underpinning their work in their published material.

References

Adam, F. & Fitzgerald, B. "A Framework for Analysing the Evolution of the IS Field - Can IS Become a Stable Discipline?", In: Coelho, D.J., Jelassi, T., Konig, W., Krcmar, H., O'Callaghan, R. & Saaksjarvi, M. (eds.), *Proceedings of the 4th European Conference on Information Systems*, pp. 17-32. Lisbon, 1996.

Allen, D. & Ellis, D. "Beyond Paradigm Closure in Information Systems Research: Theoretical Possibilities for Pluralism", In: Galliers, R., Carlsson, S., Loebbecke, C., Murphy, C., Hansen, H.R. & O'Callaghan, R. (eds.), *Proceedings of the 5th European Conference on Information Systems*, pp. 737-759. Cork Publishing Ltd, Cork, 1997.

Atkinson, P. "Some Perils of Paradigms" *Qualitative Health Research*, 5(1), 117-124, 1995.

Avison, D.E. "The Search for the 'Discipline' of Information Systems", In: McKenzie, G., Powell, J. & Usher, R (eds.), *Understanding Social Research: Perspectives on Methodology and Practice*, pp. 87-100. Falmer Press, London, 1997a.

Avison, D.E. "Action Research in Information Systems", In: McKenzie, G., Powell, J. & Usher, R (eds.), *Understanding Social Research: Perspectives on Methodology and Practice*, pp. 196-209. Falmer Press, London, 1997b.

Barrow, P.D.M. & Thomson, H.E. "Choosing Methods for Information Systems Research", In: Avison, D.E. (ed.), *Proceedings of the 2nd UKAIS Conference*, pp. 239-251. McGraw Hill, Maidenhead, 1997.

Bartlett, D. & Payne, S. "Grounded Theory- Its Basis, Rationale and Procedures", In: McKenzie, G., Powell, J. & Usher, R (eds.), *Understanding Social Research: Perspectives on Methodology and Practice*, pp. 173-195. Falmer Press, London, 1997.

Bryman, A. *Quantity and Quality in Social Research*. Routledge, London, 1988.

Bulick, S. *Structure and Subject Interaction*. Marcel Dekker, New York, NY, 1982.

Coffey, A. & Atkinson, P. *Making Sense of Qualitative Data*. SAGE Publications, Thousand Oaks, CA, 1996.

Corbin, J. & Strauss, A. "Grounded Theory Research: Procedures, Canons and Evaluative Criteria" *Qualitative Sociology*, 13(1), 3-21, 1990.

Cornford, T. & Smithson, S. *Project Research in Information Systems*. MacMillan, Basingstoke, 1996.

Denzin, N.K. & Lincoln, Y.S. "Entering the Field of Qualitative Research", In: Denzin, N.K. & Lincoln, Y.S.(eds.), *Handbook of Qualitative Research*, pp. 1-17. SAGE Publications, Thousand Oaks, CA, 1994.

Dickson, G.W., Benbasat, I. & King, W.R. "The Management Information Systems Area: Problems, Challenges and Opportunities", In: *Proceedings of the 1st International Conference on Information Systems*, pp. 1-8. 1980.

Drew, C.J. *Introduction to Designing and Conducting Research* (2nd ed.). Mosby, St. Louis, MO, 1980.

Galliers, R.D., Mylonopoulos, N.A. Morris, C. & Meadows, M. "IS Research Agendas and Practices in the UK", In: Avison, D.E. (ed.), *Proceedings of the 2nd UKAIS Conference*, pp. 143-171. McGraw Hill, Maidenhead, 1997.

Hoffman, M. "Is There a Logic of Abduction?", In: *Proceedings of the 6th Congress of the IASS-AIS International Association for Semiotic Studies*, 1997 (Also available at: [http://www.uni-bielefeld.de/idm/mhoffman/abduct.htm]. Site visited: 29/10/98.

Kaplan, B. & Duchon, D. "Combining Qualitative and Quantitative Methods in Information Systems Research: A Case Study" *MIS Quarterly*, 12(4), 571-586, 1988.

Kerlinger, F.N. *Foundations of Behavioral Research*. Holt, Rinehart & Winston, New York, NY, 1970.

Kuhn, T.S. *The Structure of Scientific Revolutions* (2nd ed.). University of Chicago Press Chicago, IL, 1970.

Kuhn, T.S. *The Essential Tension*. University of Chicago Press Chicago, IL, 1977.

Leininger, M. "Current Issues, Problems, and Trends to Advance Qualitative Paradigmatic Research Methods for the Future" *Qualitative Health Research*, 2(4), 392-415, 1995.

Mingers, J. "Combining Research Methods in Information Systems: Multi-Paradigm Methodology", In: Galliers, R., Carlsson, S., Loebbecke, C., Murphy, C., Hansen, H.R. & O'Callaghan, R. (eds.), *Proceedings of the 5th European Conference on Information Systems*, pp. 760-776. Cork Publishing Ltd, Cork, 1997.

Orlikowski, W.J. "CASE Tools as Organizational Change: Investigating Incremental and Radical Changes in Systems Development" *MIS Quarterly*, 17(3), 309-340, 1993.

Peirce, C.S. *The 1903 Harvard Lectures on Pragmatism*, 1903. (Also appeared in *Pragmatism as a Principle and Method of Right Thinking*, Turrisi, P.A. (Editor), State University of New York Press, NY, 1997.

Peirce, C.S. *Collected Papers, Vol 6*. Harvard University Press, Cambridge, MA, 1935.

Senn, J. "*The Challenge of Relating IS Research to Practice*" Information Resources Management Journal, 11(1), 23-28, 1998.

Smith, R. & Pitman, J. "Long-Run Dynamic Change in Economic Systems: Implications of an Emergent Information and Communications and Technology Paradigm", In: Dunn, S.P., Fontana, G., Forde, C., Jenkins, E., Petrick, K., Roy, A., Slater, G. & Spencer, D. (ed.), *Proceedings of the 2nd Annual Postgraduate Economics Conference*, pp. 3-22. University of Leeds, Leeds, 1997.

Stenhouse, L. "What Counts as Research?" *British Journal of Educational Studies*, XXIX(2), 103-113, 1981.

Warren, L., Hitchin, L. & Brayshaw, M. "IS: The Challenge of Neo-Disciplinary Research", In: Avison, D.E. (ed.), *Proceedings of the 2nd UKAIS Conference*, pp. 187-194. McGraw Hill, Maidenhead, 1997.

Willer, D. & Webster, M. "Theoretical Concepts and Observables" *American Sociological Review*, 35, 748-757, 1970.

Wilson, J. "Preconditions for Educational Research" *Educational Research*, 40(2), 161-167, 1998.

CHAPTER 8

MISSION IMPOSSIBLE? PLURALISM AND MULTIPARADIGM IS RESEARCH

Matthew Jones
University of Cambridge

Abstract

Recent contributions to the debate in the IS and organisational literature on research paradigms have suggested that multi-paradigmatic research is both possible and desirable. In this paper it will be argued that this view is unsustainable if we accept that paradigms should be philosophically self-consistent. A critical analysis of allegedly multi-paradigmatic IS research is presented and three responses to paradigmatic diversity discussed. It is argued that pluralism need not mean relativism, nor preclude communication between incompatible paradigms. A dialogical model of paradigm interaction is proposed and its implications discussed.

1   INTRODUCTION

> *Alice laughed. "There's no use trying," she said, "one can't believe impossible things.""I daresay you haven't had much practice," said the Queen. "When I was your age, I always did it for half-an-hour a day. Why, sometimes I've believed as many as six impossible things before breakfast."*
> *(Lewis Carroll, Alice Through the Looking Glass)*

The issue of whether it is possible for IS researchers to engage, individually, in work in more than one research "paradigm" and whether, collectively, it is desirable for them to do so has been a regular theme in the IS literature (Allen & Ellis, 1997; Gable, 1992; Kaplan & Duchon, 1988; Landry & Banville, 1992; Lee, 1991; Mingers, 1997). This debate may be seen as reflecting similar discussions in related research fields such as organisational studies (DeCock & Rickards, 1995; Deetz, 1996; Gioia & Pitre, 1990; Hassard, 1991; Jackson & Carter, 1991, 1993; Parker & McHugh, 1990; Reed, 1985; Weaver & Gioia, 1994; Willmott, 1993) around the four "paradigm" framework of Burrell & Morgan (1979) (hereafter B&M) and their claims that these represented fundamentally incommensurable positions.

A number of the IS contributors have argued that B&M's incommensurability thesis is flawed, and hence that multiparadigmatic research is possible, and probably desirable. The aim of this paper is to explore the reasoning behind these arguments and to show how they are based on a number of confusions. It will be argued that some forms of multi-paradigmatic research within a single intervention are not possible, unless (like the Red Queen in *Alice Through the Looking Glass*) we suspend normal criteria of philosophical consistency. The implications of this position for IS research will be explored.

2   ALL PARADIGMS GREAT AND SMALL?

The confusions which beset discussion of research paradigms in the IS field are often attributable to weaknesses in B&M's original argument. Before we can begin to assess the feasibility of multi-paradigmatic IS research we therefore need to understand these problems.

The first, and probably most fundamental, problem arises from limitations of B&M's framework. In attempting to categorise all sociological and organisational research within a 2x2 matrix, B&M took considerable liberties in reducing differences to just two dimensions (objective/subjective, order/conflict), and insisting that particular types of research fall unambiguously on one side or the other of their dichotomies. As   B&M admit, their selection of ontology and ideology as the primary distinguishing feature of research methods neglects significant epistemological and praxiological issues and may also be argued to oppose two inconsistent dimensions which could not be expected to provide the basis for a robust classification. Arguments based solely on critiques of B&M's flawed framework would therefore appear insufficient to sustain the case for multi-paradigmatic IS research.

A further legacy of B&M evident in debates in the IS field, has been their (acknowledged) loose usage of the term paradigm, which they adopted from Kuhn (1962). Thus, as Willmott (1993) argues, B&M's usage is not only inconsistent with Kuhn, who himself employed more than 21 different meanings (Masterman, 1970), but also contradicts some of his key assumptions about the dynamics of theory development in the natural sciences which would challenge their strong incommensurability argument. This is not to argue that Kuhn's model of the scientific process is correct, but that, if debates about "multi-paradigm" research are to be meaningful, then the term needs to be clearly defined. At minimum this would seem to require that research paradigms[i] comprise a reasonably consistent set of beliefs about the nature of the phenomena being studied. As the discussion above has illustrated, however, it is not clear that this is the case for B&M's quadrants.

As B&M discuss, any piece of research involves a complex assemblage of assumptions which they characterise in terms of several oppositions: nominalism *vs* realism; anti-positivism *vs* positivism; voluntarism *vs* determinism; ideographic *vs* nomothetic theory; order *vs* conflict. As Archer (1988) argues, however, this is a simplification, and the key dimensions of ontology and epistemology may be seen as comprising three, rather than two, positions. Thus the ontological choice is not simply between external realism and subjective idealism, but may also include internal realism, which views reality as an inter-subjective construction of the shared human cognitive apparatus. Similarly, on the epistemological dimension Archer identifies positivism (facts and values are distinct and scientific knowledge consists only of facts), non-positivism (facts and values are intertwined and both are involved in scientific knowledge) and normativism (scientific knowledge is ideological). While evidence may suggest that some combinations of these assumptions are more plausible than others, for example nominalist, voluntarist, anti-positivist, and ideographic or realist, determinist, positivist and nomothetic, it is not clear that other combinations are necessarily inconsistent (Hammersley, 1992). Thus a researcher could be an internal realist, normativist, voluntarist and ideographic or internal realist, normativist, determinist and ideographic depending on the degree to which they attributed influence to social structure or human agency. The complete adumbration of these alternative positions is beyond the scope of this paper. It is sufficient for the present argument, however, to show that there may be several possible combinations, and almost certainly more than the two (positivist and interpretivist) around which much IS debate revolves (Walsham, 1995).

The number of possible combinations, however, would seem to be limited by the mutual exclusivity of certain assumptions. For example it would seem difficult to be a subjective idealist and also a positivist. Some combinations may also be impossible because they would involve simultaneous belief in incompatible positions. For example, a researcher must decide whether they believe that reality is subjective, objective or inter-subjective, or whether they are engaged in establishing context-specific patterns or law-like generalisations. To suggest that such choices can be avoided is to dismiss the need for researchers to adopt a coherent philosophical position. Similarly, to argue for the serial use of multiple paradigms within a single piece of research, as Hassard (1991), Deetz (1996) and Mingers (1997) appear to advocate, would require the researcher to engage in a philosophical *volte face* on some central aspect of their belief system. As Parker & McHugh (1990) suggest, this would seem to imply either: that core beliefs can be changed as an act of will; that the researcher is capable of "authentically" feigning alternative beliefs; or that they have multiple personalities which dominate at different times. At some level, therefore, some forms of multi-paradigm research would be ruled out, as not all consistent sets of assumptions are mutually compatible.

Whether this precludes communication between these paradigms will be returned to later, but we may note that this definition is rather narrower than is sometimes found in the IS and organisational literature. Thus, as Hammersley (1992) illustrates, despite the widespread reference, even in apparently "respectable" circles (eg Brannen, 1992; Cresswell, 1994), to "qualitative" and "quantitative" paradigms, the types of data collected by researchers does not determine their philosophical assumptions. Similar problems arise with the use of paradigm as a synonym for a wide variety of other terms such as research methodology, research approach, (data-gathering) method, and IS development or management science methodology. Thus, although particular methodologies, approaches, or methods may normally be aligned with particular philosophical positions, they do not (*contra* Bryman, 1992), of themselves, constitute a coherent paradigm, nor does this habitual alignment necessarily preclude their use within another paradigm. Nominally "multi-paradigm" research in such contexts would therefore only be problematic insofar as particular combinations of methods, approaches or methodologies could be shown to be precluded by incompatible philosophical assumptions.

In arguing that some paradigms are incommensurable, this position clearly contradicts the views of proponents of multi-paradigm research such as Lee (1991) and Mingers (1997). What is more, these proponents would seem likely to suggest, it appears to fly in the face of practical evidence of a number of cases of successful multi-paradigm research. Before considering the theoretical and practical implications of the position it would thus seem necessary to respond to these objections. In order to do so we will analyse four studies which have been cited as examples of multi-paradigm research in order to see how they would be understood within the position outlined above.

2.1   Evidence of multi-paradigm research?

The first example of allegedly multi-paradigm research, although not identified as such by the authors, is Kaplan & Duchon (1988). This study illustrates how the combination of qualitative and quantitative methods does not involve paradigmatic choices. Thus, although Kaplan & Duchon discuss both positivist and interpretive perspectives and their association with quantitative and qualitative methods, the combination of methods is presented as providing a "richer contextual basis for interpreting and validating results". Interviews and observations were used to gain understanding of the context and to develop questionnaire items. Subsequent qualitative analysis of interview data was used to develop an interpretive model which suggested additional variables for quantitative analysis. In paradigm terms, therefore, although the authors' specific philosophical assumptions are not discussed in detail, it would appear that quantitative data was treated as supplementary evidence for an interpretive study.

A second example of mixed methods is provided by Gable (1994) on the integration of case study and survey methods. Here the philosophical position is predominantly positivist, emphasising "natural controls", triangulation, and the construction and testing of a causal model. The case is seen as a preliminary, exploratory pilot study aimed at identifying variables and relationships which could then be expressed as hypotheses. Although Gable suggests that the case study may also provide "rich detail to aid in the interpretation of quantitative findings" and as an "aid in identifying alternative *ex post* models" this would seem to suggest an inconsistent epistemological stance since such *post hoc* theoretical adjustment is incompatible with the principles of hypothesis testing

(Moser & Kalton, 1971).

A more complex example is provided by Markus (1994). She uses both a specific hypothesis test, of information richness theory, and an interpretive analysis of archival data of email use supplemented by interviews. The falsification of hypotheses might seem to suggest a positivist epistemology and indeed the survey was carefully designed to conform with the precepts of theory-testing. In the analysis, however, the disconfirmation of the hypothesis is just the starting point for an extended interpretive analysis. Thus, the discussion and conclusions emphasise that individual level theories do not provide an adequate explanation of observed behaviours and that constraints and capabilities of technologies in practice are not determined by material characteristics, but are subject to social influence. In paradigmatic terms, therefore, the survey results are not seen as providing a complete, objective description of email use, but as requiring supplementation by more qualitative data to understand the phenomena. Nor are the findings interpreted as supporting law-like generalisations.

The final example, Lee, (1991), is perhaps one of the most developed attempts to challenge the incommensurability thesis and is widely cited in the IS literature. It claims to provide an integrated framework for combining positivist and interpretivist research based on a triangular model of the relationship between the subjective understanding of social actors, the interpretive understanding of the social researcher and the positivist understanding of the same (or possibly a different) researcher, each of which mutually reinforce each other.

Lee argues that interpretive researchers develop their understanding of social phenomena through access to the subjective understanding of social actors. This understanding may be verified by reference back to the subjective understanding. The positivist researcher then uses the interpretive understanding as the basis for developing a theoretical understanding of the phenomena which reflect the subjective understanding (as interpreted by the researcher). This positive understanding is then used to develop predictions which are tested by reference to the actual behaviours of the social actors, deriving from their subjective understanding. The use of the framework is illustrated by reference to a study of the criminal justice system which combines interpretive analysis, based on six months of participant observation, with multiple regression analysis.

Although Lee argues that he fully incorporates both positivist and interpretivist approaches, there are a number of significant problems with this model which suggest that paradigmatic differences are not so easily overcome. Perhaps the most serious difficulty from an interpretivist perspective is the suggestion that the positivist understanding corresponds to the interpretive understanding and that disconfirmation of a positivist hypothesis can be used to revise the interpretive understanding. Quite apart from the implicit suggestion that the positivist understanding provides a "truer" and "more scientific" appreciation of social phenomena, this assumes that an interpretivist researcher would accept an hypothesis test as an appropriate guide to the revision of an interpretive understanding, especially without reference to the understanding of the social actors. The criminal justice case discussion provides little help in this respect since the original "interpretive understanding" was not derived from empirical interpretive research, but was an assumption of a particular theoretical model. At best, therefore, it would seem that this claim is not proven. From a philosophical perspective we may also draw attention to the contradiction between the positivist view of social actors, which, as Lee states, sees them as "puppets" with specifiable responses to known opportunities and constraints, with the interpretive view of knowledgeable agents with an awareness not only of their own condition, but also, in principle, of the researchers' interpretations. For a single researcher to sustain both beliefs about social actors simultaneously would, as Parker & McHugh (1991) have argued, seem inconsistent.

The analysis of the four papers would suggest, therefore, that these apparent examples of multi-paradigm research are either single paradigm studies, according to the definition presented here, or involve unsustainable philosophical positions. It must be acknowledged, however, that this conclusion represents a particular interpretation from a particular, interpretive, viewpoint. While this indicates that a decisive refutation of the claims of multi-paradigm proponents is not possible given the different assumptions and definitions employed, it also points us towards a number of broader implications of the position to which we will now turn.

3   INCOMMENSURABILITY, INTERESTS AND PLURALISM

The debate about multi-paradigm research in the IS and organisational literature is notable for the heat that is generated around apparently esoteric issues. To understand the reasons for this it is necessary to appreciate what is at stake. Thus, behind the philosophical arguments there are powerful interests at work. These may be considered in relation to three alternative responses to the "problem" of paradigmatic diversity: paradigmatic unity; metatheoretical transcendence and pluralism.

3.1   Paradigmatic unity

Perhaps the most straightforward debate, in which differences in interests are highlighted, relates to paradigmatic unity. This goes back to the origins of the social sciences and Comte's attempt to establish a science of society on the same model as that of the natural sciences. Proponents of paradigmatic unity tend to argue for methodological unity, or monism (Landry & Banville, 1992), suggesting that the methods of the natural sciences provide the only reliable way to acquire knowledge, and that all social scientists should therefore adopt them. This is seen as necessary to ensure the academic credibility of the social sciences and their development from a current state of paradigmatic immaturity towards consensus and a cumulative knowledge base. This view has been forcefully expressed in organisation science by Pfeffer (1993, 1995). A similar argument has been advanced in the IS field by Backhouse et al (1991).

Such arguments have, not surprisingly, evoked strong reactions on two main fronts.

The first has been to challenge the notion of the methodological unity of the natural and social sciences by appeals to the importance of the subjective experience of social actors (including researchers themselves) and their agency, in understanding social phenomena. For proponents of this view, all social research is "irretrievably hermeneutic" (Giddens, 1993). The second reaction has been to see the methodological unity argument as a more or less crude attempt by functionalist/positivist researchers to reinforce their dominance of the organisational (Gioia & Pitre, 1990) and IS (Orlikowski & Baroudi, 1991) research communities, especially in the USA. While some opponents of this perceived positivist "takeover bid", such as Van Maanen (1995a, 1995b), have questioned the practical possibility of imposing such uniformity and have argued that it would suppress "style, breadth, theoretical and methodological innovation" in organisational research, others have seized on the B&M framework to argue for the impossibility of consensus. As Reed (1985) noted, B&M may be read as proposing the view that functionalism was just one of four, equally valid paradigms and that each should, and could, develop independently. We will return to criticisms of this position in the discussion of pluralism below, but for the moment we simply note that paradigm incommensurability is embroiled in an academic controversy as a purported bulwark against functionalist hegemony.

3.2   Metaparadigmatic transcendence

For opponents of paradigmatic unity who are uncomfortable with B&M's isolationist position, an alternative solution to the problem of paradigmatic diversity has been to argue for the use of a meta-paradigm perspective which transcends the differences between the quadrants. Gioia & Pitre (1990) and Weaver and Gioia (1994) have been leading advocates of this approach, drawing on the work of Giddens (1993). Structuration Theory, it is argued, by recasting structure and agency as a duality rather than a polarised dualism, offers a metatheory which can provide a bridge between the competing paradigms, enabling the "self-stultifying incommensurability thesis" to be overcome (Weaver & Gioia, 1994:565).

As Gioia and Pitre (1990) acknowledge, however, retreating to the metatheoretical high ground does not escape the underlying paradigmatic divisions. A metaparadigmatic position will necessarily be "rooted" in the assumptions of one particular paradigm, reflecting the 'typical' stance of the individual researcher. Although they suggest that this bias may be overcome by "multiple viewers, preferably from multiple paradigms" (Gioia & Pitre, 1990: 597), all this would appear to do is to raise the paradigmatic debate to a new level (itself requiring metaparadigmatic transcendence - and so on *ad infinitum*?). Gioia & Pitre's appeal to Giddens would also seem problematic given his essentially idealist position, which sees social structures as "virtual orders" only ever existing as "traces in the mind". To suggest, therefore, that Structuration is compatible with all paradigms is to ignore central features of Giddens's argument. For example, as DeCock & Rickards (1995) note, that both Giddens and Functionalists both use the term structure does not mean that they are referring to the same concept. Indeed, the quite specific, and idiosyncratic, meaning of structure adopted by Giddens is precisely intended to avoid such conflation.

3.3   Pluralism

If paradigm transcendence is not possible and unity infeasible, then pluralism, the belief that "truth admits of more than one valid formulation" (Ford, 1990), must be accepted. Watson (1990) identifies four types: perspectival; pluralism of hypotheses; methodological; and archic. Perspectival pluralism suggests that individuals do not experience the same world and thus that each of us has their own reality. It therefore admits of no common reality and would suggest that different views may be genuinely incommensurable. Pluralism of hypotheses suggests that there is a single reality, but that different opinions about it are possible. Such opinions may be incompatible, but incompatibility will disappear as truth is discovered. Methodological pluralists also suggest that there is one truth, but that individual perspectives provide only partial access to it. Different views are not ultimately incompatible, since reality is such as to justify and relate these partial views. For archic pluralists, reality is constituted by the inquirer, so that each philosophy has its own reality. As it is mind that constitutes the real and mind is shared, then mutual intelligibility is possible as individual perspectives reflect essential possibilities of reason.

Although not phrased in his terms, Watson's types may be used to classify the different pluralist positions in the debate on research paradigms. Perspectival pluralists would adopt the "let 1,000 flowers bloom" position of radical post-modernism. In denying the priority of any metanarratives with which to adjudicate between positions, "anything goes" (Feyerabend, 1975). All paradigms are equal and the researcher is entirely free to pursue whatever approach they wish. While it could be argued that this may promote innovation and heterodoxy, it is precisely the danger against which the paradigmatic unitarists warn. Moreover, as Norris (1996) argues, such relativism has corrosive ethical and political consequences which negate its apparently emancipatory rhetoric. In accepting pluralism, however, we need not abandon rationality (Roth, 1990), and, as Watson shows, there are alternatives.

Pluralists of hypotheses would seem likely to adopt a contingent approach to paradigm choice. Here it is a matter of "horses for courses". Contingency advocates recognise a limited number of methods as valid, and argue that the right choice depends on the particular research question. While this is clearly a less restrictive position than paradigmatic unity, it often carries the assumption that research questions have an intrinsic character for which certain methods are best suited and that convergence toward a common understanding is the goal.

Methodological pluralists, such as Mingers (1997) would suggest that different approaches provide only partial access to a complex reality. A mixture of methods is therefore necessary and ultimately reconcilable. As has been discussed however, such an approach risks philosophical inconsistency.

Archic pluralism would seem to suggest two possible outcomes, one of which is presented by proponents of paradigm incommensurability, where each paradigm develops in splendid isolation. Critics of this paradigmatic apartheid (Reed, 1985; Willmott, 1993), however, suggest that in defending the principle of "equal, but different", advocates such as Jackson & Carter (1991) risk stifling productive debate. Moreover, as Deetz (1996) argues they also protect the dominant paradigm from critical engagement. Watson (1990) proposes that archic pluralism does not mean that formulations are ultimately incommensurable, compatibility can be manifested in "mutual intelligibility and translatability" from one position to the other. Such a dialogical model of the relationship between paradigms does not require that there is agreement. As Willmott (1993) puts it "an engagement [with other paradigms] can also provide a useful abrasive on which to sharpen one's blade, without necessarily stimulating or satisfying a desire to plunge it into one's adversary", more constructively perhaps, Geertz (1980) comments that "given the dialectical nature of things we all need our opponents".

4   CONCLUSIONS

Where, then, does this position leave us? If, in requiring paradigms to be philosophically internally consistent we reject complete paradigm commensurability but allow for inter-paradigm dialogue, what implications does this have for research practice?

First, we must accept that each paradigm stands in a relation of "reciprocal priority" (Ford, 1990) to others. This is evident in practice in the way that interpretivist researchers argue that positivist research always involves interpretation, or positivist researchers see interpretivists as striving (ineffectively?) towards reliable knowledge. Each understands the other in its own terms. Claims of innate superiority of particular perspectives thus need to give way to recognition of the internal coherence of paradigms and of the ways in which they develop their particular knowledge claims. As Deetz (1996) argues, different orientations research different phenomena, asking different questions, for different reasons.

Secondly, although, as Deetz (1996) notes, most researchers are not purists, their work unavoidably carries assumptions and responsibilities. Researchers therefore need to develop a thorough understanding of their philosophical position and of the questions and claims that drive their work, both to be clear about the knowledge claims they make, but also to evaluate critically the claims of others. In this, the provocations of their "opponents" may serve not just as a corrective against complacency, but also, if claims are clear and criticism well-informed, as a source of constructive insight. This view is supported by Landry and Banville (1992) who argue that the discipline this imposes should be seen as beneficial. As Deetz (1996) notes, however, communication between paradigms is rarely on an equal basis and typically places additional demands upon the minority. While such imbalances cannot be wished away, effective communication would seem to require equal discipline among positivist researchers in being clear about their assumptions.

Finally, despite Deetz's argument that the "ideal research program" would involve a complementary relation between orientations, manifested in a rotation through incompatible approaches, thorough understanding is likely to come from extended engagement with a particular position. "Multiperspectivalism", Deetz (1996:204) argues, "often leads to shallow readings". Although his does not preclude paradigm "conversions" (Mingers, 1997), it suggests that such paradigmatic multiligualism is not easily achieved. As Deetz himself acknowledges, "good scholars have deep commitments", which, he suggests, are related to particular "conceptions of the social good and preferred ways of living". Methodological choices, properly made, thus have deeper significance which would not seem to be readily traded for analytical convenience and IS researchers might take heed of the advice of Polonius in Shakespeare's Hamlet: "unto thine own self be true".

References

Allen, D. & Ellis, D. (1997) Beyond paradigm closure in information systems research. In: Galliers, R.; Murphy, C.; Hansen, H.; O'Callaghan, R.; Carlsson, S. & Loebbecke, C. (Eds) *Proceedings of the 5th European Conference on Information Systems, Cork, Ireland, June 19-21, 1997.* pp760-776.

Archer, S. (1988) 'Qualitative' research and the epistemelogical problems of the management disciplines. In: Pettigrew, A. (Ed)*Competitiveness and the Management Process* . Oxford: Blackwell, pp256-302.

Backhouse, J.; Liebenau, J. & Land, F. (1989) On the discipline of IS. *Journal of Information Systems*, **1** (1), 19-27.

Brannen, J. (1992) Combining qualitative and quantitative approaches: an overview. In: Brannen, J. (Ed) *Mixing Methods: Qualitative and Quantitative Research.* Aldershot: Avebury, pp3-37.

Bryman, A. (1992) Quantitative and qualitative research: further reflections on their integration. In: Brannen, J. (Ed) *Mixing Methods: Qualitative and Quantitative Research.* Aldershot: Avebury, pp57-78.

Burrell, B. & Morgan, G. (1979) *Sociological Paradigms and Organisational Analysis.* Portsmouth, NH: Heinemann

Cresswell, J.W. (1994) *Research Design: Qualitative and Quantitative Approaches.* London: Sage

DeCock, C. & Rickard, T. (1995) Of Giddens, paradigms and philosophical garb. *Organization Studies*, **16** (4), 699-704.

Deetz, S. Describing differences in approaches to organization science: rethinking Burrell and Morgan and their legacy. *Organization Science*, **7** (2), 191-207.

Feyerabend, P. (1975) *Against Method*. London: Verso

Ford, J.E. (1990) Systematic pluralism. *The Monist*, **73** (3), 335-349

Gable, G.G. (1994) Integrating case study and survey research methods: an example in information systems. *European Journal of Information Systems*, **3** (2), 112-126.

Geertz, C. (1980) Blurred genres: the reconfiguration of social thought. *American Scholar*, **49**, 165-179.

Giddens, A. (1993) *New Rules of Sociological Method* (second edition). Cambridge: Polity

Hammersley, M. (1992) Deconstructing the qualitative-quantitative divide. In: Brannen, J. (Ed) *Mixing Methods: Qualitative and Quantitative Research*. Aldershot: Avebury, pp39-55.

Hassard, J. (1991) Multiple paradigms and organizational analysis: a case study. *Organization Studies*, **12** (2), 275-299.

Jackson, N. & Carter, P. (1991) In defence of paradigm incommensurability. *Organization Studies*, **12** (1), 109-127.

Jackson, N. & Carter, P. (1993) Paradigm wars: a response to Hugh Willmott. *Organization Studies*, **14** (5), 721-725.

Kaplan, B. & Duchon, D. (1988) Combining qualitative and quantitative methods in information systems research: a case study. *MIS Quarterly*, **12** (4), 571-586.

Kuhn, T. (1962) *The Structure of Scientific Revolutions*. Chicago: Chicago University Press

Landry, M. & Banville, C. (1992) A discipline methodological pluralism for MIS research. *Accounting, Management and Information technology*, **2** (2), 77-97.

Lee, A.S. (1991) Integrating positivist and interpretive approaches to organizational research. *Organizational Science*, **2** (4), 342-365.

Markus, M.L. (1994) Electronic mail as the medium of managerial choice. *Organization Science*, **5**(4), 502-527.

Masterman, M. (1970) The nature of a paradigm. In: Lakatos, I. & Musgrave, A. (Eds) *Criticism and the Growth of Knowledge*. Cambridge: Cambridge University Press, pp59-89.

Mingers, J. (1997) Combining research methods in information systems: multi-paradigm methodology. In: Galliers, R.; Murphy, C.; Hansen, H.; O'Callaghan, R.; Carlsson, S. & Loebbecke, C. (Eds) *Proceedings of the 5th European Conference on Information Systems, Cork, Ireland, June 19-21, 1997*. pp760-776.

Moser, C. & Kalton, G. (1971) *Survey Methods in Social Investigation* Aldershot: Gower.

Norris, C. (1996) *Reclaiming Truth*. London: Lawrence & Wishart

Orlikowski, W. J. and Baroudi, J. J. (1991) Studying information technology in organizations: research approaches and assumptions, *Information Systems Research*, **2** (1), 1-28.

Parker, M. & McHugh, G. (1991) Five texts in search of an author: a response to John Hassard's 'Multiple paradigms and organizational analysis'. *Organization Studies*, **12** (3), 451-456.

Pfeffer, J. (1993) Barriers to the advance of organizational science: paradigm development as a dependent variable. *Academy of Management Review*, **18** (4), 599-620.

Pfeffer, J. (1995) Mortality, reproducibility, and the persistence of styles of theory. *Organisation Science*, **6** (6), 681-691.

Reed, M. (1985) *New Directions in Organizational Analysis*. London: Tavistock.

Roth, P.A. (1987) *Meaning and Method in the Social Sciences*. London: Cornell University Press.

Van Maanen, J. (1995) Style as theory. *Organisation Science*, **6** (1), 133-143.

Van Maanen, J. (1995) Fear and loathing in organizational studies. *Organization Science*, **6** (6), 687-692.

Walsham, G. (1995) Interpretive case studies in IS research: nature and method. *European Journal of Information Systems*, **4** (2), 74-81.

Watson, W. (1990) Types of pluralism. *The Monist*, **73** (3), 350-365.

Weaver, G.R. & Gioia, D.A. (1994) Paradigms lost: incommensurability and structurationist inquiry. *Organization Studies*, **15** (4), 565-590.

Weaver, G.R. & Gioia, D.A. (1994) Paradigms lost vs paradigms found. *Organization Studies*, **16** (4), 704-705.

Willmott, H. (1993) Breaking the paradigm mentality. *Organization Studies*, **14** (5), 681-719.

Willmott, H. (1993) Paradigm gridlock: a reply. *Organization Studies*, **14** (5), 727-730.

---

[i] Deetz (1996) proposes the term discourse as an alternative to paradigm. Although this has the advantage of avoiding further confusion with Kuhn and B&M, so much of the debate uses the term paradigm that it will be retained to maintain comparability.

CHAPTER 9

THE PARADIGM DEBATE IN INFORMATION SYSTEMS RESEARCH

David Allen and David Ellis
University of Sheffield

Abstract

The current debate over the 'identity crisis' the field of Information Systems has led to an increasing calls from a number of researchers for the development of a common 'intellectual core' and common set of related methodologies. Currently the consensus seems to be that researchers in the field of information systems typically adhere to one or another broad schools of thought. There is debate as to the extent to which there can be communication or commensurability between the work of those in the different schools. Researchers arguing for the strong incommensurability thesis in information systems research hold the view that inherent differences in ontologies and epistemologies reflected, for example, in the claim of the incompatibility of quantitative and qualitative research methods within the same research design, make commensurability between work informed by the different paradigms impossible. The call seems to be made by a number of researchers for 'harmony and convergence' around a single paradigm out of pragmatic considerations because by doing this the field will become stronger. These arguments are made largely on the basis of the early work of Thomas Kuhn reflected in the work of Burrell and Morgan. This paper will attempt to trace the emergence of this debate from the breakdown in the consensual functionalist approach to information systems which dominated research in the 1970's and early 1980's through the paradigm framework of Burrell and Morgan in the 1980's and early 1990's through to the present polemic over the hegemonic influence of discrete paradigm based approaches, review the principal arguments for and against paradigm commensurability encountered in information systems research, and consider their implications in relation to the calls for methodological pluralism in research design.

1   INTRODUCTION: HOMOGENITY OR HETEROGENITY IN INFORMATION SYSTEMS RESEARCH?

The theoretical position in IS research is one, as Visala (1991) Checkland and Holwell (1998) most eloquently point out of fragmentation and unco-ordination. Cumulative traditions are rare and the field is divided into a number of different schools and trends. In common with those in the field of organisational studies, these schools often perceive themselves as based upon opposing theoretical precepts. A parallel can be drawn with the field of organisational theory where there are:

> *"... discontinuities in basic philosophical assumptions. Problem focus and conceptual frameworks are seen to generate deep-seated fissures in the intellectual fabric of organisation theory. The latter tends to be viewed as a highly fragmented field of study lacking any overarching intellectual coherence or sense of historical direction." (Reid, 1992: 36)*

The communication between the different schools has been described, mainly, as based on a aggressive refutation of each other's theories, (Olaisen, 1991). Reid, memorably describes these as warring camps of 'paradigm warriors' intent on emasculating, if not destroying, the accumulated intellectual resources and powers of opposing factions." (Reid, 1992: 37)

This has been identified by a number of IS researchers as a fundamental weakness in the field of Information Systems research and one which will challenge its ability to survive as a distinct discipline. This belief has most recently been articulated by Adam and Fitzgerald (1996), who, although not arguing for a monistic paradigmatic position in IS, have argued that;

> *"There is also a very real risk that, unless the IS field can move towards becoming a stable and distinct discipline with its own intellectual core and accepted research protocols, traditional IS research issues may be 'reclaimed' by other disciplines who regard these areas as more properly their remit." (Adam and Fitzgerald, 1996: 17)*

There has been much debate on the philosophical underpinnings of IS research (Cf. Probert and Beeson 1997), whether IS could or should be described as a discipline (Probert 1997, Spaul 1997, Jones 1997) and a number of attempts have been made to map the intellectual structures of the field (Checkland and Holwell 1998). Yet, in common with a many other disciplines only a limited number of frameworks for mapping the intellectual structures of information systems research have been proposed. In the field of Information Systems Burrell and Morgan's (1979) has played, and continues to play, a critical role in determining and maintaining intra-disciplinary boundaries. Despite criticism of Burrell and Morgan's (1979) framework, and the proposal of alternatives such as that of Hirscheim, Klein and Lyytinen (1992, 1995,1996), the predominant framework used has been Burrell and Morgan's (c.f. Hirschheim and Klein 1989, Wood-Harper 1995, Klein and Lyytinen 1995, and Iivari 1991).

Burrell and Morgan categorise research in organisational studies and sociological studies into four discrete paradigms - functionalist, radical humanist, radical structuralist and interpretative. Although, the interpretation of this framework by researchers within the IS field seems to be far from Burrell and Morgan's initial conception, the general framework has, in the Information Systems field, become the accepted orthodoxy. Researchers now tend to place themselves within a paradigm explicitly (or implicitly) accepting the underlying assumptions of this framework. Research into IS traditionally has tended to fall into the 'functionalist' paradigm. Despite the calls for a broadening of the theoretical basis of the subject, the situation has not changed substantially.

Thus the framework through a process of reification, is now a 'reality'. Closure comes not only from the intended ideological stance but also by 'playing the game' inherently accepting Burrell and Morgan's terminology, interpretations of philosophical concepts and language. In this sense the researcher falls into the a bounded paradigm almost by accident rather than by design. The acceptance of this framework negates any possibility of meta theoretical innovation. Burrell and Morgan state for example that their four paradigms are based upon;

> "...mutually exclusive views of the social world. Each stands in it's own right and generates its own distinctive analyses of social life. With regard to the study of organisations, for example, each paradigm generates theories and perspectives which are in fundamental opposition to those generated in other paradigms." (Burrell and Morgan, 1979: p viii)

They argue that not only are the paradigms incommensurable at a basic philosophical level but that this means that any attempt to combine methods across paradigms is invalid; 'A synthesis is not possible, since in their pure forms they are contradictory, being based on at least one set of opposing meta theoretical assumptions' (Burrell and Morgan, 1979: 25). Each paradigm having different ontological, methodological, and epistemological foundations and embodying divergent views of human nature. It is this belief in incommensurability, either explicit or more often implicit and assumed which has formed the critical argument against any form of synthesis, integration or unity between any aspect of the paradigms.

Burell and Morgan's position was to a great extent based upon their interpretation of Kuhn (Ellis 1994, Kuhn 1961, Masterman 1970). According to Kuhn's early work, the existence of conflicting schools is a symptom of the pre-paradigmatic stage of a science. Conversely, the presence of a theoretical consensus over a paradigm for a field of study is taken by Kuhn as a sign that it has reached the stage of a mature science. That every science exists and develops by virtue of a shared paradigm. Roth (1989) makes the point that, many social scientists have taken the fact that there is no dominant paradigm in the social sciences as a reason why there is no normal science in the social sciences and therefore a lack of revolutionary breakthroughs As social scientists have striven to achieve a consensus of opinion in order to move their field from a pre paradigmatic stage they have thus taken a unitary stance on methodology.

A further implication, following from their interpretation of Kuhn's work is that a paradigm change is also taken as only occurring in a revolutionary, not evolutionary, way. This also negates the ability of the researcher to work between paradigms or incrementally move towards another paradigm. Despite the recent argument advanced by Burrell (1996) that they used the revised, and more open, Kuhnian concept of paradigm within Sociological Paradigms and Organisational Analysis, they ignore the implications of Kuhn's later work, which as Hirschheim points out can be used as a basis for contingent methodological pluralism. In short the incommensurability thesis combined with selective reading of Kuhn's concept of a paradigm provides a tool for creating and maintaining barriers within the discipline. It is an example of a disciplinary instrument. Which can be used as a tool to;

> "bind...people to their own ideas and to create docile bodies who do not question..." (Walsham, 1996: 14).

Not only do Burrell and Morgan oppose pluralism from a theoretical and practical viewpoint but also they oppose it from a ideological viewpoint, stating:

> "...Contrary to the widely held belief that synthesis and mediation between paradigms is what is required, we argue that the real need is for paradigmatic closure. In order to avoid emasculation and incorporation within the functionalist problematic, the paradigms need to provide a basis for their self-preservation by developing on their own account." (Burrell and Morgan 1979: 397-398)

Our concern is that in the IS field the paradigm debate, rather than allowing different positions to develop on their own terms, as Burrell and Morgan argue, is leading to segmentiation without communication and the possibility of the hegemony of one position.

The 'paradigm debate' is an 'ideological' struggle, based on the belief that until the field has reached a heterogeneous methodological position it will not advance, a point clearly articulated in, for example, the work of Adam and Fitzgerald's (1996). Morgan points out that -

> "Paradigm diversity is most often interpreted as threat by those organisational scientists committed to well-established models and methods for understanding the generation of knowledge as gradual, cumulative, well - ordered process." (Morgan 1993: 13)

The debate became a ideological struggle in a second sense, as Aldrich points out -

" ...all of the perspectives I have reviewed have achieved significant standing today because, at their core, they have groups of dedicated researchers working on empirical research to test hypotheses derived from the perspectives. They read one another's papers, hold conferences, and issue edited volumes collecting recent empirical work.... In the process of constructing theory groups they have bounded themselves, and organisational boundaries can be extremely difficult to surmount. The groups work very hard at emphasising how they differ from one another, and investigators have a stake in stressing their incompatibilities." (Aldrich 1992: 37).

It is perhaps ironic that this framework provides a coherent basis for the 'purist or supremacist functionalists' (e.g. Donaldson, 1996), forcing others who perceived themselves as working within alternative paradigms to further segment themselves, isolate themselves and thus perpetuate and intensify the 'paradigm wars'.

2   INTER-PARADIGM COMMUNICATION AND METHODOLOGICAL PLURALISM

An key argument for incommensurability is that, because linguistic symbols take on different meaning across paradigms, there can be no possibility of direct translation from one paradigm to another, and, therefore, there can be no communication across paradigms (Burell and Morgan 1979). Thus many of the protagonists seem to talk 'past' each other rather than to each other. This lack of communication has been traditionally linked to the 'fact' of the mutually exclusive nature of the paradigms within which the different researchers work. The argument derives from Quine's (1960, 1970) thesis of the indeterminacy of translation and the absence of a meta-language for such. This thesis has been used as the basis for an argument for methodological pluralism by Roth (1989). The argument being that the problem of incommensurability is one of translation - so that, in principle, it is not possible to assert that opposing theories are incommensurable, because of the lack of any language independent way of demonstrating the possession of common schema or set of beliefs. This is linked to relativistic arguments in that the aim of the researcher is seen as being not to ascertain the one right answer but the best, most empirically adequate account that can be given at the time. Thus the choice of framework is dependent upon pragmatic not logical grounds. Aldrich (1992) points out

"... if one adopts a more pragmatic - dare one say 'post-modern'? - approach and asks simply, 'Do the three groups talk to each other?', the answer is 'Some of the time'. They even occasionally work on similar problems, though the similarity is often obscured by different descriptive vocabularies." (Aldrich 1992: 37)

However as Mangham (1994) states -

> *" Many of us are unable to talk to economists, psychologists, sociologists, philosophers or political scientists because we do not understand their languages...Few people contributing to or interested in organisational studies show fluency in the language of any discipline." (Mangham 1994: 36-37)*

Yet the use of 'common sense language' is often put forward as an impediment to the development of 'primitive' state of IS as a 'discipline'. The creation of a common technical language, used with scholarly precision, has been identified by Checkland and Holwell (1998: 54) as a desirable characteristic which they argue would enable ideas to be expressed with greater clarity and help to stimulate better debate in the IS field. We would argue that the use of *non-technical* language is critical to the successful development of IS.

Hassard (1995) argued that Wittgenstein's later work (1953) (the *Philosophical Investigations* theory of language games) provides an analytical basis for undermining the strong incommensurability thesis. Wittgenstein's notion of language games and, in particular, the distinction between technical and non-technical language games is used to undermine strong incommensurability theses and advance arguments for commensurability. Hassard argues that

> *"...this reading of Wittgenstein argues that as our perceptual limitations are empirically established, the rules and convention of our 'meta-language in use' allow us to deal, not only with a present language-game, but also with a new language-game into which we may be trained. The emphasis is not on a sudden gestalt-switch which allows us to see the light, but rather...of established perceptual arrangements which facilitate a transfer of allegiance." (Hassard 1995:86)*

Emphasizing the commonality of the non-technical language which underpin the technical language games, it is argued that the existence of the common non-technical language means that at some level there must be a degree of commensurability between theories described in the technical language which can be determined by reference to concepts and criteria from the non-technical language. Weaver and Gioia (1994) also argue that

> *"although there may be errors of comprehension and failures of communication... there is no reason to believe that such difficulties are endemic to theoretical, meta-theoretical and methodological debates"(Weaver and Gioia 1994:585).*

In this respect communication is theoretically possible, practically undertaken, and, ideologically, not only critical for the development of the field but a prerequisite.

The incommensurability thesis used in the IS field based on Burrell and Morgan, 1979 can be seen as repressing innovation, synergy and the advancement of the field. Willmott

(1992) succinctly points out from the organisational studies field:

> *"In sum, Sociological paradigms and organisation analysis provides a valuable heuristic device...However, by denying the presence (and the possibility!) of approaches that are neither exclusively 'subjective' nor 'objective', and which are not governed solely by the principles of 'regulation' nor by those of 'radical change', Sociological Paradigms exerts an inadvertently repressive force as it denies the very possibility of analysis that is much more sensitive to the ambiguous and contradictory nature of social reality than is allowed by its own one-dimensional vision of the mutual exclusivity of paradigms." (Willmott 1993: 49)*

The argument for commensurability is linked to the long standing debate on the use of both qualitative and quantitative research methodologies in a single research design, which has been spluttering in the Social Sciences since the idea was raised by Campbell and Fiske in 1956. Increasingly it has been linked to the paradigm debate and the thesis, suggested by Burrell and Morgan (1979), that qualitative and quantitative research methods represent opposing dichotomies. As Galliers (1985) and Ngwenyama (1991) have noted the choice of qualitative or quantitative methodology has been explicitly linked to the paradigm debate and the thesis has been eagerly drawn upon by the opposing sides of the 'functionalist' and 'interpretative' camps. However, Morrow argues for the integration of qualitative and quantitative approaches in the same research design as

> *"...nothing about qualitative research, regardless of the form it takes, necessarily precludes the use of quantitative representations or non-qualitative formal methods. Ethnographers and historians can and do count things." (Morrow 1994: 207).*

Morgan (1980) one year after Sociological Paradigms was published called for methodological pluralism as a diversity of viewpoints rather than competing paradigms. Banville and Landry (1989) from the Information Systems field point to the inappropriate monistic view of MIS and call for methodological pluralism as the acceptance of the legitimacy of other paradigms. Lee (1991), who may be described as leading supporter of 'methodological pluralism' in the Information Systems field has similarly argued for an acceptance of the

> *"...methodological legitimacy of the procedures of each approach, apart from the legitimacy of their integration and collaboration." (Lee 1991: 343).*

3   EPISTEMOLOGICAL ARGUMENTS FOR PLURALISM

Methodological pluralism is inherently contentious, which ever discipline it is applied in (Holland 1990, Parker and McHugh 1991). O'Brien (1992), for example, has argued for greater rigor rather than "retreating into a comfortable methodological pluralism" in economics. In its most recent incarnation based upon 'post-modernistic' philosophy methodological pluralism stands as a direct attack upon the theoretical closure of the paradigms. It undermines the orthodox analysis based upon interpretations of Kuhn as promulgated through Burrell and Morgan's (1979) framework. As such it undermines the very basis upon which the 'paradigm wars' have been fought. It thus gains the opposition of, on one hand, both mainstream `interpretative' researchers (e.g. Lincoln and Guba 1985) and 'radical' (e.g. Henwood, and Pidgeon 1995) and mainstream 'functionalist' researchers (e.g. Jackson and Carter (1991), and Donaldson, (1988, 1996)).

One of the key reasons methodological pluralism has been argued to be valid is epistemological. Iivari (1991) argues, epistemological assumptions have been understood as "the nature of Scientific Knowledge about the phenomena to be investigated". Watson (1990) distinguishes four types of epistemological basis for pluralism:"(1) perspectival pluralism, resulting from differences in the perspective of the knower, represented by Nicholas Rescher; (2) pluralism of hypotheses, resulting from different hypotheses about the one reality, represented by Stephen Pepper; (3) methodological pluralism, resulting from different formulations of a truth that transcends them all, represented by Wayne Booth; and (4) archic pluralism, resulting from the different principles by which philosophies may be constituted, represented by Richard McKeon." Mangham notes of organisational studies;

> "In one area - epistemology - some contributors to organisational studies
> are impressively fluent. They can articulate the positions of the 'objectivists'
> and the 'subjectivists' with a fine discrimination. Some of them know their
> Foucaults from their Lyotards, some even speak Bachelard with the best of
> them and even risk a word or two of Derrida. One or two appear to speak
> Wittgenstein, but on the whole it is the same story, a limited command of the
> language with a poor sense of underlying grammar. There is little evidence
> of an ability to read, let alone talk, Davidson or Rorty, Quine, Putnam or
> Margolis." (Mangham 1992: 38).)

This is also true of the information systems field where epistemological development is particularly stunted. A number of researchers in the IS field have developed epistemological positions which are based on perspectival pluralism arguing from an interpretative viewpoint that each individuals perceptions dictate the way in which they perceive the one external reality. As Checkland states "...we perceive the world through a filter of - or using the framework of - the ideas internal to us; but that the source of many (most?) of those ideas is the world outside" (1995, p20). This view has been articulated by a number of different researchers in Information Systems (c.f. Checkland (1995)) however in each case it has led to a 'unitary' methodological stance. Pettigrew's research is perhaps the exception to this rule. Pettigrew has pioneered the use of multiple methods across paradigms both in his early (1973) and later work Pettigrew, Ferlie and McKee (1992). He used a combination of longitudinal participant and direct observation, interviews using multiple interviewers across levels of hierarchy within an organisation, questionnaires, content analysis of internal documents and historical analysis as early as 1973.

Weaver and Gioia (1994) similarly argue that communication between paradigms is possible because paradigms deal with selectively bracketed aspects of organisational or social phenomena each paradigm constitutes a legitimate part of a larger scheme. This position is based on Giddens Structuration theory (1979, 1984), which they argue offers a solution to the problem of the irreconcilable nature of paradigms and therefore of qualitative and quantitative methodologies (Hassard 1988, 1991, 1994, 1995) Giddens Structuration Theory has also been used by Weaver and Gioia, (1994) as a way of resolving the problem over the irreconcilable nature of paradigms and therefore of qualitative and quantitative methodologies. They suggest that this meta theoretical perspective provides a position from which researchers can invoke different assumptions, pursue different goals, ask different research questions, use different approaches but be involved in research with commonalities despite such diversities.

The epistemological debate has recently turned from polemic over the relative merits of the different methods and there appears currently to be a rapprochement, a reconciliation, perhaps out of exhaustion rather than philosophical belief. This has also led to the serious consideration of pluralistic approaches, by a number of researchers (Lee 1991, Orlikowski and Baroudi 1991, Gable 1994, Hirschheim 1985, Kaplan and Duchon 1988).

4   CONCLUSION

This paper has discussed the various theoretical and practical approaches to methodological pluralism in information systems research and the influence of the framework of Burrell and has had on the direction of research in the information systems field. Burrell and advance arguments for paradigm closure or exclusivity which derive from Kuhn. Later writers have drawn directly on that framework and the ideas of Kuhn and other writers to either attack or buttress the claims and counter claims of paradigm exclusivity or methodological pluralism. However, it is accepted, not least by Kuhn himself, that his original deployment of the concept of a paradigm was deeply ambiguous. Masterman identified twenty one different senses in which Kuhn had employed the term which she classified into three broad senses - metaphysical; sociological and artefact/construct. Kuhn, responding to Masterman's critique, agreed that he had used the term in at least two different senses and that, philosophically, the latter sense was the more fundamental. The first of these meanings he referred to as the sociological sense, while the second, with its reference to exemplary past achievements, was equivalent to the sense of the artefact or construct concept of a paradigm as outlined by Masterman.

Kuhn re-formulated his original argument to distinguish between, on the one hand, the broad constellation of beliefs, values and techniques that were shared by the members of a scientific community, the disciplinary matric, and on the other, to the concrete puzzle solutions, or exemplars, that are employed as model problem situations for that research community. It is the exemplar that Kuhn considered to be closest to his original concept of a paradigm, the primary philosophical sense, and the sense which was fundamental for paradigm based research and the development of normal science. Burrell and Morgan, however, invert this order, as the title of their work indicates, and treat the broader sociological sense as primary. What this means, in effect, is that the reference to the technical philosophical debate on paradigm commensurability may, strictly speaking, be irrelevant to the debate in the information systems field which derives from the employment of the concept of a paradigm in the sociological sense. This gives the debate in the field a curious flavour as the references, and referents, vacillate between the technical philosophical and the sociological, and as the ideas and writings of those philosophers who have contributed to or propounded ideas which have a bearing on the technical debate are cited in context of the sociological one.

The intractability of the paradigm debate in the information systems field then may then stem not only from the mixture of similar but different discourses but also from the consistent reference from the sociological debate back to the technical philosophical one. In this sense the character of the debate in information systems research is not like that encountered in the history or philosophy of science but rather like that encountered in theological, or, more strikingly, scholastic discourse. The adoption of a particular tradition, position, stance or interpretation, concerning the nature of information systems research is buttressed by arguments from authority. In the scholastic tradition that authority would be sought for in the scriptures and the writings of the divines. In information systems research this is substituted by references to classic cannons and authors.

The apparently technical and philosophical character or tone of much of the debate diverts attention away from the irrelevance of most of it to the question in hand. This is not whether, Kuhn, Quine, Wittgenstein, Giddens, or whoever, were methodological pluralists but whether the information systems field is, could or should be. Put starkly Burrell and Morgan's work was sociologically not philosophically oriented and intended. The effect of firing the sociological ordnance out of the philosophical cannon was probably not even consciously intended. However, by grounding the argument ultimately back in the technical philosophical discourse the sociological nature of the argument was disguised and in the resultant confusion this point was lost and the paradigm debate degenerated into an arid scholastic dispute based on a subtle but pervasive confusion of different academic genres and discourses. In this respect it is important that the paradigm debate in information systems research is recast and re-examined against its proper sociological backdrop if it is to be used to genuine effect in the determination of the future shape of the discipline rather than to shore up a superstructural scholasticism which detracts attention from examination of the real nature of its foundations and concerns.

References

Checkland, P., Holwell S. (1998) *Information, Systems and Information Systems: making sense of the field* Chichester: John Wiley and Sons

Probert, S. (1997) *The Actuality of Information Systems* in Mingers, J., Stowell, F. (1997) (Eds.) Information Systems: An Emerging Discipline? Mc Graw Hill: London p 21-57

Spaul, M. (1997) *Discipline and Critique: The Case of Information Systems* in Mingers, J., Stowell, F. (1997) (Eds.) Information Systems: An Emerging Discipline? Mc Graw Hill: London p 63-91

Jones, M. (1997) *It all depends what you mean by discipline...* in Mingers, J., Stowell, F. (1997) (Eds.) Information Systems: An Emerging Discipline? Mc Graw Hill: London p 97-113

Adam, F., Fitzgerald, B. (1996) A Framework for analysing the evolution of the IS field - can IS become a stable discipline? in Coelho, D.J., Jelassi, T., Konig, W., Krcmar, H., O'Callaghan, R., Saaksjarvi, M. (Ed) (1996) *Proceedings of the 4th European Conference on Information Systems.* Lisbon/Portugal July 2- 4. 1 17-32

Aldrich, H.E. (1992) Incommensurable paradigms? Vital Signs from three perspectives *in* Reed, M., Hughes, M. (eds.) *Rethinking Organisation: New Directions in organisation Theory and Analysis.* Sage London 17 - 46

Banville, C., Landry, M. (1989) Can the field of MIS by Disciplined? *Communication of the ACM* 32 (1) 48-60

Bryant, C.G.A., Jary, D (1991) *Giddens' Theory of Structuration: a critical appreciation* London: Routledge

Burrell, G. (1996) Normal Science, paradigms, Metaphors, Discourses and Genealogies of Analysis. in Clegg, S.R., Hardy, C., Nord, W. *Handbook of Organisation Studies:* 642 - 659

Burrell, G., Morgan, G (1979) *Sociological Paradigms and Organisational Analysis.* Heinemann

Checkland, P., Scholes, J. (1995) *Soft Systems Methodology in Action* Chichester: John Wiley

Donaldson, L. (1988) *In defence of Organisation theory: a reply to the critics.* Cambridge: Cambridge University Press.

Donaldson, L. (1996) *For Positivist Organisational Theory,* London: Sage

Ellis, D. (1994) Paradigms in Information Retrieval Research in Kent, A., Williams, J.G., Hall, C.M., Kent, r. (1994) *Encyclopaedia of Microcomputers Volume 13.* Marcel Dekker Inc

Gable, G.G. (1994) Integrating Case Study and Survey Research Methods: An Example in Information Systems *European Journal of Information Systems* Vol. 3, No 2. 112- 126

Galliers, R.D.: In search of a paradigm for Information Systems Research. In: Mumford, E., Hirschheim, R., Fitzgerald, G., Wood-Harper, A.T. eds. *Research Methods in Information Systems: Proceedings of the IFIP WG 8.2 Colloquium Manchester Business School 1994.* Elsever Science Publishers B.V North Holland (1985). 281-297

Hassard, J. (1988) Overcoming hermeticism in organisation theory: an alternative to paradigm incommensurability *Human Relations* 41, 3, 247-259

Hassard, J. (1991) Multiple paradigms and organisational analysis: A case study *Organisation Studies* 12 2 279-299

Hassard, J. (1994) Postmodern organisational analysis: Toward a Conceptual Framework. *Journal of Management Studies*. Vol. 31 no3 May. 303-324

Hassard, J (1995) *Sociology and Organisation Theory: Positivism, Paradigms and Postmodernity.* Cambridge Studies in Management Cambridge University Press. UK.

Henwood, K., Pidgeon, N. (1995) Remaking the Link - Qualitative research and Feminist Standpoint Theory in Feminism and Psychology, 5, 1, 7-30

Holland, R. (1990) The paradigm plague: prevention cure and inoculation *Human Relations* 43 23-48

Hirschheim, R.A. (1985) Information Systems epistemology - an historical perspective In: Mumford, E., Hirschheim, R., Fitzgerald, G., Wood-Harper, A.T. eds. *Research Methods in Information Systems: Proceedings of the IFIP WG 8.2 Colloquium Manchester Business School 1984.* Elsever Science Publishers B.V North Holland (1985) 13-36

Hirscheim, R, Klein, H.K., Lyytinen, K. (1992) *Control, Sense-Making and Argumentation: Articulating and Exploring the Intellectual Structures of Information Systems.* Working Paper WP24 Department of Computer Science. University of Jyvaskyla

Hirschheim, R.A, Klein, H.K., Lyytinen, K. (1995) *Information Systems Development and Data Modelling: Conceptual and Philosophical Foundations* Cambridge University Press: Cambridge

Hirschheim, R.A, Klein, H.K., Lyytinen, K. (1996) Exploring the intellectual structures of information systems development: a social action theoretic analysis. *Accounting Management and Information Technologies. 6 (1/2) 1 -65*

Hirschheim, R.A, Klein (1989) Four paradigms of Information Systems Development. *Communications of the ACM* 32(10) 1199-1216

Iivari, J. (1991) A Paradigmatic Analysis of Contemporary Schools of IS Development. *European Journal of Information Systems* 1, 249-272.

Jackson, N., Carter, P. (1991) In defence of paradigm incommensurability *Organisation Studies* 12, 1 109 - 127

Kaplan, B., Duchon, D. (1988) Combining Qualitative and Quantitative Methods in Information Systems Research: A case study. *MIS Quarterly.* 12. no 4 571-586

Klein, HK, Lyytinen, K. (1995) The Poverty of Scientism in Information Systems. In: Mumford, E., Hirschheim, R., Fitzgerald, G., Wood-Harper, A.T. eds. *Research Methods in Information Systems: Proceedings of the IFIP WG 8.2 Colloquium Manchester Business School 1994.* Elsever Science Publishers B.V North Holland, 133-156.

Kuhn, T. S. (1961) *The Structure of Scientific Revolution.* Chicago: The University of Chicago Press (Second Edition 1970)

Lee, A.S. (1991) *Integrating Positivist and interpretative Approaches to Organisational Research. Organisational Science Vol2 Part 4. 342-365*

Lincoln, Y.S., Guba, E.J. (1985) *Naturalistic Inquiry.* Newbury park, C.A: SAGE.

Mangham, I.L. (1994) Speaking in Tongues Organisation: the interdisciplinary journal of organisation theory and society. 1(1) July 1994 35-38

Masterman (1970) The nature of a paradigm. In Lakatos, I., Musgrave, A (ed.) *Criticism and the Growth of Knowledge* Cambridge University Press, Cambridge *59- 89*

Morgan, G. (1980) Paradigms, Metaphors and Puzzle Solving in Organisation Theory. *Administrative Science Quarterly* 25, 4, 605 - 622

Morgan, G. (1993) Paradigm diversity in organisational research in Hassard, J., Pym, D. (eds.) *The Theory and Philosophy of Organisations: Critical Issues and New perspectives* Routledge: London 13-30

Morrow, RA, Brown, DD (1994) *Critical theory and methodology*. Sage Publications

Ngwenyama, OK (1991) The Critical Social Theory Approach to Information Systems: Problems and Challenges. In: Nissen, H.E., Klein, HK, Hirschheim, R., eds. *Information Systems Research: Contemporary Approaches and Emergent Traditions*. Elsever Science Publishers B.V North Holland. 267-280

Orlikowski, J.W., Baroudi, J.J. (1991) *Studying Information Technology in Organisations: Research Approaches and Assumptions. Information Systems Research*. Vol. 2. No 1 pp 1 - 28.

O'Brien, D.P. (1992) Economists and Data *British Journal of Industrial Relations* 30, 2, 253-285

Olaisen, J. (1991) Pluralism or Positivistic Trivialism: Important trends in Contemporary Philosophy of Science. In *Information Systems Research: Contemporary Approaches and Emergent traditions* 235-361 Elsevier, Amsterdam. (ed. Klein, H.K., Nissen, H.K. Hirschheim, R)

Parker, M., McHugh, G. (1991) Five Texts in search of an author: A response to John Hassard's Multiple paradigms and organisational Analysis *Organisation Studies* 12 4 451-456

Pettigrew, A., Ferlie, E., McKee, L (1992) *Shaping Strategic Change: Making Change in Large Organisations. The Case of the National Health Service*. Sage: London

Pfeffer, J. (1995) Mortality, Reproducibility, and the Persistence of Styles of Theory. *Organisation Science* 6 (6) 681-686

Quine, W.V. (1960) *Word and Object* Cambridge: MA

Quine, W.V (1970) On the Reasons for Indeterminacy of Translation. *Journal of Philosophy* 84 5-10

Reid, M.I. (1992) *The Sociology of Organisations: Themes, perspectives and Prospects* . Harvester Wheatsheaf.

Roth, A.P. (1989) *Meaning and Method in the Social Sciences: A Case for Methodological Pluralism*. Cornell University Press: New York

Van Maanen, J. (1995) Fear and Loathing in Organisational Studies. *Organisation Science* 6 (6) 687-696

Visala, S (1991) Broadening the Empirical Framework of Information Systems Research. In: Nissen, H.E., Klein, H.K., Hirschheim, R., eds. *Information Systems Research : Contemporary Approaches and Emergent Traditions*. Elsever Science Publishers B.V North Holland 347-369

Walsham, G., Han, C.K (1990) *Structuration Theory and Information Systems Research*. Management Studies Research paper: University of Cambridge.

Walsham, G (1993) *Interpreting Information Systems in Organisations*. John Wiley & Sons, Chichester.

Walsham, G. (1996): The emergence of interpretivism in IS research, *Information Systems Research*, 6 (4) 376-395.

Watson, W. (1990) Types of Pluralism *The Monist: An international Journal of General Philosophical Inquiry*. Vol. 73. No.3 July

Weaver, G.R., Gioia, A.D. (1994) *Paradigms Lost: Incommensurability Vs Structurationist Inquiry*. Organisation Studies Vol. 15. No 4 pp 565 - 589

Wildermuth, B.M. (1993) Post-positive research: two examples of methodological pluralism. *Library Quarterly*, 63, 4, 450-468.

Willmott, H. (1993) Beyond paradigmatic closure in organisational enquiry Hassard, J., Pym, D. (eds.) *The Theory and Philosophy of Organisations: Critical Issues and New perspectives* Routledge London 44- 63

Wood-Harper, T (1995) Research Methods in Information Systems: Using Action Research. In: Mumford, E., Hirschheim, R., Fitzgerald, G., Wood-Harper, A.T. eds. *Research Methods in Information Systems : Proceedings of the IFIP WG 8.2 Colloquium Manchester Business School 1994.* Elsever Science Publishers B.V North Holland.

Wittgenstein, L (1953*) Philosophical Investigations,* Basil Blackwell: London .

Acknowledgements:

The authors would like to acknowledge the detailed and constructive comments of Matthew Jones of Cambridge University and of Martin Parker of Keele University. An earlier draft of this paper was presented at the European Conference on Information Systems in 1997

CHAPTER 10

AN ANTI-ESSENTIALIST READING OF INTRANET DEVELOPMENT: WHAT IS THE ROLE OF TECHNOLOGY?

Edgar A Whitley and Shervin Bouzari
London School of Economics and Political Science

Abstract

This paper describes research in progress that seeks to conceptualise the role of technology in information systems research. In particular it explores the anti-essentialist stance proposed by Grint and Woolgar in relation to the first implementation of corporate intranets and the technologies that were available at that time.

1   INTRODUCTION

The question of how to conceptualise technology has been addressed by various schools of research in information systems. This paper describes work in progress that contributes to this debate drawing on themes from recent debates in the social sciences.

At one extreme in the information systems debate is the computer science community which considers technology to be the goal of its research activities. Its aim is to develop new forms of technology which address existing problems or are able to change our world so that new issues and problems become predominant. As examples, research in computer science has led to the development of timesharing operating systems, graphical user interfaces and open systems like the internet that allow many different computers to interact seamlessly.

The management school approach has a different perspective. It typically takes technology as a given and tries to determine ways in which it can transform the operations of the organisation so that it can remain profitable and competitive. Thus attempts have been made to align information technology with business strategies or to reengineer the operations of the organisation inorder to make significant cost savings.

Interpretivist research, which adopts the stance *"that knowledge is a social construction, and that our theories concerning reality provide ways of making sense of the world rather than discoveries about the world which represent absolute truth"*

(Walsham 1993 p. xiii) also considers technology, although the way it conceptualises technology is not as clear cut as that found in the management or engineering literature.

This paper explores the different conceptions of technology found in interpretivist research and, in particular, focuses on anti-essentialist ideas which would seem to fit within the tenets of interpretivist research (Klein and Myers 1999) but which are often not taken in that way. These anti-essentialist ideas are applied to the context of an intranet project in Boeing and the implications of this reading are then discussed in some detail before areas for further research are described.

2   DIFFERENT INTERPRETATIONS OF TECHNOLOGY

If we look at the broadly interpretivist literature, we find a wide range of interpretations of the information technology component of information systems. This section reviews some of the main interpretations.

Monteiro and Hanseth (1995), for example, argue that we should be *"specific about the technology"*. In order to move beyond the cliche that technology is a crucial factor that enables and amplifies the changes in organisational structures (p. 326) they argue that it is necessary to explore the particular ways in which it actually shapes these changes. Whitley and Darking (1994) make a similar point, giving examples of the particular ways in which the particular choice of technology affects the capabilities of the resulting information system.

Another approach is given by Vidgin and McMaster (1995) who adopt the maxims of science studies (typified by Latour (1996)) and include non-human stakeholders in their analysis of a problematic information system. In this way, they incorporate technology and give it as strong a voice as human stakeholders in the discussion of the system.

Sahay *et al.* (1994) advocating a *"relativist approach to studying the social construction of information technology"* accept that information technology is not an *"objective phenomena with known properties or dimensions"* (Sahay, *et al.* 1994 p. 248). They then state, however, that *"information technology is more interpretively flexible than production technology, allowing users to reinvent it for uses that were originally unintended"* (Sahay, *et al.* 1994 p. 250). This implies that information technology has some special flexibility that is not found in production technology. Even if computer systems are open to multiple interpretations, production technology is not, a point reinforced when they state that *"(U)nlike well-known physical stimuli, information technology may evoke interpretations and produce social consequences that are unprecedented"* (p. 251) again privileging information technology.

3   ANTI-ESSENTIALIST CONCEPTIONS OF TECHNOLOGY

These differing descriptions of technology in information systems vary across a number of dimensions: Is the technology a given or is it something which is socially shaped? Is the technology totally flexible or is there something inherent to the particular form of technology which shapes / enables / constrains its application?

This paper will take one particular area of this debate and explore how it helps us in our world making activities in understanding information technology. The position which will be adopted is an anti-essentialist one, a position which argues that there is *nothing* essential to information technology, or any technology for that matter.

This position is perhaps best articulated by Keith Grint and Steve Woolgar in their book "The machine at work" (1997). They describe their approach as coming from an agnostic's doubt *"why do we take so little for granted in the social sciences and so much for granted in the natural sciences? More pragmatically for this text, what happens when you apply the scepticism normally reserved for social relations to technology?"* (p. 37).

In order to address this doubt, they propose adopting an approach found in literary analysis of texts which suggests that everything is in the 'reading'. Thus, they argue, the technology is only found in its reading by the users of the technology. It is the users who give it meaning, who determine what is to count. They accept that there may be conventions that shape how things are to be seen, but these are merely conventions which can be changed. They illustrate this with regard to the question of whether guns kill people. By taking an anti-essentialist perspective on this question they highlight the changing conventions about when people are considered to be dead. *"Does death, then, mean the absence of pulse, or fixed dilated pupils, or the absence of brain activity, or something else?"* (p. 162). Advances in medical technology mean that the thresholds for each of these criteria have changed in recent years. Furthermore, decisions about what is meant by fixed dilated pupils or the absence of brain activity are socially determined.

Anti-essentialist accounts therefore argue that we should not look to inherent features of the technology to explain things, rather all the explanation should come from the social context in which they are used. Moreover, essentialist arguments which presume some intrinsic features of the technology weaken possible critiques of technology. By assuming intrinsic features of the technology, it is no longer as convincing to argue against technological determinism (Smith and Marx 1994). This criticism can also be applied to many "social constructivist" arguments which typically talk of stability after periods of controversy; after allowing social factors to have their say, the inherent features of the technology come to dominate.

This is not to disregard those analyses which demonstrate that political influences are often found inscribed in the technology (Winner 1980) (Tiles and Oberdiek 1995) but rather to play down the deterministic role that they have in the resulting activities.

4   A CASE STUDY

The anti-essentialist position is, conceptually at least, rather an extreme one. In the context of new technologies, it is not arguing that *"(O)nce the machine works people will be convinced"* but rather that *"(T)he machine will work when all the relevant people have been convinced*" (Latour 1987 p. 10). Is there any empirical support for such an argument? This section will outline the introduction of an intranet in Boeing and explore it from an anti-essentialist perspective.

4.1   Intranets

Intranets are a relatively recent development and can be described as a small-scale version of the internet inside the organisation (Hills 1996). Sprout (1995) refers to intranets as internal corporate web pages produced by applying web technologies to share information within a particular organisation.

The main characteristic of intranets, therefore, seems to be that they are the application of internet (more typically web based) technologies within organisations. As such they provide, through a web browser, a single, consistent interface between different applications in the organisation. The use of internet software also means that the system is relatively flexible as the open standards underlying the web technology (Krol 1992) mean that suitable browsing software is available on most machines. Similarly, the hardware connections between the machines are standardised using internet protocols.

In most cases, the easiest way to set up an intranet is simply to provide TCP/IP connections and suitable browsers on all machines in the organisation and provide suitable interfaces to existing applications--typically through the dynamic creation of HTML formatted pages. More sophisticated applications may also take advantage of the device independent programming language Java, found in most web browsers.

4.2   Intranets in Boeing

One of the earliest implementations of a corporate intranet was found in Boeing (Moeller 1996) (Lloyd and Boyle 1998). According to these reports, Boeing was one of the pioneers of Intranet implementation with the first projects begun in late 1993. The project began with a number of engineers and scientist at Boeing experimenting with the earliest versions of the Moasic browser and navigating through the then infant world wide web. According to Moeller (1996) the network now runs 300 servers that are used by 20000 employees.

At the time that Boeing began to implement its intranet, advanced, reliable browsers were not available and much of the company's time was spent evaluating the technologies, adapting them to their requirements and waiting for suitable encryption functionality to become available.

5   AN ANTI-ESSENTIALIST READING OF THE ORIGINS OF INTRANETS

In order to be able to properly understand the Boeing case, it is necessary to understand the wider context of intranet and internet development at the time that Boeing began its project. This will enable us to appreciate the extent to which internet technology was widely available and the sophistication of the browsers that were being used in the implementation.

The origins of the internet go back to the late 1960s (Krol 1992) (Hafner and Lyon 1996) although its growth in popularity came much later. This can be shown in a number of ways, for example, Figure 1 shows the growth in the number of internet hosts (data taken from http://www.nw.com). A clearer picture of the popular growth can be seen in Figure 2 which shows newpaper interest in the internet. It records the number of articles mentioning the word "internet" when searching the FT-Profile newspaper database. This database contains full text articles from leading British and International newspapers. Whilst there is limited coverage of newspapers for the 1980s, the growth of interest in mid 1990s is such that any distortion caused by the limited early coverage is unlikely to be significant.

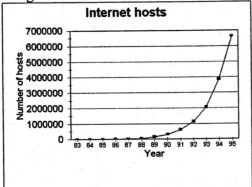

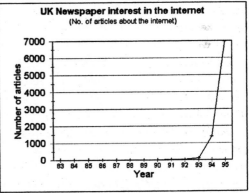

Figure 1: Growth in the internet

Figure 2: Growth in popular interest in the internet

Both graphs clearly demonstrate that the main increase in interest in the internet took place in 1994/1995. Before then, interest in the internet was limited to researchers and scientists rather than organisations and the public at large.

Thus, at the time that Boeing began their project (1993) usage of the internet was still rather limited and specialised. It was not a tool that was widely used by individuals and organisations, rather it was a research tool restricted to a few sophisticated users.

Boeing were developing their intranet using web browsers. The world wide web was conceived by Tim Berners-Lee in 1989 and the first web browser was developed in 1990. Other web browsers, such as Cello for Windows and Viola for X-Windows were released in 1992. In 1993 Marc Andreessen wrote the initial Mosaic browser (Rai, *et al.* 1998) and in 1994 he went on to cofound Netscape Communications with Netscape Navigator released that same year. Microsoft's Internet Explorer was only released in 1995 (Berghel 1998).

Thus, when Boeing was first experimenting with the using web technology for its intranet, the only software that was available was programs like Cello and the first versions of Mosaic. These initial software releases had limited functionality, were often relatively slow (especially in comparison to current browser software) and were likely to include significant faults. Certainly when Netscape was launched, new versions of the beta software were being released on a very regular basis as new functionality and fixes were introduced.

By undertaking a similar search through the FT-Profile newspaper database, the earliest uses of the term "intranet" (apart from an intra bank settling system) in the popular and trade presses suggest that intranets originated in late 1994. Moreover, many organisations did not consider the early software (Mosaic and Netscape 1.0) as suitable for use yet Boeing seemed prepared to begin to use these packages.

If we look at this situation from an essentialist perspective, then it is very difficult to explain why Boeing began its intranet project at this time. They were developing a system on the basis of a relatively new technology (internet), using unstable early software as the interface for the system at a time when the concept of intranets had not been formalised. The users of the system would be using something they hadn't heard of (there would be no "buzz" about using the internet at work), in an environment that was prone to many annoying program crashes and a generally limited and slow service. These are hardly ideal circumstances for introducing a new innovation. Indeed, an essentialist reading (*"Once the machine works people will be convinced"*) would suggest that the proposed new system would fail miserably.

And yet Moeller (1996) states that there are 300 servers that are used by 20000 employees. How can this come about? At this point, the anti-essentialist reading becomes more convincing. The technology came to be adopted *despite* the limitations in the initial versions. The slow service and the crashing software, the "essential" parts of the technology, were not taken into consideration, rather the potential (*"what we can read into it"*) was what drove the development. This is clearly a management rather than technology question and as such runs the risk of project escalation (Keil 1995). If we are to take a reading where we focus on the potential rather than the technology then we are taking a strong anti-essentialist position. Any weakening means that explanations for why the technology has taken off *have* to take into account and explain why the project succeeded despite the fact that there was considerable evidence indicating that "essential" parts of the technology were failing to provide the required service.

6   CONCLUSIONS AND FURTHER RESEARCH

This paper has reviewed a number of ways in which interpretative researchers have conceptualised the role of technology. These have ranged from those who view it as something that is inherently more flexible than other forms of technology, through those who feel that the particularities of it enable and constrain what can be achieved with an information system, to those who argue that there is nothing essential to any technology.

This anti-essentialist position was then taken and used to analyse a case study of a particular new form of technology, namely intranets. By using published descriptions of an intranet project and combining these with an understanding of the context in terms of hardware and software that existed at the time, it was possible to see that the intranet project was begun and maintained in the face of contrary evidence suggesting that it should be curtailed. As we have seen, an anti-essentialist reading of the situation, which suggests that there is nothing inherent in the technology that affects how it is used, seems particularly convincing in this situation.

There are clearly limitations to the study presented. The case of intranet adoption described is based on secondary sources. A far more detailed study, which had access to primary sources would enable a far more precise picture to be painted. By linking the exact dates at which the intranet project was initialised with the particular releases of web browsers available at that time, a far more detailed understanding of what the technological constraints limiting the acceptance of the infrastructure could be found. This would give a far clearer indication of the extent to which technological factors were explicitly ignored in allowing the project to continue.

A more forward looking study would examine a technology being adopted at a particular point in time, rather than reviewing historical data. By observing (but not participating in) management decisions on new technologies, useful grounded data on the usefulness of anti-essentialist ideas could be found.

The ideas expressed in this paper have important implications for wider information systems research. Certainly, issues of project escalation (Keil 1995) and information systems failure (Holmes and Poulymenakou 1995) (Mitev 1996) would be very different when viewed from an anti-essentialist perspective.

References

Berghel H (1998) Who won the Mosaic war? *Communications of the ACM* **41(10)**, 13-16.

Grint K and Woolgar S (1997) *The machine at work: Technology, work and organization.* Polity Press, Cambridge.

Hafner K and Lyon M (1996) *Where wizards stay up late: The origins of the Internet.* Simon & Schuster, New York.

Hills M (1996) *Intranet business strategies.* John Wiley & Sons, London.

Holmes A and Poulymenakou A (1995) Towards a conceptual framework for investigating information systems failure. In *Proceedings of the Third European Conference on Information Systems* 805-823, Athens, Greece.

Keil M (1995) Pulling the plug: Software project management and the problem of project escalation. *MIS Quarterly* **19(4)**, 421-447.

Klein H K and Myers M D (1999) *A set of principles for conducting and evaluating interpretive field studies in information systems* (To appear in MISQ, preprint) Last accessed: 29 October Last updated: October 1998 Address: http://www.auckland.ac.nz/msis/isworld/MMyers/Klein-Myers.html

Krol E (1992) *The whole internet: User's guide & catalog.* O'Reilly & Associates,

Sebastopol, CA.

Latour B (1987) *Science in action: How to follow scientists and engineers through society.* Harvard University Press, Cambridge, MA.

Latour B (1996) *Aramis, or the love of technology.* (trans. Catherine Porter) Harvard University Press, Cambridge, MA.

Lloyd P and Boyle P (1998) *Web-weaving: Intranets, extranets, and strategic alliances.* Butterworth, Heinemann, London.

Mitev N N (1996) More than a failure? The computerized reservation systems at French Railways. *IT and People* **9(4)**, 8-19.

Moeller M (1996) Boeing network takes flight with pioneering Intranet project. *PC Week* **13(7)**,

Monteiro E and Hanseth O (1995) Social shaping of information infrastructure: On being specific about the technology. In *Information technology and changes in organizational work* (Orlikowski W J, Walsham G, Jones M R and DeGross J I eds.) 325-343, Chapman & Hall, London.

Rai A, Ravichandran T and Samaddar S (1998) How to anticipate the Internet's global diffusion. *Communications of the ACM* **41(10)**, 97-106.

Sahay S, Palit M and Robey D (1994) A relativist approach to studying the social construction of information technology. *European Journal of information systems* **3(4)**, 248-258.

Smith M R and Marx L (1994) *Does technology drive history? The dilemma of technological determinism* . The MIT Press, Cambridge, MA.

Sprout A (1995) The internet inside your company. In *Fortune,* **27,**November,

Tiles M and Oberdiek H (1995) *Living in a technological culture: Human tools and human values.* Routledge, London.

Vidgen R and McMaster T (1995) Black boxes, non-human stakeholders and the translation of IT through mediation. In *Information technology and changes in organizational work* (Orlikowski W J, Walsham G, Jones M R and DeGross J I eds.) 250-271, Chapman & Hall, London.

Walsham G (1993) *Interpreting information systems in organisations.* John Wiley & Sons, Chichester.

Whitley E A and Darking S (1994) Information Systems: Social Technology in Social Systems. In *Proceedings of the Second European Conference on Information Systems* 771-776, Nijenrode University Press, Nijenrode University, The Netherlands.

Winner L (1980) Do artifacts have politics? *Daedalus* **109,**121-36.

CHAPTER 11

ARCHITECTURAL DISCOURSE FOR INFORMATION SYSTEMS

J Dobson, M Martin, M Bonatti and M Morganti
University of Newcastle; ITALTEL R&D Labs, Italy

Abstract

We examine the concept of architecture as a response to the requirements of a society to create technical systems and organisational structures to support social, commercial and administrative relationships, and the discourse of the architect in constructing such a response. The very concept of society implies the institutionalisation of such relationships and it is a characteristic of these institutionalised structures that, most of the time, there is no requirement to make many aspects of intentions, policies and values explicit in the architectural discourse. Under stable conditions, it is both safe and efficient to rely on implicit understandings based on the practical experience of both requirements owners and solution providers. When changes take place within a society which invalidate these understandings, communication between problem owners and solution providers tends to break down. In such circumstances, a dialogue can be re-established only on the basis of a clear distinction between the structure of problem space and the concepts used to explore it on the one hand, and the solution language on the other. We show the form of an architectural discourse which can be used to establish a dialogue which bridges this linguistic gap.

1   ARCHITECTURES AND COMPLEXES

The first task which faces us in this exploration is one of definition: we must establish the sense in which we are using the term "architecture". We talk about the architecture *of* something, so we cannot separate a definition of architecture from some definition of the range of things that it can be generated through its use.

The concrete or abstract products of the application of a well founded and appropriate architecture have properties intended by the architect: the purpose and value of an architecture is to achieve predictability, creating things which are fit for an envisaged purpose and which exhibit systematic properties. It is the responsibility of the architect to ensure that the envisaged properties are an appropriate and acceptable response to the requirements of the owners and users of the product of the architectural process.

In this paper, we are concerned with a particular sort of architecture capable of generating a particular class of construct which we will call an information system. The context in which such systems are conceived, designed and deployed we call a socio-technical complex and such systems, once deployed, themselves become part of the complex in which they were produced. We shall in the main concentrate on those complexes where the technical components constructed using information, computing, control and communications technologies (ICT), though we believe our approach to be more generally applicable.

Complexes, which include some resources which have been systematised and others which have not, contain two types of components: *social* ones, comprising people and their cultural, political and economic contexts and constructs, and *technical* ones, comprising technological artefacts and other resources. To stress the point: we are not concerned with purely technical systems or with human organisations such as enterprises or markets, but with composition of these two types of system into purposeful structures which we term socio-technical complexes. The architectural problem is thus one of co-optimisation: it is not a matter of optimising the social system alone or the technical system alone but of optimising their combination. Thus the architectural process may result not only in an evolution of the structure of a complex; it may also result in shifting the boundary between those aspects which are systematised and those that are not. The outcome of an architectural discourse may be the generation and institutionalisation of new meanings and new values within the socio-technical structure, which implies emergent change rather than mere development or elaboration. This raises fundamental questions regarding the evaluation of architectural discourse because there can be no stable demarcation between the subjects and the objects of such a process.

How, then, does the term architecture apply to a socio-technical complex? Our view of architecture is that it can only be understood in terms of both a construct and a process, and therefore it is the dual aspects of discourse as a linguistic framework for prescription and description of a construct on the one hand and discourse as a communicative process between people on the other, which is most useful in exploring the richness of the concept of architecture. We will define the scope and structure of the architectural discourse by considering how it is situated in relation to society, sectors and technologies; and we shall lay down some general principles governing the structure of architectural discourse in relation to system components constructed from ICT components — i.e. information systems.

We see society as being structured into a number of different contexts, which we term sectors, in which activities are subject to a particular set of interpretations and evaluations. Each sector is characterised by concerns about particular classes of relationships and resources. A sector is a cluster in which intra-sectoral (commercial and administrative) relationships are stronger than inter-sectoral relationships. There are many such sectoral contexts and their boundaries are fluid; examples are commerce, education, healthcare, entertainment, government, defence, and so on. Sectorisation is one of the most useful ways of classifying socio-technical complexes and the architectures used to sustain them. From the viewpoint of this paper, we shall consider each sector as constituting a separate domain of discourse.

Within each sector, there is an important distinction to be made between its structural part and its infrastructural part. The former corresponds to the roles and activities which are taken to be specific to the sector and which in fact define it, whereas infrastructural roles and resources may be shared or re-used in a number of different contexts. In any particular sector, what is considered to be structural and what is considered as infrastructural may change due to economies of provision or changes in social convention: there is no fixed demarcation. At any one time, it is characteristic of the infrastructure that it is considered as consisting primarily of resources (including, of course, human resources) whereas the structure is defined primarily in terms of social relationships. (For more on structuring as a explanation of continuity in social systems, and resources as structured properties of social systems, see Giddens [Giddens 1984].)

Structural and infrastructural requirements are not the only inputs to the architectural discourse; there are also constraints and capabilities generated from technological and engineering considerations. Since we are concerned with information, control and communications technologies, such constraints and capabilities may be classified in terms of the storage, processing, transmission, sensing, manipulation, presentation of information.

Technologies are offered to address these capabilities either individually or in combination. One of the most notable influences on sectoral architectures has been the convergence of technologies, meaning that more and more of these basic information handling capabilities have been delivered by the same technology: computers and communications based on micro-electronics. It is this convergence that has given rise to the need to re-investigate the problem-oriented aspects of an architecture whose job is to support socio-technical complexes.

2   SUMMARY OF ARCHITECTURAL DISCOURSE

In this section we present a framework for conducting architectural discourse. It is based on three dimensions which define a space within which different aspects of the architectural process and role relationships of the architect may be positioned. These dimensions are:

- Architectural *language and discourse,* which ranges over a set of
- Architectural *projections*, each of which delivers a set of
- Architectural *transparencies.*

We propose precisely five levels of language and stages of architectural discourse and precisely five projections; there are many transparencies.

In the case of information systems, a similar framework has been presented by

Zachman [Zachman 1987]; but although the structure there outlined agrees with ours, the detail is too oriented to information (or computing) applications and is not entirely appropriate to (tele)communication service systems. The same point can be made concerning the structurally similar Open Distributed Processing approach [ISO 1993]. What has happened since these approaches were elaborated is that there has been a convergence between applications and services and ICT systems are configured from both types of component. We therefore need to generalise and extend these previous approaches, since we believe that some rather more abstract cognitive processes are at work here, which also have relevance outside our domain of ICT systems: see for example Jacques [Jacques, Gibson *et al.* 1978], Brachman [Brachman 1985], Humphreys [Humphreys 1986] and Piaget [Piaget 1978].

An architecture is required when there is something new to be built. If the problem is simply one of extending what is already in existence — bricolage — then there is no real need to employ an architect, since it is both safe and efficient to rely on implicit understandings based on the previous experience of the requirements owners and solution providers.

Where, however, the changes that take place are sufficiently fundamental to invalidate these understandings, or where what is to be built is radically new, communication between problem owners and solution providers tends to break down. In such circumstances, a dialogue can be re-established only on the basis of a clear distinction between the structure of problem space and the concepts used to explore it on the one hand, and the solution language on the other. It is the structure of this discourse that we shall investigate.

The architect's role is necessarily Janus-like, combining engagement with the client and engagement with the builder. Each of these engagements is facilitated through a set of architectural models and a form of discourse, whose purpose is to transfer some models to the client and some to the builder. This transference is crucially important. The client must assume ownership of the client models, because only so can the client maintain responsibility for the requirements.

So one problem for the architect is how to design two sets of models (problem, solution) such that each set can be transferred to its appropriate owner (client, builder) and the relationship between the sets can be clearly demonstrated. Such design and demonstration is an integral part of what we mean by architectural discourse.

3   THE FORM OF ARCHITECTURAL DISCOURSE

Architectural discourse is concerned with the articulation of problems and policies and their resolution and implementation through the formulation of solutions. Since the entire process which makes use of a systems architecture is extended in time and space and involves a large number of participants, it is essential that the intermediate and final results are expressed, preserved and interpreted correctly and consistently: the purpose of architectural discourse is to provide appropriate inputs to, and records of, policy making and design.

We shall propose the form of a general language in which architectural discourse can be constructed, with particular application to the case where the universe of discourse is socio-technical complexes with ICT components.

What we here mean by 'form' will, we hope, become clear; but we are not proposing a syntax or even a vocabulary. Rather, we are showing something which is more abstract: the general structure of such a language, and how it may be related to a particular vocabulary and syntax. The general structure reflects the structure of systems and the process of languaging; a particular vocabulary and syntax is chosen according to the type and needs of the particular system being architected.

Whatever process the architectural discourse follows, it involves five different sorts of language in which statements in the discourse are expressed and cognitive processes which are involved. If the discourse is to make progress, then the participants must be able to assign the text of previous stages and of current presentations to one of the following levels of expression:

Level 5: Problem articulation.
The form of expression here is natural language and "rich pictures" and the content includes concerns, interests, values; in fact, anything that a problem owner or policy maker may wish to say in trying to articulate the matter of concern. Clearly, level 5 expressions are not a fit input into an engineering process but only to a problem structuring process. "The system must be secure" is an example of a level 5 expression because security can mean many different things depending on what is of value to the stakeholders. The statements at level 5 are part of a problem articulation process, and the cognitive operations are probably beyond language.

Level 4: Problem structuring.
The objective of level 4 discourse is to define a set of frames of discourse which can provide the basis for a shared semantic. The process which takes us from level 5 to level 4 is semiotic in nature and explicatory in effect. It succeeds when the policy maker recognises not only that requirements and interests have been satisfactorily re-expressed but that the concepts established at this level do not restrict the expression of evolution of policy and utility. There will be many frames at level 4, corresponding to different areas of concern expressed at level 5. The cognitive operations are those of a problem structuring process.

An example of a level 4 expression is that, to be secure, the system must maintain the separation of information domains, corresponding to a secure military system, or (as an alternative) it must provide traceability so that any change can be associated with a known agent external to the system, corresponding to a secure financial system. We have thus left axiological values behind at level 5 and now have expressions which are a fit input into a process of specification.

Level 3: Establishing the syntactic structure (or model) within which solutions may be specified and evaluated.

A level 3 expression presents a theory of a solution to a problem or requirement expressed at level 4, and takes the form of some kind of logical calculus. There is a range of logical and syntactic forms available and different ones have been appropriated in different architectural domains. They may be based on formal languages, high level application oriented languages or simulation tools. An appropriate calculus must be selected for each frame defined at level 4 (representing one particular component of the problem as expressed at level 5). A spreadsheet model is a good example of a level 3 structure, as is a formal specification in some defined logic.

Level 2: The exploration and evaluation of options.

This level of discourse exercises or interprets each level 3 structure or calculus in order to evaluate its properties and consequences. Thus, "what if" questions applied to the spreadsheet or the evaluation of a specification for liveness or closure belong at this level. Clearly, the type of evaluation which can be undertaken depends entirely on the form of the corresponding level 3 descriptions or models.

In general, what is being explored at level 2 is the relationship between the operations in the calculus established at level 3 and activities or responsibilities in the world which are being modelled by the calculus. For example, identifying the opportunities for cost reduction or estimating the risk of taking a particular business stance, are activities that can be supported by operations conducted in a spreadsheet model. The quality of conclusions drawn or decisions made at level 2 depend on how well the limitations and assumptions of the model are understood.

Level 1: Assigning referents to solution abstractions or signs.

Activities at this level establish the correspondence between the terms within a level 3 structure and entities in the real or proposed world. It also involves assigning or estimating values for parameters which are relevant in design and policy trade-offs and selections. Examples of level 1 activities include deciding what real-world entities are to be represented by particular spreadsheet variables or assigning numerical values to parameters.

The presentation of these levels does not imply a synoptic view of progress in the definition or application of an architectural discourse: the exchanges which take place, and the text generated, often contain material from different levels. What the levels do is to provide a basis for categorising, interpreting and comparing the different sorts of models, descriptions and formulations presented within different engineering traditions and cultures; thus they operate as an hermeneutic framework within which we can analyse current architectures.

In what follows, it is important to remember that these levels refer to the cognitive processes that take place during the process (which generates the discourse) of constructing and using an architecture. They do not relate to the components and systems with which the architecture deals, nor to the context within which the architecture is situated. In order to discuss these components and contexts, we need a set of abstractions, which following ODP [ISO 1993] we shall term *projections*.

4   PROJECTIONS

In the general case of socio-technical complexes, a single analytic frame or related set of level 4 concepts proves insufficient to say all the different sorts of things that need to be said. The process at level 4 is ontological in nature involving the application of a limited set of categories in order to set bounds on some aspect of the problem and solution spaces. There is a tension between the need for accessibility and tractability of the representation of architectural models and the complexity of the phenomena and ideas which are their subject. A projection provides simplification through abstraction. It may be complete with respect to its coverage of the system and its environment, but a single projection is necessarily incomplete with respect to the architectural discourse as a whole.

The ANSA project was the first architectural research to propose five specific "projections" which were claimed to provide complete coverage of information processing systems. The specific projections of *enterprise, information, computation, engineering* and *technology*, were defined by ANSA and taken up in the Open Distributed Processing standards. However, we now suggest that these are examples of a more generic concept. The more general formulation of the five projections and examples of domain specific embodiments are:

An enterprise projection which deals with rights and responsibilities.

A instrumental projection which provides an abstract framework to link acts, intended to create and discharge responsibilities, with actions on resources.

A behaviour projection which is concerned with defining functionality. Computation represents a particular case of a behaviour projection for information systems. Other conceptualisations of behaviour may be appropriate in control, communications or transaction architectures.

A design projection which deals with the organisation and co-ordination of components and the allocation of functions to resources. In the broad concept of the socio-technical architecture, this must include the design of workflows and operational procedures as well as the design of the technical systems that support them.

A physical projection which is concerned with the physical capabilities and limitations of the resources, both material and human, to be deployed in the proposed solution.

Before we consider each of these generalised projections in more detail, we must introduce the concept of a *transparency*. This is an architectural tool which allows us to abstract from a particular system concern within a projection, and treat it separately in policy definition and design processes. Location transparency, for example, allows the functionality of a system to be defined without any commitments as to where, within a distributed implementation, functioning components will be located. Location can then be treated later as a matter of (changeable) policy or design optimisation.

A projection is therefore, defined in terms of
- the class of policy issues and concerns it encompasses,
- concepts and language it supports and
- the transparencies which it provides to manage complexity.

Together, the five generic projections represent a framework within which all the different aspects of information systems associated with socio-technical complexes may be articulated. In the following sections we will examine each of them in more detail, but there are three general points to make first.

1.   Architectural models, as we define them here, cannot be limited to the specification of solutions as a set of physical, design and behaviour projections; they must also be able to specify the interpretations which are intended to be placed on states and behaviour of the described socio-technical system. The concepts used in a model expressing intended interpretations must include responsibilities and obligations, rights and duties, because, in the creation of such systems, these also are distributed and allocated as well as functions and resources. The enterprise and instrumental projections defined below provide the means to create such models of intended interpretation. In the case of institutionalised solutions, these intentional aspects may remain implicit, and consequently there may be no need for an architecture (as we are here using the term).

2.   In reasoning about the allocation and organisation of responsibilities, we require a theory of composition and analysis which yields insights into conflicts and synergies of interest and which supports the identification and characterisation of failures of intention. These capabilities have direct correlates in the analysis of the behavioural and structural aspects of physical systems.

3.   Finally, an important line of thought which underlies this approach to architectural thinking is the use of architectural models in dependability analysis. The idea of multiple projections arose, in part, from attempts to find some way to categorise and analyse the many modes of failure in complex systems. Failure (real or hypothesised) has the effect of forcing reconsideration of where the boundaries of the system lie; typically they have to be expanded in both time and space in order to explain and manage failure. The projections are a way of delineating a set of spaces in which system boundaries can be drawn and redrawn.

4.1   The enterprise projection

The enterprise projection concerns the structuring of responsibilities, rights and obligations. The transparencies that it provides mask the existence of organisational boundaries and the scope of roles for individuals. This allows us to consider what responsibilities there are, and how they are related, separately from how we combine and allocate them. The projection supports the exploration of issues such as the internalisation or externalisation of organisational relationships and the distinctions between contractual, co-operative and competitive relationships.

The notion of responsibility is key to the enterprise projection, since one of the main purposes of models created in this projection is to reason about such things as the relocation of responsibilities as a result of decisions to allocate functions to human or to systems resources. For example, in a ship whose automatic defences have been armed, simply to say that the gun has been assigned "responsibility" for defending the ship against attacking missiles, is to ignore complex problems of division of responsibility between (at least) the designer of the gun, the ship designer, the watch officer, the ship's commander and the commander-in-chief. The allocation of responsibility becomes a particular issue in the presence of failure, as for example, if the gun were to shoot down an off-course civil aircraft under the mistaken impression (if that is what guns have) that it was about to attack the ship.

4.2   The instrumental projection

The instrumental projection is concerned with the representation, preservation and exchange of the intermediate and final results of exchanges between responsible agents. The exchanges, which we call "conversations", are defined in this abstraction in terms of sequences of acts. For example, the acts associated with information include generate and interpret and acts associated with resources include allocate and consume.

An instrument corresponds to a physical resource which serves to link intended acts with performed actions. The word is thus to be interpreted almost in a legal sense (e.g. a contract) rather than in a scientific or medical sense. Persistent instruments take the form of documents or records while ephemeral instruments may be embodied in the use of connections and channels. For example, we may commit to a purchase by shaking hands or signing a contract or saying so on the telephone or by clicking a button on a browser and, in each case, the action and corresponding resource are taken to have instrumentalised the act.

The transparencies offered in this projection concern the dependability of instruments, that is to say, the extent to which a particular instrument will furnish reliable evidence of the corresponding act and agent. Again, it is failure mode analysis that reveals what characteristics of dependability are required of a particular instrument. The projection also offers representation transparency allowing the architect to consider languages, symbols and data structures which relate to the information carrying aspects of an instrument separately from the performative and evidential aspects which relate to the job that the instrument does in communication protocols.

4.3   The behavioural projection

This projection is concerned with the specification of functions of the technical system and also of organisational processes performed by role holders such as its users, operators and maintainers. Different sets of functions and procedures are significant in different architectural contexts.

Where the overall solution is dominated by information processing, the actions which are of most interest are reading, writing, creating, transforming and destroying data. In such cases, the systems-oriented behaviour projection is expressed in terms of computation. In a control environment, sensing and manipulating of physical resources are also significant while in a transaction architecture, actions such as co-ordinate, commit and roll-back are important. The behavioural projection of a telecommunications architecture is concerned with actions such as connect, transmit, receive and disengage.

The transparencies afforded by the behavioural projection depend on whether the behaviour is considered primarily as computation, control, transaction or communication. Typically, a computational view masks real timing issues, and may mask location, replication and migration as well as other transparencies. Similarly a control view of behaviour may take a simplified view of presentation, a transaction view may ignore accuracy of numerical computation, and a communications view may treat data structure as a transparency.

We have identified four behavioural domains: computation, transaction, control and communication. Socio-technical architectures have, so far, been simple in the sense that one or other of these domains has been treated as dominant and the others either ignored or relegated to being transparencies at the behavioural level or at a logically lower design level. For example, information systems have been able to treat communications as 'mere plumbing' while communications architectures have treated computation as an application issue and therefore out of scope. Sectoral convergence in the information infrastructure seems to be calling many of these traditional architectural demarcations into question.

4.4   The design projection

The design projection is concerned with the disposition of real resources to execute the behaviours defined in the previous projection. The wider concept of socio-technical architectures provides for the division of the functions in a solution between system resources and human resources. It is the trade-offs of these allocations and of the disposition of resources within the systems and organisational domains themselves which are represented, evaluated and justified in the design projection. It also provides for tracing the consequent chains of responsibility in both the definition, design and development epochs and in the operational epoch. So, a design projection encompasses systems design as well as the design of organisational structures and work flows.

There are many design transparencies appropriate to different applications domains. For example, in the area of fault tolerant systems, component replication may be offered as a transparency; in a system with mobile elements, location transparency may be significant.

4.5 The physical projection

The physical projection represents the characteristics of the material used in construction. Parameterisation of performance is the transparency which is supported in this projection and this applies to both systems implementation technologies as well as to human resources. So concepts of ergonomics and operator or user performance are included here. The physical projection provides the inventory of acceptable solution components, the rules which control their deployment and documents the constraints that they place on the design process.

5 CONCLUSION

Hitherto, the boundaries of the information, telecommunications and broadcast sectors have remained relatively stable and sectoral approaches to the architectures of the infrastructure have proved adequate. Architectural processes and architectural languages have, until recently, operated effectively within the bounds of the specific sectors in which they have evolved. As a consequence, the market structures within which sectoral infrastructures were provisioned and within which structural activities were conducted, have remained sufficiently stable to maintain the validity of the shared assumptions and understandings of both suppliers and purchasers of the technical components of socio-technical complexes.

Concepts such as the Information Society and the Global Information Infrastructure (GII) represent a challenge to the sectoral status quo. They imply a convergence at the structural and infrastructural levels across traditional sector boundaries. This challenge is exposing the limitations of the individual architectural processes and languages particularly in the following respects:

- There is a general inadequacy in the ability to support the architectural discourse of problem definition across multiple sectors; sectoral architectures rely on implicit or superficial representation of structural roles and relationships because there has not until now been a need to articulate them explicitly or in detail.

- Sector architectures have a built-in scope, treating some issues as platform or infrastructure and others as part of the application or user domain, and there has been general agreement, within a sector, on the location and characterisation of this boundary. Re-scoping an architecture proves to be threatening to these established structuring conventions.

- Within the scope of a sector architecture, there is a built in prioritisation of issues and concerns appropriate to its domain. These priorities may not correspond to those of other contexts of application in other sectors.

- The nature of the complexity which is the focus of attention varies between sector architectures as does the particular types of uncertainties they manage. This can represent an insuperable cultural barrier between architects and engineers from the different traditions.

If our thesis is valid and the challenges presented by the GII require a fundamental reappraisal of architecture, then we must engage in a exercise which has previously been conducted relatively infrequently. It is fraught with a number of deep philosophical problems which are usually, and quite rightly, ignored in the interests of progress and practicality. However, we may need some sort of map of these problems if we are to address the challenges of creating a Global Information Infrastructure which could support and sustain an Information Society.

6   REFLECTION

In developing our architectural approach and in exploring the methodological principles which underpin it, it is easy to make the mistake of assuming that discoveries and insights at more fundamental and abstract levels will be recognised and appreciated by those who are concerned with practical, real life problems. What is relevant to the architect in the role of mediator between problem space and solution space is not necessarily of interest to the denizens of either domain. And what is relevant to the methodologist in the construction of a particular architectural framework may not necessarily be of material interest to the architect who exploits it. This is not to deny that awareness and understanding of the theoretical underpinnings of a method can be an important element in its use; but it is neither necessary nor sufficient and, in practice, can serve as a distraction and obstacle to progress.

So for the architect to ask other roleholders what they think of an architecture or even whether they think it is relevant and valuable, may prove a misleading enquiry. Asking them what value they derived from the architectural discourse as they experienced it, may seem to them to be a more relevant question; but this, of course, leaves open the issue of whether the benefit is associated with the architect or with the method and material being used.

It is clear that the enterprise, instrumental and computational models, while being of some interest, are often not seen as the most significant benefit derived from the approach advocated in this paper by the engineers or by business planners and problem owners. The end users of the applications and information systems developed often have no contact at all with models created in the various projections. Our experience as architects, however, is that discussion between ourselves and our clients consistently raises interesting and fruitful questions and improved understanding of the problems and

CHAPTER 12

ONLY WORDS: A FRAMEWORK FOR ANALYSING THE DISCOURSE OF IT OPERATIONS PERSONNEL

Sue Nielsen
Griffith University, Australia

Abstract

This paper describes a four dimensional framework for analysing discourse, based on the work of Fairclough (1992) and Halliday and Hasan (1985) which enables close attention to be paid to the features of the discourse and the interpretation of the meaning of the discourse within the immediate context and the wider organisational context. The framework is illustrated by reference to a sample of discourse from a longitudinal study of the Operations Group of an Information Technology Centre in an Australian university. The paper attends to issues in discourse analysis such as the problem of bounding the text and also the need to balance the understanding of features of the discourse, with understanding of features of the social context. The framework is proposed as a useful approach to understanding change in the IT environment.

1   INTRODUCTION

In Information Systems research there has been increasing interest in the part which language plays in shaping the activities and context of information systems development and use. For example, Walsham (1993) states that *'The formation of IS strategy can be viewed as a process of continuous discourse'* (p. 157). This paper describes a framework for analysing discourse which enables close attention to be paid to features of the discourse and to the interpretation of the meaning of the discourse within its immediate context and within the wider organisational and social context. This approach assumes that the 'reality' of information systems development and use is socially constructed, continuing the tradition of IS research by Boland (1991), Walsham (1993) and others.

This paper also discusses the use of this framework in a longitudinal study of change management in the Operations Group (OG) of a university Information technology Centre in an Australian university. The study commenced with an intensive three month uncovered possibilities and options that had not yet been considered. It is this aspect which now seems to us to be of most benefit in our approach. Because we can trace a path from organisational possibility to a computational framework comprehensible to engineers, our architectural approach is doing the job it is supposed to. It is bridging between two universes of discourse, even though from within either of those universes, the overall scope and value of the architecture may only be partially discerned.

References

Brachman (1985) R.J. Brachman, "On the Epistemological Status of Semantic Networks", in *Readings in Knowledge Representation,* ed. R. J. B. a. H. J. Levesque, pp. 192-215, Morgan Kaufmann, Los Altos, CA, 1985.

Giddens (1984) A. Giddens, *The Constitution of Society* , University of California Press, 1984.

Humphreys (1986) P.C. Humphreys, "Intelligence in Decision Support", in *New Directions in Research on Decision Making,* ed. H. J. B. Brehmer, P. Lourens and G. Seron, pp. 333-361, Elsevier Science Publishers (North-Holland), Amsterdam, 1986.

ISO (1993) ISO, *Open Systems Interconnection, Data Management and Open Distributed Processing, Draf ODP Trading Function,* Report No. ISO/IEC JTC 1/SC21/WG7/N880, International Standards Organisation, 1993.

Jacques, Gibson et al. (1978) E. Jacques, R.O. Gibson and D.J. Isaac, *Levels of Abstraction in Logic and Human Action* , Heinemann, London, 1978.

Piaget (1978) J. Piaget, *The Development of Thought* , Blackwell, Oxford, 1978.

Zachman (1987) J.A. Zachman, "A Framework for Information System Architecture", *IBM Systems Journal,* vol. 26, no. 3, pp. 276-292, 1987 .

period, which involved shadowing a key informant for about twenty five hours, observing the other OG staff at their work, conducting discourse based interviews with staff and attending meetings. The study continued for another two years, including attendance at most staff meetings, but with less intensive observation of staff (approximately 3 to 4 times per month.). The study terminated when the Information Technology Centre (ITC) was restructured and the staff from the Operations Group were dispersed into other sections. The focus of the study was on how the Group managed change to the organisation of their IT support services and the development and implementation of an information system to support their Help Line telephone service.

A particular text, considered as pertinent to the development of the Help Line system, is used as an example in this paper. In this text, my key informant, "June" is describing a particular procedure to me. She is interrupted by a telephone call, but then returns to take up her description where she left off. The supervisor overhears the topic of discussion and joins in. After the supervisor leaves, June seeks affirmation that I did understand what she was talking about. The text is provided in the Appendix, and is referred to hereafter as the OG text.

2   A FOUR DIMENSIONAL APPROACH TO DISCOURSE

Discourse analysis has developed differently in a number of disciplines, according to the interests, expertises and purposes of the users. Generally, approaches to discourse analysis can be distinguished according to whether the expertise and major focus is on the language or the social context, and can be criticised accordingly. Discourse analysis within the field of linguistics is criticised for neglecting the 'content' of texts, and the lack of expertise in the social context (Thompson 1984). Conversely, many social theorists can be criticised for their lack of understanding of the importance of the structural features of language, using approaches such as content analysis which may assume that the frequency of occurrence of a word or phrase signifies something about its meaning. A considerable body of research has been carried out in information systems research using speech-act theory (Iivari et al 1998), but this approach has also been criticised for lack of attention to context (Janson and Woo 1996).

This paper discusses the approach developed by Fairclough (1992) who attempts to draw together language analysis and social theory in a way that will be *particularly useful for investigating change in language and will be useable in studies of social and cultural change'* (p. 1) Fairclough proposes to show how discourse processes develop in different ways as the social contexts change. He also takes a critical perspective. The dialectical relationship between discursive and social practices is not always overt and as new meanings are invested in conventional language structures, the meanings can be difficult to elucidate. This reinforces the idea that language does not offer a transparent window to reality, but continually shifts in its relationship to other social practices.

A four dimensional approach to discourse was adopted in this study, based on the work of Fairclough (1992) and Halliday and Hasan (1985). Fairclough sees any piece of discourse as *'being simultaneously a piece of text, an instance of discursive practice, and an instance of social practice'* (p. 3). The 'text' dimension is concerned with analysis of features of the text. The 'discursive practice' dimension specifies the ways that texts are produced and understood. *'The 'social practice' dimension attends to issues of concern in social analysis such as the institutional and organisational circumstances of the discursive event and how that shapes the nature of the discursive practice.'* (p. 3).

In order to provide a better link between the text and its immediate context I have extended Fairclough's conception of discourse by incorporating aspects of the approach taken in systemic linguistics by Halliday and Hasan (1985).

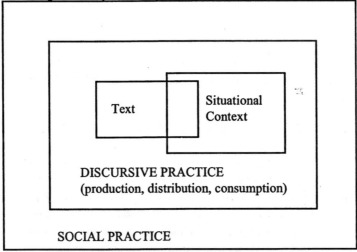

Figure 1: Four dimensional conception of discourse
(adapted from Fairclough 1992, p.73)

Such a link is important where the analyst wishes to make a rich description of the discourse practices of a group of people as well as viewing these practices within the wider context. This approach also avoids the possible criticism of the discourse analysis being too general and providing too little analysis of the situated practices. The situational context dimension of discourse is concerned with the relationship between features of the text and the immediate context. How this situational context is conceptualised depends on the view of the functions of language. Halliday and Hasan (1985) propose three contextual variables, based on three functions of language. (By the "function" of language is meant the constructive and constitutive effects of language.) In other words, any discourse simultaneously represents firstly reality or experience (what is going on), secondly, the relationships between the participants (who is taking part) and finally, the relationship between the text and other texts which precede or follow it. The OG text can therefore be understood as being firstly about what happens to reports on outstanding calls, secondly about the relationship between the author, the key informant

(June) and the Supervisor (Averil) and lastly about the way such conversations are conducted, including their relationship to other discourse in which such topics are discussed (for example, meetings).

This approach to discourse assumes that our initial understanding of what texts mean may be contradicted by reference to the contexts within which the texts are produced. Klein and Truex (1995) explain it thus ' *The preliminary examination of a text may suggest a very different reading until one considers the wider context* ' (p. 28). In the example they discuss their initial reading of a text which was contradicted by reference to the immediate context, but looking at the larger context, their initial reading was determined as correct. This paper will discuss each of the dimensions; text, situational context, discursive practice and social practice, using the OG text as an illustration.

3   TEXT AS A UNIT OF ANALYSIS

The assumption that a text is meaningful only within its context implies the bounding of a text. Klein and Truex (1995) identify the problem of the bounding of the text as one of the issues in IS research using discourse analysis as: *'how to track the links among discernible streams of meanings in the text'* (p. 39). The authors   explain this as a concern because they often found themselves *'wanting to follow a set of interactions in a direction which is not part of the method as current [ly] devised ... It would be meaningful ...to follow lines of argumentation as they evolve ...'* (p. 39) To overcome these 'superficial' boundaries between units of text, which might prevent the analyst from pursuing connections between texts, I have used an approach based on the notion of intertextuality and cohesion - textual resources that mark out the boundaries of a text and show that it is integral (Halliday 1985). The cohesive resources used in the OG text are shown in the Appendix.

The intertextuality of the OG Text with others is established in several ways, for example, by the initial question, "Can I ask you again about this business of outstanding calls?" which refers to my earlier attempt to gain an understanding of the procedure of dealing with outstanding calls. This intertextuality of texts assists us to understand more completely the meaning of specific texts by showing the relationships between texts. For example, we might say that we understand that a problem is important because it is talked about so much. An examination of intertextuality allows us to seek reinforcement for our interpretation of meaning by looking at the cohesiveness of our data. Single instances of language are not picked out and held up to be of special significance unless their status is supported by the cohesive resources of the text. The units of text are also distinguished by their consistency with the situational context and the significance of features of the text can also be affirmed by observations of the context of situation, which will be dealt with in the next section.

4   FEATURES OF THE TEXT AND THE SITUATIONAL CONTEXT

By context, is meant that which occurs along with the text. Context may therefore be "sequential context" - the text which precedes and follows the text and "situational context" which is the totality of practices and so on (such as a family meal) of which the text is a part. However, the relationship between the text and the context is not necessarily straightforward. Although the context should reduce the ambiguity of a text, the interpretation may remain ambivalent.

Halliday and Hasan (1985) propose three contextual variables, based on their three functions of language referred to in section 2; that is, ideational meaning, interpersonal meaning and textual meaning. The contextual variables are realised by particular features of the text. This approach shows how features of the text reflect and support particular uses which language and other communicative acts serve. In brief, features of the context are realised by features of the text, as follows.

Firstly, there is the *field* of discourse, which indicates the sphere of activity in which the text is situated. In the case of written documents, the field of discourse is the subject matter, whereas in work and similar situations, the field of discourse has more to do with actions surrounding the discourse. The field of discourse as part of the contextual configuration, is realised in the text by experiential components of the language expressing processes, names (participants in processes) and circumstances associated with the process. These features are the most obvious in any discourse because they appear to be 'about' something. '*Our most powerful conception of reality is that it consists of "goings-on"* (Halliday 1985, p. 101)

Halliday and Hasan (1985) categorise processes as material, mental and relational. Material processes represent the field of discourse in terms of action and event. One effect of using the material process is to make the attribution of responsibility clear. For example:

June*: "I'm just telling S [Author's name] that we don't do that"*

Mental processes are used to express opinions or to indicate feelings and thoughts. For example:

Averil: *"I think it should be discussed"*

Relational processes (attributive and identifying) involve the linking of a noun and an adjective by the verb 'to be' or a similar verb. This weakens or removes the sense of action or experience, and attribution of agency or responsibility for actions or opinions is deemphasised. For example:

June: *"it wouldn't be any use"*

Secondly, there is the *tenor* of discourse, which is concerned with who is taking part in the text. This categorisation assumes that the forms of expression chosen will reflect the relations between participants, for example long-term, non-interchangeable social relations (such as superior and subordinate), and interchangeable relations such as the speech roles of speaker/hearer. The tenor of discourse is realised by interpersonal elements in the text, primarily, personal pronouns and modality (reference to the judgement of the speaker).

The choice of personal pronouns expresses emphasis or focus, which can be put upon or deflected from an individual in the text. The choice also shows relations between participants. For example, the following expression is typical of the way that the supervisor addressed staff, both in meetings and in general discussion:

> Averil: *"We'd better bring it up, though"*.

Modality refers to the judgement of the speaker/writer, expressing degrees of probability, usuality and commitment. Low modality occurs when the speaker reserves judgement, expressed by usages such as "may", "perhaps", "possibly"; high modality by terms such as "will", "highly likely", "certain". In the text example, the supervisor often used expressions featuring low modality, such as

> Averil: *"Well, I don't know ... I think it should be discussed."*

Finally, there is the *mode* of discourse, which concerns the role assigned to language, and enables the text to be comprehensible within the situation. One way in which this is realised is by the thematic features of the text, which show what the text is about. In general, in the English language, the 'theme' of a text occurs in the first position of a text unit (e.g the sentence). The identification of what is thematic in different texts and discourses gives some indication of what speakers and writers wish to emphasise in their communication. For example, in the OG text personal pronouns often occur as themes. To understand the importance of these themes, we need to consider the idea of Discursive Practices.

5   METAPHOR AS DISCURSIVE PRACTICE

It is an assumption of this paper that the interpretation of meaning cannot rest at the level of situational context. It must be considered within the wider contexts of discursive practice and social practice (as indicated in Figure 1). One example of discursive practice - that of metaphor will be discussed in relation to some of the expressions from the OG Text.

The identification and interpretation of metaphors in discourse is a widely used analytical tool in several fields including information systems research, to uncover sets of assumptions underlying organisational practices (e.g. Kendall and Kendall 1993, Walsham 1993). However, there are some difficulties with the notion of metaphor, particularly regarding what is figurative and what is literal. In brief, metaphor refers to the transfer of meanings from one context (such as a social practice or linguistic text) typically associated with the lexical or syntactic usage, to another context not typically associated with those usages. To some extent all language may be viewed as metaphorical, since it operates in an arbitrary relationship to what is signified. The value of identifying language as metaphorical is simply to show that there are different ways that texts realise meanings within particular contexts. When a usage strikes us as novel or unusual we regard it as metaphorical. The significance of metaphor in expressing meaning therefore depends on what is considered typical, and this must be considered diachronically.

For example, when a metaphor is first used it appears striking and novel, and its association with the other context is overt and informative. However, as the usage is adopted it loses its novelty and operates in a more covert manner. Its creative power diminishes and its constraining power increases. (Lakoff and Johnson 1980). For example, the use of 'head' for head of state, head of the family, and so on, no longer seems metaphorical.

Let us consider metaphor in relation to one of the expressions from the OG Text.

Averil: *"I think it should be discussed"* *(A Mental Process followed by a Relational Process)*.

In this study, I found this expression to be a distinctive expression used by the Supervisor both in conversation with her staff and at the regular meetings. It is 'thematic' in the Supervisor's discourse with Operations staff. To understand whether this expression was used metaphorically, alternative expressions that could have been used appropriately in this type of situation (a conversation between a Supervisor and staff) need to be considered. For example, the following usages would also realise the same *field* of discourse.

"We will discuss it" (A material process)

"It will be discussed" (A relational process)

However, these expressions would realise a different *tenor* of discourse, by expressing a different relationship between the Supervisor and the Operator. They would also realise a different *mode* of discourse (a different way of conducting conversations).

In order to check which of these usages might be considered typical within the wider organisational context, I conducted discourse based interviews with members of the Operations Group which confirmed the typicality of this expression ("I think it should be discussed") and its appropriateness in a workplace which espoused ideas such as participative management and participatory design of information systems. However, an examination of management practices in the Information Technology Centre provided a different view on the consistency of this usage. Hence the relationship between the discourse and the context was viewed as problematical.

The notion of discursive practices assumes that there is a dialectical relationship between text and context: not only does the context create the text - the text also creates the context. In using a communicative expression the speaker/writer commits herself to supporting and reaffirming the tradition from which the expression derives. In creating new discursive practices she may modify that tradition or replace it. In their association of unlike domains, metaphors as discursive practices are often instantiations of contradictions in the wider context. In the above example from the OG Text, I found a contradiction between the use of forms of expression denoting participation and consultation, and the wider context of organisational change in the university. In other words, the discourse of participative management operated metaphorically and covertly; it cloaked a lack of real participation and consultation. The persistence of such discursive practices may be resisted. *'How a particular domain of experience is metaphorized is one of the stakes in the struggle within and over discourse practices'* (Fairclough 1992, p. 195). However, there was a fair degree of cynicism amongst the Operators about the misfit between their perception of the way that the Group tried to work (in a participative manner) and their actual ability to have an influence on decisions which affected them.

6   SOCIAL PRACTICE AND DISCURSIVE CHANGE

The approach to analysis described so far consists of firstly an attempt to interpret the meaning of texts within their immediate situational context and secondly to identify particular discursive practices and their relationship to the wider context in which they occur. The final stage involves an analysis of how discursive change constructs and is constructed by social change, in other words an examination of the relationship of the discourse to the wider social context.

The social context may be theoretised in many ways. The critical discourse analysis perspective suggests that that discourse is *'shaped by relations of power, and invested with ideologies'* (Fairclough 1992 p. 8) and that *'language itself is becoming a target for change'* (p. 5) Fairclough identifies three intertwined tendencies in discursive change: democratisation, commodification and technologisation. Suggestions in the OG Text of these three trends are briefly discussed.

Democratisation means the removal of overt markers of inequality between groups of speakers. This has been shown in Australia (and many other countries) by the increasing use of informal language in different social situations. For example, the use of low modality and personal pronouns rather than formal modes of address indicated democratisation of the work place for the Operations staff, which was in line with the espoused ideas of participative management and participatory design. However the tendency towards democratisation is complicated by the tendencies of commodification and technologisation.

Commodification is the tendency to reconceptualise in commercial terms domains which are not normally associated with the production, distribution and consumption of commodities; for example education has had the language of production and thereby the associations of production applied to it, through the language of business. Social relations are formed by associations between service providers and clients, vendors and customers. In this study, the increasing reference to university work in commercial terms caused confusion about the nature of the relationship between the OG staff, students and other university staff. This relationship was seen on one hand as collegiate (through the use of democratic forms of discourse) and on the other hand as commercial.

Technologisation refers to the tendency towards increased control over more and more of people's lives. In discourse terms, this refers to the appropriation of one set of discursive practices, such as narrative or conversation, to another purpose. Fairclough reminds us that these tendencies enter into different articulations with the social practices and are therefore *open to different political and ideological investments'*(1992, p. 9) In this study it appears that democratic discourse was appropriated to serve a drive towards commercialisation. This was also indicated during the period of the study by the renaming of the various groups in the ITC to show a client focus. Overall, the study found a tension between the everyday discourse of the Operations Group and the work practices developing as the university moved towards commercialisation. However, because of the strongly democratic nature of the Operators discourse which was confirmed by reference to the situational context, this tension was only revealed through careful examination of the discourse within the wider organisational context.

7   CONCLUSION

The study of the Operations Group was undertaken to make a rich description of the sense making of a group of IT personnel undergoing a rapid rate of change in the way which they provided IT support services. The approach taken to the study involved developing a form of discourse analysis which enabled a close link to be made between the discourse of the Group and the immediate and wider context within which they worked. A fuller visualisation of the framework used for analysis is given below and shows some of the features attended to in this paper. Arrows have been added to the figure to show how the analyst moves attention from the text to the wider context seeking confirmation of the interpretation.

This framework provided benefits in terms of the deepening understanding of the complex relationship between the way that people talk and write and the context which gives their expression meaning. However, the interpretation can never be considered as complete, because new texts are continually being produced which may give new meaning to preceding texts. A useful analogy to this process is the writing of a story. The author ends the story when she thinks a significant closure has occurred, or when the window of opportunity closes. But the characters hypothetically live on after the 'ending' and may accomplish further closures.

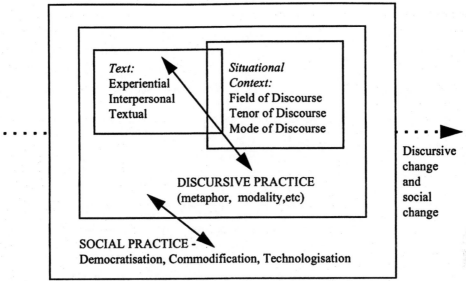

Figure 3: The framework for analysis

References

Boland, R. (1991) "Information system use as a hermeneutic process", in H.E. Nissen, H.K. Klein & R. Hirschheim (eds.) Information Systems Research: Contemporary approaches and emergent traditions. North Holland, Amsterdam.

Fairclough, N. (1992) Discourse and social change. Polity Press, Cambridge,.

Halliday, M.A.K. (1985) An Introduction to Functional Grammar. London: Edward Arnold.

Halliday, M and Hasan, R. (1985) Language, Context and Text: Aspects of language in a social-semiotic perspective. Deakin University Press, Burwood, Vic.

Janson, M.A, and Woo, C.C. (1996) "A Speech Act Lexicon; an alternative use of speech act theory in information systems" Information Systems Journal, 6, pp. 301-329

Iivari, J., Hirschheim, R., and Klein, H.K. (1998) "A Paradigmatic analysis contrasting information systems development approaches and methodologies". Information Systems Research, 9 (2) pp. 164-193

Kendall, J.E., and Kendall, K.E. (1993) "Metaphors and methodologies: living beyond the systems machine" MIS Quarterly, June, pp. 149-171

Klein, H.K. and Truex, D.P. (1995) Discourse Analysis: A Semiotic Approach to the Investigation of Organizational Emergence, (to appear in "The Semiotics of the Workplace" edited by P.B. Anderson & B. Holmquist).

Lakoff, G. and Johnson, M. (1980) Metaphors we live by. University of Chicago Press.

Thompson, J.B.(1984) Studies in the theory of ideology. Polity Press, Cambridge.

Walsham, G. (1993) Interpreting Information Systems in Organisations. John Wiley & Son, New York.

Appendix

The types of cohesive resources which operate in the OG Text include: reference to a topic or person (e.g. "can I ask you again", "where was I?",); substitution ("that" "she", "it" - indicating that the same person/subject is being discussed); conjunction ("if", "and", "but", "though"); lexical cohesion (e.g. synonyms - such as "list" and "report", "calls" and "jobs"). -

Author: Can I ask you again about this business of outstanding calls? What do you do about that - I'm not quite sure ... what you said in the meeting...

June: Well, we have this report we print off every morning, the LX506 - a list of calls that haven't been closed off.

(June is interrupted by a Help Line telephone call)

June: Where was I? Oh yes, the LX506, well what we're meant to do is call everyone to find out where their job's got to.. is it finished, has anyone contacted them, or what. But really, I can't spend the whole morning ringing these people... I mean, some of these jobs go on for days...

Author: Is it any use, do you think, having it in the manual, then? What about new operators, what would you advise them to do?

June: I'd tell them, we just don't do it, we don't have time. Aha, there's Averil listening in.

(Averil - the Supervisor - is passing by and looks over the top of the partition)

I'm just telling S [Author's name] that we don't do that.

Averil: What! The LX506? I didn't know that - that hasn't been agreed. What's happening with the outstanding calls then?

June: If they're not finished in a few days, they always come up again as new requests, or someone phones in, but it just doesn't happen like that. There's always a reason for the job going on and the person knows that.

Averil: Well, I don't know ... I think it should be discussed ... at the next meeting. How many outstanding calls are there right now?

June: Not many, otherwise we'd hear all about it from upstairs. But, look, it wouldn't work, if we had to call everyone every day, it wouldn't be any use.

Averil: What about keeping a note on the report, so the next operator ...

June: No one would use it.

Averil: We'd better bring it up, though.

(Averil continues on to her original destination)

Author: How long have you been printing out this report?

June: Since the system started, I think. Don't you agree, wouldn't you say, its really a waste of time - all those calls and everyone getting sick of us ringing them.

Author: Perhaps you could ring them much later - but it certainly looks like a lot of work.

(Author breaks off here to avoid giving any more suggestions and turns to another topic from the meeting)

CHAPTER 13

GROUNDED THEORY: I MENTIONED IT ONCE BUT I THINK I GOT AWAY WITH IT

Debra Howcroft and Jim Hughes
University of Salford

Abstract

Despite the increasing attention paid to interpretivist research, there has been a tendency to focus on the epistemological as opposed to the methodological level, with a noticeable absence of practical guidance. Whilst many researchers may feel confident about the philosophical underpinnings of their research strategy, such confidence erodes when faced with the prospect of analysing the raw materials emanating from their study. Limited sanctuary can be found, however, with Grounded Theory, an interpretive research method from the social sciences that has also been usefully applied in the field of information systems (IS). It is a method that provides practical guidelines and procedures for the collection and analysis of qualitative data. This paper outlines the historical development of Grounded Theory, from its roots in sociological studies, to its current use in IS research. A framework is presented which situates Grounded Theory in terms of its use in IS research and also considers the underlying assumptions of the researchers that utilise it. It becomes evident that there are inconsistencies in both the understanding and the application of the method. Parallels can be drawn with established research in the IS development methodologies field, which has concentrated on the application and limitations of formalised methodologies in real-world organizational contexts. This research area is implicitly drawn upon to provide insight into the application of Grounded Theory as a methodology to support the process of conducting interpretive research.

1   INTRODUCTION

There is an enduring debate within the IS field concerned with the positivist and interpretivist research traditions (Fitzgerald and Howcroft, 1998). Undoubtedly, positivism has been most influential, with much of the published research being centred upon positivistic assumptions (Kaplan and Duchon, 1988; Orlikowski and Baroudi, 1991). However, a mounting appreciation of the essentially social nature of IS has led some researchers to adopt research approaches which focus primarily on human interpretations and meaning (Walsham, 1995). As a consequence, interpretive approaches are being employed in an increasing variety of ways in IS research (Klein and Myers, 1999; Lee et al., 1997; Nissen et al., 1991).

For researchers who adopt an interpretive research strategy a more focussed, and possibly problematic, issue is that of selecting appropriate research methods to complement the chosen strategy. When presented with unstructured, non-numeric data derived from an interpretive research study that utilises techniques such as interviews, observation or action research, there is a noticeable absence of practical guidance for carrying out interpretive research. Perhaps one of the outcomes of this absence of detailed guidance, is the tendency to confound different methods. Indeed, with IS research, there is a popular misconception that interpretive research can be equated with qualitative research and all the associated procedures for qualitative analysis (Myers, 1997).

In terms of practical methods, Grounded Theory is prominent amongst the various research strategies recommended for the conduct of interpretive research (Myers, 1997). The next section proceeds by tracing the historical development of this methodology. The use and adoption of Grounded Theory in IS research is then presented in a framework which outlines the type of project and also the underlying assumptions of the researchers. The framework highlights some of the inconsistencies in both the understanding and the application of the method. To enable further understanding of the value of Grounded Theory in IS research, the authors implicitly draw upon research from the well-established field of ISD methodologies, in order to provide insight into the application of Grounded Theory as a practical method to support interpretive research. Finally, some recommendations for the application of Grounded Theory are proposed.

2   GROUNDED THEORY – A HISTORICAL PERSPECTIVE

Grounded Theory or as it is more properly titled 'The Discovery of Grounded Theory' (Glaser and Strauss, 1967) is a method for the collection and analysis of qualitative data. It derived as a means of formalising the operation of the principles of analytic induction first suggested by Znaniecki (1934) and later elaborated by others such as Robinson (1951) and Denzin (1970). In this method conceptual properties and categories may be 'discovered' or generated from the qualitative data by following a number of guidelines and procedures. There are two critical stages of Grounded Theory identified by Glaser and Strauss. Firstly that of 'constant comparative analysis', a procedure for the identification of conceptual categories and their properties which may be embedded in the data and secondly what they call 'theoretical sampling' which is both a category enriching and disconfirming procedure. These are depicted in figure 1.

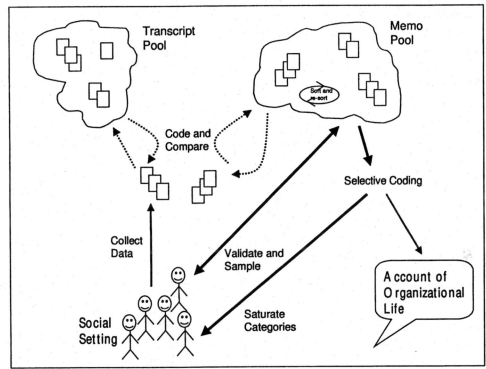

Figure 1: Grounded Theory Procedures

Glaser and Strauss' (1967) original work had three main purposes. Firstly, it was intended to offer the rationale for theory that was 'grounded', that is to say generated and developed through the inductive analysis of data collected during research projects. The use of the term theory is used in the sense that it refers to empirical models devised on the basis of data. When the method was first introduced it was a departure from traditional functionalist (Parsons 1964, 1966) and structuralist (Merton, 1963) theories, which were largely deductive. The second aim was to suggest the procedures and the reasons for them and the third aim was to propose legitimacy for careful qualitative research. Interestingly, the final aim has been achieved to the extent that Grounded Theory underpins many models of qualitative research (Dey, 1993).

The main application areas of Grounded Theory were most notably in Glaser and Strauss' own research into status passage (dying) (Glaser and Strauss, 1970). Other areas included medical or nursing related areas such as experiences with chronic illness (Charmaz, 1980), the management of a hazardous pregnancy (Corbin, 1992) and homecoming (Hall, 1992). Additionally much work has been done with respect to guidance on the use of method. Most notable amongst them include Turner (1983), Martin and Turner (1986), Strauss (1987), Charmaz (1983), Strauss and Corbin (1990).

Grounded Theory differs from other approaches to the analysis of qualitative data because of its emphasis on theory. Strauss and Corbin (1994) maintain that theory consists of

> "plausible relationships proposed among concepts and sets of concepts.......Researchers are interested in patterns of action and interaction between and among various types of social units (i.e. actors)......They are also much concerned with discovering process - not necessarily in the sense of stages or phases, but in reciprocal changes in patterns of action/interaction and in relationship with changes of conditions either internal or external to the process itself" (Strauss and Corbin, 1994)

In reply to criticism that their definition of theory may be too austere or formal they note two important aspects of Grounded Theory

> "First, theories are always traceable to the data that gave rise to them...Second grounded theories are very 'fluid' because they embrace the interaction of multiple actors, and because they emphasise temporality and process" (Strauss and Corbin, 1994)

The method of Grounded Theory has spread to many other disciplines including research in IS, and Strauss and Corbin (1994) regret that the method now 'runs the risk of becoming fashionable'. They assert this even though they accept that the procedures have evolved over the years throughout the research and experience of Grounded Theorists and the authors allow for this development as an aid to creativity. It may be surmised that it is not the development of the method that is their concern but the lack of control that they increasingly have over its diffusion. They identify the main risks of this diffusion of the method as firstly the lack of conceptual development of processes and the over-emphasis on open coding rather than theoretical coding which conceptualises how substantive codes relate to each other. They attribute much of this what they term 'misuse of method' to the overemphasis in the original (Glaser and Strauss, 1967) work on the inductive aspects of the method. Their own stress is on the significance of grounded theories and on the importance of theoretically sensitised and trained researchers. Some weight may be given to their arguments since it is clear that even the title of their method, which was the title of the original book - The Discovery of Grounded Theory - is widely misunderstood. The method is concerned with discovering theory that is grounded in social settings. The title of the original book reflected this; it is not a book about their discovery of a method that they called Grounded Theory. The misconception is so widespread that the method is now commonly known in its shortened form.

Those who choose to use Grounded Theory may consider that since the divisions amongst the original co-authors are so great the difference in stress in the use of the method by others is only to be expected. This schism between Glaser and Strauss

(Glaser, 1992) as to the focus of Grounded Theory is presented as a personal attack by Glaser. Unfortunately this distorts the academic argument which, simply put, criticises the Strauss and Corbin's (1990) version of Grounded Theory as discarding the tenets of emerging theory which is the basis for induction and replacing it with forcing theory from pre-given or determined frameworks. Whichever position a researcher may take, it is clear that the impact of the discourse suggests that the door is open to adaptation of the method. In the next section we consider the use of the Grounded Theory method in IS research.

3   A FRAMEWORK FOR THE USE OF GROUNDED THEORY IN IS RESEARCH

This section is concerned with the use of Grounded Theory in IS research projects. In order to clarify the analysis, the characteristics of the projects and the underlying assumptions of the researchers are tabulated in Table 1. The authors accept that the projects do not represent a definitive account of the use of Grounded Theory in IS research, rather they typify the ways in which Grounded Theory has been used in a variety of projects. The entries in each section are summaries of those that have been reported by the project authors. They are not our interpretation of how Grounded Theory was used - nor would we claim authority. Although we would point out that when considering the use of Grounded Theory in the IS field there are *inconsistencies* in the understanding of the method as there are in the application of the method. The framework illuminates a number of issues concerning the use of Grounded Theory in IS research.

- The projects range from those concerned with organisational change (Orlikowski, 1993; Pries-Heje, 1992) to those concerned with the practical use of the method to inform knowledge based systems design (Oliphant and Blockley, 1991; Galal and McDonnell, 1997)
- For some the full blown use of the method is important (Pidgeon, Turner and Blockley, 1991) whilst for others the use of specific procedures helps to overcome deficiencies in another research strategy (Baskerville and Pries-Heje , 1995 and 1998; Hughes, 1998a) or selectively change the method to suit the purpose of the research (Calloway and Ariav, 1991; Fitzgerald, 1997)
- The underlying assumptions made explicit by the authors range from qualitative-interpretive (Howcroft, 1998) to qualitative-positivist (Pries-Heje, 1992). The latter to the extent that the project's author explicitly commends the method for its meeting the criteria of good science. Although interestingly these criteria are not rigorously pursued.
- Grounded Theory is used as a method alongside others (Orlikowski, 1993; Toraskar, 1991) and also used entirely on its own (Calloway and Ariav, 1991)
- These raise a number of questions for the use of Grounded Theory in IS research. Is

there some 'correct' way of using Grounded Theory? Is there a research paradigm in which Grounded Theory 'fits'? What validity can be given to the concerns of Strauss and Corbin (1994) about the need for sensitised and trained (experienced) Grounded Theorists? As a means of addressing these questions we consider aphorisms from the literature associated with formalised IS Development methods and methodologies, since we consider that there are lessons about Grounded Theory and its use in IS research that can be learnt from such a treatment.

	Research project	Underlying assumptions / perspectives	Adaptations to Grounded Theory method made explicit
Toraskar (1991)	To evaluate the product of IS design.	Grounded Theory is in the tradition of hermeneutic methods of analysis and prediction.	Ignores evaluative criteria.
Calloway and Ariav (1991)	To explore how IS designers perceive the use of design tools during systems development.	Grounded Theory can be used as a method of data reduction alongside Content Analysis.	Ignores evaluative criteria. Uses seed categories rather than inductive generation of all categories.
Pidgeon, Turner and Blockley (1991)	For conceptual analysis in knowledge elicitation.	Grounded Theory provides rich conceptual models that accurately describe data. The evaluative criteria provide necessary rigour.	Follows the method.
Oliphant and Blockley (1991)	Design of a knowledge based advisor on the selection of earth retaining structures.	Grounded Theory provides a hierarchical model from which knowledge based rules can be derived.	Follows the method.
Pries-Heje (1992)	An investigation into barriers for the use of computer-based tools in ISD.	Grounded Theory provides systematic techniques to develop substantive theory that meet the criteria of 'good' science	Follows the method
Orlikowski (1993)	Development of a conceptual framework for understanding organizational issues surrounding the adoption and use of CASE tools.	Grounded Theory adopted because of its inductive, contextual and processual characteristics useful in considering change	Follows the method alongside other methods to triangulate findings
Baskerville and Pries-Heje (1995; 1998)	To study methods and tools in order to improve problems that exist in software product development.	Grounded Theory increases the rigour in the theory development portion of action research.	Limited theoretical sampling. Predetermined core categories. Reorientation of early coding to evaluate and learn about predetermined core category.

	Research project	Underlying assumptions / perspectives	Adaptations to Grounded Theory method made explicit
Fitzgerald (1997)	A field study of the use of systems development methodologies in practice.	Grounded Theory increases rigour and traceability during theory development.	Use of seed categories.
Galal and McDonnell (1997)	A case study of an automated document management system for the legal domain.	Grounded Theory supports rigorous analysis of qualitative data. Adopted for the evolution of a first requirements' model.	Follows the method integrated into KBS engineering techniques.
Hughes (1998a)	A data analysis method used for requirements determination.	Grounded Theory provides useful procedures to elicit situated requirements within an ethnomethodological perspective.	Use of seed categories. Use of software package to aid analysis. Ignores evaluation criteria.
Howcroft (1998)	An interpretive study of the nature and characteristics of Internet usage.	Grounded Theory offers a systematic and traceable method for inducing patterns from the raw data.	Use of seed categories.

Table 1: Use of Grounded Theory in IS Research

4   INSIGHTS INTO THE USE OF GROUNDED THEORY IN IS RESEARCH

In order to shed light on this situation, the literature associated with formalised IS development methodologies has been drawn upon. This research area was selected because its core concern is with providing a fuller understanding of the strengths and limitations of the application of formalised methodologies as an aid to the development process. Therefore, this research domain offers valuable insights as regards the application of Grounded Theory to the qualitative research process. This is presented under the headings of four propositions. In each case, the proposition will be outlined in general terms, this will then be discussed in the context of its relevance to the application of Grounded Theory in IS studies.

4.1   Developers have Various Levels of Experience
Much of the IS literature regards systems developers with derision and they are often used as scapegoats for many of the recurrent systems development problems (for a review see Fitzgerald, 1996). As a means of alleviating this, formalization of practice is presented as a universal 'cure-all' for many of the ills that have plagued the systems development community (Wilson and Howcroft, 1996). Fitzgerald (1996) notes that whilst this bias in the literature may not reflect actual practice, nevertheless it still influences it by implicitly supporting the adoption of methodologies. This perhaps explains why 'novice' developers rigidly adhere to the reductionist framework which methodologies provide, opting for 'adaptive reaction' (Wastell, 1996) as they become

more skilled and experienced. Indeed, Wastell (1996) confirms the view that methodologies may act as a useful crux for the novice developer, particularly given the stressful nature of systems development (Wastell and Newman, 1993), yet as their experience develops, there is a real danger that the methodology becomes a fetish at the expense of personal and critical reflection. Empirical studies reveal that as developers evolve over time, they adopt methodologies in a far more pragmatic way (Fitzgerald, 1997).

This view of skill levels in systems development is similar to that provided by the Dreyfus brothers in their critique of artificial intelligence (Dreyfus and Dreyfus, 1986). They present a 5-stage model of skill acquisition, beginning with the inexperienced novice and graduating to the expert. Their view is based on a holistic approach to situational understanding and they present a strong case for tacit knowledge and intuition, both of which are identified as critical features of expertise in unstructured problem areas. This re-orientation towards a 'knowing how rather than a knowing what' strongly centres upon intuition and experience, as opposed to a knowledge of facts and the rules for relating them. Hughes (1998b) echoes these themes when he stresses that systems developers should be encouraged to articulate tacit knowledge rather than simply focus upon learning the theory of methodologies.

Analogies can be drawn with the use of Grounded Theory. Research conducted by Baskerville and Pries-Heje (1995; 1998) - who could appropriately be labelled experts in the Dreyfus' model - provides an example of how aspects of Grounded Theory are consciously avoided in order to maintain the richness of the action research project that is central to their research study. As IS experts, particularly in the area of action research, they deliberately select elements of Grounded Theory to support areas of uncertainty in their research, yet choose to ignore the elements that would detract from the richness of the study. Furthermore, for those researchers who use seed categories or initial categories to inform their analysis (Calloway and Ariav, 1991; Fitzgerald, 1997) it may reasonably be argued that they are drawing upon their previous experience to provide a basis for current work.

4.2   The Formation of Mental Constructs

In his work on ISD methodologies, Jayaratna (1994) identifies four elements that are present within any problem-solving context: the problem situation, the problem solver, (developer), the problem solving process (methodology), and the evaluation. In any given context in the problem solving process, the problem solver will utilise their mental constructs to influence their thinking processes and actions. These mental constructs influence their own sense-making and decision-making activities and thus explain the ways in which a methodology is used differently by one person as compared with another, and indeed as compared with the original proponents of the methodology.

This research is relevant when considering the application of Grounded Theory, since it raises issues relating to the diffusion of the method and the users of the method. If it is accepted that Grounded Theory lacks any overarching philosophical perspective (Dobbie and Hughes, 1993), then perhaps the qualitative data analysis which proceeds is attributable to the researcher's own mental constructs as opposed to the method itself. This would therefore relegate the use of Grounded Theory to no more than a set of useful guidelines which aid the interpretive researcher, rather than a model of research *per se*. Indeed, Strauss and Corbin (1994) scathingly comment that Grounded Theory runs the risk of becoming fashionable and somewhat faddish as more researchers use it as a cover-all for any research method that attempts to collect and categorise qualitative data. Perhaps this absence of so-called rigour in the method adoption could more appropriately be attributed to utilisation of mental constructs that help the sense-making process when faced with such a quagmire of data.

4.3   Methodologies are Tailored to the Contingencies of a Situation

Most of the currently available systems development methodologies are founded on outdated concepts which emerged in the period from about 1967 to 1977 (Fitzgerald, 1997). Empirical research supports the contention that the profile of the development environment is very different from that faced in the past when these methodologies were first promoted. For example, the faster 'metabolism' of today's business environment means that developers do not have the luxury of being able to follow all the detailed steps in a monolithic methodology. Consequently, many methodologies are neither followed rigorously nor uniformly (Fitzgerald, 1996), rather they are tailored to the contingencies of the particular organizational context and problem situation.

With the examples provided in Table 2, it can be seen that only a limited number of research projects follow Grounded Theory prescriptively (e.g., Galal and McDonnell, 1997; Pidgeon et al., 1991). Perhaps one explanation could be that rather than attribute this to deficiencies or ignorance on the part of the researchers, researchers consciously intervene and 'cut and paste' aspects of the method which are relevant to the study in question. The desire to follow the method in a painstaking and meticulous manner can overwhelm other, perhaps more important considerations. To follow the method religiously could result in rigour at the expense of relevance. Therefore, rather than scornfully point to the corruption of Grounded Theory, it may be more appropriate to highlight the successful deployment of interpretive and intuitive skills which contribute towards enabling the method to 'work' for any given research project.

4.4   Methodologies Serve as a 'Comfort Factor'

Fitzgerald (1994) noted that methodologies might well be used "as a comfort factor to reassure participants that 'proper' practices are being followed". Wastell (1996) develops this point further by considering that methodologies operate as a social defence, providing security for systems developers operating within the acute stresses of systems development. He compares the learning of methodologies with the psychoanalytic concept of transitional objects: they provide psychological support until the novice gains sufficient confidence to tackle problems independently. As experience develops, the methodology becomes internalised and the novice graduates to expert, discarding the transitional object *en route*.

Parallels can be drawn with the stressful and uncertain nature of conducting qualitative and interpretive research, particularly for inexperienced researchers. One can see that the use of an established and widely used model of qualitative data collection and analysis such as Grounded Theory may well serve as a 'comfort factor' or transitional object. The method provides a useful set of procedures and guidelines which can be followed by less experienced researchers. As their level of expertise progresses, they become emboldened to tackle more complex problems and the techniques of Grounded Theory can be employed with increasing discretion and flexibility.

5   SUMMARY AND CONCLUSIONS

The aim of this paper has been to consider the value of Grounded Theory as an aid to interpretive research. Given the paucity of practical guidelines, Grounded Theory is a useful vehicle for structuring the process of conducting qualitative data analysis. The history of the development of Grounded Theory is somewhat chequered and this is reflected in the various ways in which the method has been diffused. This is clearly evident in the various ways in which Grounded Theory has been used in IS research. In order to make sense of these inconsistencies, the literature from the area of IS development methodologies was consulted in order to provide insight into understanding the use of methods in real-world situations.

Having briefly summarised the main points of the paper, it is now worth reflecting on possible implications. The four aphorisms outlined earlier have direct counterparts in these discussions:

1. Grounded Theory provides a useful template for novice researchers and as such serves as a comfort factor for the stressful and uncertain nature of conducting qualitative research.
2. Grounded Theory facilitates the use of seed categories for experienced researchers.
3. Grounded Theory acts a support for the utilisation of the researchers mental constructs during the sense-making process.
4. IS researchers successfully intervene and use their interpretive and intuitive skills to make the method 'work'.

These points suggest a different scenario for the evaluation of Grounded Theory in IS research, one which acknowledges the crucial role of the individual researcher attempting to find their way through the labyrinth of uncertainty. Maybe we can now reject the inflated view of Grounded Theory as a methodology to be blindly adhered to and instead consider it as a reliable means of data analysis.

References

Baskerville, R. and Pries-Heje, J. (1995) 'Grounding the theory in action research' in Doukidis, Galliers, B., Jelassi, T., Kremar, H. and Land, F. (eds.) *Proceedings of the third European Conference on Information Systems*. Athens. Greece. pp. 837-848.

Baskerville, R. and Pries-Heje, J. (1998) Grounding Action Research, *Journal of Accounting, Management and Information Technologies* (forthcoming)

Calloway L J and Ariav G (1991) Developing and using a qualitative methodology to study relationships among designers and tools, in Nissen H-E, Klein H, Hirschheim R (1991) *Information Systems Research: Contemporary Approaches and Emergent Traditions*. Proceedings of the IFIP WG 8.2 Working Conference, Copenhagen, 14-16 December. North-Holland, Amsterdam, 175-193.

Charmaz, K. (1980) 'The construction of self pity in the chronically ill' *Studies in Symbolic Interaction*. Vol. 3 pp. 123-145.

Charmaz, K. (1983) 'The Grounded Theory Method: An Explication and Interpretation' in Emerson, R.M. (Ed.) *Contemporary Field Research*. Waveland Press Inc. Illanois, USA. pp. 109-126.

Denzin, N. (1970) *The Research Act*. Butterworths. London.

Dey, I. (1993) *Qualitative Data Analysis: A User-Friendly Guide for Social Scientists*. Routledge. London.

Dobbie M and Hughes J (1993) Realist ethnomethodology and grounded theory: a methodology for requirements determination in information systems analysis, *Proceedings of the First British Computer Society Conference on Information Systems Methodologies*, Edinburgh, 311-321.

Dreyfus H and S (1986) *Mind Over Machine*, Blackwells, Oxford.

Fitzgerald, B. (1994) The Systems Development Dilemma: Whether to Adopt Formalised Systems Development Methodologies or Not? in Bates, W. (Ed) *Proceedings of Second European Conference on Information Systems*, Nijenrode University Press, Holland, pp. 691-706.

Fitzgerald B (1996) Formalized systems development methodologies: a critical perspective, *Information Systems Journal*, 6:1, 3-24.

Fitzgerald, B. (1997) The Use of Systems Development Methodologies in Practice: A Field Study, *Information Systems Journal*, Vol. 7, No. 4.

Fitzgerald B and Howcroft D (1998) Towards dissolution of the IS research debate: from polarization to polarity, *Journal of Information Technology*, 13, 313-326.

Galal and McDonnell (1997) Knowledge_based systems in context: a methodological approach to qualitative issues, *AI & Society*, 11, 104-121.

Glaser, B. (1992) *Emergence vs. Forcing: Basics of Grounded Theory*. Sociology Press. Mill Valley, California.

Glaser B G and Strauss A (1967) *The Discovery of Grounded Theory: Strategies for Qualitative Research*, Aldine Publishing, New York.

Glaser , B. and Strauss, A.L. (1970) *Status Passage*. Aldine. Chicago.

Hall, C. (1992) 'Homecoming: the self at home' Unpublished doctoral thesis, University of California, Dept. of Social and Behavioural Sciences.

Howcroft D A (1998) Spanning the spectrum from utopia to dystopia: an interpretive field study of the nature and characteristics of Internet usage, PhD thesis, UMIST.

Hughes, J. (1998a) The Development of the GIST (Grounding Information SysTems) Methodology: Determining Situated Requirements in Information Systems Analysis. Ph.D. Thesis. Information Systems Research Centre, University of Salford, Salford, UK.

Hughes, J (1998b) Selection and evaluation of information systems: the gap between theory and practice, *IEE Proceedings on Software*, 145: 4, 100-104.

Jayaratna N, *Understanding and evaluating methodologies*, McGraw-Hill, 1994.

Kaplan B and Duchon D (1988) Combining qualitative and quantitative methods in information systems research: A case study, MIS Quarterly, December, 571- 586.

Klein H and Myers M (1999) A set of principles for conducting and evaluating interpretive field studies in information systems, *MIS Quarterly*, Special issue on intensive research, forthcoming.

Lee A S, Liebenau J and DeGross J (1997) *Information Systems and Qualitative Research*, Chapman & Hall, London.

Martin, P.Y. and Turner, B.A. (1986) 'Grounded Theory and Organizational Research' *Journal of Applied Behavioural Science*. Vol. 22(2) pp. 141-157.

Merton, R.K. (1963) Social Theory and Social Structure. Free Press. Glencoe.

Myers M (1997) Interpretive research in information systems, in Mingers J and Stowell F (1997) (eds.) *Information Systems: An Emerging Discipline?* McGraw Hill, London, 239-266.

Nissen H-E, Klein H, Hirschheim R (1991) Information Systems Research: Contemporary Approaches and Emergent Traditions. *Proceedings of the IFIP WG 8.2 Working Conference*, Copenhagen, 14-16 December. North-Holland, Amsterdam.

Oliphant, J. and Blockley, D.I. (1991) 'Knowledge-based system: Advisor on the Earth Retaining Structures' *Computers and Structures*. Vol. 40(1) pp. 173-183.

Orlikowski W J (1993) CASE tools as organizational change: investigating incremental and radical changes in systems development, *MIS Quarterly*, 17:3, 309-340.

Orlikowski W J and Baroudi J J (1991) Studying IT in organizations: research approaches and assumptions, *Information Systems Research*, 2:1, 1-28.

Parsons, T. (1964) 'Evolutionary Universals in Society' *American Sociological Review*. Vol.29(3). pp. 339-357.

Parsons, T. (1966) *Societies: Evolutionary and Comparative Perspectives*. Prentice-Hall. Englewood Cliffs.

Pidgeon N.F. ; Turner, B.A. and Blockley, D. I. (1991) 'The use of Grounded Theory for conceptual analysis in knowledge elicitation' *International Journal of Man-Machine Studies*. Vol. 35(2) pp. 151-173.

Pries-Heje, J. (1992) 'Three Barriers for Continuing Use of Computer-based Tools in

Information Systems Development : a Grounded Theory *Approach' Scandinavian Journal of Information Systems*. Vol. 4 pp. 119-136.

Robinson, W.S. (1951) The Logical Structure of Analytic Induction' *American Sociological Review*. Vol. 16(6) pp. 812-818.

Strauss A (1987) *Qualitative Analysis for Social Scientists*, Cambridge University Press, Cambridge.

Strauss A and Corbin C (1990) *Basics of Qualitative Research: Grounded Theory, Procedures and Techniques*, Sage, California.

Strauss A and Corbin C (1994) Grounded theory methodology: an overview, in Denzin N K and Lincoln Y S (eds.) (1994) *Handbook of Qualitative Research*, Sage, London, 273-285.

Toraskar K (1991) How managerial users evaluate their decision support: a grounded theory approach, in Nissen H -E, Klein H, Hirschheim R (1991) (eds.)*Information Systems research: Contemporary approaches and emergent traditions*. Proceedings of the IFIP WG 8.2 Working Conference, Copenhagen, 14-16 December. North-Holland, Amsterdam.

Turner, B.A. (1983) 'The use of Grounded Theory for the Qualitative Analysis of Organizational Behaviour' *Journal of Management Studies*. Vol. 20(3) pp. 333-348.

Walsham G (1995) Interpretive case studies in IS research: nature and method, *European Journal of Information Systems*, 4, 74-81.

Wastell D G (1996) The fetish of technique: methodology as social defence, *Information Systems Journal*, 6:1, 25-40.

Wastell D G and Newman M (1993) The behavioural dynamics of information systems development: a stress perspective, *Accounting, Management and Information Technology*, 3, 121-148.

Wilson M and Howcroft D (1996) New Directions for Systems Analysts: Lessons Drawn from the Application of Multiview, in Jayaratna N and Fitzgerald B (eds.) *Lessons Learned from the Use of Methodologies*, 271-286.

Znaniecki, F. (1934) *The Method of Sociology*. Farrer and Rinehart. New York.

CHAPTER 14

RESEARCH INTO INFORMATION SYSTEMS IN PUBLIC SERVICES: SOME IMPLICATIONS FOR RESEARCH METHODOLOGY

Jim Cowan
Wandsworth Social Services

Abstract

This short discussion paper presents quite basic perspectives from which to view ISTs in public services. Much of the attention has been focused on one of these perspectives which seeks to relate organisation and IST. This view also has tended to consider large scale systems on an organisation wide basis. The paper presents some philosophical considerations under the general heading of 'sociorationalism' which might underpin research into other ISTs in different public sector contexts. These might include ISTs which are being developed within organisations like Social Services and which may be supporting 'people services'. By comparison such systems might be quite 'localised' to a function and be close to the front end of the organisation and service delivery. The presentation of this material raises further issues about the concepts used to evaluate ISTs in public services. Some specific methodological issues are raised to do with attaching boundaries to underlying perspectives while remaining alive to and being able to draw on methodological developments well away from IST research.

1   INTRODUCTION

My research is being conducted as a practitioner with a quality assurance brief in Wandsworth Council's Social Services Department. Part of this work is also the subject of a PhD registered with Southbank University and is about information systems and meeting the needs of service users. Stage 1 of the work has used a modified grounded theory approach to reconsider some of the concepts used to evaluate ISTs in public services, suggesting that the notion of 'gain' may have application. This has brought to forefront the need to construct a view of how actors define and shape organisational realities, including ISTs. Sociorationalism is one such account and may offer a relevant perspective from which to view ISTs in some public service contexts.

2   PUBLIC MANAGEMENT

If we look at the kind of emphasis being placed on IST developments in public management at present, quite a lot of attention is going on large scale, often civil service, 'electronic admin' e.g. administrative services/entitlements electronically available. This prompts several questions which in turn lead into the methodological and philosophical points I would like to contribute.

1.   These developments in 'electronic admin' seem scarcely relevant to local personal/demand led services like Social Services, Youth services etc where it is not 'electronic admin' but services which centre on interactions, and where both tangibles and intangibles play a vital part in the quality of services (e.g. daycentres, youth clubs/projects, community care etc).

2.   You don't have to go to too many conferences to hear local government saying the civil service agenda for ISTs doesn't really connect with the local public service agenda. I wonder if there is more to this than a kind of `sour grapes`. I don't think it is just that local services have disproportionately less need for `electronic admin`. What lies within this reaction may be something more fundamental about basic perspectives on IST, which are not really being made explicit.

3.   One of the triggers suggesting there may be something more to this has, for me, been to hear the stark contrast between the central government spokesperson interpreting `service user responsiveness` as `electronic admin`, kiosks etc. On the other hand, those from local government seem to have been looking for ways to become both user focused and while doing this to create much needed internal organisational change through the IST development. The local public services view has been very sceptical about BPR as a vehicle for achieving internal change (as have academics).

4.   This in itself might suggest a critical look at the available perspectives on IST in public management.

5.   When asked what they are looking for by way of internal organisational change quite traditional organisational development concepts begin to be employed. For example, how 'value added' can be taking place internally. What is suggested is not just a vacuum of IST perspective but also of public management concept.

6.   Increasingly managers of public services face a reality not confined to just managing people and budgets. Managers are having to face up to responsibilities for control over information, to the extent that it might be seen as a third, basic resource. They may well have devolved budgets with which to pay for such developments and it may not be a large scale organisation wide information system that is needed. The conditions in public management , from this viewpoint, may be `ripe` for substantial IST development: however it is questionable whether existing perspectives and

concepts really empower public managers to feel able to or to want to make use of the possibilities. It is also questionable that current perspectives will enable public managers to utilise or harness the potentials available through modern IST.

3   THREE BASIC PERSPECTIVES

There is a case for saying the time has only just come (and it has not come in all public organisations by any means) when managers could be looking to shape what gets done with the ISTs without being so influenced in their thinking by the technical perspective of IT professionals. This technical approach to ISTs, mediated by IT professionals can, without intending to, at worst alienate managers or at best simply not tap into their pre-occupations and the things that are really motivating them. In general a technical perspective towards IST does not really offer a way forward for operational and senior managers that connects with their managerial agendas.

A perspective has also developed which explores the relationship between the technical and the organisational. Nolan's early six stage view of how ISTs evolve from initiation to full maturity within organisations was one well known example of relating the technology to the organisation in a systematic way (Nolan, 1979). Since then Nolan has developed, from the IST experience, a radical, `total organisation` change process for senior managers (Nolan R L and Croson, 1995). Although there is an empirical basis to these prescriptions there does seem to be an element of an ongoing comparison between what kind of organisation could be developed (based on extensive IST use) and the current organisation. One of the inherent difficulties is that public managers tend not to be making this comparison. They tend to be understandably pre-occupied with the current framework.

This is indeed reflected in a rather different approach to the relating of organisation to IST undertaken by Bellamy, Taylor, and Willcocks. These authors have almost all focused on the larger, high profile, civil service computerisation projects. Like Nolan, they too express the sense of frustration at how organisational realities serve to damp down IST potential. Willcocks has highlighted the importance of "human resource, cultural, and political issues" while Bellamy has emphasised a need not to simply reproduce the existing organisational framework but to harness the potential for change inherent in ISTs (Willcocks, Currie and Jackson, 1997; Horrocks and Bellamy, 1997).

These perspectives do not seem very promising in the sense of offering a way to engage managers in what they are seeking to do so that IST use becomes better developed. There might be several base line conditions for even being able to consider such a possibility. Such conditions might include things like;
1.   Acceptance of managerial responsibilities for control over information i.e. this becomes an accepted part of the management process
2.   The availability of software which managers can see enables them to address their concerns.

3.   A developmental presence able to straddle the management-IT divide and work in
     an empowering and enabling way with staff and managers.
   However this is an overly simple list which would need to be further developed.
   What is of interest in this approach is that it starts with, as it were, the 'constructs' of
managers, embedded within an organisational reality. As a perspective, it has more to do
with reality as personally as well as collectively constructed. Rather than locating the
view just with individual managers, the approach places it with the collectively of public
managers in specific organisational contexts. We might call this a 'sociorationalist' view
(explained below). It is important not to confuse this third perspective with human
computer interaction or socio-technical. It does not seek to focus on the human-computer
interaction either individually or on a larger scale. It is with the collectively of managers
and within what it is they are trying to do that is the prime focus i.e. technology is not
triggering or driving the agenda to do with getting control over information.
   This distinction between three perspectives, in the public management context, raises
the possibility that at least three perspectives towards ISTs might be co-existing within
the one organisation.

4   EVALUATIVE CONCEPTS:'VALUE ADDED'

The problem with value added is that it has been used by writers such as Porter to
identify the specific contribution of functions/teams/units within an organisation to the
end result delivered to customers. In a public management context, there are at least two
problems with this;
1.   There are governance and accountability processes which can't meaningfully be
     talked about in this service delivery way
2.   Value added does not specify a shift in management process.
   It is about shifting management process while at the same time meeting users needs
differently that is at issue here. The information system is the intermediary process.
   Rather than focusing on managers as individuals the perspective in this article is to
consider managers as a collective body within an organisation and to be looking for ways
to develop the management processes operated by them to the direct benefit of service
users. A concept is needed which can encapsulate what can happen when managers
change the way they address the needs of service users by harnessing new information
available through ISTs. In this situation managers are `coming from` the perspective of
seeking improvement in end results for service users, rather than a more inward looking
preoccupation with the service delivery arrangements.
   Distinguishing between perspectives, in the public management context, also the
raises a question about attempts to research an inter-relating plurality of perspectives?

5   UNDERPINNING THE THIRD PERSPECTIVE?

A technical perspective, might be said to have methodological affinities, very broadly with positivist orientations. The organisational-technical view, as represented in public management literature, has tended to reflect a more interpretative orientation. In other contexts, this might not be the case. The sociorationalist view is thoroughly interpretivist.

The significance of identifying this third perspective does not simply lie in its apparent potential to drive IST development from managerial agendas. Methodologically it would also seem to offer the potential to connect individual cognition and its 'organisational expression', where 'organisational expression' might well include the ISTs developed.

At this point it is necessary to refer to some of the relevant theory;

> *"Ones actions appear to be vitally linked to the manner in which one understands or construes the world of experience" (Gergen, 1982:17).*

According to Gergen the positivist mode of enquiry is fundamentally incapable of dealing with the human being's ability to act reflexively in relation to what is taken from one's past and to autonomously envision alternatives.

> *"Acceptance of a cognitive orientation at the theoretical level flies in the face of the logical empiricist's conception of science....i.e. the capacity of the individual to respond to meaning or conceptualisation of a stimulus rather than the stimulus itself, essentially frees the individual from stimulus control" (Gergen, 1982).*

More recently, this viewpoint has been developed into sociorationalism with the view that;

> *"Social phenomena are guided by cognitive heuristics, limited only by the human imagination: the social order is a subject matter capable of infinite variation through the linkage of ideas and action " (Cooperrider and Srivasta, 1987:139)*

Implied within this then is the view that 'reality', in this case, information systems, is literally constructed, created and recreated within the view brought to the reality by the actors creating it. Furthermore

> *"..a body of literature that views organisations as social constructions iterations of interpretative attributions by its members...there is (also) a body of literature on social cognition that demonstrates that positive images or projections of future possibilities can result in social processes of organising which enact shared construction of reality..." (Johnson and Cooperrider, 1991).*

From these theoretical roots, a direct connection between individuals and social processes of organising is being made. Moreover it is being made within an overall theoretical framework which is much less 'problem oriented' than much writing about IST in public management and indeed has affinities with contemporary developments such as 'appreciative enquiry' (See Cooperrider references).

While this has been a necessarily brief snapshot of an epistemological position, it would be interesting to see what the implications might be for information systems research methodology and for practitioners. This sort of epistemology has been developing both for social research and for change/development in action settings. On the social research front, an obvious implication is that this view may encourage attempts to identify public managers *'cognitive heuristics'* and the possibilities for change. For IST practitioners and managers, it might be of interest to note that appreciative development and change methods have originated from global social change organisations. IST in public services has tended to be viewed at its most negative as a kind of 'disaster faster'. While the potential to apply the technology to greater effect in public services would seem to be considerable these sociorationalist underpinnings do at least seem to offer both researchers and practitioners a framework consistent with gaining greater understanding about the potential for improvement in IST use in public services.

6 BOUNDARY ISSUES

There are innumerable combinations of research methods in relation to innumerable possible topics. However, there are fewer basic perspectives. In the above, coming from an 'information systems in public management' context, several distinct perspectives have, albeit crudely, been identified. Would it be more fruitful to attach the pluralism to the 'few' perspectives rather than to the multiple methodology-topic combinations of research, when seeking to draw boundaries?

A second implication from the above is to ask whether boundary drawing is consistent with making appropriate use of emerging methods being developed elsewhere. Sociorationalism has developed out of substantive cases argued for interpretivism. Appreciative enquiry has in part emerged out of critiques of action-research and problem-oriented methodologies. Given these sorts of development (and others) in research methodology generally, will IST research `boundary drawing` be consistent with drawing appropriately on the range of available methodological orientations and methods?

References

Cooperrider, D. and Srivasta, S. (1987). `Appreciative Enquiry in Organisational Life`. In Woodman, R. and Pasmore, W (eds.). *Research in Organisational Change and Development.* Vol. 1:129-169. Greenwich,CT: JAI Press.

Gergen, K. (1982) *Toward Transformation in Social Knowledge*. New York:Spring-Verlag.

Horrocks, I. Bellamy, C. (1997) 'Telematics and Community Governance: Issues for Policy and Practice'. *International Journal of Public Sector Management*, vol. 10, No 5:377-387.

Johnson, P and Cooperrider, D. (1991) Finding a Path with the Heart. Research in Organisational Change and Development. Vol. 5:223-284.

Nolan, R.(1979) 'Managing the Crisis in Data Processing'. Harvard Business Review, March/April: 115-126.

Nolan, L. and Croson, C.(1995) Creative Destruction. A Six Stage Process for Transforming the Organisation. Harvard Business School Press.

Willcocks, P. Currie, W. Jackson, S.(1997) 'In Pursuit of the Re-Engineering Agenda in Public Administration'. Public Administration, vol. 75, Winter: 617-649

CHAPTER 15

THE SUBSTANTIVE SUBJECT OF IS RESEARCH - THE M-A MODEL

Colin Dougall
Napier University Business School

Abstract

This paper presents a model of what it takes to be the substantive subject of IS research as a fusion of Maturanian organisation-structure and Aristotelian form-matter. It is argued that an inadequate conception of such a subject is a major weakness of Winograd and Flores' earlier attempt at a synthesis of Maturana and Heidegger and is responsible for the difficulties social researchers in general have faced in attempting to port autopoiesis theory to the social domain. Maturanian metaphysics as expressed in autopoiesis theory is briefly discussed and a number of theoretical difficulties noted. The relevant areas of Aristotelian metaphysics are discussed as a way of resolving these difficulties and the M-A model is presented as a synthesis of the two. The paper concludes with pointers to further research.

1   INTRODUCTION

In his 1974 paper Maturana (Varela et al. 1974) argues that contemporary biology has no adequate conception of the proper substantive subject of biological research due to its overemphasis on particular phenomena taken in isolation. The same criticism can be made against the emerging discipline or science of IS. By focusing on particular research themes taken in isolation we lack an adequate conception of the substantive subject of IS research. In biology it is difficult to conceive of such a thing as 'pure' research divorced from the biological subject as, for example, there can be in the mathematical sciences. Similarly, it is difficult to conceive of such a thing as 'pure' IS research divorced from its proper subject. It is uncontroversial to state that the proper substantive subject of IS research is the social system conceived as information system.

2   THE SUBSTANTIVE SUBJECT OF IS RESEARCH

Were Aristotle alive today he would probably regard IS as one of the 'special sciences' with its own special subject area carved out from the rest of reality and with its own special premises and taken for granted axioms. As well as being able to conceive of such compartmentalised 'special sciences' Aristotle could also conceive of a universal science. The universal science, what Aristotle designates *first* philosophy, is the science of being *qua* being which Grene (1963) describes as '*par excellence the science of the causes, the science of form, the science most to be desired, the science the possession of which is wisdom*'. Where the special sciences study the 'intrinsic coincidents' of their taken for granted subject, first philosophy, the universal science, studies just such as is taken for granted - a subject with essential properties. Any philosophising of IS ought to begin by confronting this and raising the question as to what is its taken for granted subject and what sort of thing it is. This is not merely to ask after the special subject area of IS. Rather it is to ask after, as Aristotle would put it, that of which everything else is said but which is itself not said of anything. The biologist studies just those intrinsic coincidents that qualifies his subject as a biological subject and which constitutes his subject area. Similarly the IS scientist studies just those intrinsic coincidents that qualifies his subject as an IS subject and which constitutes his subject area. The particular intrinsic coincidents the IS scientist studies are just those as listed in the call for papers for this conference, just some of which are Knowledge Management, Organisational Intelligence, Knowledge Based Systems, IS Design, IS Modelling, IS Evaluation, and so on. Each of these however is grounded in the underlying taken for granted subject which in the case of IS is the social system conceived as information system. Such a view of social systems can be taken either as metaphor or as being a strong claim as to the essential nature of such systems.

Philosophising IS can be seen then in part at least as an attempt at laying bare the nature of this subject. This of course is once more to raise the 'being' question. In recent years a particular reformulation of this has been attracting the attention of social researchers which has its roots in autopoiesis theory as initially elaborated by Varela et al (1974) and Maturana (1975) in the early 1970's. Maturana reformulates 'What is Being?' as 'What is Organisation?' and in raising this sort of question and in this way his focus turns from that of the field biologist to that of the metaphysician or 'first philosopher'. His answer to this question is to be found in his elaboration of autopoiesis theory as outlined in his scientific papers dating from this period to the present day. Social researchers working under the rubric of 'social autopoiesis' have been attempting to generalise Maturana's answer (autopoiesis theory) so as to make it more readily applicable to the social domain and so make accessible to the social researcher many of Maturana's insights into the workings and nature of complex systems. To date however there has been little consensus as to how successful this has been. Winograd and Flores (1987) made an early attempt at synthesising the ideas of Maturana with those of Heidegger into a coherent programme for IS design and although they made no claims as to whether or not business systems or corporations such as IBM or General Motors could be said to be autopoietic, their characterisation of such systems as 'networks of communications' has a distinctly Luhmann-esque feel to it. Heidegger took issue with Aristotle as to the appropriate way of raising the *being* question. In raising it as 'What is Substance?' Heidegger believed Aristotle to be responsible for our current 'inauthentic' and technological understanding of *being* and his project can be seen in large part as leading us away from this and back to a more 'authentic' understanding. Heidegger would presumably have made the same sorts of criticisms against Maturana as he does against Aristotle since 'What is Organisation?' is not a completely different question from 'What is Substance?'. One of the weaknesses of Winograd and Flores' project is that they never realised this, or at least if they did they choose to ignore it and consequently failed to see that the answer to this sort of question (in its reformulation) describes a substantive subject.

3   THE SUBSTANTIVE SUBJECT OF AUTOPOIESIS THEORY

If we take metaphysics generally to mean the statements the scientist makes regarding the broad structures of reality then Maturanian metaphysics admits of two sorts of 'unity' which, as particular spatio-temporal entities, populate and ground metaphysical reality. These are respectively (i) the simple unity and, (ii) the composite unity. In distinguishing an entity's components we simultaneously distinguish its structure which Maturana defines as just such physical components and the relations among them. Of the latter a subset of them is used to describe the entity's organisation. Organisation refers to the relations between components whereas structure is *actual* relations and *actual* components. Although the relations that describe organisation are a subset of those used to describe structure they are not synonyms. All the components of an autopoietic systems are produced internally by the system itself and there are no 'inputs' or 'outputs' except energy, hence the terms 'self organising' and 'self producing'. Since such systems have no inputs or outputs they are best described as closed systems. Given this closedness property there can be no unmediated access to nor contact between the system and any external environment. An implication of this is that in systems with a nervous system there can be no distinction between hallucination and reality. An autopoietic unity is capable of bearing and surviving change (structural perturbations) and hence of maintaining identity by virtue of its structural plasticity. What persists throughout the change process is organisation and this persistence is explainable in terms of 'structural compensations'. Any change in a composite system is a structural change determined by the properties of its components. This means there can be no "instructive interactions". An environmental action cannot determine its own effect on a structure determined system.

Such is the substantive subject of autopoiesis theory - a hylomorphic unity of organisation (the universal *in* the particular) and structure. In the application of autopoiesis theory to social systems we can treat particular systems as autopoietic in a purely metaphorical sense. Such an approach allows for the unproblematic use of many of the insights afforded by Maturana and Varela's work on the nature of complex systems and can be of immense help in explaining many of the more puzzling facets of organisational life. Proponents of 'social autopoiesis' however argue that autopoiesis is an accurate characterisation of social systems and is applicable other than metaphorically (Zeleny 1985, Robb 1989, Luhmann 1986).

Zeleny is uncompromising in his assertion that social institutions (which he takes to include families as well as business corporations) are autopoietic. The dominant theme running through his work is that of using the autopoietic model to explain or at least to somehow validate, Hayekian "spontaneous" social orders. It is one thing to assert "social autopoiesis" however, and quite another to "prove" it. It is in giving a reasoned and coherent account of this we find the major weakness of Zeleny's work. Autopoiesis theory has its genesis in biological research and uses the physical model of an organic cell to demonstrate the proof and validity of its arguments. However in using the physical model of autopoiesis Zeleny has to show how social phenomena are governed by the same physical relations as an organic cell. In the end his arguments degenerate into haggling over what is and what is not "alive" and not surprisingly has failed to convince his critics.

The autopoietic subject in Robb's work finds its expression as a "supra-human autopoietic system". Robb (1989) claims that such systems emerge spontaneously from the interaction of other mostly human autopoietic systems and may exert a malign influence on us. Since such suprahuman systems, which may be nested many levels deep, exist on a higher 'logical level' we are therefore powerless to intervene in their activities or to exert any control over them. While this may seem fanciful in his published work he never gave up on this idea. In his later papers he claimed to have "fleshed out" his ideas to include particular business practices or processes and although they seem to have added more gloss than substance they do contain a grain of truth - Robb's "supra-human autopoietic system" is in fact the substantive subject we have been referring to above. Although Robb was dimly aware of this he lacked the proper analytical tools to further elaborate.

Luhmann's work is probably the most extensive, coherent, and rigorously worked out in this area. With Luhmann the autopoietic subject finds its expression as a communicative act, i.e., as pure communication separate from the concrete host systems (organic bodies) whose lot it is to carry out such communicative acts. This is about as far removed from the original conception of autopoiesis as it is possible to get. In spite of its rigour and subtlety Luhmann's candidate subject meets very few, if any, of the formal requirements of autopoiesis theory and ultimately has to be viewed as something other than an autopoietic subject.

The conclusion that we can draw from this is that social models of autopoiesis fail if they stick too closely to the physical model because social systems do not follow the same physical laws as organic cells (Zeleny) and that they fail if they are too distant from the physical model and hence do not to meet the formal requirements of the theory (Robb and Luhmann). What is unquestioned so far is that autopoiesis theory is internally consistent. If we look closer at Maturana's central theoretical terms however we can find a number of difficulties and inconsistencies. Firstly, Maturana never says what a unity is a unity of and neither does he offer a clear account of how something comes to be a unity. There are good reasons for thinking that it can't be a unity of its organisation and structure since organisation is treated as a subset of structure in a concrete entity. Consequently his use of the terms 'unity' and 'entity' obscure rather than clarify whatever it is that these terms are meant to convey or explain. We may of course object to this and claim that a unity is after all a unity of its organisation and structure. This however only pushes the problem further up the line since as we noted we have no account of how a thing comes to be a unity. For something to count as a case of genuine unity a minimal condition is that it must be a unity of *different* or heterogeneous stuffs. An apple can't be considered a unity of two half apples – this would render the notion of unity vacuous. Admittedly Maturana does say that organisation and structure are not synonyms. It is difficult however to see how he can make this stick. It may of course be argued that Maturana does not problematize 'unity'. In reply to this the textual evidence is that he does.

Secondly, it is difficult to see what Maturana means by denying synonymy between organisation and structure when we can advance strong reasons for believing to the contrary. In saying that organisational relations are a subset of structural relations he seems committed to a relation of synonymy. The vowels are a subset of the letters of the alphabet and there is a relation of synonymy between any vowel and any consonant since they are the same sort of thing. In similar fashion there would seem to be a relation of synonymy between organisational and structural relations since they too are the same sorts of thing. In saying that organisation and structure are not synonyms he seems committed to a relation of homonymy between them since clearly paronymy can be ruled out. This difficulty is left unresolved.

Thirdly, if structural relations are *actual* relations what sort of relations are organisational relations? The obvious candidates are relations of constitution, specification and order. A problem arises with this however if Maturanian organisation is taken as a relational construct, which it seems to be. Relational entities owe or are dependant for their existence upon their relata and cannot in any way be said to be explanatory or constitutive of them. To give just one example, 'cousin' is a purely relational term. What the 'cousin' relations constitute, specify or order is at best the linguistic term 'cousin' and not the ontological real that can instantiate 'cousin'.

Fourthly, it isn't at all clear that organisational persistence is explainable in terms of structural activity. Structural change is determined by structural properties. By the same token, organisation has to *persist* through change by means of its *own* properties. Appeals to structure cannot explain this since any explanation will or ought to be in terms of what it is about *organisation* that makes it the sort of thing that can persist. If we grant Maturana his argument that there are no 'instructive interaction' between an autopoietic unity and its external environment, then by that selfsame token there can be no 'instructive interactions' between structure and organisation. A structural action can never determine its own effect on organisation. Structural plasticity is an account of how something can change – it is on the wrong explanatory side of the model (see below).

Lastly, what sort of thing *is* organisation? For Maturana science, and hence scientific knowledge, is of the universal and not the particular. Indeed we only recognise living things as living things in virtue of our recognition of the universal 'organisation' in them (Varela et al 1974). If we cannot recognise such a universal organisation in whatever it is we distinguish then it is an unanalysable bundle of properties of which we can say little. In view of this it is tempting to think of organisation as a simple universal. In attempting to interpret Maturana on this point Mingers (1995) suggests this is one way of looking at it: '*The distinction between structure and organisation is between the reality of an actual example and the abstract generality lying behind all such examples*'. Viewed thus organisation is indeed some sort of abstract generality arrived at via what philosophers call a one-over-many argument. Yet in light of the role Maturana assigns it, the constitutive and explanatory force he ascribes to it, and its absolute centrality and pivotal role in his metaphysics, the suggestion is that it ought not be taken as such. We have good reason for arguing that as a biologist the distinctions he makes are real distinctions, real items in his ontology and not simply linguistic predications.

4   ARISTOTLE'S SUBSTANTIVE SUBJECT

To on pollachos legetai - 'being', Aristotle tells us, 'is said in many ways'. Aristotle raises the 'being' question as 'What is Substance?'. Substances can be taken universally as species, e.g., horses, men, dogs, cats, and so on (Aristotle calls these primary substances), or as particulars, e.g., *this* dog, *this* man, *this* horse, (Aristotle calls these secondary substances). Aristotle takes primary substance, and the spatio-temporal entities (taken universally) it is the substance of, to be the true and proper objects of scientific knowledge. In his early metaphysical theory of the *Categories* Aristotle presents us with his first analysis of substance. As a metaphysical theory the *Categories*, as the name suggests, categorises things under the most general categorial headings which Aristotle lists in *Cats. IV*. These have come to be rendered respectively as the categories of substance, quantity, quality, relation, place, time, position, state, action, affection. The *Categories* also presents us with Aristotle's theory of predication whose aim, by giving an account of the correct application of words to things, is to make clear the difference between what a thing *Is* as opposed to what it *Has*. In the *Categories* this distinction appears as the difference between 'said-of' and 'present-in' and is used to distinguish cases in which a word may be applied to something in virtue of what that something *Is* as opposed to what it *Has*. This roughly splits into what is *essential* to something as opposed to what is merely *accidental*. Of the ten categories the first, substance, is the most important in the ontology. Primary substances represent ground zero and are the most basic and fundamental items in the ontology. They are what are called substances 'most strictly, primarily and most of all'. Aristotle carried this substance/accident distinction over to the *Physics*, a work largely concerned with change in natural organisms, where he was to make his celebrated form-matter distinction. In this same work he also adverts to an alternative formulation, namely potential/actual although he offers little by way of clarification on this subject. This is one of the tasks he sets himself in the *Metaphysics*.

What something is, what it most essentially is in its being is identified with substance and hence form and not with matter. However 'being as substance' is only one of the four kinds or ways of being that Aristotle discusses in the *Metaphysics*. The other three are (i) accidental being, e.g., when the pale man is musical we can say 'the musical is pale' – Aristotle dismisses this as of no consequence to science, (ii) being as truth and falsity, and (iii) being as potential/actual. On these three only the last is of primary interest. In the *Physics* Aristotle had reached the conclusion that his form-matter-privation formula was one way of solving the problem that had dogged his predecessors, namely how something can come to be from what is not. But he also adverted to an alternative formulation, namely potential/actual. In his account of potential/actual Aristotle recognises that there are degrees of potentiality. In the *De Anima* he speaks of a subject's being potentially something either because (a) it is made out of the right sort of stuff or (b) it has the potentiality to engage in something at will. The sort of potentiality described by (a) is best thought of as a remote potentiality or possibility whereas the sort described by (b) is best described as a proximate potentiality. To convert a remote potentiality into a proximate potentiality requires growth, training or instruction and involves an alteration of the subject. The potential/actual distinction arises naturally enough out of Aristotle's concern with explaining change and persistence. What explains a subjects going from being not-F to F (say from being unmusical to musical) is the subjects potentiality for becoming F (musical). Further, this potentiality must be a persistent feature of the subject unaffected by external conditions. Were this not the case a subjects potentialities would be relatively transient and suffer a dilution of the explanatory power Aristotle ascribes to them. Aristotle sharply differentiates between *potentiality* and *possibility*. If potentiality just is possibility then if x is possibly y and y is possibly z then by transitivity we might argue that x is possibly z. Aristotle however would reject this as a proper potentiality. The raw chemical soup of the earth may possibly be the matter of flesh and blood and flesh and blood may possibly be the matter of a fully fledged human being. However the distance or connection between this raw chemical soup and the compound unity that is a human being is too remote to count as a *potentiality* - in stating what a thing is 'we must state its most proximate causes'. Aristotle's motivation in restricting the range of potentiality in this way lies in his belief that potentiality has explanatory power. Reference to potentiality explains change by reference to *persistent* features of the subject of change. Since these are persistent features it follows that if x is capable of F at period t and if nothing changes in x between period *t* and *t1* then *x* is still capable of *F* at *t1*. This is true regardless of any external changes in *X*'s environment.

In organic subjects that 'exist by nature' acquiring and exercising potentialities involves various processes and conditions whose causes are internal. In natural organisms the only thing that satisfies or fulfils the conditions for potentiality is the actual organic body itself. However in identifying potentiality with matter in this way the potentialities are potentialities for change. This presents Aristotle with a problem: if potentialities are potentialities for change then actuality, and hence form, will be some sort of change also. But Aristotle identifies form with substance and therefore with the persisting subject. This is Aristotle's problem as expressed by (Irwin 1995): '*If the account of potentiality and actuality is to support his claims about form and substance, he needs to loosen the connection between potentiality and change, and to show that an actuality may be a persistent state rather than a change or episode*'. Aristotle's solution is to separate out the whole of movement (Aristotle's term for change) which was originally conceived of as the locus of both potency *and* actuality from actuality itself. He does this in Book IX of the *Metaphysics* where he distinguishes between what he calls an *energeia* (activity) and a *kinesis* (process), a distinction which turns on the difference between complete and incomplete actions. Complete actions do not lie at the end of a process, as does a cake from baking, hence they are not changes or episodes.

While separating out movement from actuality may sound reasonable in situations such as baking a cake or walking to Athens, how is it applicable to natural organisms, say human beings *qua* those natural organisms whose lives seem characterised by almost constant change and whose processes are their vital activities? The solution is to conceive of form as *first* actuality and *second* potentiality (Aristotle calls the form of a human being its Soul [*psuche*]). Since form is actuality and Soul is the form of the human body it follows that Soul is the actuality of the human body. Aristotle distinguishes different grades of actuality. In bringing this distinction into focus Aristotle uses the example of knowledge and its exercise. Ones knowledge is an actuality since in acquiring it we go from being a potential knower to being an actual knower. All that is left is to actively exercise this knowledge in contemplation. This suggests to Aristotle that merely being in possession of knowledge is only a first level actuality. Actively exercising it is a higher level of actuality. By analogy organisms live at different levels of activity. Being awake is to be actively living whereas sleeping, by way of contrast, is to be only minimally alive. Soul is the same sort of actuality as being in possession of knowledge or sleeping: it is only a first actuality. As well as being a first actuality with respect to a material body Soul is also a second potentiality with respect to the vital activities of such a material body. If we make the equation between form and organisation and between matter and structure we can bring all of the above together into the model of fig.1. below. This model, which I have called the M-A model (Maturana-Aristotle) brings together Maturana's notion of organisation with Aristotle's notions of form-actual. In doing so it purges organisation of its relational character and brings to form-actual Maturana's important notion of organisational closure. It also brings together Maturanian structure with Aristotelian matter-potential. Structure is broadened so as to include Aristotle's perceptible/intelligible distinction regarding matter. Following Aristotle and Maturana its asserts both the priority of act over potency and the ontological dependency of accidents of substance on substance. Lastly, with the clear separation of organisation and structure a more coherent picture of Maturanian unity emerges.

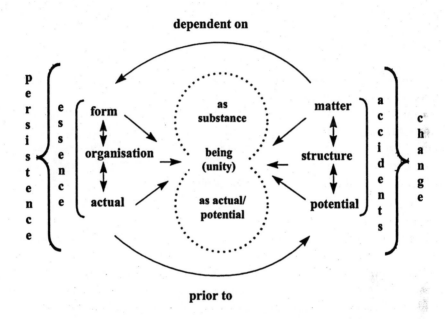

Fig. 1. The Substantive Subject of IS Research - The M-A Model

In terms of the above model the substantive subject of IS is to be found on the persistence side, i.e., it is organisation-form-actual. One of the difficulties with the above model from the social autopoiesis perspective lies in the matter-structure-potential side. A formal requirement of autopoiesis theory is that all material system components be produced by the system itself. This does not seem to be the case with the social model. The solution to this is to adopt Aristotle's broader conception of matter. Aristotle separates matter (*hule*) into perceptible matter (*hule aisthete*) and intelligible matter (*hule noete*). Perceptible matter is straightforward enough and it can be thought of as the basic material elements through elementary compound stuffs such as bricks and stone to more refined compounds such as blood and marrow right up to and including "an organised body, potentially having life in it". Aristotle doesn't give a particularly helpful example of what he means by 'intelligible matter' although it seems clear that what he is getting at or trying to pick out is the generic conformation that underlies 'divergent final differentiations' of whatever it is that is under consideration. Furth (1988) gives an example of bovine head-forms. The head-forms of the American Bison and Tibetan Yak are 'divergent final differentiations' of the more generic underlying bovine head-conformation (dubbed *bucephalic* by Furth). Here the generic underlies the more specific as 'intelligible matter'. Furth has argued that in the case of social systems the perceptible matter consists of the people who periodically fill the roles while the intelligible matter consists of the roles or offices specified in the constitution of the system. Such roles or offices are no different in principle from the roles that the organs of, say, a human body fill (or en-matter).

5   CONCLUSIONS

Having arrived at a conception of the substantive subject of IS research questions naturally arise as to how useful it is and how it is to be applied. Along with the further elaboration of its key terms application and evaluation is of course the next step. Such questions will ultimately be decided by how researcher-friendly the model proves to be as a conceptual framework within which to problematize and raise the issues of the day. Winograd and Flores have already given a pointer as to how we might proceed. How we actually proceed is the task of further research.

References

Furth, M. (1988) Substance, Form and Psyche: An Aristotelian Metaphysics. CUP, Cambridge, USA.

Grene, M. (1963) A Portrait of Aristotle. Thoemmes, Bristol, UK.

Heidegger, M. (1977) The Question Concerning Technology. In D. Krell (Ed.), Martin Heidegger: Basic Writings, pp287-317, Harper San Francisco, USA.

Irwin, T. (1995) Aristotle's First Principles. Clarendon, Oxford, UK.

Luhmann, N. (1986) The Autopoiesis of Social Systems. In F. Geyer and J. van der Zouwen (Eds.), Sociocybernetic Paradoxes. Sage, London, UK.

Maturana, H. (1975) The Organisation of the Living: A Theory of the Living Organisation, Int. J. Man-Machine Studies, 7, pp313-332.

Mingers, J. (1995) Self-Producing Systems: Implications and Applications of Autopoiesis. Plenum, London, UK.

Robb, F. (1989) Cybernetics and Suprahuman Autopoietic Systems, Systems Practice, vol. 2.

Varela, F., Maturana, H., & Uribe, G. (1974) Autopoiesis: The Organisation of Living Systems: Its Characterisation and a Model. Biosystems. 5. pp187-196.

Winograd, T., & Flores, F. (1987) Understanding Computers and Cognition: A New Foundation for Design. Addison-Wesley, Wokingham, UK.

Zeleny M. (1985) Spontaneous Social Orders, Systems Science, II(2), pp117-131.

CHAPTER 16

MANAGING INFORMATION SYSTEMS PROJECTS THE NEED FOR A NEW APPROACH

Roger Elvin
Cranfield School of Management

Abstract

Whilst information systems and technology (IS/IT) investments have always caused business change to some degree, the main purpose of many of today's IS/IT projects is to change the business and/or organisation in some significant way. However, most organisations' approaches to managing IS/IT developments have changed little in the last 15 – 20 years and are heavily dependent on methodologies of IS/IT development and associated project management principles. This paper argues that these methods contain out-dated assumptions about the nature of the business environments in which the projects are conceived and delivered. These assumptions are exposed and it is shown how they can lead to common experiences of project dissatisfaction. The paper goes on to propose the basis for a new framework that is more in line with the realities of today's organisational environments. The significant implications of this new framework for the management of IS/IT projects are discussed and plans for further research to explore the issues described.

1   INTRODUCTION

In a previous paper (Ward et al. 1998), we proposed a new framework for the management of IT-enabled change projects. This framework was derived empirically from case study research with our sponsors in the Cranfield IS Research Centre. In that paper, we described a programme of action research with our sponsors that, through an analysis of difficulties they typically experienced when managing IT-enabled change projects, gave rise to the new framework for the management of such projects.

The sponsors of our research had powerful reasons for wanting a new framework. They are all large UK companies (or UK subsidiaries of multi-national companies) and, despite having standardised on in-house systems development methodologies, they were not satisfied that they were consistently delivering value for money from their IS projects. They all felt organisational pressure to deliver benefits from IS/IT investments against a backcloth of stakeholder cynicism or antipathy in an environment of unprecedented business change. When surveyed (Ward et al. 1996), less than 50% felt that their existing systems development methods were producing satisfactory results.

The purpose of this paper is not to describe the framework further but to propose a rationale for it. This will be done by exposing the in-built assumptions of the development methods that the IT profession has been using for the last 20 years. It will be argued that these assumptions are no longer valid and that to remove them we need to adopt a different perspective of the problem.

2   LIMITATIONS OF EXISTING METHODS – THE IN-BUILT ASSUMPTIONS

Historically, the IT profession's systems development methods were designed to bring the coding problem of the Seventies and Eighties under control. The basic principles were adopted from other engineering disciplines with an emphasis on delivering a working IT application (to specification, time and cost). Furthermore they were developed in an era of less dynamic business change and built on many examples of benefits harvesting through automation of the *status quo*. This had led to an implicit view that an IT application is an asset with inherent value. Furthermore, in the earliest applications of IT, it had been straightforward to abstract the design of the application from the business activity with any re-design of the latter being simply an incremental enhancement of the current system (often manual). Moreover, since the business environment was changing only slowly if at all, the only obstacle to obtaining a complete, comprehensive and stable set of requirements for the IT application was finding a competent systems analyst. Lastly, as the impact of the IT application on the organisation was well-bounded (usually within a single department) and the organisational context in which the department operated was likely to remain relatively unchanged throughout the lifetime of the project, it was possible to do a complete analysis and design exercise prior to commencement of programming. In such a project environment, the relationship between the business and the IS/IT specialists could be transactional in the sense that once the requirements for the IT application had been agreed, the IS/IT specialists had little need for further contribution from the business until the IT application had been developed and system tested. The project manager's main task was then to ensure that a comprehensive plan was produced and delivered in the sure and certain knowledge that if she/he did so, the intent of the project would be satisfied.

As successful projects were those in which these issues were controlled and understood, they became the benchmark for success. All of the underlying assumptions inherent in such an environment (see table 1) were then carried forward into the system development methodologies that were developed in the late Seventies and early Eighties. Although rooted in a business environment that has now ceased to exist, they can still be seen to guide the conduct of IS projects in our sponsor organisations. In effect, they form an implicit belief system about the way IS projects should be organised and managed.

• The IT asset has inherent value • The design of the IT asset can be abstracted from the business activity • The design of the business activity is an incremental enhancement of the status quo • A complete, comprehensive and stable set of requirements for the IT asset can be gathered prior to its design • The relationship between the business and the IS/IT specialists can be 'transactional'	• The organisational impact of the IT asset is well-bounded, and • The organisational context of the IS project is static and hence: – completion of project plan will satisfy the project intent – once requirements have been specified, the business can withdraw from the project until implementation – project management can be directive/"hands-off"

Table 1: The in-built assumptions

The consequences of this belief system could be readily observed in our sponsors' projects. Faith in the inherent value of the IT asset meant that, irrespective of the nature of the business problem (or opportunity) underpinning the intent of the project, delivery of the IT asset became very rapidly the main objective of the project and its principal focus of attention. So strong was this focus that the project manager was generally an IS/IT specialist whose goal was to deliver the IT asset to specification, to time and to budget. If a business case was produced at all, the business benefits were articulated solely to satisfy the sponsor organisation's investment appraisal criteria.

Belief in the incremental nature of change and in the ability to abstract and model the essence of business activity from observations of how work is currently performed has, in effect, defined both the rôle of the systems analyst as an IS/IT specialist function and the characteristics of the tools and techniques of that function. This can be seen in our sponsor projects to lead to a 'transactional' relationship between the business user and the IS/IT specialist. The distant nature of the relationship (at both a project and organisational level) inhibited a synergistic sharing of expertise, knowledge and purpose.

The methods used by the IS/IT specialists were rational in the sense that there existed an expectation that either a true consensus about the project's objectives would emerge or that any trade-offs between organisational sub-units could be resolved logically for the greater good of the organisation (or, failing that, by executive decision). Two of the projects ran into difficulties when rationality required that powerful sub-units to cede power or responsibility to another. The sub-units delayed the projects while developing counter-arguments to resist the potential loss of political power.

The belief that, once initiated, the IS project could be isolated from events occurring elsewhere in the organisation led to a number of negative outcomes. In one case, the IT asset was delivered as planned but became irrelevant as a major organisational change occurred during the project and a newly formed organisational sub-unit on which successful implementation depended refused to participate. In another, changes in the business environment surrounding the project undermined the original requirements capture. Because of the distant relationship between the business and the IT specialists, the project was slow to realise what was happening and the implications of the changes.

The negative outcomes described above arose even though all parties were well-intentioned and generally followed what they considered to be at least good practice (if not actually best practice). It is the contention of this paper that a major cause of inadequate IS project performance is the out-dated assumptions that have been designed into the IS project methods commonly in use today and which implicitly guide much of present IS project behaviour. It is now time to re-evaluate these assumptions to create methods more in tune with the business realities that our sponsors are now clearly experiencing.

3   FOUNDATIONS OF A NEW APPROACH

Our new approach is based on three principles. The first is the philosophy that business benefits arise from changes in business activity that the application of IT enables and not from the IT asset itself. This notion was put forward by Earl, 1992, and has been taken up and given concrete form in the benefits management methods developed in recent years (Ward et al. 1996). The second principle follows from this philosophy and is that we need to conceptualise our projects at a higher level of abstraction than that of the requirements of the IT asset. We need a perspective that embraces the total domain of the problem, encompassing both the business activity and the IT application that enables (or perhaps constrains) it. The perspective must encompass the recursive relationship between business activity and its enabling IT. The capability of the enabling IT makes possible new opportunities for activity design which in turn establishes the requirements for the IT asset whose design enables or constrains the activity design ... and so on. A veritable chicken and egg situation!

The third and final principle is that IS projects should be viewed as business interventions rather than primarily as an exercise to engineer an IT asset. This concept is described more fully in Ward et al (1998). For the purposes of this paper, it is sufficient to say that its realisation (figure 1) embraces a number of ideas:

- organisations are dynamic entities with a natural evolution in a changing context
- there exists in the minds of some members of the organisation the idea that the current state of evolution is in some way problematic and they have an intent to solve the 'problem'
- they have, or develop, a picture of a state of the organisation - the outcome or ideal future situation - in which this 'problem' does not exist
- they initiate action designed to bring about the desired outcome
- the action may, however, bring about an outcome different from the desired outcome and so further action may become necessary.

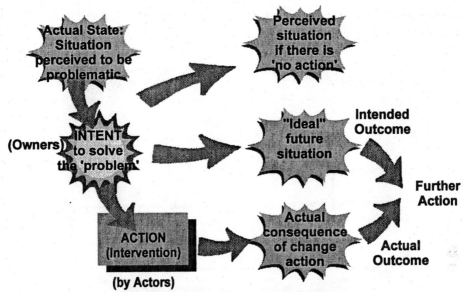

Figure 1: IT & Change - a Rich Picture

To operationalise these ideas we have adopted a modified version (figure 2) of the model of change management developed by Pettigrew & Whipp, 1991, (and similar to that used by Willcocks and his co-workers (Willcocks et al. 1994a,b,c) as a basis for IS project risk analysis). The key components of this model (which is described more fully in Ward et al (1998)) are:

- an *intent* to solve a 'problem'
- the *content* of change *ie* what has to change to solve the problem
- the *process* of change *ie* how the changes are to be brought about
- the *outcome* that is envisaged to satisfy the intent
- the *context* of the intervention *ie* the historical, internal and external factors that will influence and be influenced by the project.

4   THE INHERENT DIFFICULTIES

Using these models as the basis of our project framework we can see that we should expect, during the course of the IS project, to encounter a number of areas of difficulty:

- clarifying and agreeing the intent
- initially envisioning the intended outcome
- responding to evolving perceptions of the intended outcome, as a result of:
    - stakeholders' learning
    - changes in the organisational context of the project
- responding to the effects that changes in the organisational context will have the content of change

- expansion of the scope of the content increasing the risk that the content will not deliver the required outcome.

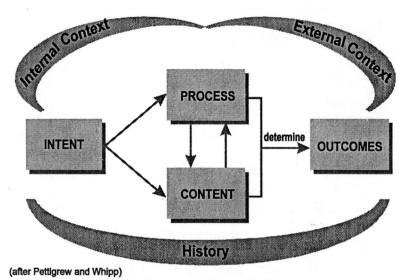

(after Pettigrew and Whipp)

Figure 2: A Change Model

We can now readily see why our sponsors encountered difficulties in their projects. Without a clear statement of intent, it was not possible to specify an acceptable outcome and, furthermore, the projects were initiated without any clear success criteria. In the absence of the latter, delivery of the IT application (to whatever specification was produced, whether acceptable to the business or not) became, by default, the only means by which the IS/IT specialists could determine completion of the project. By viewing the project as an "IT project", the business failed to envisage the outcome beyond accepting a statement of requirements for the IT application that had not been thought through because the business context in which the IT application was to be set had not been designed. Furthermore, as the business had not bought into the process of change, they saw no problem in re-assessing their requirements as the project progressed. Lacking a clear view of the outcome and with an incomplete content of change, both combined with a process of change owned only by the IS/IT specialists, the project was then particularly susceptible to changes in the business context which had the potential to make outcome, content and process at best in need of modification and at worst irrelevant in business terms.

Such difficulties are the natural consequence of the nature of IS projects within the context of significant business change. They are not an aberration from some ideal model of IS project management nor is their appearance necessarily a manifestation of professional incompetence. Rather they are the natural aspects of today's IS project management environment and therefore need to be managed as such. What is needed is a framework for managing IS projects that accepts and accommodates this reality.

5   IMPLICATIONS FOR THE MANAGEMENT OF IS PROJECTS

Understanding and accommodating these inherent difficulties has a significant impact on the nature of the project management task, requiring behavioural and attitudinal changes on the part of all the major stakeholders in the project - senior management, business management and users, and the IS/IT specialists.

5.1   Maintaining a tolerance for uncertainty and learning
Until the outcome has been clearly specified and it has been shown how the features of the outcome will satisfy the intent, it is not possible to be precise about benefits, costs and timescale. Senior managers, in particular, are frequently reluctant to accept this reality and the uncertainty and risk that it implies.

5.2   Taking the time to explore the problem domain before taking action
The necessity to understand the intent and the organisational context in which it has been set and to design an acceptable outcome implies the need to take the time to do the requisite analysis. This conflicts with a macho (or perhaps desperate), 'let's get on with it' attitude on the part of both the business and the IS/IT specialists, driven by the pressure for results from senior management.

5.3   Carrying out a complete design of the outcome, encompassing both the business activity and the requirements of the IT asset
Accepting the concept of the mutual inter-dependence of the business activity and the IT asset that enables it, requires a recognition on the parts of both the business and the IS/IT specialists that they cannot design their components in isolation and that the creation of an environment of joint ownership and collaboration is necessary. The major implication for senior management is the necessity of releasing key personnel - and even themselves perhaps - from day-to-day operations to carry out this activity.

5.4   Making the changes to the business activities
IS projects involving significant degrees of business change require that change to be planned and executed with the same degree of formality as that of the development of the IT asset. Moreover, not all business changes will be dependent on the IT asset. There will be many supporting or enabling changes which will be independent of the IT asset and which can and must be carried out before the IT-enabled change can take place.

The project must contain and encompass the activities in the business needed to bring about the changes, with the requisite allocation, ownership and management of those activities and their intended outcomes. These are clear business responsibilities that must be owned, managed and resourced as such.

5.5   Expecting and reacting to a changing context
A large project in a changing business environment cannot exist in isolation. Its very

existence will affect the context in which it is operating. Moreover, it is very likely to be dependent on other initiatives going on in the business. Consequently, it should not come as a great surprise if contextual factors demand modification of some aspect of the project (intent, content, process or outcome) during its lifetime. Acceptance of this situation demands that it be managed and processes put into place to expect and look for the impacts and to adapt to them as necessary. The longer the duration of the project and the greater its impact on the organisation, the more important it becomes that senior management accept and undertake this responsibility.

5.6 Applying control through output measures (the benefits) rather than input measures (activity and resources)

The project can be claimed to be complete, when:

a) the content is delivered (*ie* all of the planned changes have been made)
b) when the desired outcome (and the expected benefits therefrom) has been achieved
c) the intent, or an agreed modification thereof, has been satisfied.

Traditional approaches to managing IS projects rely primarily on (a) above. In recent years, benefits management methods (Ward et al. 1996) have emphasised item (b). In reality, all three are necessary. The implication of this is that the task of managing IS projects becomes more complex, requiring the active collaboration *in the process of control* of the project team members (who will focus on (a)), business managers (who will focus on (b)) and senior managers (who will focus on (c)). This implies the need for a multi-level project management team carrying out a variety of management rôles. In this environment, success criteria become more diverse and need to be tied more to benefits, outcome and intent than to content and process (*ie* specification, plan, time and cost). Moreover, the assessment of scope change needs to be made against the benefits realisation plan rather than the specification or activity plan.

6   CONCLUSIONS AND FURTHER RESEARCH

IS projects have had, for many years, a poor reputation for delivering to time, cost and specification. The importance of IS/IT to today's business environment is difficult to deny. It therefore behoves both business and the IT profession to find ways of reliably delivering benefits from IS/IT investments. Systems development methods commonly in use today were developed during the Seventies and Eighties to solve problems in business environments very different to those of today. Although successful in some circumstances, our methods have clearly failed to deliver success 'across the board'. Many classic cases of IS project failure demonstrate their limitations when dealing with large projects and/or significant business change. Moreover, as several generations of very able IT professionals have struggled to achieve successful outcomes with current methods, the finger must surely be pointed at the methods rather than professional incompetence. There is therefore a compelling case for the need for new thinking about the methods which organisations use to deliver IS projects.

In this and our previous paper (Ward et al.1998), we have developed and described an "IT & Change Framework" derived from a new perspective of the IS project management 'problem'. So far, this framework has proven useful as a diagnostic tool in the process of making sense of the behaviours we have observed in actual projects and the outcomes that have been the consequence of those behaviours. Our next step is to be a programme of action research, consisting of both passive and active interventions, to test the thesis that our framework constitutes a model of best practice for the conduct of IS projects. In carrying out this research we will have two complementary goals:

- to enhance the body of practical knowledge and experience that currently constitutes accepted best practice in the management of IS projects
- to create frameworks and theories that make sense of observable behaviours and their respective outcomes, in either a diagnostic or predictive sense, within a variety of project contexts.

The second objective will attempt to provide a rationale for why best practice (the goal of the first objective) actually works.

References

Earl, M. J., "Putting IT in its Place: a Polemic for the Nineties", Journal of Information Technology, 7, 1992, pp. 100-108

Pettigrew, A. and Whipp, R., *Managing Change for Competitive Success*, Blackwell Business, 1991

Ward, J. M., Taylor, P. and Bond, P., "Evaluation and Realisation of IS/IT Benefits: an Empirical Study of Current Practice", European Journal of Information Systems, February 1996

Ward, J. M. and Elvin, R., "A New Framework for Managing IT Enabled Business Change", Proceedings of the 3rd UKAIS Conference, Lincoln, 1998

Willcocks L. and Griffiths C., "Predicting the Risk of Failure in Major Information Technology Projects", Technical Forecasting and Social Change, 47:2 , 1994, pages 213-236

Willcocks, L. and Margetts, H., "Risk and Information Systems: Developing the Analysis", in *Information Management: the Evaluation of Information Systems*, Willcocks, L. (ed.), Chapman and Hall, 1994, chapter 11

Willcocks, L. and Margetts, H., "Risk Assessment and Information Systems", European Journal of Information Systems, **3**, 2 (1994), pages 127-138

CHAPTER 17

IS DEVELOPMENT METHODS AND TECHNIQUES: THEIR CURRENT AND FUTURE USE FOR DESIGNING DSS

Ian Allison and Gurmak Singh*
The Nottingham Trent University, *Wolverhampton Business School

Abstract

System development methodologies have been used to support the development of information systems (IS) for decades. In order to consider the improvements for the future of IS used for decision making, a survey of UK organisations was undertaken to establish which methodologies and design techniques are currently used. The results of the study are presented and discussed. The findings show that most organisations are now applying structured methodologies and scientific approaches within their IS projects. The paper evaluates the approaches used and looks at how they could be improved to provide decision-makers with better support tools in the future.

1   INTRODUCTION

Computer-based information systems (IS) now allow companies to analyse the business, along with its environment, and formulate and check that it achieves its goals (Avison and Fitzgerald, 1995). They do this through providing information to those who need it, but Sakthivel (1992) found that IS often do not meet the users' needs due to ineffective development methods. Research into the use of methodologies has been covered from many perspectives: the increase in the number of commercially available methodologies (Chatzoglou, 1997); methodologies not being used in their entirety (Fitzgerald, 1996); methodologies not being universally applicable (e.g. Avison and Taylor, 1997); contingency approach to the use of methodologies (Avison and Fitzgerald, 1988); methodology use by experienced developers (Lee and Kim, 1992; Kozar, 1989). However, Wynekoop and Russo (1997) still found a *'paucity of empirical research addressing the use or efficacy of SDMs [systems development methodologies] in practice'* (p56). This research addresses these issues by providing an empirical study of the development methods and techniques used for identifying users' requirements. The paper builds on the earlier research into methodologies but also provides a foundation for research direction into pragmatic tools employed by the practitioners.

1.1   Research Methodology

The data collection was conducted through a mail questionnaire survey. The target population comprised developers of IS used for decision-making in the UK. The main objectives of the survey were:

- to determine which SDM and design techniques are used for designing decision support systems (DSS);
- to discover how the techniques used help to identify users' decision-making approaches and information requirements;
- to identify areas for further research into, and development of, SDM for user-centred information systems.

In order to achieve good questionnaire design, the methods and ideas for adopted by others were applied (e.g. Hoinville and Jowell, 1978; Salant and Dillman, 1994). Also, established texts in the field were used to maximise the common understanding of terms used (e.g. Avison and Fitzgerald, 1995; Flynn, 1992), and a draft version was reviewed by colleagues and practitioners. To ensure maximum response, the questionnaire was kept to two sides of A4 and therefore required only a few minutes to complete. The questionnaire was mailed to three hundred UK based organisations and posted to suitable electronic-mail discussion groups. The postal population was extracted from the Times 1000 (Barrow, 1996) and local contacts involved in IS development.

There are limitations with this research method. In particular, the views and answers given by the respondent may be only appropriate for that person or their project/system. Other designers on different projects within that organisation could use alternative methods. In an attempt to overcome this problem, respondents were encouraged to pass on copies of the survey to colleagues. For e-mail distributed questionnaires it is difficult to tell whc has received the questionnaire and people are more likely to just delete the mail as it is less personal than an individually addressed paper version. The response via this channel was small, but contributed to the findings.

1.2   The Response

Seventy-six questionnaires were returned (postal: 69 (23% response rate); e-mail: 7). All percentages shown in the study are based on the number of responses received for a given question, unless shown otherwise. Figure 1 summarises the business backgrounds of the firms who took part in the survey. These were mainly organisations of significant size over half had more than a thousand employees. The vast majority of responses were from the main developer of the system (42%) or the project leader/IS manager (40%). Other responses came from a member of the development team. In seven percent of cases an end-user responded.

The questionnaire was aimed at developers who were involved in designing and building information systems used for decision-making, rather than corporate databases. Applications included in the response included: flight tracking; analysis of emergency services; monitoring progress against targets; managing fleets of vehicles; stockbroker support; analysis of business data using a data-warehouse; resource scheduling.

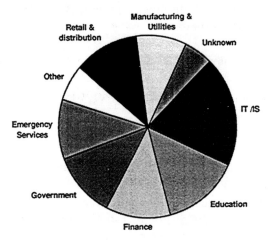

Figure 1. Respondents by Business Type

Information is considered to be processed data that has meaning in some context (Lewis, 1994). The systems above provide this ability to transform raw data into meaningful information through analytical tools as well as flexibility in displaying the results. Most were paper or screen based reports, others used internet and intranet technology to provide the information. Many were numerical or textual in format but others used graphical displays such as geographic information systems or simulation tools, or a variety of formats via multi-media technology.

2   DEVELOPMENT METHODOLOGIES AND TECHNIQUES USED

Sakthivel (1992) defines a systems development methodology as *'a collection of organised methods to develop computer based information systems'* (p141). It should be capable of developing a variety of systems and supporting the different tasks during the development cycle. Despite the backlash against SDM (Avison and Fitzgerald,1995) seventy-eight percent of projects were using one (see figure 2). A few organisations had created in-house methodologies, which were based on standard design techniques. Others had used a combination of methodologies in the one project. In this case, where the methodologies were named specifically then figure 2 has an inclusion under each method, otherwise they are shown under the 'mixture' column.

Chazoglou and Macaulay (1996) found that software houses and consultancies were far more likely to use a methodology than industrial organisations. Our survey did not reflect this polarity, with less than a quarter of the organisations not using a specific methodology. There are no consultancies in the sample and IS /IT organisations are mainly technology suppliers rather than software houses.

Traditional development methodologies have used scientific problem solving methods to develop information systems. Information requirements and screen designs have dictated approaches and methodologies such as STRADIS and SSADM have elaborate and sophisticated ways of designing data structures. Currently the dominant methodology, especially in larger organisations, is SSADM with forty percent of organisations using it. Iterative methodologies and approaches are also widely used. Rapid application design (RAD) was applied by twenty-one percent of the respondents. Prototyping was used by a majority of projects (61%), often as an approach to checking the requirements within the chosen SDM.

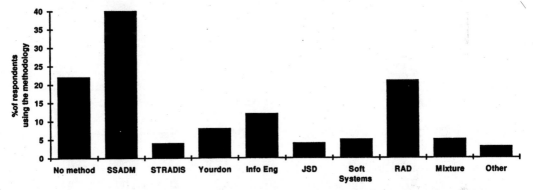

Figure 2. Methodologies used for developing information systems

Table 1 shows the design techniques that were used. A small number of organisations stated that they had applied a soft systems methodology, but often this appeared at odds with the techniques used (or not used). Only one respondent had applied object-orientated analysis and another organisation had created a purpose built model for developing multi-media systems. The de facto standard appears to be data flow diagrams often supported with structure diagrams. Respondents considered entity modelling helpful, especially where the design was likely to result in a database solution as it *'can be adapted for use during end-user interviews to identify necessary data stores'*. One questionnaire stated that process modelling was *'best carried out through interviews / observation and trial and error reiterative techniques esp[escially] prototyping'*. Others noted that all these techniques help to decompose the problem and *'help to simplify an apparently complex requirement, and identify nuances that make for complexity'*.

Visual languages, screen design tools, desktop databases and spreadsheets, and decision support generators were all used to facilitate the dialogue with end users by allowing speedy changes to the system. Project management tools were widely used by respondents (32%) irrespective of methodology, but CASE tools were used distinctly more by those applying a named methodology (36%) compared with those not using a methodology (12%).

Technique Applied	% of organisations utilising the approach
Data Flow Diagrams	75
Screen Prototyping	61
Structure Diagrams	49
Entity Modelling	49
Structured English	20
Object Modelling	17
Decision Trees/Tables	17
Storyboarding	13
System Life Cycle	13
Action Diagrams	13
Matrices	12
Rich Pictures	8
Conceptual Modelling	4
Root Definitions	0
None of the above	4

Table 1. Techniques used for the design of information systems

3   ESTABLISHING END USERS' REQUIREMENTS

One of the most difficult aspects of IS design is deriving the information needs of the decision-maker. Table 2 shows the variety of communication techniques for establishing user requirements applied by organisations. Not surprisingly, nearly all companies utilised face-to-face interviews to identify the needs of the user, often supported by telephone conversations. Respondents considered these as *'vital'* in gathering the requirements. Many respondents noted that eliciting user opinion was difficult, and that users were insecure and confused about what they wanted. To get the most out of interviews they need to be structured and used in conjunction with joint application design (JAD) sessions. Nearly half of organisations are applying the principles of JAD. The advantage of this technique is that it builds a team spirit and sense of joint ownership between the key stakeholders, thereby helping to produce a complete and harmonised set of requirements. One respondent stated that *'joint application design was positively received'* by their users. A sentiment supported by many others. However, it was also noted that this was often a *'long-winded process'*. Other benefits stated by the respondents included the involvement of the end user, which helped to develop good working relationships and user ownership or *'buy-in'*.

Another well-established and popular approach to establishing user preferences was through the inclusion of a user (or a key functional specialist) in the design and development team. Whilst it was clear that including users does cause a logistical problem in obtaining their time, respondents felt it was worth it because users *'feel that it is their system as they designed it!'* The involvement of users in this way was normally supplemented with prototyping techniques. An alternative attitude was expressed in some quarters, that is end users' decision making characteristics had *'no real impact .....as the users were very much led by us'*.

Communication Methods Used	% of organisations adopting the approach
Face-to-Face Interviews	97
Seminars / Joint Design	46
Questionnaires	43
Observation	34
Telephone Discussions	26
Video-Conference	8
Previous system / documents	7
User secondment	5
E-mail	1

Table 2. Methods used to Establish User's Requirements

3.1 Impact Of End User Characteristics On The Design Of Information System

Cognitive psychology has gained a strong influence in the design of information systems and research has shown cognitive styles to have an important place in the development of information systems. Twenty-five percent of the questionnaires received stated that the cognitive style(s) had been identified within the development. It appears that where cognitive style was identified, it was mainly through an informal process of assessing people's preferences rather than trying to analyse their decision making approach in any scientific way.

The majority of systems were designed with little or no consideration of the character of the end user(s). Less than a third of respondents believed end-user characteristics had had an impact on the design. The factor taken into account most was the age of the user. Why this should be is unclear unless it is simply believed to relate to IT literacy, another key factor identified, with younger people often considered to have more confidence with computers. Respondents selected a variety of other user characteristics that were taken into account in the design: academic achievement; ethnic/cultural background; user's first language; social vocation and job type; and gender. Why some of these are considered important and whether they are real or perceived differences in how people use IS is worthy of further research on its own.

Table 3 summarises the impact of the decision making approaches had on the design of the information systems. Again, it can be seen that a considerable number indicated that they had not taken these characteristics into account for the design. Where designers had considered the impact of the users' approaches to decision making, different user groups showed different needs. In many cases the need to have a global view of a problem was important as the decision process involved tackling many parts of the problem together. Others preferred to break down the information into smaller, well-distinguished items. It is important that SDM and the design techniques available provide simple, scientific mechanisms for designers to establish these requirements, otherwise they are presumed or derived in an ad-hoc fashion.

	Major (%)	Significant (%)	Minor (%)	None (%)
Prefers to breakdown data/information into smaller parts	25	17	21	37
Seeks well distinguished data items	8	37	20	35
Does not like system and routine	7	16	40	38
Is an analytic and prefers organised data items	12	35	25	28
Needs to see the whole problem	26	42	13	19
Tackles many parts of the problem together	25	38	18	19

Table 3. The impact of end users' approach to decision making on the design of IS

4   DISCUSSION AND CONCLUSION

The survey identified the methodologies and techniques that are being used to develop information systems. It showed that traditional structured (or hard) approaches continue to dominate the field. Even where companies are not applying a named methodology, elements of the hard methodologies were ubiquitous. The survey also supported the view that methodologies are not fully adhered to in practice (Fitzgerald, 1996).

The dominance of hard approaches could be because of a bias within organisations, government mandate, the supporting tool, the training available and the availability of experienced staff and the research literature (Fitzgerald, 1996). Alternatively, software developers are more comfortable with the technical and logical processes within traditional hard methodologies rather than dealing with the psychological and organisational aspects of other forms of system design. Indeed there are, of course, many advantages to a formalised methodology. However, Wastall & Newman (1993) state that methodologies are not universally applicable to all problems. Designers and managers need to select the methodology and techniques appropriate to their situation (Allison, 1996). Inappropriate, repetitious use of the same methodology may be comfortable but is likely to lead to systems developed within the wrong straitjacket.

Today's business environment is characterised by rapid pace of change, requiring developers to produce systems quickly. Tools are available that encourage end-users to build their own systems and that support developers in incremental development. New methodologies are being created that allow faster development. Methodologies such as RAD have placed the users at the front of the development process and have helped to encourage a participative approach. These approaches have received wide acclamation, mainly due to reduction in development time. However the RAD approach, like those before it, fails to explicitly encapsulate end-users' cognitive characteristics and it is not a new approach, relying on existing techniques to implicitly consider the user's requirements (Singh, 1996). According to Chatzoglou and Macaulay (1996) when a SDM is used developers are more confident about the quality of information requirements captured than when no methodology is used. They found that iterative and user centred methodologies increase the confidence more significantly then data centred approaches.

How do the current methods support the development of user-centred information systems? Fitzgerald (1996) argues that there is inadequate recognition of developer-embodied factors in formalised development methodologies. It is the authors' concern that there is also a lack of user-embodied factors. Systems developers are recognising the need to humanise systems in the way they interact with their users. Most of the development is still traditionally scientific emphasising the use of ideas such as objectivity, rationality and optimality, hence precluding the use of humanistic design components such as subjectivity and creativity. Researchers are looking for ways of engineering requirements so that they are 'right'.

Design is a creative process and requires the cognitive activity of the designer. To simply reduce systems development to a set of logical steps from requirements capture to a solution based on those requirements, misses the synergy created between designer and user. As Fitzgerald (1996) states *'it is important, therefore, not to lose sight of the fact the it is people, and not methodologies who actually develop systems'* (p16). Research has shown that methodologies are often not chosen on merit but *'simply for reasons of history or familiarity'* (Chazoglou and Macaulay, 1996, p218). The question designers need to ask themselves is 'are my methods appropriate to the situation?'

Systems are required that actively provide decision-makers with the information that they can use in a way that is suitable for their needs and decision-making style. To achieve this Lewis (1994) suggests an IS developer *'requires an understanding of the cognitive frameworks by which organisations and individuals perceive the world and themselves'* (p.100). The systems development community needs an improved understanding of the type of support users need for unstructured decision-making (Islei et. al., 1997). Rationalist IS designers often find it difficult to understand why any rational manager would not use their system (Wilson and Wilson, 1994). Actual human behaviour however often deviates from the normative view of decision-making when faced with the complexity of real problems (Klien and Methlie, 1995).

The survey showed that most designers do not identify users' cognitive styles as part of the design activity. However, the ideas behind cognitive psychology are, in part, applied intuitively by designers. It is known that as developers gain domain knowledge the development is more likely to be successful (Davis & Olson, 1985) suggesting that it is the cognitive style of the designer that is important in current development rather than that of the user. Another popular approach to establishing user preferences was through the inclusion of a user (or a key functional specialist) in the design and development team. By including them in the team their observations are continually built into the design. Allingham and O'Connor (1992) found that user satisfaction with the final system tended to be higher for those who had been involved. However, involving users in IS projects can lead to conflict, as vested interests can take over (Newman and Robey, 1992). This conflict can create a sub-optimal systems design and can also cause delays as a result of having to deal with multiple user groups (Land and Hirchhheim, 1983).

So what about the future? Incorporating user characteristics more formally in the design process IS methodologies would help to reduce the dependence on the designer's intuition and domain knowledge. Further research is required to identify how this is best achieved. To avoid creating a uniform interface, organisations and researchers need to consider how the individual aspects of users' decision making styles can be captured. It is difficult to see how this will be solved for a very large user base unless the systems can be flexibly adapted to a variety of approaches. To achieve this, the design and tools need to allow for a variety of views of the data. One organisation had solved this by 'designing a solution (i.e. warehouse) rather than a system with set screens and reports'. Due to the overhead involved, not all users or organisations will want the bother of building individually tailored environments each time a new user is introduced to the system. However, it may be possible to produce a small number of standard views, which could be selected quickly to build a semi-tailored view.

In conclusion then we can see that traditional thinking still pervades the IS development environment. Researchers need to help practitioners by showing how this can be changed. Practitioners need to question whether their approach is the best fit for the task.

References

Allingham, P. and O'Connor, M. (1992) 'MIS success : why does it vary amoung users?' Journal of Information Technology, 7, pp.160-168.

Allison, I.K. (1996) 'Executive information systems: an evaluation of current UK practice' International Journal of Information Management, 16,1, pp.27-38.

Avison D.E. and Fitzgerald G. (1988) Mutiview. Blackwell, Oxford.

Avison, D.E. and Fitzgerald,G. (1995) Information systems development : methodologies, techniques and tools (2nd Ed.). McGraw-Hill, Maidenhead.

Avison D.E. and Taylor, V. (1997) 'Information Systems development methodologies: A classification according to problem situation.' Journal of Information Technology, 12, pp.73-81.

Barrow, M. (1996). The Times 1000. Times Books. Compiled by FT Extel. London.

Chatzoglou, P.D. and Macaulay, L.A. (1996) 'Requirements capture and IS methodologies.' Information Systems Journal, 6, pp.209-225.

Chatzoglou, P.D. (1997) 'Use of Methodologies: an empirical analysis of their impact on the economics of the development process' European Journal of Information Systems, 6, pp.256-270

Davis, G. and Olson, M. (1985)   Management information systems: conceptual foundations, structure and development. McGraw-Hill, New York.

Fitzgerald, B. (1996) 'Formalized systems development methodologies: a critical perspective' Information Systems Journal, 6, pp. 3-23.

Flynn,D.J. (1992) Information systems requirements, determination and analysis.

McGraw-Hill, Maidenhead.

Hoinville, G. and Jowell, R. (1978) Survey Research Practice. Heinemann, London.

Islei,G., Lockett,G., Cox,B., Gisbourne,S. and Stratford,M. (1997) 'Decision support systems for strategic decision-making and performance measurements.' In Managing IT as a strategic resource, Willcocks,L.P., Feeny, D.F. & Islei,G. (eds), McGraw-Hill, Maidenhead, pp.94-115.

Klien, M.R. and Methlie, L.B. (1995) Knowledge-based decision support systems (2nd Ed.). Wiley, Chichester.

Kozar, K. (1989) 'Adopting Systems Development methods: an exploratory study.' Journal of MIS, 5, 4, pp.73-86

Land,F and Hirchheim,R. (1983) 'Participative systems design : rationale, tools and techniques' Journal of Applied Systems Analysis, 10, pp.91-107.

Lee, J and Kim, S. (1992) 'The relationship between procedural formalization and LIS success.' Information and Management, 22, pp.89-111.

Lewis, P., Information-systems development. Pitman Publishing, 1994.

Newman,M and Robey,D. (1992) 'A Social Process Model of User-Analyst Relationships' MIS Quarterly 16,2, pp.249-266.

Sakthivel,S. (1992) 'Methodological requirements for information systems development' Journal of Information Technology, 7, pp.141-148.

Salant, P. and Dillman, D.A. (1994) How to conduct your own survey. Wiley, Chichester.

Singh, G. (1997) 'Designing information systems using cognitive styles' In procedures of 2nd UKAIS Conference, Avison,D. (ed), McGraw-Hill, Maidenhead, pp. 265-272.

Wastall,D. & Newman, M. (1993) 'The behavioural dynamics of information systems development : a stress perspective' Accounting, Management & Information Technology, 3, 2, pp.121-148.

Wilson,F.A. & Wilson,J.N. (1994) 'The role of computer systems in organizational decision making' The Information Society, 10, pp.173-180.

Wynekoop, J.L. & Russo, N.L. (1997) 'Studying system development methodologies: an examination of research methods' Information Systems Journal, 7, pp. 47-65.

CHAPTER 18

THE ROLE OF COMPONENTS IN ELECTRONIC COMMERCE: A STAGES OF GROWTH MODEL

Stephen F King
Leeds University Business School

Abstract

This paper addresses the "componentisation" of organisations. Using case studies of four large UK-based organisations, the paper shows that component-based development (CBD) can be interpreted narrowly, as a way of building software-based systems rapidly from reusable components, or more widely as an organisational design approach which embraces not only software, but also business processes, core capabilities and the outsourcing of components to specialist suppliers. The movement from small components to large ones is framed as a stages of growth model with the case study organisations positioned at different stages. As growth progresses the focus of design moves from software and IT through business processes to finally reach the customer. Here we see CBD merge with electronic commerce, and the dominant issue is no longer how to get the software components to work together but how to use IT to increase the total life-time value (LTV) of the customer relationship.

1   COMPONENTS GREAT AND SMALL

There has been a long history of research into object technology. From the early days of SIMULA67 and Smalltalk modelling a system as a set of communicating objects has been intuitively attractive. Objects can, in principle, be used to model any type of organisational entity, from a button on a computer screen to a whole organisation which communicates with other organisation objects to form a business community. In practice, object technology has remained very much the province of the IT specialist in most organisations. And so, whilst benefits have been claimed for this new approach, the benefits have been localised to the IT systems and have thus had a limited impact on the organisation as a whole.

More recently, there have been attempts to move objects up the corporate agenda, in particular by identifying business objects (Spurr *et al*, 1994; TI, 1996) which are significant components of business process reengineering exercises (Jacobson *et al.*, 1995; Taylor, 1995). Techniques such as Use-Case analysis have been used to link objects to business processes by showing how the process stimulates a set of related objects to work together to deliver a product or service. The components of a business process may be individual staff, departments, computer systems, outside organisations etc. Furthermore, King (1998) has proposed a link between component-based development (CBD), in the form of expressive systems, and the burgeoning use of Enterprise Resource Planning (ERP) packages. In this view, package modules represent large-scale software components which can be customised to a company's business processes.

Thirdly, there are links also to the growing outsourcing movement. Outsourcing, rather like CBD has progressed from a focus on IT and IS to the business process level. In this high-level scenario, business processes (and the associated systems) are outsourced to a supplier who specialises in refining the processes and systems and customising both to the unique needs of the client organisation. Thus processes become components which can be reused across a number of client organisations. The last strand in the story is electronic commerce. In particular, the related concepts of mass customisation and relationship marketing (Peppers & Rogers, 1997). According to these authors, IT has a key role to play in business development because it can be used by an organisation to:

1. Remember who its customers are and what they need.
2. Enable mass customisation of products and services to meet those needs flexibly, as needs change.
3. Provide a delivery channel for satisfying those needs and providing feedback.
4. Encourage a cycle of organisational learning based on needs identification and satisfaction.

In order for this vision of the future to work, an organisation must have flexible business processes and flexible information systems. The key dimensions of flexibility being the ability to deliver new, customised products and services, via an adaptable delivery and feedback channel, to meet changing customer requirements (Plowman, 1994; Peppers & Rogers, 1997). The component approach promotes flexibility by enabling rapid reuse of systems and processes in response to changing customer requirements. The key issues are the degree to which the reused components need to be customised in order to deliver the product or service, and the ease of customisation.

2   RESEARCH APPROACH

The foregoing discussion points to a need to describe how component-based development is undertaken in organisations, and what type of components are used. If, as supposed, different organisations adopt different approaches, then we need to ask why and to what effect? This is an exploratory study, attempting to map out a broad area of future research. Therefore, a case study approach has been adopted, focusing on organisations that exemplify very different approaches to "componentisation". In the following case studies quotes from staff involved are interspersed with the narrative.

3   THE CASE STUDIES

3.1   The Insurance Company ("Componentise" systems, then reuse across business units)

This company, a top 5 European insurance firm, undertook an IS strategy study in 1991. The study looked at how data was managed across the various business units, how systems development was carried out and how a systems "blueprint" might be created to meet future business needs. The study, like many of its kind, was driven by the corporate headquarters and assumed that local business unit differences could be reconciled in order to produce a single "correct" corporate data model. And, like many such studies, the project eventually ground to a halt due partly to the acquisition of another insurance company in 1993 and also the demands from the business units that the centre stop planning and "*do something*".

This called for an alternative approach. Instead of driving top-down, development was driven bottom-up for a selected business unit: Commercial Insurance. The corporate data model was put to one side, and the new system requirements were based on the functionality of the existing Product and Underwriting system used in Commercial. This system indicated which elements of the corporate model were relevant, and these elements were "componentised" by combining data with associated procedures to form "wrapped" objects within the computer-aided software engineering (CASE) tool repository. The CASE tool was then used to generate COBOL code; not an object-oriented language.

The result was the creation of eight "business objects", or subsystems, which made all references to other systems and components via methods and message passing. Business objects covered most business activities including the Product and Underwriting management system which allows insurance products to be defined and underwriting rules maintained in a database; the Business Enquiry System which routes customer calls to an agent and captures customer details and the Back Office System which handles contracts administration, including quote conversion, adjustments and renewals.

These business objects, in turn, share a number of common services, or "enterprise objects" including security authorisation, location management and services. In total some 17% of the code was reused across the eight business objects. Furthermore, after taking 70 developer-years of effort to develop the Commercial systems, it is estimated that only a further two developer-years of effort will be needed to customise the systems for the International Insurance business unit. The benefits claimed for the new

Commercial systems are many including improved *customer focus* via a single point of contact with the ability to negotiate on-line and re-run scenarios when quoting for new business; rapid development of *new products* with minimal system alteration (a few weeks as opposed to many months) and *rapid skilling* of new staff via the underwriting "knowledge base" enabling novice underwriters to operate at expert level after six months instead of several years.

3.2   The Manufacturing Company (Buy-in components for integration and information sharing)

Our second case is similar to the Insurance Company. Here a large manufacturer of male fragrances, part of a massive multi-national group, was attempting to implement a consistent information platform Europe-wide in order to aid information flow around the company and to provide real time, consistent management information. Instead of opting for bespoke IS development, the company has opted for the Enterprise Resource Planing (ERP) package, SAP R/3. Whilst the company had a large and competent IT department, R/3 was chosen ahead of bespoke development because of its "*tremendous functionality*", "*80% coverage*" of both core and support activities and the potential to integrate data across business units.

The company is mid-way through a four-year implementation programme and has found that information flows have improved, but that the package is a "*very complicated, data hungry system*". It takes over two years to get a team member up to speed with the package. In general, business processes have been changed to fit the package rather than vice versa due to the complexity of changing the code and the concerns that code changes will not be supported when the next release comes along. The only significant change has been to develop some simplified data-entry screens in-house, although there are fears that these will not be supported by future upgrades to R/3. Additional benefits include Year 2000 compliance and the facility to update the current version to handle the Euro. But R/3 is not "best of breed" in every area; the project manager for example cited the planning element as a particular weak-link. And the product is not bug-free, although support from SAP was viewed as "*good*", and the frequency of upgrades was a cause for concern, although they do not have to be taken.

This account is in accord with other ERP experiences (Davenport, 1998). The package offers tremendous functionality in its established manufacturing marketplace. The promise of integration and improved management control is very attractive, but the implementation effort required is great and the organisation, despite its size and IT competence dare not alter the package too much – it's simpler to alter the business processes instead.

3.3   The Building Society (Everything is a component: people, processes and systems)

Our third case study builds on both of the previous cases. Like the Insurance Company, the Building Society has undertaken significant bespoke IS development in recent years, and has embraced object thinking, if not object technology. Like the Manufacturing firm, business processes have been changed also. The major difference is in the holistic nature of the changes. The first two organisations have adopted an IT-driven approach to change. The focus is systems first, then adapt the processes and the people to fit the new systems. In contrast, the Building Society, driven by a restless, visionary chief executive officer (CEO) has adopted a top-down approach to change starting with the organisational culture, mindset and language, moving on to the core business processes and finally updating the IT to support the new processes.

At the process level, the customer engagement process has been completely overhauled. It is described by a simple nine-stage plan: *welcome; enquire; right person, time & place; understand circumstances; agree requirements; agree solutions; fulfilment; seek future referral; assess contribution.* The aim is to reuse this high-level process scheme to deliver:

- different products
- through different channels
- for different customer circumstances.

Here, the reuse of ideas is seen as far more important than reuse of systems. Like the Insurance Company, "architectures" play a key role as *communication devices* and as *analytical tools.* The models are deliberately kept simple, with the intention that each architecture should be expressed on one side of A4 paper. In that way as many people as possible in the organisation can understand it. Process teams map their own processes using their own choice of modelling technique. Whilst this may make standardisation and comparison of models difficult, it empowers the teams to develop communication devices that suit them, and not the corporate headquarters.

IT comes into play later on, when the process maps are converted into systems by programmers identifying menus and transactions based on the stages in the process defined in the map. In addition, existing systems are used as input to new systems, so business process reengineering (BPR) has both a top-down "blue sky" element (the maps) and a pragmatic bottom-up element (the current system). Software reuse happens at a very low, technical level. PowerBuilder and Unisys Navigator objects provide some sharing of screen designs and database services but there are no high level objects such as *customer* or *product* or anything equivalent to the business and enterprise objects used by the Insurance Company.

3.4   The Customer Services Firm (Outsource your business and its component parts)

Our final case presents another large UK-based organisation which has undergone significant IT-enabled change in recent years. A few years ago, the firm was the credit-card arm of a large store chain. It was not seen as a core business, and a new CEO was appointed with the task of closing the company down. His proud boast today is that he "failed", with business growing at over 30% per annum. From an ailing business, the company has been turned around due to a strategy of providing outsourced customer management for client companies. So, instead of handling the card accounts for its parent store chain, the company is dedicated to providing an extremely comprehensive "customer management" process for a rapidly expanding list of blue chip clients. Like the Building Society, the company has chosen to focus on the front-end process of customer service, but has broadened it out to cover the complete customer lifecycle from prospecting through acquisition and service to retention and churn management. The service is provided from a 3000 seat telephone call centre which handled 57 million customer calls in 1997.

The key development here is that the focus of the business has moved on from processes to *customers*. And, like the Insurance Business and the Building Society, this has been achieved with traditional IT (COBOL, DB2 databases, mainframes). Whilst the systems have not proven to be a brake on expansion, the point is now being reached where a more flexible long-term systems architecture needs to be put in place. This will allow the company to further customise its offerings to clients, which, together with the breadth of lifecycle coverage and fast response to client demands, is a key source of competitive advantage. Therefore a programme is currently underway to migrate systems from a mainframe/COBOL environment to client-server/object technology (OT). When asked about the possible contribution of packages, the IT planning manager stated that no package supports the full customer lifecycle yet, nor could they scale-up to the demands of such a large call centre. Whilst some made a good job of integrating telephony and databases, his view was that system (and process) flexibility and control were key sources of competitive advantage and he had no wish to change his processes to fit someone else's package: *"If there's no bespoke work then you can't be adding much value for the client"*. The need to be cost effective in order to win new client business also means that the high cost of package implementation is a major deterrent, with a typical ratio of £3 of implementation charges for every £1 spent on the software being cited.

Like the Building Society, the company is currently working with low-level components such as graphical user interface objects and database access routines. It plans to create "enterprise objects" in-house (e.g. generic customer and client components) by extracting them from the code of the first large-scale OT-based project which is currently underway. The ultimate aim is to make the system so user-friendly and flexible that marketing staff can sit alongside clients and customise the system (and therefore the business process) to the client's needs via "ticklist" on the screen. This is in line with the vision of expressive systems put forward by Pawson *et al* (1995). The system will then be ready to test. Returning to the package question, a new package has been announced that promises to provide richer functionality and scalability, and, of significant importance, is based on the OT tool being used for bespoke development. Thus there are hopes that the components being developed now can eventually be integrated with the package to provide the best of both worlds: a truly flexible, customisable package that helps the company win new clients rather than proving a brake on business expansion.

4   DISCUSSION

These cases show that, whilst all four organisations are using component-based development, they have been addressing far more challenging organisational design issues in the process. Their experiences are summarised in the following model (table 1) which suggests some possible "stages of growth" in componentisation starting with an internal, systems focus and ending with an external, customer focus delivered via outsourced processes and systems.

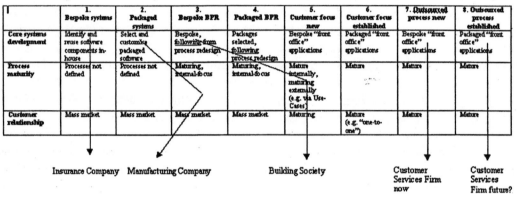

	1. Bespoke systems	2. Packaged systems	3. Bespoke BPR	4. Packaged BPR	5. Customer focus new	6. Customer focus established	7. Outsourced process new	8. Outsourced process established
Core systems development	Identify and reuse software components in-house	Select and customise packaged software	Bespoke, following from process redesign	Packages selected, following process redesign	Bespoke "front office" applications	Packaged "front office" applications	Bespoke "front office" applications	Packaged "front office" applications
Process maturity	Processes not defined	Processes not defined	Maturing, internal-focus	Maturing, internal-focus	Mature internally, maturing externally (e.g. via Use-Cases)	Mature	Mature	Mature
Customer relationship	Mass market	Mass market	Mass market	Mass market	Maturing	Mature (e.g. "one-to-one")	Mature	Mature

Insurance Company   Manufacturing Company   Building Society   Customer Services Firm now   Customer Services Firm future?

Table 1: A stages of growth model for component-based organisations

The model is based on a convergence of two technological "waves" which have been widely observed: the tendency for IS-related activity within organisations to focus initially on getting the systems to work, then to move on to provide systems that support business process redesign and finally to work backwards from customer requirements, and identify the process and system implications therein. A fourth stage has been added to these three: outsourcing. Generally, outsourcing occurs when an activity becomes sufficiently mature and standardised that it can be moved out of the organisation and provided by a supplier. Alternatively, an organisation can accelerate its internal learning process by outsourcing an immature activity, hoping to buy in "better practice" from the supplier. Outsourcing could occur at any stage in the model, but has been added as a final stage to reflect the evidence from the Customer Services Firm.

Within each stage a second technological wave occurs: the movement from bespoke systems development to package procurement as the activity/process becomes more widespread and standardised across the industry sector (Joseph & Swanson, 1998). What is especially significant about the four organisations studied here is that the systems being developed were core systems, supporting primary activities in the value chain such as the customer engagement process or the manufacturing process. Many packages to date have addresses non-core, or support, activities such as finance and human resource management (Joseph & Swanson, 1998). Clearly the business impact of component-based development and packaged software will increase where core activities are addressed. However, core activities, by their nature, tend to vary between firms and are often a source of competitive advantage. It is therefore likely that there will always be a mixture of packaged and bespoke systems development taking place as organisations seek out new advantages supported by bespoke development, whilst previous areas of advantage become industry standard practice and are thus addressed by packaged software suppliers. One future development that may impact the dividing line between bespoke and package-based development is the advent of fine-grain business objects which combine the economies of scale of packages with the capacity to be customised more closely to fit leading-edge business practice. This may enable a greater proportion of core systems to be component-based than is the case currently.

The four organisations have been mapped onto the model. The mapping is approximate at this early stage of the research, and the contents of each cell are only broadly-defined. The *core systems development* row describes the move from bespoke to packages within each stage. The mapping shows that only one out of the four organisations has so far adopted a package, SAP R/3, which may indicate the immaturity of the package market in the other business sectors: insurance, building societies and customer services/call centres. The *process maturity* row moves from immature (processes not defined), through a focus on internal processes, to finish with a clear linking of customer requirements in terms of products or services to the process steps which will deliver what is required. The Use-Case analysis technique (Jacobson *et al*, 1995) is suggested as an indicator of increasing customer-focus in process design. Finally, the *customer relationship* row indicates the importance of the customer as the key unit of analysis and is influenced by the work of Peppers & Rogers (1997) who describe how IT can be used to develop "one-to-one" relationships with customers, enabling organisations to customise their products and services precisely to individual customer needs and to move away from the "mass market"/"one size fits all" mindset. The aim is to maximise share of the customer or customer life-time value (LTV) rather than share of the market. Peppers & Rogers' work strongly influenced thinking at the customer services firm.

As might be expected, not all organisations fit neatly into one column. The manufacturing company, in adopting SAP R/3, is forced to devote considerable effort to systems customisation due to the size and complexity of the package. However, R/3 comes with an extensive set of pre-defined business processes (the Reference Model) and these force the client to addresses process issues as well as systems development. Thus systems change is accompanied by internal process change as show by the mapping. Similarly, the Building Society undertook holistic BPR and was very much aware of the need to customise processes to address different customer circumstances. However, the language was still very much BPR-focused and the key consideration was to move from a hierarchy to process teams, with customer circumstances being an important input to the redesign but not the key driver.

When studying the evolution of stages of growth models in the IS literature, Galliers & Sutherland (1991) noted how impact of the early models was reduced due to their focus purely on IT issues. These models did not speak out in the language of senior business managers. In order to address this problem, they based their model on a generic model of a business: the "Seven S" model used by McKinsey & Company. The model presented here adopts a similar perspective. The aim is not to describe in detail developments in component-based technology or ERP packages. Instead, the key message is that the term "component" does not only apply to software, but has a larger and more significant organisational meaning. Therefore a range of organisations have been chosen that may appear dissimilar initially, but exhibit a key similarity: the use of component "thinking". The four organisations presented here are particularly useful at this early stage of the research, because they exhibit a wide range of components and thus stimulate us to consider the broader, organisational implications of this technology, rather than focusing more narrowly on IT.

In its current form the model serves two purposes: firstly to define some of the key dimensions of component-based organisational design. Secondly to suggest actions that organisations might take to realise greater benefits from component-based design, by moving through the stages of growth defined here. But order of progress need not follow the model precisely. For example, some organisations may start beyond stage 1, and others may skip several stages at a time, for instance by outsourcing immature processes and systems. And there may well be good reasons why organisations do not wish to progress. For example, as the Manufacturing Company shows, implementing a large-scale ERP system is not easy. And as the Building Society showed, holistic BPR is a very demanding organisational change strategy.

5   CONCLUSION

In this paper a new model of organisational development is proposed based on case study work in four large UK-based organisations. Whilst all four firms have used elements of CBD, it is the organisational changes and opportunities that surround the new technology that are more exciting. Not only is software becoming "componentised", so too are business processes, staff capabilities and customer management. In order to deliver the promises of electronic commerce, leading firms are adopting new systems development approaches, new process development approaches and new ways of sourcing both systems and processes in order to pursue the elusive "share of the customer".

6   ACKNOWLEDGEMENTS

The author would like to thank his colleagues Thierry Demay, Lydia Lau and Brian Fish for discussions which have helped these ideas take shape.

References

Davenport, T.H. (1998) 'Putting the enterprise into the enterprise system', Harvard Business Review, July-August, pp. 121-131.

Galliers, R.D. & Sutherland, A.R. (1991) 'Information systems management and strategy formulation: the "stages of growth" model revisited', Journal of Information Systems, Vol 1, pp. 89-114.

King, S.F. (1998) 'Megapackages and expressive systems: a research agenda', Proceedings of the 3rd UK Academy for Information Systems Conference (Lincoln, 15-17 April). McGraw-Hill, pp. 381-392.

Jacobson, I., Ericsson, M. & Jacobson A. (1995) The object advantage: business process reengineering with object technology. Addison-Wesley.

Joseph, T. & Swanson, E.B. (1998) 'The package alternative in systems replacement: evidence for innovation convergence', Information Systems Innovation and Diffusion: Issues and Directions (Tor J. Larsen and Eugene McGuire (eds)), Idea Group, pp. 375-389.

Pawson, R., Bravard, J-L & Cameron, L. (1995) 'The case for expressive systems', Sloan Management Review, Winter, pp. 41-48.

Peppers, D. & Rogers, M. (1997) Enterprise one to one: tools for competing in the interactive age. Currency/Doubleday.

Plowman, B. (1994) High value, low cost: how to create profitable customer delight. Pitman Publishing.

Spurr, K., Layzell, P., Jennison, L. & Richards, N. (eds) (1994) Business objects: software solutions. Wiley.

Taylor, D. (1995) Business engineering with object technology. Wiley.

TI. (1996) Component based development fundamentals. Texas Instruments Software, Component Based Development Series, July.

CHAPTER 19

SHAPING IT THROUGH PARTICIPATION IN STANDARDS SETTING - A PRACTICABLE ALTERNATIVE FOR USERS?

Kai Jakobs
Technical University of Aachen

Abstract

The paper presents and discusses some findings from a survey of multi-national corporate e-mail users. A brief description of the methodology used is followed by a discussion of users' opinions regarding active participation in the standards setting process, as revealed by the survey. Relations between the different stakeholders of the process are identified, and the specific differences between large users and SMEs are discussed, as is the issue of why, how, where, and when users should participate. Finally, in order to make sure that standards actually meet the user community's diverse requirements, a proposal for a new standards setting process is outlined.

1   INTRODUCTION AND MOTIVATION

For some decades now Information Technology (IT) has been at the heart of virtually every organisation. More recently, electronic communication services started playing an extremely crucial role. This holds particularly for electronic mail (e-mail), which provides a fast, efficient and function-rich alternative to letter, facsimile and telephone, and which establishes the technical basis for a number of mail-enabled applications, including particularly EDI (Electronic Data Interchange).

One of the major developments in the IT sector was the move from proprietary communication systems - almost exclusively employed until the early eighties - towards 'open' systems - i.e. TCP/IP or OSI-based communication networks. However, this represented only the first step towards globally homogeneous, useful and usable communication services. Today, major issues include interoperability between these - and other - communication worlds, full implementation of the respective standards, and, particularly, integration of high-level communication services into existing IT environments.

On the other hand, international standardisation bodies such as ISO and ITU have been struggling to keep in touch with the fast developments primarily triggered by the market. New procedures (e.g. ISO's Fast Track) have been adopted, and new bodies have been founded (such as ETSI, the European Telecommunications Standards Institute) in an attempt to deliver standards specifications in a timely fashion.

From the users' point of view, employing standards-based systems and services represents one way of achieving seamless integration of different components (a 'user' is any organisation employing IT systems, as opposed to those producing or selling them). Using homogeneous proprietary systems, or maybe outsourcing IT functions, may well be considered alternative options. Ultimately, each user has to establish his actual needs and requirements, and decide which path to follow. This paper aims at providing some arguments in favour of the 'standards' path.

The findings presented are based on a survey of corporate users of electronic messaging systems. This survey was part of a larger project aiming to establish the benefits and problems of (increased) user participation in standardisation.

The remainder of the paper is organised as follows: a brief outline of the survey methodology is given in chapter two. The need for voluntary standards, especially in the field of communication systems, and what would be likely to happen without them, will be stressed in chapter three. Subsequently, issues surrounding the participation of users in the standards setting process will be discussed in chapter four. Finally, in conclusion, a proposal for a new standardisation process, which takes into account the issues identified thus far, will be outlined.

2   METHODOLOGY - A VERY BRIEF OUTLINE

The survey was done through both questionnaires and open-ended face-to-face interviews. The questionnaire used comprised four parts with a total of fourty-nine questions; the topics addressed included general expectations on, and experiences with electronic messaging services; introduction strategies; end-user related issues; envisaged or planned future developments; functional shortcomings of the systems used, if any, and how they were overcome; and attitudes towards participation in standards committees.

The sampling frame comprised large, internationally operating members of the (European) Electronic Messaging Association (E)EMA. It was assumed that large companies are more likely to be interested in messaging-related issues, as they have a more urgent need of seamless global information interchange than e.g. companies operating only within a local environment. It was also felt that membership in these organisations expresses a higher than average degree of interest in the subject. The individual prospective interviewees were senior members of IT departments, and almost all of them were responsible for the respective corporate e-mail system.

The nature of the information sought had a major impact on the design of the questionnaire. For example, the ordering of questions was not that much an issue. Whilst obviously a certain logical structure was necessary (e.g. to avoid switching back and forth between subjects), it did not really matter whether or not questions were answered in the same order they were put. The underlying guiding principle of the questionnaire was to convey as little bias as possible, as it was felt that unanticipated answers were most likely to occur. Taken together, these characteristics suggested the use of open-ended questions.

Twenty questionnaires were returned, representing a response rate of 4%. In addition, thirteen interviews were conducted. Yet, the survey did not aim at yielding statistically significant data, as the nature of the information sought is hardly quantifiable and does not really lend itself to statistical analysis. Therefore, the comparably small sample was considered not too terribly disastrous.

3   USER PARTICIPATION IN STANDARDISATION

Discussions of the issues surrounding the problem of user participation in standards setting have long been high on the agenda of both researchers and the standards setting bodies themselves. There is a general agreement that user participation is a sine qua non for a standardisation activity to be successful, particularly in the field of information technology (see e.g. (ETSI Directorate, 1992), (Hanrahan, 1995), (International Organization for Standardization, 1996)). In fact, to increase user participation is often considered as the panacea for all problems. However, very limited numbers of user representatives can be observed in almost all major international standards organisations. Looking at the list of ITU-T members, for example, is quite sobering in this respect. Within ETSI, the grand total of user group members is twenty.

3.1   The Users' View
This section reports the outcome of a survey of large, globally operating users of electronic messaging systems on their perception regarding the usefulness of participation in standards setting, and their respective approaches. Thirty companies were represented in the survey.

At a very general level, three different types of user companies may be identified with respect to participation in standardisation activities:
- Non participants: They form the largest group by far. The reasons for not participating in standardisation typically run along the lines of *"No real benefits"* and *"We are tooooooo busy for the most part".*
- Selective participants: Two (comparably small) companies reported activities in sectors they consider as being vital to their core business. However, both acted on behalf of their respective constituencies, thus representing larger market segments, similar to e.g. a trade association. In both cases, standardisation on EDI had been

recognised as being critical for the respective business domains, especially as companies in both sectors typically need to communicate with an extremely broad range of business partners and clients. Also in both sectors, there is no single influential entity that could lead a standardisation process. Thus, it seems that a sufficiently urgent need for established standards may well push even smaller companies into the standardisation process.

- Genuinely interested participants: Only two respondents had been active in different standardisation bodies because of identified corporate needs and requirements. In contrast to the companies discussed above these activities were primarily in more general infrastructure related areas (as opposed to specific, business-critical applications such as EDI). It should be noted, though, that one of these companies is a very large and pro-active user indeed, with a track record in IT standards development. Size and global operations, however, do not seem to be sufficiently strong motivators in their own rights.

On the whole, the responses suggest even less interest on the users' side to participate in standards setting than could be anticipated from earlier analyses (Jakobs et al, 1996). Interviewees typically commented that their companies do not see any business benefits in such activities. Moreover, it was felt that standardisation does not deliver. This view is not really surprising: the lengthy processes often yield specifications which cannot be directly implemented and which, if and when implemented, give no guarantee of interoperability. Accordingly, many firms in the case study simply buy their hard- and software off-the-shelf; they would naturally look to providers and vendors to come up with solutions if problems arise. A typical approach may be summarised as: *"organization is not interested in standards issues, since we purchase software from Microsoft or Microsoft compatible. Thus we are happy to let Microsoft set the standard."*

This response hints at a distinct 'not-our-business' attitude, which could be observed for a number of companies. They do not care how their system is installed, and whether or not any standards-based components are employed at all, as long as the provided functionality and connectivity are deemed sufficient. In particular, depending on just one supplier does not seem to be an issue, despite the well-known potential problems inherent to such a 'lock-in', see, e.g. (Williams, 1997). Some companies, though, had identified shortcomings they felt had to be addressed. However, they would not look to standards committees, but try and solve the problems internally.

Most of those users who go to standardisation meetings do so for knowledge gathering. It is likely that this motivation will yield committee members that can be best characterised as 'observers' (Spring et al, 1995). Only two interviewees reported a 'real' motivation on the side of their companies to participate, i.e. *"To make sure that our business are met."* Unless users feel their core business interests are at stake, they will hardly spend money on standardisation.

For one company standards committees appear to serve also as a platform for pre-development cooperation with vendors. That is to say, this company has shifted the contacts with potential vendors, at least in part, from bilateral talks into the standards setting process. This is indeed a pretty clever approach: if products have to be redesigned to meet their needs anyway, why not shift part of the work into the earliest possible stage of product development - standardisation. Moreover, they kill two birds with one stone by making sure that their requirements are considered from the very beginning, whilst at the same time having the vendors' staff on the committees work towards the company's goals.

A drawback of this approach is that only very large and influential users with sufficient purchasing power and a known reputation as being technically sophisticated will be in a position to pursue it. Another potential problem will occur if several such companies, yet with different needs and requirements, follow this approach. Yet, at the same time problems for other, smaller and maybe technically less sophisticated companies would grow, as their specific environments and needs are not necessarily identical with, or even similar to, those of the larger companies. Issues like e.g. scaling are crucial for large companies running and maintaining their own communication infrastructures, but will be of little interest to SMEs.

3.2   Relations Between Stakeholders

An analysis of the relations between the different stakeholders in the standards setting process (partly based on additional evidence from a survey of standards committee members, see (Jakobs, 1997)) reveals that user 'participation' is almost exclusively through a 'filter' of vendors and service providers.

This filter, or barrier, between standardisation and users may be supposed to not only absorb at least some of the requirements identified by users, but also to make users consider ad-hoc solutions provided by service providers or vendors. This may(!) well be acceptable if any modifications of an implementation solve the problems in a standard-compliant way. Otherwise, the newly gained functionality may well cause incompatibilities with other implementations of the same standard. In addition, this strategy will easily lead the user into a dependence upon a particular vendor or provider, thus creating a situation standards were supposed to help overcome in the first place.

If users participate at all in standards setting, they will primarily try and push their specific requirements. While typically wishing to have standards-based systems, users at the same time also want to have solutions which are adaptable as much as possible to their specific needs. Thus, clashes are pre-programmed not only between single vendors, but also between vendors and users and, ultimately, between users. Not least in an attempt to circumvent these clashes, and to accommodate their customers, vendors tend to incorporate enhancements into their products to meet actual demand. Similarly, every now and then users tend to design their own standards, which then eventually compete with their official counterparts. This happened for example in the case of EDI, where the official standard was preceded by, and has to compete with, several sector standards. Ultimately, such activities undermine the general idea of compatibility standards.

3.3   Large Users and SMEs

A distinction has to be made between large user corporations and smaller ones - SMEs - as they differ considerably in terms of IT and communication requirements, available resources and knowledge. Indeed, it has frequently been observed that SMEs do not normally participate in standardisation, a fact typically attributed to a lack of resources. It follows that measures have to be taken to enable smaller companies to contribute to the process as well. This is all the more important since SMEs are a major cornerstone of employment, and of increasing economical importance in the future (Organization for Economic Co-operation and Development, 1995).

At least in some cases leading edge users may decide to carry these requirements into the standards setting process. To have a realistic chance of success, however, their efforts have to be be backed by sufficient resources. That is to say, if they happen to be sufficiently large (i.e., for example, Boeing or General Motors) they may well be successful in pushing their requirements through. In contrast to that, less prosperous organisations will tend to consider involvement in standardisation being too costly and just not worth the effort.

Major differences between large organisations and SMEs can also be identified regarding adoption and usage of information technology. For instance, the former tend to go for systems based on 'official' standards (those produced by ITU and ISO) if and when available, whereas most of the latter opt for readily available off-the-shelf systems and services, which need to be cheap and easy to install, maintain and use. With respect to e-mail, for instance, this means that SMEs are most likely to use Internet-based services (if there is a sufficiently strong incentive to use that kind of technology at all, that is), or proprietary systems if compelled to do so by e.g. a major business partner. The non-use of services such as X.400[ii] and X.500 by SMEs is largely due to a perceived lack of knowledge and resources. This is a rather worrying indication that 'official' standards, and consequently the products implementing them, actually fail in adequately addressing the needs of major market segments for simplicity and usability. In fact, this perception, which is quite typical no matter whether or not it is actually justified, may be considered as a major impediment to a more successful uptake of standards based systems. With SMEs being a large base of potential customers, it also reveals an urgent need for simpler standards.

Funding - or rather the lack of it - is another aspect which is of particular importance to the user community. In fact, it is one of the most prominent explanations for users' abstention from standardisation. Active involvement in standardisation not only demands regular participation in meetings; additional time for preparation is also required. A standards worker will not be available to his/her employer for a considerable length of time if the engagement is taken seriously, thus incurring major expenses. Various suggestions have been made if and how funding should be provided to attract more users. Views differ widely in this respect; some claim that no special funding needs to be made available to users because they are already adequately represented on the committees, whereas others argue that additional funding should be made available by interested parties (e.g. governments), especially to enable and promote participation of smaller users.

3.4   Why, What, How, Where, and When

A number of questions directly related to the issue of user participation in standardisation need to be considered. First, why participate at all? After all, such commitment implies major expenses on the part of the user, with a very uncertain return on investment. Yet, users need to recognise that they are the ultimate sponsors of standardisation (the costs of which are included in product prices). Indeed, as customers they have a tremendous hold over the industry (a fact of which they are not necessarily aware). This holds especially in telecommunications, where the benefits to be gained from network externalities will either rapidly attract more and more users, or where their absence will throw a standard into obscurity. Moreover, users will suffer most from inadequate standards. Likewise, they will benefit from well-designed standards addressing real needs; for one, they stand to gain major benefits from backward-compatible standards, which offer a degree of protection against obsolescence. To actually reap these potential benefits, however, direct user participation in the process is essential.

What could users contribute? Two prominent areas may be identified, the most obvious one being their needs and requirements. User requirements are rarely, if ever, specified in a way that renders further discussions, refinements and elaborations in the committees dispensable. Moreover, users do not see standards as a means in itself; rather, they need systems that work smoothly in networked environments, that can easily be interconnected and are interoperable across both network and organisational boundaries. Their choices will therefore be pragmatic, and standards are only one way to achieve these goals, albeit a very obvious one. Users need to ensure that not only their compatibility needs be addressed, but also their overall 'computing' needs, i.e. those requirements that originate from their organisational and strategical environments.

The second field is somewhat similar. Users will go through a learning process when employing services. At some stage, therefore, they will be able to contribute their experiences gained from real-life day-to-day work to the process (Foray, 1995). These experiences will eventually bring users in a position to work on the technical committees, and make contributions well beyond pure requirements compilations (Naemura, 1995). At this point, however, opinions vary. Whilst some subscribe to the view that users are well able to contribute to the technical work, others maintain that the technical nuts and bolts should be left to the vendors (Alexander, 1995).

Whereas the 'why' has been addressed at length in the literature, 'how to participate' remains somewhat less touched. In general, though, there seems to be consensus that especially large users, i.e. those with an urgent need for standardised systems or services should participate directly in the technical work. However, especially for smaller companies there are obvious barriers to this form of participation, largely rooted in the lack of sufficient financial resources and knowledgeable personnel. In this case, sector representation through dedicated organisations, e.g. trade associations, is a popular suggestion. For a discussion of this question see chapter four below.

The standards setting process comprises a variety of different types of organisations, commonly and collectively referred to as 'Standards Developing Organisations' (SDOs). These include official voluntary organisations, organisations dedicated to the specification of functional standards as well as industry. Thus, 'where to participate?' is another important question to be addressed. In most cases 'the standardisation process' is considered something akin to an atomic entity, which cannot be subdivided any further. In particular, rarely is a distinction being made between organisations producing base standards and those in charge of functional standards. However, it is not entirely clear were participation is most beneficial for users. Participation in profile development would be the option of choice if interoperability of implementations were to be assured. On the other hand, there is little point in specifying a profile for a base standard that itself does not meet the requirements.

Finally, when should users participate? This problem is closely related to the question of what users can contribute to standardisation. The two genuine user domains, requirements and operating experience, seem to suggest that the crucial periods of user contributions are prior to, or at a very early stage of, a standards activity (requirements), and either following field trials - which may or may not be part of the process - or after the project has finished and products are available on the market. Whilst these suggestions appear to be straightforward, they will need additional discussion, and most likely some major changes to the standards setting process as such.

4   IN CONCLUSION - A NEW STANDARDISATION PROCESS

From the business process point of view, standardisation is an extremely simple procedure: a perceived need is identified somehow within (or possibly outside) a standards setting body; if a specified number of members subscribe to this view and offer support and commitment a work group or committee is established to provide a technical solution to the problem in question. All standards setting bodies have well-defined rules in place to guide committees from milestone to milestone until eventually the proposal is ready for voting, which is again governed by a set of precisely defined procedures. However, little is available in terms of guidelines for the management of the actual work in the committees, and no policies exist within ISO, ITU, or the IETF how to prevent a committee from being dominated by an interested party or group. In an era of multinational companies ISO's 'one country, one vote' balloting approach, for example, seems ill suited; it should not be too difficult for a sufficiently interested multinational to dominate balloting through company representatives on the single national committees, or through 'proxies', who exist in the form of standards consultants.

Moreover, nothing is being done to establish whether or not the perceived need actually justifies the effort. Given that the costs associated with OSI, for example, have been estimated at over $4 billion (Ferné, 1995) standards setting bodies would be well advised to produce a business case prior to the technical work. A major task, therefore, would be to sell the planned activity to those who would actually have to carry most of the financial burden, and who may be expected to be most interested in the final product, including particularly vendors and users. Issues to be addressed here include requirements compilation and verification, ability to meet these requirements, identification of resources required, expected stability of the standard, likelihood of meeting a window of opportunity, establishment of appropriate liaisons, etc.

To come up with a meaningful set of requirements, however, implies that users know from the outset to what use the proposed new standard will be put within their respective organisation. Whilst this will be next to impossible in most cases, at the very least it implies that corporate strategists need to be involved at least during the stage of requirements elicitation, in addition to the engineers who typically populate standards committee. Likewise, users from different types of companies (including particularly SMEs, as opposed to large organisations), and from different backgrounds have to contribute. Only if users can be assured that their requirements will establish the basis of the proposed standard can their commitment to eventually purchase products based on this standard be secured. In parallel, commitment from vendors to actually implement the standard needs to be obtained. If these prerequisites can be met it will also imply that the need for functional standards and profiles vanishes, which in turn speeds up the overall process, thus reducing the time to market.

Following these 'preliminary' activities, the standards development can commence. Based on the requirements compiled, a technical group develops a draft specification, which is returned to the user representatives for review and, eventually, approval. There may be several iterations of this sequence, with the proviso that a balance is maintained between evaluation and development. Eventually, the first version of the final specification can be released for implementation.

During the following deployment phase, operational experiences will be gained within a variety of user environments. Eventually, the accumulated experience will be sufficient to identify shortcomings of the specification. The resulting additional requirements identified will serve as input to a second cycle, during which the specification will be enhanced accordingly. Prior to this stage, the specification will be 'frozen', i.e. no changes may be made. Reassessments could be done on a regular basis, thus making standards development more reliable, and easing the task of systems planning for the user community. They would ensure the start of new specification activities if and when sufficiently strong new requirements emerge. It follows that the user community must have the right to demand the specification of a new version of a standard.

Summarising the characteristics of the proposed model of a standards setting process, it can be noted that a viability analysis preceding the actual technical work should not only make standardisation more efficient, but should also reduce the number of standards, making life easier for both users and vendors. The feedback and monitor mechanisms for users will significantly contribute to standards that meet actual requirements. The price to pay is primarily constituted by the longer overall process. Thus, the time allocated for the technical specification of a standard should be minimised, to enable timely first implementations.

References

Alexander, D. (1995) 'Infrastructure Evolution and the Global Electronic Marketplace: A European IT User's Perspective', in Hawkins, R.W. et al., editors. *Standards, Innovation and Competitiveness*. Edward Elgar Publishers.

David, P.A.; Monroe, H.K. (1994) 'Standards Development Strategies Under Incomplete Information - Isn't the Battle of the Sexes' Really a Revelation Game?, *MERIT Working Paper 2/94-039*.

ETSI Directorate, editors (1992) 'Progress on User Participation in the Standardization Process', presented at the 3rd Interregional Telecommunications Standards Conference, Tokyo.

Ferné, G. (1995) 'Information Technology Standardization and Users: International Challenges Move the Process Forward', in Kahin, B.; Abbate, J. (editors), *Standards Policy for Information Infrastructure*. MIT Press.

Foray, D. (1995), 'Coalitions and Committees: How Users Get Involved in Information Technology Standardisation', in Hawkins, R.W. et al. (editors), *Standards, Innovation and Competitiveness*, Edward Elgar Publishers.

Hanrahan, W.F. (1995) 'Standards and the Information Infrastructure', in Kahin, B.; Abbate, J. (editors), *Standards Policy for Information Infrastructure*. MIT Press.

International Organization for Standardization, editors (1996), *Raising Standards for the World - ISO's Long Range Strategies 1996 - 1998*'. http://www.iso.ch/presse/strategy/strategy.html.

Jakobs, K.; Procter, R.; Williams, R. (1996) 'Users and Standardisation - Worlds Apart? The Example of Electronic Mail', *ACM Standard View, 4(4): 183-91*.

Jakobs, K.; Procter, R.; Williams, R. (1997) 'Competitive Advantage Through Participation in Standards Setting?', Proc. FACTORY 2000: The Technology Exploitation Process, IEE Press.

Naemura, K. (1995), 'User Involvement in the Lifecycle of Information Technology and Telecommunication Standards', in Hawkins, R.W. et al., editors. *Standards, Innovation and Competitiveness*. Edward Elgar Publishers.

Organization for Economic Co-operation and Development, editors (1995), *Information Technology (IT) Diffusion Policies for Small and Medium-Sized Enterprises (SMEs)*. OECD, Paris.

Schmidt, S.K.; Werle, R. (1992) 'The Development of Compatibility Standards in Telecommunications: Conceptual Framework and Theoretical Perspective, in Dierkes,

M.; Hoffmann, U. (editors), *New Technologies at the Outset - Social Forces in the Shaping of Technological Innovations*. Campus/Westview.

Spring, M.B. et al. (1995), 'Improving the Standardization Process: Working with Bulldogs and Turtles', in Kahin, B.; Abbate, J. (editors), *Standards Policy for Information Infrastructure*. MIT Press.

Williams, R. (1997), 'The Social Shaping of Information and Communications Technologies', in Kubicek, H. et al. (editors), *The Social Shaping of the Information Superhighways*. European Commission DGXIII, Luxembourg.

[ii] Although rarely visible, X.400 systems are still being used internally by many large organisations.

CHAPTER 20

VIRTUAL ORGANISATIONS AND THE CUSTOMER: HOW 'VIRTUAL ORGANISATIONS' DEAL WITH 'REAL' CUSTOMERS

J Hughes[*], J O'Brien[†], D Randall[‡], M Rouncefield[*] and P Tolmie[*]
*Lancaster University, †Xerox Research Centre Europe, and
‡Manchester Metropolitan University

Abstract

This paper reflects on the results of a long-standing ethnography of customer-facing work within a large retail Bank. Features of the contingent and skilful nature of that work, in an institution undergoing large scale organisational change, are documented and used to comment on aspects of working with 'virtual customers' within an organisation that might be seen as moving towards the model of the 'virtual organisation'.

1   INTRODUCTION: 'VIRTUAL ORGANISATIONS' AND THE CUSTOMER

This paper details a range of fieldwork observations undertaken in various organisational units of a large retail bank. These descriptions are intended to provide some analytic purchase on aspects of responsiveness to customers and 'customer-facing' work in highly distributed, or 'virtual' organisations.

Whilst we entertain some doubts about the explanatory value of the notion of the 'virtual organisation' the concept is intended to denote an organisational form that addresses major transformations in the social, economic and technological environments in which organisations now operate. These 'virtual' organisational arrangements consist of networks of workers and organisational units, linked by information and communication technologies (ICTs), which flexibly co-ordinate their activities, and combine their skills and resources in order to achieve common goals. One such common goal is an increasing focus upon customers. These so-called 'post-Fordist' relations are instantiated in Burton's (1994) perceived shift in financial services from a 'telling' to a 'selling' culture: *"There has evidently been a shift from organisational cultures which were conservative, reactive and cautious, and where the main element of the job was administration. Contemporary financial service personnel are required to be proactive, entrepreneurial and possess a high level of interpersonal skills and marketing expertise"* (Burton, 1994, p 5).

Our interest is with describing such relational issues and considering how they can be handled in the 'virtual organisation'.

2   METHOD: 'DATA DRIVEN SOCIOLOGY' - ETHNOMETHODOLOGICALLY INFORMED ETHNOGRAPHY

The method employed in this study, ethnomethodologically informed ethnography (Button & King, 1992; Hughes et al, 1994) places methodological emphasis on the rigorous description of the situated practices through which a settings' activities are produced and accomplished. Its aim is to observe and describe the phenomena of 'everyday life' independently of the preconceptions of received sociological theories and methods. Thus, attention is focused upon the study of *doing the work* and the general advantage claimed for ethnography lies in the 'sensitising' it promotes to this real world character and context of work. The distinguishing characteristic of this approach is the researcher's relatively anonymous and unmotivated immersion in the milieu of study and the provision of 'thick descriptions' of the circumstances, practices, conversations and activities that comprise the 'real world' character of everyday work settings: *"to treat practical activities, practical circumstances, and practical sociological reasonings as topics of empirical study, and by paying to the most commonplace activities of daily life the attention usually accorded extraordinary events, [it] seeks to learn about them as phenomena in their own right"* (Garfinkel, 1967).

A central feature of the ethnographic approach is the recognition of the situated character of work; that even in the most apparently routine activities workers need to use their judgement and discretion in response to the various contingencies that arise in the course of the working day; and that 'typically' the accomplishment of these work tasks involves a range of tacit skills and local knowledge that often goes unrecognised; skills which may become visible only in circumstances of failure and customer complaint. Consequently, ethnographic methods seek to uncover and describe what might seem routine or commonplace features of the sociality of work and its organisation; how the work 'gets done'. This approach to work as socially organised is designed to illuminate the rationale brought by people at work to the various tasks, the 'problems', and so on that they are confronted with in the course of their daily working lives. This paper therefore describes in some detail how customer-facing work in financial services is actually done, drawing on examples taken from eight years research within financial services and offering suggestions about what features of these interactions may prove consequential for customer-facing work in 'virtual' organisations.

3   CUSTOMER-FACING WORK

A commonly observed feature of branch work in the Bank is that cashiers have to deal with each customer without knowing in advance what their requirement will be, not just in terms of the *nature* of a request, but also in the way it is *structured*. Customers present their requirements in a variety of ways: making a series of requests at the beginning of their encounter with the cashier; inserting 'oh, by the way' questions into the course of their interaction; or alternatively waiting for the completion of the processes associated with an initial request before making a second. Customers simply cannot be relied on to produce questions in a fashion that is predictable or consistent with the institution's order of things. Nor can they be relied on to furnish all relevant information. This unpredictability of interactions with customers has relevance not only to face-to-face interaction but also to telephone enquiries and other forms of computer mediated communication, whereby trying to keep the customer satisfied is a matter of juggling a quite complex and potentially conflicting series of demands.

3.1   Demeanour Work

Customer confidence comes from the seamless, apparently unproblematic way in which bank staff are *manifestly*, demonstrably, able to do the work necessitated by customer demands and thereby produce an orderly flow of transactions. For cashiers to be seen as competent requires them to engage in a significant amount of demeanour work - routinely explaining as they go along the steps they are taking, what enquiries they are making of the screen, who they are telephoning, etc.. Competence is evident through the way the flow of interaction is maintained, without palpable gaps, in routine and minute by minute interactions.

Competence also needs to be displayed whilst simultaneously interacting with customers and using information screens. In using technology, the cashiers' interaction with the technology and with their customers must ideally render the technology 'invisible'. However, navigating through screens and reading the information they contain is time consuming, leading to difficulties in conducting smoothly flowing conversations with clients. Problems interrogating the database and deciphering information can erode customer confidence. Related to this, the fundamental problem of information screens is that the information they convey is typically structured according to the flow of transactions, not to the flow of enquiries. A customer's orientation to a given enquiry, however, will be driven by a particular context. It is the absence of context sensitivity that creates difficulties in interrogation. This in turn disrupts the flow of visibly competent work. Whilst customer satisfaction remains an issue, operatives, whether on the telephone, or using video conferencing systems, will still have to contend with various sources of unpredictability. Hence efficient use of the technology and interaction with customers has to be successfully managed simultaneously. In the act of processing transactions, the competent operative must routinely 'weave' use of the technology into the flow of interaction with customers such that the relevant expertise and skill is made visible.

An example of this issue relates to use of the teleconferencing kit (a commercial, ISDN-based, desktop video conference system, with dedicated database and communication software) that had been installed in the 'Telehelp' section of the Insurance division of the Bank. The role of the Telehelp team was to give insurance advice to customers. One highly visible feature of the work with the videolink was the extent to which staff were required to 'talk through the technology', both to alert the customer to what was going to happen next - 'the screen will go fuzzy'; 'it will take a couple of seconds for this information to be transferred to you' etc. - and to explain the everyday meaning of technical insurance terms. This process is illustrated in the following abbreviated observation of the videolink in use:

> *1. Preparing PC1 for use. - in response to call from branch ... 2. Call through on link - 'what can I do for you?' ... 3. Branch intros customer ... 4. Takes customer details - using screen - filling in form on screen - surname, initials, postcode, house number ... 5. Transferring info - explains about picture 'going fuzzy' ... 6. Buildings insurance - asking questions - rebuilding costs etc ... 7. Transferring info - explains about screen 'going fuzzy' again - talks about 'features and benefits' - additional insurance. freezer food; 2 million owner liability etc - makes postman and slate 'joke'.*

Apart from preparing the customer for the screen 'going fuzzy' the operator also deploys one of the standard 'jokes' for explaining the importance of a £2 million owner liability feature in the policy in order to mediate between the technical insurance and legal language of 'owner liability' and the everyday world. This is done through the device of *"what would happen if one of your slates fell on the postman's head when he was delivering?"*. Of course this issue of 'translation' and of coping simultaneously with both the technology and the customer happens with other technologies and in other contexts but the difficulties that ensue should not be underestimated. Observations document the sheer *frequency* and *regularity* of this kind of 'demeanour' work . Accomplished use of the technology necessitates operator's spending a great deal of their time reassuring customers and navigating them through the work.

3.2   Knowledge Of The Customer

The unpredictabilities of customer facing work are demonstrably manageable, and handled in ways which indicate the sometimes hidden skills of ordinary operatives. One such way is the use of 'local knowledge' - a particular knowledge of the circumstances of the customer, their business and their account that often represents a short-cut to processing. The following extract indicates how some of this 'local knowledge' is deployed in a lending interview. In this particular case the Lending Officer is considering an approach to borrow money to purchase a hairdressers:

LO: "What can I do for you?"
C: ".. been hairdressing for 10 years... we've seen premises .. we were enquiring about money.."
LO: "Where is it?"
C: "Its on ...
LO: "What figures are we talking?"
C: ".. 68K .. the Building Society say its worth 65... we think it'll come down.."
LO: "..first question - what have you got to put into it?"
C: ".my own home.. that's all .. we haven't really got any ideas.."
LO: "For a commercial proposition to get off the ground we're looking at a third..."
C2: " do you think if we got a more realistic figure .. we would stand a chance?"
LO: " There's nothing wrong with purchasing property.. (but) I'd be thinking more on the lines of 30.. The first question on my pad is the contribution .. if it was 30 and you were putting in 10 then I'd think of it..."
After the interview.
LO: " You've go to be cruel to be kind.. there's no way I'm going to lend the 68K with no contribution from them .. the risk is all with the Bank.. (after looking at the) initial contribution I didn't delve any further .. The problem is ... I know her account is crap.. there's an enforcement order on... its a waste of time .. I spend an hour going through them.. (the proposition) wasn't really thought through.. (its) back of a fag packet stuff.."

The 'skill' that Lending Officers routinely deploy in customer interviews, as well as the detailed 'local knowledge' of their customers and the running of their accounts indicates the extent to which decision-making in the Bank, despite an emphasis on procedure and the range of sophisticated computer support, often comes down to 'gut feeling'. As one Lending Officer put it *"a lot of it is just gut feeling.. the only other thing you've got is how the account has run historically and income and expenditure breakdowns ..and they cant tell you anything.."*. Lending on 'gut feeling' clearly benefits from the kind of detailed local knowledge of the customer commonly found in the branches. The point we are interested in is the extent to which such local knowledge, developed in a branch with a few thousand customers, is likely to be a useful resource in everyday work in a highly centralised and distributed organisation - a 'virtual organisation' - where the customer base is nearer one million.

4   CUSTOMER WORK AND THE "VIRTUAL ORGANISATION'

This section uses our current fieldwork to examine 'customer-facing' work in situations which do not involve actual face-to-face communication. Here we attempt to address some of the intriguing issues of co-operating with 'absent' customers - co-operating with the 'customer in the machine' - that have resulted from the massive organisational changes and changes in consumer behaviour that Burton (1994) suggests have occurred in financial services in recent years.

Like many other financial institutions, the Bank from which the fieldwork observations are drawn has started to transform its 'traditional' organisation to enable it to meet increasing competition in the financial markets. This strategic plan has been implemented in various ways; most obviously through a general and comprehensive restructuring involving the centralisation and standardisation of processes and the creation of specialist centres, such as Lending Centres, Service Centres, and Securities Centres, all servicing an increasing number of 'high street' Customer Service Branches.

The overall aim of the Bank's strategic plan was to transform the organisational culture from a predominantly 'administrative' one to a 'selling and service' culture. While the rationale of these changes is 'organisational' it is also dependent on extensive use of IT to 'reconfigure the organisation' through its application in data analysis and processing, communication, and decision support. The centralisation process itself requires much greater co-ordination and IT support, networked systems of accounting, relational databases, and 'expert' systems are seen as essential. Financial institutions have long been in the forefront of such use of distributed computer systems. Recently they have begun to explore greater use of IT to support decision-making, quality control, and customer services. The notion of the 'virtual customer' is one promoted and enabled by this developing use of IT.

'Virtual customers' are representations 'on file' and increasingly 'in the machine' of 'types' of customer endowed with utilisations of bank products, spending and income patterns along with protocols representing the 'rationalities' governing customer behaviour. Information contained in customer files, and increasingly through perusal of computer records such as the '836' (a breakdown of the working of the customer's account over the year) and the 'Customer Notes' (a record of every contact between the Bank and the customer), was used to construct a 'picture' of the customer which then played a part in the interaction between the customer and various bank managers. This increasingly computerised record was valuable not simply for attributing blame. Through its procedural implicativeness in informing and guiding the actions of others, it constituted an important component in the individual worker's 'sense of organisation' - enabling them to quickly grasp not only of 'what had happened' but also 'what to do next'.

A dramatic illustration of this is contained in the next example when one business manager who was covering for another's illness suddenly received a phone call asking for an increased loan to pay off the Inland Revenue. As he looked through the customer record the Business Manager had to come to a rapid understanding of 'what's going on', make a quick decision and offer a reasonable justification for his actions:

1. Looking at file - emergency (phone call from customer) - doesn't know the file. Customer is heavily borrowed and not generating the income. ... Discussion of case - .. Well, its a bit of a problem really because I don't know the file ... its a pretty meaty file I don't know it..so I have to very quickly look and try and sort of acquaint myself with what's going on and what's been arranged in a short space of time ... But basically, he's heavily borrowed ... forget the money on clients accounts because that's not his money ..but he's got a private loan acc of 38 a business loan acc of 20 and bus OD ..umm..of 29 there's a lot of borrowed money there ..on a business and clearly he's having difficulty in servicing it all ..now I don't know what they were all for.. I really..I mean I would if it were my own file I would know it having done it and researched it ..I could find out by reading it..but don't really have too much time to do that........but you know, isn't it ridiculous ..saddling.. themselves with all that level borrowing.....its 90000..and they can't deal with the thing..

4.1   Reconfiguring The Customer

As the bank began its reorganisation there was a recognition of some of the tensions that would develop between a policy of centralisation and a desire to continue to look like a local 'high street' bank. This tension manifested itself in numerous ways, most notably in the conflict between 'relationship management' (managing accounts according to what is 'known' about the customer as the result of a long-standing relationship) and management according to expert risk grading and assessment packages; and especially in the tension between responding to the customer and 're-configuring the customer'. This was partly resolved at the level of the account with accounts deemed 'core' or 'mass market' being largely managed 'by the machine'. However, even important business accounts were subjected both to various expert risk grading packages - such as GAPP - and to a formal process of report. Furthermore, customers in the mass market could make complaints that demanded a personalised, managerial response.

The centralisation process has been driven by a variety of factors. One of these is an attempt to ensure standardisation and consistency in decision-making and procedure not only through increasing reliance on the technology but through attempts to re-configure customers and staff. As one Lending manager put it, *"...whether you go into a branch. or apply for a loan . in Manchester or in Southampton .. you should be treated the same way.."*. This involved developing a set of expectations as to how accounts should be handled which emphasised the application of standard procedure as opposed to the more personalised approaches of the past. So, for example, a standard set of templated letters were developed to send to accounts that were 'out of order', accompanied by a 'script' to be used whenever customers complained.

Of course this did not guarantee that customers would respond to computer generated letters informing them of the state of their account in the same impersonal way. For instance, one customer responded to such a letter in the following manner: *"Might I enquire as to what particular charm school gave you your wonderful way with sarcasm and barefaced cheek! You were bloody rude... I demand, by return an apology"*.

As one manager pointed out the attempt to ensure consistency and, importantly, the attempt to write in 'plain English' has not always been appreciated by customers, especially long-standing ones.

These examples suggest some initial tensions in the 'customer care' process in the large, centralised units, but it should not be thought that 'skilful' demeanour work was totally absent. Demeanour work was just as observable in mediated communications such as telephone work - often referred to as 'smiling down the telephone'. However, given the much greater customer base of these units, such demeanour work was unlikely to be facilitated by 'local knowledge' of the customer. What *does* become important in such customer facing work is orientation to the customer record - in effect attentiveness to the 'virtual customer' represented in organisational records of various kinds - and attentiveness to unravelling the history of a customer's account or complaint using the available technology. In these circumstances issues of representation and standardisation of the customer record become especially important for organisational actions.

4.2   Getting To Know The 'Customer In The Machine': Categorisation And Standardisation

In the context of the Bank, many managers have effectively become a locus of change: balancing and resolving at a practical level the tensions involved in reconciling the centralisation of processes and administration with the decentralisation of customer services and 'selling'. These managers are consequently obliged to reconcile organisational realignments with changes in consumer behaviour such as the increasing disappearance of customers from the banking hall and the growth, for example, in telephone banking and the use of ATMs. As one manager commented; *".. whereas in the past the branch manager could stand in the banking hall and recognise ten of his customers .. now he might not know any of them.. ".* For the branch manager this creates an interesting problem:

> *"If you take out the non-customers and you take out the business customers, and you take out the runners... if you take out that lot, then you take out the customers of other branches, I'm actually seeing very, very few of my own... customers. So then we got to say 'where are the rest of them?' because I can produce a printout that says I've got fourteen thousand customers. And that was the answer to it: 'How well do you know your customers?' 'Not very well". Some of them have credit balances of twenty, thirty thousand pounds. And we never see them. We've never even heard of them... "*

This branch manager can see - 'in the machine' - that he has 14,000 customers on a computer printout, but most of them he never sees. Yet the computer tells him that they are his customers so they must be there. The problem then becomes how do you sell your products to someone you never see?.

For the Bank one answer to this problem has been a strategy entitled 'Managing Local Markets' (MLM), a sales approach focused within the bank's CSBs and Business Centres where face-to-face customer contact has been retained. Initially all staff underwent an exercise to develop some understanding of what they needed to know about customers which involved going out and finding what lay 'beyond the walls' of the bank. Employees went out in the streets on walkabouts and drivearounds, collected newspaper cuttings, advertisements of house sales etc, trying to assess the character of their particular area and gain some measure of the competition. At the point of application MLM is computer driven. Customers are categorised into 5 basic categories - A+, A, B, C and D - the A+'s being the "super accounts" and the Ds being the ones that "cost money to run". These categories are based upon a thorough knowledge of the customer's dealings with the bank, the nature of their credit balances, the running of their account, credit cards, investments, mortgages, insurance etc. In practice large numbers in the B and C categories necessitated further classifications. Customers are variously listed as being: 'Retireds'; FIYAs (Financially Independent Young Adults); YSs (Young Singles); and Mid-Markets, BOFs (Better Off Financially) and WOEs (Well Off Establisheds) who are all aged 31 to 50 with the classification being based on the amount of money that passes through their accounts. This process of categorisation can be refined even further as the following fieldwork extract where a manager is elaborating further about MLM:

> .... what we intend to do is to literally look at these very narrow groups so we may actually go to the computer ... where we may actually be able to say 'Right what we want to have a look at, we want to have a look at those customers which are classified as Mid-Market, that are aged between thirty one and thirty three, that's this little group, that have a risk grade of one to five on their account so that we know they're good accounts, and that perhaps live in a particular area ... And that should produce a target group of something in the region of say fifty accounts

The target products in MLM - insurance, pensions or whatever - tend to be ones that are currently in focus throughout the bank, and a complimentary sales drive operates under the banner of 'Business as Usual' where they attempt to sell the same products to the people they do see regularly. To establish the ones they don't see they use the customer database to discover their normal mode of contact with the bank.

MLM has a number of important implications. Computer derived models of market segments are being used to devise a whole set of organisational and marketing rationales. These underlie an increasing number of management activities and decisions and the way they are achieved. Additionally efforts are underway to arrive at ever better depictions of customers within the machine. There are at least two issues worthy of consideration here. One of these is the representational nature of such virtual customers and how they are arrived at and engaged with from day to day. The other is the question of how managers (and others) negotiate some sort of 'fit' between 'virtual customers' and the 'real' customers they see over the counter or talk to on the phone.

5   CONCLUSION

In describing the various activities associated with customer-facing work within the Bank the intention of this paper is to highlight the accomplished and skilful nature of such work. Furthermore, our studies suggest that 'real world' activity in customer services, whether or not it is computer-mediated, requires appreciable 'sense-making' work on the part of operatives. As organisations seemingly move towards increasingly distributed and 'virtual' forms of working the recognition of the varied skills involved in customer-facing work seems likely to place particular and increasing burdens not only on the technology of the organisation but also on its training regime.

We can see in the above observations that, regardless of the presence of electronically-mediated artefacts in such work, a great deal of its actual achievement boils down to the skilful adaptation of pre-existing interactional competencies such as those embodied in things like demeanour work, handling the unpredictable, and the relevant use of local knowledge. Whilst staff will regularly turn to 'virtual' representations of customers in the context of their day-to-day work, these amount to no more or less than sophisticated bodies of information. The real skill, or artfulness, in customer-facing work resides in embedding those bodies of information in experience in such a way as to make them specifically relevant to necessarily situated and contingent circumstances, a contingency recognised in notions such as lending on 'gut feeling'. So, whilst it is possible to wax lyrical about ever more virtual, transient and flexible patterns of co-ordination it is important to recognise that at some point these ideals will need to make contact with situated, manifestly 'real' work where what matters is the interactional competences through which distributed resources can be brought to bear. Ultimately, then, 'virtual' organisations need to give close attention to providing appropriate technology, and training, for the contingent character of such interactionally-focused work.

References

Anderson, R., Sharrock,W.W., and Hughes, J. (1989), "Working for Profit: The Social Organisation of Calculation in an Entrepreneurial Firm", Avebury, Aldershot.

Bloomfield, B.P., Coombs, R., Knights, D., and Littler, D., (1997) Information Technology and Organizations: Strategies, Networks, and Integration, Oxford University press

Burton, D., (1994) Financial Services and the Consumer, London, Routledge

Button, G., and King, V., "Hanging around is not the point: Calling Ethnography to Account", paper to the Workshop on Ethnography and CSCW System Design', Toronto, Nov, 1992.

Garfinkel, Harold, (1967), Studies in Ethnomethodology, Polity Press, Cambridge

Gaver, W., (1992) "The Affordances of Media Spaces for Collaboration", in 'Sharing Perspectives', Proceedings of CSCW '92, Toronto, Nov 1992, ed. Turner, J. and Kraut,

R., ACM Press

Heath, C., and Luff, P., (1991) "Collaborative Activity and Technological Design: Task Coordination in London Underground Control Rooms", in 'ECSCW '91', proceedings from the 2nd European CSCW Conference, Sept 1991, Amsterdam, ed. Bannon, L., Robinson, M., and Schmidt, K., Kluwer Academic Press

Hughes, J., Randall, D., and Shapiro, D., (1993), "From Ethnographic Record to System Design", in Computer Supported Cooperative Work: An International Journal

Hughes, J. A., King, V., Rodden, T., and Andersen, H. (1994) "Moving out from the control room: Ethnography in system design". In Proceedings of CSCW '94, Chapel Hill, North Carolina.

Knights, D., (1997) 'Governmentality and Financial Services: Welfare Crises and the Financially Self- Disciplined Subject', in G. Morgan and D. Knights, Regulation and Deregulation in European Financial Services, Basingstoke, Macmillan

O'Reilly, J., (1994) Banking on Flexibility, Aldershot, Avebury

Ouchi, W.G., 'Markets, Bureaucracies, and Clans", Administrative Science Quarterly, Vol 25, March 1980

Randall, D. and Hughes, J. A. (1994) "Sociology, CSCW and Working with Customers", in Thomas, P (ed) Social and Interaction Dimensions of System Design. Cambridge University Press Cambridge.

Suchman, L. (1987), "Plans and Situated Actions: The problem of human - machine communication", Cambridge: Cambridge University Press.

(Research acknowledgements: the ESRC 'Virtual Society?' program project 'Where the 'Virtual' Meets the 'Real': management, skill, and innovation in the virtual organisation'; the 'DTI/EPSRC funded initiative in CSCW; the DTI/EPSRC SYCOMT Project No. GR/J53409; and the NCR funded project 'Building the Virtual Bank').

CHAPTER 21

THE IMPORTANCE OF SOCIAL AWARENESS IN GLOBAL INFORMATION SYSTEMS

Tanko Ishaya and Linda Macaulay
Department of Computation, UMIST

Abstract

The purpose of this paper is to highlight the importance of social awareness in global information systems. We present a conceptual design framework developed from case study results and analysis of some groupware systems. The systems used are web based shared workspace, desktop video conferencing, and Ventana electronic meeting system. The framework categorises social awareness into availability, identity, trust building, and activity. The elements are presented and consolidated with existing models in the literature. The framework constructed is being used to develop a prototype for global information systems.

1 INTRODUCTION

Global communication is increasingly an essential component of work. Many organizations are dispersed or have affiliations around the world, with workers in many different time zones. In this setting, work is organized either by project or by the expertise of individuals rather than by the conventional physical location. Recent research findings show that people need knowledge of their co-workers identity, location, activities, and intentions to enable them to work together more effectively. (Olson and Bly 1991; Dourish and Bellotti 1992; Bly et al., 1993; Gutwin, C. and Greenberg, S 1997). Thus, the issue of awareness is paramount for a successful collaboration.

One definition of Awareness is *"the understanding of the activity of the others, which provides a context for your own activity"* (Dourish and Bellotti 1992). In this paper we define awareness as the understanding and knowledge of others and what they are doing to provide a context for your own activity. We argue that knowledge of just the activities of others does not provide people with a sufficient context for their own activities.

Many approaches have been used in order to provide awareness within collaborative systems and many tools exists today, e.g. PORTHOLES (Dourish and Iris 1992) and PEEPHOLES (Greenberg S 1996). The most useful approach we found in the literature is that described by Gutwin and Greenberg (1997), where they identified awareness types and defined a framework for workspace awareness. The types of awareness described are:

- Workspace awareness
- Organizational awareness
- Situation awareness
- Informal awareness
- Structural awareness
- Social awareness

The focus of this paper is on social awareness. By which we mean communal awareness provided by physical proximity, even by casual encounters in the hallway, such as who is there, what are their names, what are they doing, if they are talking to someone, if they can be disturbed and what their feelings are. Gutwin and Greenberg (1997) defined it as the information that a person maintains about others in a social or conversational context. It is the knowledge of an individual and group we maintain in order to facilitate group work. Social awareness is central to any form of awareness, since work within any group could be described as a social phenomenon. Therefore, it is very important to achieve a deep understanding of the nature of social activity. Without such knowledge a collaborative tool might work against social norms.

The importance of social awareness in co-operative working has been identified by among others Moran & Anderson (1990), Gaver (1992) and Muhlbach et al., (1995). Despite this, social awareness has not yet been fully studied from the viewpoint of information systems design. Existing work seems fragmented, each view providing only certain elements of what we describe as social awareness. In this paper, we develop a framework of social awareness from an analysis of the investigation carried out on some groupware systems, consolidated by bringing together much of what has been suggested about social awareness in the literature. The framework divides social awareness into four categories, namely Availability, Identity, Trust Building and Activity.

The reminder of the paper is divided into four sections. Section two presents a summary of the investigations undertaken. Section three presents a framework based results of the investigation . Section four discusses the framework and draws on current literature to define some requirements. Section five presents some conclusions and points to future work.

2   INVESTIGATION

In order to develop a proper framework of social awareness, we carried out a case study of a group of information systems students who used three different groupware systems to perform specific tasks. The three systems reflected three categories of use:

Asynchronous-remote; Synchronous-remote; and Synchronous-local.

The subjects were forty two Information Systems students, four tutors, and the lecturer on a course called 'CSCW and Software Engineering' in the Department of Computation, UMIST. The students all had previous experience in team work. They were divided into four groups each with a tutor. Below is a description and social awareness analysis for each of the three systems.

2.1   Web based shared workspace- BSCW

This uses an asynchronous-remote form of communication, a shared web-based workspace system, called Basic Support for Co-operative Working (BSCW) (Bentley et al., 1997). The system supports collaboration in heterogeneous environments (a different-time different-place situation). Each student used the workspace to provide discussion ideas and other related issues. Thus, an on-line threaded discussion took place on particular guided topics throughout the course. It was also used as a repository for CSCW course documents, course notices, and meeting schedules.

Through observation and analysis of students' feedback, a summary of social awareness issues supported by BSCW is as follows:

BSCW1.1   Information about individual names including their email addresses.
BSCW1.2   Information about what has been done and when it was done.
BSCW1.3   Information about changes that have been made
BSCW1.4   Information about group activity.
BSCW1.5   Explicit information on a set of feelings about an idea e.g. annoyance.
BSCW1.6   Historic information on the presence of users and their activities.

A further set of social awareness issues which BSCW could not support were identified from students feedback. These are:

BSCW2.1   Information about individual location.
BSCW2.2   Information about individual skills, abilities and experiences.
BSCW2.3   More information about member identity e.g. language background.
BSCW2.4   Information about presence of members working on the same document at the same time.
BSCW2.5   Information about individual intentions.
BSCW2.6 Information about individual commitments.

2.2   Desktop video conferencing (DVC)

This uses a synchronous-remote form of communication. It is a medium where both audio, video and data are transmitted, allowing collaborative working through shared applications. The software used in this study was the White Pines CU-SeeMe. CU-SeeMe enables videoconferencing with another site located anywhere in the world. By using "reflector" software, multiple parties at different locations can participate in a CU-SeeMe conference, each from their own desktop computer.

The subjects were the same as in 2.1. However, this time they were divided into groups of three. A collaborative task was designed involving software engineering activities; brainstorming, prioritizing and diagramming. Since one of the aims of the study was to simulate remote collaboration, the three participants in each group were placed in a different location. The task was two hours long including practice time and completion of a questionnaire.

A summary of social awareness issues observed to have been supported by DVC is as follows:

DVC1.1   Information about member presence and availability shown through a shared window and the use of audio.

DVC1.2   Information about member identity. Through the use of voice and video.

DVC1.3   Information about member expressions through gaze, facial expressions and body movements.

DVC1.4   Information about member location.

DVC1.5   Information about changes being made through the whiteboard.

DVC1.6   Information about group factions and politics.

DVC1.7   Information about activities and events which occur in the background.

Analysis of students feedback revealed that most of the issues provided are at poor quality. Issues that DVC needed to support were identified as follows:

DVC2.1   More information about member identity. Displaying video clips of people does not provide enough information about individuals' identity.

DVC2.2   Information about individual feelings.

DVC2.3   More information about individuals' physical appearance, since DVC does not capture the whole of an individual body.

DVC2.4   More information about peoples' expressions.

DVC2.5   Information about commitment and willingness to share information. Awareness of certain information should be at will and on demand.

DVC2.6   Information about group cohesiveness.

2.3   Ventana Electronic Meeting System (VEMS)

This uses a synchronous-local form of communication. In general, group meetings are dominated by the loudest personalities, or by those with the highest standing. Because of this, every voice in the group is generally not heard. Other problems with focus groups include having the time to express all the ideas generated by the group. These aspects of domination and time have been mitigated by the use of Ventana Electronic Meeting System, which enhanced group decision-making process by helping participants brainstorm a list of ideas anonymously and all at the same time and quickly capturing quality ideas.

The Ventana system uses the familiar concept of a meeting. There is normally a group leader who uses a public display at the front of the room to give directions or discuss interesting points about the work the group has done. An agenda is first created, listing the activities to accomplish, such as brainstorming, categorizing ideas, and voting.

Social awareness issues supported are summarized as follows:

VEMS1.1   Physical availability since members are usually in the same room.
VEMS1.2   Provides an identity of each of the participating members.
VEMS1.3   Shows tasks to be performed.
VEMS1.4   Makes changes visible to all members.

Despite the advantages of the system, it supports only one aspect of collaborative work, namely meetings. More so, it does not support global meetings. Students feedback identified the following which VEMS should further support:

VEMS2.1   Information about individual abilities
VEMS2.2   Information about individual feelings, emotions and aspirations.
VEMS2.3   There should be flexibility in providing information

After identifying social awareness issues for each of the three systems, the subjects had brainstorming sessions in order to derive the categories from which social awareness is to be conceptualized. The aspects were grouped (see Table 2.1) to derive the four categories availability, identity, trust building, and activity.

3   THE FRAMEWORK

The framework presented in Figure 1 is based on the four categories of social awareness identified in Table 2.1. The elements are structured into four categories and directions.

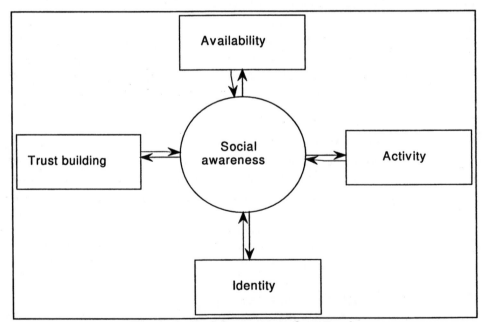

Figure 1: Social awareness framework.

Element Ref.	Information about presence	Information about members	Information about commitment	Information about activities.
BSCW1.1		√		
BSCW1.2				√
BSCW1.3				√
BSCW1.4				√
BSCW1.5		√	√	
BSCW1.6	√			√
BSCW2.1	√			
BSCW2.2		√	√	
BSCW2.3		√	√	
BSCW2.4	√			
BSCW2.5		√		
BSCW2.6			√	
DVC1.1	√			
DVC1.2		√	√	
DVC1.3		√	√	
DVC1.4	√			
DVC1.5				√
DVC1.6		√	√	
DVC1.7			√	√
DVC2.1		√		
DVC2.2			√	
DVC2.3	√	√		
DVC2.4			√	
DVC2.5			√	√
DVC2.6			√	
VEMS1.1	√		√	√
VEMS1.2		√		
VEMS1.3				√
VEMS1.4				√
VEMS2.1		√	√	
VEMS2.2		√	√	
VEMS2.3				√
Category	Availability	Identity	Trust building	Activity

Table 2.1 Four categories of social awareness

4   DISCUSSION

The categories described in the framework are 'Availability' for which the elements identified are those that show members' presence; 'Identity' for which the elements are those that create in members the knowledge of individuals (this usually takes place within the first two or three meeting sessions); 'Trust building' for which the elements are those that members need to know about one another to keep the group moving;; and 'Activity' for which the elements involve knowing what others are doing. Each of these is presented in more detail, followed by a non-exhaustible lists of elements.

4.1   Availability

Availability is the extent to which the presence of individual group members can be perceived in a system. Mathew Lombard and Teresa Ditton (1997) described it in terms of intimacy and immediacy, which includes physical proximity, eye-contact, intimacy of conversational topic, amount of smiling, and other behaviors to establish an equilibrium between conflicting approach and avoidance forces. Its importance in group collaboration was emphasized in Ackerman (1996). It is the degree to which a system can produce seemingly accurate representations of objects, events, and people; representations that look, sound, and feel like the "real" thing; impressions of sharing space with those at remote physical sites Muhlbarch (1995). See Rocco, Elena(1998), Lomberd and Ditton(1997) for a review of presence in media systems. In computer-mediated communication, availability is a perceptual illusion (Lomberd and Ditton 1997). The following table is a description of some of the elements identified that need to be provided in this category.

Elements	Related Questions	Sources
Presence	Who is around? Are they visible? Are their visual and vocal expressions clear?	Ackerman '96 Mulhbearch '95
Proximity	How close are they?	Lamberd' 97
Intimacy	Can they be contacted? Is there any feeling of togetherness?	Lamberd '97 Argyle '65
Immediacy	How immediately can they communicate? Can they see things happening?	Argyle '65
Location	Where are they? Are they in different parts of the globe?	Gutwin '97 & Susan '96
Environment	Is it a mediated environment? Can they interact with larger groups?	Biocca & Levy '95
Visibility	What is the viewing distance? What is the image quality and size?	Mulhbearch '95

Table 4.1 Availability elements

4.2   Identity

During the case study, we identified individual and group identity as vital for both normal face-to-face and mediated interaction. It was identified as the first collaborative element that enhances respect for individual norms and values. Studies, for example, by Rocco (1998), emphasized how group identity can enhance co-operation even if communication occurs electronically. Group identity is also recognized as a pre-requisite for long-lasting trust-based co-operation (Sally 1995). The question is, what is it, and what do we need to know about group identity? Many definitions can be found in the literature all revolving around what are referred to as the characteristics of an individual. Most of these include individuals' name, sex, age, affections, state of health, attitudes and values (Tubbs 1992). Below is the table describing identity elements.

Elements	Related Questions	Sources
Name	What are their names?	Tubbs '92
Sex	Are they male or female?	Tubbs '92
Age	How old are they?	Tubbs '92
Origin	Where do they come from?	?
Intentions	What are their intentions?	Tubbs '92
Attitudes	What are their attitudes and values?	Tubbs '92
Health	What is their state of health	Tubbs '92

Table 4.2 Identity elements

4.3   Trust building
Trust is a prerequisite for success when a collaborative task involves risk of individualistic or deceitful behavior by others. In both mediated and non-mediated communication, trust is usually measured by the degree of co-operation between collaborating team members. Uncertainty and vulnerability are high within mediated communication since there are no standardized procedures or guaranteed control on individual behavior. In this situation, trust and commitment are the only common mechanisms for group co-operation.

Field evidence (Olson 96) shows that people are reluctant to use computer-mediated systems for collaboration, because lack of face-to-face contact reduces trust and commitment. This was further proved in Rocco's investigation 1998, where trust only succeeded in face-to-face communication or an initial face-to-face meeting for virtual groups. However, our case study revealed that about 90% of individuals could not trust one another even after three prior face-to-face meetings. Trust was observed to have emerged within groups only after a series of successful collaborations. It was however, observed that initial face-to-face meeting can stimulate a greater understanding of individual identity. Trust needs touch, contact and interaction. The question is how can trust be built into global virtual teams where there is no prior familiarity with each other and no prior shared past experiences.

In this category, we described elements and those aspects that make people build trust with one another during face-to-face meetings. The elements are described in table 4.3

4.4   Activity
Activity awareness is the knowledge of what one is doing. Its importance for a successful collaboration has been emphasized by Dourish and Belloti (1992). The concept of activity within this social context is used to ensure that individuals' activity is relevant to the group's activity as a whole. It is a social aspect because people generally want to know others' activities, which also serves as a motivating factor for their own activities.

This overcomes the problem of co-ordination (Fish et al 1988 in Dourish and Belloti 1992). Elements for which we need to be aware in the activity category are described in table 4.4.

Elements	Related Questions	Sources
Skills	What are their skills?	
Experience	How much experience have they got/need?	
Culture	What are their beliefs? What are their cultural differences? Are there cultural effects?	Robins '95
Expectations	What are the individual and group expectations?	
Values/Attitudes	What are their values and attitudes?	Sally '95
Language	Are there language differences? Are their language concepts different?	Gutwin '97
Health	What are their states of health?	
Commitment	How committed are they?	Olson '96
Confidence	Who do I confide in? Who do I rely on?	
Responsibility	Who is responsible for what?	
Security	Are we secure?	

Table 4.3 Trust building

Elements	Related Questions	Sources
Activity level	Is there an activity going on? Can I join the activity? Who initiated it?	Gitwin '97
Actions	What are they doing?	Gutwin '97
Changes	Are there changes? Where are changes being made?	Gutwin '97
Objects	What objects or resources are they using?	
Deadlines	What are the deadlines?	
Relevance	How relevant is the activity ? Is it relevant to personal goals?	
Nature of activities	Are the activities group or personal tasks?	

Table 4.4 Activity elements

5   CONCLUSION AND RECOMMENDATIONS

The framework presented here focuses on four basic issues of social awareness. We have extended Gutwins' concept of social awareness by not only classifying it into four categories but also describing elements for each of the categories. Rather than focusing just on social awareness issues of availability and peoples' activities, this study reveals that member identity and trust building is vital for virtual communication. This classification is not only a technique for designing social awareness tools but is also useful for classifying and evaluating existing tools. We identified social awareness elements for each of the four categories and possible questions that could lead to identifying user requirements. In general, this study suggests the need to provide social awareness in virtual environments.

We are planning a long-term user study to evaluate these elements in a wider context and to decide how to gather and display the information via the interface for virtual collaborating teams. The main questions we want to address for further research include the following: what cues can we use for social awareness? how can we provide sufficient clues about others and the environment so that groups can develop a feeling of social awareness? what information about others do we really need? what representations can we use for people and how can people use them to communicate their expressions? how can these representations be personalized? what norms, conventions and mechanisms must be considered to insure privacy, trust and security of this private information? how would global managers build trust among team members scattered from Manchester to Lagos? what are those issues that make people build on trust during face-to-face meetings? and how would those issues be mediated?

References.

Ackerman, M S and Starr, B. (1996) " *Social activity Indicators for Groupware*" in Computing Practices. June 1996. pp 37-42

Bentley, R., Appelt, W., Busbach, U., Hinrichs, E., Kerr, D., Sikkel, S., Trevor, J., and Woetzel, G. (1997) *Basic support for Co-operative work on the World Wide Web*; In Internal Journal of Human-Computer Studies: Special issues on innovative applications of the World Wide Web; Academic Press; Spring 1997.

Dourish, P. and Bellotti V. (1992) Awareness and Co-ordination in Shared Workshops. In Proc. of *CSCW'92* (Toronto, Canada), ACM Press, 1992. pp 107-114

Dourish, P . and Bly S. (1992) "Portholes: Supporting awareness in a distributed work group," Bauersfeld P., Bennett J., and Lynch G., editors, Proc. Conf. *on Human Factors in Computing Systems* (INTERCHI'92), SIGCHI,. ACM Press, New York, NY, May 1992. pp 541-547

Greenberg, S (1996). Peepholes: Low cost Awareness of one's community. In *Conference companion of CHI'96*. pp 206-207

Gutwin, C., and Greenberg, S (1996). Workspace Awareness for Groupware. In Proc. Of *CHI'96* (Vancouver, British Columbia, Canada), ACM Press 1996. pp 208-209

Konrad Tollmar, Ovidiu Sandor and Anna Schomer (1996) Supporting social awareness @work. Design and Experience, to be published in the Proc. of *CSCW'96*, Boston, Massachusetts, November 16-20, 1996. pp 298-307

Linda Macaulay, Greg O'Hare, Paul Dongha, Stev Viller. (1994) Co-operative Requirements Capture: Prototype Evaluation. In *Computer Support for Co-operative work*. (Eds) Kathy Spurr, Paul Layzell, Leslie Jennison and Neil Richards. John Willey & Sons Ltd 1994, pp 169-194.

Mathew Lombard and Teresa Ditton (1997). At the Heart of It All: The Concept of Telepresence. *Journal of Computer Mediated Communication Volume 3 Issue 2* September, 1997.

McDaniel, E. Susan. (1996) Providing awareness information to support transitions in remote computer-mediated collaboration. In proc. *CHI 96*. 1996. pp 57-58

Muhlbach, L., Bocker, M., & Prussog, A. (1995). Telepresence in videocommunications: A study on stereoscopy and individual eye contact. *Human Factors, 37(2)*, pp 290-305.

Robbin, A. Harvey, and Finley Micheal (1995). *Why teams don't work: (What went wrong and how to make it right)*. Peterson Guides, Inc. USA.

Rocco, Elena, (1998). Trust Breaks Down in Electronic Contexts but can Be Repaired by Some Initial Face-to-Face Contacts. In proc. *CHI 98*. 1998. pp 496-502

Rodden, T. (1996). Populating the Application; A model of awareness for co-operative applications. In Proc. *Intl Conf. On CSCW*. Nov 1996. pp 87-96,

Salim, S, S and Macaulay, L,A. Groupware: What You See Is What You Need? In proc (*HCI International '97*), San Francisco, California, USA August 24-29, 1997. pp 53-56

CHAPTER 22

INVESTING IN HUMAN CAPITAL: STUDYING WORK GROUP TRUST AND COHESION THROUGH COMPUTER SIMULATION

Rosane Pagano
Manchester Metropolitan University

Abstract

Cohesiveness has long been regarded as a vital characteristic of effective work groups. The difficulty for analysts has been in moving beyond the subjective perceptions of group members in modelling the dynamics of how that cohesion might be achieved, and how it might be related to participants' traits. The research reported in this paper addresses the difficulty by constructing a computer-simulated microworld of group work. The proposed basis for this simulation model is a revised, more rigorous conception of "trust". The purpose of this enclosed system - the microworld - would be to experiment with different human scenarios, modelled according to certain well-defined principles of trust, in a group work situation. It is argued that such experimentation serves to provide insights into which scenarios, involving specific combinations of work-group member profiles, would make the more cohesive teams.

1   INTRODUCTION

For building today's learning organisation, the importance both of microworlds (Senge 1993) and of thinking systematically (Checkland 1994) are often emphasized. A computer simulation, by its very nature, encourages system thinking. It requires for its existence that the boundaries of the whole, of the ensemble, are made explicit. The building of a computer simulation requires careful reflection on the delineation of such boundaries, on the inclusion or the exclusion of particular elements by determining their relevance to the system. Simulation is an effective tool for strategic decision making. Systems that are too critical or too obscure to be studied analytically can be successfully modelled by simulation approaches (Badiru 1993).

This paper proposes that three principles of trust be incorporated in a model that is to be used as the basis for constructing a computer simulated microworld of group work. The purpose of this enclosed system - the microworld - is to experiment with different human scenarios, modelled according to those principles of trust, in a group work situation. This experimentation would serve to gain insights on which scenarios (more specifically, combinations of human profiles) would make the more cohesive teams.

The simulation model focuses on one social trait: the trust accredited to individual team members by the other members of the team. Trust is arguably of particular relevance to the success of any work group (Castelfrani 1998). Furthermore, this model postulates that trust emerges from three persistent characteristics of each individual team member and from the contextual interaction among members of the team. These characteristics constitute the participant's profile, and persist for the length of time the group is working together, which is the time frame of the simulation. Trust itself, however, can be regarded as perceptibly changeable for the duration of the team members' interactions.

Work-group and team-based organisation structure has proved critical in organisational effectiveness, highlighting the importance of a cohesive team (Katzenbach 1993). In the everyday meaning of the term recorded by the Concise Oxford Dictionary, cohesion is "the tendency to stick together, to remain united." In the spirit of this definition, the view adopted here is that trust facilitates inter-actions and a history of trust brings union — in other words, cohesiveness. Hence we can identify a cohesive (and therefore likely to be effective) team as the one where every member of that team achieves high and equitable levels of trust among its members. The aim of this investigation, then, through the simulation of different scenarios, is to aid attempts to answer the following questions:

- how long, in terms of a scale embedded in the simulation model, does it take for a team to achieve cohesion? More importantly, how does this length of time compare to the time taken by other teams with different profiles? We designate as response time the measure of time that it has taken to reach the situation where every team member exhibits equitable levels of trust.
- how do differences in profile, that is different intensities of each individual characteristic of the profile, affect the response time? More importantly, how different combinations of profiles affect the response time?
- how does the team size (the number of participants) affect the response time?

The following sections present in more detail the foundations of this simulation model, first by describing how a team member is represented in the system and secondly, by describing how the environment within which they interact is represented.

2   TRUST - THE BASIS FOR GROUP COHESIVENESS

Related studies on the simulation of social behaviour have highlighted a number of social traits as critical to a desirable modus operandi of the group, generally referred to as team work. For example, traits such as social power (Castelfrani 1990), need of help (Cesta 1993) (Miceli 1994), commitment (Castelfrani 1993), and social norms (Conte 1993) have been identified. Besides these, trust has also been the topic of substantial studies that demonstrate its importance in social interactions and group behaviour (Deutsch 1962) (Deutsch 1973) (Luhmann 1979) (Castelfrani 1998).

The literature of the social sciences offers some well-known definitions of trust between humans. Giddens (1990), for example, described trust as *'confidence in the reliability of a person or system, regarding a given set of outcomes or events, where that confidence expresses faith in the probity or love of another, or in the correctness of abstract principles'*. This definition seems to corroborate our view that the concept of trust is determined by a complex outcome of inter-actions between persons in systemic roles, where the individual attributes of those persons are in turn affected by given social constraints or principles.

Besides pointing out the relevance of trust to group interaction, several investigative studies have also attempted to make explicit the building blocks of trust. For example, trust as a function of utility (Deutsch 1962) (Deutsch 1973), of complexity and risk (Luhmann 1979) (Koller 1988), of performance and ability (Castelfrani 1998). Such studies have helped advance the representation of trust in computational environments in fields such as CSCW and MAS. Some other examples are (Jones 1997), (Arion 1994), and (Furuta 1992). More needs to be said though about 'computational trust', and even more needs to be said about 'computational trust' in simulation for strategic decision-making.

To build computational environments to support or represent team work, it is first necessary to distinguish explicitly two categories among those traits. One is the category of social and changeable features such as trust and performance. These vary in intensity as interactions with other participants occur. The other category is that of individual and relatively persistent features ('time invariant' or persistent at least for the duration of the group interaction) such as individual competence and individual commitment. These are designated as the characteristics of the team member's profile, or simply the profile.

Secondly, it is necessary to state the set of principles that govern how a particular trait affects every other trait over time. People's individual and persistent characteristics should be explicitly represented. Further work is required regarding the time scale on which these traits manifest themselves; how their intensity varies in relation to every other.

Several studies in organisational behaviour have drawn attention to a number of contingency factors that improve managers' ability to build effective teams. For example Hackman suggests that managers should "engineer" groups and influence group cohesiveness by manipulating "sources of ambient stimuli" (Hackman 1992). Most important of all in this 'engineering' process are "the people who compose the group" and hence, by implication, the individual characteristics of every participant. The consequences for group behaviour of all participants' characteristics taken together (not just any single one) are of major significance.

The model presented in this paper focuses on trust as the key concept for group cohesiveness and ultimately for group effectiveness. The relevance of trust to work group behaviour has long been recognized by researchers in the field of organisational behaviour (Bartolome 1989). Also, in his long-term work in simulation of social behaviour and in computational intelligence, Castelfrani has argued for the crucial importance of trust in social interactions and therefore in multi-agent systems (Castelfrani, 1998). Although the relationship between cohesiveness and effectiveness is more complex than a straightforward correlation, research has shown that generally highly cohesive groups are more effective than less cohesive groups (Robbins, 1994).

The notion of cohesiveness is a collective and an emergent one - it results from the togetherness of the team members - and therefore more difficult to be applied by managers in anticipating the effectiveness of a work group. It is therefore desirable to make explicit those 'contingency factors', at the level of individual team members, that influence cohesiveness and effectiveness, for they are usually more easily estimated and quantifiable. This would facilitate manager's task of engineering groups so that cohesiveness and effectiveness would emerge.

In this study, the observable outcome of the simulation is the degree of trust accredited to each team member over a period of time. Here a time period is composed of one or more 'time units', each unit being defined as the time required for one interaction. We take levels of trust as an indicator of cohesiveness and infer a degree of effectiveness (Hollon 1977). It is expected that a team becomes cohesive (and more effective) as every member of the team exhibits a <u>high</u> and <u>equitable</u> degree of trust over that period of time. Hereafter a team member will be referred to as an agent.

3   THE DETERMINANTS OF TRUST

In this model, 'trust on the agent' is defined as the trust accredited to the agent by every other member of the team as a whole, and not by any single other member. Therefore trust becomes an attribute of the individual agent.

It is postulated that the perceived degree of trust accredited to an agent is a three party trust (what one might call the building blocks of trust), each emerging from one of the three persistent characteristics of that agent (profile). These are basic trust, motivational trust and contextual trust. The basic trust is the trust derived from the agent's competence and previous experiences. The motivational trust is the trust derived from the agent's commitment regardless of the context. The contextual trust is the trust derived from the responsiveness of the agent at each interaction with another agent in a specific context.

To understand those characteristics, one has to consider the relationship between trust and performance. The building blocks of trust relate to the agent's performance level through every characteristic of the profile. The relationships are as follows:

- the basic trust of the agent at any given time $T_B(t)$ is determined by the agent's general performance level $P(t)$, modified by the first characteristic of the profile that we designate by degree of competence K.

$$T_B (t) = K x P(t)$$

- the motivational trust of the agent at any given time $T_M(t)$ is determined by the variation in performance level from one interaction to another ($P(t) - P(t-1)$), modified by the second characteristic of the profile that we designate by degree of commitment J. This means that any 'sudden' change in performance (large variation in performance level within one interaction) is very likely to affect the motivational trust accredited to the agent. Note that it is less likely that changes in performance would affect basic trust on the grounds that it is less likely that the agent would have lost its competence in one interaction.

$$T_M (t) = J x (P(t) - P(t-1))$$

- the contextual trust is much more susceptible to the interaction in context. The increment in contextual trust at each interaction is determined by the agent's general performance level, modified by the third characteristic of the profile that we designate by the degree of responsiveness I. The evolution of contextual trust over time is of most interest to be observed during the simulation and can be expressed as follows:

$$T_C (t) = T_C (t-1) + I x P(t)$$

The three persistent characteristics of the profile are then the degree of competence, the degree of commitment, and the degree of responsiveness. It is worth noting that although this formulation uses what seem to be the same notions of basic, general and contextual trust as developed by Jones (1997), our modelling approach differs from Jones's in the way that trust is determined and quantified. Jones does not explicitly represent the time line nor does he explicitly represent the effect of individual profile characteristics in his determination of trust. Similarly, although in broad lines we take Castelfrani's view (Castelfrani 1998) that trust is a function of performance, our modelling approach differs from his in the way that trust is to be determined and quantified. As with Jones, Castelfrani does not explicitly account for the time line and the characteristics of every profile.

We assume that the three profile characteristics (persistent for the time of the interactions) are independent of each other. This means that there is assumed to be no causal relationship between any two of them. For example, the fact that a team member has a high degree of commitment does not necessarily imply that she or he will have high or low degree of competence, nor high or low degree of responsiveness. The next section discusses how the agent's inter-actions build up the trust placed on the agent.

4   MODELLING THE ENVIRONMENT: THE INTER-ACTIONS

In his work "Computational Intelligence", Poole (1998) identifies six modes of using agent models. The uses of agent models can be in embedded mode, in simulation mode, in verification mode, in optimization mode, in learning mode and in design mode. In simulation mode, the one of interest in this context, a model of the environment is used as well as the model of the agent. The agent interacts with a model of the environment (an abstraction of some aspects of the world) rather than with the environment itself. Therefore building a model of how the agents inter-act is not only required but also is crucial to test the agent's specification.

The simulation environment presupposes a wider social context where effective interaction is facilitated through conversation. In order to build the simulation model, an analogy was drawn between group work and conversational moves. Consider specifically a meeting centred on group discussion. In this view, people co-operate within the work process through coherent discourse. The conceptual framework of discourse analysis (Sinclair 1979) was drawn upon to model the inter-actions between team members.

The analysis of discourse has been approached from a number of different disciplinary perspectives. The approach that is deemed to be the most relevant for the purposes of this model is that derived from research done in the field of sociolinguistics. It attempts to study larger linguistic units (beyond the sentence or beyond the clause, depending on the grammatical model being deployed) such as occur in conversational exchanges. It is concerned with language in use in social contexts, particularly with interaction between speakers. Language, action and knowledge are inseparable as we use language for social interaction. Several different factors determine the appropriateness of utterances used in different social contexts. Discourse analysis uses observable social data, that is, field-work observations of the ways people use language. It seeks a coherent view of language that takes into account connected utterances in everyday use and questions what functions are served by utterances in a particular type of speech event.

It is the aim of such analysis to provide recognition criteria for the coherence of conversational exchanges. To illustrate this point, consider the following example adapted from Stubbs (1983). A client has joined two consultants in a pub, and they have bought him a drink, although they do not already know him. The two consultants have been talking for some minutes, the client listening, then one of them says (with the client's response following):

Consultant: You're not saying much.
Client: (Pause.) I'm just enjoying my Guinness.

The problem for discourse analysis is to specify how these two utterances are heard as coherent, that is, how the client's response comes to be seen as appropriate and relevant. It cannot be explained by reference to the syntax and semantics of single sentences. Discourse sequences imply predictions in terms of propositional content. Since we are dealing with predictions and expectations, it is understandable that any resulting model of discourse would involve considerable abstraction from particular empirical conversational data.

Two important points from discourse analysis are taken into account when modelling the agent's inter-actions, which can be regarded as the equivalent of conversational moves:

- Conversation is highly variable, but interpretative rules are invariant. Each utterance implies constraints and therefore provisionally classifies the utterance following it. Each utterance is preclassified into categories before it ever occurs independent of its semantic meaning, though the speaker can still choose whether to follow this classification or not. It is the hearers' interpretations that create the coherence of discourse, whether to support or to reject the preceding utterance.
- Conversational moves suggest the general concept of exchange. The sociolinguistic model of discourse implies that meaningful conversation happens in turns. An exchange comprises an initiation, where the possibilities are open-ended, followed by utterances that are pre-classified and therefore increasingly restricted. The exchange may be regarded as an information unit or the minimal interactive unit.

The concept of exchange is central to discourse analysis. In the model of discourse developed by Sinclair and Coulthard, a basic exchange structure is proposed. Given any utterance, does it predict a following item, is it in itself a response to preceding items, or does it mark an initial boundary of a relatively large unit? Such an approach leads to the conceptualisation of a small number of minimal interaction categories, which includes the following moves: initiate (I); respond (R); respond-initiate (R/I); and feedback (F). Stubbs discusses the extent of the applicability of the above structure and supports the model with extensive observational data (Stubbs 1983). For example, consider the request for information given below:

Subject	Utterance	Classification
A:	what time does this period end is it ten	I
B:	quarter past	R
A:	quarter past oh that's all right	F

Clark (1996) defends the thesis that 'language use is really a form of joint action. A joint action is one that is carried out by an ensemble of people acting in co-ordination with each other. Doing things with language is ... different from the sum of a speaker speaking and a listener listening. It is the joint action that emerges when speakers and listeners ... perform their individual actions in co-ordination, as ensembles.' He suggests that an individual act is to be distinguished from an individual participative act. He also remarks on the difference between a joint act and a joint action. A joint act is an event occurring in a single moment in time. A joint action is a process that unfolds in time, a sequence of joint acts that are co-ordinated in time.

In this simulation model we abstract from particular conversational data and extend the basic exchange-structure proposed by Sinclair to establish the possible conversational moves, that is the inter-actions, between team members (agents). Agents may act in one of two ways at any given time: to speak or not to speak. Each act, which is part of a joint action, is associated with a particular category of utterance, which then defines the utterance pairing along the lines of a speech act. They are: "Speak to Initiate" (s-I), "Speak to Respond" (s-R), "Speak to give Feedback" (s-F), "Listen and Hold waiting feedback" (l-H), "Listen and Mute" (l-M).

At each cycle of the simulation, a transition (conversational move) occurs for every agent. Each agent performs a speech act, which may be identical to the previous one. The conditions for a participant to change from one utterance to another are governed by the basic exchange unit of discourse, that is, by the preceding use of a certain necessary type of utterance. When the transition occurs the agent produces the appropriate type of utterance. In this simulation model the valid set of utterances are extensions of the Sinclair-Coulthard taxonomy of utterances.

Joint Act	Taxonomy of Utterances
speak	Initiation
speak	Response / Initiation
speak	Feedback
speak	Response
hold	Mute
listen	Mute

In accordance with the rules of discourse the following constraints apply to the simulation model:
- there cannot be repetition of the same pair in two consecutive cycles, <u>except</u> l-M.
- s-R/I must be preceded by s-I from a <u>different</u> agent.
- s-F must be preceded by h-M from the <u>same</u> agent.
- s-R must be preceded by s-I from a <u>different</u> agent.
- at any given time only one agent is in state s.
- h-M must be preceded by s-I from the <u>same</u> agent.

The form of discourse analysis used here was originally derived from the conversation between two agents, that is, a one-to-one interaction. An important point to note about this simulation model is that it extends the analysis, in the sense that it applies the rules of discourse to a one-to-many situation (the group).

Above all, it is necessary to make explicit the connection between the principles of trust and the inter-actions. People's estimates of the amount of trust they can place on an agent are based on the agent's actions in a given context. Actions are observable outputs on which one can base one's evaluation of trust. Therefore one can weight certain acts or 'act categories' according to the intensity with which they build up the trust accredited to the agent. For example, the simulation user can reward with higher levels of trust a Feedback act category, as this type of act is deemed to enhance the cohesiveness and effectiveness of the group. Another way of evaluating trust is by the principles involving social traits and individual profiles, as discussed in the previous section. However, this is the other side of the same coin - trust - and can be expressed by the following equality relation:

$$T(t) = T_B(t) + T_M(t) + T_C(t)$$

The overall trust accredited to an agent through its actions must be equal in intensity to the trust originating from its social traits and from the individual persistent characteristics of its profile, as they are indeed 'two sides of the same coin'.

5   SIMULATION SCENARIO

The simulation is being developed in an agent-oriented language - a Strictly Declarative Modelling Language (SDML), which is in fact a computer simulation environment. The concept of team member has been mapped into the computational agent embedded in the language. The interested reader can refer to (Moss 1998).

The simulation user is expected to input into the simulation program the profile of each agent that provides the persistent characteristics of each team member: individual commitment (J), responsiveness (I) and individual competence (K). The simulation user is also expected to associate levels of trust with categories of acts performed by the agent. The outcome of the simulation is the evolution of contextual trust over time for each agent, as that is the element of trust that is the most affected by the presence of other agents.

A preliminary version of the simulation model indicates that different sets of the persistent characteristics of each agent (the JIK factors) lead to different response times across the group as a whole, that is, different lengths of time are needed for the group of agents to achieve a steady state of communication (Pagano 1996). Such a 'steady state' means that all agents exhibit a high and equitable degree of trust after that period of time, and when that happens the group can be said to be stable. Some choices for the values of the JIK factors cause instability; that is, no 'plateau' of trust is achieved and the group is said to be unbalanced. These preliminary investigations have been carried out for a group of three agents. Even this seemingly small grouping has generated results of sufficient interest to justify the choice of simulation for the purposes of exploring the work-group model, and to suggest that further development of the model is appropriate.

References

Arion, M., Numan, J., Pitariu, H., Jorna, R., (1994) "Placing Trust in Human-Computer Interaction." *7th European Conference on Cognitive Ergonomics*, Bonn.

Badiru, A.B., Pulat, P.S., Kang M., (1993) "DDM: Decision support system for hierarchical dynamic decision making." *Decision Support Systems* 10 1-18, North-Holland.

Bartolome, F., (1989) "Nobody trusts the boss completely - now what?" *Harvard Business Review*, March-April.

Castelfrani, C., (1990) "Social Power: a point missed in Multi-Agent, DAI and HCI." *Decentralized A.I.*, Elsevier Science Publishers, pp. 49-62.

Castelfrani, C., (1993) "Commitments: from individual intentions to groups and organizations." *A.A.A.I. Workshop*.

Castelfrani, C. and Falcone, R., (1998) "Principles of Trust for MAS: cognitive anatomy, social importance, and quantification" *Inter Conference on Multi-Agent Systems*.

Cesta, A. & Miceli, M., (1993) "In Search of Help: strategic social knowledge and plans."*12th International Workshop on Distributed Artificial Intelligence.*

Checkland, P., *System Thinking, System Practice*, John Wiley, 1981.

Clark, H., *Using Language*, Cambridge University Press, 1996.

Conte, R. and Castelfrani, C., (1993) "Norms as mental objects: from normative beliefs to normative goals." *Technical Report*, Instituto di Psicologia, Social Behavior Simulation Project.

Deutsch, M., (1962) "Co-operation and Trust: some theoretical notes." *Nebraska Symposium on Motivation*, Nebraska University Press.

Deutsch, M., (1973). *The Resolution of Conflict: constructive and destructive processes.* Yale University Press.

Furuta, K. and Kondo, S., (1992) "Group Reliability Analysis." *Reliability Engineering and System Safety* 35, pp 159-167.

Giddens, A., (1990) *The Consequences of Modernity*. Stanford University Press.

Hackman, J.R., (1992) "Group Influences on Individuals in Organizations." In *Handbook of Industrial & Organizational Psychology*, vol.3, Consulting Psychologists Press.

Hollon, C. and Gemmil, G., (1977) "Interpersonal trust and personal effectiveness in the work environment", *Psychological Reports*, 40.

Jones, S. and Marsh, S., (1997) "Trust in CSCW." *SIGCHI Bulletin*, 29 (3) July, pp. 40.

Katzenbach, J.R. and Smith, D.K., (1993). *The Wisdom of Teams: creating the high-performance Organization.* Harvard Business School Press, Boston.

Koller, M., (1988) "Risk as a determinant of trust", *Basic and Applied Social Psychology*, 9(4), pp 265-276.

Luhmann, N., (1979). *Trust and Power*, John Wiley.

Luhmann, N., (1990) "Familiarity, confidence, trust: problems and alternatives." In *Trust*, Basil Blackwell.

Miceli, M., Cesta, A., Rizzo, P., (1994) "Autonomous Help in Distributed Work Environments." *7th European Conference on Cognitive Ergonomics*, Bonn.

Moss, S., Gaylard, H., Wallis, S., Edmond, B., (1998) "SDML: a multi-agent language for organizational modelling", *Computational Organisation Theory*, vol.4, no.1, pp 43-69.

Pagano, R., (1996) "Talking shop: engineering group support in team work - a simulation model", *Technical Report*, MMU Department of Business Info Technology.

Poole, D., Mackworth, A., Goebel, R., (1998) *Computational Intelligence*, Oxford Press.

Robbins, S., (1994). *Organizational Behavior*, Prentice-Hall.

Senge, P., (1993) "Microworlds: the technology of the learning organization", *The Fifth Discipline*, Century Business.

Sinclair, J., Coulthard, M., (1979) *Towards an Analysis of Discourse*, Oxford Univ Press,.

Stubbs, M., (1983). *Discourse Analysis*, Basil Blackwell.

CHAPTER 23

A REVIEW AND APPLICATION OF THE CRITICAL SUCCESS FACTORS CONCEPT FOR RESEARCH ON THE INFORMATION SYSTEMS DEVELOPMENT PROCESS

Tom Butler and Brian Fitzgerald
Telecom Eireann, University College Cork

Abstract

The Critical Success Factors (CSF) concept has been widely applied by both practitioners and researchers in several areas within the field of information systems (IS). Rockart's (1979) CSF method was the first to be used in IS research; it is interpretive in character and it has been employed in several studies since. Rockart's CSF approach captures the teleological nature of social action; therefore, following Visala (1991), it can be used in conjunction with the hermeneutic method to conduct interpretive research on the systems development process and its related environments. A review of the relevant literature revealed that the systems development process has not been the subject of CSF research using Rockart's (1979, 1982) original interpretive method. The primary objective of this study was to determine the systems development-related CSFs of social actors involved in the systems development process, i.e. IS function management, project managers, developers, and users. The findings of this study have contributed to the cumulative body of research on CSF concept by highlighting its utility as a fruitful approach for research on the systems development process, and to the extant body of research on the systems development process by illustrating empirically its complex multidimensional nature and by providing fresh insights into the challenges that face both developers and users in their task of developing organisational IS.

1   INTRODUCTION

Critical success factors are those few things that must go well for an individual or an organisation to ensure success in a business undertaking: consequently, they represent those organisational, managerial, or individual activities that must be afforded particular and continuous attention so as to achieve the level of performance necessary to achieve desired goals. This simple concept has been applied in a wide variety of forms, by both practitioners and researchers, within the information systems (IS) field. However, a review of the CSF research literature reveals that the concept has not been employed to any great degree in research on the topic of information systems development.

This study applied Rockart's original interpretive approach to examine the CSFs for systems development. Bullen and Rockart (1986; p. 384) argue that the application of the concept requires the possession of a thorough understanding of *"the industry, the specific company, and the job being performed by the manager being interviewed."* Similarly, the Ives *et al.* (1980) research framework indicates that research on the systems development process must take cognizance of the influence of social actors in the development, organisational and external environments. As indicated, the focus of the present application of the CSF concept was to delineate a set of CSFs for the systems development process. The primary objective of this study was to determine the systems development-related CSFs of project managers, developers, and users involved in the development process in order to arrive at what Bullen and Rockart (1986) have termed as a 'collective' set. This 'collective' or 'candidate' [Barat, 1992] set of CSFs was further analysed arrive at a 'generic' [Rockart, 1979] set for the systems development process. The views of IS function management were also sought in order to indicate their role in shaping the IS development environment and, hence, in influencing the trajectory and outcomes of the systems development process itself. This holistic approach satisfied the criteria laid down by Bullen and Rockart (1986) and by Ives *et al.* (1980) and` led to the desired in-depth understanding of the phenomenon.

2   THE CSF CONCEPT

The use of a CSF approach for IS planning was developed at MIT's Sloan School of Management. Subsequently, Rockart (1979) employed the method to determine the key information needs of top executives. However, the conceptual foundation of the CSF concept can be traced to the writings of Aristotle:

> *"Now the cause of action (the efficient, not the final cause) is choice, and the cause of choice is desire and reasoning directed to some end."*[iii]

Aristotle thus describes the teleological nature of human action and in so doing he illustrates that social actors choose particular means to achieve desired ends. A more recent antecedent of the concept may be found in the writings of Baron Von Clausewitz[iv]. Von Clausewitz held that the more competent and successful military commanders focused their available resources on the few battles of significance, whereas, the less competent commanders dispersed their forces throughout the entire battle front: he termed this the principle of "concentration of forces".

The genesis of the critical success factor approach in a managerial context, that incorporates a role for information system, was first delineated by Daniel (1961; p. 111) who argued that an IS should focus on small group of *"success factors"*, the *"key jobs must be done exceedingly well for a company to be successful."* Other seminal contributions are to be found in the writings of Anthony et al. (1972) who reported that CSFs were different across organisations, and also between managers within individual organisations; Zani (1970) illustrated that key success variables (e.g. CSFs) might identify the most important elements of a firm's success and, thereby, help specify priorities for IS development; and King and Cleland, (1975) argued that critical decision areas[v] had a major role to play in information requirements analysis and in the design of information systems. The work of the later researchers prompted researchers in the IS field to investigate the informational role of CSFs [see Mooradian, 1976; Rockart, 1979]. This research found a home in MIT and culminated in Rockart's seminal paper on the subject in 1979.

The CSF approach, as conceived by Rockart, is essentially an information systems planning methodology for top level management. However, he later used the approach to conduct research on the roles of IS executives [Rockart, 1982]. Rockart (1979; p. 217) defines critical success factors as:

> *"The limited number of areas in which results, if they are satisfactory, will ensure successful competitive performance for the organisation. They are the few key areas where "things must go right" for the business to flourish. If the results in these areas are not adequate, the organisations efforts for the period will be less than desired."*

The CSF method thus attempts to make explicit these areas, and their associated information needs, such that IS appropriate to these requirements can be planned and developed. Bullen and Rockart (1981) later extended the application of the CSF concept to other managerial levels within an organisation. Focusing on the organisational information systems planning process, they suggest that the CSFs of managers at multiple levels within an organisation be obtained so as to arrive at a 'collective' set for the entire organisation. This 'collective' set is also aggregated to arrive at what Rockart (1982, 1979) terms a 'generic' set. Information resources and activities are then targeted at enabling the enterprise to realize these 'collective' and 'generic' CSFs.

Since the original application of the CSF concept and method for defining the information needs of business executives [Rockart, 1979], the CSF approach has been applied by both practitioners and researchers in a number of areas. Bryers and Blume (1994; p. 53) report that *"both academics and practitioners have accepted the top-down CSF approach as an appropriate planning methodology."* Slevin et al. (1991) indicate that most of the literature on CSFs focuses on the planning utility of CSFs and/or the integrative result of tying the IS function more directly into specific performance measures for the overall organisation. Figure 1 has been created to provide a more dynamic illustration of the precise relationship of this research to the IS development process. In the upper left-hand portion of this figure, researchers such as Rockart (1979) have used the CSF method to determine the planning and information needs of business executives. The remainder of this diagram focuses on CSF studies within the IS function itself, and illustrates areas within the IS function that have been the subject of investigation.

2.1   Research on CSFs Specific to IS Development

As can be seen from Figure 1, several studies have focused specifically on systems development. Sumner and Ryan (1994) identified a number of CSFs associated with information systems development in their field study of CASE (Computer Assisted Software Engineering) usage. A composite set of 23 text-book-like CSFs were derived from lists in survey responses from just 23 developers across a range of different organisations; the CSFs are grouped under the SDLC-related headings of requirements analysis, systems design, detailed systems design and systems implementation. It is clear that the 23 CSFs identified merely constitute a 'candidate set' of CSFs [Barat, 1992] for the development process; further analysis is required if a 'generic' set of CSFs [Rockart 1979, 1982] for the process is to be arrived at. A set of 8 CSFs were reported by Nandhakumar (1996) in an interpretive case study on the development of an EIS in one organisation: these CSFs related to *market conditions* and *technological innovation* in the business environment, *hierarchy and relationship with executives* and *company policies* in the organisation, *systems security* and *technical resources* in the IS function environment, and *screen design conventions* and *standards on report format* within the development team itself. However, although the study attempted to capture the complex social dimension to the process, only 2 CSFs were reported for the development process *per se*. An earlier study by Krcmer and Lucas (1991) focused on identifying the key factors in the development of strategic IS; factors such *as recognising and sizing on opportunities, cost justification, need for a sponsor, marketing the application, building on existing infrastructure,* and *possessing a customer-oriented view* were said to characterise the successful development of strategic IS. Finally, Phan *et al.* (1995) identified a set of 13 CSFs for the project management of software projects.

It is clear from the foregoing that a coherent set of CSFs for the IS development process has not emerged form previous efforts to operationalise the concept in what is regarded by many to be the core of the IS field [cf. Cotterman and Senn, 1992; Hirschheim, Klein and Lyytinen, 1996]. In addition, it is widely argued that the systems development process is not well understood [Lewis, 1994; Cotterman and Senn, 1992; Turner, 1987]. This then constitutes what Lincoln and Guba (1985) as a state of affairs that begs for additional understanding—it is, in effect, the research problem. The proposed research objective of identifying a comprehensive set of CSFs for the systems development process attempts to contribute towards a 'resolution' of this problem.

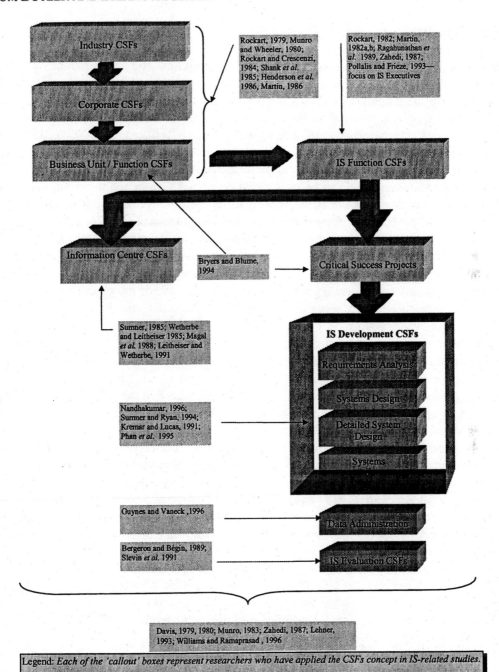

Figure 1: Research Focus of Studies on the CSF Concept and Method

3   THE RESEARCH APPROACH

Information systems development is regarded as complex and ill-structured activity [Walsham, 1995; Sol, 1992; Kling, 1992]: complex, because of the large variety and cardinality of system components, and ill-structured as a consequence of *"the variety of often-conflicting goals and objectives of system stakeholders, and a large, possibly infinite, set of alternative courses of actions and solutions"* [Kumar and Welke, 1992; p. 258]. Hence, it is argued to be a social rather than a technical process [Land, 1992; Land and Hirschheim, 1983]. On the one hand, both the process and outcomes of the systems development endeavour is said to be influenced by policies made and decisions taken by managers in the IS development environment; furthermore, developers participate in this decision making process and they implement the decisions made [Aaen, 1986]. On the other hand, both the trajectory and outcomes of the systems development process are said to be heavily influenced by social actors in the organisational environment [Butler and Fitzgerald, 1997; Kumar and Welke, 1992; Markus, 1983].

The actions of social actors participating in the IS development process are teleological in nature, and a research approach that captures this dimension of social behaviour is therefore advocated [Visala, 1991]. A teleological explanation of an actor's planned behaviour runs something like; *"A wants p; A knows that without doing a, he cannot obtain p; So A sets about doing a"* [Visala, 1991; p. 353; cf. Aristotle, 1962]. In fact if one considers **p** as the objective or goal of a social or organisational act, then **a** may be regarded as a CSF for **p**'s attainment; this indicates that the CSF method may be employed to operationalise the teleological approach. Furthermore, in his extension of the Ives *et al.* (1980) research framework, Visala (1991) argues that a hermeneutic research approach is also required to complement the recommended teleological approach. Other researchers within the IS field have also argued for a hermeneutic approach to the investigation of IS development-related phenomena [see Myers, 1995; Kanungo, 1993]. Rockart (1979) describes his CSF approach as being interpretive in orientation, as the aim of the method is to capture an individual's *'world view'*. Therefore, when used in conjunction with the hermeneutic method, the CSF approach presents itself as an appropriate vehicle for research on the systems development process and its related environments. Several weaknesses have been associated with the operationalisation of the CSF concept and method [see Williams and Ramaprasad, 1996; Davis, 1979,1980]. The ontological, epistemological and methodological perspectives of the hermeneutic approach are argued to provide an appropriate framework within which to address these weaknesses [cf. Davis 1979].

Hermeneutic philosophy posits that the goal of the interpretive act is to arrive at an understanding of the phenomenon under study [Gadamer, 1975; Bauman, 1978]. Briefly, and in the context of this study, hermeneutics concerns itself with interpretation of social action, the objective being to make sense of such action in the context in which it occurs and, thereby, contribute to an understanding of socially-based phenomena such as systems development [Myers, 1995; Kanungo, 1993; cf. Ricoeur, 1971]. The hermeneutical philosophy of Gadamer (1975) and Ricoeur (1981) informed the hermeneutic method employed in this study, while Madison's (1988) methodological principles for the interpretive process helped operationalise the method.

3.1.1   The Case: Telecom Eireann's IT Directorate

The unit of analysis in this study is the IS function—the Information Technology Directorate (ITD)—of a large Irish telecommunications company, Telecom Eireann. The ITD is comprised of six operational divisions, four of whom undertake systems development for the parent organisation. The IT Director may be categorised as an IS executive following the criteria defined by Pollalis and Frieze (1993) and described by Rockart (1982). Two managerial layers report to the director; IS function managers and their systems development project managers.

In keeping with the original CSF method, a qualitative, case-based research strategy was adopted for the study. This strategy involved an exploratory case study design with four embedded units of analysis—four systems development projects. Purposeful sampling was employed throughout [Patton, 1994; Marshall and Rossman, 1989]. The case design utilised has been described by Yin (1989) as 'post-hoc longitudinal research'.

Research into the selected case and its embedded units was conducted through the use of individual interview and documentary sources over a period of two months. The Ives et al. (1980) research framework posits that research into the development process should take cognizance of the environments in which it is embedded. Bullen and Rockart (1986; p. 384) argue that the application of the concept requires the possession of a thorough understanding of *"the industry, the specific company, and the job being performed by the manager being interviewed."* Accordingly, a total of 38 interviews took place with social actors in several development-related areas viz. development project managers and developers in IS development project teams; IS function management in the development environment; and social actors in the organisational environment—user representatives and user project managers were considered to be representative of 'world views' in the relevant user constituencies. Thus, following Lee et al.'s (1991) injunction regarding the management of self-report bias in studies on IS development, both user and developer 'world-views', and hence a comprehensive set of IS development-related CSFs, were apprehended.

4   RESEARCH FINDINGS AND ANALYSIS

The CSFs for the IS development process were first determined through an application of the CSF and hermeneutic methods in order to determine the 'world views' and CSFs of development project managers, developers, and users. These are described in the following sub-section. Following, recommendations made by Ives et al. (1980) in their research framework, and later by Visala (1991), this study took cognizance of environmental influences on the trajectory and outcomes of the development process. Hence, the IS development-related perspectives of the IS executive and his IS function management team were first ascertained; this provided the necessary context for the integrative analysis conducted in the latter part of this section on the 'collective' or 'candidate' [Bullen and Rockart, 1986; Barat, 1992) set and 'generic' (Rockart, 1982) sets of CSFs.

4.1   A 'Generic' Set of CSFs for the IS Development Process

Research on the CSF concept illustrates that CSFs can be both general and specific; this dimension to the concept indicates that, depending on the unit of analysis, CSFs may be industry wide, specific to an industry, or common across organisations in that industry; they may be particular to a functional unit within an organisation or be common across several functional units; common to several individuals or specific to an individual's role within an organisation [Bullen and Rockart, 1986; Rockart, 1979]. Therefore, it follows that some of the CSFs for the systems development process will be common across all development projects—i.e. be 'generic' CSFs [Rockart, 1982] or 'critical core' CSFs [Pollalis and Frieze, 1993]—and others will be project-specific [cf. Rockart, 1982, 1979; Bullen and Rockart, 1986; Williams and Ramaprasad, 1996]. The aggregation of project-specific CSFs gave rise to a 'candidate' set of CSFs for systems development as it occurs in this organisation [see Barat, (1992), Bullen and Rockart, (1986) and Boynton and Zmud, 1984]. Therefore, a meta-analysis conducted on the basis of a cross-project aggregation and ranking of 21 'collective' or 'candidate' CSFs that emerged from the initial analysis of CSFs for the four development projects studied surfaced a 'generic' sub-set of nine CSFs for the IS development process in Telecom Eireann. The research data on each of the development projects indicated that the 'generic' CSFs chosen have been influential in shaping the development process in each and, also, in determining development outcomes—the rank order of this set of CSFs indicates the degree of emphasis placed on them by both developers and users alike.

The 'generic' set of CSFs illustrated in Table 1 are considered as being the salient component phenomena of the IS development process in the organisation under study. However, the identification of these phenomena is insufficient in explicating their relationships either to each other or the ISD process as a 'whole'. Therefore, the data requires further analysis with respect to the existence of interrelationships between the CSFs as exogenous and endogenous components of the systems development process. This detailed analysis is performed in the following sub-section.

Rank	CSFs for the Information Systems Development Process	Environment
1	Low level user representation/participation at all stages of the ISD process.	Development process
2	Project estimation, planning, tracking to agreed targets, coordination and control of project activities.	Development process
3	Obtaining an appropriate level of vendor support.	External Environment

Rank	CSFs for the Information Systems Development Process	Environment
4	Spend adequate time on end-user requirements analysis.	Development process
5	The use of prototyping techniques/case tools to determine and refine user requirements.	Development process
6	Ensuring that business client/end-user industrial relations (IR)/change management issues related to the ISD process and product are resolved.	Organisational Environment
7	Having a committed project sponsor.	Organisational Environment
8	The availability of structured development methods and supporting case tools environments.	IS Function Environment
9	Overcoming project technical obstacles.	Development Process

Table 1: A 'Generic' Set of CSFs for the Development Process

4.1.1 An Integrative Analysis of the CSFs for IS Development

The network analysis[vi] conducted in Figure 2 illustrates a network of influences between the CSFs that constitute the 'candidate' set for the development process. Primary focus is given to role of the 'generic' sub-set of CSFs, these are illustrated in gray. The unbroken arrows indicate a strong level of influence between the 'generic' and 'non-generic' CSFs that constitute the 'candidate' set, the broken arrows signify a weaker level of influence between these CSFs, double-sided arrows indicate a reciprocal relationship. The following analysis explores the development process from the perspectives offered by this figure. An initial examination of Figure 2 reveals that the 'generic' CSFs fall into two distinct but interrelated groups (illustrated by the medium- and light-gray boxes). The point of intersection between these two groups is the CSF that deals with project management issues (shown in dark gray). Of note here is that, in comparison to other 'generic' CSFs, this latter CSF exhibits a higher degree of influence on other CSFs. For example, the activity of project estimation and planning influences, and is influenced by, the time spent on requirements analysis. A reciprocal influence exists between this CSF and the need for adequate developer and user resources, and the issue of developer and user team coordination and control.

It was clear that a successful outcome to the requirements analysis endeavour (time limitation issues aside) was influenced by the siting of the development team within the user community, developer and end-user resources made available for the process, and developer awareness of business issues/perspectives. The   need   to   site   the development team within the business community is a 'candidate' CSF for successful IS development; however, particular emphasis was also placed on this aspect of systems development by IS function managers. For example, it was revealed that IS function managers—in conjunction with managers in the business constituency—exert an exogenous influence on the outcome of the requirements analysis. In two of the projects studied, IS manager had instituted a policy of siting development teams within the user community, the outcome of this policy decision had a direct bearing on the quality of user requirements in the projects studied.

The network analysis reveals that although project management activities are influenced by the use (or not) of prototyping and structured development methods in systems development, these two CSFs form a network of influences with other CSFs. The latter CSFs constitute part of the group of 'generic' CSFs on the lower left-hand area of Figure 2. An examination of this group of CSFs reveals that they are primarily technical in nature, although, there are underlying social dimensions to them.

Obtaining an appropriate level of vendor support is often critical to a development team's efforts in overcoming technical obstacles to successful ISD—areas such as interconnectivity between different IT platforms is one particular issue that surfaced in this study. IS function management adopted a policy of providing corporate IS through the adoption and integration of application-based packages'; this impacted on the type of vendor selected, and the level of vendor support available to development teams. Hence, its is clear from this that IS function management policies shape and influence the development environment process. Vendor support for structured methods, prototyping and CASE tools also influenced the effective use of such products for systems development.

An inspection of the group of 'generic' CSFs (shown in medium-gray) in the centre and upper half of Figure 2 also reveals a complex network of interrelationships between both 'generic' and 'candidate' CSFs. In development projects where it is vital to have a committed project sponsor, it was found that the existence of such an individual had a positive influence on the level of user participation, the time spent on user requirements, change management, the activities of the development steering group and, finally, development project resources. IS function managers also placed special emphasis on this dimension of the development process; for example, IS managers were in the process of introducing a Project Charter to fully formalise the relationship of between the project sponsor and the development team in each development project.

The existence of user participation in systems development strongly influenced the outcome of the requirements analysis, and had a weaker influence on change management issues. In relation to the latter point, it was evident that user participation alone did not guarantee the successful negotiation of problematic IS development-related change management issues. Effective change management was also seen to influence the level of end-user training and associated computer literacy skills during implementation. Project managers, IS function management, and business managers were all heavily involved in one way or another—either formally through institutional mechanisms or informally through the development process itself—in addressing change management and implementation-related issues.

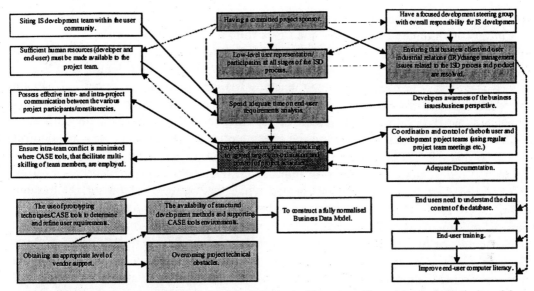

Legend: Each of the above boxes represents a 'candidate' CSF for the ISD process. The grey boxes signify the 'generic' set of CSFs for the ISD process. The existence and direction of an arrowed line indicates that a CSF "influences" another. The arrows with broken-lines signify a weaker level of influence.

Figure 2: A Network Analysis of 'Candidate' and 'Generic' Sets CSFs for the IS Development Process

The foregoing analysis has illustrated that an explanation of the IS development process can begin with an explanation of any one of its component phenomena, that is its CSFs. However, one soon finds that in order to explain fully—and, thereby, understand—the role or influence of a component phenomena on the development process, one must include or examine other related component phenomena or 'parts' within the context of the 'whole'—that is, the IS development process itself. Thus, in hermeneutic terms, the circular structure of understanding is revealed, whereby, the comprehension of a little understood phenomenon commences by the identification and explication of its component phenomena, their interrelationships, and contexts [cf. Gadamer, 1975; Ricoeur, 1981].

5   DISCUSSION AND CONCLUSIONS

This paper has provided a comprehensive analysis of the CSFs for the IS development process in one organisation. In so doing, it has contributed to the cumulative body of research on both the CSF concept and method and in the area of systems development.

The CSF method, however operationalised and applied, can fall prey to the accusation of being reductionist; and, indeed, this is true of many studies where CSFs have been presented without reference to the necessary contextual data that would illustrate how, as important 'parts', they contribute to an understanding of the socially constructed 'whole' of the phenomenon of interest. This deficiency was addressed in this study as the application of the hermeneutic method—in conjunction with several analytic techniques employed—highlighted the fact that the CSFs form an integral part of the complex web of social conditions and factors that characterise both the systems development process and IS function management activities [cf. Kling and Scacchi, 1982; Kumar and Welke, 1992]. Therefore, in explicating what this study has identified as the 'generic' CSFs for the development process in the organisation studied, the research findings have illustrated that IS development CSFs are closely interrelated; furthermore, they influence each other in a reciprocal manner and the strength of this influence can vary. In addition, it is clear that the CSFs cannot be considered in isolation from their socio-structural and contextual dimensions if their full impact on related social phenomena is to be comprehended—this was clearly delineated when the 'generic' CSFs for the systems development process were subjected to a network analysis. It was also evident that 'non-generic' or 'candidate' CSFs give context and meaning to the 'generic' set. Here too was further evidence of the complex web of interrelationships between both 'candidate' and 'generic' CSFs as component phenomena of the development process. All this implies that researchers should not treat CSFs as discrete component phenomena when presenting and analysing research findings in relation to the phenomenon under study.

CSFs have been conceptualised in different ways by researchers: Rockart (1979,1982) and Bullen and Rockart (1986) refer to individual, collective and generic CSF sets, and to the temporality of certain CSFs. In a related vein, Barat (1992) illustrates the existence of a candidate set of CSFs from which a specific or generic set is drawn. Zahedi (1987) comments on the existence a hierarchy within a particular set of CSFs. Nandhakumar (1996) to the existence of causal connections, interrelatedness and dynamic nature of influences between factors within the social context. Finally, Williams and Ramaprasad (1996) posited four different levels of criticality for CSFs, and three sets of dichotomous attributes. With the exception of certain aspects of Williams and Ramaprasad's (1996) conceptualisation, this study has provided empirical validation for previous conceptualisations of the concept. CSFs were shown to be specific to individuals and development projects, yet when aggregated to form a collective or candidate set, and then ranked, a generic set emerged in all cases. The generic/candidate dimension, coupled with the grouping of generic CSFs indicates the hierarchical nature of CSFs. Because the development process is dynamic in nature, CSFs were also seen to possess a temporal dimension. Relative causality, interrelatedness, the dynamic influences between CSFs were all apparent from the network analysis conducted on the 'generic' and 'candidate' CSFs. So too were elements of Williams and Ramaprasad's (1996) levels of criticality and dichotomous attributes associated with CSFs.

As indicated, the CSF concept was successfully operationalised in this study for research on the systems development process. However, Rockart's (1979) original interpretive method has been augmented, as per Visala's (1991) recommendations, by the joint use of teleological and hermeneutic approaches to research on the systems development process. Hermeneutic theory and method was shown to provides an important adjunct in the application of the CSF concept, especially in interpreting the 'world views' of managers, developers, and users. It also proved to be a valuable research tool in the analysis of the research data. In conclusion, this study has contributed to the cumulative body of research on the CSF concept and method by highlighting its utility as a fruitful approach for research on the systems development process. The study has also shed new light on process by which information systems are developed by illustrating empirically its complex multidimensional nature and by providing fresh insights into the challenges that face both developers and users in their task of developing organisational IS.

References

Aaen, I. (1986). Systems Development and Theory - In Search of Identification. In Quality of Work Versus Quality of Information Systems, Report of the Ninth Scandinavian Research Seminar on Systemeering, Lund Universitet, 203-223.

Anthony, R.N., Dearden, J., and Vancil, F. (1972). Management Control Systems, Irwin, Homewood, IL.

Aristotle (1962). The Nicomachean Ethics, English Translation by H. Rackam, 2nd Edition, London: Heinemann.

Barat, J. (1992). Scenario playing for critical success factor analysis. Journal of Information Technology, 7, 12-19.

Bauman, Z. (1978). Hermeneutics and Social Science: Approaches to Understanding, Hutchinson and Son, London.

Bergernon, F. and Begin, C. (1989). The Use of Critical Success Factors in Evaluation of Information Systems: A Case Study. Journal Of Management Information Systems, Spring, 5(4), 111-124.

Boynton, A.C. and Zmud, R.W. (1984). An Assessment of Critical Success Factors. Sloan Management Review, Summer, 17-27.

Bryers, C.R. and Blume ,D. (1994). Tying critical success factors to systems development; A contingent analysis. Information & Management, 26, 51-61.

Bullen, C.V. and Rockart, J.R. (1986). A Primer on Critical Success Factors. In The Rise of Managerial Computing: The Best of the Center for Information systems research, Rockart J.F. Bullen C.V. (Eds.), Sloan School of Management, Massachusetts Institute of Technology, 383-423.

Butler T. and Fitzgerald B. (1997). A Case Study of User Participation in the Information Systems Process. In E.R. McClean and R.J. Welke (Eds.), Proceedings of the 18th International Conference on Information Systems, Atlanta, Georgia.

Cotterman, W.W. and Senn, J.A. (1992). Challenges and Strategies for Research in Systems Development, Cotterman, W.W. and Senn, J.A. (Eds.). John Wiley and Sons, London.

Daniel, D.R. (1961). Management Information Crisis. Harvard Business Review, September-October, 111.

Davis, G.B. (1980). Letter to the Editor. MIS Quarterly, June, 4(2), 69-70.

Davis, G.B. (1979). An Opinion..."Comments on the critical success factors method...". MIS Quarterly, September, 3(3), 57-58.

Gadamer, H. G. (1988). On the Circle of Understanding. In Hermeneutics Versus Science? Three German Views, Conolly J.M. and Keutner T. (Eds.), University of Notre Dame Press, IN, 68-78.

Gadamer, H. G. (1975). Truth and Method. The Seabury Press, NY.

Guynes, C.S. and Vaneck, M.T. (1996). Critical Success Factors in Data Management. Information and Management, 30, 201-209.

Henderson, J.C., Rockart, J.F. and Sifonis J.G. (1986). A Planning Methodology for Integrating Management Support Systems. In The Rise of Managerial Computing: The Best of the Center for Information systems research, Rockart J.F. Bullen C.V. (Eds.), Sloan School of Management, Massachusetts Institute of Technology, 257-282.

Hirscheim, R., Klein, H. and Lyytinen, K. (1996) Exploring the intellectual structures of IS development, *Accounting, Management and Information Technologies*, Vol. 6, No. 1/2, pp. 1-64.

Miles, M.B and Huberman, A.M. (1994). Qualitative Data Analysis: An Expanded Sourcebook, Second Edition, Sage Publications, CA.

Ives, B., Hamilton, S. and Davis, G.B. (1980). A Framework for Research in Computer-Based Management Information Systems. Management Science, September, 26(9), 910-934.

Kanungo, S. (1993). Information Systems: Theoretical Development and Research Approaches. Information Systems, 18(8), 609-619.

Keen, P.G.W. (1981). Information Systems and Organisational Change. Communications of the ACM, January, 24(1), 24-33.

King, W.R. and Cleland, D.I. (1971). Manager-Analyst Teamwork in MIS, Business Horizons, April, 14(2), 59-68.

Kling, R. (1992). Behind the Terminal: The Critical Role of Computing Infrastructure in Effective Systems Development and Use. In Challenges and Strategies for Research in Systems Development, Cotterman, W.W. and Senn, J.A. (Eds.), John Wiley and Sons, 365-413.

Kling, R. and Scacchi, W. (1982). The Web of Computing: Computing Technology as Social Organisation. Advances in Computers, 21, 2-90.

Krcmer, H. and Lucas, L.C. (1991). Success Factors for Strategic Information Systems. Information and Management, 21, 137-145.

Kumar, K. and Welke, R.J. (1992). Challenges and Strategies for Research in Systems Development, Cotterman, W.W. and Senn, J.A. (Eds.), John Wiley and Sons, 257-266.

Land F. (1992). The Information System Domain. Choosing Information Research Approaches. In Information Systems Research: Issues Methods and Practical

Guidelines, Galliers R.D. (Ed.), Blackwell, 6-28.

Land, F. and Hirschheim, R. (1983). Participative Systems Design: Rationale, Tools, and Techniques. Journal of Applied Systems Analysis, 10, 91-107.

Lederer, A.L. and Sethi, V. (1988). The Implementation of Strategic Information Systems Planning Methodologies. MIS Quarterly, September, 12(3), 444-461.

Lee, S., Goldstein, D.K. and Guinan P.J. (1991). Informant Bias in Information Systems Design Team Research. In Information Systems Research: Contemporary Approaches and Emergent Traditions, Proceedings of the IFIP TC8/WG 8.2 Working Conference, Nissen, H., Klein, H.K. and Hirschheim, R. (Eds.), Elsevier Science Publishers B.V. (North-Holland), 635-656.

Lehner, F. (1993). Success Factor Analysis as an Instrument for Information Management. Journal of Computer Information Systems, Spring, 58-66.

Leitheiser, R.L. and Wetherbe, J.C. (1991). A comparison and perceptions about information centre success. Information & Management, 21, 7-17.

Lewis, P.J. (1994). Information-Systems Development, Pitman Publishing, London.

Lincoln, Y. and Guba, E. (1985). Naturalistic Inquiry, Sage Publications, CA.

Madison, G.B. (1988). The Hermeneutics of Postmodernity: Figures and Themes, Indiana University Press, IN.

Magal, S.R. and Carr, H.H. (1988). An Investigation of the Effects of Age, Size, and Hardware Option on the Critical Success Factors Applicable to Information Centers. Journal Of Management Information Systems, Spring, 4(4), 60-76.

Magal, S.R. Carr, H.H. and Watson, H.J. (1988). CSFs for SC Managers. MIS Quarterly, 12(3), 413-426.

Markus, M.L. (1983). Power, Politics, and MIS Implementation Communications of the ACM, June, 26(6), 430-444.

Marshall, C. and Rossman, G.B. (1989). Designing Qualitative Research, Newbury Park, Sage Publications, CA.

Martin, E.W. (1982a). Critical Success Factors of Chief MIS/DP Executives, MIS Quarterly, June, 6(2), 1-9.

Martin, E.W. (1982b). Critical Success Factors of Chief MIS/DP Executives-An Addendum. MIS Quarterly, December, 6(4), 79-81.

Martin, J. (1986). Information Engineering Volume 2: Strategies and Analysis, Savant.

Miller, J. and Doyle, B.A. (1987). Measuring the Effectiveness of Computer-Based Information Systems in the Financial Services Sector, MIS Quarterly, 11(1), 107-124.

Mooradian, G.G. (1977). The Key Variables in Planning and Control in Medical Group Practices, Unpublished master's thesis, Sloan School of Management, MIT, Cambridge, Mass.

Munro, M.C. (1983). An Opinion...Comment on Critical Success Factors Work. MIS Quarterly, September, 7(3), 67-68.

Munro, M.C. and Wheeler, B.R. (1980). Planning, Critical Success Factors, and Management's Information Requirements. MIS Quarterly, December, 4(4), 27-38.

Myers, M.D. (1994). Dialectical hermeneutics: a theoretical framework for the implementation of information systems, Information Systems Journal, 5, 51-70.

Nandakumar, J. (1996). Design for Success?: Critical Success Factors in Executive Information Systems Development. European Journal of Information Systems, 5, 62-72.

Patton, M.Q. (1990). Qualitative Evaluation and Research Methods, Sage Publications, CA.

Pellow, A. and Wilson, T.D. (1993). The management information requirements of heads of university departments: a critical success factors approach. Journal of Information Science, 19, 425-437.

Phan, D.D., Vogel, D.R. and Nunamaker, Jr. J.F. (1995). Empirical Studies in software development projects: Field survey and OS/400 study Information & Management, 28, 271-280.

Pollalis, Y.A. and Frieze, I.H. (1993). A New Look at the Critical Success Factors in IT Information Strategy: The Executive's Journal, Fall, 24-24.

Ragahunathan, T.S. Gupta, Y.P. and Sundararaghavan, P.S. (1989). Assessing the Impact of IS Executives' Critical Success Factors on the Performance of IS Organisations. Information & Management, 17, 157-168.

Ricoeur, P. (1971). The Model of the Text: Meaningful Action Considered as a Text. Social Research, (3), Fall, 534-549.

Rockart, J.F. (1982). The Changing Role of the Information Systems Executive: A Critical Success Factors Perspectives. Sloan Management Review, Fall, 3-13.

Rockart, J.F. (1979). Chief Executives Define Their Own Data Needs. In The Rise of Managerial Computing: The Best of the Center for Information Systems Research, Sloan School of Management, Massachusetts Institute of Technology , Rockart J.F. Bullen C.V. (Eds.), 207-234.

Rockart, J.F. and Crescenzi A.D. (1984). Engaging Top Management in Information Technology. Sloan Management Review, 25(4), 3-16.

Shank, M.E., Boynton, A.C. and Zmud, R.W. (1985). Critical Success Factor Analysis as a Methodology for IS Planning. MIS Quarterly, June, 9(2), 121-129.

Slevin, D.P., Stieman, P.A. and Boone, L.W. (1991). Critical success factor analysis for information systems performance measurement and enhancement. Information & Management, 21, 161-174.

Sol, H.G. (1992). Information Systems Development: A Problem Solving Approach. In Challenges and Strategies for Research in Systems Development, Cotterman, W.W. and Senn, J.A. (Eds.), John Wiley and Sons, 151-162.

Sumner, M. (1985). Organization and Management of the Information Center. Journal of Systems Management, November, 10-15.

Sumner, M. and Ryan, T. (1994). The Impact of CASE: Can it Achieve Critical Success Factors. Journal of Systems Management, June, 16-21.

Turner, J. A. (1987). Understanding the Elements of System Design. In Critical Issues in

Information Systems Research, Boland, R.J. and Hirschheim, R.A. (Eds.), John Wiley and Sons, 97-111.

Visala, S. (1991). broadening the Empirical Framework of Information Systems Research. In Information Systems Research: Contemporary Approaches and Emergent Traditions, Proceedings of the IFIP TC8/WG 8.2 Working Conference, Nissen, H., Klein, H.K. and Hirschheim R. (Eds.), Elsevier Science Publishers B.V. (North-Holland), 347-364.

Walsham, G. (1995) Interpretative Case Studies in IS Research: Nature and Method. European Journal of Information Systems, 4(2), 74-81.

Williams, J.J and Ramaprasad, A. (1996). A Taxonomy of Critical Success Factors. European Journal of Information Systems, 5, 250-260.

Wetherbe, J.C. and Leitheiser, R.L. (1985). A survey of services, decisions, problems, and successes. Information Systems Management, 2(1), 3-10.

Yin, R.K. (1989). Research Design Issues in Using the Case Study Method to Study Management Information Systems. In The Information System Research Challenge: Qualitative Research Methods, Volume 1, Cash J.I. and Lawrence P.R. (Eds.), Harvard Business School, Boston, MA, 1-6.

Zahedi, F. (1987). Reliability of Information Systems Based on the Critical Success Factors Formulation. MIS Quarterly, June, 11(2), 186-203.

Zani, W.M. (1970). Blueprint for MIS. Harvard Business Review, Nov/Dec, 48(6), 85-97.

[iii] In Aristotle's Nicomachean Ethics (1962; Book VI. ii. p. 329) translated by H. Rackham; Rackham indicates that Aristotelian choice refers to a "choice of means, not of ends".

[iv] Cited in Rockart, 1979.

[v] It is evident from the King and Cleland's (1975) research paper that critical decision areas are basically synonymous with CSFs.

[vi] See Miles and Huberman (1994) for a description of this data analysis, display and reduction technique.

CHAPTER 24

APPLYING THE FOUR-PARADIGM THEORY TO INFORMATION SYSTEMS RESEARCH

Donal J Flynn and Zahid I Hussain
Department of Computation, UMIST

Abstract.

The research we are currently conducting concerns a large NHS hospital in Yorkshire. Our research goals are to apply theories of social behaviour relevant to IT to seek to explain the factors which, in this hospital, shape the structure and process involved in obtaining the requirements for an information system. One theory in which we are currently interested is the four-paradigm theory for developing information systems (Hirschheim, Klein and Lyytinen 1995). We describe theory elements, how we operationalised the theory to apply to the hospital, and discuss early results, showing the prevalence of the functionalist and neohumanist paradigms among hospital stakeholders, to show the relevance of this theoretical approach to our research situation.

1   INTRODUCTION

We are currently conducting research in a large NHS hospital in Yorkshire. This hospital is seeking to use IT as part of a project to integrate several day clinics into one clinic in a single location; part of this integration process is concerned with the development of an information system (IS) to support certain aspects of the new clinic's procedures. We are interested in developing and testing theory to support social aspects of this integration process.

Our research goals are, firstly, to apply theories concerning social behaviour relevant to IT to seek to explain the factors which, in this hospital, shape the structure and process involved in obtaining the requirements for the IS. We anticipate that, by focusing more on the social (rather than the technological) nature both of the requirements development activity as well as that of the eventual system, we will generate proposals for newer methods for the development of requirements that will better satisfy the needs of users of IT systems. Within our wider work we are using several theories in an attempt to present several points of view, in the belief that more than one theory may result in a richer account. Secondly, we hope to refine theory through practical experience of its applicability.

One of the theories in which we are interested, quoted widely in IS research, is what we term the four-paradigm theory of information system development due to Hirschheim, Klein and Lyytinen (1995); we refer to these authors subsequently as HKL. Our aim is to ascertain, for key stakeholders, their paradigmatic assumptions concerning the way in which they develop requirements for the new IS. We intend to link these assumptions to the results of stakeholder interviews in an attempt to investigate the extent to which they shape their views of the process of requirements construction.

The aim of this paper is to briefly discuss the results of the research, which has recently begun, and to present the approach we are taking in terms of the operationalisation of the theory and its likely applicability to the research setting. We describe our research method and the hospital context, the HKL paradigms, paradigm operationalisation and some preliminary results, concerning the prevalent paradigms found among the stakeholders and our views on their relationship to the process of requirements construction.

2   RESEARCH METHOD AND HOSPITAL CONTEXT

The most suitable research method for applying the theory was the case study, as this would enable us to acquire a good understanding of the hospital. Regular visits to the hospital were made to gather data and learn common organisational myths, tales, stories and rumours. A number of other research approaches supplemented the basic method, for example, un/structured interviews, non/participant observation, unstructured questionnaire and secondary literature research.

The project involved the merge of seven geographically and procedurally separate day clinics into one clinic in a single location over the period September 1997 - September 1998; the development of a computer-based IS was only a part of this integration process. Five teams were formed to develop and implement the requirements for the clinic (including the new IS) and a brief summary of their work is as follows:

- Strategic group - supervises the work of four other teams and makes decisions.
- Operational team - drafts operational policy and decides the way the new clinic will operate including treatment areas, clinical methods and rules, clinic security and staff reporting structure.
- Documentation team - drafts forms and documents that will be needed in the new clinic. Administration team - decides on the new administration system for all the new specialities in the clinic.
- IT team - designs, implements and evaluates the IT system for the clinic.

2.1   Description of HKL four-paradigm theory

"The most fundamental set of assumptions adopted by a professional community that allows its members to share similar perceptions and engage in commonly shared practices is called a 'paradigm'. Typically, a paradigm consists of assumptions about knowledge and how to acquire it, and about the physical and social world" (Hirschheim and Klein 1989). HKL suggested that a wide range of assumptions were held by individuals involved in the development and implementation of IS in organisations. Such assumptions are critical as they affect the process and product of IS development as well as they way in which IS are used. They grouped similar types of assumptions together into four paradigms of IS development, based on the four paradigms of social research due to Burrell and Morgan (1979). One of their aims was to demonstrate the current imbalance of IS development approaches towards only one of these paradigms, the functionalism paradigm. The HKL (1995: 48) paradigm map is shown in figure 1.

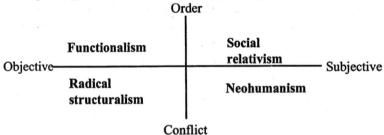

Figure 1: Four paradigms for IS development

2.1.1   Operationalisation of HKL in the research situation

HKL assumptions - The four paradigms arose from two dimensions, shown in figure 1, that grouped together related sets of assumptions viewed by Burrell and Morgan as characterising approaches to social research within organisations.

The first dimension was concerned with four assumptions that they located along a subjective-objective dimension. These assumptions concerned: (1) ontological, (2) epistemological, (3) human nature and (4) methodological issues. At the objective end, these assumptions treated the social world as a hard, external, objective reality; at the subjective end, the subjective experience of individuals in their creation of the social world was emphasised, including ways in which the individual creates, modifies and interprets his or her world, usually by interaction with others. The second dimension was concerned with assumptions about the social world located along an order-conflict dimension. Towards the order end, the social world was seen as stable, cohesive and integrated, where the status quo was continually maintained or changed only slowly and where differences and conflict were largely absent; this view emphasised society's protection of individuals. Towards the conflict end, the social world was seen as unstable and divided, where the status quo changed rapidly and where conflict and dissension were the norm; this view emphasised society's restriction of individuals.

As we felt that the assumptions were at the heart of the theory, we decided that we would operationalise them by basing a set of questions on them and using these in a questionnaire to ascertain assumptions held by hospital stakeholders. To minimise the length of the questionnaire we constructed five basic questions, based on the ontological, epistemological, human nature (subjective-objective dimension) change and conflict (order-conflict dimension) assumptions. We omitted the methodological assumption as this is stated as being determined by the other subjective-objective assumptions.

In order to determine what paradigm was indicated by a given stakeholder response, we prepared a set of reference answers to each question for each of the four paradigms. Although HKL provide some guidance on the paradigms the reader may infer some of our bias from the interpretations of the assumptions and their position on the dimensions.

To reduce any difficulty in interpreting open responses to the questions, we decided on multiple choice responses, where, for each question, the four choices of answer presented to the respondent were summaries of our reference answers. This however ran the risk of no one answer fitting the perception of an assumption held by any particular respondent.

2.1.2   Five basic questions

1. *Ontological. Do you see your organisation as having a relatively objective existence or as a collection of beliefs and values of the individuals who control the organisation?*
   This question targets ontological assumptions whereby an organisation may be seen as a "solid" entity, albeit based on beliefs, or as a network of individual beliefs, some of which are shared.

2. *Epistemological. Do you view the nature of knowledge in your organisation as tangible or intangible?*
   Some epistemological assumptions hold that there is hard/tangible knowledge about the organisation or society, which exists as 'hard data' and can be acquired through positivist means. An alternative assumption is that much knowledge is intangible and is made up of common beliefs, where it can be learnt through subjective experience and continual interaction.

3. *Change. Do you see your organisation as one where fundamental changes occur frequently or only rarely?*
   This question is aimed at revealing whether fundamental organisational change is perceived as a frequent phenomenon and to what extent are workers used to such changes occurring frequently.

4. *Conflict. What role does conflict play within your organisation?*
   Some assumptions emphasise the role of conflict within organisations whereas others focus more on organisational stability. Conflict may be viewed as positive, with the potential to make improvements, or as negative, threatening stability and the status quo. For example, conflicting views on the usability aspects of an information system

may be seen as positive by those who want to change the system and are looking for evidence to support their case.

5. *Human nature. How important is it for workers to determine some or all aspects of their work at your organisation?*
This is aimed at eliciting assumptions concerned with the relationship between human beings and their environment. On the one hand, a deterministic view is that humans are products of their environment whose behaviour is conditioned by external circumstances; this contrasts with a voluntaristic perspective where "free will" is important, attributing to humans a more creative role where they may be masters of their environment.

3   RESULTS

3.1   Interviews and questionnaire responses

We obtained agreement from six stakeholders to respond to the questionnaire. Of these, two gave us only verbal responses as they stated they were not willing to record their views in this written form. We felt that this was due to the fact that hospital access was given to us by a hospital executive who was senior to project team management, who may have felt, despite assurances, that written questionnaires might find their way somehow to this executive.

The respondents' roles were managerial level and were: IT executive, system manager, project manager, organisational manager, clinic manager (a doctor) and the clinic registrar. Thus, our respondents were mainly top/middle management of the project. Several of these managers refused to allow us to interview their junior staff on the teams. We felt that this was due to their perception that staff views might contradict management responses, there was a lack of time due to immediate pressures, or both.

3.2   Paradigms present

We discuss each of the five questions, showing the paradigms revealed by their answers.
Ontology. Most respondents viewed organisations as having a physical existence (functionalism), with one viewing them as made up of company beliefs and shared values (neohumanism). A major reason why respondents saw their organisation as a physical entity was that they believed that management was not possible unless there was a concrete structure. They saw physical existence in terms of certainty, good planning, good logic and predictability. For example, the clinic manager stated: "Most certainly, it is a concrete structure". It appeared that most respondents ticked this option almost without thinking.
Epistemology. Three paradigms were revealed in response to this question: functionalism, social relativism and neohumanism, with three respondents stating that knowledge was tangible. One reason for this was that most perceived the hospital as being dominated by written guidelines that they saw as being necessary. In addition, there is a tradition in the NHS to follow the rule-book on all matters.

Change. The three previous paradigms were again revealed here, with most respondents selecting functionalism, despite being engaged in a substantial change exercise. This response mainly came from more senior management who were advocating change and would hope to personally succeed by gaining acceptance of the need for change among staff. The change venture had strong external drivers and was justified as being efficiency driven that would improve and maintain the status quo; the hospital was undergoing a merger with another hospital and issues of autonomy and influence, although not formally stated, were on many respondents' minds.

Conflict. Three paradigms, radical structuralism, social relativism and neohumanism, emerged here, with most stating that conflict created differences that needed to be reconciled. All respondents saw the need for differences and conflict as a means to allow new clinic requirements to be generated and they encouraged this for the change process to proceed.

Human nature. Two respondents stated that everything is pre-planned on the workers' behalf (functionalism), while four stated that individuals are intelligent beings and should be seen as capable of making their own decisions (neohumanism). This was due probably to the fact that most of the respondents were senior managers who had some degree of freedom in their decisions. During interview the project manager commented "Well, I think I'm capable of making my own decisions, otherwise I wouldn't be here".

Summary of results. Overall, the responses to the ontology, epistemology and change questions suggested a predominantly functionalist paradigm among these respondents, with the conflict and human nature questions revealing a predominantly neohumanist paradigm. No respondent selected more than one response to a given question: if a respondent employed different paradigms this was revealed by responses to questions.

4   DISCUSSION OF RESULTS

The functionalist and neohumanist paradigms were the most prevalent among the respondents. The functionalist paradigm was revealed by beliefs that the clinic was characterised by rationally defined structures, standards, work patterns and communication; in addition, ideological structures, informal laws and obligations were also perceived. For example, junior doctors should only work certain number of hours a week and only perform certain operations (usually minor). However, in reality there was a hidden expectation for the junior doctors to work double the number of their contracted hours and to perform many tasks that were outside their contract.

The neohumanist paradigm was revealed by stakeholders' beliefs that their personal motives, values and views were important in bringing about changes. For example, the unit manager, a mother, proposed that there should be a children's corner in the new clinic. After negotiation her idea was accepted and a budget drawn from the building decorations fund.

4.1   Requirements construction process
Functionalist and neohumanist perspectives

This section will reflect on the process whereby the IS requirements for the day clinic have been constructed from the functionalist and neohumanist perspectives. The results presented previously show that both paradigms were present in those involved in constructing the requirements. The requirements construction process may be characterised by two factors: (1) team-led (2) informal and unstructured. The five project teams described earlier brainstormed, discussed, investigated and finally decided on the requirements. No requirements construction method was explicitly adopted, and no team member "brought along" any method with which they had previously been involved or had heard about. During the brainstorming sessions team members made suggestions about new ways of operating and functionality required from the IS. These suggestions were either accepted or rejected by the other team members. Useful ideas were accepted and discussed further, where the practical usefulness and the conformance of the ideas to the NHS standards and policies were considered. If an idea conformed to this NHS framework and was believed to be useful then further investigation was carried out by nominated team member(s) who checked in more detail the conformance of the idea to the NHS framework and other factors.

The brainstorming process can be regarded as subjective, the results of which were then checked against the objective NHS framework. If the idea conformed to the framework then certain stakeholders were asked to investigate its use further, which is a subjective action. If the investigation revealed the benefits of using this idea then it was included in the new clinic policy that was part of the general hospital policy framework.

Therefore the subjective aspects involved were the stakeholder's status, personal influence, skills, and roles within the project sphere. The functionalist aspects involved were: organisational standards, policies, functional needs, specifications, funding, past projects and the influence of external bodies.

5   CONCLUSIONS

HKL noted that the practitioner community have moved on to incorporate non-functionalist paradigms in their IS development methods. In our study, we found that, in the requirements construction process, hospital stakeholders use methods for developing requirements that are clearly influenced by the neohumanist as well as the functionalist paradigms. For example, different stakeholders had different views about the nature of the new clinic as the context for the IS; functionalism would assume the existence of one status quo to which all concerned subscribed. Another example concerns the functionalist view that knowledge is objectively available; again, team development showed that requirements had to be constructed by a (sometimes arduous) process of discussion.

Paradigms are thus archetypes and methods may display features of more than one paradigm. A rich set of paradigms was required to take into account social as well as technological issues. Certainly from a structuration theory perspective (Giddens 1979) that attempts to integrate such paradigms, one would expect to find situations where social structure influences human interaction as well as those where interaction produces new structure. For example, functionalist assumptions are shown in stakeholder awareness of NHS guidelines acting as "objective" constraints on the requirements process to produce requirements that conform to these guidelines. From an interaction perspective, neohumanist assumptions are evident from decisions taken to create a climate whereby team discussions can generate proposals for change to the status quo. Continual conflict between these two assumptions is limited in the hospital as NHS guidelines are on a high level of abstraction compared to clinic requirements.

There are several elements of the requirements method used in the hospital that indicate the features of a seventh generation "emancipatory" approach as proposed by HKL. Based on the paradigm of neohumanism, such an approach sees systems development as a social process that "focuses on emancipation ... and takes its motivation from the work of Habermas' (1984) Theory of Communicative Action" (HKL: 39). We reach this conclusion as it appeared to us that the managers of the project established team meetings as "vehicles ... to overcome obstacles to free and undistorted communication" (HKL: 39) where rational and emancipatory discourse was possible when discussing requirements, mainly by emphasising the need for "mutual understanding for all its users" (HKL: 39). There was evidence from interviews that stakeholders were encouraged to suggest requirements that made their job easier or more fulfilling. The reasons for this were perhaps mainly pragmatic: several independent clinics had to be integrated and no one person knew how all the clinics operated.

However, we see three difficulties in making this a strong claim: firstly, stakeholders may give the impression to researchers that such emancipatory discourse is taking place, whereas in fact they are inwardly constrained by issues such as hospital politics. Secondly, as systems development invariably takes place within boundaries (eg budgetary, NHS guidelines) of one sort or another, how "loose" should such boundaries be for conditions to favour the presence of emancipatory discourse? Thirdly, we have not really thought out the criteria we used for judging the "degree of emancipation" underlying, for example a speech act in a requirements meeting. Perhaps HKL found a similar problem when they attempted, as they state without success, to find a neohumanist method with which to illustrate their concepts.

A preliminary conclusion with respect to improvements to requirements methods is that they should be concurrently multi-paradigm: that is, they should not merely allow for several paradigms to exist in a serial manner but should allow several to exist at the same time. It was interesting that questionnaire respondents did not select more than one answer to a question, thereby ostensibly ruling out the possibility that they might have a multi-paradigmatic view on one question. However, they appeared to be comfortable with such a view over different questions.

We found the HKL four-paradigm theory broadly applicable to our research situation, on the basis that respondents were able to relate the meanings of the paradigms (based on our reference answers) to their perspectives. However, we feel that we have not differentiated strongly enough between the neohumanist and social relativist paradigms. We shall amend this in another NHS hospital where we are conducting similar research.

We have presented a rather simplistic, high-level picture of the requirements process in the hospital as influenced by the two paradigms. HKL note that it is complicated to show how the paradigms are actually reflected in systems development, as they are "largely implicit and deeply rooted in the web of commonsense beliefs and background knowledge which serve as implicit 'theories of action'" (1995: 49). However, we intend to adopt the HKL solution of "generic stories" which may enable us to have more insight into key aspects of the process. For example, the importance of conformance to NHS standards will lead us to explore the influence of those individuals who possessed, had access to or pretended to be aware of such key knowledge. We also intend to explore occasions where, during requirements construction, conflict occurred between neohumanist ideals of free communication and emancipation of individuals and functionalist characteristics of hierarchical communication and the priority of organisational needs over those of individuals.

References

Burrell G and Morgan G (1979) Sociological paradigms and organisational analysis, Heinemann, London.

Dickson G W et al (1977), Research in Management Information Systems: the Minnesota Experiments, Management Science 23(9), 913-923.

Giddens A (1979) Central problems in social theory, Macmillan, London.

Hirschheim R and Klein H K (1989) Four paradigms of information systems development, Communications of the ACM 32(10), 1199-1216.

Hirschheim R, Klein H K and Lyytinen K J (1995) Information Systems Development and Data Modeling: Conceptual and Philosophical Foundations, Cambridge University Press, Cambridge.

Hirschheim R and Klein H (1994), Realizing Emancipatory Principles in Information Systems Development: The Case for ETHICS, MIS Quarterly 18(1), March, 83-109.

Ives B et al (1980), A Framework for Research in Computer-based Management Information Systems, Management Science 26(9), 910-934.

Lyytinen K and Hirschheim R (1988), Information Systems as Rational Discourse: an Application of Habermas' Theory of Communicative Action, Scandinavian Journal of Management 4(1/2), 19-30.

Walsham G (1993) Interpreting Information Systems in Organizations, Wiley, Chichester.

CHAPTER 25

THE 'INFORMATION CONTENT' PROBLEM OF A CONCEPTUAL DATA SCHEMA AND A POSSIBLE SOLUTION

Junkang Feng
University of Paisley

Abstract

A research problem, namely the 'information content' of a conceptual data schema for an information system is looked at in this paper. It argues that the lack of clearly expressed 'information content' of a conceptual data schema is responsible for some well known difficulties in data modelling and analysis. What is required for solving this problem is then discussed. Then this paper shows that existing methods and techniques in the literature surveyed do not seem to have solved this problem. Finally a possible solution to this problem is outlined.

1 WHAT IS THE PROBLEM AND WHY IS IT WORTH A SOLUTION?

That a database is constructed for representing information is acknowledged by most of the writers of the literature surveyed. For example, Elmasri and Navathe (1994), Batini et al (1992), Hawryszhiewycz (1991), Halpin (1995), Hull and King (1987), Vetter and Maddison (1981), Loucopoulos (1992 in Loucopoulos and Zicari 1992 page 4), and Mortimer (1993). Vetter and Maddison (1981, page 7) say that one of the aims of database design is that all types of *information* can be stored in the database, and the conceptual data schema is a '*single common reference point*' of the information resources of an organisation (ibid., page 72). Elmasri and Navathe (1994, page 451) maintain that the problem of database design is designing the structure of a database to accommodate the *information* needs of the users in an organisation for a defined set of applications. Batini et al (1992, page 6) say that a conceptual schema is invaluable as a stable description of the database *content*. Mortimer (1993) says that *information* is the life blood of business and organisation (ibid., page 7) and that the quality of information a database provides has been defined as giving the user what they want and not what they ask for (ibid., page 12). Halpin (1995, page 2) maintains that stages in information systems engineering such as requirements analysis, database design, forms development etc. are all underpinned by the notion of *information*, since all deal with it in one way or another. Halpin says also that his formal object-role model (FORM) is for the formulating of the *information structure* of a database application (ibid., Preface).

These goals and aims are, however, *'very hard to accomplish and measure'* (Elmasri and Navathe 1994, page 451). Designing databases is 'a very difficult, complex and time-consuming task' (Kahn 1985 in Yao 1985 page 1). An optimal design of a database is difficult to achieve (Su 1985). Vetter and Maddison (1981, page 1) say that 'the definition (of database design objective) is simple; the execution is difficult'. The hardest part of designing a database is finding out exactly what is needed (Salzberg 1986, page 9). Especially, Batini et al (1992, page 144) say that

> *'It is very difficult to formally define the <u>information content</u> of the schema or prove that the information content of two schemas is identical.'*

Note that in the above a few paragraphs, the italic and underline are mine. Bubenko (1986) commented in 1986 that a comprehensive theory of information systems development that was forecast in 1970 by Auerbach had not been materialised. The field at that time was characterised by having hundreds, even thousands of methodologies, a gap between the invented and the practise, the problem of the identity of information systems and so on. Twelve years on, the situation is still being seen as *'confused'* (Checkland and Holwell 1998). The problem of the information content of a conceptual data schema is at the centre of information systems design. Like many issues in this field, it appears that this problem is yet to be solved.

2   WHAT IS REQUIRED FOR SOLVING THIS PROBLEM?

A formal information system will inevitably use some data storage mechanism to store data. Information will be derived from the stored data. The structure of the data storage mechanism will be specified by a conceptual data schema. So a conceptual data schema determines the 'data' basis of a formal information system. We will define the 'information content' of a conceptual data schema to be the infons ('infon' is a formal model of items of information proposed by Devlin (1991), which will be described later) that can be derived from the data storage mechanism defined by the schema. Information occurs in an agent's mind. Information stemming from the data in a data storage mechanism is unlimited. From the point of view of information systems design however, we want to make sure that the information that can be derived from the data storage mechanism includes the information that the system is designed to provide. We will term the latter 'required information'.

Thus, to solve the 'information content' problem will require a mechanism whereby three tasks can be fulfilled. The first one is the formulation of required information from human purposeful activities. The second is the derivation of a conceptual data schema from the formulated required information. And finally the third one is the analysis of a conceptual data schema in terms of whether the required information can be derived from the data schema. That is to say, to solve this problem, it seems to be useful to develop a mechanism for the construction of a conceptual data schema whose 'information content' is such that the required information can be derived from a data storage mechanism. And the conceptual data schema specifies the data structure of the data storage mechanism. To develop such a mechanism, a fundamental prerequisite seems to be the separation of data and information.

3   ADEQUATE SOLUTIONS WERE NOT FOUND IN THE LITERATURE

The lack of adequate solutions to this problem is demonstrated by difficulties in many aspects of conceptual data design for formal information systems. In the next section, we will look at three of them, which are concerned with the treatment of information, semantic modelling, and the quality of a conceptual data schema. First we will look at how 'information' is handled in the database design literature surveyed, as it appears that the aforementioned prerequisite has not fully recognised and used in database design literature.

3.1   'Mystical fluid' in database design literature

The purpose of conceptual database design is to describe the information content of the database (Batini et al 92, page 6). But the very element 'information' has been treated in the database design literature that we surveyed like a kind of *'mystical fluid'* (after Stamper 1985). That is, information is used as an intuitive term and taken for granted, not a subject for a scientific enquiry. The nature of it is not clearly defined, and particularly there is no concrete form for capturing it. This prevents the 'information content' from being expressed accurately and studied thoroughly in the first place. This in turn is probably because of the lack of a realisation in the database design field that data analysis is a type of inquiry, in which the concept of information should play a central role.

Most database design methodologies take information and data as synonyms and use them interchangeably, for example Date 1994, page 4. A conceptual data schema is produced through abstraction and conceptualisation from user requirements by using semantic models. Such a schema sometimes is indeed called *'information model'* (Shlaer and Mellor 1992, Flynn and Diaz1996) or information-structure perspective (ISP) (Kahn 1985). Halpin (1995, page 5) says that ER is the most widely used semantic model, which might be used as an 'information model'. King and Mcleod (1985, in Yao 1985 page 115) say that semantic database models attempt to logically structure the information in a database. Kahn (1985, in Yao 1985 page 10) takes attributes and *'non-decomposable groups'* as *'elementary piece of information'*. When data is taken as information, data processing becomes information processing. For example, Mortimer (ibid., page 133) takes DFD as a graphical representation of the flow of information.

In the database design literature information is also sometimes defined as *'facts'* (Mortimer 1993 page 7, Halpin 1995 page 5) and it is said that information must be informative and have meaning, that is, it informs (Mortimer 1993 page 8). But definitions like these do not help much because, as Stamper (1985) points out, these definitions appeal to mentalistic notions such as 'meaning', 'knowledge', 'idea' and 'concept', which are themselves as difficult or even more difficult to define. As a result, in the database design literature that was surveyed within this work information required by the user does not have a concrete form. Hence methodologies cannot address the issue of 'required information being provided by the database' with exactitude. After the information requirements analysis phase, the issue of information is quickly forgotten and data becomes the thread throughout the rest of database design process.

3.2   Difficulties in semantic modelling

The dominant approach to conceptual data design is using a semantic model to formulate users' information requirements. The literature and our own experience show that there are some difficulties with this approach. These difficulties can be divided into two categories, namely the *'design product'* and the *'design process'* – following IFIP WG 8.1's idea (Olle et al 1991, page 2).

At the 'design product' side, IFIP WG 8.1's CRIS conference series (Olle et al 1986, 1991) include many criticisms on IS methodologies. For example, when commenting on conceptual modelling in general, Rolland and Cauvet (1992) say that existing conceptual models are not rich enough for enforcing ISO's conceptualisation principle and often ill-defined and difficult to use. Bubenko (1986 in Olle et al 1986 page 296) says that concepts advocated by many methodologies are *'fussy'*, not precise and/or well defined. It is difficult to know which ones to use, and how to use them in different, less trivial design situations.

A prominent problem on the 'design product' side with semantic modelling is its *'non-determinism'* (Hawryszhiewycz 1991) or *'semantic relativism'* (Brodie 1984). Halpin (1995, page 322) says that given the informal nature of the initial step in modelling the universe of discourse, it is not surprising that humans often come up with different ways of describing the same reality. King and McLeod (1985, in Yao 1985 page 121) say that a significant problem in database design is that the designer is faced with a large number of arbitrary degrees of freedom in modelling. Su (1985, in Yao 1985 page 152) observes that there are often several alternative ways of modelling user's information requirements. 'Semantic relativism' permits different views of data to coexist and evolve. While this supports logical data independence and modelling flexibility, semantic relativism also causes confusion and uncertainty in semantic modelling.

Another problem is the misinterpretation of a conceptual schema (King and McLeod 1985, in Yao 1985 page 124). Halpin (1995, page 8) points out that the direction of a relationship in an ER schema can be easily misinterpreted. Howe (1983) identified a number of misinterpretation types concerning the connections within an ER schema, and called them *'connection traps'*.

At the 'design process' side, there seem more problems than the 'design product' side. It is equally important or even more important to provide the designer with a design procedure, which tells the designer how to develop a model step by step using the metaconcepts and the notation (Mearsman and Falkenbery 1995 in Halpin 1995 Forward). However, as Rolland and Cauvet (1992 in Loucopoulos and Zicari 1992 page 27) say, very little attention has been paid to the conceptual modelling process. Semantic modelling work at the object level, rather than a 'record' level as record-oriented models do. The issue of identification of objects or data entities is an important part of a semantic modelling process. Su (1985 in Yao 9185 page 156) says that proper data entities need to be identified and defined to best reflect user's view of the database, and says *'the selection of a good design of entity types is very important.'* But the 'design process' of IS methodologies is taken as the stages of the life cycle by, for example, IFIP WG 8.1's CRIS conference series (Olle et al 1986, 1991), which ignore this issue. So very little attention has been paid to this. Semantic models normally do not provide guidance for finding relevant objects. Lewis (1995 in Stowell and West 1995 page 193) says that the identification of entities is one of the problems with data analysis as an ontological approach.

3.3 The quality of a conceptual data schema

The conceptual data schema determines what information can be represented by an information system, so the quality of the schema is crucial. And yet, only a notably small number of works in those that were surveyed pay some attention to this issue. Bubenko (1986) observes that many software systems lack qualities normally associated with good engineering designs, and that determining their validity and correctness is a serious problem. Bubenko pointed out that one of the problems that had not been considered was how to verify the correctness and consistency of a conceptual specification (ibid.). Rolland and Cauvet (1992 in Loucopoulos and Zicari 1992 page 34) say that elimination of ambiguity, inconsistency and incompleteness in a conceptual schema is difficult. They observe that the impotence of schema validation is widely recognised by most developers but still there is a lack of formal theory for efficiently carrying out validation (ibid., page 11). Meye (1985) lists *'seven sins of the specifier'*, including contraction, ambiguity, and wishful thinking. Flynn (1998, page 413) defines the quality of an information system as the developing of a system that meets the requirements of the user.

The most common checking step for consistency seems to be cross-references between different perspectives such as the data, process and behaviour perspectives (Olle et al 1991, page 75). But any consistency checked this way is *'very much a matter of individual preference rather than consistency in a mathematical sense'* (ibid.). The quality factors that are nearest to an explicitly defined information content of a conceptual schema in the literature surveyed is the set put forward by Batini et al (1992). This set includes *completeness, correctness, expressiveness, readability, minimality, self-explanation, extensibility* and *normality* (ibid, page 139-43). Of these quality factors, completeness, correctness, and minimality are particularly relevant to information requirements. The completeness is concerned with whether relevant user requirements are represented in the schema. The correctness is concerned with whether concepts (entities, relationships etc.) are used according to their definitions. The minimality is defined as every aspect of the requirements appearing only once in the schema. Redundancy depends on syntax and meaning of a schema (ibid., page 146). Meaning is hard to define precisely. A problem with these definitions is that information requirements are not defined formally so the quality factors are difficult to be quantified.

One prominent quality factor of a conceptual data schema is its capability of supporting database transactions. Hull and King (1987) say that the specification of database dynamics is the structuring database manipulation primitives into transactions. Kahn (1985 in Yao 1985 page 5) defines '*process requirements*' as the definition of the data manipulation process of the ensuing system. And yet, Su (1985 in Yao 1985 page 153) observes that little has been done on the specification, analysis, and modelling of corporate constraints and processing requirements. Many more recent textbooks on database design do not address this issue, for example, Halpin 1995 and Date 1995.

3.4   Summary of the literature analysis

The analysis above shows that the fundamental prerequisite for solving the defined problem, namely the separation of data and information was not fully recognised in database design literature surveyed. The works in database design literature surveyed do not seem to have the concept of 'formulating information flows in a human purposeful activity'. Most of them are concerned with processes and data that are required by the processes. Some work such as Lewis (1994, 1995) does use the concept of 'human purposeful activity', but information formulation does not seem to be their concern. As for how to derive 'data level' constructs from formulated information, a common approach is to use a semantic model in a 'straightforward' way. No systematic method for deriving them from analysing information was found. The concept of 'information bearing capacity' of a data schema was found neither adequately recognised nor defined. The quality of a schema is relevant to this problem, but very few works among the surveyed address this. Those who do have not defined their quality factors on an explicit 'information' basis. So the conclusion we have reached is that the literature surveyed does not seem to have provided a satisfactory solution to the defined problem. In the rest of this paper we will outline our mechanism for tackling this problem.

4   THE PROPOSED MECHANISM IN OUTLINE

As said earlier the separation of information and data is a prerequisite for solving this problem. We adopt semiotics principles (Stamper 1997) and Mingers' idea (1995) about a sense making system - a *'meaning system'*.

The foundations of our mechanism are: Mingers' framework of sign, information and meaning (1995), Barwise's *'situation theory'* (Barwise and Perry 1983), Devlin's *'information flow theory'* (1991), Predicate logic and Harel's higraph (1988). The proposed mechanism consists of three components. We will give a belief description for each of them in turn.

4.1   Formulating required information in human purposeful activities

We take the view that information only occurs in the mind of an agent who is capable of and conducts perception and cognition, and information can be expressed in some way. We will assume that information is made up of items of whether certain given objects posses a certain property or a relationship in a certain context, which we call 'item of information'. An item of information consists of two parts – a statement of the alleged fact that certain given objects posses a certain property or relationship, and a context within which the statement is true. We suggest using a formal concept 'infon' (After Devlin 1991) to model the 'statement' by using a *predicate* expression:

```
Individual(a₁,…,aₙ)∧TemporalLocation(t)∧SpatialLocation(l)∧Polarit
y(1)∧r(a₁, …, aₙ, l, t, 1)
```

This view is not exactly the same as that of Mingers' (1995). That is, our term 'information' is similar to Mingers' 'meaning', not his 'information'. We will put human actors in purposeful activities at the centre of attention. Around the actor there are a number of *situation types* (Barwise and Perry 1983). The situation types are connected by *info connections* and/or *actions*. These constitute a mechanism of formulating *information flows* (Devlin 1991) around human activities, through which *required information* and *raw data*, which are embedded in the infons, will be identified. The information content of a conceptual data schema is formed from the infons that capture the required information.

4.2   Constructing a conceptual data schema from raw data

Because the raw data are a collection of signs from which required information is derived, a conceptual data schema constructed from the raw data in a certain way should be able to bear required information. The question is to find the certain way. The idea is to formulate and then analyse the usage of the raw data items in relation to elementary activities in order to classify them and find the relations between them. To this end, the raw data items need to be consolidated first with a view to making them mutually exclusive, as they may overlap or one may include another. We will model raw data as *object types* (Devlin 1991), which are specified by using infons and situations. So the consolidating process is that of analysing infons and situations. Then the usage of raw data items is formalised by using a set of *parameters*. Through calculation of the parameters, raw data items are classified and clustered. As a result data level constructs will emerge, and therefore a conceptual data schema will be formed.

4.3   Representing 'required information' with a conceptual data schema

The conceptual data schema formed through the previous stage is a preliminary and crude one in terms of whether it indeed represents the required information. The final stage of the proposed mechanism is to analyse and make sure that a quality schema be constructed. This requires looking at a data schema's 'information bearing capacity'. In order for a data schema to be able to bear formulated required information, it is necessary that:

a) Every object type found in the formulated required information (which is in the form of infons and situations) is represented by one or more *data entity types* in the data schema; and

b) Every instance of an *info unit* in the formulated required information is represented by at least one *topological connection structure* in the data schema.

   To this end, the proposed mechanism includes the analysis of the topological structure of a conceptual data schema by using Harel's higraph, and the analysis of the relationship between *info units* of the formulated required information and the *topological connection structure* of a conceptual data schema. Through these three stages the information content of a conceptual data schema is identified, formulated, and contained (represented) by the schema.

5   SUMMARY

This paper has defined a research problem, namely 'the information content of a conceptual data schema'. This term is widely used in database literature, but in general it is used informally and loosely. The main reason for investigating this problem is that it is crucial for a formal information system but does not seem to be addressed adequately in the literature. It was argued that the cause of this inadequacy is that information has been treated as mystical fluid in database design literature. Solving this problem should improve a number of major aspects of conceptual data design. The first one is the alleviation of difficulties in semantic modelling. The second one is the improvement of such quality factors as completeness, correctness and minimality of a conceptual schema. This paper then outlined a proposed mechanism for tackling this problem. The mechanism consists of three components, namely the formulation of required information, the construction of a data through analysing raw data's usage, and the analysis of the information bearing capacity of a data schema.

References

Barwise, J. and J. Perry, (1983) Situations and Attitudes, Bradford Books, MIT Press.

Batini, C, S. Ceri, and S.B. Navathe (1992) Conceptual Database Design: An entity-relationship approach Benjamin/Cummings, Redwood City in Calif.

Brodie, M. L. (1984) 'On the Development of Data Models', in On Conceptual Modelling, Brodie et al (eds), Springer-Verlag, New York.

Bubenko jr, J.A., (1986) 'Information Systems Methodologies - A Research View', in Information Systems Methodologies: Improving the Practice, T W Olle, H G Sol, A A Verrijn-Stuart (ed), IFIP WG8.1 working Conf proc , North-Holland.

Checkland, P., and S. Holwell, (1998) Information, Systems and Information Systems, John Wiley & Sons, Chichester, New York.

Date, C. J. (1995) Introduction to Database Systems, 6th ed., Addison-Wesley, Reading, Massachusetts.

Devlin, K. (1991) Logic and Information, Cambridge University Press, Cambridge.

Elmasri, R. and Navathe, S. B., (1994) Fundamentals of Database Systems, 2nd ed., Benjamin/Cummings, Redwood City, California.

Flynn, D., (1998) Information systems requirements: determination & analysis 2nd ed, McGraw-Hill.

Flynn, D., and F. Diaz, (1996) Information modelling: An international perspective, Prentice-Hall Inc Englewood Cliffs, New Jersey.

Halpin, T., (1995) Conceptual Schema & Relational Database Design, Prentice-Hall Inc. Australia.

Harel, D., (1988) On visual formalisms, ACM Communications, Vol 31, No 5, May 1988

Hawryszhiewycz, I.T., (1991) Database analysis and design 2nd ed, MacMillan publishing company.

Howe, D.R., (1983) Data analysis for data base design, Edward Arnold.

Hull, R., and R. King, (1987) 'Semantic Database Modelling: Survey, Applications, and Research Issues', ACM Computing Surveys, Vol 19 No 3 Sep 1987.

Kahn, B.K., (1985) Requirement specification techniques, in Principles of Database Design, Vol 1 Logical Organisations, S.Y. Yao (eds), Prentice-Hall.

King, R., and D. McLeod, (1985) Semantic Data Model in Principles of Database Design, Vol 1 Logical Organisations, S.Y. Yao (eds), ,page 115, Prentice-Hall.

Lewis, P., (1994) Information-systems Development, Pitman, London.

Lewis, P., (1995) 'New Challenges and directions for data analysis and modelling', in Information Systems Provision: The Contribution of Soft Systems Methodology, Stowell, F. eds. McGraw-Hill, London.

Loucopoulos, P., (1992) 'Conceptual modelling', in Conceptual Modeling, Databases, and CASE - An Integrated View of Information Systems Development, P Loucopoulos, and R Zicari (eds), John Wiley & Sons, Inc, New York, Chichester.

Meyer, B., (1985) 'On formalism in specification', IEEE Software, 1985 Jan pages 6-26.

Mingers, J., (1995) 'Information and meaning: foundations for an intersubjective account', Info Systems J, 5.

Mortimer, A., (1993) Information structure design for databases - A pratical guide to data modelling Butterworth-Heinemann ltd.

Olle, T.W., H.G. Sol, and A.A. Verrijn-Stuart (eds), (1986) Information Systems

Methodologies: Improving the Practice, IFIP WG8.1 working Conf proc , North-Holland.

Olle, T.W., J Hagelstein, I G Macdonald, et al., (1991) Information systems methodologies: A framework for understanding, Addison-Wesley Publishing Company, Wokingham in England.

Rolland, C., and C. Cauvet, (1992) Trends and Perspectives in conceptual modelling, in Conceptual Modeling, Databases, and CASE - An Integrated View of Information Systems Development, p. Loucopoulos, and R Zicari (eds), John Wiley & Sons, Inc, New York, Chichester.

Salzberg, B. J., (1986) An introduction to database design, Academic Press College Division, Orlando.

Shlaer, S and Mellor, S. J., (1988) Object-Oriented Systems Analysis: Modelling the World in Data, Yourdon Press, Prentice Hall Building, Englewood Cliffs, New Jersey.

Stamper, R.K., (1985) Towards a theory of information, Information: Mystical fluid or a subject for scientific enquiry? The Compter Journal, Vol.28 No 3, 1985, pages 195-202.

Stamper, R. (1997) 'Organisational semiotics', in Information systems: An emerging discipline? eds Mingers, J. and Stowell, F. McGraw Hill, London.

Stowell, F. and West, D., (1994) Client-led Design, McGraw-Hill, London.

Su, S.Y.W. (1983) 'A semantic association model for corporate and scientific-statistical databases', Inf. Sci. 29, pages 151-199.

Vetter, M., and R.N. Maddison, (1981) Database design methodoly, Prentice-Hall Inc., Englewood Cliffs, New Jersey.

Yao, S.B., (1985) Principles of Database Design, Vol 1 Logical Organisations, Prentice-Hall Inc., Englewood Cliffs, New Jersey.

CHAPTER 26

IMPROVING SYSTEM HANDLING IN RETRIEVAL SYSTEMS BY INTEGRATING A VISUAL COMPONENT

BE Bürdek, M Eibl and J Krause
College of Design, Offenbach; Social Sciences Information Center, Bonn; University of Koblenz,

Abstract:

The Boolean query, so popular in document retrieval, causes great problems for users. Various approaches to the elimination of these problems by means of visualisation create new problems. Less than convincing metaphors, and the inadequate and hard-to-interpret forms of representation, impair the usability of these visualisation techniques. This paper discusses the critical aspects of visualisation in document retrieval systems, and presents a new approach to the solution. The general design strategy employed are findings from software ergonomics and aspects of interface and media design.

1   INTRODUCTION

The Social Sciences Information Center in Bonn is maintaining several databases containing heterogeneous data of the social sciences. In 1995 the project GESINE was launched with the stated goal to build one information system integrating the different databases. GESINE is based on a common relational data model. The user of GESINE will have the impression to search only one large database.

GESINE will offer several different search interfaces in order to meet different search strategies and levels of user experience. Those search interfaces include a search form, a natural language interface, a search grid and the here presented visualisation. Before integrating the visualisation in GESINE it is being tested as a stand alone application using the GIRT-database (*German Indexing and Retrieval Test Database*) which is an extract of SOLIS (document database) and FORIS (project database) both maintained at the Social Sciences Information Center.

In 1997, a co-operation agreement was made between the College of Design, Offenbach, the Institute of Computer Science, University of Koblenz and Social Sciences

Information Center. The stated goal was to bring software ergonomics and interface and media design closer together in order to combine the cognitive but anaesthetic solutions of software ergonomics with the stylistically well-thought-out but less effective ones of interface and media design, and to find common solutions that do justice to both sides. The visualisation presented here was conceived as part of this co-operation.

2   CONSIDERATIONS CONCERNING THE DESIGN

The visualisation presented in this article is designed to employ a certain search strategy which is to be described firstly: The visualisation makes two basic assumptions about the use of Boolean search logic in document retrieval systems. Firstly, a user for whom working with such a system is only a means to an end (e.g. library information systems at universities) has great difficulty with the concept of Boolean algebra, and therefore produces too many invalid queries. The more specifically he wants to express his need for information, and the more complex his query becomes, the greater the probability of errors. There are several factors behind this, like for example the difference between the natural-language and the Boolean use of "OR", the difficulties in the Boolean "NOT", or the complexity of nesting with brackets. Here, a visualisation of the query can help free the user from the strictly logical ballast of the Boolean search, and allow him intuitive access.

The second assumption has to do with the search strategy of document retrieval systems. Normally, the user first formulates a broader query, and has the system show how many documents have been found. Their number decides whether the user displays the documents or reformulates the query, to narrow or widen the result. He therefore uses the number of documents found to determine the quality of his query.

The following example of a query illustrates this strategy: assume a user wants to write a paper dealing with the topic of sociological family research, and needs information about the effects of the spouse's employment on the family's housekeeping. As this aspect is only a small part of the actual paper, the user wants to read as little about it as possible. He enters the following query at the system:

```
descriptor = 'woman' & descriptor = 'occupation'
```
to see whether there are any documents available on this topic. And, sure enough, the system displays:

```
130 documents found
```
He tries to narrow down the query:

```
descriptor = 'woman' & descriptor = 'occupation' &
descriptor = 'private household'
```
The system now displays:

```
0 documents found
```
This is decidedly too few for the user, and he reformulates his query as follows:

```
descriptor = 'woman' & descriptor = 'occupation' &
descriptor = 'family'
```

The system now displays:
```
50 documents found
```
This is too many documents for the user, but he can see that he is on the right track. To further narrow down his query, he considers how interesting it would be to know what the husband does while the wife is working:
```
descriptor = 'woman' & Descriptor = 'occupation' &
descriptor = 'family' & descriptor = 'man'
```
To his satisfaction, the system now says:
```
5 documents found
```
This is a number that the user can comfortably peruse more closely, and he has the documents displayed. This is the basic search strategy, which reaches the result by iteratively reformulating the query. The queries used here were very simply formulated. If the remaining Boolean operators are used as well, the iterative process is prolonged accordingly.

3   DESIGNING THE VISUALISATION

Considering existing systems in visual document retrieval like InfoCrystal (Spoerri 1994), Vibe (Korfhage 1991), LyberWorld (Hemmje 1993), Vineta (Elzer&Kohn 1997) leads to three basic questions concerning the representation of terms and documents in a visual interface. In the search for a suitable form of representation, we cannot avoid answering these questions first:

1) Should the documents be presented singly or bundled? The individual representation of the documents can express the relevance of each document more distinctly. Bundling documents in general means, first of all, reducing data. The individuality of the documents is abandoned in favour of their categorisation. Bundled representation helps to avoid ambiguity more easily, and drastically reduces the complexity of the presentation. Orientation and reorientation after entering new search arguments is facilitated by a bundled representation.

2) Does it make sense to employ the attraction metaphor, which is done by Vineta, VIBE and InfoCrystal? Figure 1 shows a schematised diagram of the attraction metaphor. In the corners we find four search terms A, B, C and D. The two relevant documents Doc1 and Doc2 are placed between the search terms according to their relevance. Since Doc1 is relevant to search term A as well as to search term B, it is „attracted" to these two. Therefore, it is placed between them. The attraction metaphor works quite well for document Doc1 but ambiguities appear concerning Doc2. Is it relevant to terms A and C or to terms B and D or even to all four of them? Presenting several documents or several document sets with different relationships leads to superposition. In order to handle ambiguities systems using the attraction metaphor are commonly designed mobile. The user is enabled to move the search term icons.

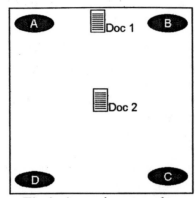

Fig.1: Attraction metaphor

But then again he has to spend time and cognitive resources judging the repositioning of the document icons. The problem with the attraction metaphor is that they seem to be the most „natural" way of representing relevance in a visualisation but in reality they are incapable of representing the relationships without ambiguities. A visual formalism can avoid such a shortcoming.

3) Should a two- or three-dimensional representation be used? When representing the elements of an n-dimensional space, it seems appropriate to use the greatest number of dimensions that a human being can handle cognitively. On the other hand, if one has to "flatten" the n-dimensional space anyway to make it representable, would it not make more sense to go the whole hog and reduce it to a less complex, two-dimensional structure? The inclusion of the third dimension sharply increases complexity. Because the three dimensions are squeezed together to two again on the screen, the representation is in no way simplified. The aim of visualisation, however, should be to make complex situations easy to handle.

The reason for using the third dimension are the ambiguities caused by the attraction metaphor. But the fact that ambiguities crop up later in the three-dimensional representation does not mean that no ambiguities crop up. It would, however, be desirable to create a visualisation that remains unambiguous in its representation, independent of dimensionality. As Roppel 1996: 147 et seq. demonstrates, the apparent advantage of the third dimension with regard to focus-context visualisation and space-saving is achieved at the expense of serious problems with interaction. The much heralded simplification of orientation is non-existent. The arguments of the 3D advocates are therefore untenable.

We decided in favour of a 2D visualisation based on a visual formalism using a bundled representation of the documents. On this concept we designed and discussed more than 40 draughts under the aspects of software ergonomics and of interface and media design. The purpose was to demonstrate that the two schools could, after all, be combined to advantage.

4   THE VISUALISATION

Consider a person in need for information about the promotion of women in leading positions in business. Figures 2-4 show the newly created visualisation, and how it can be used to build up a query in stages.

Fig.2.a-c: Building up a search

The initial state of the visualisation is an angle under which the user can enter the first search argument. The ▮ is the button of a dropdown list. After entering a search term *woman* the number of documents found (*2857*) appears on the right side inside the angle. (In the example shown, the search criteria are descriptors. In reality, the user can choose between titles, authors, year, etc.) A second input field is placed below the first one. As soon as the user has entered more than one argument, all possible combinations of the search criteria appear right of the input fields. In figure 2.b the only possible combination of the search terms *woman* and *promotion* is *woman AND promotion* (190 documents) represented by the document set icon on the right. The relationship between the search arguments and the document set icons is coded by colour.

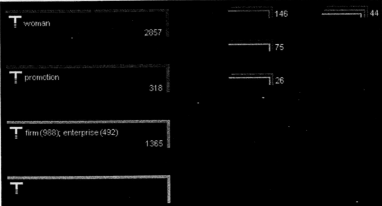

Fig. 3: Structure of a query: three search arguments

As demonstrated in figure 3 the system also accepts search arguments consisting of more than one search term in one single input field: In figure 3 the third search argument consists of two terms and is to be read as *firm OR enterprise*. 988 documents are found for *firm*, 492 for *enterprise* and 1365 for *firm OR enterprise*. Thus, the right handed document set icon contains 44 documents for the query *woman AND promotion AND (firm OR enterprise)*.

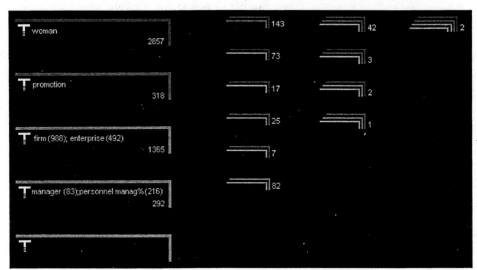

Fig. 4: Structure of a query: four search arguments

In figure 4 the search term *personnel manger* is truncated to *personnel manag* by using the %. If the user wants to see all the terms the system found to the truncated one he can use the star (*): now all the found terms appear inside the input field.

As figure 4 clearly demonstrates the combinations of the search arguments, i.e. the document set icons, are arranged in columns according to their valence, i.e. whether they are 2-, 3- or 4-fold, etc. In the left column of document set icons we find those combinations consisting of two search arguments. The icon on the right hand always represents the one combination of the highest amount of entered search arguments, in figure 4 four.

The user can decide whether he wants distinct sets or not. If he does not need distinct sets the left column of document set icons is to be read from the top as follows: *woman AND promotion* (143 documents), *woman AND (firm OR enterprise)* (73 documents), *woman AND (manager OR personnel manag%)* (17 documents), etc.

If you consider figure 4 there seems to be something wrong with the numbers of documents: the last icon in the middle column contains one document whereas right icon contains 2 though it should be a more specific query. The reason for this is that figure 4 shows a search using the distinct set feature. Thus, the left column has to be read as follows: *woman AND promotion AND NOT (firm OR enterprise OR manager OR personnel manag%)* (143 documents), *woman AND (firm OR enterprise) AND NOT (promotion OR manager OR personnel manag%)* (73 documents), *woman AND (manager OR personnel manag%) AND NOT (promotion OR firm OR enterprise)* (17 documents), etc. Since the Boolean NOT-operator is always troublesome to novice users we made the use of distinct sets optional.

The visualisation is designed as an open one; that is, in principle, an infinite number of search arguments can be entered without requiring a change to the basic appearance of the visualisation.

The coding of the set icons is performed using colours. Using lots of terms can make identification and thus interpretation difficult. Should the user feel the need to examine the exact relationships of the individual icons after all, he only has to move the mouse over the document set icons, and all the input fields that are not related to this set are dimmed (see fig.5). This feature was highly welcomed by the test persons and is a demonstration of the superiority in speed of an interactive visualisation over a textual retrieval interface.

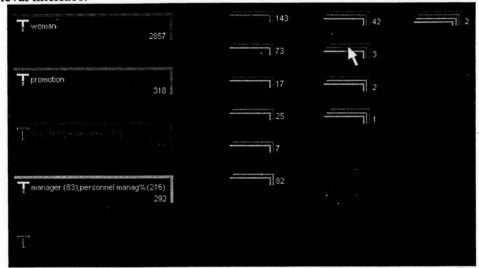

Fig.5: Moving the mouse over a document set icon

The feature works vice versa as well: moving over an input field hides all irrelevant document set icons. A variety of further tools help the user to achieve an even more exact definition of the sets than would be possible with Boolean logic. For example, he can click on each separate set icon to display authors and titles, and a ranked list of all the descriptors of the documents in the set. He can thus ascertain the contents of the documents and the possibility of further queries.

5   EXTENDED VERSION

Boolean retrieval is only one among many possible retrieval models for data search. We wanted the visualisation to be *open*, not only concerning the visual appearance (see above) but also concerning the supported retrieval models. Thus, we implemented a second retrieval model: the probabilistic retrieval model.

The main principle difference between Boolean and probabilistic retrieval is the dealing with relevance. Whereas Boolean retrieval differs in a strictly binary way between relevant and not relevant, probabilistic retrieval computes degrees of relevance: Documents are organised in a list by their assumed degree of relevance to a query. The cluster hypothesis however allows to cluster several documents and allot them the same degree of relevance. We will employ this hypothesis in order to extend our visualisation.

The relevance of the single document clusters is defined by the relevance of the search arguments user to define them. The relevance of the search arguments again is determined by the relevance of its search terms. Their relevance is computed by the *Inverse Document Frequency*-function (IDF). The IDF is based on the assumption that specific terms describe a user need more precisely and therefore lead to more relevant documents. In fact, broad terms lead to search results with high recall, whereas specific terms lead to search results with high precision. An example: If one uses the term *car* to describe a query he will get lots of documents and lots of them he does not want. If he uses the more specific term *Austin Mini* he will get only view documents, but he is probably going to read all of them.

Figure 6 demonstrates the aligning of the relevance along the X-axis. The more relevant a term is considered to be the more it slides to the right. Therefore the term *promotion* (318 documents) is placed right of the term *woman* (2857 documents) which is less specific and therefore seen as less relevant. If a search argument consists of more than one search term, the arithmetic mean of the IDFs of the search terms are taken.

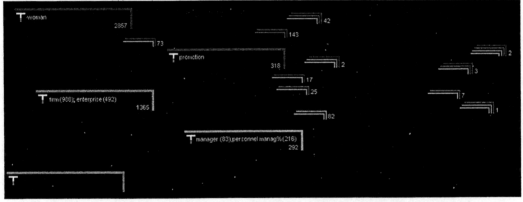

Fig.6: Probabilistic version using the inverse document frequency (IDF).

This function is certainly not too elaborate but we use it in order to demonstrate that the visualisation is not only usable for strict Boolean combinations but in principle also extendible to more sophisticated and up-to-date retrieval approaches.

Since this is a wholly statistical approach the user is allowed to interact with the visualisation. By moving the input fields he can determine which search arguments he himself considers to be more important.

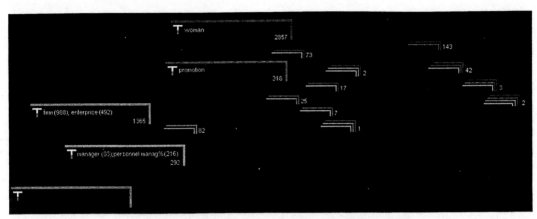

Fig.7: Probabilistic version after user interaction.

Figure 7 shows the visualisation after user interaction: The user has moved the blue input field *woman* to the right and the green input field *manager OR personnel manag%* to the left. By doing so, he increased of the blue term and decreased the importance of the green one. The document set icons are replaced according to the new relevances.

6   USER TESTS

The Social Sciences Information Center is planning to provide the German Indexing and Retrieval Test database (GIRT) (cf. Frisch & Kluck 1997) for the evaluation of retrieval systems. So far two retrieval systems (Messenger and freeWAISsf) have been tested using the GIRT database and nine related search topics. In order to maintain comparability the visualisation has been tested according to the rules of GIRT. Eight professional database searchers participated at the test. Since the result set was limited to 30 documents, recall values were quite low.

Concerning the recall and precision values the visualisation (recall: 15,2%; precision: 60,7) is placed between Messenger (recall 17,5%; precision 62,8%) and freeWAIS (recall 13,8%; precision 58,3%). The probabilistic version of the visualisation led to astonishing good results (recall 16,9%; precision 67,7%) even though it employes just very simple probabilistic ranking methods.

The evaluators were asked to answer some questions about their experiences with the visualisation. They could answer using a scale from -3 (negative) to +3 (positive). They considered the handling to be quite easy (+1,29) and the appearance of the document sets very clear (+2,38). The optical appearance of the visualisation was appreciated (+2,63). Though they did not find the speed of work enhanced (0,0) they commonly said that this would depend on the underlying topic. Concerning the speed, the answers were very divergent: they reached from -3 up to +3. Confidence in the retrieval result was high (+1,88). All in all the visualisation was highly accepted (+2,13).

7   CONCLUSION

Research on visualisation in document retrieval is still in its infancy. It is very difficult on account of the abstract character of query logic. Nevertheless, it is possible to find visualisations which hold out the promise of good user acceptance and also take account of aesthetic criteria. The here presented visualisation is designed openly concerning the appearance as well as the retrieval model it is based on. It does without metaphors, and is strictly formal from a visual aspect.

References

Elzer, P., Krohn, U. (1997) 'Visualisierung zur Unterstützung der Suche in komplexen Datenbeständen.' Proceedings of the HIM '97 - „Hypertext - Information Retrieval - Multimedia". Dortmund, 1997 p.27-38.

Frisch, E., Kluck, M. (1997) 'Pretest zu Projekt German Indexing and Retrieval Testdatabase (GIRT) unter Anwendung der Retrievalsysteme Messenger und freeWAISsf.' IZ-Arbeitsbericht Nr.10, Bonn.

Hemmje, M. (1993) 'LyberWorld - Eine 3D-basierte Benutzerschnittstelle für die computerunterstützte Informationssuche in Dokumentmengen.' GMD-Spiegel, No.1, p.56-63.

Korfhage, R. (1991) 'To see or Not to See - Is That the Query?' SIGIR'91, p.134-141.

Nardi, B.A., Zarmer, C.L. (1993) 'Beyond Models and Metaphors: Visual Formalisms in User Interface Design.' Journal of Visual Languages and Computing, No.4, p.5-33.

Olsen, Kai A. (1993) 'Visualization of a Document Collection: The Vibe System.' Information Processing & Management, Vol.29, No.1, p.69-81.

Roppel, S. (1996) 'Visualisierung und Adaption: Techniken zur Verbesserung der Interaktion mit hierarchisch strukturierter Information.' PhD thesis, University of Regensburg, Germany.

Spoerri, A. (1994) 'InfoCrystal: Integrating Exact and Partial Matching Approaches through Visualization.' RIAO'94, New York (NY), 1994, p.687-696.

CHAPTER 27

COMPUTATION OF UNCERTAINTY IN INFORMATION SYSTEMS

J Korn
Middlesex University

Abstract

The subject-predicate form attached to special verbs is introduced as a carrier of a quantity of information with meaning. An information system is described as an assembly of interacting objects intended to bring about mental changes in selected objects called receivers of total information which is regarded as a product. Uncertainty is introduced into operation of objects and interactions through modifiers, adjectival and adverbial phrases, which all together are modelled into a computable formalism. The formalism consists of a diagram from which predicate logic sequences are deduced carrying specific kinds of uncertainty.

1 INTRODUCTION

The notion of information and its historical development has been discussed (Korn1998). A quantitative information theory culminated with Shannon's work. The work of Bar-Hillel and Devlin concerned semantic information. A more philosophical direction of development was taken by authors such as Dretske.

The topic of information systems seems to be concerned with modelling and design of assemblies of people, computers and hardware interacting in terms of information bearing entities such as orders, invoices, letters and so on. Information systems are seen to operate in human activity situations like commercial, manufacturing and other types of organisations (Hawryszkiewycz 1988, Flynn, Diaz 1996). The identity of the topic of information systems in terms of a recognised body of knowledge has not been established yet (Anon 1995, Checkland,Holwell 1998). There are a number of approaches to the development of models, perhaps the most common is based on data flow analysis leading to a formal model of processes and entities.

In the literature the concept of information by and large appears to be discussed without reference to information systems and vice versa. Once a model of an information system is prepared there is no way to manipulate the model and to introduce uncertainty associated with the operation of human beings and machines. There is no means to introduce dynamics into such model.

The objective of this paper is to suggest a concept of information incorporating meaning and quantity that fits into an information systems theory and to outline such a theory based on linguistic modelling and leading into systems design (Korn 1996a).

2   CONCEPT OF INFORMATION

Development of a concept of information as the term is understood here, begins with reference to perception. Living things and through them, organisations (beehives, groups of animals, families, political, social, commercial, manufacturing organisations) have contact with the outside world by means of sense organs and instruments, means of their extension. Sense organs are physical objects which require a small but a finite amount of power for their operation. These organs are usually delicate so as to minimise their power consumption. Parts of the world appear to the sense of vision in their entirety as combinations of geometrical, material, numerical and possibly energetic properties (Korn 1995, Korn 1996b). Other senses receive only a partial view. These properties are perceived through the intervention of power from light or moving air for vision or sound, for example. The concept of property is defined in physics, natural language allows a much wider use but in much the same sense as in physics (Korn 1996b).

If we close a sense organ, the mind through the brain, can form visual images (Johnson-Laird 1988) in terms of properties. The mind can also create images independently of the world. Visual images can be reproduced as sketches, paintings, sculptures or other structures using a combination of properties as listed above called 'informatic'. These are called iconic models.

A problem with iconic models is that they refer to parts of the world in their entirety. Such models cannot be used for :

1. Expressing a view, an opinion, indicating or making a statement about a part of the world and issuing instructions.
2. Asking questions.
3. Manipulating images other than changing their spatial position. Reasoning and operating rules is not possible.
   These mental feats can be accomplished by symbols.

Using the notions of property and symbol, when considering a part of the world we can separate one or more properties from an image, or its iconic model, rather than viewing it in its entirety and assign symbols to the separated property and the rest of the image. In general, we have arrived at the concept of subject-predicate. When the subject-predicate symbolism is used for expressing a view (1st feat) then we speak of information.

The subject-predicate arrangement is intended to represent a physical object and a property/feature or an event and a feature. In natural language the first is realised by the predicate being an adjectival phrase whereas in the second case the predicate includes a verb phrase.

The subject-predicate form is best known in the symbolism of natural language. However, it is used in other ways of communication such as body language and signs.

A symbol is constructed from a combination of geometrical, material and possibly energetic properties so as to be perceived by a sense organ. The construction is arbitrary but once agreed on, must be carried out to close specifications otherwise the symbol would not be recognised. Thus, the construction is realised by purposive systems. The meaning of a symbol refers to the relation between the symbol and what it is intended to represent. Since a symbol is an arbitrary mark, an object or an event, its meaning must be learnt either ostensively or by being told about it or by guessing.

In general, we can distinguish concepts expressed as symbols which are directly observable through a combination of properties and those which can be concluded from observation i.e. theoretical constructs.

Information as a message which is understood and accepted by a receiver, is used by a sender to exert specific influence on the mental state expressed in terms of properties, of a receiver. Thus, the subject-predicate form is attached to special verbs capable of carrying a message and representing influence (Korn 1996b) as adjectival or verbal subordinate clause. For example, 'waiter *indicates* to the guest that *the restaurant is full*'.

The result of influencing the mental state can take the forms :

1. The mental state itself changes. For example, in *'The building society notified the young couple that their application for a mortgage had been approved'* it is likely that the couple's mental state changes from anxious to relieved.

When we perceive information the function of the sender and receiver is the same. For instance, *'The man has noticed that his neighbour is untidy'*.

2. The mental state changes so as to initiate action. For example, in *'The government announced to the country that it intends to ration petrol'* the mental state of people is likely to change so as to initiate a rush to buy petrol. Sending and carrying out instructions comes under this category of influence leading to the exercise of 'skilled power'.

A message usually contains more than one subject-predicate form called here the unit of information. To be able to accomplish a specific task, total information, just like a kind of energy, has to be constructed from a number of meaningful units of information. A letter with a request, for instance, should contain total information. Data are numerical part of a predicate, often used in technical discourse.

A message carried by interaction called influence (Korn 1996b) between a sender and a receiver involves : a medium, message carrier and meaning. For instance, the medium can be realised by light, vibration of air, orders, invoices or letters. The term 'message carrier' includes symbols such as natural language or Morse code, the meaning of which must be agreed between a sender and a receiver. These five constituents of delivering a message with information involve uncertainties.

3   CONCEPT OF INFORMATION SYSTEM

Physical objects, the relevant objects of surroundings and the activities of these objects, together are called an observed situation, or a scenario. A theoretical object is regarded as a conjunction of properties (Korn 1996b) one or more of which emerges depending on the situation in which the object happens to be. Such a property is referred to as contingent. Activities are seen as interactions between theoretical objects. The model of such objects, their contingent properties and interactions is called a situation. We can identify one, or more, objects in an observed situation the mental state of which is to be changed. This state is described as contingent properties, happy, sad, ignorant and so on. An information system is an assembly of objects with the task to deliver total information required to accomplish the change. Here we are concerned with modelling situations with information systems.

Total information delivered by an information system to an identified object called the 'receiver', is regarded as a product which has to be designed (Korn 1996a). Information carried in a letter, for instance, has to be constructed so as to achieve the expected effect. The system-product-receiver chain has emerged. When the product is a kind of energy or an artifact, the term 'receiver' is replaced by that of 'user'.

Interaction in an information system is called influence which carries the appropriate information and modelled as a verb with a subject-predicate form attached. Theoretically influence requires zero physical power. In practice, however, information is carried by a medium. In this case the medium itself may be treated as a part of the structure of the situation i.e. collection of objects and their interactions.

4   MODELING INFORMATION SYSTEMS WITH UNCERTAINTY

Total information is a designed product which is delivered by an information system to a receiver to achieve a specific change in mental state expressed in terms of properties. Thus, an information system operates in accordance with a purpose (Korn 1996a) and involves living things, predominantly people and organisations. In such observed situations qualitative rather than quantitative properties or features which are important and available. These properties are attached to objects with potentially unpredictable behaviour yet usually operating as a part of a structure which may be regarded as permanent over some time. Departments in a factory or in a supermarket, a small shop or office are examples of this type of situation. Thus, although people, operating as components or objects within say a department, regularly carry out much the same functions, their day to day performance may vary as a result of changes in mood and health, of ambitions and effects of domestic and other circumstances. In general, variations of relevant characteristics of any kind which we may like to assign to an object, are bound to affect its performance or behaviour in some way leading to alterations in an anticipated outcome. This applies to animate and inanimate objects such as a car engine.

In addition, the operation of a purposive system invariably involves decision making not only at a basic but at organisation level. Decision making implies reasoning with some form of logic based on information about objects in an environment such as competitors, resources, suppliers, and markets. Decision making can also be based on the results of comparison and more complicated calculations. Some of the reasoning can involve vague terms which can be handled by fuzzy logic (Korn, Huss, Cumbers 1993).

We can see that in human activity situations there are objects with a low degree of anticipation of repeatability of certain of their features. These objects exhibit fluctuating behaviour. For these reasons, apart from social difficulties, experimentation with human activity situations is not fruitful. An appropriate model of such situations can only have conditional predictability : we can say that if objects have certain stipulated properties and behave in a certain way then the model can be used for prediction of an outcome. We intend to use natural language as the basis for the development of modelling human activity situations since it can handle the features just outlined. Having suggested the required empirical generalisations (Korn 1996b), here we intend to show how the symbolism of linguistic modelling is used.

4.1   Uncertainties in information systems

We have asserted that transmission of a message involves five components : a sender, a receiver, a medium, a message carrier and meaning. There is a variety of uncertainties associated with each of these components. There are also difficulties with the design of total information. We are not certain about the kind and quantity of information which would be necessary to successfully accomplish a mental change in a receiver. Designing total information and its medium is much more uncertain than that of energy and the medium for carrying it. Here we only intend to show a formalism for including uncertainties associated with fluctuating properties, logical operations and calculations, filtering and decision making by comparison.

The method described here uses a story, a narrative or an appraisal of a situation expressed in declarative sentences of natural language, as the starting point for modelling situations. Natural language is rich in metaphors, cannot be manipulated for prediction and for the application of computing, thus, it cannot be used directly. Linguistic analysis has to be introduced with the function (Korn 1996b) :

1.   To identify context-free sentences with verbs, initiating and affected objects.
2.   To identify the verbs which carry the appropriate interaction.
3.   To reduce linguistic complexities into a combination of one or more stative and dynamic clauses of one-or two-place sentences called 'basic constituents'.
4.   To identify the modifiers, or properties, of nouns and verbs within a basic constituent. Modifiers make a sentence situation-dependent and carry the uncertainties considered here.
5.   To identify clauses for modelling the structure of a situation and those which carry

information i.e. the special verbs carrying subject-predicate clauses.

Context-free sentences with modifiers can be diagrammed (Korn 1996b) showing structure, input and output objects. Uncertainty can be introduced in the following way :

1. Graded adjectives : Modifiers are expressed in terms of adjectival and adverbial phrases. The majority of adjectives admit variation, or grading, of the concept which they represent. For example, the concept 'comfort' can be graded as very comfortable, comfortable, uncomfortable. Others like 'square' cannot be graded.

The function of grading an adjective, or an adverb, is to explore the effects of day to day variation of properties of objects and interactions like moods, illness, personal problems and others on the performance of an otherwise stable structure.

2. Measure of grades : Each grade of an adjective can be assigned two numbers. The first number between $0-100$, expresses the significance of a property and grade as far as the outcome of basic constituent is concerned. This outcome will be defined as the consequent of the appropriate logic implication. The second number between $-1 - +1$, is intended as a measure of certainty that an object has a particular grade of a particular property. All numbers are based on subjective assessment.

3. Personality profiles : An object or an interaction can have more than one modifier, each can be graded and a measure assigned to it. For example, we can say 'The trained secretary is willing to work'. This is expressed as

'Secretary,(training(high,80/.8,low,40/.6)),(willingness(strong,90/.7,weak,50/.6)). showing concepts, grades and measures.

Each grade under a concept can be matched to another grade under a different concept, here we have four possibilities : high, strong; high, weak; low, strong; low, weak. Anyone of these possibilities is defined as the personality profile. For example, we can say that 'Secretary's training is low but his/her willingness to work is strong' (To an extent described by the corresponding numbers).

4. Certainty factor (cf) : This is described as the level of belief in a hypothesis in the light of available evidence. We compute the cf by dividing the sum of the first numbers weighted by the second numbers by the sum of the former. Thus, the cf for 'low, strong' is given by $(40x0.6 + 90x0.7)/(40 + 90) = 0.67$ which means that this particular possibility is '*probable*' (Durkin 1994).

5. Gates : The occurrence of an outcome can be subject to conditions of some quantity being greater or smaller than another. A value of the cf can be used for this comparison. In decision making an outcome may be subject to conditions expressed by 'if...then' kind of statements or the result of calculations. These manipulations are included in 'calculating properties' (cp).

6. Purposive systems : The operation of such systems is extremely pervasive among living things at the micro and macroscopic level. Here we use a purposive system to generate a condition for further propagation of a property.

4.2 Symbolism

Linguistic analysis of a story leads to a collection of one- and two-place sentences with dynamic verbs. Such a sentence carries the initiating and affected objects and their modifiers as properties : driving (dp), enabling (ep) and calculating (cp) together with a verb as interaction (in) and its adverbial modifier. Based on assumptions, a sentence is expressed as logical conditionals which can be represented as a diagram (Korn 1996b).

A diagram generates logic sequences with no uncertainty. Uncertainty is introduced through perturbations using the factors described in the previous section.

The following symbolism is intended to capture the preceding description by including the identity of an object and interaction, kind of property/adverb, topology of objects and uncertainty :

$$\text{zp(on,rp,lp,(prop}_i\text{(mod}_j\text{))) (.)} \rightarrow \text{(.)in(vn,do,ao,(adv}_k\text{(mod}_m\text{)) (.)} \qquad 1.$$

$$\text{in(vn,do,ao,(adv}_k\text{(mod}_m\text{)) (.)} \land \text{wp(on,rp,lp,(prop}_i\text{(mod}_j\text{))) (.)} \rightarrow$$
$$\text{(.)ap(on,rp,lp,(prop}_i\text{(mod}_j\text{))) (.)} \qquad 2.$$

where ap – acquired property (Korn 1996b), z – d and/or a, w – e and/or c and/or a, on – object name, rp,lp – reference, live positions which specify the topology of the situation, prop – property concept, mod – grade and numbers, vn – verb name, do,ao – initiating,affected objects' position, adv – adverbial concept, $i = 1,2,...I$ and for each 'i', $j = 1,2,...J$, similarly for k and m. The brackets with dots are for cf.

To indicate topology eqs.1,2 reduce to

$$\text{zp(-,x)} \rightarrow \text{in(x,-)} \qquad 3.$$
$$\text{in(-,y)} \land \text{wp(-,y)} \rightarrow \text{ap(-,-)} \qquad 4.$$

where the dashes and x, y stand for numerals standing for rp and lp.

4.2.1   An example

The following text describes an observed situation : 'Customer sends an order specifying the required items to manufacturer where it is received by a clerk who verifies it if it is complete. The clerk returns an incomplete order to customer. The clerk checks that all items are available at the local depot. If the answer is yes, the clerk generates a local delivery advice for the order. If it is no, he prepares a transfer delivery note. The store uses the local delivery advice to prepare delivery and delivery docket at the local depot and to send transport request to vehicle scheduler to arrange a vehicle to deliver the ordered items'.

Only one sentence '..clerk checks that...' satisfies the description of concept of information. The other sentences indicate the medium presumed to carry information.

The story yields nine context-free sentences the first four of which are : 'Customer sends order', 'Order is received by clerk', 'Clerk changes status of order' an additional sentence, 'Order is verified by clerk'. Their diagram is shown in Fig.1 with properties and interactions indicated. For example :

```
dp(1,1) - customer : buying habits ; frequent, occasional,
standing ; long, recent,
in(1,2) - sends : sending ; quickly, slowly, where : manufacturer,
```

showing graded adjectives and adverbs introducing uncertainty into the situation. Some of these have been added intentionally to the story.

From Fig.1 logic sequences describing the topology of the situation as eq.3,4 can be derived :

dp(1,2)→in(1,2)   5.
in(1,2)∧ ep(2,2) → ap(3,3)   6.

and so on for 18 expressions.

There are two comparisons in the story : '..verifies it if it is complete..' and '..If the answer is yes..'. These are taken into account by 'cp' properties and logical 'OR' function and shown at objects 7 and 9 in Fig.1.

Further to Fig.1, the situation with objects 1 to 8 is considered in more detail. Using the format of eqs.1,2, in order to compute uncertainty, personality profiles, graded adjectives/adverbs and certainty factors are introduced. Thus, the first two terms of the logic sequence corresponding to eqs.1,2 are

dp(customer,1,1(buying(frequent,90/.8,occasional,60/.7)),
(standing(long,70/.8,recent.70/.6)))(..)   →
(..)in(sends,customer,1,order,2(sending(quickly,slowly)),
(where(manufacturer)))(..)   7.

in(sends,customer,1,order,2(sending(quickly,slowly)),
(where(manufacturer)))(..) ∧
ep(order,2,2(dispatch(recorded,100/.3,ordinary,90/.7)),
(items(required,100/.8)))(..)
→(..)ap(order,3,3(sending(sent)))(..)   8.
.... and so on for 10 expressions.

In general, the logic sequences a sample of which is given by eqs.7,8, contain the topology, objects, interactions, their modifiers and all the factors required to introduce uncertainty into a situation. With reference to eqs.1,2,7,8 the personality profile of an object consists of a combination of grades and numbers. For example, the customer's personality profile has two components and four combinations.

From combining the grades the personality profile can be made variable and a certainty factor (cf) can be calculated for each variation. Such cf is then written in the brackets empty so far. For example, in eq.7 'long' and 'recent' can be combined with each of 'frequent' and 'occasional'. Thus, for instance, 'frequent,90/.8,long,70/.8' gives a cf = 0.8 which was obtained by dividing the sum of weighted whole numbers by their sum i.e. (90x0.8 + 70x0.8)/(90+70).

Cf = 0.8 means that the 'customer is *almost certainly* long standing and a frequent buyer' (Durkin 1994).

Using the idea of variable personality profiles, eqs.1,2, through their particular cases such as eq.7,8 can be expanded and each variation is also combined through the logical operations of 'AND' and implication. Introducing numerals, eqs.7,8 can be written as

  dp(1,1,1(1,2),2(1,2))(..) →   (..)in(1,2,1(1,2),2(1,2))(..)   9.

giving 4x2 = 8 possibilities and in

```
(1,2,1(1,2),2(1,2))(..) ∧ ep(2,2,1(1,2),2(1))(..) →
(..)ap(3,3,1(1))(..)
```
10.

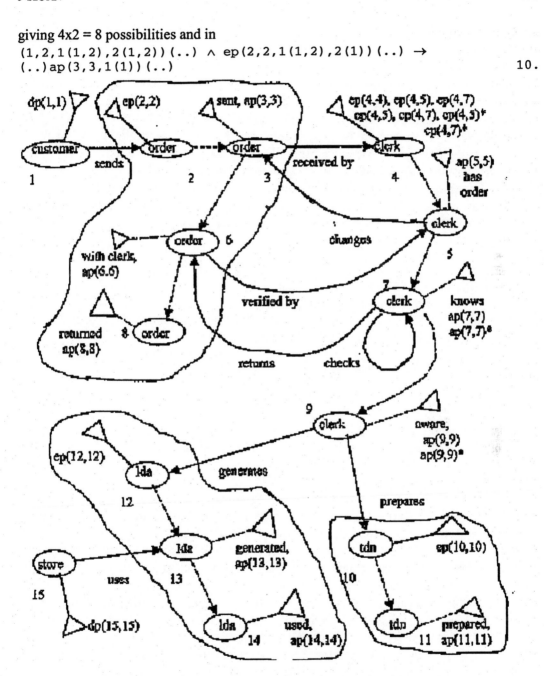

The contours indicate changes of state of products as a result of interaction.
Figure 1: Diagram of situation

giving 8x2 = 16 possibilities.
.... and so on for 10 expressions.

The number of possibilities expands very rapidly. Using all 10 expressions and with reference to Fig.1, in terms of the acquired properties the situation can occupy any of the following states : ap(3,3) = 16, ap(5,5) = 32, ap(6,6) = 512, ap(7,7) = 98304 and ap(8,8) = 100663296. The expansion of possibilities can be kept within limits by explicit, purposive systems which introduce acceptability criteria. For example, only possibilities with cf greater than a specified figure, are allowed to propagate further.

In the absence of other criteria, all states occur with equal probability if unchecked. For calculating particular values of cf, we choose the first state and inserting the cf for the rule after the implication sign (Durkin 1994), we can write

```
dp(1,1,1(1),2(1))(.8)→ (.9)in(1,2,1(1),2(1))(.72)                    11.
```

```
in(1,2,1(1),2(1))(.72) ∧ ep(2,2,1(1),2(1))(.55) →
(1)ap(3,3,1(1))(.55)                                                  12.
```
.... and so on for 10 expressions.

The result is ap(8,8,1(1)) = 0.55 which says that 'the order *maybe* returned' (Durkin 1994). If the personality profile of the 'customer' in 'dp' is allowed to vary to 'occasional,recent', for instance, with all other conditions remaining the same, it turns out that the result remains unchanged.

References

Information systems as a discipline, Systemist, v17, n1, 1995.

heckland, P., Holwell, S., *Information, Systems and information systems : Making sense of the field*, J. Wiley, Chichester, 1998.

Durkin, J., *Expert systems*, Macmillan, NY, 1994.

Flynn, D.J., Diaz, O.F., *Information modelling*, Prentice-Hall, London, 1996.

Hawryszkiewycz, I.T., *Introduction to systems analysis,design*, Prentice-Hall, NY, 1988.

Johnson-Laird, P.N., *The computer and the mind*, The Fontana Press, London, 1988.

Korn, J., Huss, F., Cumbers, J., Systems modelling with natural language and fuzzy logic, Systems science addressing global issues, ed.F. A. Stowell et al. Plenum Press, NY, 1993.

Korn, J., Theory of spontaneous processes, Structural Engineering Review, v7, n1, 1995.

Korn, J., Domain-independent design theory, J. Engineering Design, v7, n3, 1996.

Korn, J., Linguistic modelling of situations, Systemist, v18, n4, 1996.

Korn, J., Linguistic modelling of information systems, Proc of PAIS II Symposium, U. of West of England, Bristol, UK, 27-29 July 1998.

CHAPTER 28

DEALING WITH UNCERTAINTY AS A SUCCESS FACTOR FOR DECISION SUPPORT SYSTEMS: A PRELIMINARY INVESTIGATION

Nelly Todorova
University of Canterbury, New Zealand

Abstract

The paper focuses on the relationship between dealing with uncertainty and success of Decision Support Systems. Such relationship cannot be considered in isolation since it is interrelated with other aspects of DSS success. To include all aspects a multidimensional framework model has been presented. The potential role of uncertainty based on review of relevant literature and qualitative research in large UK businesses has been discussed in its context to justify the need for further research.

1 INTRODUCTION

The extensive growth in the Decision Support Systems (DSS) market indicated by the results of recent surveys (Computer Personnel, 1997) shows that senior managers recognize the increasing importance of DSS for company success and competitiveness. With the growth of investment in and use of DSS it becomes increasingly important to understand the reasons behind success or failure of DSS.

There has been extensive research in the area of IS/DSS success and various factors affecting it (e.g. Alavi and Joachimstaler, 1992; DeLone and McLean, 1992; Udo and Davis, 1992). One potential factor that has been discussed but not investigated is dealing with uncertainty. Previous research considers uncertainty mainly as a task attribute and it is mostly related to the level of difficulty. The purpose of this paper is to investigate uncertainty as a dimension of all factor constructs –task, user, system, industry and organization. First a IS/DSS success model has been formulated combining success factors discussed in the literature. Then forms of uncertainty are presented and their relation to success factor categories is discussed to justify the need for further investigation. Finally, preliminary results of a qualitative research are discussed within the framework model.

1.1   IS/DSS success model

Reviews of previous research in the area of DSS success (Alavi and Joachimstaler, 1992; DeLone and McLean, 1992; Udo and Davis, 1992) show conflicts, confusion and inconsistency between the results of various studies. "Thus the extent to which the existing body of research reflects substantial and cumulative development is not entirely clear" (Alavi and Joachimstaler, 1992). One reason for this problem is the diversity in DSS success research. Researchers have viewed DSS success from a number of perspectives using varying measures and factors of success. Thus comparisons are difficult to make and "the prospect of building a cumulative tradition [is] elusive" (DeLone and McLean, 1992). The purpose of this study is not to test the various factors but rather to organize all of them in a model. As a result of an extensive literature review, DSS success factors and measures are integrated into a framework model of multidimensional constructs (Fig. 1):

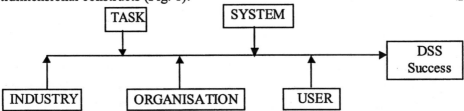

Figure 1: Multidimensional DSS success model

Success factors are distributed as dimensions of these constructs as follows:

- Task- structure, uncertainty, interdependence and variety
- System- type and origin of application, ease and length of use, timeliness, accuracy and relevancy of output.
- Industry- type, industry growth, strategic position, generic strategy, degree of competition
- Organization- management support and involvement, user training, user involvement
- User- organizational level, experience, technical knowledge, expectations and attitudes towards DSS.

Some factors have been tested and evaluated, others are stated only as potential factors. The need for further research to construct and evaluate an integrated model has been recognized in a number of studies. For the purpose of this research to investigate the potential of dealing with uncertainty as a dimension of success factors all dimensions have been included in the model.

While studies related to success factors are relatively rare and consider isolated factors, there has been a considerable research effort to organize all categories of success measures. DeLone and McLean (1992) review 180 articles and present a taxonomy consisting of 6 categories of success. The authors suggest interdependencies between the categories and conclude there is a need for further development and validation. Seddon (1997) modifies the model to eliminate some of the conceptual confusion. In this study the dimensions of DSS success are DSS use, perceived usefulness, user satisfaction and individual impact as defined in Seddon's model (1997). DSS use is not treated as a measure of success but as a necessary event leading to individual and organizational impact. All success dimensions considered in this study are investigated as perceived by users.

1.2 Dealing with uncertainty as a potential success factor

Decision making under uncertainty is a field investigated from different angles by researchers representing various disciplines such as mathematics, psychology, economics, operations and management. This section discusses in brief the main research directions taken. First, there is a need to explain what is meant by uncertainty since there are numerous conceptualisations of the term in the literature. Argote (1982) notes that "there are almost as many definitions of uncertainty as there are treatments on the subject" and Downey and Scolum (1975, quoted in Lipshitz, 1997) suggest that "the term uncertainty is so commonly used that it is all too easy to assume that one knows what he or she is talking about when using the term".

A survey of the literature shows that this confusion in definitions is not due to the lack of a theoretical framework or the existence of conflict in definitions (as is the case with DSS and DSS success). The diversity of definitions shows the multidimensional nature of uncertainty which is not recognized by some authors. Uncertainty is not a homogenous concept. There are diverse types and sources of uncertainty which have been meaningfully classified according to their issue (what the decision maker is uncertain about) and their source (what causes this uncertainty).

	All expected information is present	Some expected information is absent
All incorrect information is absent	Accurate	Incomplete
Some incorrect information is present	Incompatible	Approximate

Table 1: Hunter's classification of information

There are a number of classifications that place and structure all types of uncertainty (e.g. Klir and Folger, 1988; Smithson, 1981; Motro and Smeths, 1995; and Hunter, 1996). Since there are no significant conceptual differences or conflicts between them, Hunter's classification (1996) will be presented as an example, "intended to indicate possibilities rather than be definitive". Table 1 presents Hunter's classification of information according to the presence or absence of expected and incorrect information. Using that classification the meaning for uncertainty is determined as follows- uncertainty exists in information when it is incomplete, incorrect or approximate.

Hunter's classification is by no means the only organization of uncertainty types. There are a number of others and some even indicate possible relationships between the various types. For example Montro and Smeths (1995) suggest that the more complete the information is the less accurate it is. For the purpose of this research it is necessary to be familiar with the existing classifications but not necessary to choose one. Since the nature of the research is exploratory and inductive it is important to recognize the uncertainty dimensions when they are provided by the users' interviews.

To justify the choice of uncertainty as a subject of investigation as a potential factor affecting the success of DSS a brief overview of the main general research directions in decision making under uncertainty is presented. They could be divided in three main areas (Moskowitz, 1990):

1. Foundations and theoretical underpinnings- this research has been performed in the areas of behavioural psychology and focuses on the construction of axioms of rational behaviour which allow a decision maker to choose consistently and maximize expected utility.
2. Application and implementation- this broad term includes three main research areas: assessment and measurement of a DM's beliefs and tastes; optimization under uncertainty; development of DSSs to facilitate the use of decision analysis methodologies.
3. The role of uncertainty in microeconomic theory- focuses on determining the effect of DM's uncertainty and risk attitude on the behaviour of the firm or organization.

When all the above areas are considered in the light of the research of DSS success it is clear that they are closely related. The first area (1) and the measurement of DM's beliefs are related to user's attributes; optimization techniques and their incorporation in DSS are essential part of the system and task attributes and the role of uncertainty on the organization's behaviour is closely related to the organizational attributes. Therefore, it comes as a surprise that uncertainty forms have not been investigated as dimensions of the factors affecting the success of DSS.

Uncertainty in its various forms is repeatedly stated as a potential influence on DSS success in the most recent studies but its involvement is theoretically unsupported and there has been very little empirical work done. (Sanders and Courtney, 1985; Holt, 1988; Kydd, 1989; Udo and Davis, 1992; Guimaraes et al, 1992; Walsham, 1993; Yoon et al, 1995; Etezadi-Amoli et al, 1996). Most of the statements regarding the potential role of uncertainty are based on personal opinion (Holt, 1988; Kydd, 1989, Walsham, 1993) or one company study (Yoon et al., 1995) or on one question related to uncertainty in an instrument (Guimaraes et al, 1992) and all authors consider uncertainty only as an aspect of the task attributes.

Most authors suggest uncertainty as a possible dimension of task difficulty and task structure variables. The literature regarding these variables is very scarce and inconclusive. Problem structure is associated only with the repetitiveness of the problem. The very scarce empirical work on task difficulty as a success factor concludes that task difficulty is directly and positively related to user satisfaction. Users find DSS more useful when they assist them in more difficult and complex situations. Since uncertainty is a major part of complex decision situations it is logical that it should have some impact on the success of a DSS. Yoon et al. (1995) argue that "despite widespread belief in the importance of the many variables underlying problem difficulty there is practically no empirical research testing their relationship".

Kydd (1989) considers addressing uncertainty during the implementation phase as a major success factor of a project. Three out of four of the dimensions in the "Quality of Output" variable defined by Etezadi-Amoli et al. (1996) (accuracy of the output information, completeness of the output information and ease of understanding of the output) are in effect forms of uncertainty in information. The results showed Quality of Output to be the most important of the factors considered in the study.

In conclusion, the literature suggests dealing with uncertainty as a potential factor influencing the success of DSS. However, these statements are not empirically and/or theoretically supported. The term uncertainty is not explained in most studies and others connect it with other terms such as repetitiveness. Also, most studies include uncertainty only as a dimension of a task attributes variable. Again as argued above, interrelations between dealing with uncertainty and other influence factors are not considered. Therefore there is need to investigate uncertainty as a construct of dimensions incorporated within the various factors influencing the success of DSS. Then this impact needs to be evaluated to form a foundation for a conclusion on the role of dealing with uncertainty as a factor affecting the success of DSS.

1.3   Research approach

At the first stage of the research a questionnaire survey was mailed to randomly selected large companies in UK (more than 500 employees) and replies were received from 117 companies. The main purpose of the questionnaire survey was to provide the information, on the basis of which companies were to be selected for interviews. The questionnaire was intended to identify relevant issues regarding the success of DSS and factors influencing it. The criteria for selection was a maximum variety of successful DSS used and influence factors involved. The questions included all aspects of the integrated success framework developed from the literature

The questionnaire survey provided the necessary data to select the database of companies using successful DSS with the required variety of industry, user, system, task and organizational attributes. Also, it provided some preliminary results regarding factors affecting DSS and the potential role of dealing with uncertainty as one of them.

In logical continuation, the second stage of the research concentrates on the objective to develop and evaluate uncertainty as a multidimensional factor affecting the success of DSS. To facilitate this objective in part, the aim of the open ended interviews is to explore and identify the aspects of uncertainty influencing the success of DSS and to place them as dimensions of the DSS success framework. Although there have been some initial indications of interrelations between those aspects the main focus of the interviews is to provide a rich picture of all possible uncertainty influences.

The companies in which the interviews were held were selected according to the attributes provided by the survey. Two representatives of each company were interviewed – typically one of them has been a senior IT manager and the other one an experienced user of the DSS. The users have been chosen whenever possible to be with different background and IT experience. The system to be discussed has been selected to be used throughout the organization and to have been implemented relatively recently but at the same time with enough experience to be established (normally 2-3 years).

The interview guide was divided into two main parts. The first part consisted of topics related to factors affecting the success of DSS. The aim was to obtain the users' views on factors and measures of success and extract from that information uncertainty dimensions without leading questions. The interviews concluded with discussion of users' perceptions of uncertainty. This provided the user's definition of uncertainty.

2   PRELIMINARY ANALYSIS OF THE INTERVIEW MATERIAL

Twenty interviews have been completed and the analysis of the data is still ongoing. This paper presents some preliminary results and indications. The results have been mapped on the framework model.

2.1   Success of DSS
As in the literature, replies to questions related to the success of DSS are the most straightforward. This is the only construct that hasn't been related to uncertainty so far. Standard replies associate the success of DSS with tangible benefits- financial benefits due to savings of time, savings on salary pay "since we do not have to pay highly qualified staff", increased profits from better quality of decisions. However, it's interesting to note that all participants pointed some intangible benefits as most important- reducing of stress as "the responsibility is shared", better quality of decisions, better and faster service to customers. It's also interesting to note that it was confirmed that in many cases the use of DSS is not voluntary and therefore it cannot be accepted as a valid measure of success.

2.2   External environment aspects
Factors influencing DSS success associated with the unpredictability and uncertainty in the external environment have been recurring and are most interesting. One of the companies have been sold from one large business to another three times for the last 5 years. That has lead to constant uncertainty about the "strategic aims" and changed the system requirements and specifications even if its primary aim has stayed unchanged (approximate). Uncertainty related to changes in the political situation in Europe and UK has influenced directly the success of a DSS used in a large bank. This factor is

interrelated with the specific industry type since "the financial world is always dependent on the political situation"(incomplete). As related to that the geographical location of the business was also stated to be of importance for the reducing of uncertainty and so indirectly influences the success of the system. The occurrence of unpredictable events (Princess Diana's funeral and car accidents on M1 were given as examples) were viewed to be of considerable importance to the DSS success in a hotel and travel business since the system is not able to deal with them.

2.3   Organizational aspects

In this category management involvement is the most popular aspect discussed in the literature. The authors argue that the involvement of management in the implementation and use of DSS has a direct positive influence on the success of DSS. However, from the interviews, there appear to be two aspects in this factor. So far the findings indicate that it is indeed beneficial if the management has supported the implementation of the system. But there are no indications that the use of the systems by managers at senior level affects the success of DSS. The argument in the literature for this relationship is that if they use DSS directly managers are more inclined to support their implementation and renovation. However, with the growth of the use of IT in most recent years that does not seem to be the case. Some of the interviewed senior representatives of the companies admit that they do not use DSS ("we open a bottle of champagne if we have an actual report printed straight from the system without explanations"). However they recognize the need of DSS and the advantages they bring to the organizations. Thus although they are not actively involved in the use of the system they support its use within the organization.

There is a need for more investigation into the influence of the user training on the success of the systems. Although all of the researched companies have organized formal training sessions for personnel, this factor seems to be directly interrelated with the background of the user. In one of the companies the system analysts had to learn on their own but this fact doesn't appear to have influenced the success of their system.

A very interesting aspect of the organizational environment was raised by a representative of a branch of an American company in Britain. According to him the nationality of the owners of the company has a great impact on the performance. He argues that since "the Americans are achievers" they demand more from their staff. Also, they are more willing to make large investments in the decision support systems and that affects its success.

2.4   User related factors

There are strong indications that the uncertainty created by the lack of understanding of the DSS due to the user background is an important factor in the DSS success framework. However, this factor appears to be dependent on the organizational level of the user. Users at senior level complained that the systems are too complicated and they can not understand "what is going on inside" and so they can't trust the system. At the same time users at operational level who admitted they were not sure how the system works, were happy to accept the results given by it.

2.5   System aspects
There were many indications of the importance of the capability of the DSS to deal with forms of uncertainty. Most of the users referred to capabilities of the system to deal with incomplete and inconsistent input data. Also, in one of the cases it was pointed out that there was so much data that it creates confusion as to how to be used while the computer can process it without difficulty and in much shorter time.

2.6   Task related aspects
There is an argument in the literature whether the extent of uncertainty present in a problem has a positive or negative effect on the success of DSS. While some authors argue that the degree of uncertainty make users more reluctant to use the system (Guimaraes et al, 1992) others speculate that the ability of the system to deal with uncertainty would encourage its use (Yoon et al, 1995; Etezadi-Amoli et al, 1996). The wording of the arguments suggests that the conflict of opinions is based on the different focus of the two "camps". While the first one concentrates on the negative presence of uncertainty, the second focuses on the ability to deal with that presence. In fact both sides are possibly making the same argument but saying it in a different way. So far the preliminary findings indicate that the ability of a DSS to deal with task uncertainty has a positive influence on the success of DSS. Many of the interviewed users stated features of the system dealing with uncertainty as an important contribution to their user satisfaction and the benefits perceived by them.

3   CONCLUSION

There are indications in the existing literature that dealing with uncertainty is a potential factor affecting the success of decision support systems. However this statement has not been empirically or theoretically supported. To allow for interrelations between success factors a model has been constructed (Fig. 1) organizing the main success constructs and their dimensions. Some of the dimensions have been extensively researched and tested, others still need further evaluation. Therefore the model is by no means a completed effort. All aspects of the model are treated as potential causes or results from uncertainty. The preliminary results of the interview data suggest uncertainty dimensions in each factor construct that need to be evaluated and tested further. So far dealing with uncertainty has been considered as a feature of the system related to a task attribute. However, the analysis of the data shows a more considerable influence of uncertainty dimensions incorporated in the industry, organization and user constructs. Organizational changes bring uncertainties that have negative effect on user satisfaction and perceived usefulness and affect user attitudes and expectations. System quality is also influenced as the change in the organizational aims changes the user requirements. Uncertainty associated with business competitiveness has been perceived by users as a positive factor leading to greater motivation for utilization of DSS resources and increased user satisfaction. Ineffective user training leads to uncertainty related to the system features and the need for its use. Some organizations have recognized these factors and have implemented techniques for dealing with uncertainty to support successful DSS implementation. Others have realized the impact of dealing with uncertainty as a result of failure of DSS. Based on all these experiences the paper suggests uncertainty dimensions incorporated into a DSS success model and provides directions for future research in the area.

References

Alavi, M. and E. Joachimsthaler, "Revisiting DSS Implementation Research: A Meta-Analysis of the Literature and Suggestions for Researchers", *MIS Quarterly,* vol. 16, p.95-113, 1992.

Argote, L., "Input Uncertainty and Organizational Coordination in Hospital Emergency Units", *Administrative Science Quarterly*, vol. 27, p420-434, 1982.

Baird, B., *Managerial Decisions under Uncertainty*, John Wiley & Sons, 1989.

Barki, H. and S. Huff, "Change, Attitude to Change, and Decision Support Systems Success", *Information &Management*, vol. 9, p.261-268, 1985.

Brewer, P. et.al, "Managing Uncertainty", *Management Accounting,* vol. 75, p39-45, 1993.

Chong, V.K. and K.M. Chong, "Strategic Choices, Environmental Uncertainty and SBU Performance: A Note on the Intervening Role of Management Accounting Systems", *Accounting and Business Research*, vol. 27, p. 268-276, 1997.

DeLone, W. and E. McLean, "Information Systems Success: The Quest for the Dependent Variable", *Information Systems Research,* vol. 3, p60-95, 1992.

Etezadi-Amoli, J. and A. Farhoomand, "A Structural Model of End User Computing Satisfaction and User Performance, *Information and Management*, vol. 30, p65-73, 1996.

Gaglio, S., P.P Puliafito, M. Paolucci and P.P. Perotto, "Some Problems on Uncertain Knowledge Acquisition Rule Based Systems", *Decision Support Systems*, vol. 4, p307-312, 1988.

Ghosh, D. and R. Manash, "Risk, Ambiguity and Decision Choice: Some Additional Evidence", *Decision Sciences*, vol. 28, p81-104, 1997.

Horowitz, I., "Decision Making and Estimation-induced Uncertainty", *Managerial and Decision Economics*, vol. 11, p.349-358, 1990.

Kydd, C., "Understanding the Information Content in MIS Management Tools", *MIS Quarterly,* vol. 13, p277-290, 1989.

Motro, A. and P. Smets, *Uncertainty Management in Information Systems: from Needs to*

Solutions, Kluwer Academic Publishers, Massachusetts, 1997.

Raymond, L. and F. Bergeron, "Personal DSS Success in Small Enterprises", *Information & Management*, vol. 22, p.301-308, 1992.

Ribeiro, R., Powell, P. And J. Baldwin, "Uncertainty in Decision Making: An Abductive Perspective", *Decision Support Systems*, Vol. 13, p183-193, 1995.

Sanders, G. and J. Courtney, "A Field Study of Organisational Factors Influencing DSS Success", *MIS Quarterly*, vol. 9, p.77-93, 1985.

Seddon, P., "A Respecification and Extension of the DeLone and McLean Model of IS Success", *Information Systems Research*, vol. 8, p240-253, 1997.

Tsoukias, A., "A Qualitative Approach to Face Uncertainty in Decision Models", *Decision Support Systems,* Vol. 12, p287-296, 1994.

Udo, G.J. and J. S. Davis, "Factors Affecting Decision Support Systems Benefits", Information and Management, Vol. 23, p359-371, 1992.

Youn, Y., T. Guimaraes and Q. O'Neal, "Exploring the Factors Associated With Expert Systems Success", *MIS Quarterly,* vol. 19, p.83-106, 1995.

CHAPTER 29

AN INTELLIGENT AGENT-BASED METHODOLOGY FOR LEGACY INFORMATION SYSTEMS INTEGRATION

Joaquim Filipe, Bernadette Sharp and Kecheng Liu
Escola Superior Tecnologia / IPS, Staffordshire University,
Staffordshire University

Abstract

This paper describes an on-going project which approaches the problem of legacy information systems integration by establishing an agent network, based on the following technologies: (i) Semiotics and Deontic Logic - which provide the tools for representing business norms and social behaviour, and (ii) Distributed Artificial Intelligence and Multi-agent Systems - which provide a framework to interpret, model and communicate norms and behaviour across different sectors of the organisation.
The agent network architecture includes three kinds of agents: (i) knowledge wrappers, (ii) personal assistants, and (iii) a meta-agent that is responsible for centralising organisational information and for resolving semantic conflicts amongst other agents.

1 A CONCEPTUAL FRAMEWORK FOR INFORMATION SYSTEMS INTEGRATION

Successful business organisations must create a knowledge sharing infrastructure to support and co-ordinate their business processes. Within many organisations knowledge sharing is hindered by the legacy of their information systems and the inability to extract vital information from a huge mass of heterogeneous data sources. Often, applications are designed to perform their individual tasks without ever acknowledging the presence of other applications. Eventually, strategic planning and organisational requirements lead to the need to use data and services among different systems and, consequently, to co-ordinate and integrate these systems. Coping with this objective clarifies that a system is more than the simple sum of its parts.

However, the organisational information systems based on isolated departmental systems of the past are changing into more integrated environments. This is due not only to the software industry maturing, making greater use of off-the-shelf components and generic solutions, but also to an increasing demand for integrated information services, with open architectures [11].

The integration task can be modelled by a layered framework [11] containing three major components: enabling technologies, integration architectures, and global integration. Enabling technologies are the prerequisites for system integration, and include software engineering concepts and tools, the use of databases in different forms of applications, and the adequate subsystems networking. Integration architectures describe the interconnection and usage of the building blocks that form the system. Global integration addresses the co-ordination and fine-tuning of the system at the user interface and semantic levels.

Our approach focuses on the problem of interconnecting parts, required by the need to characterise and improve existing solutions – legacy systems analysis and integration. The conceptual framework used to instantiate the architecture is based on the message-passing paradigm, with special attention to a specific enabling technology, namely the multi-agent system paradigm from Distributed Artificial Intelligence.

2   SEMIOTICS AND BUSINESS PROCESS MODELING

Semiotics was founded as a formal theory of signs by Peirce [12], which has established three distinct fields of semiotics: syntax, semantics and pragmatics. Stamper [15] added three more levels to this theory, creating a framework which could be characterised as depicted in figure 1.

Andersen [1] defined computer semiotics as a "branch of semiotics that studies the special nature of computer-based signs and how they function in use." The semiotic approach to computing emphasises the importance of the integration of computers in social reality. As explained in [9] this is very important to make computer-based systems fit into a business organisation and integrate information technology with the social aspects that enable the successful fulfilment of business goals. Sometimes there is a risk of applying highly sophisticated technology without a clear understanding of the information circuits and information systems already in place.

Using the semiotics framework to cover the main stages of systems lifecycle, a collection of methods has been defined, which can be applied to all the systems development activities along the systems development lifecycle. These were developed under the MEASUR research programme – Method for Eliciting, Analysing and Specifying User Requirements [16]. In the current project, we are mainly interested in formalising one of these methods: the norm analysis method and in studying a new approach to communication and meta-systems analysis and integration, all based on Artificial Intelligence ideas.

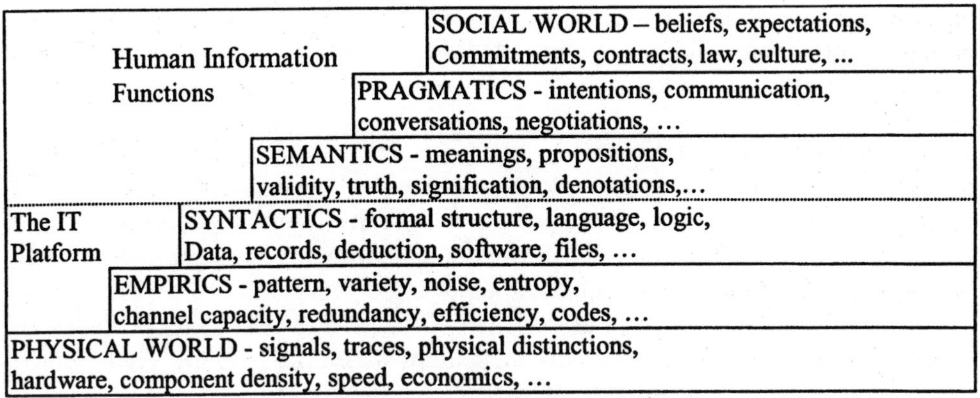

Human Information Functions	SOCIAL WORLD – beliefs, expectations, Commitments, contracts, law, culture, ...
	PRAGMATICS - intentions, communication, conversations, negotiations, ...
	SEMANTICS - meanings, propositions, validity, truth, signification, denotations,...
The IT Platform	SYNTACTICS - formal structure, language, logic, Data, records, deduction, software, files, ...
	EMPIRICS - pattern, variety, noise, entropy, channel capacity, redundancy, efficiency, codes, ...
	PHYSICAL WORLD - signals, traces, physical distinctions, hardware, component density, speed, economics, ...

Figure 1 – Semiotic Framework

In our project we try to use an intelligent agent society approach, based on the semiotic theory of social communication, formalised with the help of a logic for normative knowledge representation, namely deontic logic. The adopted approach views a business process as a process-oriented network of intelligent agents connected solely by conversations [5]. The agent can represent external agents such as customers, regulators or suppliers, and internal agents such as staff, departments, or systems. We treat these communications as semiotic acts between agents, formalised using speech-act theory [14].

3   DEONTIC LOGIC

Deontic Logic is the logic of obligations. It studies the normative use of language and is useful to reason about normative vs. non-normative behaviour [10].

Sometimes the distinction between normative and actual behaviour is not clear, in systems specification. This precludes the specification that some behaviour is illegal but nevertheless possible. However, in certain circumstances, it is very important to specify what should happen if such illegal but possible behaviour occurs. This is facilitated by the use of deontic logic.

The usual axiomatisation of Deontic Logic derives from a Tarskian Logic [17] where Kripke structures are superimposed [8]. The resulting logic is called the standard system of deontic logic, or KD. This name refers to a classification of modal logic systems defined by Brian Chellas [2]. Actually this is a modal logic with possible-worlds semantics, where an Obligation modal operator (O) is defined. However, this deontic logic system is prone to certain types of paradoxes when there are contrary-to-duty obligations involved (obligations that refer to sub-ideal situations). However, most of these paradoxes can be eliminated if the concept of "default obligation" is introduced, together with the related concepts of defeasibility that lead to the overshadowing or cancelling of certain obligations when others are enforced [6]. This requires combining deontic logic with default logic [13].

3.1   Deontic Logic and Agents

There is a small number of tentative applications of Deontic Logic to the Distributed Artificial Intelligence field, including the development of languages such as ERAE. Dubois [3] combines deontic logic with action logic, where it is possible to tell which agent(s) take responsibility in each situation change.

A deontic dyadic operator, proposed by Von Wright [18] has been used, which expresses the correlation between (a) the state in which the world is when an action has been completed and (b) the state in which the world would be if the agent had not interfered but remained passive. Von Wright has generalised his theory of actions so that it is possible to consider the presence of two or more agents in the application domain. The theory of actions becomes therefore also a theory of co-operation of agents. The development of this approach is proceeding under project ICARUS - an European Community supported program. Deontic action logic and temporal reasoning over deontic logic is also developed by Fiadeiro and Maibaum [4], in the area of multi-component computer systems specification.

4   MULTI-AGENT SYSTEM ARCHITECTURE

The current paper proposes a specific agent architecture, which has the specific purpose of enabling knowledge sharing and co-operative problem solving in a legacy systems environment. These systems are often too important and expensive to be replaced, and yet unable to be used enterprise wide.

There are three types of agents in the network: Wrappers, Personal Agents and Meta-Agents. Wrappers are the gateways between legacy systems and modern information systems. They consist essentially of APIs (Application Programming Interfaces) that encapsulate legacy systems inside abstract software layers, compatible with the communication protocols used by modern systems. These agents act, in a modern network, as front-ends for the legacy systems they encapsulate; Personal agents are functional software units, with characteristics of intelligent agents, acting on behalf of their owners, with complex internal structures that are easier to describe using abstractions such as beliefs, desires and intentions. These agents can be located throughout the organisation at machines with heterogeneous operating systems or they can be mobile agents.

However, the use of a meta agent does not necessarily imply the use of a common database. Hsu et al [7] developed a two-stage Entity-Relationship Model with mapping algorithms for consolidating user views, a knowledge base, information administration facilities and meta-data management.

5   A CASE STUDY

At the Polytechnic Institute of Setúbal, a case study was developed, concerning one of the library information circuits, namely the book acquisition process. The general model depicted in figure 3 was used.

5.1   Architecture level
The library has a book database supported by dBase tables. This database managing system is a legacy application resident in a PC computer system, on the MSDOS operating system, with no network connection. The formal accounting of all book acquisitions is kept separately, in another department, using the organisation's general accounting application. That application is supported by a terminal-based VAX/VMS platform. Finally, members of the staff have Windows machines, and are connected to the network, where they have access to Windows NT servers, UNIX servers and Netware servers.

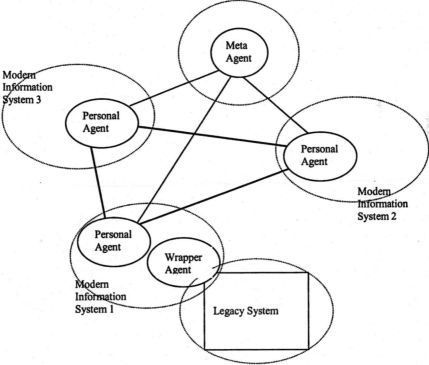

Figure 3 – Overall System Architecture

5.2   Knowledge Wrappers

In this case study two different wrappers were identified, namely the one that encapsulates the book database, and the one that encapsulates the accounting system. The first one required an ancillary Windows machine with networking capability, where the wrapping agent is implemented. The connection between the two machines is achieved by serial port communication, using a kind of terminal emulation software that was developed in Delphi, in the Windows machine, using a serial communication software component. The second wrapper was developed for the VMS system, also using a terminal emulation application, developed in Delphi. Whilst the wrapper hides from the external network most of the accounting system details, it can interface with external agents, offering a protocol or application programming interface (API), by which it can accept a limited but sufficient number of commands and types of queries, translate them into the legacy system native code, and produce back answers in the standard communications protocol format.

The wrappers were developed using Delphi 3, an object oriented rapid application development software tool. This development tool provides a serial communication component that could be used to establish a channel between a personal agent, placed in a gateway machine (connected and accessible to the other agents in the modern network) and the legacy system, which was connected to the gateway machine via serial port communications. Dedicated software had to be developed for interfacing with each legacy machine.

5.3   Personal Agents

Personal agents are acting in the organisational network on behalf of users who are ultimately responsible for these agents. Personal agents are intelligent agents that are designed to perform routine tasks which require moderate reasoning skills. These agents are built using very abstract software concepts. It is usual to describe them using mental attitudes, such as the BDI architecture model, which is based on the combination of Beliefs, Desires and Intentions. This model ascribes mental attitudes to agents in order to make it easier to discuss the specification and analysis of intelligent agents, by using an adequate abstract level of discussion.

On the implementation side, these agents consist of processes, supported by an object-oriented multi-thread programming language, namely JAVA. The use of JAVA as an infrastructure in the framework enables the easier integration with legacy systems and databases, because JAVA generates portable code allowing agents to run in most operating systems.

The overall architecture of an agent is shown in figure 4 (inspired by the JAFMAS agent architecture). JAFMAS is a software package that defines many constructs that simplify the task of agent construction and communication. It provides some basic communication, interaction and co-ordination mechanisms to application developers.

The protocol layer provide for direct agent-to-agent communication, as well as "broadcast" to a class of agents ("multicast"). Whenever communication difficulties arise, the meta-agent intervenes to perform semantic unification. A similar notion of central agent is a recommendation produced by FIPA (Foundation for Intelligent Physical Agents), which may very well become a standard, in autonomous agent architectures.

The linguistic layer defines a message structure for communication, which is based on the principles of Speech Act Theory. A semiotics stance provides an adequate conceptual framework for analysing and defining the social behaviour of the organisation, because all co-ordinated problem-solving results from conversations (semiotic acts).

The social model of an agent defines the way it interacts and co-ordinates with other agents in the system, in order to bring about a coherent solution.

5.4   Internal Agent Architecture

Each agent is a knowledge-based system, with an internal architecture constituted by a knowledge base, an inference engine and a communications interface.

The knowledge base and the inference engine are essentially modified versions of the forward chaining engine commonly found in expert systems, in order to accommodate the necessary deontic knowledge and also the communication environment.

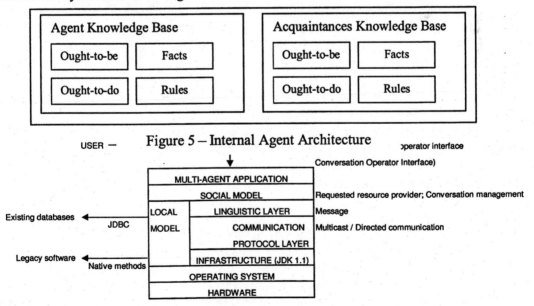

Figure 5 – Internal Agent Architecture

Figure 4 – Application architecture

An important aspect that must be take into account when designing a deontic knowledge base is the separation between sentences of the form ought-to-be and sentences of the form ought-to-do. Ought-to-be represents what is commonly accepted as ideal, but without ascribing its responsibility to a specific agent. These sentences are usually not action oriented, and therefore are included in the agent knowledge base as a general guidance to the agent behaviour. Sentences of type Ought-to-do represent actions to be performed, in the ideal situation, by a specific agent. Although the agent can choose not to perform these recommended actions it will have to take responsibility for any norm violation. In particular it must consider the impact of contrary-to-duty norms that will become active due to a primary norm violation.

Each agent maintains a self-KB and an acquaintances-KB. Each KB has 2 parts: the deontic part and the factual part. In the deontic part of the KB the agent must represent all propositions of the form ought-to-be and ought-to-do that it believes are their obligations; in the factual part of the KB the agent must represent all facts and rules it believes in.

The deontic part of the knowledge base is a cornerstone of the current work, therefore it deserves an additional explanation. It is of utmost importance to differentiate between ought-to-do and ought-to-be, or many paradoxes are bound to occur in deontic reasoning. The problem is that the theory of oughts typically expressed in standard deontic logic is impersonal, whereas when actions are to be represented it is important to ascribe responsibilities to specific agents. Following a suggestion of Meinong and Chisholm, the modal operator ought-to-be can be combined with the agency operator STIT (see to it that) in order to provide a clear semantics for ought-to-do, without the need to have two different ought operators, which could be confusing. The result is a proposal that the formula *Ought:[a stit: A]* can be taken to express the claim that *a ought to see to it that A*, or that *a is obligated to see to it that A*.

An interesting thing to note is that *Ought:[a stit: A]=>Ought:A* is valid. This seems to be a nice result since it means that the agent is never obliged to waste its time bringing about a state of affairs that, in itself, need not hold.

Another interesting result is that (using the modal belief operator *possible*) it is possible to have *Ought:A* and *Possible:[a stit:A]* without *Ought:[stit:A]*. This means that although it is desirable A, and the agent *a* has the ability to bring it about, the action to do it remains an agent's choice. Impersonal oughts do not imply personal obligations.

5.5   Meta-Agent

Besides working as a meta-data system, as described above, providing an integrated and standardised view of the data resources of the system, the meta-agent is also aware of global organisational norms and procedures, and is a referee for inter-agent problems, resulting in norms violation. The meta-agent is also knowledgeable of the idiosyncrasies of wrappers and personal agents, being therefore helpful also in resolving semantic problems in communication interactions between other agents. The meta-data system doesn't centralise all data. It does centralise however, the messages exchanged between agents, providing for adequate semantic integration.

6   CONCLUSIONS AND FUTURE WORK

The main research topics, related to integrating legacy information systems in organisations, have been outlined. Since these systems usually are agents of an information society where humans are also interacting agents, it is important to understand how software agents are able to relate to human agents. Semiotics provides a stance and a methodology for representing and capture organisational knowledge, specially normative knowledge. Distributed Artificial Intelligence provides a technology, which can be understood as a development of object-oriented systems, namely agent-based systems, that provides a framework for dealing with systems integration as a co-operative problem solving agent society. Organisational agents relationships can often be modelled by contracts that define mutual obligations – this is adequately represented with deontic logic.

We are currently researching the problem of integrating deontic logic with intentional systems using a variant of BDI logic, in order to enable the specification of agent wrappers for legacy systems in corporate information systems as well as the formalisation of social aspects concerning the overall framework.

References

Andersen, P. A Theory of Computer Semiotics: Semiotics approaches to Construction and Assessment of Computer Systems, Cambridge University Press, Cambridge, Mass., 1990.

Chellas, B.F. Modal Logic-An Introduction. Cambridge University Press, Cambridge, MA, 1980.

Dubois, E. "Use of Deontic Logic in the Requirements Engineering of Composite Systems," in: Deontic Logic in Computer Science, J. Meyer and R. Wieringa (Eds), J.Wiley&Sons, 1993.

Fiadeiro, J. and Maibaum., T., "Temporal Reasoning over Deontic Specifications," in: Journal of Logic and Computation, 1 (3), 1991.

Graham, I., "Modeling Business Processes with Agents," Object Magazine, vol.7, no.9, p21-3, 1997.

Horty, J. Deontic Logic as Founded in Nonmonotonic Logic. Annals of Mathematics and Artificial Intelligence 9, 1993.

Hsu, C., M.Bouziane, W.Cheung, J.Nogues, L.Rattner, and L.Yee, "A Metadata System for Information Modelling and Integration," in Proceedings of the 1st International Conference on Systems Integration, Morristown, 1990.

Kripke, S. A. "Semantic analysis of modal logic in normal propositional calculi". In: Z. Math. Logic Grundlagen Math. 9, 1963.

Liu, K. Semiotics Applied to Information Systems Development, Ph.D. thesis, University of Twente, Enschede, Holland, 1993.

Meyer, J. "A Different Approach to Deontic Logic: Deontic Logic Viewed as a Variant of Dynamic Logic". In: Notre Dame Journal of Formal Logic, 29(1), 1988.

Mylopoulos, J. and M. Papazoglou, "Cooperative Information Systems," IEEE Expert, Vol.12, No.5, 1997.

Peirce, C. Collected papers of Ch.S. Peirce, edited by Hartshorne and Weiss, Cambridge, Mass., 1960.

Reiter, R. A Logic for Default Reasoning. In: Artificial Intelligence 13, 1980.

Searle, J. Speech Acts – An Essay in the Philosophy of Language, Cambridge University Press, Cambridge, 1969.

Stamper, R. Information in Business and Administrative Systems, John Wiley & Sons, 1973.

Stamper, R., K. Althaus and J.Backhouse, "MEASUR: Method for Eliciting, Analysing and Specifying User Requirements," Computerised Assistance during the Information Systems Life Cycle, Olle, Verrijn-Stuart and Bhabuts (Eds), Elsevier-Science Publishers, Holland, 1988.

Tarski, A. Logic, Semantics, Metamathematics: Papers from 1923 to 1938, Clarendon Press, Oxford, 1956.

von Wright, G.H. Deontic logic. In: Mind (60), 1951.

CHAPTER 30

INFORMATION TECHNOLOGY TRENDS IN WAFER ENGINEERING, APPLICATION OF DATA MINING TECHNIQUES TO ASSIST IN PROCESS CONTROL

WM Gibbons and TM Scott
University of Ulster

Abstract

Ad hoc techniques are no longer adequate for sifting through vast amounts of data and are giving way to data mining and knowledge discovery for turning corporate data into a competitive business advantage. The commercial demand for the latter developed when companies realised the valuable resource that was hidden and undisturbed within their masses of data, and the economic advances that could be achieved were it harnessed and used in support of business decisions. This paper focuses on the significance of using data mining techniques and tools to generically enhance applications within the manufacturing industries utilising a user-centred approach. It describes how data mining methods are currently being used in a high-tech manufacturing facility to identify fundamental second order process control parameter relationships currently responsible for causing process variance within manufacturing operations. A case study is presented providing a brief insight into the application area of this research, including an outline of the current work in progress. The research knowledge presented in this paper is based on the 'on-plant' experiences gained as a participant of a data mining application in one of the larger magnetic recording manufacturers in Northern Ireland.

1   INTRODUCTION

Contemporary organisations are inundated with data, however, they have little information, even less knowledge, and perhaps no wisdom. Many companies simply hold data in record or archive format, therefore, potentially, valuable information hidden within these databases remains untapped, (McClean & Scotney, 1996). The sheer volume of data held in corporate databases, in particular, is already too great for manual analysis, and as the information within them grow, the problem is similarly compounded.

Previously, organisations failed to solve business problems due to the deficit of available data, however, to date, the problem has been reversed, as there is a plethora of obtainable data in many of today's modern organisations. Accordingly, the challenge is to find ways of distilling these large volumes of data into valuable information. Data mining and knowledge discovery in databases is an increasingly popular approach to providing an intelligent solution to this voluminous data problem. Knowledge discovery in databases is an umbrella term describing the variety of activities available for making sense of data. The term is utilised to outline the process of detecting and extracting and interpreting useful patterns and trends in. The KDD process incorporates many phases of which data mining is just one of a list of essential steps to ensure that useful information is derived from the data. Data mining is the automatic extraction of information from data, encompassing the application of a range of computing algorithms to volumes of data and the interpretation of the patterns generated by these algorithms, (Fayyad et al, 1996). The information extracted is a summary or distillation of the original data that may illuminate new and unexpected characteristics within the newly mined data.

The aim of this paper is to emphasise the application of suitable knowledge discovery (KDD) and data mining (DM) techniques within the manufacturing industry. These techniques possess the potential to enhance process control, yield learning and overall performance, as the results illustrates, within the magnetic recording engineering case-study presented. The primary phase of a data mining in manufacturing related framework is presented, summarising the strategic factors and enabling technologies that are essential for a business to conduct a data mining application. Research currently being conducted in this area is outlined in brief and results to date discussed.

2   CASE STUDY: WAFER ENGINEERING IN MANUFACTURING

The case-study described in this section involves one of the largest magnetic recording manufacturing industries. This particular organisation is engaged in the time critical fabrication of data storage products on a global basis. The facts and knowledge presented in this case-study have been obtained as a participant in a live implementation project currently in progress.

Improving process control to enhance performance, ameliorate product quality and increase productivity is an important consideration within any manufacturing industry. Accordingly it is critical to find efficient methods of both performing and achieving this acumen. The fabrication and production of components carried out within a manufacturing facility requires a vast number of complex and meticulous processes. Such extensive manufacturing operations are often carried out in clean-room environments and employ continuous quality and precision controls. A major difficulty with process control in the manufacturing industries is the extensive quantity and complexity of data and procedures involved within the fabrication process, (Shim & Mathon, 1993). In this particular case study, magnetic recording engineering involves the collection of large quantities of real-time data on various composite operations within the production process. Often, process data is collected from more than one database, hence problems analysis and decomposition are laborious tasks. The complexity and magnitude of operations performed in the fabrication process, inevitably impacts upon process control, making it a cumbersome procedure. Current methods of process management employed within this manufacturing case study, such as SPC (statistical process control) and feedback control models, have proved to be inefficient in providing adequate information management to enhance process control. This has caused a reduction in product quality and productivity in this particular manufacturing industry as engineers are unable to exercise controlled changes due to the limited real-time framework involved. As a result, temporal and monetary detriment have increased in this high cost, time critical environment. This case study highlights the complexity and intricacy involved in wafer manufacturing processes and emphasises the need for new process control management methods. These needs are addressed in the following section, which discusses the current research in progress within this environment.

3   CURRENT RESEARCH

Compared to most discrete manufacturing industries, semiconductor wafer fabrication encounters composite process, quality and performance control difficulties. Some of these specific challenges include:

- a large number of process steps (approximately exceeding 250 process steps per product).
- a high re-entrant process flow (lots visit the same equipment multiple times).
- an intermixture of single wafer and lot-based process operations.
- the batching of multiple lots that share process recipes and processing times.
- some process steps have material life thresholds that predict when subsequent processes must take place - failure to comply, yields produce scrap or rework.
- equipment alignment and calibration issues which require some process steps to return to the exact piece of equipment, or variant thereof, that processed the lot in a previous critical step.

These constraints must be considered by planning and scheduling systems when making crucial business decisions. If the constraints are not represented in the planning system, the actual performance of a facility compared to the planned performance can result in a significant degree of error. Additionally, as the semiconductor device design evolves, new process constraints are continuously added, making the planning process more complex. To date the manufacturing process has become so complex that the number of constraints, their interrelations, and the need to consider numerous scenarios is more than humans can handle without sophisticated computer-based tools to assist them, (Shim & Mathon, 1993).

Research currently being conducted in conjunction with the case study discussed in section two involves two major objectives with the potential to improve manufacturing process control. These are outlined below:

1. Primarily, the identification of fundamental second order process control parameter relationships currently responsible for causing process variance within magnetic recording manufacturing operations.

2. Secondly, the development of a generic, user-centred, practical data mining framework to enable the application of future data mining projects in manufacturing.

Both aspects of this research are outlined in brief in the following sub-sections.

3.1   Identification of second order process control parameters

The first aspect of current research in this area involves the identification of second order process control parameters. The case study discussed in section two outlines the major process control, time delay and yield problems prominent in the magnetic recording industry in particular, including the intricacy of the process operations. One such operation involves plasma machines, which are widely utilised during critical steps within the thin film recording head and semiconductor manufacturing processes. The complexity of the physics involved and inability to monitor the plasma characteristics on a real-time basis makes the control of this process equipment very difficult.

Work is currently being carried out, in accordance with the manufacturing case study, on one of the most critical process steps during the manufacture of thin film recording heads. Figure 1 illustrates the processes and parameters involved. Statistical process control is applied to measured results before and after the plasma processing step (Meas1 and Meas2) of the manufacturing process and at the final test results (Ftest), respectively.

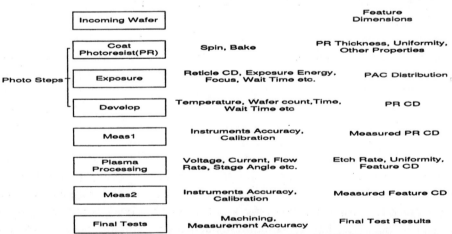

Figure 1: Illustrates the process steps & parameters involved in the Ftest operation

Figure 2 depicts the various control loops involved in this critical process operation. The objective of these controls are to achieve the final test results (Ftest) within the product specification or target measurement.

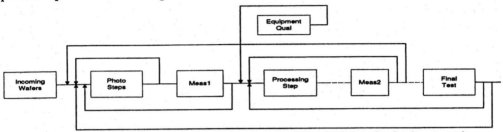

Figure 2: Illustrates the control loops involved in obtaining the final test results

The drawbacks of the current method are immense, primarily because SPC is applied off-line which means that the corrective actions are taken after the out-of-control actions have occurred. Secondly, the feedback time between the point at which the SPC charts are analysed and the process step is controlled constitutes an extremely lengthy control loop. Similarly, the feedback time between Meas2 and the processing step concerned may range from two to four days. Feedback between the final test results (Ftest) and the processing step can range from anything up to five weeks. When a fault is discovered, substantial quantities of wafers may have already been processed on these machines, resulting in these wafers becoming redundant.

As part of this research project, real-time equipment information is collected and sent to a central database. The real-time equipment parameters involved are characteristically auto-correlated and cross-correlated, rendering traditional SPC approach no longer valid. As a result of the vast amount of data generated for each individual run (over a hundred parameters) and also the inherent non-linear nature of the plasma process, difficulties arise and it becomes extremely laborious for an engineer to analyse such volumes of data using basic statistical software. Consequently, a more effective and systematic approach is necessary, (Fan & Wu, 1995).

Current research has illustrated that a greater level of process control can be achieved using a predictive model. This may be accomplished by applying multivariate or neural network analysis techniques on process data, including production lot history data, in-line physical measurement data, real-time equipment data, equipment maintenance data and end-of-line product test and final yield data. This model may be integrated within a real-time knowledge-based-system to provide engineers with real-time run-to-run control in a user-friendly format using feedback and feed-forward control predictive models.

Due to the complexity of the equipment parameters involved and the highly correlated nature between them, it was necessary to employ multivariate analysis techniques such as Principal Component Analysis (PCA), (Esbensen et al, 1994). This is a powerful technique which applies data reduction techniques on highly correlated data variables, whilst simplifying the analysis process Everitt & Dunn, (1994). An in-depth analysis was carried out on over one hundred parameters using the Unscrambler software's (by

Camo) PCA technique.

A predictive model was built using The Unscramblers multivariate analysis technique Partial Least Square Regression (PLS) and a feed-forward backpropagation three layer neural network (Esbensen et al, 1994). PLS was used to primarily reduce the dimension of the data, the results of which were used as input for the neural network. This approach succeeded in accelerating the training time of the neural network and also reduced the chances of over-training.

Three different models were built and explored individually. In the first model process parameters included wafer feature dimensions, photo step process parameters, plasma machine data, Meas1 and Meas2, were used to model and predict the final test results (Ftest). Promising results were obtained as illustrated by figures 3 (a & b).

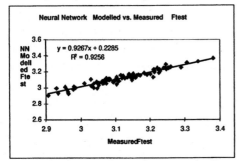 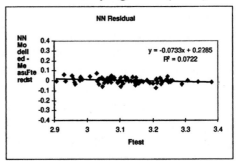

Figures 3 a & b : Illustrates the Ftest results of the neural network predictive model

The accurate prediction of the final test results at this stage has incurred two significant benefits. Primarily, the neural network modelled results (using ISL's Clementine software) proved to be a superior final predictor to the final test results in comparison to Meas2 results, providing a better level of control. Secondly, as a result of accurately predicted final test results at Meas2, it has been established that the lengthy control loop prior to this step is redundant.

In the second model, all input parameters except Meas2 are used to model the final test results. As a result, as soon as the plasma processing step was over, it was possible to predict the final test results and take corrective action for the next wafer in line if required. To date, it was not possible to implement control action for the next wafer waiting to be finally tested as equipment performance could only be assessed after Meas2 is noted. Results of the second model have also incurred additional benefits as it enables control to be taken immediately after the processing step without waiting for the Meas2 results, thus reducing the control loop by up to four days. Another advantage incurred by this model is that Meas2 and associated process steps may also be eliminated which would shorten the overall process cycle time and reduce line yield losses at these steps.

In the third model, modelling is conducted immediately after Meas1 using previous run equipment data. This model demonstrates that preventative actions can be taken so that the expensive action of scraping or reworking wafers could be avoided, achieving run-to-run control in the process.

At the moment, this research is in the process of working towards implementing these models to be part of the final testing (Ftest) control strategy. As part of a previous research project, a real-time knowledge-based-system was specifically developed for the engineers to provide them with automated SPC chart and alarm generation. The predictive models will eventually be integrated into this knowledge-based-system to provide engineers with real-time information to make data analysis and interpretation more efficient.

Implementation of predictive models has proved that they have the potential to achieve real-time run-to-run control when utilised as a process control mechanism within the manufacturing environment. These models have not only reduced the length of the control loop considerably, but they also provided a better level of control for the critical parameter final test results (Ftest). The integration of these models within a real-time knowledge- based-system will make analysis and interpretation of vast amounts of data feasible on a real-time basis. The possible elimination of certain process steps not only constitutes a more condensed cycle time, it also reduces line yield loses at these particular steps. Since these predictive models are characteristically generic, they may be applied it to other process operations and areas within the manufacturing environment.

3.2 User-centred data mining framework

Semiconductor manufacturing is characterised by it's increases complexity. Improving this situation is even more challenging, especially for the engineer who must monitor manufacturing control. This has resulted in a need for a business and user-centred approach to defining a practical process structure for future data mining projects. The second aspect of this research concerns the completition of the development of a generic, user-centred, practical data mining framework to enable the application of future data mining projects in manufacturing to benefit from the experience of previous projects. This framework consists of eight major steps as illustrated by figure 4.

Each phase will consist of a series of iterative steps that should be ensued by the user, expert and business in order to facilitate a successful data mining application. This framework is generic in nature, therefore it may easily be applied within other manufacturing sectors. However, for the purpose of this paper, detail presented on the first phase – business oriented strategic factors and enabling technologies, is specifically adapted towards the electronics industry in particular.

The first phase of this process structure provides a framework defining a series of strategic factors and enabling technologies that modern fabs must employ to facilitate data mining in order to enable optimal control of their manufacturing processes. The necessary strategic factors of this phase are considered, followed by the essential enabling technologies.

Strategic practices may be categorised into four basic types of practices at which a fab must excel in order to realise excellent manufacturing performance. These categories are outlined below, they must possess:

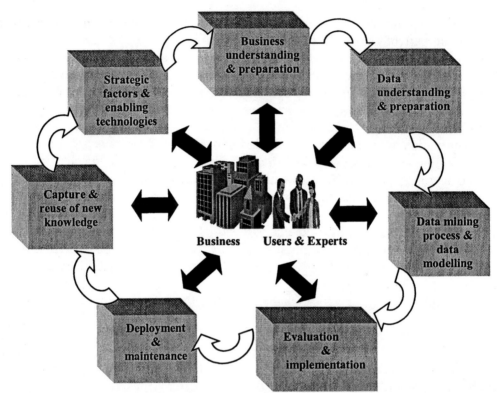

Figure 4: Illustrates the phases of the user-centred practical data mining framework

1. Computer systems that provide strong process control, excellent data collection and analysis capabilities. It must be able to expeditiously pinpoint the causes of yield loss and the sources for losses of wafer throughput. The fab must be able to recognise when processing is being done incorrectly, or better yet, prevent misprocessing entirely with equipment controls, system controls and procedural checks.

2. An organisation that not only executes the manufacturing processes well, but is also proficient at problem recognition and problem solving.

3. The internal technical talent as well as the requisite support from vendors to expeditiously make modifications to product, process and equipment in order to implement changes that have been identified by problem-solving efforts as desirable or necessary to improve manufacturing performance.

4. Effective procedures for managing the introduction of new process flows, machines and products. The economic life of many of these is on average, three to four years with unit prices for the products in particular, declining rapidly over this period. Therefore, it is economically important to introduce new process flows and it's equipment as soon as possible so as to realise good yields and high throughput of the

process flow early in it's life. As a result, this will quickly assist in the control of better yields and future wafer throughput.

Manufacturing covers a broad spectrum of industries each with it's own special production methods, however, a manufacturing organisations must possess the following enabling technologies implemented among their existing systems in order to accommodate data mining

- The incorporation of a datawarehouse on top of the IT landscape to profit from the OLAP technology.
- The provision of distributed and heterogeneous data access, using ODBC.
- Appliance and manipulation of parallel hardware and data access technologies to ameliorate performance and also yield scalability.
- The use of multi-dimensional servers which can act to pre-cluster data and also improve data access performance.
- A number of modern reporting tools to verbalise, tabulate or visualise knowledge.

Digesting millions of data points, each with tens of hundreds of thousands of measurements are generally beyond a scientists human capability. This tedious and time-consuming task can be turned over to data mining techniques for data reduction, as data mining functions act as an interface between the user and large datasets. Data mining has the potential to computationally extract previously unknown and potentially useful information from data. It asks questions about an organisation, that members of the organisation have not thought to ask and it also has the capacity to discover relationships within data that reports and human analysis can not effectively reveal. The potential benefits of the application of data mining techniques are colossal provided the correct tools and techniques are used. Due to the unrealistic volumes of data available within many organisations today, data mining offers a realistic solution to an otherwise impossible manual data analysis task.

4   CONCLUSION

The case study presented in this paper has emphasised the need to employ tighter process control techniques in manufacturing processes in the form of data mining techniques. This research has illustrated the need for a business and user-centred approach to defining a practical process structure for future data mining projects. A brief outline of this proposed eight phase framework was discussed in detail. It has also demonstrated the benefit of using neural network and multivariate analysis techniques to assist in process control and the identification of second order process control parameters using predictive models. Results to date have demonstrated that predictive models can achieve run-to-run control when utilised as a process control mechanism. This research has highlighted that data mining may most profitably be used in manufacturing to identify areas where improvement exercises should be directed such as in process control as manufacturing organisations are continually striving to cut the operating costs of their manufacturing processes. In such an environment the application of data mining techniques is therefore best directed at achieving this goal as, *"data holds and hides decision-making knowledge, freeing this knowledge is the key to increased performance, service excellence and business success in the information age"* (Shim & Mathon, 1993).

References

Esbensen, K Midtgård, T, Schönkopf, S (1994) *Multivariate Analysis in Practice,* Camo AS, Trondheim.

Everitt, B & Dunn, G, (1994) "Reducing the Dimensionality of Multivariate Data: Principal Components and Correspondence Analysis", in *Applied Multivariate Data Analysis,* Edward Arnold, London.

Fan, H-T & Wu, S, (1995) "Case Studies on Modelling Manufacturing Processes Using Artificial Neural Networks", Journal of Engineering for Industry, Vol.117, No.3, PP.412-417, 1995.

Fayyad, U, Piatetsky-Shapiro, Smyth, P & Uthurusamy, R (1996) *"Advances in Knowledge Discovery and Data Mining",* AAAI Press.

McClean, S & Scotney, B, (1996) "The data mining report", Unicom Seminars Ltd, Middlesex.

Shim, K & Mathon, A, (1993) "Simulation of Manufacturing Models and it's Learning with Artificial Networks", PROC of International Joint Conference on Neural Networks, Vol.1, pp991 - 994, 1993.

CHAPTER 31

THE ROLE OF REPOSITORIES IN INTEGRATING INFORMATION SYSTEMS AND ENTERPRISE KNOWLEDGE

Nektarios Georgalas
British Telecom Labs

Abstract

Unstable market conditions oblige enterprises to embark on changes in their business practices in order to remain competitive. To enhance the success factor of the change an organisation needs to have clear and well-specified knowledge of its entire domain. Additionally, the organisation must own information systems that are flexible, evolvable and able to effectively store, manage and manipulate the knowledge, even on fluid changing conditions. The present paper studies the role repositories play in integrating patterns of knowledge with the enterprise IS. The analysis is conducted in the context of a component-based environment that is built around a knowledge repository. Initially, we investigate the aspects of knowledge needed be represented within an enterprise. Then, we describe three models, namely, Enterprise, Information Systems and Legacy Model, which manage to capture all the facets of knowledge. Special emphasis is given to the construction of the Legacy Model. Through this model the repository, actually, manages to integrate IS and Enterprise Knowledge. Finally, an example is described to practically present the elaborated ideas.

1 INTRODUCTION

Over the past decade an enormous change has been realised in the market forces that influences the traditional business practices. This change has been brought about because of different requirements, such as social, political, technical and economic, and exerts pressures on enterprises to respond in a timely and cost effective way. Information system (IS) developers are challenged by this fluid conditions to implement systems that can meet the requirements of modern organisations.

Furthermore, enterprises experience the effects of the integration and evolution of Information Technology (IT). Organisational IS are transformed/re-engineered in order to align with the IT trends. However, the likelihood of success in every attempt of change is directly dependent on the capacity of the organisation to *effectively* manipulate the Enterprise Knowledge. Companies should invest in technologies and apply approaches that would ensure:

- Thorough acquisition of knowledge about the organisational systems and the types of information they manage
- Explicit specification of this information in conceptual models and storing such that it can be transferable, exchangeable and thus a shareable resource among the enterprise stakeholders
- Effective integration, re-using and management of the knowledge in order to drive successfully the evolution of legacy and the development of new IS.

In this paper we focus on the role repositories play in providing viable integration solutions for the enterprise IS and knowledge. Investigating repositories into the context of the DELOS component environment we aim at presenting their efficient integrating capabilities for systems and knowledge. Following a short introduction of DELOS (section 2), the paper discusses the multidimensional aspects of the enterprise knowledge and the models that capture it, namely, *Enterprise, Information Systems* and *Legacy Model* (section 3), the way the legacy model is produced and integrated with the other models (section 4) and an example that practically exhibits all the analysis. Finally the paper concludes with a number of observations (section 6).

2   A COMPONENT-BASED ENVIRONMENT

In an attempt to provide the grounds for the development of flexible Information Systems we implemented DELOS, a component-based infrastructure (Klimathianakis et al, 1997). The idea behind DELOS is the fabrication and deployment of *network-centric* applications that are built up by co-operative software components (SC) which communicate exploiting network services. The main innovation in DELOS is the employment of a central semantic repository that aims at overcoming the problem of insufficient meta-data management other component-based environments occur. Each software component is specified in the repository by means of a behavioural model that describes the states the component may get into. Similarly, the repository stores the configuration models for each DELOS application in order to describe the way its constituent components interact. It is obvious, hence, that the DELOS repository is key for the smooth operation of the environment.

The framework's repository is based on the *Semantic Index System (SIS)* (Constantopoulos et al, 1994). The SIS is a persistent storage mechanism based on an object-oriented semantic data model. It implements the *TELOS* knowledge representation language (Mylopoulos, 1992). The primitives that build up the knowledge base are *individuals* that represent entity classes and *attributes*, which declare binary and one-way relationships between individuals. The semantic mechanisms supported by the repository are:

- *classification*, or inverse *instantiation*, by which individuals or attributes can instantiate classes belonging to a higher abstraction level. That gives the flexibility to have hierarchies of abstraction. In SIS the classification is unbounded and defines an infinite hierarchy of abstraction levels called T (for the lowest), S, M1, M2 etc
- *generalisation*, or inverse *specialisation*, by which classes of the same abstraction level can construct isA hierarchies
- *aggregation*, or inverse *decomposition*, by which composite (alternatively known in literature as aggregate or structured or complex) objects can be represented.

The contents of SIS can be retrieved by means of a query interface that provides search through multiple and recursive conditions as well as navigation search across the entire semantic network (Dadouris et al, 1995a), (Dadouris et al, 1995b). A query can reference both schema and meta-schema levels. An example of SIS is given in Fig. 1.

3   A CONCEPTUAL INTEGRATION BASIS FOR IS AND ENTERPRISE KNOWLEDGE

The implementation of a structural or process Change within the organisation's scope more or less involves the re-engineering of the legacy or the development of new IS. In this situation, the knowledge needed be represented relates to:

- the environment in which the system will function and the ways the system will interact with other entities within its context
- the information the system will be expected to store and its conceptual relation with the rest of the Enterprise context
- the method, approach or framework upon which the design process progresses
- the design rationale that describes the reasons behind certain decisions taken
- the system's design models that will guide its implementation and maintenance phase and
- the operational data that will reflect the changes occurred in the business processes.

The aforementioned aspects describe the multi-dimensional space where the Enterprise Knowledge is captured. These different dimensions are related to either the IS or the information per se. Both, IS and information, occur the need for efficient modelling and management of meta-data. IS meta-data describes issues like the behaviour of software components, the configuration of specific applications or system designs. Meta-data for the organisational information involves methods to model operational data, methods to model business processes and structures, ways of working and design rationales. All in all, we gather that the Enterprise Knowledge aspects move along 3 basic lines:

- knowledge pertinent to the *description of business processes and structure* (this knowledge body is produced by applying business modelling methods),

- knowledge that is *stored and tightly-coupled with the company's legacy systems* (mostly handled by the company's Operations Support Systems), commonly known as *operational* or *raw data*, and
- knowledge relevant to the *specification of the business IS components*.

The repository of our component-based environment assembles descriptions of all the facets enterprise knowledge is composed of. It provides for sufficient management of meta-data through the supported hierarchy of abstraction layers. Consequently, the repository guarantees, by all means, the *conceptual* integration of IS (third category) with high-level (first category) and low-level (second category) knowledge.

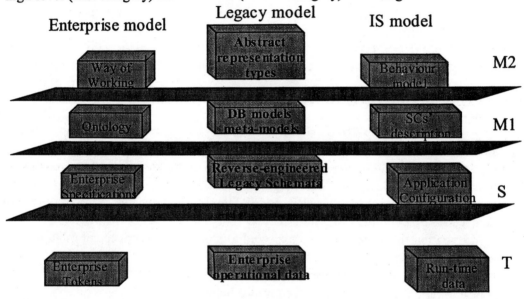

Figure 1: The repository's contents

The repository's contents are represented as 3 different models, namely the *Enterprise Model*, the *Legacy Model* and the *Information System Model*. All are tightly integrated and scope over four levels of abstraction, the Meta-meta level (M2), the Meta level (M1), the Simple class level (S) and the Token level (T). Levels M1 and M2 refer to meta-data, independent of any specific enterprise. Levels S and T correspond to specific enterprise data. A presentation of the repository's contents is given in Figure 1.

3.1 Enterprise Model

The *Enterprise Model* is concerned with specifications of the structure of an enterprise. The term is used to collectively refer to all the respects pertinent to the modelled universe of discourse. It encompasses conceptual schemata that depict goals, requirements, designs of business processes and structures that specify formally an enterprise domain. The conceptual representations at the M2 level give a generic description of a Way of Working (WoW). Actually, they specify the design rationale behind the business analysis methodology used. The M1 level provides meta-models that conform to the M2 WoW model and specify a certain method to describe design artefacts. Particularly for our framework, a generic methodology has been invented called *Enterprise Requirements Analysis* (ERA) (Loucopoulos et al, 1996) which consists of a set of meta-models aiming at capturing any knowledge aspect within an enterprise. The M1 meta-models enable the user to represent the particular domain schemata of different enterprises at the S layer of the repository. Finally, business data (tokens) occupy the T-level.

3.2   Information System Model

The *Information System Model* describes the SCs, the application configurations and the applications execution. M2 hosts the behaviour meta-model, which highlights the Way of Working of a SC. This is the Finite State Machine model mentioned in the description of DELOS. M1 contains the descriptions of the implemented SCs that comply with the behaviour model. The components may co-operate to configure specific applications that perform automated tasks in the enterprise environment. These configuration schemata reside on the S level. The T layer is used for the run-time data produced during an application's execution. The co-existence of IS models with Enterprise models and data in SIS achieves the integration of IS and enterprise knowledge enabling a smooth transition from domain concepts, requirements and knowledge to pragmatic system implementations.

3.3   Legacy Model

The *Legacy Model* is primarily concerned with detailed specifications of the information that is managed by the organisation's *legacy* systems[1]. The legacy frequently lacks analytical design documentation of how the information it handles is structured. Hence, legacy entities, associations and constraints remain hidden and tightly-knitted with the business logic within the applications. Our framework adopts a method of 3 steps aiming at building up the Legacy Model. The method is described in section 4 while here we present the structure of the model within the repository.

Schemata that model the legacy information are introduced into the S-level. Business stakeholders that apply ERA may identify within the new models concepts that acquire sense in the ERA context. Hence, links could connect legacy classes with the ERA meta-models presenting a newly discovered volume of knowledge that, along with the *Legacy*, may be considered as part of the *Enterprise model*. Fig.1 presents T-level as containing the Enterprise Legacy records. In real terms, these records remain residents in the legacy DMBSs and are not physically replicated in the repository. What Figure 1 actually aims at is to pinpoint the records conceptual gravity and positioning in relation to the rest of

---

[1] The name of the model (*Legacy*) is attributed to the legacy DBMSs

the repository models. That is, that the legacy records carry the same conceptual abstraction as the *Enterprise tokens* do in the *Entrerprise Model*. From a physical point of view, however, while the records are produced by business operations and hence, as stated, reside in several database systems, the tokens intend to serve the business modelling process and therefore populate the SIS. The Legacy DBMSs may support different data-models for structuring the operational data, such as relational, hierarchical, network, object oriented. The M1-level hosts meta-models that specify the semantics used by the data-models. Links between the M and S schemata manage to pertain the database identity of the legacy entities and to give information on *where* (the network location) and *how* (the form) the legacy classes are stored in a certain DBMS. Finally, the M2-level is populated by classes of abstract data representation types. These types provide a generic "guide" (*rationale*) of how data representation models are constructed independently of proprietary, method-specific features[2].

4   KNOWLEDGE FROM DATA

Before contriving the Legacy Model, the DELOS environment could provide access only to the information stored in the repository. In this situation other types of stores, which kept the operational data, remained neglected by tools performing within DELOS. This was mainly because DELOS initially aimed at the development of new systems and did not target to embracing the legacy. Nonetheless, the environment's design was extensible enough to encourage the deployment of a method that would manage its unification with legacy systems. The method has been presented in (Georgalas, 1998b). Here, we summarise the basic steps of it.

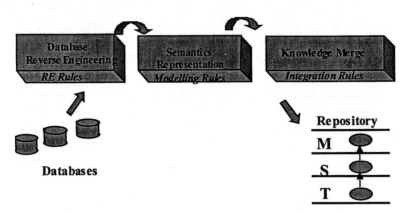

Figure 2: Building the Legacy Model

---

[2] The development of such meta-meta-model is currently under progress.

In the first step, the method's objective is to acquire knowledge about the types of persistent information stored and managed by the organisational IS. This objective is achieved by closely analysing and reverse-engineering the legacy. This is a laborious process considering the fact that in the past decades companies used data management systems where data logic was tightly coupled with business logic. For this reason, database reverse-engineering requires a methodological strategy that will enable the unveiling of concealed concepts. In (Georgalas, 1998a), we thoroughly examine the case of relational databases and we describe a set of rules that provide for the detection of such concepts. Actually, this particular rule set assists in the identification of semantic formations in structured data. Despite the specialisation of the study there were valuable generic lessons learned, especially from the work carried out at the second stage of the method.

The second step involves the representation of the extracted knowledge. We used the TELOS knowledge representation language, which is the syntax supported by the framework's repository. A set of potential modelling alternatives using TELOS semantics was proposed for the reverse-engineered concepts. This work resulted in advancing the logical schemata of databases into conceptual. The advantage of TELOS is the simple, however expressive, semantics set it supports and its capacity to explicitly express *constraints*. Manipulating the TELOS semantics to describe relations (tables) we generalised and concluded that it is possible to realise a minimum set of semantics which may represent the logical data structures databases organise their data by. That is, the experience gained in the second step of our method founded the basis for a deeper investigation of the issue of such *Abstract Data Types* which, essentially, are captured in Fig. 1 at the fourth level of the Legacy Model.

The final stage of the method relates to the integration of the Enterprise Knowledge. After enhancing our understanding about the types of information the organisation manages with its systems, we are at the position to interrelate and group the concepts into different domains. These domains might be *disjoint* i.e. they might handle different types of information, or they might be *overlapping* i.e. there is information commonly shared by more than one domain. Assuming the example of a service providing company, the *customer domain*, which includes information related to business customers, appears to be disjoint with the *business management domain*, which is involved with business management type of information. However, the customer domain may be overlapping with the *billing domain* since billing systems need manipulate customer information to provide a consistent billing service. A different type of integration achieved is what we call the *viewpoint integration*. As it has already been mentioned, classes belonging to the S-level schemata of the Legacy Model can instantiate meta-classes residing at the M-level of the Legacy Model but can also be associated with M meta-classes of the Enterprise Model if they acquire sense in the *ERA* context. In other words, reverse-engineered classes can be viewed from a Data-Model and an Enterprise Ontology's viewpoint (see Fig. 1). This is an asset provided by the repository through the support of abstraction layers. A good example is given in section 3.3.

5   AN EXAMPLE

A simple example is presented in this section in order to realise practically the aforementioned ideas. The case is illustrated in Fig.3.

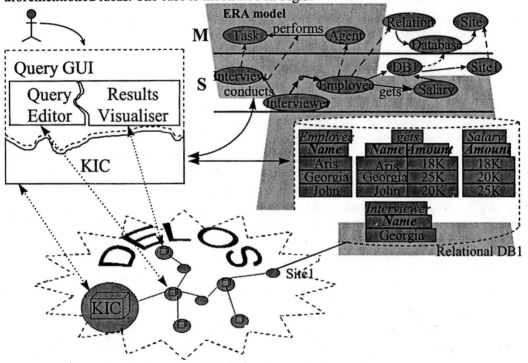

Figure 3: An example

Let us call *DB1* a relational database that resides on *SITE1*, a node of the company's network. Assume DB1 hosts only 4 tables: *Employee, Salary, gets* and *Interviewer*. By reverse-engineering the relational schema we get three entities and two entity associations that form the *Employee gets Salary* and *Interviewer isA Employee* conceptual model. This model will be introduced in the S-level of SIS and corresponds to the *Reverse-Engineered Legacy Schema* of the *Legacy Model*. The user may run an application that customises the SIS editor (Fig.3) in order to populate the SIS. The TELOS code used for this purpose is:

```
TELL Individual Employee in S_Class
      end Employee
TELL Individual Salary in S_Class
      end Salary
TELL Individual Interviewer in S_Class isA Employee
      end Interviewer
TELL Attribute gets
```

```
Components
        from: Employee
        to: Salary
in S_Class
end gets
```

Two meta-models appear on M. One is part of the *ERA ontology* (*Enterprise Model*) and the other describes features of the relational data-model -it corresponds to the *DB meta-model* of the *Legacy Model*. The class *Employee* of the reverse-engineered schema is simultaneously an instance of the ERA and the relational meta-model. The legacy schema is extended with classes, which provide information about the database the entities belong to and its location across the network. Specifically, we have represented that *Employee* exists as a *relation* in a *database, DB1*, which resides on a network *Site, Site1*.

In this example we avoided depicting into SIS specifications of the illustrated DELOS components. Instead, the figure presents the way an application is configured and runs in the environment. The particular case describes a query mechanism that consists of a *query editor* where the user edits his/her query, the *Knowledge Integrator Component (KIC)* (Georgalas, 1998a) where the query is processed and a *results visualiser* that visually displays the query results to the user. The components co-operate closely to perform the application's operations although they may reside on different network sites.

6   CONCLUSION

Our framework utilises a knowledge repository and a component-based environment in order to integrate IS with high- and low-level knowledge of an Enterprise. The intertwining of operational information meta-descriptions, through the reverse-engineered schemata, with business models and IS specifications achieves the integration of systems and knowledge at a conceptual level. Additionally, the configuration of applications, which may access the repository and the legacy systems accomplishes the integration at a functional level.

The Enterprise, by using this framework, manages to add value to its operational data. This happens because the raw data is mirrored in the repository through the reverse-engineered schemata, although it adheres to be structured in flat data-stores. This arrangement enriches the horizontal structure of the data with a vertical dimension of analysis and process that is granted by the hierarchy of abstraction layers the repository supports.

This framework does not emerge as a panacea for all the stated problems it is called to address. It makes, however, a substantial contribution by bringing into the game repository technology as the substantial means for the integration of IS and knowledge. We hope the ideas put forward could be of assistance to others.

References

Bernstein, P.A. Dayal, U. (1994) 'An Overview of Repository Technology', Proceedings of the 20th VLDB Conference, Santiago, Chile.

Bernstein, P.A. (1997) 'Repositories and Object Oriented Databases', Proceedings of BTW Conference, editors Dittrich, K.R. and Geppert, A., Springer-Verlag, Ulm, Germany.

Bubenko, J.A. (1996) 'Enterprise knowledge management and Organisational Learning', Proceedings of the "Requirements Engineering in a Changing World" Workshop in CAiSE96, Crete, Greece.

Constantopoulos, P., Doerr, M. (1994) The Semantic Index System: A brief presentation. On-line at http://www.ics.forth.gr/proj/isst/Systems/sis.

Dadouris, C. Dorr, M. (1995a) "SIS-Programmatic Query Interface. Reference Manual", Working Paper#3, Institute of Computer Science, Foundation for Research and Technology, Crete, Greece.

Dadouris, C. Dorr, M. Kizlaridou, S. Prekas, N. (1995b) 'SIS-Query Interpreter: An Interactive program to Use PQI functions', Institute of Computer Science, Foundation for Research and Technology, Crete, Greece.

Darling, C.B. (1996) How to integrate your Data Warehouse. On-line at http://www.datamation.com/Plugin/issues/1996/may15/05beval1.html.

Georgalas, N. (1998a) Enterprise Data and Knowledge Integration using Repository Technology. MPhil Thesis, Information Systems Engineering Group, Department of Computation, UMIST, Manchester, UK.

Georgalas, N. (1998b) 'Can Operational Data become the driving force for Business Change?', Proceedings of the Conference in New Information Technology (NIT98), Athens, Greece.

Klimathianakis, P. Loucopoulos, P. (1997) 'DELOS - A Repository Based Environment for Developing Network Centric Applications', Proceedings of the 9th International Conference CAiSE97, Barcelona, Spain.

Loucopoulos, P. Kavakli, E. Louridas, P. Prekas, N. Tzanaki, A. (1996) 'The Enterprise Requirements Analysis (ERA) Approach', Information Systems Engineering Group, Dept of Computation, UMIST, Manchester, UK.

Mylopoulos, J. Borgida A., Matthias J., Koubarakis M. (1990) 'TELOS: Representing Knowledge About Information Systems', ACM Transactions on Information Systems, Vol. 8, No 4.

Mylopoulos, J. (1992) 'Conceptual Modelling and Telos' in "Conceptual Modelling, Databases and CASE", editors Loucopoulos, P., Zicari, R., Wiley Publications.

CHAPTER 32

CONTEXTUALIZATION IN COMPUTER - MEDIATED COMMUNICATION: THEORY INFORMS DESIGN

Dov Te'eni and David G. Schwartz
Bar-Ilan University

Abstract

Dispersed organizations rely on distributed information processing, communication and collaboration. But this requires thoughtful information processing and rich communication. This paper begins with a discussion of the communication process and then focuses on one particular communication strategy – contextualization. In contextualization, the action 'bottom line' is augmented with context information drawn from the organizational knowledge base. We then describe the design of a system, we call HyperMail, that supports contextualization. HyperMail is designed to enrich e-mail with knowledge taken from the organizational knowledge base.

1   THEORY

Today's organizations must rely on thoughtful communication and learning (Schein, 1993). Although sophisticated information technology is rapidly becoming a necessary tool in dispersed organizations, it cannot guarantee success for at least two reasons. One is that common technology is not always designed to cope with states of high uncertainty and high novelty that are characteristic of today's diverse environments (Daft & Lengel, 1984) nor are they capable of supporting thoughtful communication and learning (Boland, Tenkasi & Te'eni, 1994). Two, technology alone cannot overcome some of structural communication problems that arise in communication across organizational cultures.

A better understanding of inter and intra-organizational communication is needed to inform designers of information technology how to better support thoughtful communication beyond the routine exchange of data found in common electronic data interchange. We therefore look not only at the media of communication (fax, e-mail etc.) but at the message too. By message we mean the organization of the material communicated: the amount of material transmitted and its structure. Clearly, a comprehensive picture of communication must include both messages and media. Moreover, a deeper understanding of communication should clarify how people decide on a message and media. Thoughtful communication is needed not only because of higher complexity in the message communicated (Galbraith, 1977), but also because of the knowledge differences between the communicating parties. For example, communication between different organizational cultures, e.g., engineers versus managers, requires elaborate messages and descriptions of context (Schein, 1993). Given the need for thoughtful communication, it is disturbing to find very little guidance on how to provide it.

1.1   A model of communication in organizations
A learning organization can be modelled as a system in which actors act on evolving knowledge. For example, Boland et. al. (1994) characterized knowledge as the collection of actors' interpretations of the relevant world and argued that communicating these interpretations will support actions. Communication can play a crucial role in translating learning into action if it is effective (Levitt & March, 1996). We expand this general direction of communication for action to define specific goals of communication.

We present here a general framework for placing goals of communication (to be defined below) into a broader view of organizational communication. These are the elements of the proposed model:
1.   Environmental factors: two classes of given inputs: i) task and situational factors, and ii) individual characteristics;
2.   Communication process: a goal oriented process of communication, which includes communication strategies and two design variables: message and media;
3.   Communication impact in relation to its goal.

Each element is now described briefly (see Te'eni & Schwartz, 1998, for a more detailed description). Communication can be evaluated in terms of 1) the product of communication in relation to its function, and 2) the receiver's understanding of the message in relation to the sender's intentions for the communication. Habermas' (1981) theory of communicative action can be used to examine the validity of each communicative act. A communicative action assumes four conditions to be valid:
1.   it is comprehensible so that the receiver can understand the sender,
2.   it is true so that the receiver can share the sender's knowledge,
3.   intentions are expressed truthfully so that the receiver can trust the sender,
4.   the communication is appropriate within some normative context so that the receiver can agree with the sender within this value system.

The starting point of the communication process is the goals of organizational communication such as commanding action, controlling action and influencing. Given some goal in mind, the process of communication continues with 1) the selection of communication strategies for exchanging the message, 2) the choice of media, and 3) the design of messages.

Strategies. Communication strategies are means for achieving communicative goals. One such strategy is *contextualization*, i.e., building an explicit and multi-layer interpretation of the issue as opposed to concentrating on the task-related information, the 'bottom line' message. Context is usually built of layers around the core message that explain how an action can be performed, or how it can be decomposed into sub-actions, what is the motivation for the action, what information may be related to the message, alternative interpretations etc. Contextualization is necessary when the message may be misunderstood (Gumpertz, 1982).

Given this and other strategies, one can hypothesize on when a strategy is appropriate for a given goal. For example, contextualization may be necessary for the goal of thinking collectively but not for monitoring communication. Furthermore, armed with such knowledge it is feasible to design a system that supports the communication strategies, as we demonstrate below.

Media. There is today a variety of communication media available to the sender including letters, memos, faxes, oral communication by phone, face-to-face, e-mail and more. Media Richness Theory (Daft and Lengel, 1984) classifies these media according to level of interactivity, number of channels supported, capacity to transmit high-variety languages, and ability to personalize messages.

Message. The message is the organization of information communicated. We characterize a message by the amount of explicit information it carries and the degree of its organization. A high degree of message organization provides the clarity necessary for communicating complex information. Anything that comes in the way of a highly structured and clear message reduces the degree of organization. For example, personal notes in the middle of some explanation may be important to create a positive attitude with the receiver but reduce the degree of organization.

Our model determines the conditions that require contextualization. For example, when the sender and receiver work in two different functions (e.g., engineering and marketing), there is a higher probability of misunderstanding due to different perspectives and therefore contextualization is required. Similarly, when the task is unstructured, contextualization is required. Moreover, contextualization affects and is affected by message and medium. Contextualization requires structured messages and is best communicated with interactive media. Our goal in this paper is to assume that the model is given and to see how it can be applied.

1.2 Contextualization and organizational knowledge

Contextualization must rely on organizational knowledge for two components: 1) knowledge to provide the additional layers of context around action, and 2) knowledge to identify the conditions in which contextualization is recommended. We assume here that organizational knowledge is explicit and available. This assumption is of course extremely naïve and outright wrong in many cases. However, learning organizations are realizing the importance of making knowledge available (Nonaka & Takeuchi, 1995). Moreover, new technologies such as expert support systems, intranets, document (including e-mail document) management are making it feasible to store knowledge in an accessible fashion. We assume therefore the knowledge is stored in some organizational memory, and that it can be linked to ongoing communication (i.e., through e-mail).

Organizational memories (OM) provide a way to preserve, distribute, and reuse the knowledge accrued by an organization. The integration of email and OM can be used to strengthen the "weak ties" identified above and remove a number of threats to effective communication. Using organizational memory as a basis, we are investigating and developing different mechanisms that, leveraging the OM, contextualize electronic communication. By combining organizational memories with electronic mail communications, we can achieve richer communications to decrease the probability of misunderstanding. Central to the success of such a combination is the collection and use of meta-knowledge. We further define an Organizational Memory as follows: *An Organizational Memory consists of a (semi-formal) organizational knowledge base and a (formal) set of meta-knowledge that can be applied to that knowledge base.*

Thus there are two key components here: (1) a knowledge base, which has been the subject of decades of AI research; and (2) a well-defined set of meta-knowledge - another well-worn AI technique, yet one that has yet to be fully leveraged in the context of Organizational Memories. Neither, in and of itself, should be considered an OM. It is through the combination of the two that OM can be applied in the industrial setting to which we refer.

1.3   On The Relationship between communication and organizational memory

Sierhuis and Clancey (1997), emphasize the centrality of people to the task of knowledge management in an organization - not only while constructing the OM, but in properly using it as well. Sierhuis and Clancey are most explicit in this regard "knowledge cannot be disembodied from the people and the situation". Indeed, this line of thought applies directly to communication in which the communicator decides what knowledge to transfer. But the task of assessing the knowledge held in common by members of a community of communicators, be they branch managers in a chain of department stores, or clothing designers and sewing production managers in a textile manufacturer, is complex and involves a variety of knowledge structures and judgmental processes.

The discussion of communication invalidity is now linked to organizational memory. As presented in Table 1, each threat to valid communications can be diffused to varying degrees through the use of organizational memories. Comprehensibility problems may be supported by translations, explanations and structure. Truth or accuracy problems can be supported by more details or explanations. Problems of trust need to be addressed by explaining intentions and the context of actions. Problems of appropriateness need to be addressed by discussing norms and shared values.

There have been efforts to address the interpretation of email messages through highly structured and formalized email mechanisms (see, for example, Kimbrough and Moore 1997). However these attempts involve replacing English with some theoretically sound formal language - achieving semantic accessibility at the expense of semantic richness - and are thus not relevant to this discussion.

Threat to Validity in Communications	Role of OM in Diffusing the Threat	Necessary Component of Organizational Memory
Comprehensibility	Provide supporting and background materials	Primary OM content
Truth	Indicate consensus and similar interpretations across the organization	Shared Semantics indications
Trustworthiness	Provide supporting and background materials in context of sender and recipient	User-specific meta-knowledge
Appropriateness	Provide supporting and background materials	User-specific meta-knowledge and shared semantics.

Table 1: Diffusing threats to valid communications

2   DESIGN

To illustrate the application of these concepts to actual design, we report on the development of the HyperMail system. The development of *HyperMail* follows suggestions by Kantor (1994), that similar to other problems that have been dealt with by AI, the field of OM requires solutions that are domain-specific, not unlike the need for domain-specific intelligence found in expert systems and other AI technologies. This approach becomes apparent in our use of management-specific meta-knowledge as a facilitator to improve on more traditional information retrieval and ranking techniques. The use of meta-knowledge as a facilitator in integrating the knowledge of multiple participants has been the focus of much DAI research (see, for example, Schwartz 1995) in a two-tiered object-meta architecture, and more recently in a three-layer architecture (Abecker et al. 1998) for Organizational Memory applications.

2.1   Defining the Organizational Memory

Organizational memories can take many forms and be implemented based on many different software environments. Our assumption in this analysis, and our work with HyperMail, uses an Internet-based organizational memory that consists of URL-addressable HTML pages. The creation of such an OM can be a formidable task and it is not at all clear from the literature what information should or should not be included.

A primary component of the OM used by HyperMail is an organizational ontology. An ontology is an explicit specification of conceptualization which can take the form of a shared vocabulary to ensure users of the OM have the same intended meaning when using a term. Ontologies are generally hierarchical, starting with high level that are decomposed into easily understandable or identifiable terms. For an ontology to be useful in the long-term, it must allow for modifications to reflect the changing use of terminology. The use of standards in the development of an ontology is particularly important if the ontology is to be shared outside the organization.

Ontologies are particularly useful in an organizational setting as they provide a measure of authoritative knowledge – knowledge that has undergone some form of confirmation. A reusable ontology is an important part of an organizational memory and can provide some of the primary OM content necessary to address the *threat of comprehensibility* identified above. One intriguing possibility is the use of *collaborative* ontologies (Farquhar et al. 1997) as a component of an internet-based OM.

An ontology, however, is but a small part of a complete Organizational Memory. As demonstrated by Abecker et al (1998), a complete OM may include some or all of the following components: Ontologies/thesauri, Semi-structured documents, Informal documents, Databases, Contacts to employees, and Old business practice instances.

The OM used by HyperMail initially consists of a conceptual ontology, semi-structured documents, and databases.

2.2   Accessing the Organizational Memory Through Meta-Knowledge

Electronic mail, like any other free-text document, represents informal knowledge, yet it does include some useable formal knowledge, namely the identification of the sender, the identification of the recipient, and a timeframe reference. Our goal at this stage is not to treat the email message as part of the organizational memory, but rather to use it as the informal launching point for entry into the organizational memory.

The identification of the sender and recipient of an email message is of paramount importance. Knowing this allows us to access a wealth of user-specific meta-knowledge that can be used in focusing access to the organizational memory.

The meta-knowledge used by HyperMail consists of two main components - user profile information and shared semantics information. Both of these reside in a highly-structured relational database. There are clearly other mechanisms and methods that can be used to handle the meta-knowledge (higher order logics come to mind), however the relational database mechanisms provide both sufficient expressiveness and acceptable performance for the queries necessary to support our particular use of the Organizational Memory. The (formal) meta-knowledge serves as the link between the (informal) email communications and the (semiformal) HTML-based organizational knowledge base.

Storing and maintaining information regarding the shared semantics of a given concept is a fundamental requirement of any OM system. Our implementation of shared semantics provides a mechanism by which a member of the organization, upon viewing a knowledge item relevant to a given concept, can either ascribe to or disassociate himself from the association presented by the system. By ascribing to a given knowledge association, the user is indicating that he shares the semantic representation of that item with whomever else has ascribed to that representation.

The corporate knowledge bases being used by HyperMail consist of both semiformal and informal knowledge. The informal knowledge exists in the form of Word documents and files from other computing applications (such as spreadsheets), text documents, and graphical images. Semiformal knowledge exists in the form of tagged HTML documents and historical email messages (whose semiformal aspect was described above). These documents are indexed and searched using an industry-standard mechanism.

2.3   Contextualization through Meta-knowledge

Establishing shared semantics is just the first step in harnessing meta-knowledge to effectively access an organizational memory. The use of meta-knowledge in support of organizational communication goes beyond the determination of shared semantics and can extend to deeper contextualization.

The use of contextualization in organizational memories has been addressed by Ackerman (1993) but not within the context (for lack of a better word) of organizational communications.   Ackerman refers to context information about the specifics of the sender/receiver attributes as well as the task characteristics prevailing at the time of the knowledge generation. We shall refer to this type of context information as situational context. He argues that contextual information must often be dropped when building an organizational memory, in order to generalize the information. He further states that:

> *"The removal of contextual information, including the writer's implicit knowledge of the reader, is required to make the information understandable across organizational boundaries".*

In establishing the "correct" level of context, we would argue that while context may be removed from organizational memories, it should not be discarded. On the contrary – by distilling contextual information and retaining it in the form of meta-knowledge, we can achieve Ackerman's goal of generalizable organizational memories, without losing our ability to recontextualize that knowledge when the application so demands. Enhance email communication is just such an application. Having removed context in order to add longevity to the knowledge, we must then recontextualize that knowledge to add meaning to communications. Note however that Ackerman refers only to situational context but not to another type of context information that we address, which has to do with explanations of why and how an action is taken.

Examples of situational context regarding a given item in the organizational memory may include attributes such as: 1) Time/date of knowledge item (KI) creation/ modification, 2) Name of KI author, 3) Title of KI author, 4) Current project of KI author (at time of KI creation), 5) Number of years KI author is with the company, 6) Number of years KI author is in current position, 7) Department of KI author.

Consider, for example, a multi-national textile manufacturer with offices in Tel-Aviv,

Cario, London, and Amman. There is a need to reconcile differences in meaning given different business realities. T400 is a computerized loom and the memo shown in Figure 1 is from a senior engineer in the machine maintenance department. It originally read as follows:

To:	Machine operators
From:	N. Jenire
Re:	T400 maintenance schedule

Please note that our analysis has shown an increased maintenance schedule results in lower defects/recall rate. All T400 maintenance schedules should be adjusted to be bi-monthly.

Figure 1: Scotland memo

The salient message can be divided as follows:

T400 maintenance is bi-monthly; There is a justification for the T400 maintenance schedule.

Situational context implicit in this message includes:

Author: N. Jenire	
Position:	Senior Engineer
Department:	Plant Engineering
Years on Job:	14
Years in current position:	4
Time/Date of KI creation:	19/6/1998
Department location:	Scotland

A context-free organizational memory will only provide the salient message. This message may be generally useful, but occasionally misleading — say, in the case of the Cairo factory where T400 maintenance is already done each month due to the weather conditions — and there is clearly no intention of making the maintenance period longer.

A corresponding memo, as shown in Figure 2, is directed to the Cairo operation:

To: Machine operators	
From:	M. Handess
Re: T400 maintenance schedule	

Please note that our analysis has shown an decreased maintenance schedule results in higher defects/recall rate. All T400 maintenance schedules should remain monthly.

Figure 2: Cairo memo

The salient message can be divided as follows:

T400 maintenance is monthly; There is a justification for the T400 maintenance schedule.

Situational context implicit in this message includes:

Author:	M. Handess
Position:	Senior Engineer
Department:	Plant Engineering
Years on Job:	12

```
Years in current position: 3
Time/Date of KI creation: 19/5/1998
Department location:      Cairo
```

Removing situational context from both items, results in contradictory knowledge in the organizational memory. The only way this contradiction can be resolved is by reintroducing the contextual knowledge and using it to access the correct knowledge item.

If the contextual knowledge is so important to understanding, why then do we want to remove the contextual knowledge in the first place? First of all, the contextual knowledge is not necessarily present, or obvious. There may be a concerted effort involved in identifying and collecting the context. So "removing" context is only one of the possible scenarios.

Even if the contextual knowledge is present, we must differentiate between the benefit of having the contextual knowledge removed from the core knowledge – what Ackerman refers to as "reduced context", and the benefit of having that context available separately to reason over. The need to formalize knowledge and remove social cues and group references points to reducing context – and indeed that is the motivation of most of the work in this area.

For the purpose of enriching communication, however, the main benefit is having the context available to reason over. This means that the context does not have to be removed from the original knowledge item, but rather replicated in a usable form to help guide us to the proper use of that knowledge in the future.

Treating situational context as meta-knowledge accomplishes that task. When available, it is culled from the core knowledge item, and when it is not available, it must be created as an integral part of the OM creation process

Proper application of the contextual knowledge will result in an email message from a Cairo-based manager regarding the T400's performance being linked to the memo in Figure 2 rather than that of Figure 1.

2.4   HyperMail Human-computer interaction

In this section we describe the human-computer interaction design in HyperMail. Figures 3 presents a sample session. The recipient of an email message uses a standard Web browser to view and interact with the email message. We begin with a screen showing a message with an analysis of terms that appear in the organizational memory. We later extend the dialog to include support for broader contextualization as discussed above.

There are three types of actors involved in any use of HyperMail: (1) the email author; (2) the email recipient (which may actually be a set of recipients); and (3) the contributor of any portion of the Organizational Memory referred to by the enhanced email. We refer to these three respectively as: Author, Recipient, and Contributor. Each type of actor encounters different functionality and a different interface when interacting with HyperMail. The following scenario describes a typical use of HyperMail illustrating the role of Author.

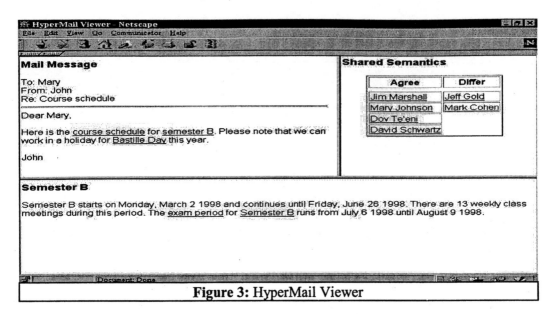

Figure 3: HyperMail Viewer

- Using a regular email client editor, John wants to send email to Mary.
- When John presses SEND, a dialog appears asking him if he wants to "Enhance" his email.
- The dialog presents three choices: Enhance and Send; Enhance and Preview; Just Send It.
- The process of enhancing the email parses the email text to identify any concepts located in the Organizational Memory. The selection and ranking of the identified concepts is based on a correlation between the user-specific meta-knowledge about the sender, and similar knowledge about the recipient. The identified text is augmented with a link to the appropriate spot in the OM. An HTML version of the email message is created wherein the OM entries are presented as links.
- In Preview mode, the author has extensive powers to modify, delete, or augment the links suggested by the system. The need for this functionality was pointed out early on by our field subjects.

The author scenario demonstrates a most basic level of contextualization, i.e., displaying definitions of terms created in the past under other circumstances and instances of using the term in other contexts. Moreover, the right-hand frame in Figure 4 is a good example of making the user aware of potential problems in communication

The result is that the user has a fine level of control of the extent of obtrusiveness or transparency granted to the system. One possible enhancement for the future is the definition of topic-based levels of context. With topic-based levels of context, the user could define high levels of contextual knowledge display for topics he is less familiar with, and a low (or no) level for topics in which he has a high degree of expertise.

3   CONCLUSIONS AND FUTURE WORK

We have presented an ongoing research project that aims to develop a communication support system called *HyperMail*. Our research encompasses both theory building and systems building. We demonstrated the link between theory and system design through one strategy within the model, namely the strategy of contextualization. Other strategies for improving communication (i.e., reducing the chance of misunderstanding) exist and should also be analyzed. Given a strategy, the conditions and goals in which and for which the strategy is effective, it is possible to design the appropriate support. The second half of the paper described our attempts in designing *HyperMail* to provide such support, within the general direction of contextualizing e-mail on the basis of organizational memory.

The next phase of our research is to implement the system and conduct a longitudinal field study at the multi-national company we are working with. We are currently tackling with building the organizational memory. Once it is partially constructed, the system will be installed at the organization we are working with. We believe that once operative, the organizational memory will begin to grow by sheer use. Our initial findings of communication processes with regular e-mail suggest that our model is appropriate and that individuals do employ the contextualization strategy under the predicted conditions. Furthermore, we have detected failures in communication that can be traced back to conditions that we suspected would be of higher probability of errors. We are therefore optimistic that we can build the knowledge base for determining when and how HyperMail should intervene and support communication.

References

Abecker, A., Bernardi, A., Hinkelmann, K., Kühn, O., & Sintek, M. (1998), Toward a Technology for Organizational Memories, *IEEE Intelligent Systems*, Vol. 13, No. 3, pp 40-48.

Ackerman, M.S., (1994), Definitional and Contextual Issues in Organizational and Group Memories, *27th Hawaii International Conference of System Sciences*.

Boland R, Tenkasi R and Te'eni D. (1994) Designing information technology to support distributed cognition. *Organization Science*, 5(3), 456-475.

Daft R.L. and Lengel R.H. (1984) Information richness: A new approach to managerial behavior and oganization design. In L.L. Cummings and B.M. Staw (Eds.) *Research in Organizational Behavior*, 6, Greenwich, CT: JAI, 191-233.

Farquar, A., Fikes, R., & Rice, J. (1997). The Ontolingua Server: a tool for collaborative ontology construction, *Int'l J. Human-Computer Studies*, 46, 707-727.

Habermas J. (1981) The theory of communicative action, Boston: Beacon.

Kantor, P.B., (1994) Information Retrieval Techniques, in M.E. WILLIAMS editor, Annual Review of Information Science and Technology (ARIST), **29**, pp. 53-90, American Society for Information Science.

Kimbrough, S. O., & Moore, S.A. (1997). On Automated Message Processing in Electronic Commerce and Work Support Systems: Speech Act Theory and Expressive Felicity, *ACM Transactions on Information Systems*, Vol. 15, No. 4, pp. 321-367.

Nonaka I and Takeuchi H. (1995). *The knowledge-creating company*. Oxford: Oxford University Press.

Schoop M (1997). Habermas and Searle in hospital: A description language for cooperative documentation systems in healthcare. In Dignum F, Dietz J (Eds.) *Communication Modeling – the Language/Action Perspective*. Computing Science Report 97-09, Eindhoven University of Technology, Eindhoven, 117-132.

Schein E H (1993). On dialogue, culture, and organizational learning. *Organizational Dynamics*, Winter, 40-51.

Schwartz, D.G. (1995). *Cooperating Heterogeneous Systems*, Kluwer Academic Publishers.

Sierhuis, M. & Clancey, W.J. (1997). Knowledge, Practice, Activities, and People, *Proceedings of the AAAI Spring Symposium on Artificial Intelligence in Knowledge Management*,http://ksi.cpsc.ucalgary.ca/AIKM97/AIKM976Proc.html

Te'eni D. & Schwartz D.G. (1998). A cognitive-affective model of organizational communication. Working Paper. Graduate School of Business, *Bar-Ilan University*, Ramat-Gan, Israel, 52900.

CHAPTER 33

THE POTENTIAL OF INTRANETS AS A TOOL FOR KNOWLEDGE MANAGEMENT: THE NEW CHALLENGE FOR IS PROFESSIONALS

Gelareh Roushan and Milena Bobeva
Bournemouth University

Abstract

This paper presents the findings of the current stage of an ongoing research on the evolving role of intranets. The paper explores the potential of intranets as a knowledge management tool. We build on previous work on information relationship management as a new responsibility for IS professionals and on research on the critical factors for the development and exploitation of effective intranets. We observe the expansion of intranets adoption and earlier examples of intranets as tools for knowledge management. In addition, we describe three case studies in support of our supposition on the current role of this type of enterprise-wide information system. Furthermore, we investigate the potential of using intranets as a tool for the facilitation and management of corporate and individual intelligence. Concurrently we acknowledge the increasing recognition of knowledge management as a strategic necessity for business competitiveness in the contemporary highly dynamic and information intensive business environment. We postulate that while intranets have the potential to transform the traditional IS function to incorporate knowledge creation and utilisation, they present a further challenge for IS professionals.

1 INTRODUCTION

Over the last decade a number of definitions have been developed to describe information systems (IS), intranets and knowledge management. However, for the purposes of this paper we use the following definitions:

- Information systems = The set of computerised and non-computerised systems and their underlying technologies, which are used in an organisation to address the information requirements of the business activities.

- Intranets = Enterprise-wide systems based on internet protocols, standards and technologies which could incorporate or provide access to other information and communication systems used in the organisation.
- Knowledge Management = The processes and systems used to create, deploy and manage corporate learning and expertise.

In recent years a significant degree of research has been carried out examining and predicting the evolving role of IS (Ward et al 1996). In this paper we develop this further by presenting our vision of the evolution of intranets as information systems.

Intranets present a phenomenon which has gained considerable recognition as information and communication tools enabling businesses to transcend geographical and time barriers. We start with a review of the current role of the intranets as enterprise-wide information systems, using three examples of ongoing projects on intranet development. Later, we address the notion of sustaining competitive advantage through management of organisational and individual knowledge and postulate that intranets hold the potential to facilitate the creation, utilisation and management of knowledge. In considering intranets as a gateway to unlimited information resources, we argue that they provide a mechanism to interrogate, capture and optimise explicit knowledge. However, the real challenge for the business and academic world is to comprehend tacit knowledge and enable its reuse and communication through the use of information and communication systems, such as intranets. This poses even greater demand on IS professionals by expanding their responsibilities to incorporate knowledge management. In conclusion we present some future research questions for the consideration of the IS community.

2   INTRANETS

Intranets, the new generation enterprise-wide information systems, are being increasingly adopted in organisations, providing the opportunity of instant access to accurate, consistent and coherent information for corporate members all over the world. They hold the potential to facilitate the development of organisational intelligence and its administrative and decision-making processes through sharing expertise and knowledge. Furthermore, intranets offer an informal way for multimedia enriched communication to be adopted to suit different user personalities.

A research by KPMG Management Consulting in 1998 (KPMG 1998), suggests that 48% of respondents stated that their organisation currently had an intranet; and 37% of respondents were planning to install an intranet in the next three years. Another research conducted in the same year suggests that 59% of US and 38% of European organisations adopted intranets (International Data Corp. 1998). The same research estimates that some 77% of US and 75% of European organisations expect to be using intranets next year.

Despite the diversity in the results, which is a natural result of the different research population samples, these statistics illustrate the extent of intranet adoption. It is the speed of expansion in intranet utilisation as well as the degree of IT involvement that formulated the focus of the attention of this research on the evolving role of information systems professional. Some go as far as stating: *'Seldom has a technology hit the IT world harder or faster that intranets'* (James 1998).

From a pure technological perspective, intranets are corporate networks that apply the Internet protocols, standards and technologies, e.g. Web browsers, Web servers and firewalls. We evaluate intranets from an Information Systems perspective, that stresses intranet applications as enterprise-wide information systems that could incorporate or provide access to other information and communication systems used in the organisation. Hence, we support the view of intranets as an enhancement to the information systems infrastructure (Guengerich et al. 1997), introducing the potential for interoperability, flexibility, dynamic reconfiguration and ease of use, alongside financial, marketing and strategic benefits (Campbell 1996).

3   KNOWLEDGE MANAGEMENT

In the recent past the importance of the role of information as an asset (Hawley1995) has continued to evolve into the power of knowledge and the call for a new breed of senior manager responsible for intellectual capital (Houlder 1996).

It was primarily the ongoing quest in maximising the opportunities for an organisation to achieve and maintain competitive advantage that resulted in knowledge becoming the key competitive factor in organisations (Prahalad & Hamel 1990). Similarly, the concept of learning organisations that led to increasing discussion in the concept of knowledge, in particular, organisational knowledge (Nonaka 1994, Spender 1996) played a key role in the increasing attention paid to knowledge management.

The degree of current discussions (Nonaka 1994, Spender 1996, Davenport 1996, Chase 1997, Kidd 1998) in the area of organisational knowledge illustrates the role of this commodity, knowledge, as a key competitive tool.

The concept of knowledge management has been examined from a number of angles, such as Nonaka & Takeuchi (1995) who developed theories to discuss the relationship between strategic management and knowledge management.

Similarly, the role of IS professionals is considered as a key aspect to be considered when discussing the concept of knowledge management. Wang (1998) proposes that ' *to get started on turning information into knowledge, you'll have to focus in on key goals and find the right role for IS in building and maintaining the system'*.

Wang (1998) expands on the role of IS in knowledge management by further asserting that '*knowledge management is often defined as the ability to get the right information to the right people at the right time'*. Wang argues that this is what IS should have been about from the beginning and states that the reason for the lack of success in achieving a knowledge management system by IS is due to the "haphazard way" in which communication networks have grown.

We carry forward these ideas by postulating that the evolution from information to knowledge management has to be considered in two stages: the first one focusing on the use of information and communication systems for knowledge management of explicit knowledge, and the second, focusing on enabling knowledge management of tacit knowledge. We use Snowdon's (1998) definitions for the purposes of this research. He defines explicit knowledge as reusable in a consistent and repeatable manner; and defines tacit knowledge as *something that we simply know, possibly without the ability to explain*.

In our current research we focus on the use of information and communication systems, and in particular intranets, for enabling the management and optimisation of explicit knowledge of organisational issues.

4   INTRANETS AS FACILITATORS FOR KNOWLEDGE MANAGEMENT

4.1   The centres of expertise

We have reviewed the current intranet practices of companies such as Arthur Andersen, McKinsey and Company, KPMG, Workspace International et al., that pride themselves on their consultancy expertise in knowledge acquisition and sharing. The common feature of these companies practises is that they recognise the three major sources of knowledge: experience, education, and research. Some of these companies, e.g. Arthur Andersen with their KnowledgeSpace® (Andersen 1998) take that further by inviting their Web site visitors to subscribe to the services they deliver through their intranet. Both businesses and individuals could benefit online from joining one of the virtual communities they support and using resources tailored to their needs or sharing expertise. Members are offered access to research findings and the most important news of the day edited to meet their information, or to a knowledge base in a particular area, e.g. financial assistance, gas and oil trends. Adding value to educational and consultancy practises and communication channels is one of the major benefits that well established consultancy companies are looking for in the employment of contemporary information and communication technologies, such as intranets.

4.2   Initial Case Study Results

In an effort to examine the potential of intranets to facilitate knowledge management, we present a summary of initial findings of three case examples (**Table 1**). Confidentiality prevents us naming the companies, hence, they are referred to as 'Case A', 'Case B' and 'Case C'. All the companies have adopted intranets.

From the examples presented it becomes evident that the common aim for adopting an intranet in these organisations has been to improve internal communications. We argue that the communication should not be limited to information communication but expanded to include knowledge communication.

Case A: The company primarily embarked on intranet technology to improve internal communications within the organisation. However, once the initial stages of intranet adoption were completed the company has been determined to make the maximum benefit of their intranet information systems. It is this awareness, to achieve more from the intranet, and the technology infrastructure in place that we envisage the potential for the intranet to develop into a knowledge transfer tool.

Case B: As in Case A, this company adopted intranets to improve communication internally within the organisation. However, as well as the high speed expected in sharing information, the company mentions sharing of learning and experiences. This foresight, in our belief is a fundamental prerequisite for a knowledge transfer tool. Although in its initial stages users are currently undergoing education as intranet requires a new way of working and change management.

The importance of sharing non-tangible results, such as experience and learning, leads us to deduce the potential for this company to consider knowledge management more explicitly.

Case C: This company goes a step further than a general improvement of internal communication and focuses on teamworking and information sharing amongst working groups. However, their aims and expected income seem to be quite explicit and indicate that the company already envisages the role of their intranet to go beyond an information dissemination tool to incorporate methods of sharing best practice. This verifies the role of the intranet, within their business environment, to more than just potential, but a tool already facilitating knowledge transfer.

Although the three companies used in the case studies operate within diverse sectors of the market they all use intranets primarily to improve their internal communication. They also share the vision for a future expansion of their intranet to encapsulate external business partners and a wider application of sharing best practice. However, it seems that the company described in Case C is more active in promoting sharing of best practice and takes advantage of intranets in understanding of process and strategy.

The overall picture suggests a conscious effort from companies to encourage maximum benefit of current technology in practice with a forward insight into future potentials.

	Case A	Case B	Case C
Nature of Business	Supermarket retailer	Major international advertising and media strategy company	IT consulting
Aim	Internal communication (e.g. telephone book, store details, pricing strategies, merchandising briefs, internal news and views) Quicker and cheaper communication, save paper Expand into extranet to include functionality (e.g. linking to suppliers)	Internal communication (email, an employee directory, internal news bulletins, feedback, sales figures) Sharing best practices, case studies, discussion forums, research papers, articles on the environment they work in Overview of customer process (e.g. Unique Selling Point (USP)) Faster dissemination of information and sharing of learning and experiences	Internal communication (including email), process documents database Teamworking applications, shared presentations and white papers Customer information databases, project databases Discussion forums and bulletin boards
Expected Outcome	Improved communication Speedier information dissemination Reduction in paper and printing	Improved communication Sharing of best practices, case studies	Improved communication, less 're-inventing of the wheel' Sharing of experience Better teamworking Better understanding of process and strategy
Potential KM tool	Company keen to move forward with the intranet to gain maximum benefits, but haven't identified the mechanisms yet.	Adoption of applications such as discussion forums (referred to as 'shared learning' applications')	Adoption of applications such as Virtual work rooms Discussion forums

Table 1: Intranet projects

5   CURRENT RESEARCH

5.1   Exploring the Potential of Intranets to Facilitate Knowledge Management

The current stage of the research builds on previous research on information relationship management as a new stage of responsibilities of IS (Rolfe et al., 1997) and critical factors for the development and exploitation of effective intranets (Bobeva et al, 1997). We maintain that the future implications for IS professionals must be concerned with the management of the transformation of the self servicing individualistic exploitative information relationships towards contributing to knowledge creation and transfer relationships. As part of our research in this area, we also examine the future role of Information Systems professionals as corporate knowledge managers.

This research focuses on exploring the potential of intranets to add value to organisational and personal knowledge management through fostering a sense of partnership and ownership. We have identified that technological achievements such as intranets are much more precious in their ability to improve the connections and communications between people within and across organisations, rather that in their capacity to store and process information. At this stage, we seek collaboration with experts in business analysis, organisational politics and psychology of human networks to establish a framework of common denominators to explore the potential of intranets to build and maintain the intellectual assets of an organisation.

6   CONCLUSION

The role of IS professionals continues to be vital in managing the corporate information resources. It has evolved by adopting an enterprise-wide vision of information management which in its advantageous forms incorporates gateways for business partners information systems. We have previously maintained that the future implications for IS professionals must be concerned with the management of the shift away from the self servicing individualistic exploitative nature of information processing, which now is becoming a project theme for many organisations. We adhere to the notion that the role of IS specialists is expanding towards information relationship management, through contribution to knowledge creation and transfer relationships.

Furthermore, we reflect on the explosion of intranets development and hypothesise on their evolution from an enterprise-wide information and communication tool into a potential knowledge management base. In conclusion, we suggest further collaborative research in the innovative management of explicit knowledge through appropriate application and utilisation of technology.

References

Andersen, A. (1998) KnowledgeSpace® WWW site. Available at *http://www.knowledgespace.com*

Bobeva, M., Roushan, G. and Rolfe, R. "Double Vision: Intranet Ideals and Realities" BIT Conference, Manchester, UK, November 1997.

Campbell, I., "The Intranet: Slashing the Cost of Business", Preliminary report, International Data Corporation, 27 November 1996.

Chase, R.L., "Knowledge Management Benchmarks", The Journal of Knowledge Management, Vol. 1, No. 1, September, pp. 83-92, 1997.

Guengerich, S., Graham, D., Miller, M., McDonald, S., Building the Corporate Intranet, Wiley Computer Publishing, John Wiley and Sons, Inc., 1997.

Hawley, R., "Information as an Asset", The Hawley Committee on behalf of KPMG IMPACT programme, 1995.

Houlder, V., "The Power of Knowledge", Financial Times, 2 September 1996.

James, G., "Intranets Give New life to BPR", The Intranet Journal, 8 September 1998.

KPMG, Intranet Research Report 1998, KPMG UK Management Consulting, 1998. Available   at: http://www.kpmg.co.uk/uk/services/manage/research/knowmgmt/index.html

Nonaka, I., A Dynamic Theory of Organisational Knowledge Creation, Organisation Science, Vol. 5, No.1, February 1994.

Nonaka, I., and Takeuchi, H., The Knowledge Creating Company, Oxford University Press, 1995.

Parahalad, C.K. and Hamel, G., " The Core Competence of the Corporation", Harvard Business Review, 68 (3): 79-91., 1990.

Rolfe, R., Bobeva, M. and Roushan, G., Information Relationship Management in Electronic Commerce UKAIS Conference, Southampton, UK, April 1997.

Spender, J.C., "Competitive Advantage from Tacit Knowledge? Unpacking the Concept and its Strategic Implications", Organisational Learning and Competitive Advantage (edited B Moingeon, A Edmondson), pp.57-73, 1996.

Wang, J., "Building a Knowledge Management System", Netscape World, April, Available at http://www.netscapeworld.com/ned-04-1998/ned-04-knowledge.html, 1998.

Ward, J., and Griffiths, P., Strategic Planning for Information Systems, Wiley, 1996.

CHAPTER 34

KNOWLEDGE MANAGEMENT: ARE WE MISSING SOMETHING?

P Hildreth, P Wright and C Kimble
University of York

Abstract

As commercial organisations face up to modern pressures to downsize and outsource they have lost knowledge as people leave and take with them what they know. This knowledge is increasingly being recognised as an important resource and organisations are now taking steps to manage it. In addition, as the pressures for globalisation increase, collaboration and co-operation are becoming more distributed and international. Knowledge sharing in a distributed international environment is becoming an essential part of Knowledge Management (KM). In this paper we make a distinction between hard and soft knowledge within an organisation and argue that much of what is called KM deals with hard knowledge and emphasises capture-codify-store. This is a major weakness of the current approach to KM. This paper addresses this weakness by exploring the sharing of 'soft' knowledge using the concept of communities of practice.

1   INTRODUCTION: MANAGING KNOWLEDGE – THE CHALLENGE

Three major issues facing organisations are globalisation, downsizing and outsourcing and all three have implications for knowledge sharing and management. Downsizing and outsourcing (Davenport and Prusak, 1998) mean a reduction in personnel. As people leave, organisations have come to realise that they take with them valuable knowledge. Globalisation is a separate issue which affects most organisations in some form (Castells, 1996). Many organisations are now undergoing some form of structural change to cope with the increased internationalisation of business. For example, Castells (1996) has observed the emergence of what he calls the Network Enterprise, made up of several organisations of different sizes working together. These changes mean that information and knowledge have to be shared between individuals and companies who perhaps never expected to work together. As globalisation impacts upon organisations, they are finding they have to turn to international teams to maintain an essential flexibility (Manheim, 1992). These teams may find themselves operating in different locations, which means that groups need to share knowledge asynchronously between different locations.

The challenges posed by downsizing, outsourcing and globalisation are those of knowledge loss and distributed working. There is clearly a need to manage such knowledge and Knowledge Management (KM) claims to address this. This paper will explore the state of KM and distinguish between 'hard' and 'soft' knowledge. It will argue that soft knowledge is an aspect of KM that is currently under-explored. The paper will also report on research being done to examine the role of this part of KM in the distributed international environment.

2   MANAGING HARD KNOWLEDGE

Much of the KM literature has a common view of knowledge that continues to concentrate on the capture-codify-store cycle of management. In this sense, KM does not seem to have moved on from what was previously termed Information Management. For example, the view of knowledge as being 'hard', that is codifiable, has led to attempts to extract knowledge from one group of 'experts' so that it can be used by another, less skilled, group. However, the results of such expert systems have been disappointing (Roschelle, 1996; Davenport and Prusak, 1998).

Another 'hard' knowledge approach aims to support, as opposed to replace, the knowledge worker. With this approach, knowledge is codified into operating procedures or other forms of instruction for action. Orr (1990) reported a study of copier repairers who had manuals containing the procedures to be followed when repairing a copier. These were laid down by the designers and catered only for the problems foreseen by them. However, there were occasions when problems occurred that were not covered by the procedures. The repairers tackled such problems by creating 'workarounds'. Workarounds in this context constituted an example of what we refer to in this paper as soft knowledge.

Despite its evident problems, the management of 'hard' knowledge is now well established and there are many tools and frameworks available for this form of KM. The soft knowledge embedded in the day-to-day working practices of groups is much less amenable to a capture-codify-store approach. Some researchers have begun to recognise the challenges raised by soft knowledge (e.g. Macintosh (1998); Buckingham Shum, 1997) but there is a need to understand more fully the nature of soft knowledge and the means by which it might be managed

3   MANAGING SOFT KNOWLEDGE

There is a wide body of literature that suggests that there are 'softer' types of knowledge (Nonaka, 1991; Kogut and Zander, 1992). This knowledge is less quantifiable (Kidd, 1994; Skyrme, 1998) and cannot be captured, codified and stored so easily. Examples of such knowledge might include tacit knowledge that cannot be articulated, internalised experience and automated skills, internalised domain knowledge and cultural knowledge, embedded in practice.

Soft knowledge is acquired through the praxis of work and consequently when an organisation loses staff, the soft knowledge that is lost cannot easily be replaced. As companies have cut out layers of middle management they find that they have lost the people who knew who to approach for specific problems; how to deal with different people and who best to use for different tasks. In short, people who knew how to make things happen. The loss of such personnel creates a problem for organisations as they move to cheaper, less knowledge-rich, workers.

As a first step towards the management of such knowledge we need to understand the social processes that govern its construction and its sustenance in an organisation. Lave and Wenger (1991) suggest that soft knowledge is created, sustained and shared through communities of practice by a process called legitimate peripheral participation (LPP). They describe how groups are regenerated by newcomers joining and eventually, replacing existing members. The newcomers learn from "old-timers" through co-practice that is graduated, permitting them to undertake more central and critical tasks. In so doing, they not only learn the domain skills associated with the practice but they also learn the language of the community, its values and its attitudes. Through this kind of participation newcomers move from peripheral positions to more central ones and in so-doing are transformed into old-timers. Membership is legitimated though participation and participation is legitimated through membership.

Seely Brown and Duguid (1991), have extended Lave and Wenger's community of practice model and applied it to technological communities. Their example is based on Orr's description of the work of copier repairers given above (Orr 1990, 1997). When a problem could not be solved by adherence to the manual, or when newcomers had difficulties, they would enlist the help of colleagues. By applying their shared experience, they would arrive at a solution to the problem. But such solutions were not then forgotten, the new knowledge was shared with other members by what Orr describes as the telling of 'war stories'. War stories not only represent the soft knowledge of the community, but their telling also serves to legitimate a newcomer as they move from peripheral to fuller participation. Members will be assayed by the stories they tell and the stories in which they feature. We can discern three trajectories of soft knowledge construction in these communities. Firstly there is the gathering of domain knowledge (for example, how to solve a particularly tricky diagnosis problem). Secondly, the construction of knowledge of work practices specific to the community (For example, knowledge of an individual machine's idiosyncrasies and how they are catered for). Finally there is the knowledge that the community constructs about the competencies of its members. To quote from Orr directly,

> *"Once war stories have been told, the stories are artefacts to circulate and preserve. Through them experience becomes reproducible and reusable.... They preserve and circulate hard won information and are used to make*

*claims of membership or seniority within the community. ...They also amuse
instruct and celebrate the tellers' identity as technicians. Such tellings are
also demonstrations of one's competence as a technician and therefore
one's membership in the community." Orr (1997) p.126.*

These examples illustrate some of the essential characteristics of soft knowledge in
communities. Soft knowledge is embedded in the practices of, and relationships within,
the group. Secondly, the source of the legitimacy of the knowledge differs from hard
knowledge. 'Hard knowledge' is accepted as legitimate by virtue of the formal authority
of the designer of the system or the author of the procedure. Soft knowledge becomes
accepted by virtue of informal authority and consensus within the group. Although
newcomers might have a degree of hard domain knowledge, their soft knowledge only
develops as they move from being newcomers to fully-fledged members of the
community.

From the point of view of managing soft knowledge in a global industry, one of the
striking features of the above examples of communities of practice is that their members
are co-located and that the learning and the construction of soft knowledge is a situated
activity. This raises the question of whether this co-location is essential to the way that
communities of practice share soft knowledge. The next section reports on two case
studies that explore this question by studying work in distributed international
environments.

4   THE CASE STUDIES

The central questions driving the studies were:
- Can a community of practice exist in the distributed international environment?
- How can the sharing of soft knowledge be supported?

4.1   Case Study 1
The case study was undertaken with Watson Wyatt, an international actuarial
organisation, and was conducted in two parts.

The first part was a survey collecting factual information. A questionnaire was issued
to 1500 staff in the UK and Europe. Five hundred and sixty-seven were returned (a
response rate of 37.8%). The questionnaire looked for respondents who:
- are in regular contact with colleagues/peers doing similar jobs;
- talk with colleagues to solve problems;
- share projects with other colleagues;
- swap anecdotes/experiences with colleagues;
- learn from discussions with colleagues.

These five metrics were used as indicators of membership in communities of practice
and were also divided into 'same location' and 'other locations' in order to differentiate
between co-located and distributed communities. Using the above it was possible to

identify potential examples of soft knowledge being shared in a community of practice.

The second stage consisted of semi-structured interviews with 22 staff based in two sites. The aim of the interviews was to obtain richer data regarding the types of communities of practice with which people were involved.

4.2   Case Study 2

The second case study took place in the research arm of a major international company. A week was spent with the UK part of a management team for IT support. The other part of the management team was located in the USA. The UK team was identified as having a number of features that were characteristic of a community of practice.

Much of the work is undertaken in the UK and USA cores but the group has full face-to-face meetings approximately twice a year. In between face-to-face meetings, the group communicates by electronic media – e-mail, video, voice mail and Microsoft NetMeeting. The group finds that after a period of time the relationship 'decays' until the next face to face meeting. The UK core consists of four members – an overall manager and three managers of specialist teams within the IT group. These members have equivalents in the USA core (Figure 1)

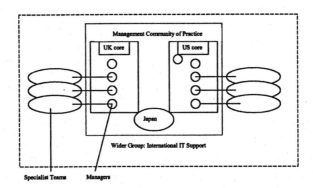

Figure 1: Structure of Group in Case Study 2

A week was spent observing the day to day work of the community members discussing aspects with them and sitting in on meetings.

5   RESULTS

5.1   Case study 1

The questionnaire stage of case study one confirmed the existence of communities of practice in the organisation, and that there was a distributed aspect to them. Interviews supported this general view. A key finding that emerged from case study 1 concerned the development of evolution of groups to a community of practice in a three-stage process:

1) Distributed communities of practice can evolve either from initial informal contact between members or from an official imposed grouping

2) The community of practice may create a link with other *individuals* at other locations who do similar work. These people will possibly be members of other communities of practice. Star and Griesemer (1989) adopted the notion of 'marginals' to describe people who are members of more than one community. Here we have two different types of marginal. There are the people who are members of more than one community – but who seem able to help in sharing knowledge across community boundaries. The other is the person who functions on the geographical periphery of the community of practice. This is in contrast to a traditional community of practice where newcomers function on a social periphery.

3) A community of practice evolves. The group might create links with another group, possibly abroad, which also functions as a community of practice.

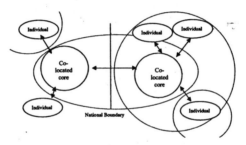

Figure 2: Physical Development of the Communication Links

The findings of case study one provide encouragement for the view that communities of practice can be sustained in distributed international environments. However, at least in the case of Watson Wyatt, these distributed communities are not entirely distributed. The legitimation of newcomers, with no previous domain knowledge, through participation, appears to take place in those co-located cores. Although LPP was key to the regeneration and evolution of the communities of practice of Lave and Wenger (1991) it does not appear to be key to the distributed aspect of communities observed here. In order to explore how soft knowledge sharing is achieved through the communications media it was clear that further data was needed regarding the interactions and practice of such a community.

5.2 Case study 2

In case study two, we explored how a distributed international community of practice supported soft knowledge in a social network and the role that communications media played in this. Over the four days we observed several face-to-face meetings in the UK, and meetings between the distributed communities, using a variety of communications media.

The community of practice in the second study matched perfectly the model shown in Figure 2. There was a co-located core in the UK and one in the USA. Additionally there was an individual member in Japan. The group had evolved by making the links between the two cores and the member located in Japan. The members of this particular community of practice all had a degree of domain knowledge. The learning a newcomer required was concerned with knowledge of group specific terminology, such as who is expert in which field, different roles and ways of working.

Given the apparent role that face-to-face meetings and situated learning play in the construction of soft knowledge, it might be expected that video conferencing would be the media of choice for the distributed community. However, of far greater importance was speed of interaction. As a consequence, telephone conferencing was popular choice of medium for communications between distributed members. Telephone conferencing was often used in conjunction with NetMeeting to support the sharing of documents.

We observed the telling of war stories both in face-to-face meetings and using telephone conferencing and NetMeeting. For example, the UK core were experiencing a difficulty with a technical problem and the US core pointed out that they had already solved the problem and were willing for the UK part of the community to leverage their experience.

In some cases, war stories were stimulated by the discussions around a planning document that the UK core was constructing. The planning document was a shared artefact under construction and its purpose was to make explicit the UK work plan. However, it also served as a catalyst for collaboration both within the UK group and between the UK and the US. The UK had access to a similar document produced in the US and this was used to help construct a document that would be meaningful to the US group. The UK group not only used the US document to help design the UK one, but they also used it to anticipate possible differences in understandings between the two groups. The planning document can be seen as hard knowledge under construction, but in this process, soft knowledge implicit in other documents and in the group's experience was used. An example of this was the discussion of the planning document in an e-meeting between the UK and US cores. The planning document served several purposes here. Each item in the plan was discussed in turn, the cursor of NetMeeting being used to indicate the current item being discussed. Some items stimulated discussions about opportunities for collaboration between the UK and the US. It served to support discussions about problem solving and the identification of experts in the US that may be able to help the UK and vice versa. Problem solving took the form of identifying previous experience with similar problems. Collaborative solutions and collaborative work plans emerged from discussions around this shared artefact. The hard knowledge represented in the planning document supported the construction of soft knowledge between the distributed groups.

NetMeeting was also used to create minutes of meetings. These were constructed in real time in the shared space of NetMeeting. This meant that people had visibility of what was getting in to the minutes as the meeting progressed and could suggest changes at the time of construction. This avoided the problem highlighted by some authors and increased the trust and confidence of the members. (Cicourel, 1990; Lipnack and Stamps, 1997); *"Sometimes you think the guy that wrote the minutes was at a different meeting"* (Case Study interviewee)

6   DISCUSSION

In exploring possible use of IT to support this under-explored area of KM the case studies have highlighted some interesting issues. Electronic media are constantly being compared with face-to-face in a race to replicate all the cues of face-to-face. The second study in particular indicated that video does not offer much more than the phone and that it is speed of interaction and the use of a shared artefact which are more important in this context. Instead of seeing some media as inferior to others we should be aiming to use the right media for the right task, as indicated by Lipnack and Stamps (1997), with the extra rider of in the right context.

We found the existence of distributed communities of practice but they did not operate in a totally distributed manner — there was an evolutionary aspect to them in that they evolved from co-located cores. Examples of LPP were seen in the first case study but were restricted to co-located situations. This structure was mirrored in the community of practice studied in the second case study. Perhaps LPP does not translate well alone into a distributed environment and perhaps something else is necessary.

Face-to-face communications remain an essential part of communication for communities operating in a distributed environment. The communities of practice that were found in the commercial setting are not totally distributed: they are evolving from co-located cores. Community members appear to need face to face contact to maintain impetus when communication is then restricted to electronic media. The face to face element increases trust and members reported feeling they knew their communication partners better having met them. There were two strong relationships reported in the second case study which had developed over electronic media, however the feeling was that these had taken a long time to develop and were rare occurrences.

In the second case study, an artefact played a role in knowledge creation as community members applied knowledge and it functioned to share embedded soft knowledge. It was interesting to note the use of shared artefacts to aid communication between distributed members, which also seems to support soft knowledge sharing and creation, can serve as catalysts, focal points and embodiments of soft knowledge.

7   CONCLUSION

This paper has reported preliminary results from two case studies on the sharing of soft knowledge in distributed communities of practice. For case study two in particular, there are still many useful findings to be gleaned from the corpus of data. One of our primary aims for this paper was to determine whether distributed groups currently in existence demonstrated any of the characteristic features of the more familiar co-located communities of practice reported in the literature. Our initial results in this regard are promising and suggest both similarities and differences between co-located and distributed communities.

Our findings extend the concept of peripherality introduced by Lave and Wenger as one of three key aspects of communities of practice. For them peripherality was couched in terms of legitimacy of membership and practice. While this is undoubtedly true in the distributed groups observed in our cases studies, physical and temporal peripherality where also factors that mediated the practice and the quality of interaction.

The exchanging of war stories and the sharing of artefacts via telephone conferencing and NetMeeting also has many similarities to the way in which this occurs in co-located teams. In both cases they have been shown to serve as vehicles for the exchange of soft knowledge, and there is some suggestion in our data about how some kinds of soft knowledge can be made hard through a process of consensus making via shared artefacts.

The area of Distributed Cognition (Hutchins, 1995) provides us with interesting ideas about the use of artefacts. Star (1989), Star and Griesemer (1989) and Sandusky (1997), develop this further with the notion of boundary objects which cross boundaries between communities. These could be useful methodological devices in that they focus attention on the transition between communities.

At the heart of the case studies so far is an unanswered question. This concerns why distributed teams feel the need for face to face meetings and what they mean when they talk of collaboration 'decaying' without such meetings. We might look here to the question of what factors effect the sense of identity of individuals as members of the community. Maybe there are social factors involved, where what is meant by social is quite literally the enjoyment of socialising with like-minded others. As was quoted earlier, Orr (1997) talked of how war stories "amuse, instruct and celebrate the tellers' identity as technicians". Such factors may be a vastly under-rated resource for the sustenance of soft knowledge in an organisation.

References

Buckingham Shum S (1997). Negotiating The Construction and Reconstruction of Organisational Memories Journal of Universal Computer Science Vol. 3 No 8 Special Issue pp899-928

Castells M (1996). The Rise of the Network Society. Blackwell Malden Massachusetts

Cicourel A (1990). The Integration of Distributed Knowledge in Collaborative Medical Diagnosis. In Galegher J Kraut R E and Egido C (Eds) Intellectual Teamwork. Social and Technological Foundations of Cooperative Work Lawrence Erlbaum Associates pp221-242

Davenport T and Prusak L (1998). Working Knowledge. How Organizations Manage

What They Know. Harvard Business School Press

Hutchins E (1995) Cognition in the Wild MIT Press

Kidd A (1994) The Marks are on the Knowledge Worker. In Adelson B Dumais S & Olson J (eds.) CHI '94 pp186-191

Kogut B and Zander V (1992). Knowledge of the Firm Combinative Capabilities and the Replication of Technology. Organization Science vol. 3 No.3 August

Lave J and Wenger E (1991) Situated Learning. Legitimate Peripheral Participation Cambridge University Press

Lipnack J and Stamps J (1997) Virtual Teams Wiley

Macintosh A (1998) Knowledge Management. On-line at http://www.aiai.ed. ac.uk/~alm/kamlnks.html

Manheim. M (1992). Global Information Technology. International Information Systems Jan 1992

Nonaka I (1991) The Knowledge Creating Company HBR Nov-Dec pp96-104

Orr J. (1990). Sharing Knowledge Celebrating Identity: War Stories and Community Memory in a Service Culture. In Middleton D. S. and Edwards D. (eds) Collective Remembering: Memory in Society. Beverley Hills CA: Sage Publications

Orr, J. (1997) Talking about machines: An ethnography of a modern job. NY: Cornell University Press.

Roschelle J. (1996). Designing for Cognitive Communication: Epistemic Fidelity or Mediating Collaborative Inquiry. In Day D and Kovacs D (eds) Computers Communication and Mental Models Taylor and Francis

Sandusky R J (1997). Infrastructure Management as Cooperative Work: Implications for Systems Design. In Hayne S C and Prinz W (eds) Proceedings of the International ACM SIGGroup Conferences on Supporting Group Work pp91-100

Seely Brown J & Duguid P (1991): Organisational Learning and Communities of Practice. Organisation Science Vol 2 No 1

Seely Brown and Duguid (1996). Universities in the Digital Age. Change pp11-19

Skyrme D (1998). Developing a Knowledge Strategy Strategy January 1998

Star S L (1989) The Structure of Ill-Structured Solutions: Boundary Objects and Heterogeneous Distributed Problem Solving Distributed Artificial Intelligence Vol 2 pp37-54

Star S L and Griesemer J R (1989). Institutional Ecology 'Translations' and Boundary Objects: Amateurs and Professionals in Berkeley's Museum of Vertebrate Zoology 1907-39. Social Studies of Science Vol 19 pp387-420

CHAPTER 35

INFORMATION SYSTEMS STRATEGY IN ADHOCRATIC BUSINESSES

Ernest Jordan
Macquarie University, Australia

Abstract

An investigation has been carried out that examines the relationship between an organisation's structure and the information systems that support its operations. Twenty-five business units in an international bank were studied in terms of organisational structure and information systems. This paper examines in detail the eight business units that were classified as adhocracies. *End user computing was commonly used as the strategy for effectively using information technology in these units. Propositions derived from the work of Mintzberg were tested and found to be of limited usefulness.*

1   INTRODUCTION

In the mid-1980s, the specific need to carry out strategic planning for the information systems (IS) and information technology (IT) infrastructure of the organisation became obvious in larger organisations as budgets increased and the impacts, both inside and outside the organisation, became more significant (Lederer and Mendelow 1986; Brancheau and Wetherbe 1987; Earl 1989).   The need increased for many when it appeared that competitors were able to achieve competitive advantage through these technologies (Wiseman and MacMillan 1984; Porter and Millar 1985). By 1996, Brancheau et al. were reporting that strategic planning was much lower on the IT manager's list of priorities, nevertheless an activity that must be carried out.

Initial approaches to the task of carrying out information systems strategic planning (ISSP) were simple models and frameworks that helped understanding and showed opportunities but did not lead to an implementable plan (McLean and Soden 1977; King 1978; Nolan 1979). Since then many methodologies have been developed that will guide the user to an IT development portfolio (Earl 1989; Lederer and Sethi 1988, Edwards et al. 1995). Most methodologies have been pragmatically developed and investigate three areas: business needs, an enhancement path for existing systems, and technology-driven opportunities. The need to ensure that the development plan fits with the organisation structure has received little attention in the established methodologies (McFarlan 1990) although it continues to receive attention from researchers (Tavakolian 1989; Iivari 1992; Drury and Farhoomand 1998).

ISSP remains complex, expensive and uncertain. Organisations that have carried out ISSP are not assured of success in developing applications of IT that will achieve competitive advantage (Earl et al. 1988). Conversely, organisations may develop successful applications without engaging in ISSP. Our aim is to evaluate a potential assessment method for evaluating alignment with organisation structure.

In looking for a theoretical foundation for ISSP, research results point towards an organisational role for information and a competitive or strategic role for information. While the competitive strategy approach has been widely researched (Sabherwal and King 1991, for example), here we examine the contribution of organisational structure, as a way of substantiating the organisational fit.

2   THE ORGANISATIONAL VIEW OF INFORMATION

There are many approaches to examining and discussing organisational structure. The analysis of that substantial literature is reviewed elsewhere (Jordan 1994, Jordan and Tricker 1995). Mintzberg's model of organisational structure is adopted as that which most clearly deals with the role of information and information systems within an organisation.

In his seminal work on organisational structures, Mintzberg (1979) breaks down any organisation into five basic parts: the strategic apex, middle line, operating core, technostructure and support staff; shown in Fig. 1.

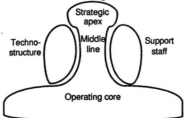

Fig.1: The Structural Components of the Organisation (Mintzberg 1979)

Mintzberg (1979) describes five distinct ways that work may be coordinated, that are used depending upon the complexity and dynamic nature of the organisation's environment, and interdependencies of the work tasks being undertaken in the operating core; namely: direct supervision, standardisation of work processes, standardisation of outputs, standardisation of skills, and mutual adjustment.

Each particular coordinating mechanism allows one of the basic parts to become the dominant, controlling part of the organisation. For each of them in turn, there is a corresponding form of the organisational structure, shown in Table 1. In recent work,

Mintzberg (1994) has adopted titles of: entrepreneurial, machine, diversified, professional and adhocracy, that we shall use here.

Control mechanism	Dominant part	Structural form
Direct supervision	strategic apex	Entrepreneurial
Standardisation of work processes	technostructure	Machine
Standardisation of outputs	middle line	Diversified
Standardisation of skills	operating core	Professional
Mutual adjustment	support staff	Adhocracy

Table 1: The five structural forms

The *entrepreneurial organisation* has direct, two-way information flows between the operational employees and the strategic apex, with most of them being informal. There is little need for a formal management information system because most of it is in the mind of the senior management. With direct supervision being applicable to all the operational employees, there is no need for formal communications. Information gathering is elementary, with external regulators such as government taxation and labour departments being driving forces. Any systems will be centralised and functional.

The *machine organisation* is appropriate for stable environments; when non-routine decisions need to be made or exceptions arise, they need to be communicated up the hierarchy to someone with the level of authority to act. The management information system is designed with that principle in mind. Summary information also flows up to higher levels so that control can be exerted and decisions can be made; which decisions in turn flow down the organisation. If designed correctly, at each point in the hierarchy there is sufficient authority to deal with the normal amount of variation, so that only exceptions need to be passed on.

Mintzberg characterises the *diversified organisation* as a collection of organisational units, usually machine organisations, under the supreme control of the headquarters strategic apex. Thus the apex of each of the component divisions becomes the middle line in the overall organisation, passing up performance information for the purpose of control. Within each division, the information flows are those of a machine organisation, except that the information requirement of the apex has been designed and specified by the technostructure at headquarters:

The *professional organisation* is one in which the standards used by the operating core are determined by outside professional bodies. Thus the technostructure does not develop a performance control system; the standards and techniques of the operating core have been established in the professional code and practice of their discipline. All the factors are in the hands of the profession, not the technostructure. There will remain information flows that follow the flow of work but they will simply be enough to effect communication with the next professional in the chain, such as in the medical referral; the next professional is expected to know what to do.

The *adhocracy* has professionally trained staff, like the professional organisation, but they are organised in organic teams to try to solve new problems, such as reported by Burns and Stalker (1966) in the British electronics industry. Within the teams, which are usually project-based, will be managers and support staff. Liaison groups will be widely used to effect coordination between groups, with mutual adjustment used within the group. Formal IS that regulate and control are not important:

> *The regulated system does not matter much either. In this structure, information and decision processes flow flexibly and informally, wherever they must to promote innovation. And that means overriding the chain of command if needs be. (Mintzberg 1979: 473*

Mintzberg describes two variants of the adhocracy - the administrative adhocracy that is concerned with problems belonging to the organisation itself, and the operating adhocracy whose problems belong to outside clients or customers. Both the administrative and operating adhocracies are decentralised such that control is within the project teams, the manager being part of the team. There is no organisation-wide control system; each team has goals of its own.

The preceding sections demonstrate that the nature and role of information is central to the study of organisations, and, just as emphatically, that the organisational structure and managerial roles are critical ingredients in the selection, analysis and design of IS. The organisational structure model of Mintzberg facilitates the understanding of information in the organisation, particularly through its examination of the flows of information, decisions and control. It is also amenable to empirical investigation.

3   RESEARCH HYPOTHESIS

The environment in which the adhocracy flourishes is characterised by instability, complexity, market diversity and hostility - conditions that are becoming more common under the influences of globalisation of markets, economic instability and proliferating information technologies (Drucker 1994). In this section a tentative hypothesis is developed by considering the impact of organisation structure on IS using the theories of Mintzberg. The fundamental functioning of the organisational structure is examined to attempt to define the generic information system that would be appropriate for it. Mintzberg gives few suggestions of the information requirements of adhocracies, except the team-based coordination.

We propose that the generic information system for the adhocracy is the network; local area networks to support the small-size unit focused on a particular function or market, and larger networks to facilitate liaison and coordination among larger groupings. Networks mimic, supplement and support the human networks that are an essential part of the adhocracy. The software on the network should vary significantly, although there is a need for some transferability and transportability. The criterion for selection of the software will be the extent to which it supports and enhances the performance of the team; in other words, the software may have to be regarded as another team member. Mintzberg identifies "non regulating and unsophisticated technical systems" as the hallmark of the operating adhocracy. An administrative adhocracy will have an information system incorporated in the background production process; it may be as explicit information or as control and monitoring information built into hardware devices.

4   METHODOLOGY

An in-depth investigation was carried out on the strategic business units of a multinational financial institution, referred to here as "Globalbank". Its practice of decentralisation of business units has enabled those units to pursue strategies that are almost independent, to such an extent that the business units can be regarded as distinct entities with a small set of organisational constraints. Thus the internal business units of Globalbank will serve as separate implementations of IS strategy, as a large sample rather than just a single one. The emergent IS strategies of adhocratic units are compared with the above propositions.

Globalbank is seen by authoritative commentators as a leader in the application of IT to banking, a position that it has held for many years. It adopted technology leadership as a strategic move in order to become more successful. As an example of its leadership, it introduced a communications network into its IT architecture long before most of its competitors; it was a strategic move that indicated its aim to expand the marketplace in which it operated. The perception of strength is not only held externally but also internally; for example, its annual reports repeatedly refer to IT as one of the strengths of the organisation. Globalbank has given great emphasis to IT over so long a period that the impacts of IT on the business, if any, will have been felt. There have been opportunities and encouragement to use IT to its greatest advantage. An IT strategy, then, has been implemented. The IT strategy can be observed through its implementation, and its effects and characteristics related to each other.

Globalbank has many distinct business units, each of which has had considerable freedom in determining its own IT strategies. Globalbank managers are expected to be aggressive in using IT wherever it is beneficial in their domain. In such a setting there is the opportunity to assess many possibly successful users of IT, to determine whether the theories of Mintzberg suitably describe the information strategy.

A schedule was established for interviewing managers of business units, using a semi-structured questionnaire. Supplementary information sources included computer system documentation, internal communications and external material, such as newspaper and journal articles. The sources are described in the following sections but references are omitted to maintain confidentiality. The principal data collection method was determined to be semi-structured interviews with a framework compiled from the extensive literature. The interview framework was designed to be directly administered by the interviewer. Questions raised in one interview could be presented to another manager in a later interview.

The interview subjects were the managers of the various business units and, when applicable, the managers of the business groups. In a few cases where operating processes were unclear or unusual, junior staff were consulted for explanation. Those staff were not targets for the questionnaire, which was aimed at managers making recommendations for IS facilities to support their business strategy. The sequence of business units investigated was customer-oriented units and then product-oriented units. After all the business units had been examined, the most senior managers were interviewed.

A wide variety of documents originating from inside Globalbank Asia Pacific was collected. It included IS documentation, ISSP documents, minutes of working meetings, inter-office memos, and formal reports dealing with IS. In addition, wider organisational material included organisation charts, standard business forms, internal publicity, recruitment and induction handouts, newsletters and company magazines.

As Globalbank is a major international organisation, references to it are frequently to be found in public media. A collection was made of newspaper reports and journal articles referring to Globalbank, which often had articles referring to the same major issues that had been revealed earlier in interviews. Newspapers were also sources for advertisements for Globalbank's services and for recruitment of staff. Major references were found in books, although they seldom referred to activity in Asia Pacific. Similarly there were regular references in such sources as *The Economist* and *Business Week*. In addition to the more journalistic articles, there were highly formalised public documents such as annual reports to shareholders, returns to statutory authorities, and invitations to participate in financial instruments and share issues.

5   STRUCTURE AND ORGANISATION OF GLOBALBANK

Globalbank's main activities in the Asia Pacific region are corporate, consumer and private banking. Corporate banking customers include businesses, government departments and other banks. Each of the businesses reports to its own superiors at head office directly. Within each country a committee coordinates certain activities and ensures that local legal requirements are met. However, the organisational structure is not hierarchical, it is a matrix based upon customers, products and geography. Thus, in the "geography" dimension, each business also reports to a regional group, which in turn reports to head office. The product dimension of the structure becomes most apparent when looking within a business area.

Although corporate banking customers are subdivided into smaller customer groups, there are product teams dedicated to providing and managing certain products, whichever customer is using them. The product teams may well cut across the boundaries between corporate, consumer and private banking. Product teams also have a reporting path to head office.

The effect of this structural arrangement is to break down Globalbank into many smaller businesses, each responsible for a small group of customers, products or geographical territories. It is described by Gonzalez and Mintzberg (1991) as the 'related diversifier' or 'shotgun' strategy, where a financial institution enters many business segments, with only loose links between them. A senior Globalbank headquarters executive describes it as a key strength, because the small business units are all available for expansion.

The manager of each of the businesses will have the job of achieving the best performance for the unit, in cooperation with others. There are many committees and other opportunities for coordination and liaison between units. Further complication is added because the manager of one unit may well have responsibilities in another area and because the individual's set of responsibilities frequently change. Each of the individual business units has been able to develop in its own way, within the general constraints posed by the organisation.

The actual area of study is the Asia Pacific corporate banking business, Corporate Banking Asia Pacific (CBAP). Note that, for confidentiality, generic names are used for business units and groups. Through decentralisation each unit in this business has had considerable freedom and opportunity to develop the IS that it needs. By studying the nature of each unit's activities and its use of IS, we can examine various implementations of a single corporate policy. In this paper only those units that were found to be adhocratic in structure are reported. Those that are customer-oriented, shown in Table 2, and those that are product-oriented, shown in Table 3.

Unit	Code	Main Customers	Typical Products
World Corporate Group	WCG	Multinational	Many
Corporate Banking Unit	CBU	Major local companies	Many
China Country Office	CCO	Joint ventures	Many

Table 2: A summary of the customer-oriented business units

Unit	Code	Main customers	Products
Treasury Marketing	TM	Many	Money market, FX
Corporate Finance Unit	CFU	Middle size manufacturers	Corporate equity
Project Finance Unit	PFU	Large organisations	Capital project finance
Institutional Investment	IIM	Large organisations	Pension funds
Tax Management Unit	TMU	Multinationals	Tax management

Table 3: A summary of the product-oriented business units

5.1   IT services in the Asia-Pacific region

The organisation of IT service provision mirrors the business units. The corporate, consumer and private banking organisations have their own IT services groups, and there is a regional group (Asia Pacific IT, APIT) which can support any unit, country or product. In many countries the local IT group (ITG) carries out some systems development for APIT, and *vice versa*. Any unit in CBAP must seek the assistance of its local ITG for any of its IT requirements. If they are not provided directly by either APIT or ITG, one of these units will manage the project and ensure that it meets corporate standards and fits into the existing systems. However, to a great extent it is the responsibility of the business unit to determine its own IT requirements and to decide on the amount of funds that may be allocated to new systems. It reinforces the notion of the decentralised business units being independent decision-makers.

6   ANALYSIS

Extended case descriptions for the units, including their IT functions, are available from the author by electronic mail. Differences from the earlier propositions need to be understood, either as "random" variation, reasonably insignificant differences, or as differences caused by some other factor that was not part of the experiment, or as faults in the propositions.

As this paper aims to examine in some detail the use of information systems with adhocratic organisations, we report only on those units. The other business units are reported elsewhere (Jordan and Tricker 1995).

There are eight business units classified as adhocracies:

World Corporate Group, WCG,   Corporate Banking Unit, CBU,
China Country Office, CCO   Institutional Investment Management, IIM,
Tax Management Unit, TMU,   Project Finance Unit, PFU,
Treasury Marketing Office,   TMO, Corporate Finance Unit, CFU.

They are all operating adhocracies that deal with customers' problems. In all units professional staff are employed who use their skills more on unique cases or projects than on routine action, although there is some routine in all of their work. There is much dealing with other professional or expert staff in different domains of expertise. Creativity, originality and the ability to coordinate with other disciplines are key attributes for staff in these areas. In all areas standard professional skills are used but a variation is found in WCG where Globalbank has created its own profession of the WCG specialist, looking after major global organisations. They are only interchangeable with WCG specialists from other countries.

CBU and CCO are concerned with setting up new business, while TMO even has a transaction processing function (highly automated) in the unit. All units are concerned with the design and/or the marketing of products. CBU creates management information for its own use. There is little use of IT to directly support staff activities beyond the use of PCs to model alternative proposals. The Globalbank electronic mail network is used in all units to work with people in other locations. It is critical to the success of WCG, TMU, PFU and the CCO. The existence of an international telecommunications network permits the processing that WCG and CCO bring to market. Specific software that enhances the functioning of the staff in used in TMU, IIM and TMO, with the most sophisticated software used by any of the groups being in TMU. General-purpose software, such as PC packages, is used for enhanced performance of PFU, CFU and WCG. Because CFU's networks extend outside Globalbank, cellular telephones are used more extensively than in other business units. Thus the dominant forms of information systems found were end-user computing and electronic mail, together with a variety of network-based applications.

The above shows that the propositions developed from the examination of Mintzberg are generally supported but they give little explanation of the differences between the IT developments in the units. The strongest support for the propositions is given in CCO, WCG, PFU, CFU and TMU.

6.1   Results

Overall then, the propositions are seen as being under-developed but a useful basis for further examination. It is perhaps indicative of the competitive, dynamic and evolving nature of banking in the present era that eight business units (out of 25 studied) were found to be operating as adhocracies. None of the units presented explicit use of information systems that was inconsistent with the propositions, but the explanatory power of the propositions was weak. Apart from the notion of (human) networking and interaction with other experts, there are few concrete statements in Mintzberg's theory. End-user computing was highly developed in the adhocracies, and in different ways in different units, but the Mintzberg's theories have no precise proposals that could be tested.

7   SUMMARY AND CONCLUSIONS

The general problem for an organisation to decide in which areas to develop IS and IT may be approached through ISSP. A body of knowledge and experience suggests that the best information strategy depends on many organisational and environmental factors. The alignment of IS strategy with the business needs has been an important issue to many organisations in their adoption of ISSP. The starting point of this investigation is that the business need must be moderated by the organisational structure in order to best determine the IS strategy.

The existing literature in IS development is particularly concerned with the problems of big business and the design of IS to suit their needs. Such organisations often would be classified as machine organisations or diversified organisations. Elsewhere we have reported that their generic IS descriptions suggested by Mintzberg are strongly supported (Jordan and Tricker 1995). Similarly, the professional organisations follow the hypothesised descriptions well, although there is significant variation among them. Entrepreneurial organisations are not so simple as theory suggests and for such units, conclusive results have not been found beyond the inadequacy of existing theories.

However, we have found that simply considering Mintzberg's theory is insufficient to deal with a form of organisational structure that is becoming more common, the adhocracy. Our results show that this organically functioning, creative business unit benefits from a wide variety of information technologies, most particularly networks and small systems and models developed by the users – end-user computing. Further research is needed to develop an extended model to cover the wide range of adhocracy organisations.

References

Brancheau, James C. and James C. Wetherbe (1987) 'Key Issues in Information Systems Management,' *MIS Quarterly*, **11**, 1, Mar., 23-45

Brancheau, J.C.; Janz, B.D. and Wetherbe, J.C. (1996) 'Key Issues in Information Systems Management: 1994-5 SIM Delphi Results', *MIS Quarterly*, **20**, 2, 225-242

Burns, Tom and Stalker, G.M. (1966) *The Management of Innovation (2nd ed.)*, Tavistock Publications, London

Drucker, Peter F. (1994) *Post-Capitalist Society*, HarperCollins, New York

Drury, D. H. and Farhoomand, A. (1998) "Comparisons of Alignment in Managing Information Systems", in Baets, W.R.J. *Proceedings of the Sixth European Conference on Information Systems*, IAE Aix-en-Provence, 1056-1070

Earl, Michael J. (1989) *Management Strategies for Information Technology*, Prentice Hall Intl, Hemel Hempstead

Earl, Michael J.; Feeny, David; Lockett, Martin and Runge, David (1988) 'Competitive Advantage Through Information Technology: Eight Maxims for Senior Managers,' *Multinational Business*, **2**, Summer, 15-21

Edwards, C.; Ward, J. and Bytheway, A. (1995), *The Essence of Information Systems, 2nd Ed.* Prentice Hall International, London

Gonzalez, Maria and Mintzberg, Henry (1991) 'Visualizing strategies for financial services,' McKinsey Quarterly, **2**, 125-134

Iivari, J. (1992) 'The organizational fit of information systems', *Journal of Information Systems*, **2**, 3-29

Jordan, E. (1994) "Information Strategy and Organisation Structure," *Information Systems Journal*, **4**, 4, October 1994, pp. 253-270.

Jordan, E. and Tricker R.I. (1995) "Information Strategy: Alignment with Organisation Structure," *Journal of Strategic Information Systems*, **4**, 4, December 1995, 357-382.

King, William R. (1978) 'Strategic Planning for MIS,' *MIS Quarterly*, **2**, 1, Mar.

Lederer, Albert L. and Mendelow, Aubrey L. (1986) 'Issues in Information Systems Planning,' *Information & Management*, **11**, 245-254

Lederer, Albert L. and Sethi, Vijay (1988) 'The Implementation of Strategic Information Systems Planning Methodologies,' *MIS Quarterly*, **12**, 3, Sep., 445-461

McFarlan, F. Warren (1990) 'The 1990s: The Information Decade,' *Business Quarterly (Canada)*, **55**, 1, Summer, 73-79

McLean, Ephraim R. and Soden, John V. (1977) *Strategic Planning for MIS*, Wiley-Interscience, New York, NY

Mintzberg, Henry (1979) *The Structuring of Organizations: A Synthesis of the Research*, Prentice-Hall, Englewood Cliffs, NJ

Mintzberg, Henry (1994) *The Rise and Fall of Strategic Planning*, Prentice-Hall, Englewood Cliffs, NJ

Nolan, Richard L. (1979) Managing the crises in data processing, *Harvard Business Review*, **57**, 2, Mar.-Apr., 115-126

Porter, Michael E. and Millar, Victor E. (1985) 'How Information Gives You Competitive Advantage,' *Harvard Business Review*, **63**, 4, July-Aug., 149-160

Sabherwal, Rajiv and King, William R. (1991) 'Towards a Theory of Strategic Use of Information Resources: An Inductive Approach,' *Information & Management*, **20**, Mar. 191-212

Tavakolian, Hamid (1989) 'Linking the Information Technology Structure with Organizational Competitive Strategy: A Survey,' *MIS Quarterly*, **13**, 3, Sep., 309-317

Wiseman, Charles and MacMillan, Ian C. (1984) 'Creating Competitive Weapons from Information Systems,' *Journal Business Strategy*, **5**, Fall, 42-49

CHAPTER 36

ANARCHIC IS AND BUSINESS ALIGNMENT STRATEGIES: TOWARDS A CONFIGURATIONAL MODEL

LCK Ma, JM Burn and R Hackney
City University of Hong Kong, Edith Cowan University, Manchester Metropolitan University

Abstract

The alignment of Information Systems (IS) strategy with business strategy is the most commonly suggested approach for the strategic management of IS. This paper reports on a study, which addresses four major limitations which have been identified from this literature. Specifically, IS strategic alignment is usually not well-defined, there has been little empirical evidence to establish appropriate measures, the significance of its benefits have remained largely undetermined and guidelines for the implementation of an effective alignment strategy are largely non-existent. This paper develops a configurational model of IS strategic alignment that evaluates not only the internal consistencies between IS strategy and business strategy but also contingency approaches for different types of IS strategic alignment. Qualitative analyses from a survey and multiple case study evaluations were undertaken which identified good practices and pitfalls to avoid in IS strategic planning, as well as the change processes in the migration from one alignment type to another. The authors argue that there is a need to match users' information management experience against the IT department's capability to develop and deliver high quality information systems. The evidence from this paper suggests that there is no one best way to achieve such an alignment and a constant reassessment of organisational boundaries is necessary through the anarchic alignment strategies proposed.

Keywords: *IS Strategy, IS Alignment, IS Management, Organisational Configurations, IS Success*

1   INTRODUCTION

Over the last decade many surveys and some empirical studies have supported the notion that strategic alignment of IS with organisational strategies is critical if organisations are to gain competitive advantage (Watson & Brancheau, 1991; Brancheau et al, 1996; Neumann et al 1992; Chan and Huff 1992; King 1988; Sambamurthy et al 1993; Earl 1993, Ward and Griffiths, 1996). However, there is little consensus with regard to the approach which should be used to achieve this strategic fit and indeed some scepticism that there is a universal "best" approach (Hackney, 1996; Yetton, 1997; Burn, 1997; Sauer & Burn, 1997). These researchers suggest that it is inappropriate to assume that IS strategic alignment will automatically improve the chances of IS effectiveness and improved organisational performance through the notion of "fit". More recently a number of authors have also identified various factor (i.e., senior management support, IT function assessment, etc) for successful congruence between IT and the business but there has been little comment on how such changes can be implemented (Dutta, 1996; Earl, 1996; Earl & Sampler, 1998; Horner & Benbasat, 1996).

This paper reports on a longitudinal study over the last four years and from the results of a very detailed survey conducted at several different levels within 74 organisations. It develops a configurational theory of strategic alignment, which not only extends the boundaries of "fit" but allows for continual movement and re-alignment. The results suggest that IS success is greater if the members of the organisation perceive that there is a good alignment between IS and their business needs. This model was further assessed by in-depth case studies in a number of organisations. The findings provide new guidelines which may be used to establish a continuum position on the configurational alignment model which reflects a valid IS strategy. The paper, therefore, makes an observation on the issues involved through the implementation of IS.

The contribution of this paper is to propose a theory of IS success based on organisational configuration, users' perceived needs and information management experience. It supports the IT department's capability to develop and deliver high quality IS strategic planning (ISSP) to achieve business performance (Feeny & Willcocks, 1998). The paper also provides practical guidelines on how to achieve alignment and how to identify their success within the organisational framework. Finally it challenges traditional assumptions of alignment and proposes models which could be viewed as anarchic by proponents of the "IT for competitive advantage" school.

2   IS STRATEGIC ALIGNMENT CONFIGURATIONAL MODELS

A number of strategic alignment models were evaluated within this study to develop a comprehensive framework (Henderson and Venkatraman, 1989, 1993; Venkatraman 1985, 1989; Chan & Huff 1992, 1994; Chan 1992; Ward & Peppard, 1996). The Strategic Orientation of Business Enterprise (STROBE) model (Venkatraman, 1989), and the extended strategic orientation of IS (STROIS) model (Chan and Huff, 1992) were determined to form the most useful base for measurement of IS strategic fit. Many later models build upon these ideas but commonly fail to encapsulate implementation issues (Brown & Magill, 1994). The STROBE model (Venkatraman 1989), consists of six strategic dimensions, and 29 indicators which can be used to measure the strategic orientation of the organisation as shown in Appendix 1. Against each of the strategic dimensions and items of STROBE, Chan and Huff (1992) have developed a corresponding set of 6 strategic dimensions and 29 items to determine and measure the Strategic Orientation of IS (STROIS).

The research in this paper, therefore, sought to further developed an IS strategic alignment configurational model for analysing the characteristics of particular types of alignment of business unit strategy with IS strategy via a combination of STROIS and STROBE as shown in Figure 1.

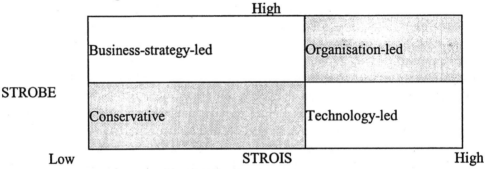

Figure 1: IS Strategic Alignment Configurational Model
(based on STROBE vs. STROIS)

A contingency approach was adopted in the formulation of the model suggesting that organisations in different alignment types may need different approaches to ISSP to more effectively address particular issues relevant to their alignment type. By matching the current strategic position of the organisation, as represented by their respective STROBE and STROIS, this study examined whether the four classifications of the matrix could fit with various IS planning models (Earl, 1993; and Sullivan, 1985), application portfolio (Venkatraman, 1991), 5-Level of IT-Induced Reconfiguration (McFarlan, 1981) and strategic grid and sector management approaches (Earl, 1989). The configurational model derived in research for this paper was also used to explore the different characteristics of various fits in alignment type: low integration (Conservative); medium integration (Middle-fit) and high integration (Organisation-led).

2.1 Conservative

The strategic orientation of "conservative" organisations is relatively low in both business strategy and IS strategy (as reflected by low scores in both STROBE and STROIS) hence:

a) Role of IS: Since the operating environment of the organisations in this category is not very competitive and the demand for IS service not high, the application portfolio is expected to be largely concentrated in local exploitation (Level 1 of Venkatraman, 1991), the support quadrant of the Strategic Grid (McFarlan, 1981) or the delay segment in the Sector IT Management (Earl, 1989). User managers are not expected to have a high demand for more sophisticated IS services.

b) ISSP: Since the business strategic orientation and IS applications in this group of organisations are support, there may be less incentive to perform formal business/IS strategic planning. Typical approaches are: (1) no ISSP (2) Stages of Growth (SoG) as suggested by Sullivan (1985) where organisations with a more stable environment tend to adopt a progressive agenda for ISSP, (3) Budgetary driven or administrative led as suggested by Earl (1993) where the objective is to allocate resources.

2.2   Technology-led
The strategic orientation of "Technology-led" organisations is reflected by low scores in STROBE but high scores in STROIS., hence:

a) Role of IS: Since the operating environment of the organisations in this category is not very competitive but the strategic orientation of IS is relatively high, the application portfolio is expected to be largely concentrated in local exploitation and internal integration (L1 & L2 of Venkatraman, 1991), the factory quadrant (McFarlan, 1981) or the dependent sector (Earl, 1993). A major concern is whether organisations with low business strategy orientation will continue to invest in IT where the expected return may not align with a conservative business strategy.

b) ISSP: Typically technology-driven or architectural approaches (e.g. Business Systems Planning) are adopted for developing technology infrastructure such as telecommunication networks, database and office automation.

2.3   Business-strategy-led
This group of "business-strategy-led" organisations demonstrate a relatively high strategic orientation of business but low strategic orientation of IS, hence;

a) Role of IS: Since the operating environment of the organisations in this category is high but the strategic orientation of IS is relatively low, the application portfolio is expected to be largely concentrated in Business Process Redesign (Level 3 of Venkatraman, 1991), the turnaround quadrant (McFarlan, 1981) or the drive sector (Earl, 1993). The major concern in this configuration is that user managers are working in a demanding business environment but the IT support may be weak.

b) ISSP: Since the business strategic orientation is high in this group of organisations but their IS applications are not very strategic, they may adopt a more business-oriented approach in ISSP. Typically, business-driven approaches (e.g. CSFs analysis) may be adopted in defining information requirements.

2.4   Organisation-led

The strategic orientation of "organisation-led" organisations is reflected by high scores in both STROBE and STROIS hence:

a) Role of IS: Since the operating environment of the organisations in this category is high as is the strategic orientation of IS, the application portfolio is expected to be largely concentrated in Levels 1-4 (Venkatraman, 1991), the strategic quadrant (McFarlan, 1981) or the delivery sector (Earl, 1993).

b) ISSP: Since the orientation of both business unit strategy and IS strategy are high in this group of organisations, they may adopt an organisation wide approach in ISSP such as the theme-based exploration advocated by Earl (1993).

2.5   Theory Extension: The Dynamics of Strategic Orientation

Mintzberg (1994) and Ohmae (1982) suggest that we should attempt to differentiate *Strategic Thinking,* which is the process to determine and identify long-term strategic direction and targets, and *Strategic Planning*, which is the process to formulate implementation strategies to bridge the gap between current strategic orientation and future strategic direction. Hence, an important step in strategic planning is to determine the current strategic position (*where you are*) and to plan the course of actions *(what the organisation should do)* towards the future strategic direction (*where the organisation wants to go*), as shown in Figure 2.

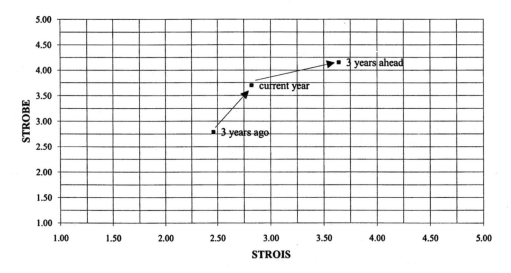

Figure 2: Movements and Direction of STROBE vs. STROIS

The trend analysis sample chart in Figure 2 illustrates that the organisation is migrating from a "Conservative Environment" 3 years ago to "Business-strategy-led" at present, and is expected to move towards "Organisation-led" 3 years ahead. These were charted for each organisation and used to identify changes in planning characteristics which would be required to enable a successful transition.

3 RESEARCH SURVEY AND ANALYSIS

The alignment of business strategy and IS strategy based on the combination of STROBE and STROIS was used to measure IS strategic fit. The test results were based on construct validity, scale reliability and comparative analysis. Having identified the realised business unit strategy and the IS strategic orientation, this study examined (a) whether organisations behave differently in the development and implementation of IS strategy and (b) whether organisations in different alignment types have different levels of IS success. A quantitative survey was applied to each organisation with three sets of questionnaires. The results of these questionnaires formed the basis for selecting appropriate organisations for case study analysis as well as for providing a rich source of information for supporting further analysis and evaluation on the effectiveness of ISSP, as shown in Table 1, through senior executive participation and Table 2 as an overview of alignment type.

Questionnaire:	A	B	C
Areas of Analysis	Strategic Planner, CEO or GM - familiar with Business Strategy and Business Performance	Senior Manager of a Department consisting of major IS Users	IS/IT Manager or CIO in-charge of IS/IT functions
STROBE	Detailed		
STROIS		Detailed	
Strategic Role of IS	✓	✓	
IS Satisfaction of IS		Detailed IS Service	Detailed IT
ISSP Characteristics			Detailed
Overall Success of ISSP	✓	✓	✓
Overall Satisfaction IS	✓	✓	✓
Business Performance	✓		

Table 1: Participation of Senior Executives

Alignment Type	Count
Business-strategy-led (B)	16
Conservative (C)	26
Organisation-led (O)	19
Technology-led (T)	13

Table 2: Organisations by Alignment Type

An analysis was conducted on Chief Information Officers (CIOs') perceived effectiveness of ISSP and ISSP success by Chief Executive Officers (CEOs) and general managers (GM). These findings were then used as the basis to develop a model showing the configurational characteristics of ISSP and related to an analysis of IS success factors and the overall organisational satisfaction with IS, as shown in Table 3.

Satisfaction with IS Service	Mean by Alignment Type				
	B	C	O	T	Mean
CEO/GM	2.67	2.25 L	3.36 h	2.67	2.69
User Manager	3.03 L	3.23	3.63 h	3.38	3.32
CIO	3.50	3.23	3.53	3.46	3.41

(LSD test: "h" scores > "L" scores within the Same Row at significance level .05)

Table 3: Alignment Type and Overall Satisfaction with IS Service

CEO/GMs from the "conservative" group had significantly lower average scores than their counterparts in the "organisation-led" group. User Managers from the "business-strategy-led" group had significantly lower average scores than their counterparts in the "organisation-led" group. Although there is no significant differences in the average scores of CIOs' "overall satisfaction with IS Service", the average score from the "organisation-led" group is also the highest. After analysing the IS Success items from the comparison of their mean scores, the items with significantly high mean scores and significantly low scores were grouped under "More Satisfied with or Better in" and "Less Satisfied with or Weak in" respectively. As expected, User Managers from both "business-strategy-led" and "conservative" groups (with low STROIS) indicated a lower level of IS Success, particularly in the "business-strategy-led" group. User Managers from both "organisation-led" and "technology-led" groups indicated strong satisfaction with IS.

3.1   Configurational Characteristics of the Business-Strategy-led Group

Although the CIOs perceived many effective indicators in ISSP (e.g. good top management support, funding of both ISSP and the Implementation of IS plan) general managers were less satisfied with IS (e.g. poor quality of systems and poor IS contribution). There was an obvious "misfit" between ISSP and IS implementation between the two interest groups.

Perceived ISSP Effectiveness (CIOs)	Perceived IS Success (General Managers)
More Effective Indicators	More Satisfied with or Better in
Better Planning and Control of human, software & hardware requirements	(no obvious item)
Top management commitment in Implementing IS plans	Less Satisfied with or Weak in
	IS delivered on-time
Analyse resource constraints and contingency plans	Relative Functional Quality of IS
Quality of Inputs from Users	Relative Technical Quality of IS
Funding for the implementation of IS plan	Ability of IS staff to customise (develop in-house)
Funding for the IS strategic planning Process	systems
Improvements on IS strategy planning processes	Application of IS to advance CSFs
Better appreciation of the business unit's overall Information Needs	IS contribution to improving Profitability
	Relative IS contribution to managerial effectiveness
Greater exploitation of IS opportunities for gaining	IS contribution to operational efficiency

Perceived ISSP Effectiveness (CIOs)	Perceived IS Success (General Managers)
competitive edge	Relative Alignment of IS Plans with Business Needs
Less Effective Indicators Analyse telecommunication requirements	

Table 4: Configurational Characteristics of Business-Strategy-led group

3.2   Configurational Characteristics the Conservative Group

There was a fairly good match between "ISSP" and "IS Success" as shown in Table 5. The CIOs in this group considered that ISSP was less effective and the User Managers were less satisfied with IS! In other words, a "conservative fit" was a good "fit" with regard to alignment but an unsatisfactory approach to develop successful ISSP or IS.

Perceived ISSP Effectiveness (CIOs)	Perceived IS Success (General Managers)
More Effective Indicators (no obvious item)	More Satisfied with or Better in (no obvious item)
Less Effective Indicators (in most items, especially the following items) Appreciation of business unit's information needs Quality of Inputs from Users Top Management support Funding for ISSP and its Implementation BPR for implementation of IS plans	Less Satisfied with or Weak in IS contribution to improving Profitability Systems development tools Relative Alignment of IS Plans with Business Needs Application of IS to advance CSFs Relative IS contribution to operational efficiency End-users' ability in defining business information requirements

Table 5: Configurational Characteristics of Conservative Group

3.3   Configurational Characteristics the Organisation-led Group

Perceived ISSP Effectiveness (CIOs)	Perceived IS Success (General Managers)
More Effective Indicators *ISSP Team*, especially team leader Better Integration of business and IS plans Involvement and Quality of Top management support Approval of new IS follows recommendations of ISSP BPR and restructuring of business unit for implementing IS plan Better appreciation of the business unit's overall Information Needs Review alternative strategies Assess internal strengths and weakness of our current IT environment Assess business opportunities and threats associated	More Satisfied with or Better in *End-users' ability in defining business information requirements* Application of IS to advance CSFs IS contribution to improving Profitability Relative Functional Quality of IS Relative Technical Quality of IS IS delivered on-time IS delivered within budget Alignment of IS Plans with Business Needs Less Satisfied with or Weak in (no obvious item)

Perceived ISSP Effectiveness (CIOs)	Perceived IS Success (General Managers)
with IS Quality of Inputs from Users Quality of Inputs from strategic business planning to IS strategic planning. Participation of IS managers in strategic business planning. Less Effective (no obvious item)	

Table 6: Configurational Characteristics of Organisation-led Group

There was a good match between "ISSP" and "IS Success" as shown in Table 7. This indicates that there was a high integration of STROBE and STROIS and the "fit" was perceived by both groups as appropriate.

3.4   Configurational Characteristics the Technology-led Group

Perceived ISSP Effectiveness (CIOs)	Perceived IS Success (general Managers)
More Effective Indicators (no obvious item) Less Effective Indicators Selection of Application Portfolios Top Management support and involvement Quality of Inputs from Top Management Planning and control of human, software and hardware resources Top Management Commitment in the Implementation of IS plans Re-structuring the chosen business unit for the implementation of IS plan	More Satisfied with or Better in Relative IS contribution to operational efficiency Relative IS contribution to managerial effectiveness Systems development tools Relative Alignment of IS Plans with Business Needs Relative Functional Quality of IS Less Satisfied with or Weak in End-users' ability in defining business information requirements IS delivered on-time

Table 7: Configurational Characteristics of Technology-led Group

There was a complex situation when matching "ISSP Effectiveness" and "IS Success" as shown in Figure 6, since it again showed a "misfit" yet one in which the General Managers were satisfied despite the apparent lack of effectiveness in ISSP! Interestingly, general Managers considered that their staff (end-users) had inadequate ability in defining business information requirements. This was clearly a good explanation of the misfit in the "technology-led" group. This may be explained by the fact that much of the development in such an environment will be user driven - they had the technology and so would use it. Whether they were using the technology in support of top management plans was open to question. Possibly top management had been overtaken by technology and were unsure of their expectations

From the data analysis in Figures 3 to 6, it can be observed that there were significant differences between perceived "ISSP Effectiveness" and perceived "IS Success". Both "business-strategy-led" and "organisation-led" groups, (high STROBE), were operating in a more demanding business environment, and hence, considered planning as important. However, both "technology-led" and "organisation-led" groups, (high STROIS), saw enhanced user satisfaction and improved operation efficiency as important. Furthermore, the following four "fits" were identified:

1. Good fit: alignment in ISSP with satisfactory level of IS found in "organisation-led" group.
2. Conservative fit: low satisfaction with ISSP and low expectation of IS found in "conservative" group.
3. IS-Misfit: effective ISSP but low IS success found in "business-strategy-led" group.
4. Business-Misfit: ineffective ISSP but relatively strong IS success found in "technology-led" group.

These differences between perceived or "intended strategy" and actual or "realised strategy" suggested a need to explore these models further in order to define particular criteria for success and develop a more comprehensive model combining both ISSP and IS implementation.

4   CASE STUDY ANALYSES

In the initial selection of organisations, the main criteria was to determine the highest scores in ISSP success, ISSP process and IS where the chosen organisation represented the typical characteristics of the alignment type. A major constraint, however, was that most organisations were "too busy" or reluctant to participate in case study interviews and that some managers revealed limited information, especially in the area of business strategy. Four case study analyses (one in each alignment type) are reported as shown in Table 8.

Organisation Code	BBB	CCC	OOO	TTT
Alignment Type	Business-strategy-led	Conservative	Organisation-led	Technology-led
Industry	Banking	Certified Public Accountants	Public Authority	Transport and Storage
Number of Employees	over 600	over 50	over 40,000	over 200
Number of Employees in IT	over 30	4	over 200	15
Business Unit studied	Consumer banking	Certified Public Accountants	A large hospital	Shipping
No of Employees in SBU	over 300	over 50	over 1,000	over 40
Interviewee Positions	GM of SBU OM of SBU MIS Mgr BBB	CEO Audit manager	Hospital CEO CIO of OOO Systems Mgr	CEO GM MIS manager

Table 8: Summary of Case Organisations' Characteristics
Business-strategy-led case: Although a profitable bank only had slightly above-

average scores on ISSP approach and IS success, it was selected because the responding managers were very supportive of the interviews and the bank was also a typical case of the alignment type.

Conservative case: An accounting and auditing firm was chosen because it had the highest scores in ISSP success and IS success among Conservative organisations and good support was also available from the CEO and the Audit manager.

Organisation-led case: A public authority was chosen because it had the highest scores in ISSP process and IS success among Organisation-led organisations, and good support was also available from the three respondents.

Technology-led case A shipping company was chosen because it had the highest score in importance of ISSP process among Technology-led organisations and both the CEO and CIO were very supportive of the research.

4.1   Strategic Business Planning (SBP) and Information Systems Strategic Planning (ISSP)

Many SISP studies (Earl 1993, Lederer & Mendelow 1986 and Bowman et al. 1983) have raised a concern that the availability of (formal) business plans for SISP cannot be assumed nor their communication to the concerned managers. This is particularly true from the case study analyses as only OOO's CIO had ready access to the business plans. The other three CIOs did not have direct access and had to obtain indirect inputs either from the CEO or other senior managers. OOO followed the "organisational" approach in ISSP as advocated by Earl (1993). Both CCC and TTT were aware of the role of IST in the organisation and were satisfied with the reactive ISSP approach. However, BBB was more concerned about its ISSP process because of their high dependence on IT.

Organisation: Item	BBB	CCC	OOO	TTT
CIO reporting to	General manager	CEO	CEO	CEO
CIO's involvement in business planning	No direct involvement but with informal discussion with managers SBUs	No direct involvement but with informal discussion with the CEO	Member of planning team	No direct involvement but with informal discussion with the CEO
Strategic business planning process	Formal	Informal	Formal	Formal
Coverage of business planning	5 years	1-2 years	5 years	2 years
ISSP Process	Informal	Informal	Formal	Informal
Coverage of ISSP	1-2 years	ad-hoc	5 years	ad-hoc
ISSP Approach	budget driven and business-led	reactive	Theme-based exploration	reactive
ISSP Success	Average	Successful	Successful	Successful
IS Success	Average	Good	Very Good	Good

Table 9: Summary of Findings from Multiple Case Study Analyses

4.2   Link between SBP and ISSP

Based on the case study analyses, the CIO's rank was seen as an important factor in providing the linkage between SBP and ISSP. Only the CIO from OOO (out of the four cases) who held the title of Deputy Director), had direct involvement in SBP. The informal inputs of business plans from the CEO or senior managers to the CIO were considered by the CIOs in both BBB and TTT to be ineffective (although better than nothing) and a constraint to effective ISSP. The CIOs wanted to participate in SBP. As anticipated by the configurational model, managers in OOO were highly satisfied with the success of IS services due to good alignment. Managers in BBB were not satisfied with IS services because the banking environment demanded good IS service/support in order to compete but the IS department could not perform as expected. The CEOs in both CCC and TTT were fully aware of the role of IS in their organisation and hence satisfied with IS in general.

Organisation	BBB	CCC	OOO	TTT
Coverage of ISSP planning	1-2 years	ad-hoc	5 years	ad-hoc
ISSP Process	Informal	Informal	Formal	Informal
ISSP Approach	budget driven	reactive	Theme-based exploration	reactive
ISSP Success	Average	Successful	Successful	Successful

Table 10: Summary of ISSP Success

Organisation	BBB	CCC	OOO	TTT
IS Success	Fair	Average/Good	Very Good	Average/Good

Table 11: Summary of IS Success

4.3   Evaluation and Future Outlook

It is interesting to note that with the exception of the business-strategy-led case, all the

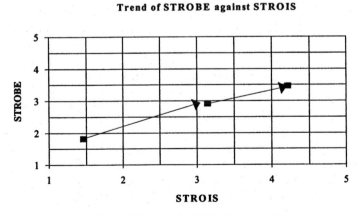

Figure 3: Trend of STROBE vs STROIS for four Cases

other three cases have passed through or around the "middle-fit" zone in the chart.

Organisation:	BBB	CCC	OOO	TTT
Legend in Chart:				
Alignment Type (3 years ago)	Business-strategy-led	Conservative	Conservative	Conservative
Alignment Type (current year)	Business-strategy-led	Conservative	Organisation-led	Technology-led
Alignment Type (3 years ahead)	Organisation-led	Conservative	Organisation-led	Organisation-led

Table 12: Movement of Alignment Types in Four Cases

Due to dissatisfaction with their previous IS services in BBB and TTT, these two organisations replaced their EDP Manager with a more senior MIS Manager (two and three years ago respectively). The MIS manager of BBB (business-strategic-led) had better banking application experience than its previous EDP manager and was more open-minded in accepting open-systems, packaged applications and outsourcing (leading to higher capability of IT services). The MIS manager of TTT (technology-led) had better IT knowledge than its EDP manager but limited business knowledge. These changes seemed to reinforce their present configurational characteristics and to cater for their expected migration to the organisation-led configuration.

5   CONCLUSION

IS strategic alignment is a complicated phenomena which cannot be easily evaluated without a deep understanding of the organisation and its processes in both business strategy planning and ISSP. Also, inputs from multiple stake-holders within the same organisation are necessary in order to assess the effect of alignment from multiple perspective. There is not necessarily a single definition of "best" alignment but various types of alignment.

The cases support four types of alignment with very different configurational characteristics which may be appropriate. Aligning within these four types can result in

   a) a fit between STROBE and STROIS
   b) a misfit between STROBE and STROIS
   c) a misfit between strategy of alignment and the configurational needs
   d) a fit between strategy of alignment and the configurational needs

All four alignment configurations may present an appropriate model for an organisation depending on:

   • The extent of IT dependency within the organisation
   • Current IT capabilities
   • Users' knowledge and experience in information management.

As these factors change, it is important for organisations to learn how to realign to a more appropriate model in the most effective way. The alignment chart for each case clearly illustrates "where they are" and "where they expect to go to". This directional guidance is perhaps more important than analysing the alignment fit. This may involve a strategy of change through more than one model using a "middle-fit" as a change vehicle. The specific factors and associated items associated with success have been clearly identified in Table 4-7 to assist organisations in the implementation of effective changes and the development of long-term strategies.

This paper has proposed, therefore, one paradigm for the successful alignment of IS with the rest of the business organisation through a conceptual anarchic strategy and a practical configurational model.

References

Brown, C V & Magill, S L (1994) Alignment of the IS Function with the Enterprise: towards a model of antecedents, *MIS Quarterly*, December, pp 371-403.

Burn, J. M. (1997) A Professional Balancing Act: Walking the Tightrope of Strategic Alignment in Sauer and Yetton (eds). *Steps to the Future Fresh Thinking on the Management of IT-Based Organizational Transformation*, Jossey-Bass, p. 55-88.

Chan, Y.E. (1992) Business Strategy, Information Systems Strategy, and Strategic Fit: Measurement and Performance Impacts, *PhD Dissertation*, (UMI), University of W Ontario.

Chan, Y.E. & Huff, S.L. (1993) Investigating Information Systems Strategic Alignment, *ICIS*, p.345-61.

Earl, M.J. (1993) Experiences in Strategic Information Systems Planning, *MIS Quarterly*, March, p.1-24.

Earl, M J (1996) Integrating IS and the Organisation: a framework of organisational fit, in Earl M J (Eds)., Information Management: the organisational dimension, *Oxford University Press*.

Earl, M J & Sampler, J L (1998) Market Management to Transform the IT Organisation, *Sloan Management Review*, Summer, pp 9-17

Feeny, D F and Willcocks, L P (1998) Re-Designing the IS Function Around Core Capabilities, *Long Range Planning*, Vol 31, No 3, pp 354-367

Hackney, R A (1996) Sustaining an Information Systems Strategy, *1st Annual UKAIS Conference*, Cranfield University, 10-12 April

Henderson J. & Venkatraman, N. (1989) Strategic Alignment: a process model for integrating Information Technology and Business Strategy, *Sloan Working Paper*, October, [3086-89].

Horner, B. & Benbasat, I. (1996) Measuring the Linkage between Business and Information Technology Objectives, *MIS Quarterly*, March, p.55-82.

King, W.R. (1988) How Effective is your Information Systems Planning, *Long Range Planning*, 21:5, p.103-12.

McFarlan F.W. (1981) Portfolio Approach to Information Systems, *Harvard Business*

Review, September, p.142-50.

Miles, R.E. & Snow, C.C. (1978) Organisational Strategy, Structure, and Process, *McGraw Hill.*

Mintzberg, H. (1994) The Fall and Rise of Strategic Planning, *Harvard Business Review,* January, p.107-114.

Neumann, S.; Ahituv, N. & Zviran, M. (1992) A Measure for Determining the Strategic Relevance of IS to the Organisation, *Information & Management,* May, p.281- 99.

Ohmae, K. (1988) Getting Back to Strategy, *Harvard Business Review,* 66:6, p.149-56.

Rockart, J.F. Earl, M.J. & Ross, J.W. (1996) Eight Imperatives for the New IT Organization, *Sloan Management Review,* Fall, p.43-56.

Sauer, C. and Burn, J. M. (1997) The Pathology of Strategic Alignment, in Sauer and Yetton (eds). *Steps to the Future Fresh Thinking on the Management of IT-Based Organizational Transformation,* Jossey-Bass, p. 89-113.

Sambamurthy, V.; Venkatraman, S. & Desanctis, G (1993) The Design of InformationTechnology Planning Systems for varying Organisational Contexts, *European Journal of Information Systems,* 2:1, p.23-35.

Sullivan, Jr. C.H. (1985) Systems Planning in the Information Age, *Sloan Management Review,* Winter, p.3-12.

Venkatraman, N. (1989) Strategic Orientation of Business Enterprises: the construct, dimensionality and measurement, *Management Science,* 35:8, p.942-62.

Venkatraman, N. (1991) *IT-Enabled Business Reconfiguration, in Scott-Morton (ed.), The Corporation of the 1990's,* Oxford University Press, p.122-58.

Ward, J & Griffith, A (1996) Strategic Planning for Information Systems, John Wiley (2nd Edition)

Ward, J & Peppard, J (1996) Reconciling the IT Business relationship: a troubled marriage in need of guidance, *Journal of Strategic Information Systems,* Vol 5, No 1, pp 37-65

Yetton, P. W. (1997) False prophecies, Successful Practice, and Future Directions in IT Management, in Sauer and Yetton (eds). *Steps to the Future Fresh Thinking on the Management of IT-Based Organizational Transformation,* Jossey-Bass, p. 27-54.

6   APPENDIX 1

Dimension	STROBE Items
Aggressiveness	1. We sacrifice short-term profitability to gain market share.
	2. We frequently cut prices to increase our market share.
	3. We have a strong preference to set prices below competition.
	4. We seek market share positions at the expense of cash flow.
Analysis	1. Use of Management information and control systems
	2. Use of Manpower planning
	3. Use of Performance appraisal of senior managers
	4. We emphasise effective co-ordination among our functional areas

Dimension	STROBE Items	
	5.	We require a great deal of factual information for our day-to-day decision making.
	6.	When confronted with major decisions, we typically develop thorough analyses.
Defensive	1.	Use of Cost control systems
	2.	Use of Production/operations management techniques
	3.	Emphasis on product/service quality.
	4.	Making significant modifications to the technologies in our business operations.
Futurity	1.	Forecasting key indicators of operations
	2.	Tracking significant general trends
	3.	Use of "What-if" analysis of critical issues
	4.	Our criteria for resource allocation generally reflect long-term considerations.
	5.	We emphasise long-term research to provide us with future competitive edge.
Proactiveness	1.	We are constantly seeking new opportunities related to the present operations.
	2.	We are usually the first ones to introduce new products/services in our market(s).
	3.	We are constantly on the look out for business that can be acquired.
	4.	We pre-empt our competitors by expanding our capacity ahead of them.
	5.	Our operations in later stages of life cycle are strategically eliminated.
Riskiness	1.*	Our new projects are approved on a *stage-by-stage* basis rather than with *blanket* approval.
	2.*	Our mode of operations is generally more risky than our competitors.
	3.*	We usually adopt a conservative view when making major decisions.
	4.*	We tend to support projects where the expected returns are certain.
* = reverse scored	5.*	Our business operations have generally followed the "tried and true" paths.

Adapted STROBE Dimensions and Indicators (after Venkatraman 1989 and Chan 1992).

CHAPTER 37

AN INTEGRATED APPROACH TO ENTERPRISE MODELLING – A PRACTICAL PERSPECTIVE

AK Athwall and R Moreton
University of Wolverhampton

Abstract

The main objective of Enterprise Modelling is to derive a common view of the organisation to be based on an information management and business strategy perspective. This paper reports on current PhD research programme, which has led to the development of a theoretical framework to develop an Enterprise Model. The model aims to provide a stable foundation for information systems development by offering consistency and traceability from the strategic to the operational level. Three different organisations were selected to evaluate this framework. The paper presents the validation process and its outcomes, which demonstrate the applicability of the model under very different organisational environments.

1   INTRODUCTION

It is widely reported that most organisations, both in the public and private sectors, have undergone considerable change during the last decade, and there are no signs of abatement in the pace and nature of organisational change (Pettigrew 1985; Nolan 1987; Carnell 1990; Belmonte 1993). Information systems (IS) can provide the foundation for successful change but it is widely recognised that IS have not kept pace with the changing environment. This requires a fresh approach to the subject of information systems development methods.

The main objective of Enterprise Modelling (EM) is to derive a common view of the organisation. This research project has developed a theoretical framework for arriving at an Enterprise Model using object-oriented techniques (Athwall, 1996 and Athwall & Moreton, 1995) and the objective was to determine the usability of the framework within different organisations and establish the benefits from its use.

The first part of this paper gives a brief outline of the approach, followed by a brief description of the three organisations in section 2. The third section describes the validation process in some detail, followed by a discussion of its applicability in three organisations which differed in terms of their core business, size and approach to the development and use of information systems.

1.1 An Integrated Approach to Enterprise Modelling

This approach is based on Zachman's Information Systems Architecture (1987), Shelton's OOBE (1994) and the Object Management Group's Reference Model (Hutt, 1994). Table 1 shows this association and the second column depicts the overall structure, which contributes towards the Business Core Model - comprising of a set of vertically integrated models, which provide connectivity, and traceability from business goals through to implemented business objects.

ZACHMAN'S ISA	OOBE	OMG Reference Model
Scope	Strategic Model	Strategic Modelling
Enterprise	Enterprise Model	Analysis Modelling
System	Operational Model	Design Modelling
Technology	External Model	Implementation Modelling
Components	Implementation Model	Construction

Table 1: Different Perspectives of an Enterprise Model

The suggested approach incorporates the main concepts from the above three models. Figure 1 shows this approach which is mainly concerned with developing a high level perspective of the organisation or of selected department(s) of the organisation. The top two layers of table 1 are fully utilised in this approach and as Lehman (1997) suggests that a high level understanding and representation of the needs of a business and of relevant organisation processes in context are required.

This framework encompasses the consolidation of organisational structure, information flows within the organisation, definition of an Object Model (a combination of Process Model and Data Model), and common definitions of objects/classes across all Business Areas (BA) within an Organisation. The steps illustrated in figure 1 are fully explained in a previous paper (Athwall, 1996).

1.1.1 Validation Phase - Context

Three different organisations were selected to determine the validity and usability of the theoretical framework and also what benefits could be achieved by its use. The three organisations were a large NHS hospital, a medium-sized Building and Maintenance Company, and a small firm of Property Consultants. The hospital case study, in a public sector setting, was the main source of detailed analysis. The other two private sector organisations were used for comparative purposes.

The NHS Hospital was built in the late 1980s on a greenfield site, serving a population of 200,000 in a semi-rural setting on a new industrial development area. It has 350 beds; employ 1200 people with an annual turnover of over £30 million.

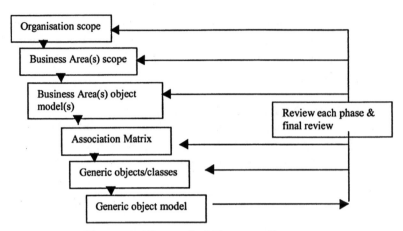

Figure 1: Theoretical Framework

It is a complex organisation comprising a wide range of services and staff from a multiplicity of professions with differing skills. Different departments within this hospital can be treated as disparate business areas; for example the Imaging Directorate has its own business plan, budget and staffing responsibility. Several business areas (departments) were identified - namely Finance, Outpatients (several different clinical areas), Accident and Emergency, Radiology and a General Practice associated with the hospital to carry out this work.

The Building and Maintenance Company was launched in the early 1990s and has expanded rapidly to become one of the leading, fast reactive maintenance companies in the Midlands. It provides a complete set of services covering various trades within a 50-60 miles radius of its location. Currently, it has 20 office-based staff and 50 field-engineers. It has an annual income of more than one million pounds.

The company offers trade work in different areas that include building, plumbing, painting, decorating, carpentry, electrical, gas maintenance and many other repair services. The company has a functional structure based on the following activities: Operations; Finance; Purchasing/Warehouse; Personnel and Contracts. Each department has its own manager who reports directly to the Managing Director.

The Property Consultancy is based in the Midlands but offers its services nationally. It has a core team of ten members and in addition to this, it has a network of at least 50 specialist consultants on its register and their expertise is called upon as and when required. The firm offers two distinct services. The first is Managing Properties (renting/letting) for the residential and commercial markets. The second is buying and selling land and properties for Commercial businesses. The first service is a small-scale venture whereas the second service is the largest generator of income that accounts for several million of pounds.

The firm does not have a traditional functional structure; hence the Business Areas were not clearly definable. Having a very flat structure, areas of responsibilities are shared out amongst senior members. It has an integrated computer system and the required information is accessible to all who needed it, apart from financial accounts which were the domain of the Managing Director and the Company Secretary.

1.1.2   The Validation Process

Preliminary work started with the NHS hospital in March 1996. The hospital was already working closely with the university in planning and eventually implementing a networked integrated system to support many of its IT needs. Several systems, such as the Radiology System, Accident and Emergency System are linked through the Patient Master Index System (PMI), which is based at another hospital in the region. The PMI is not owned by the hospital as it is shared by several hospitals within the region. It is planned that any new initiatives relating to IT will be managed by the hospital's own IT department and future plans include the implementation and management of an integrated system within the hospital.

The Information Department initiated this investigation. This department provides financial data to the Finance Directorate for the production of monthly reports. These reports are sent to the different directorates detailing monthly income and expenditure. The brief was to analyse the current practices in producing these monthly reports from the Ledger System, which was part of the Income and Budget System.

The hospital's Patient Administration System (PAS) links into PMI and it records all patient-related activity data. The Information Department is able to download the data required from PAS and bring it together using a database and a spreadsheet packages. A hard copy is sent to the Accounts Manager to produce the required reports, as it has no network connection with the Financial Directorate. The Accounts Manager uses the same spreadsheet package which is installed on a stand alone PC and enters the selected data to produce the required reports. Eventually, the same data has to be entered into the Ledger System again to generate the end of year Financial and Audit reports.

This highlighted the duplication of effort, storage of data in three different systems, thus proving a very costly exercise to the hospital. The duplication of data directed the analysis into a detailed study, which documented a common set of data requirements. If this data was captured once and stored centrally, it could then be utilised by the different applications within the hospital. An intermediate solution was found immediately by having the reports from the Information Department on a floppy disk, which enabled the Accounts Manager to download the required data, thus cutting out a days work. It was found that the Ledger System had a facility by which information could be imported/exported from the spreadsheet package, which made further savings in time resource.

This exercise proved to be a success and it was completed in June 1996. The Information Department decided to analyse several different departments in terms of their data requirements. The framework to develop an Enterprise Model was put forward to the Information Manager and it was decided to study the activities in terms of processes and the related data requirements of each department to determine what similar data items existed. This study would take several months as a number of departments were identified.

The validation phase began in July 1996 and was concluded in April 1997. The above mentioned departments were studied in detail according to the steps indicated in the framework. This proved a time consuming exercise as information was gathered through interviews, observations and existing documentation. Interviews were conducted with senior management, clinicians - consultants, nurses and the reception staff. At times availability of personnel proved difficult because of their other commitments. Each department identified a key person, who could then verify what was being done.

The analysis resulted in the production of object models for each department, documenting their data in terms of objects. Once this step was completed, object models were compared and it was clear that the same data were required by different departments to carry out their functions. Close examination also indicated that specific data items were known by different names, for example home address was recorded simply as address, patient address or home address. Where the data requirements were the same, these objects were identified as Core Objects. A sample set of core objects is shown in table 2.

Enterprise Generic Objects/Classes		
Business Areas	**Core Objects**	**Others**
Finance	GP	Contract
Imaging	Referral Source	Non-Contract
Accident & Emergency	Admin Team	Health Authority
Outpatient clinics -	Clinician Team	Daily Log
Breast	Nurse Team	GP Practice
Back	Consultant Team	GP Fundholding
Cardiology	Clinic Specialty	GP non fundholding
Haematuria	Clinic Type	Support Team
Admissions -	Waiting List	GP Team
Emergency	Appointment Schedule	Hospital
Planned	Appointment Type	Bed Bureau
Waiting List	Patient	
GP	Out-pat	
	Day-pat	
	In-pat	
	Other-pat	
	Pat Activity	
	Medical Condition	
	Symptom	
	Prescription	
	Treatment	
	Report	
	Referral	
	Discharge	
	Diagnostic	
	Resource	
	Ward	
	Ward-Bed	
	Admission	

Table 2: A sample of derived set of Generic Objects for the NHS Hospital

The existing systems, which were disparate, showed duplication in terms of processes, data and data storage. The end product of this analysis is displayed in figure 2. The central section (EO) represents a core set of generic objects, common to all/most Business Areas, to fulfil their business activities. The BAOM layer, shows objects specifically related to a particular Business Area and the SOM layer documents system or application specific objects.

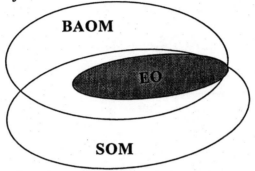

Figure 2: Enterprise wide Objects
EO   : Enterprise-wide Objects
BAOM : Business Area Object Model
SOM   : System Object Model

The framework successfully leads to a set of core or foundation objects/classes. A high level perspective is provided by the first two layers (EO and BAOM) of EM. The derived set of generic objects will not remain static, as the set will probably grow to reflect the changing nature of business requirements.

The Building and Maintenance Company formed the second case study and a similar approach was taken. This started in October 1997 and it was concluded in January 1998. Different departments were identified as Business Areas, and these were studied in detail to establish information flows, processes and data requirements. Some functional areas were already computerised and the company was looking towards extending the existing system such that it should result in an integrated computer system. A set of generic objects is shown in table 3 and these should form the basis for extending the system.

The third organisation was contacted in February 1998 and the study was completed in June of the same year. The theoretical EM framework could not be utilised fully as the organisation structure was very different from the other two organisations. The organisation already had an integrated computer system in place, so this framework was to audit the existing processes and data. The main focus was to discover whether the user/owner perception matched and the required functionality was provided by the integrated system. Any anomalies discovered could then be modified.

Generic Set of objects/Classes		
Business Areas	**Core Objects/Classes**	**Other Objects/Classes**
Operations	Customer	Time Sheet Record Book
Finance	Customer-Type	Pay Details
Contracts	Field-Engineer	Paid Book
Warehouse/Purchasing	Skill-Code	Requisition Sheet
Personnel	Service	Requisition Book
	Service-Type	Purchase Requisition
	Job sheet	Employee
	Quotation	Office worker
	Time-Sheet	Job Description
	Job Authorisation	Vacancy
	Supplier	Advert
	Purchase Requisition	
	Purchase Order	
	Stock item	
	Hire Request	
	Hire Equipment	
	Hire Company	

Table 3: A sample of derived set of Generic Objects for the Handy-Man Ltd.

Generic Set of objects/Classes		
Business Activities	**Core Objects/Classes**	**Other Objects/Classes**
Property Management:	Property	
Renting	Property category	
Letting	Residential	
	Commercial	
	Rent	
	Rent category	
	Payment	
	Payment category	
	Correspondence	
	Invoice	
	Reminder	
	Statement	
	Statement type	
	Client	
	Tenant	
	Landlord	
	Etc.	

Table 4: A sample of derived set of Generic Objects for Managed Properties.

Instead of Business Area analysis, business activities within the firm were identified, for example renting and letting. Each business activity was studied in detail to establish the processes involved and the related data requirements. The same principles were applied as in building a BA Object Model. In this case, the object model developed related to different Business activities. The generic set of objects (or entities) was already in place within the integrated computerised system and these were verified. Table 4 gives a sample set of generic of objects.

2   DISCUSSION AND OUTCOMES

Different authors give different definitions of an 'Enterprise'. In this research project, the following definition has been derived from Olle et al (1991), Whitten et al (1994), Alter (1996) that Enterprise is *"an organisation contains business areas, the enterprise links these business areas, their activities and related data and information flows"*. The organisational theory has modelled enterprises in terms of structure, functions, management view, employee view, etc. Wortmann (1993). The enterprise perspective identifies the organisational activities for which IS support is required. The people perspective defines the personnel involved, their responsibilities and their roles. The information/data perspective defines the information that an organisation is required to store, process and make available in a standard format, which is secured against unauthorised access. The application/process perspective defines the functions that IS are required to provide to support the organisational activities. The technology perspective defines the computing and communication infrastructures, which should meet the organisational, IS requirements.

Katz (1990) states that the term EM can be used to describe a number of different aspects of a business: financial, manufacturing, information and data requirements, flow of information and data across business functional areas, etc. EM can be performed at both higher and lower levels depending upon the degree of detail required and it has the purpose of redesigning an organisation or redesigning existing system development techniques.

The aim was to provide a stable foundation for information systems development by offering consistency and traceability from the strategic to the operational level. The framework achieves this by carrying out BA analysis that provide a high level understanding and representation of the relevant business processes and data requirements within that context. It also gives an insight into the manner in which these act and interact. The essential lesson learnt is that it provides a global view and comprehensive insight as to how different BAs interface and have similar type of data requirements. The objective was fulfilled as this framework did achieve its goal by determining a common set of objects which at a later date can form the basis for future IS development.

Three different organisations were selected to evaluate this framework. Although the first case study achieved the desired results but it was not enough to state that the framework could be applied in other organisations. Two other organisations were identified for further validation. It was applied rigidly within the second case study and the results were favourable. In the third organisation, it had to be tailored, as there were no strict organisational structure. So, the framework can be applied in its entirety or it can be tailored thus giving the user some flexibility.

When looking towards future systems development, the generic set of objects should become the building blocks. Then the required details would be implemented in relation to the required functionality. This integrated approach also offers uniformity and traceability in the system development process as it makes use of the generic set of core objects.

It helps to provide a tangible reference to analysts and designers alike, to compare the objects, their purpose and their relationships. The core objects would also prove useful across business process boundaries. Leach (1998) emphasises the same point by stating that common business objects can be used as the foundation between applications. The following set of benefits could be achieved, for example:

- The framework proves to be a good vehicle for communication with the developers and individuals.
- This approach allows the analyst to think through the overall strategic system strategy and determine how a core set of objects can be developed. This is supported by Mannion (1998) that these core objects are identified by examining business processes, IT applications which support those processes and picking out the ones which appear in each application.
- This core set of objects then will be used as the basis for future systems development and detail is engendered as the system development process begins, thus reducing costs and development time. Karbach et al (1997) states that business objects are extremely useful for fast and reliable development of new applications. As the core set of objects are defined and developed generically, gains are achieved through reuse and Mannion (1998) supports this view that reuse can be provided across different applications which support the business.
- An organisation can also benefit as the core set of objects and classes can be stored in an object library or a repository for future use. This will assist with system development and help to reduce development time and associated costs.
- The growth or modification can take place in a systematic and an orderly fashion as it would help the developers by providing an immediate tangible reference point against which to compare the changes needed.

3   SUMMARY

A survey in Computing (1998) stated that 'IT purchases should deliver business goals', which indicates that organisations of today are not looking for short term solutions to meet a functional need, but for systems which support wider business activities. For organisations to survive in the global market, systems developed should deliver their integrated core business activities rather than disparate functions. In order to do this, a holistic view of organisational activities must be developed. The results from the work with three organisations confirm that an Enterprise Model can be derived using the framework developed in this research project. The framework can be applied from a single department to multiple departments, as well as a whole organisation. This model achieves a holistic perspective by determining a common base of generic objects, which provide a firm foundation of future requirements for the systems development.

References

Alter, S. (1996). "Information Systems - A Management Perspective". The Benjamin/Cummings Publishing Company, Inc.

Athwall, A. K. (1996). "An Integrated Approach to Enterprise Modelling". Object Technology 96 conference (25-27 March); Oxford, England.

Athwall, A. K., Moreton, R. (1995). "Object-Oriented Technology and Enterprise Modelling". BCS ISM - 3rd conference on Methodologies - September.

Belmonte, R. W.; Murray, R. J. (1993). "Getting Ready for Strategic Change". Information Systems Management. Summer.

Carnell, C. A. (1990). "Managing Change in Organisations". Prentice Hall.

Computing (1998). "Business goals dominate IT buying". Computing. VNU Publication. 13 August.

Hutt, A., editor. (1994). "Object Analysis and Design -Comparison of Methods". John Wiley & Sons Publication.

Karbach, W; Noack, J; Kittlaus, H. (1997). "Leveraging a Large Banking Organization to Object Technology". ICSE 97, Boston, MA, USA.

Katz, R. L. (1990). "Business/Enterprise Modelling". IBM Systems Journal, Volume 29, No.4, pp509-525.

Leach, E. (1998). "Counting on Components". Conspectus. Prime Marketing Publications Ltd. March.

Lehman, M. (1997). "Process Modelling - Where Next". ICSE 97, Boston, MA, USA.

Mannion, M; Keepence, B. (1998). "Software Jigsaw". The Computer Buletin. BCS. September 1998.

Nolan, R. L. (1987). "What Transformation is, in Stage by Stage". Nolan, Norton and Co, Boston, MA. Vol 7, No 5.

Olle, T. W.; Hagelstein, J.; Macdonald, I. G.; Rolland, C.; Sol, H. G.; Van Assche, F. J. M.; Verrinj-Stuart. (1991). "A Information Systems Methodologies". Addison-Wesley Publishing Company.

Pettigrew, A. M. (1985). "The Awakening Giant: Continuity and Change in ICI". Blackwell, Oxford Press.

Shelton, R. E. (1994). "Object-Oriented Business Engineering". Object Expo, New York. June 6-10.

Shelton, R. E. (1994). "Business Object Management". Object World, UK. June 21-23.

Whitten, J. L.; Bentley, L. D.; Barlow, V. M. (1994). "Systems Analysis and Design Methods". Irwin, Inc.

Wortmann, J. C. (1993). "Enterprise Modelling: purposes and means". IFIP. pp 613-623.

Zachman, J. A. (1987). "A Framework for Information Systems Architecture". IBM Systems Journal, v. 26, no. 3.

CHAPTER 38

THE INTEGRATION OF INFORMATION TECHNOLOGY (IT) INFRASTRUCTURE WITH NEXT-GENERATION BUSINESS PROCESS RE-ENGINEERING (BPR): A PROPOSED MODEL OF BEST PRACTICE

Majed Al-Mashari and Mohamed Zairi
University of Bradford

Abstract

This paper discusses a proposed model presenting the implementation of next-generation BPR through IT infrastructure support from a complete and integrated perspective. The model is represented by key drivers and four essential core components found to be critical to successful outcomes from the introduction of change based on BPR principles. The basis of the model is supported by empirical studies and widely reported experience on the order of criticality of each of the elements discussed. The central theme of this paper argues that an IT infrastructure that covers aspects of IT infrastructure composition, strategic alignment, effectiveness measurement, re-engineering and migrating legacy systems, IS integration and IS function competence, is essential and critical for effective implementation.

1 INTRODUCTION

Despite the fact that some practitioners consider BPR a management fad which will die like other fads, research has shown that BPR is very much alive and well. A recent survey of Chief Information Officers (CIOs) reports that facilitating and managing BPR is the second most important issue of information systems (IS) management (Brancheau *et al.*, 1996). A Scottish study of BPR practice and a comparative analysis of major surveys in past years reveals that the levels of BPR implementation are: 40% in Scotland, 69% in North America, 75% in Europe, and 27% in the UK (Sockalingam and Doswell, 1996). The ninth annual survey of North American CIOs reveals that the average company launched 3 BPR projects with 82% level of success, and 63% of surveyed companies expected BPR projects to increase in number in future years (Deloitte & Touche, 1998).

However, because of the exponential advancement in enabling integration and global technologies such as the Internet, and the enterprise resource planning (ERP) packages, e.g., SAP (Deloitte & Touche, 1998), the increasing awareness of the importance of change management and process management-related issues (Deakins and Magill, 1997), and the growing interest in viewing BPR as a strategic change activity (Huizing *et al.*, 1997), there appears to be a shift towards a more holistic BPR approach which recognises the importance of processes and technology and their integration in business vision, structure and relationships, resources and culture (Andreu *et al.* 1997; Watts, 1995).

While arguing that BPR remains a critical engine of growth and renewal as we look toward the next millennium, and drawing on a comprehensive review of key reports, research studies and major surveys related to BPR, this paper proposes a model for next-generation BPR based on a holistic view (Figure 1) and shows how it can be implemented effectively. Beside the discussion of the various constituents of this model, a particular emphasis is placed on the potential of IT infrastructural components in this context.

2   AN OVERVIEW OF THE MODEL AND THE VALIDATION OF ITS BASIS

The model described in the following sections is based on the premise that effective implementation of organisational change using the BPR approach and supported by IT means requires attention to certain key elements and their inter-connectedness and integration. The proposed model is composed of 8 elements, illustrated in Table 1, and each is elaborated on in the following sections.

Model Element	Purpose in BPR	Empirical Supporting Evidence
Change Drivers	Triggering change	CSC Index (1994)
BPR Strategy	Describing a plan for change that goes in line with the overall business strategy	Mitchell and Zmud (1995) Huizing et al. (1997)
Benchmarking	Shaping up the strategic direction and determining change attributes	Zairi and Sinclair (1995)
Degree of Change	Translating BPR strategy into a detailed change portfolio that combines a variety of change scales	Andreu et al. (1997) Kettinger et al. (1997)
Methodical Components	Providing a suite of working plans, techniques, and software tools to deal effectively with various activities in BPR	Carr and Johansson (1995) Kettinger et al. (1997) El Sawy (1997)
Integration Components	Sustaining the benefits gained from the introduction of BPR-related change	Zairi and Sinclair (1995)
Socio-Technical Components	Facilitating the insertion of newly-designed processes and structures into the working practice, and minimizing organisational resistance	CSC Index (1994) Zairi and Sinclair (1995) Carr and Johansson (1995)

Model Element	Purpose in BPR	Empirical Supporting Evidence
IT Infrastructural Components	Enabling the implementation of redesigned processes by offering higher degrees of integration among business functions	Mitchell and Zmud (1995) Duncan (1995) Brancheau et al. (1996)

Table 1: Description of The Model Key Elements' Purposes and Supporting Evidences

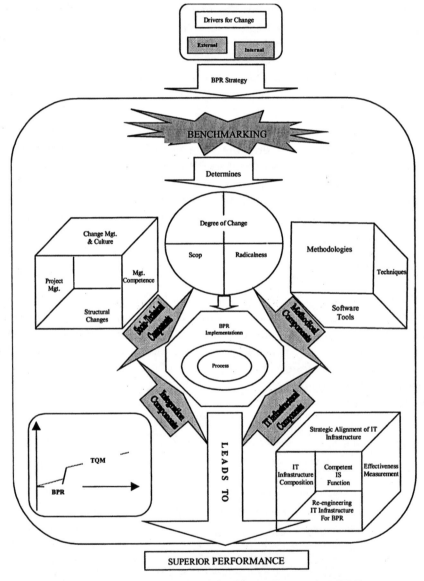

Figure 1: A Holistic Model for Next-Generation BPR

3   ELEMENTS OF NEXT-GENERATION BPR MODEL

3.1   BPR Drivers

BPR drivers can be classified into external and internal drivers. External drivers are related mainly to the increased level of competition, the changes in customers' needs, IT and government regulations and policies. Internal drivers are mainly related to changes in organisational strategies, structure, processes and capabilities.

3.2   BPR Strategy

As business strategy determines objectives and guidance on how organisational capabilities can be best utilised to gain competitive position, BPR strategy accordingly guides the alteration of tasks and flows into integrated processes (Mitchell & Zmud, 1995). Variance in how tasks are performed and the flow of material, people, and information is a source of competitiveness (Hammer, 1990). Therefore, a consideration of strategic context of growth and expansion, creating a top-level strategy to guide change, and careful alignment of corporate strategy with BPR strategy (Guha *et al.*, 1993) are crucial to the success of BPR efforts. An effective strategic discourse will determine how BPR can be implemented and the related change successfully absorbed by the organisation concerned.

3.3   Benchmarking

Benchmarking highlights the negative gaps in performance and enables suitable actions to be taken in all areas to maximise the level of performance needed to be the best in the class (Zairi, 1992). It can play a critical role in shaping the strategic direction to be adopted for change introduction using BPR as it helps organisations to make informed decisions about the type of change to be introduced, highlights areas of change and prioritises them (Zairi, 1995). It is also an effective tool for determining process objectives and identifying innovative process attributes (Davenport, 1993b). Through a comprehensive gap analysis, benchmarking assists in determining the degree of radicalness of the change program concerned.

3.4   Degree of Change

3.4.1   Change Scope

Depending on the desired degree of change, BPR can be implemented at different scopes and levels. These range from narrow processes to changes that go beyond the organisation's boundaries, e.g. to include business partners, customers and suppliers. Process scope (Andreu et al., 1997), relationships between IT application levels and business processes change (Venkatraman, 1994), and type of change orientation (customer and shareholder) (Cypress, 1994) are the major determinants of process change scope. However, models such as those of Venkataraman (1994) provide flexibility in offering a range of scopes of change, i.e. inter-functional, intra-functional and inter-organisational.

3.4.2   Level of Radicalness

A BPR effort can be considered as radical if it takes a "clean-slate" approach and breaks the old way of doing business. Accordingly, the level of radicalness can be seen as the extent to which BPR efforts are innovative and how difficult the learning process is (Andreu *et al.*, 1997).

With the shift towards combining different scales of change, i.e. TQM, BPR and business transformation, as part of one improvement strategy, level of radicalness has been very useful in establishing a clear and detailed change portfolio that ensures a maximum fit and alignment between all types of improvement (Zairi and Sinclair, 1995).

Strategic centrality, feasibility of IT to change process, process breadth, senior management commitment, performance measurement criteria, process functionality, project resource availability, structural flexibility, cultural capacity for change, management's willingness to impact people, and value chain target, are proven useful factors in indicating the level of radicalness that a BPR should take, as well as whether the project should start from a "clean-slate" (Kettinger *et al.*, 1997).

3.5   Methodical Components

Using systematic and structured methodologies for BPR provides working plans to deal with various activities in the BPR process, facilitates motivation and training, accumulates experience in a variety of aspects of BPR and provides milestones for implementing BPR projects (Guha *et al.*, 1993). Project radicalness, structuredness of the process, level of customer focus and the potential for IT enablement has been found critical in defining BPR methodology (Kettinger *et al.*, 1997).

Taking advantage of modern modelling and simulation tools is an element of BPR best practice (Carr and Johansson, 1995). There are more than 102 BPR tools (Kettinger et al., 1997). However, both process visualisation and process analysis are key features in the success of BPR tools (El Sawy, 1997).

3.6   Integration Components

BPR integrated with Total Quality Management (TQM) can achieve better performance because no single approach is believed to be appropriate for organisational change at all times (Zairi and Sinclair, 1995).

There are four major approaches for integrating TQM and BPR: (1) wavering between TQM and BPR; (2) classifying processes based on types of changes required, whether they are radical or incremental; (3) using BPR for high-level design of processes and TQM for detailed designs; or (4) combining short-term improvement with long-term innovation within the same change initiative (Davenport, 1993b).

3.7 Socio-Technical Components

Table 2 presents the role of each socio-technical component as well as the major critical factors in each group.

Cha. Met.	Change management is needed to facilitate the insertion of newly-designed processes and structures into working practice and to deal effectively with resistance. Revision of reward systems, communication, empowerment, people involvement, training and education, creating a culture for change, and stimulating receptivity of the organisation to change are the most important factors related to change of management systems and culture.
Met. Cmp.	Sound management processes ensure that BPR efforts will be implemented in the most effective manner. The most noticeable managerial practices that directly influence the success of BPR implementation are top management support and commitment, championship and sponsorship, and effective management of risks.
Stru.	As BPR brings about structural changes, there is a clear need to determine how BPR teams are going to look, how human resources are integrated, and how the new jobs and responsibilities are going to be formalised.
Pre. Met.	Successful BPR implementation is highly dependent upon an effective BPR program management which includes building process vision, identification of performance measures, adequate identification of the BPR value, effective planning and project management techniques, adequate resources, effective process redesign, and effective use of consultants.

Table 2: Socio-Technical Components of Next-Generation BPR

3.8 IT Infrastructural Components

Besides using software tools to analyse and model business processes, IT infrastructureal enablers are also essential to implementing BPR (Duncan, 1995; Lyons, 1997). Based on their support of different business process requirements, Lyons (1997) classifies the currently available ITs into eight groups: (1) process integration and communication; (2) process coordination and control; (3) front-end data capture and validation; (4) integrated work support; (5) information storage and access; (6) document management; (7) process work support; and (8) process systems development.

The IT infrastructure is a system of artifacts, people and IT-related activities that enables organisational change (Mitchell and Zmud, 1995). Duncan (1995) describes it as a set of shared IT resources that enable current and future business applications.

Results from the CSC Index (1994) show that getting the IS and technology infrastructure in place is the most difficult aspect of BPR in both the US and Europe. This explains why building a responsive IT infrastructure was ranked top of the list of key issues in IS management in a recent Delphi study conducted by Brancheau et al. (1996).

Information plays an active role in BPR. The extent to which a change initiative is successful is determined greatly by the extent to which the needed level of appropriate information is met (Mitchell & Zmud, 1995). Therefore, IT infrastructure and BPR are interdependent in the sense that deciding information needs for the new business processes determines IT infrastructure constituents, and a recognition of IT capabilities provides alternatives for BPR (Mitchell & Zmud, 1995). However, prescriptive matches between various IT architectural designs and organisational structures fail to capture the interdependent nature of emerging organisational processes (Davenport & Short, 1990). This can be put down to a series of incorrect or inadequate decisions on various issues of the IT infrastructure, specifically its composition, alignment of its strategy with BPR strategy, measuring its effectiveness for BPR, the process of re-engineering current IT infrastructure for BPR, and the role of IS function competence in BPR efforts.

3.8.1   IT Infrastructure Constituents and Composition

An IT infrastructure is made up of physical assets (Kayworth *et al.*, 1997), intellectual assets (Broadbent & Weill, 1997; Ross, 1998a), shared services (Broadbent & Weill, 1997), and their linkages (Ross, 1998a).

An effective IT infrastructure composition process follows a top-down approach, beginning with business strategy and IS strategy and passing through designs of data, systems and computer architecture (Malhotra, 1996). Linkages between the IT infrastructure components through an enforcement of IT standards (Kayworth *et al.*, 1997), as well as descriptions of their contexts of interaction, are important for ensuring integrity and consistency among the IT infrastructure components (Ross, 1998a). The IT infrastructure shared services (Broadbent and Weill, 1997) and the human IT infrastructure components, in terms of their responsibilities and their needed expertise, are both vital to the process of the IT infrastructure composition.

3.8.2   Alignment of IT Infrastructure and BPR Strategies

According to Earl *et al.* (1997), two-way strategic alignment between business and IT is needed. However, BPR and IT infrastructure strategies also need effective alignment to ensure a successful change initiative (Kettinger *et al.*, 1997). An IT infrastructure strategy can be defined as '*a plan for directing IT resources and guiding the deployment of information resources*' (Mitchell & Zmud, 1995, p.432).

Henderson and Venkatraman (1993) propose a model of strategic alignment which uses two types of linkages, namely strategic fit and functional integration (Figure 2). The external context represents the business environment in which an organisation competes. The internal context describes the organisational structure choices, the impetus for redesigning critical business processes, and human resource management skills. This model suggests that a fit should exist between the external context of IT and its internal arrangement, and that this fit is as significant as the fit between the internal and the external contexts of business. The model also suggests an operational integration between the IT and organisational infrastructures.

Reich and Benbasat (1996) suggest a number of linkages that indicate the degree of alignment between IT and business strategies. These are also useful in indicating the extent to which both BPR strategy and IT infrastructure strategy are integrated. Firstly, the BPR strategy should contain a statement of information resources requirements. Secondly, the IT infrastructure strategy must be driven from the BPR strategy. Thirdly, the IT infrastructure strategy must be examined against the BPR strategy. Fourthly, line management has to be actively involved in the IT infrastructure strategic planning process. Next, IT managers must be actively involved in BPR planning and, finally, the two strategies must be synchronised carefully during the formulation process.

Critical to the success of BPR projects are strategic decisions related to adequate IT investment (Zairi & Sinclair, 1995) and proper selection of IT sourcing (Earl, 1996).

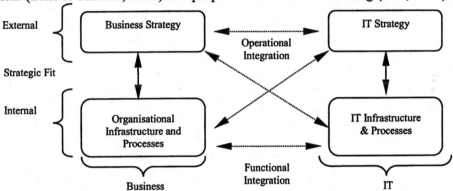

Figure 2: IT Strategic Alignment Model (From Henderson and Venkatraman, 1993)

3.8.3   Measuring IT Infrastructure Effectiveness for BPR

Measuring the IT infrastructure effectiveness for BPR is very important as it determines IT deficiencies that exist when business process information resources requirements cannot be met by the current IT infrastructure capabilities (Earl, 1997). Having feedback mechanisms to re-align the change efforts ensures that the IT infrastructure being put in place optimally supports the change process and thereby becomes fully integrated with the re-engineering efforts.

While Barki and Hartwick (1994) propose a user-centred model for measuring IS effectiveness, Pitt et al. (1995) use service quality. However, other researchers, such as Fiedler et al. (1997) and Munshi (1996), take a more holistic view of IT/IS effectiveness. Fiedler et al. (1997) constructed a web site for IS effectiveness in which brief descriptions and available resources are grouped to address several dimensions of IS success. Munshi (1996), however, identifies three dimensions for IS effectiveness namely scope, measurement, and social paradigm. However, measures can be customised from different models, e.g., Fiedler et al. (1997), to fit the specific needs of an organisation.

3.8.4 Re-engineering the IT Infrastructure for BPR

Re-engineering and Migration of Legacy Systems
BPR projects often require revamping of the IS to deliver the full potential of the re-engineered processes (Jahnke & Tjiok, 1998). However, because of the mismatch between current technology and the legacy architecture of current systems, and the need for cross-functional applications to achieve alignment with the newly-redesigned cross-functional business processes (Lyons, 1997), migrating legacy systems to new systems is a key to creating an integrative IT infrastructure. Also, Jahnke and Tjiok (1998) state that, *'legacy systems represent an important asset, containing valuable information about current practices and business rules, which might support the analysis and fact-finding stage within BPR. Reengineering legacy IS is aimed at using corporate resources in a most economic way, i.e., re-using application knowledge to a maximum extent'* (p. 43).

Technical approaches are used to re-engineer legacy systems automatically. For instance, knowledge-based technology helps software engineers to re-engineer software systems to new technology standards by automating the knowledge-intensive conversion process (Liu *et al.*, 1996). However, architectural understanding, programming language and structure of code, dependencies on special platform features and the cumulative effects of continuous maintenance all affect the ability to re-engineer a legacy system (Tilley, 1996). Therefore, the use of data architecture repositories which describe business rules, process architecture and functional architecture (Jahnke & Tjiok, 1998), and the enforcement of systems reusability, are important approaches to making the legacy systems re-engineering process easier and adaptable.

IS Integration
Earl *et al.* (1997) believe it is imperative for IT organisations to move from internal systems development towards systems integration. A recent survey of critical issues in IS management in both the US and Europe conducted by CSC Index shows that companies are still dominated by function-based software development approaches, despite their accumulating experiences in BPR for six years (Lyons, 1997). This indicates a major source of failure as the development of IS based on traditional function-based approaches does not fit the core principle of BPR, which asserts the necessity of rethinking business operations in terms of integrated cross-functional processes (Lyons, 1997).

IS integration for BPR can be viewed as the extent to which various IS are formally linked for the purpose of sharing complete, consistent, accurate and timely information among business processes (DoD, 1994). Data integration and communication networking are the most important enablers for IS integration. The new advanced techniques of database integration and the extensive communication and inter-connectivity technologies offer better mechanisms for integrating various organisational IS that support business processes with their information needs (Duncan, 1995). With the move towards open architectures and the use of client/server technology which brings together a mix of platforms, applications and multiple network configurations, there has been a greater focus on developing connectivity tools. SAP developed the R/3 systems integrator, which is now being built in most big companies like IBM and Price Waterhouse. This technology forces some re-engineering as it is used essentially to integrate major systems within the organisation, e.g., manufacturing, financial and supply chain management. There is also a growing interest in supporting integration of wide-area heterogeneous information repositories by making use of Internet and Intranet technologies.

3.8.5 The Role of IS Function Competence in BPR Efforts

Building a high performance and effective IS function to accommodate the radical shifts in both technology and business is considered a critical factor in the success of BPR efforts (Earl *et al.*, 1997). An effective IS function needs to be designed into a comprehensive and flexible structure that focuses on a number of competencies (Laud & Theis, 1997; Ross, 1998b; Gordon, 1994; Saunders & Jones, 1992) (see Table 3).

• Quality	• Empowerment through education	• Cheaper IT operations and support
• Partnerships between all parties involved in managing IT resources based on mutual trust and credibility	• Re-skilling of IT staff	• Satisfied customers
	• Motivation of employees	• Value creation
	• Better strategic planning	• Faster solution delivery
	• Continuos IS function benchmarking	• Continuos measurement of IS function effectiveness
• Adequate distribution of IT managerial responsibilities		

Table 3: Features of Competent IS Function for Next-Generation BPR

4   CONCLUSION

This paper presented a holistic model of BPR implementation using IT infrastructure support. It argued that at the heart of effective BPR implementation for next generation projects, a full integrated and balanced perspective has to be taken. In particular, the paper proposed that the following approach, if adhered to, would most likely yield the desired outcomes for optimum performance:

- Key drivers - widely supported by the body of the literature, next-generation BPR projects will be dependent on a range of internal and external drivers.
- BPR strategy - supported by many studies, BPR implementation depends on a thorough and systematic approach to strategic formulation, deployment, alignment and review.
- Benchmarking - viewed by many practitioners as an indispensable technique for determining various attributes of BPR-related change.
- Core components - four critical components represent key pillars to successful BPR

implementation: (1) socio-technical, involving change of management and structure, management support and project management; (2) methodical, necessitating the use of methodology, techniques and software tools; (3) integration, calling for integrating BPR with TQM; and (4) IT infrastructural, involving IT infrastructure composition, strategic alignment, effectiveness measurement, re-engineering and migrating legacy systems, IS integration and IS function competence.

The make-up of the proposed model suggests that this balanced approach could lead to sustainable performance and an effective introduction of change. The model offers ample opportunity for further study and is suitable for more empirical testing and validation. For instance, the following aspects could be scrutinised:

- Process-oriented IS analysis and design methods.
- IT infrastructure design and creation of value orientation.
- Integration between BPR and TQM.
- Impact of degree of radicalness on sustainable performance.
- Driving BPR through effective corporate strategy.

References

Andreu, R., Ricart, J., and Valor, J. (1997) 'Process Innovation: Changing Boxes or Revolutionising Organisations?', Knowledge and Process Management, Vol. 4, No. 2, pp.114-125.

Barki, H. and Hartwick, J. (1994) 'Measuring User Participation, User Involvement, and User Attitude', MIS Quarterly, March, pp.59-79.

Brancheau, J., Janz, B., and Wetherbe, J. (1996) 'Key Issues in Information Systems Management: 1994-1995 SIM Delphi Results', MIS Quarterly, June, pp.225-242.

Broadbent, M. and Weill, P. (1997) 'Management by Maxim: How Business and IT Managers Can Create IT Infrastructures', Sloan Management Review, Spring, pp.77-92.

Carr, D. and Johansson, H. (1995) Best Practices in Reengineering: What Works and What Doesn't in the Reengineering Process. McGraw-Hill, New York, USA.

CSC Index (1994) State of Reengineering Report. North America and Europe, Technical Report, CSC Index, Inc., London, UK.

Cypress, H. (1994) 'Reengineering', OR/MS Today, February, pp.18-29.

Davenport, T. (1993a) Process Innovation: Reengineering Work through Information Technology. Harvard Business School Press, Boston, MA, USA.

Davenport, T. (1993b) 'Need Radical Innovation and Continuous Improvement? Integrated Process Reengineering and TQM', Planning Review, May/June, pp. 6-12.

Davenport, T. and Short, J. (1990) 'The New Industrial Engineering: Information Technology and Business Process Redesign', Sloan Management Review, Vol. 31, No. 4, pp.11-27.

Deakins, E. and Makgill, H. (1997) 'What Killed BPR?: Some evidence from the literature', Business Process Management Journal, Vol. 3, No.1, pp.81-107.

Deloitte & Touche (1998) Reengineering for Results. On-line at http://www.dtcg.com/what/serv/reenres/.

DoD (1994) Corporate Information Management for The 21st Century: Enterprise Integration – Implementing Strategy. On-line at http://www.dtic.mil/c3i/bprcd/mlibtop.htm.

Duncan, N. (1995) 'Capturing flexibility of information technology infrastructure: A study of resource characteristics and their measure', Journal of Management Information Systems, Vol. 12, No. 2, pp.37-45.

Earl, M. (1996) 'The Risk of Outsourcing IT', Sloan Management Review, Spring, pp.26-32.

Earl, M, Rockart, J, and Ross, J. (1997) Eight Imperatives For Today's IT Organisation: Accommodating A Radical Shift of Responsibility. Executive Reports, Centre for Research in Information Management, London Business School, London.

El Sawy, O. (1997) Business Process Reengineering – Do software Tools Matter?. On-line at http://hsb.baylor.edu/ramsower/ais.ac.97/papers/elsaw.htm.

Fiedler, K., Grover, V., and Teng, J. (ed.) (1997) Information Systems Effectiveness. On-line at http://theweb.badm.sc.edu/grover/isworld/isoehom3.htm.

Gordon, S. (1994) Benchmarking The Information Systems Function. On-line at http://www.babson.edu/faculty/gordon/f94bench.html.

Guha, S., Kettinger, W., and Teng, T. (1993) 'Business Process Reengineering: Building a Comprehensive Methodology', Information Systems Management, Summer, pp.13-22.

Hammer, M. (1990) 'Reengineering Work: Don't Automate, Obliterate', Harvard Business Review, Vol. 68, No. 4, pp.104-112.

Henderson, J. and Venkatraman, N. (1993) 'Strategic Alignment: Leveraging Information Technology for Transforming Organisations', IBM Systems Journal, Vol. 32, No. 1, pp.4-16.

Huizing, A., Koster, E., and Bouman, W. (1997) 'Balance in Business Reengineering: An Empirical Study of Fit and Performance', Journal of Management Information Systems, Vol. 14, No. 1, pp. 93-118.

Jahnke, B. and Tjiok, C. (1998) 'Identifying IS Support Alternatives for Business Process Reengineering', Knowledge and Process Management, Vol. 6, No. 1, pp. 41-50.

Kayworth, T., Sambamurthy, V., and Chatterjee, D. (1997) A Conceptual Framework of Information Technology Infrastructure: The Critical Link of Technology Standards. On-line at http://hsb.baylor.edu/ramsower/ais.ac.97/papers/kayworth.htm .

Kettinger, W., Teng, J., and Guha, S. (1997) 'Business Process Change: A Study of Methodologies, Techniques, and Tools', MIS Quarterly, March, pp. 55-80.

Laud, R. and Thies, P. (1997) 'Great Expectations: Structuring IT Organisations That Really Deliver', Business Horizons, July-August, pp.25-36.

Liu, Z., Ballantyne, M. and Seward, L. (1996) An Assistant for Re-engineeing Legacy

Systems. On-line at http://www.spo.eds.com/edsr/papers/asstreeng.html.

Lyons, G. (1997) 'The Role of Information Technology in Enterprise Re-engineering', Knowledge and Process Management, Vol. 4, No. 4, pp. 268-277.

Malhotra, Y. (1996) Enterprise Architecture: An Overview. On-line at http://www.brint.com/papers/enterarch.htm.

Mitchell, V. and Zmud, R. (1995) 'Strategy Congruence and BPR Rollout' in Grover, V and Kettinger, W. (eds.), Business Process Change: Reengineering Concepts, Methods and Technologies, Idea Group Publishing, London, pp.428-452.

Munshi, J. (1996) 'A Framework for MIS Effectiveness', Presentation at the 1996 International Conference of the Academy of Business Administration, July 10-17, Athens, Greece.

Pitt, L., Watson, R., and Kavan, C. (1995) 'Service Quality: A Measure of Information Systems Effectiveness', MIS Quarterly, June, pp. 173-187.

Reich, B. and Benbasat, I. (1996) 'Measuring the Linkage Between Business and Information Technology Objectives', MIS Quarterly, March, pp.55-81.

Ross, J. (1998a) 'IT Infrastructure Management', Presented at the 98 annual conference of IS Management at the London Business School Centre for Resaerch in Information Management, London, UK.

Ross, J. (1998b) 'Strategic Management of IT Assets', Presented at the 98 annual conference of Information Systems Management at the London Business School Centre for Resaerch in Information Management, London, UK.

Saunders, C. and Jones, W. (1992) 'Measuring Performance of the Information Systems Function', Journal of Management Information Systems, Vol. 8, No. 4, pp. 63-82.

Sockalingam, S. and Doswell, A. (1996) 'Business Process Re-engineering in Scotland: Survey and Comparison', Business Change & Re-engineering, Vol. 3, No. 4, pp. 33-44.

Tilley, S. (1996) Perspectives On Legacy System Reengineering. On-line at http://www.sei.cmu.edu/~reengineering/pubs/lsysree/lsysree.html.

Venkatraman, N. (1994) 'IT-Enabled Business Transformation: From Automation to Business Scope Redefinition', Sloan Management Review, Vol. 35, No. 2, pp. 73-87.

Watts, J. (1995) 'An Introduction to Holistic BPR', Business Change & Re-engineering, Vol. 2, No. 4, pp. 3-6.

Zairi, M. (1992) Competitive Benchmarking: An Executive Guide. Technical Communications (Publishing) Ltd, UK.

Zairi, M. (1995) 'The Integration of Benchmarking and BPR: A Matter of Choice or Necessity?', Business Process Re-engineering & Management Journal, Vol. 1, No. 3, pp. 3-9.

Zairi, M. and Sinclair, D. (1995) 'Business Process Re-engineering and Process Management: A Survey of Current Practice and Future Trends in Integrated Management', Management Decision, Vol. 33, No. 3, pp. 3-16.

CHAPTER 39

MOTIVATION FOR INTEGRATING COMPUTER NETWORK SIMULATION WITH BUSINESS PROCESS SIMULATION

Julie Eatock, George Giaglis and Ray J Paul
Brunel University

Abstract

Many companies are disappointed with the results that investing in new IT infrastructure or BPR projects generate. This may be due to the fact that the results of implementation of a new information system are dependent on the experts' best 'guesstimates', rather than in-depth analysis. This paper identifies a need for the integration of computer network simulation and business process simulation in order to properly analyse the effect one has on the other. A simple case study is included to illustrate fundamental problems. An intermediate model, representing the information system level, is promoted to forge the link between the two other domains.

1. INTRODUCTION

Most large companies have information systems supporting their core activities, and as competitive pressures increase the dependency on these systems increases also, leading to changes in the IS infrastructure within the company. However, these changes in IS infrastructure often lead to disappointment with a failure rate up to 70%.

Business Process Re-engineering (BPR) is concerned with redesigning the business processes to improve throughput, minimise production times, reduce the number of resources etc. It has been reported (Hammer and Champy, 1993, Stewart, 1993) that the failure rate in BPR projects is over 50%.

Both these statistics are disturbing. One frequently cited problem is the fact that BPR fails to accurately predict the effects of radical changes (Hansen 1994). Many re-engineering projects advocate the installations of new computer systems to improve these processes but do not properly investigate the underlying structure of this new IS.

Designing a computer network to support the IS infrastructure is not necessarily an easy task. However, the so-called 'best' computer network may not be the best for the business as a whole. It is often the case that the cost of implementation of this comprehensive network may outweigh the advantages of its installation. If this 'best' network is installed the company may end up with an expensive system that has abilities way beyond their requirements, whilst a lower specification network may fulfil their requirements at a much cheaper cost.

The effects of installing a new IS may require that business processes change radically, but the effects of these changes on performance can be extremely difficult to quantify (Giaglis and Paul 1996, MacArthur et al 1994). It will generally be in the hands of the team of experts in charge of the business process change who will use best 'guesstimates', based on their own experiences and expectations.

Business Process Simulation (BPS) is becoming an increasingly important tool in business process re-engineering (Lee and Elcan 1996, Giaglis 1996), whilst computer network simulation (CNS) is being used with increasing frequency in the designing of computer networks (Sauer and McNair 1983). Both of these aspects can affect the design of the other, but are usually considered in isolation. In order to obtain optimal results of the entire management change process these two tools should be used in parallel (Venkatraman 1994, Fielder et al 1995, Galliers 1993, Grover et al 1994). This is not happening in practice.

Section 2 discusses some of the limitations of simulation in the business process and computer network domains. It suggests that a direct link between the two domains may exist, and explores the difficulties of forging it. Section 3 considers the fact that link between the two domains may be indirect, rather than direct, and suggests a method to link the two domains by incorporating a third domain, namely the IS level. The final sections cover discussion topics and indicate areas of further research needed on the subject.

2. SIMULATION OF BUSINESS PROCESSES AND COMPUTER NETWORKS

Business process simulation software, such as SIMPROCESS, MicroSaint, and Witness are designed to emulate the dynamics of processes and display it graphically, thus indicating visually problems within the system, such as the build-up of queues, waiting times for resources etc. This visualisation of the system in its entirety, rather than its constituent parts in isolation, can then be the origin of creative ideas for re-designing the problematic processes (MacArthur et al 1994).

Business process simulation software, although stochastic (at least to some extent), doesn't take into account the physical location of servers and workstations, or how data is stored and the ease of accessibility. These attributes of the physical network can affect the overall process. An increase in the number of inputs into the system will increase traffic on the communication links between servers and workstations. This increase in traffic may in turn cause more 'collisions' of data within the links, requiring that the data must be re-sent, which in turn causes the communication between the server and workstation to be slower. However, when designing a business process model the times allocated to the task are dependent of the number of entities rather than the amount of network traffic. For example, a company that has 1000 products on its books will have more network traffic than that which has only 100 products, even if they both receive the same number of orders per day. This is due to the number of times the product and inventory databases have to be accessed per order. This means that this increase in delay time between sending the data and receiving the reply may not be considered when modelling the process at the business level only. This error may be negligible for a single data item transaction, but may become significant if this transaction is repeated continually. In other words, a model may suggest an ability to cope with an x% increase in the number of inputs, but in reality this percentage may be significantly less, or it may lead to unexpected bottlenecks. This could lead to the disappointment that many companies experience with their new IS infrastructure.

Alternatively, the installation of a new computer system may cause business processes to change, producing an increase in performance. The problem is how can we accurately assess this increase in performance especially if this is crucial to the process as a whole. To illustrate this point, let us consider a very simple case. Company XYZ receive orders from their customers, check the order against their inventory, and despatch the goods to the customers. However, 30% of the orders received require some products that are currently out of stock. XYZ despatches the goods that are in stock and creates a backorder for the out of stock goods. This effectively increases the packing and delivery process by 30%. It is anticipated that a new computer system will improve the replenishment process, thereby reducing the number of backorders, and hence workload required. The problem is to determine the percentage by which the backorders will be decreased, and then reflect this reduction in the TO-BE model of the new business process in order to determine whether this new computer system is economically viable. As this reduction in the number of backorders is crucial to the process as a whole, the need to accurately assess it is imperative. The problem is *how* can we accurately assess the change in performance?

In order to calculate the business effects of changing the underlying IS let us assume that there is a direct link from the computer network model to the business process model figure 1. That is, if a computer network model of the proposed IT system is built, the outputs from this model can be directly fed into the business process model, accurately reflecting the changes that the new IS would produce at the BP level.

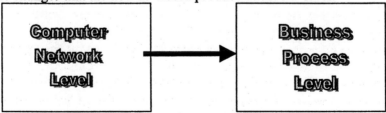

Figure 1: Relationships between BPS and CNS (Initial Hypothesis)

Two models of the above scenario were built, one that reflected the activities at the business process level, and the other that represented the new computer network that was to be installed. Figures 2and figure 3 show how one process, namely 'receive order', is represented in both models.

XYZ receive order by phone

Figure 2: The Order Taking Process (Business Level)

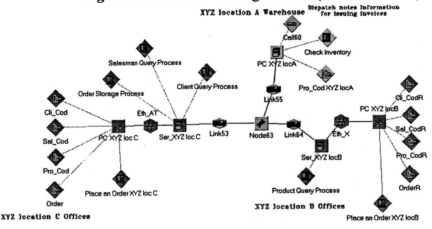

Figure 3: The Order Taking Process (Network Level)

At this point it becomes obvious that the two models are working at a completely different level of abstraction. The business process model is dealing with orders, and does not consider the products that are ordered on an individual basis, whilst the computer network is dealing with the databases, and therefore with individual products. Another problem that becomes apparent is that the network level of the model is dealing with times in units of milliseconds and seconds, while the BP level is dealing with processes in units of minutes or hours. This means that changes in the CN level model will only produce small changes in the BP level model, and may not alter the overall results. This means that the outputs from the computer network model are incompatible with the inputs of the business process level. For example, as stated 30% of the orders produce backorders, but this figure doesn't indicate how many of the products from each order are missing. At the business process level, the fact that an order produces a backorder or not is all that is relevant whereas at the computer network level, how many of the products are out-of-stock is proportional to the traffic in the communication links. This increase in traffic will affect the speed with which an order can be input into the system, thereby affecting the whole process, even though the model does not deal explicitly with products.

This is as already stated a simple example in a very simple case, but similar problems will be experienced to a greater or lesser degree in almost all other attempts to integrate models in these domains.

3. SIMULATION OF INFORMATION SYSTEMS

The difficulty of interfacing these two models requires that another model at an intermediate level is built to enable the two models to 'speak' to each other. This intermediate level represents the IS infrastructure within the business process, which the computer network will support. It should indicate the communication between workstations and servers, and how this communication will operate. For example, in the above scenario, will the whole order be taken before checking the inventory, or will the inventory be checked after each item is ordered? Figure 4 shows this intermediate level for the above scenario.

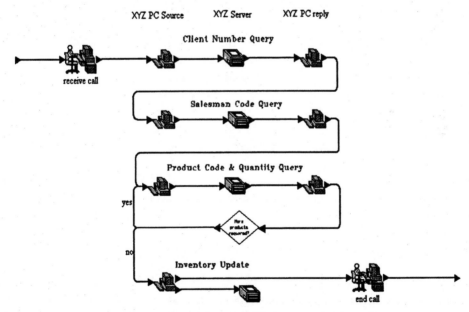

Figure 4: The Order Taking Process (IS Level)

This IS level model is not concerned with such things as modem link speeds, protocols, packet size etc, which are the domain of the network simulation model. The main purpose of this model is to identify how long the delays are between requesting information and receiving the appropriate reply reflecting the longer delays experienced with the increase in traffic on the network.

This development refines the original hypothesis, that a *direct* link between the CN and BP levels exists, to an alternative hypothesis that the link between the levels exists, but rather than being direct, they are linked through a third level, namely the IS level of the system (Figure 5).

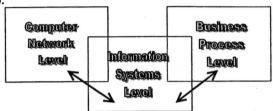

Figure 5: Relationships between BPS and CNS (Revised Hypothesis)

Establishing this link can be broken down into three stages. Stage 1 involves building a business process model by dividing the process into individual tasks, keeping the model as accurate as possible, whilst retaining simplicity e.g. receive order by phone, create despatch note. This model should then be verified and tested to check the accuracy of the results against current performance indicators. Stage 2 is then to build an IS level model of the activities identified in the BP level model into the processes that make up these activities. For example, accessing the server to identify the customer, checking stock levels etc could be processes that are combined in the 'receive order by phone' activity. Stage 3 is to break these activities down further into the computer network level to incorporate the effects of processor speeds, modem speeds, packet size, protocols, etc. that determine how the IS will conduct its communications.

The results obtained by running the computer network model, can then be incorporated into the IS level model. The IS model can then be run which will then reflect the process at both the lower level entities and higher level entities, in this case both product and order level. The information pertaining to the higher level entities (orders) can then be fed into the business process level model and this model run to determine the effects of the installation of the new computer system. Because the business process model will now reflect the lowest level of operation the results will quantify the performance change.

4. DISCUSSION AND CONCLUDING REMARKS

The advantage of using the three levels of simulation models is that a change in any of the levels will be easily reflected in the other two levels. This means that if an increase in throughput is anticipated at the business process level, the effects of this can be monitored at the computer network level to determine whether this increase in throughput will have any adverse effects. Any necessary changes could then be made at the network level to deal with these effects. Conversely, any changes at the computer network level, such as taking advantage of some new technology, can be tested at the network level and then fed back via the IS level model to the business process level model to determine the effects on the overall process. New technology benefits can be compared to the cost of installation to determine economic viability and the appropriate action can be taken, reducing the chance of companies being disappointed with new technology benefits living up to expectations.

Further refinement to the model can be made which involves re-defining the IS model as a sub-level of the BP model (Figure 6). For this to be possible the modelling tool used needs to be of hierarchical design.

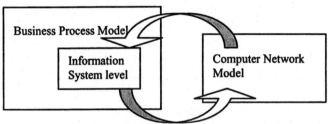

Figure 6: Integrated BP/IS level and CN model

The main advantage of this design over the previous one is that now any changes with the information system level are *automatically* reflected in the business process model, and vice versa, without the need to transfer data between the models. Using this design for the integration of the models, data now only needs to be transferred between the CNS model and the IS level of the BPS model, whilst maintaining the ability to reflect changes in the other domain. This design also reduces the number of models that are required to be built to two, but increases the complexity of the business process model. The complexity and the need to build two models, from different aspects, of one system implies that this method is only viable if the BP model is particularly sensitive to changes in the information system. This could be verified by performing some sensitivity analysis on the basic BP model.

5. FURTHER RESEARCH

This section suggests areas of further research into this topic. There is a need to build a more detailed framework of how these models should be designed from one another. This will be a more iterative approach than this paper suggests, with the network communications having an impact on the IS which will impact on the business processes as well as vice versa.

Another factor that needs to be studied is assessing the viability of building three models from differing aspects of the same problem. Is this going to be a financially viable option? The answer will depend on how accurate the results are, or indeed how much the computer network functions will affect the organisation as a whole or vice versa. Essentially, the answer to this question depends on comparing the *benefits* of having the additional information/insight that simulation can produce against the *costs* of building and using the models. It is expected that only very complex business processes and information systems may render such evaluation by simulation worthwhile at the present state. However, it is possible to build re-usable simulation model libraries that would enable modellers to pick simulation objects and assemble models in a more economical fashion that would render the method effective in most real-life situations.

A two-year research project, that commenced in April '98, funded by EPSRC, under their SEBPC program, is currently underway. The project is in collaboration with CACI products, who have supplied two of their simulation software packages "Simprocess" and "Comnet III", that are being used in the project, and OSI, who have agreed to donate a generous amount of consultancy time to the project. The ASSESS-IT project aims to develop a framework of analysis for information systems modelling, and then translate the modelling requirements into simulation structures. The purpose of this is to integrate business process and information technology simulation models in theory, and in practice by way of a case study.

For more information about the project, our industrial collaborators, and how to contact us, see our web-site *http://www.brunel.ac.uk/~cspgggg/assess/assessit.htm*

References

Fielder, K.D., Grover, V. and Teng, J.T.C. (1995) An Empirical Study of Information Technology Enabled Business Process Redesign and Corporate Competitive Strategy, European Journal of Information Systems, 4, 1, pp. 17-30.

Galliers, R.D. (1993) Towards a Flexible Information Architecture: Integrating Business Strategies, Information Systems Strategies, and Business Process Redesign, Journal of Information Systems, 3, 3, pp. 199-213.

Giaglis, G.M. (1996) Modelling Electronic Data Interchange Through Simulation: An Industry-Wide Perspective. In the Proceedings of the 8th European Simulation Symposium, Genoa, Italy, October, pp. 199-203

Giaglis, G.M. and Paul, R.J. (1996) It's Time to Engineer Re-engineering: Investigating the Potential of Simulation Modelling in Business Process Redesign. In Scholz-Reiter, B. and Stickel, E. (eds.), Business Process Modelling, Springer-Verlag, Berlin, pp. 313-332.

Grover, V., Fielder, K.D. and Teng, J.T.C. (1994) Exploring the Success of Information Technology Enabled Business Process Reengineering, IEEE Transactions on Engineering Management, 41, 3, pp. 276-284.

Hansen, G.A. (1994) Automating Business Process Reengineering: Breaking the TQM Barrier, Prentice-Hall, Englewood Cliffs, New Jersey.

Kottemann, J.E. and Dolk, D.R. (1992) Model Integration and Modeling Languages: A Process Perspective, Information Systems Research, 3, 1, pp. 1-16.

Lee, Y. and Elcan, A. (1996) Simulation Modeling for Process Reengineering in the Telecommunications Industry, Interfaces, 26, 3, pp. 1-9.

MacArthur, P.J., Crosslin, R.L, Warren, J.R. (1994) A Strategy for Evaluating Alternative Information System Designs for Business Process Reengineering, International Journal of Information Management, 14, 4, pp. 237-251.

MacArthur, P.J., Crosslin, R.L, Warren, J.R. (1994) A Strategy for Evaluating Alternative Information System Designs for Business Process Reengineering, International Journal of Information Management, 14, 4, pp. 237-251.

Sauer, C.H. and MacNair, E.A. (1983) Simulation of Computer Communication Systems, Prentice Hall, New York.

Stewart, T.A (1993) Reengineering - The Hot New Managing Tool, Fortune, 128, 4, pp. 32-37.

Venkatraman, N. (1994) IT-Enabled Business Transformation: From Automation to Business Scope Redefinition, Sloan Management Review.

CHAPTER 40

A PROCESS IMPROVEMENT FRAMEWORK FOR SMALL TO MEDIUM SIZED ENTERPRISES TAKING INTO CONSIDERATION ELECTRONIC COMMUNICATION TECHNOLOGIES

T Husein, R Moreton, A Sloane and HD Knöll *
University of Wolverhampton, * Fachhochschule
Nordostniedersachsen, Lueneburg, Germany.

Abstract

Given the rapid change in technology and market conditions, small to medium size enterprises (SMEs) are under tremendous pressure to improve their effectiveness. In order to do this, these enterprises need to analyse their business to determine relevant changes, and to determine how new technology can be successfully utilised? In particular the advances in electronic communication technologies (ECTs) offer such organisations the opportunity to use this technology to increase organisational effectiveness. To encourage SMEs to incorporate these technologies, it is important that a reasonably inexpensive, thorough and easy-to-use process improvement framework (PIF) is available to guide them through the changes. This paper aims to promote such a framework. The life cycle of the framework has the potential to involve all development stages, from strategic analysis and Business Process Reengineering (BPR) through to the continuous process improvement (CPI) of the reengineered process.

1 INTRODUCTION

Globalisation of business practices, increasing use of computers and communication technologies are beginning to redefine the nature of office work. Enterprises need to, therefore study themselves to determine what should be changed (Vogel & Glasson 1995; Grover et al. 1995; Talwar 1993). This is especially true of SMEs, which are a major provider of employment and can play a vital role in economic regeneration

(Beaver & Harris 1995). Many of these enterprises have evolved to the point where the structure and procedures are no longer in keeping with the needs of the future (Regan 1995; Zwass 1996). However, they should not be treated like small versions of large enterprises because they have a significant number of attributes, which makes them different from larger enterprises (Petric et al. 1996*)*. Some of these attributes are: little or no formal administrative structure, less formal organisational structure, limited access to resources or expertise, limited financial resources and very little or no resources are available to research or to innovate.

Technological or socio-political development compels Industries to change (Champy 1995). Globally, access and availability of information together with electronic communication technologies (ECTs) are beginning to generate a new business paradigm. It is effective utilisation of available communication technologies to convey information and to use strategically; to re-organise business processes to satisfy customer perspectives; to gain competitive edge; to accommodate and respond to changes quickly and effectively. Recent years have seen businesses benefiting from significant changes in the telecommunications environment, which have occurred mainly in the area of network services, including Fax, Electronic Mail (e-mail) Electronic data interchange (EDI) and the Internet, forming an integral part of Electronic Commerce (E-Commerce).

E-Commerce has been described variously by different authors. It is sharing information, maintaining business relationships, and conducting business transactions by means of telecommunications (Zwass 1996). It is the application of information technology to support the business processes, the exchange of goods and services, which promises to radically transform business (Kambil 1997). It is a modern business technology that addresses the needs of organisations, markets and consumers to cut costs while improving the quality of goods and services and increasing the speed of service delivery (Kalakota & Whinston 1996). It is a business strategy that seeks specific business goals, which needs a variety of Information Technologies for the purpose of transforming the relationships between businesses and opening new market opportunities (Pickerill 1993).

The move towards E-Commerce is driven by four primary forces: - the increasingly global nature of business; the growing inter-organisational and co-dependency of companies within a value chain; the need to control costs; and the desire to provide superior customer services. Lucas (1997) estimates that by the year 2000, business conducted through E-Commerce will exceed approximately 25 billion pounds per year.

Process improvement has been widely referred to in the literature as a result of BPR initiatives in the early 1990s. More recently it has been recognised that the alternative, less radical approach of Continuous Process Improvement (CPI) may be more appropriate for many organisations.

Business Process Reengineering (BPR), involves the fundamental rethinking and radical redesign of business processes to achieve dramatic improvement in critical measures of performance such as cost, quality service and speed (Hammer 1994;

Hammer & Stanton 1995; Hammer1996; Regan 1995). Though work in the field of BPR emphasises the need for a synthesis between business and technology, many studies have not taken account of the fundamental nature of electronic communication and its influence on the business environment. Continuous Process Improvement (CPI) on the other hand aims to achieve incremental, continuous improvement resulting in the streamlining of a process in the pursuit of specific objectives, for example continuous customer satisfaction. It aims to enhance the existing situation and only looks at what is required to attain the desired performance requirements.

With these rapid advances in E-Commerce many organisations are now trying to use new technology to make themselves more successful (Probhu et al, 1994; Ramarapu & Lado 1995). Hence Business Process Redesign/Reengineering has become the main issue for many companies to regain competitiveness and profitability (Wastell et al. 1994; Reponen 1994). It has been suggested that many companies are aware of the possibilities that E-Commerce can provide, but are afraid to adopt it as a medium for doing business (Bradesko 1995). This reluctance to adopt these technologies by SMEs have been widely documented and analysed (Garcia-Sierra et al. 1994; Hoogeweegen & Wagenaar 1995; Meier & Suhl1995; Gebauer 1995; Parker & Swatman 1995). Key inhibiting factors are a lack of awareness regarding these technologies; a fear-based culture; financial constraints and constraints of home market. To address this issue it is important that a reasonably inexpensive, thorough and easy to apply Process Improvement framework (PIF) is available to guide the businesses through these changes.

2   METHODOLOGY ANALYSIS.

Process Improvement (PI) and often BPR has become the key issue for companies to maintain competitive edge in an ever-increasing global market. Recent years have seen a remarkably high increase in the number of commercially available methodologies to support its implementation (Kleinberg 1995). However it has been recognised that in practice a methodological approach is often not used (Chatzoglou & Macaulay 1996) because they appear to lack clear articulation (Probhu et al. 1994).

A methodology should be a formal structured general-purpose approach to the solution of a particular type of problem (Kellener 1995) and should be an explicit mechanism for helping to solve problems. However, once there is more than one methodology for solving similar problems, an additional problem of choice is created (Jayaratna 1994). A methodology comparison provides a structured means of selection and serves to provide evidence that the initial selection was correct or that other more appropriate methodologies exists (The Object Agency Inc. 1995). There is however problems associated with methodology comparisons and in an attempt to avoid these problems, it is suggested that the following is undertaken: -
i.   use of an appropriate framework to conduct the evaluation;

ii.   a thorough review and research of the methodology including manually searching for varied terms which should then be quantified;

iii.   an appropriate definition of the methodology which is neither overly constrained or unconstrained.

It was therefore decided to use NIMSAD (Normative Information Model-Based System Analysis and Design), a general framework derived from problem solving in industry and academia. Its application to the analysis of any methodology promotes understanding the area of problem solving and evaluating the methodologies' structure, steps, and formalisation.

A number of methodologies were chosen on the basis that each claimed to be able to successfully and radically improve organisations business processes. Those included in the comparison were chosen from varying backgrounds i.e. commercial, academic, research based, etc. The comparison highlighted that the strongest methodologies in all aspects of BPR were those commercially available and coincidentally the most expensive, placing them beyond the budget of SMEs (Husein et al. 1997). The less expensive methodologies, within the budgetary scope of SMEs, often lacked strength in many important areas of process improvement and offered very little detailed documentation. The comparison yielded a new Process Improvement framework (PIF) taking ECTs into consideration and was designed to provide an inexpensive, simple but thorough alternative for SMEs to utilise.

3   DESCRIPTION OF THE FRAMEWORK.

The iterative life cycle of the framework specified has the potential to involve all stages from strategic analysis and BPR through to the CPI of the reengineered process. The framework is divided into phases, stages and steps. The three phases are - identification of process/processes requiring CPI or BPR; development of plan for reengineering; and lastly continuous process improvement. These phases are then subdivided: - initiation; investigation; design; implementation and finally manage and monitor. The stages are then further subdivided into steps, which are described below.

3.1   Phase 1. The identification of process/processes requiring CPI or BPR.
The first phase of the framework is divided into two stages: Initiation and Investigation. which are summarised in figure 1 and described below.

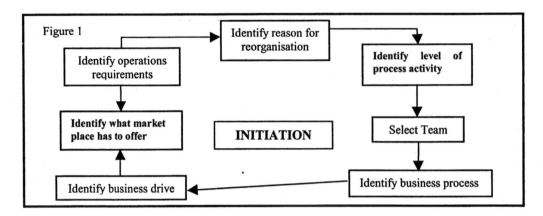

Figure 1

3.1.1   Initiation

The objectives of this stage are to identify the reason for reorganisation, the level of process activity and the process(s) requiring reorganisation. These objectives are achieved by the 7 steps.

- Identify reason for reorganisation: The reasons why an organisation may be required to reorganise its processes will vary and therefore before any action can be taken to tackle problems within existing processes these reasons need to be identified so that a plan of action can be implemented. Having established the reasons why changes are necessary, it can then be determined which level of process activity is best suited to solve the business problem.
- Identify level of process activity: Hammer (1994) and Martinsons (1995) argue that for an organisation to survive in today's competitive environment, improvement is not an option but a necessity. For organisations that seek to thrive, small incremental improvements associated with CPI are always necessary. However, occasionally the only key to success is dramatic improvement, this involves BPR, the complete rebuilding of a process (Martinsons 1995). Both CPI and BPR are necessary to drive significant advances in organisational performance, but they differ for example, in management involvement, improvement goal, implementation approach, etc. To establish which level of process activity is required a questionnaire was designed taking into account key considerations; i.e. market place changes, geographic spread, customer & supplier involvement, cost, staffing allocation, and level of urgency.
- Select team: Having established what level of process activity is required, the next step is to select a team of people who will drive the effort. The most important issue at this stage is the decision regarding team size and structure. This will vary according to which level of process activity is to be employed. The CPI team will tend to involve employees at all levels involved with the process led by a facilitator. The BPR team will tend to involve a team of experts, a management committee and task teams (Regan 1995), to handle changing organisational structure and redesigning jobs.
- Identify business process: The next step is to establish the process(s), which require

reorganisation. A process is a series of steps designed to accomplish a goal. They are three dimensional, linear in that they have starting and finishing points, width based on the number of departments involved and depth determined by the level of detail at which the process is documented. In addition processes have customers, beneficiaries and are driven by business, management and customer requirements (Regan 1995).

- Identify business drivers: Processes are the infrastructure of an organisation, the primary pipeline through which corporate work flows. Successful reengineering projects realign their processes to satisfy customer demands. The customers of the process must be identified prior to determining the customers' requirements, achieved by listing any external and internal customers who are either effected or depend on the process for information, products or service. The next step is to identify what the customers require of the process to be reengineered. This may include requirement areas such as timeliness, cost, accuracy, quantity, price, availability etc. This can be achieved via questionnaire and interview.

- *Identify what the market place has to offer:* The sixth step to take if possible is that of benchmarking, which involves the learning and discovery of how other work groups perform common processes or how other competitive or best performing organisations operate.

- Identify operating requirements: *The final step of this phase is to identify the operating requirements i.e. what needs to be achieved to meet the requirements of those driving the reengineering effort. This step will result in the identification of what the process should do, based on the customer and marketplace information gathered.*

3.1.2   Investigation

The objectives of this stage are to understand and measure the existing processes, envisage a desired state and identify weaknesses in the current performance of the processes. The following steps achieve these objects illustrated in figure 2 below.

Figure 2

- Analyse existing process: Without knowledge of the performance of the existing process, it is impossible to state with any degree of certainty whether or not process reengineering will benefit the organisation. The first step therefore is to document the "as is" process by defining and mapping out all of the tasks involved in the process to providing a clear and realistic view of the process. To document the process two basic steps should be undertaken. The first is to list all of the major process tasks. The input and the output involved in the process should be determined and everything in-between will be the tasks involved. Once the major tasks have been identified the smaller subtasks and decisions that link the major tasks together should be determined. The second step is to then create a process flowchart, which will allow visual interpretation of what happens in each step of the process.

- Identify weaknesses: At this juncture the process can now be measured to gather performance data. This will identify weaknesses and areas of where improvements can be made. The data gathered will depend on what needs to be measured e.g. the cost or the time scales to undertake each task. Hence it is important to gather data on each task of the process identified.
- Visualise new process: This step aims to focus on what the new process could be and what it could accomplish. The following questions need to be addressed: -
- How will the new process help the customer?
- How will it help the organisation?
- How will the organisational environment change?

On completion of stage 2 the vision, mission statement and the mapping of the current process will have been achieved. Having envisaged the desired state the difference between this and the "as is" state should be compared. A significant difference between the two implies BPR should be considered else CPI should be reconsidered at this stage.

3.2   Phase 2. Development of a Plan for Reengineering.

3.2.1   Design

The objective of this stage is to provide a detailed model of the reengineered process resulting in a prototype. The steps to achieve this objective are summarised in figure 3 and described below.

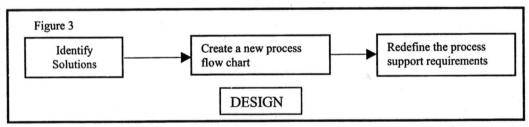

Figure 3

- Process system: During this step solutions to the weaknesses identified during stage 2 should be identified. This can be achieved by utilising the process design alternatives worksheet as described by Chang, 1995. This involves listing each key task of the process and describing how that task is currently being completed. The next step is then to identify alternative methods of undertaking the same task. These methods must be realistic and take into account the customers requirements and what the competitors provide. From here a feasibility report should be submitted.
- Create a new process flow chart: Having identified feasible solutions a new process

flow chart should be created. The mapping of the "ideal" process will result in a practical application of the planning effort. This step can be time consuming but it is important to be thorough to ensure success.

- Redefine the process support requirement: This step aims to redefine the process support requirements including people, technology and finance. During this step certain questions should be asked. These include: - can the process be made simpler? Can technology help? Can time and/or cost be reduced?
- Process reengineering includes a human element and therefore any impact the new process will have on people needs to be identified. By listing the present and future responsibilities of each job role, will provide information on new job requirements and training needs.

New technology especially that of ECT can have a large impact on the success of an organisation (Amos & Cooper 1995). During the design stage of the framework it is of paramount importance that such technologies are considered for implementation. The growing numbers of different ECT is vast and therefore makes it difficult to make decisions on what to implement. This can therefore be achieved during this step by utilising an ECT analysis tool in the form of an expert system to establish appropriate and suitable ECT, which can be utilised to maximise the potential of the reengineered process. A detailed analysis of current literature on the development of case-based reasoning was undertaken (Aamodt & Plaza 1994; Rahanu et al.1998) and then adapted to suit the necessary criteria required for developing an ECT analysis tool (Husein et al. 1998).

Case-Base Reasoning (CBR) solves new problems by adapting previously successful solutions to similar problems (Aamodt & Plaza 1994; Watson & Marir 1994; Kolodner 1993; Riesbeck & Schank 1989; Slade 1991). It has the ability to utilise the specific knowledge of previously experienced, concrete problem situations (cases), and by finding a similar past case, and reusing it in the new problem situation it provides a solution to the identified problem (Watson 1997). A second important characteristic of CBR is that it enables incremental, sustained learning, since a new experience is retained each time a problem has been solved. This makes it immediately available for future scenarios.

Finally, a cost-benefit analysis should be undertaken during this step to determine whether it is advisable to proceed to the next stage of implementation. The impact of the reengineered process on the organisation should also be considered during this step. On completion of this stage a new management plan will have been documented and the prototype of the reorganised process will have been developed ready for implementation.

3.2.2   Implementation
This stage involves the implementation of the prototype redesigned process. The objectives are to ensure the appropriate emplacement and adequate operation of the new process, which are summarised in figure 4 and described below.

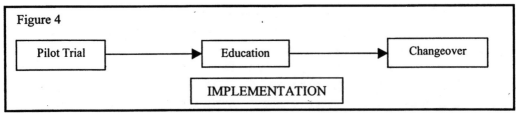

Figure 4

- Pilot trail: Before full implementation is considered a thorough pilot trial should be considered to ensure that the proposed changes would enhance the process. Upon the trial's conclusion it is important to establish the success of the new process. Data should therefore be gathered on the new process to determine whether the changes meet the desired goals. Finally it should have been identified whether it is safe to proceed to full implementation or whether adjustments need to be made first.
- Education: Before full implementation can be made all education needs should be met (Husein et al. 1996). These should have been identified and addressed during the design stage and completed by this stage.
- Changeover: The final step in the implementation stage is that of changeover to the new reengineered process where the new process should be standardised to enable acceptance and establishment within the organisation and documented along with the new guidelines. The final product of stage 4 should include a fully implemented, standardised reengineered process.

3.3   Phase 3 Continuous Process Improvement (CPI)
The final phase of the framework involves the management of the reorganised process and incorporates CPI. Here the application of tools designed to achieve incremental, continuous improvement in process cycle-times and added-value contributions, with emphasis on the elimination of waste and cost factors. The overall objective being to streamline processes in the pursuit of continuous satisfaction by meeting the demands of a business plan, performance target, to support a corporate initiative and to aid the success of a quality scheme.

3.3.1   Monitor and Manage
The stage is team-based, co-ordinated by a facilitator, who is provided with the project goals and a set of targets from which the group builds process maps and looks at target-related elements and areas. Projects only look at what needs to be achieved to attain the desired performance requirements, not the business as a whole.

   The focus of the CPI method is to enhance the existing situation, a process map is created from which improvement opportunities are identified. Any maintenance and refinements required will be identified during the problem solving stage. During the implementation stage, the education of process owners/users will be undertaken before changeover. Finally, the selected team will monitor an ongoing audit of its effects. The stages of the CPI phase are summarised in figure 5.

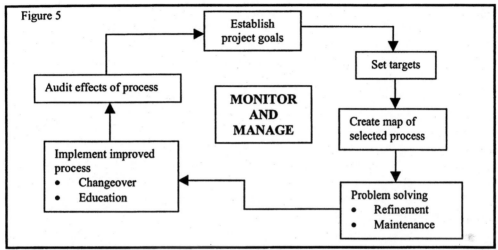

Figure 5

The process improvement framework (PIF) has been applied so far in three organisations to validate and to assess its impact. The processes implemented are still in their infancy, so it is not yet possible to assess their impact. The data collection from the reengineered processes is on going at the time of writing.

4   CONCLUSION

Technological developments, marketplace competition and business developments are all transforming the way businesses are run. As computing and communications technologies converge, and with an increasing demand for accurate and up to date information, it is essential that businesses have the best available infrastructure in place to realise and gain advantage. Enterprises are therefore increasingly looking for a range of solutions to either revolutionise or reform the way they do business.

However for many organisations, the real concern is not the burning desire to be at the foreground of change but rather not to be left behind. It has been realised that fundamental change is now essential to simply stay in the same relative position, not in order to be the leader. This is especially the case with communication technology amongst SMEs.

From the analysis of the characteristics of SMEs, the lack of knowledge and expertise is often identified as a major factor limiting the improvement of such organisations (Husein et al. 1998; Ibrahim & Goodwin 1986; Raymond & Magnenat-Thalmann 1981). Hence, if PIF is to be useful to SMEs, it is of paramount importance that it has the attributes of relatively low cost, easy to understand, and easy to follow after preliminary training. The framework presented in this paper has the necessary attributes to satisfy the above characteristics.

An ECT analysis tool, a major component of the framework, is specifically developed for SMEs, to assist them in reengineering their business processes with effective utilisation of electronic communication technologies. This tool takes into account some of the reasons that are preventing SMEs adopting communication technologies: -

- **Lack of the necessary knowledge required to implement ECT;**
- **Lack of the necessary funds to do research prior to acquiring new technology;**
- **Mistrust of IT vendors;**
- **Lack of training and education in IT generally and ECT in particular.**

To overcome these obstacles, it is imperative that impartial advice regarding the implementation of new technology is provided from independent sources. Hence, the development of an expert system as described above will promote the use of ECTs among SMEs. This acceptance is based on the recognition that a range of organisations has successfully utilised the proposed technological solution provided by this tool. It also provides impartial advice based on previous experiences described by independent researchers and in the academic literature.

References

Aamodt, A. & Plaza, E. (1994), Case-Based Reasoning: Foundational Issues, methodological variations, and system approaches. AI Communications, Vol.7, No.1, pp 39-59.

Amos J. and Cooper, J. (1995), Case studies of the NSW Government's supplying in a action, Proceeding of The 8th International Conference on EDI and Inter-Organisational Systems, Bled, Slovenia, June, pp 172-186.

Beaver, G. & Harris, L. (1995) Performance management and the small firm: dilemmas, tensions and paradoxes, Journal of Strategic change, Vol.4, No.2, pp. 38-42, 57.

Bradesko M. (1995), Electronic commerce on the Internet - facing the new media, Proceeding of the 8th International Conference on EDI and Inter-Organisational Systems, Bled, Slovenia, June, pp 243-249.

Champy, J. (1995), Reengineering Management, (Harper Collins Publishers, London).

Chang, R. (1995), Process Reengineering in Action, (Kogan Page, London).

Chatzoglou & Macaulay, (1996), Requirements capture and IS methodologies, Journal of Information systems, Vol. 6 pp: 209-225.

Garcia-Sierra A., Moreton, R & Sloane, A. (1994), EDI and SMEs: the business case, Journal of Industrial affairs, Vol.3, No.2, pp. 99-106.

Gebauer, J. (1995), Analysing the potentials of EDI for business process reorganisation - A Conceptual Framework, Proceeding of The 8th International Conference on EDI and Inter-Organisational Systems, Bled, Slovenia, June, pp 52-67.

Grover, V., Jeong, S., Kettinger, W. & Teng, J. (1995), The Implementation of Business Process Reengineering, Journal of Management Information Systems, Vol. 12 No. 1, pp. 109-144.

Hammer, M. (1994), Reengineering the corporation: - a manifesto for business revolution,
(Brealey, London).

Hammer, M. (1996), Beyond reengineering (HarperCollins Publishers, London)

Hammer, M. Stanton, S. (1995), The reengineering revolution (HarperCollins Publishers, London)

Hoogeweegen M. R. & Wagenaar R. W. (1995), Assessing costs and benefits of EDI, Proceeding of The 8th International Conference on EDI and Inter-Organisational Systems, Bled, Slovenia, June, pp 1-11.

Husein, T., Moreton R. & A. Sloane (1996), Electronic Commerce: A consideration of implementation for SMEs, Journal of Management Studies, Vol.5 No.1, pp 77-83.

Husein, T., Moreton R., Sloane A, & Knöll H. (1997), "BPR methodology comparison using Normative Information Model-based System Analysis and Design (NIMSAD) Frame", Internal Publication, University of Wolverhampton.

Husein, T., Moreton R., Sloane A, & Knöll H. (1998), An expert system utilising CBR technology, to provide assistance to SMEs to analysis their requirements of ECTs. Proceeding of the 4th SCI'98 and ISAS'98, pp: 102-108, Orlando, USA, July, Vol.2, pp 102-108.

Ibrahim, A. & Goodwin, J. (1986), Perceived causes of success in small business, American Journal of Small Business, Fall

Jayaratna, N. (1994), Understanding and Evaluating methodologies NIMSAD: A systemic framework, (McGraw-Hill Book Company Europe, Maidenhead, England).

Kalakota, R. & Whinston, A. (1996), Frontiers of Electronic Commerce, (Addison-Wesley, Wokingham, England).

Kambil, A. (1997), doing business in the wired world, Computer, May, pp. 56-61.

Kellener, D., (1995), Business programmes and information systems methodologies, Journal of information systems, Vol. 5, pp: 137-157.

Kleinberg, K. (1995), BPR Tool Categories-Multiple Choices, Gartner Group Continuous services, UK.

Kolodner, J.L. (1993), Case-Based Reasoning, (Morgan Kaufmann, London, UK).

Lucas, A. (1997), What in the World is Electronic Commerce? World Executive's Digest Technology, Summer, pp. 16-17.

Martinsons, M.G. (1995), Radical process innovation using information technology: the theory, the practice and the future of reengineering, International Journal of Information Management, Vol. 15, No.4, pp. 253-69.

Meier, J. & Suhl, H. (1995), Empirical survey of electronic data interchange applied in practice, Proceeding of The 8th International Conference on EDI and Inter-Organisational Systems, Bled, Slovenia, June, pp 47-51.

Parker, C. M. & Swatman, P. M. C. (1995), Encouraging SME acceptance of EDI: an educational approach, Proceeding of The 8th International Conference on EDI and Inter-Organisational Systems, Bled, Slovenia, June, pp 27-46.

Petric, D., Zupancic, B. & Gricar, J. (1996), Preparing Small and Medium-Sized Enterprises for EDI/EC, Proceeding of the 9th International Conference on EDI and Inter-Organisational Systems, Bled, Slovenia, June, pp.364-376.

Pickerill, J. B. (1993), Electronic Commerce: Technology in support of global business strategies, EDI Forum, Vol. 6 No. 3 pp. 64-68

Probhu, G., Nilakanta, S. & Subramanian |. (1994), Methodology for business transformation, Proceeding of 3rd International Conference on System Integration, Brazil, Vol.1 pp. 403-411.

Rahanu, H. Davies, J. & Rogerson, S. (1998), Development of a Case-based Reasoner as a Tool to Facilitate Ethical understanding, Proceedings of the 4th International Conference on Ethical Issues of Using Information Technology (Rotterdam, Holland). March, pp: 578-588.

Ramarapu, N. & Lado, A. (1995), linking information technology to global business strategy to gain competitive advantage: an integrative model, Journal of Information Technology, Vol. 10, No. 2 pp. 115-24

Raymond, L. Magnenat-Thalmann, N. (1981), Information systems in small business, American Journal of Small Business, Spring

Regan, J. (1995), Crunch Time, (Century Ltd, London).

Reponen, T., (1994), Organisational information management strategies, Journal of information systems, Vol. 4 No. 1 pp: 27-44.

Riesbeck, C. & Schank, R. (1989), Inside case-based reasoning, (Lawrence Erlbaum, USA.)

Slade, S. (1991), Case-based reasoning: A research paradigm. AI Magazine, Spring, pp: 42-55.

Talwar, R. K., (1993), Business reengineering: - A strategy driven approach, Long Range Planning, Vol.26 No. 6 pp: 22-40

The Object Agency Inc., (1995), A Comparison of Object Oriented Development Methodologies, http//www.toa.com/pub/html/mcrl.html. <accessed 12th May 1996>

Vogel, D. & Glasson, B. (1995), Electronic commerce in the international office of the future, Proceeding of the 8th International Conference on EDI and Inter-Organisational Systems, Bled, Slovenia, June, pp.308-320.

Wastell, D.G., White P. & Kawalek P. (1994) A Methodology for business redesign: experiences and issues, Journal of Strategic Information Systems, Vol. 3 No.1 pp 23-40.

Watson, I. & Marir, F. (1994) Case-Based Reasoning: A review. The knowledge Engineering Review, Vol. 9 No. 4.

Watson, I. (1997), applying Case-Based Reasoning: Techniques for enterprise systems, (Morgan Kaufmann Publishers, Inc. San Francisco, California, USA).

Zwass, V. (1996), Electronic Commerce: Structures and Issues, International Journal of Electronic Commerce, Vol. 1, No. 1, pp. 3-23.

CHAPTER 41

TECHNICAL ISSUES RELATED TO INTEGRATING MODELLING OF BUSINESS PROCESSES, IS AND COMPUTER NETWORKS

A Serrano, GM Giaglis, Ray J Paul
Brunel University

Abstract

Information Systems (IS) and Computer Networks (CN) aim at assisting organisations in realising their business objectives in a more effective and efficient manner. To achieve this goal, Business Processes (BP) and their corresponding systems and networks must be aligned. Simulation modelling in both domains (BP and IS/CN) is widely used to analyse existing operations and propose improvements. However, although it is clear that these organisational facets should be aligned, there is no direct path that bridges them in the simulation domain. This paper investigates approaches to integrating BP and CN simulation environments using IS as the link.

1 INTRODUCTION

Since it has been realised that organisations can be studied and analysed according to the business processes they perform, process-based organisational analysis has become a prominent matter of study in both the management science and Information Systems fields (Ould 1995). Processes within an organisation are not static, but they undergo changes in the same direction that the organisation moves towards achieving its objectives. Business Process Reengineering (BPR) is the management area that is concerned with the study of the behaviour of the current processes and how they affect the organisation, as well as studying the organisational environment and proposing changes on those processes that are not aligned with the organisational goals.

Business process changes can be classified as radical or soft (Kettinger et al 1997) and may cause disruptions to the organisation activities and may possibly involve significant investments in order to be realised. One way that a proposed process change can be tested without causing disruptions in the real business environment and without requiring significant investments is through modelling and simulation. Simulation can be used to predict, observe and diagnose the behaviour of a phenomenon in order to predict the impacts of changes over the event that is being observed. Such predictions are aimed, essentially, at improving performance and reducing operational costs (Curtis et al 1992). As a result, Business Process Simulation (BPS) is a technique that has been used successfully by BPR engineers.

IT, in general, is a well-known enabler of business change. For example Childe et al (1994) state that the initiative to move towards BPR in some cases originates from the IT departments. Gant (1992) sees BPR as the redesign of processes based on the potential of Information Technology. Davenport (1990) affirms that Information Technology and Business Process Redesign are transforming organisations, and that together, these tools have the potential to create a new type of industrial engineering.

Existing research has led to the conclusion that the way Business Processes (BP) and IT have been interacting is not the best that can be achieved. We argue that one of the major restrictions in finding the link between BP and IT is due to IT being considered as a single entity. However, IT is comprised of different elements and, despite the fact they interact, in practice they are studied separately. IT applied to business organisations can be split into two major areas, namely *Information Systems (IS)* and *Computer Networks (CN)*.

The relationship between BP modelling and IT is oriented much more towards Information Systems rather than Computer Networks. This relationship is illustrated by studying the most common performance measures needed by a BP model: cycle time, entity count, resource utilisation, and activity cost. Some of these need to be analysed in order to identify how they are related with IS. For example, cycle time and resource utilisation measures include value-added process time, waiting time, and transaction time. These time measures will be affected if changes to the IT are proposed. However these changes are generalised by the use of IS regardless of whether they rely on Computer Networks or not.

Computer network simulators (CNS) are powerful tools that help CN engineers to identify and predict networking problems. Some of the most important objectives of a network model are to measure the effects of increasing or reducing traffic on network performance, to measure the impacts of a link failure, to test protocols for best network performance, to choose the best design for a new communications network, and to measure the impacts of additional PCs on a LAN, and so on (Law and McComas 1996). All these measures are directly oriented to network terms, and do not indicate any direct link with the measures required by the business process models.

2   IS, THE LINK BETWEEN BP AND CN MODELS

When the design of a network is to be proposed, a network model is used to consider the pure "communication links" factors. However, network modelling does not have a direct connection with business processes. The way that BP is related to CN is through the relationship that information systems have with BP.

Painter et al (1996) have addressed this problem and proposed that a 'middle' layer is introduced between Business Processes and Computer Networks. The middle layer consists of models that depict the IT applications that run on the Computer Networks and support the Business Processes (see Figure 1). Such a layer introduces a medium abstraction level as a mechanism for bridging the gap between Business Processes and Computer Networks, and may thus prove useful in developing integrated business simulation environments

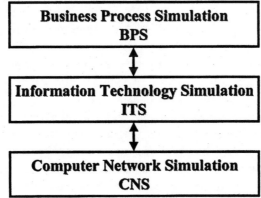

Figure 1: A Hierarchical Approach to BPS and CNS Integration (Painter et al 1996)

However, the interrelationships between BP, IT, and CN are much more complex and may have different implications for the design of successful integrated simulation environments.

The approach that will be followed by this paper implies that an IS process description can be integrated in the BP process model. Having a "graphical" description of the IS processes within the BP process will help to give a general view of the behaviour of the BP process, and when necessary, it can be analysed in more depth. The IS process description integrated in the BP model is called the Information Systems/ Business Process model (IS/BP).

3   IS AND CN DATA RELATIONSHIP

The relationship between the IS/BP level with the Computer Network model must be established in order to determine in which direction the final CN model will take. A detailed design of the communication links, flow, frequency and information storage suggested by the IS/BP model is required in order to develop a CN model.

The major purpose of the Information Systems /Business Process level proposed in this paper, is to provide the information that is needed to generate a CN model and it can be summarised in 4 general objectives:

- To indicate the composition of the data that traverse the BP model
- To indicate the location and flow of each data component
- To indicate the size, in bytes, of each component
- To indicate the frequency with which each data component is generated

One of the main tasks of information systems is to provide the facilities to obtain the value, given by the organisation, from the information available. Information differs from data in that data itself is useless until it is used with a particular meaning. Adding value to this data can be considered as one of the major tasks of management. The accuracy of assigning the correct value to the data, is the basis for management decision-making.

There is no formula that measures the value added to information; it depends on the goals and objectives of the organisations that possess it. However there are some information attributes that can be generally applied. Information attributes can be classified under five headings. These are accessibility, relevance, comprehensibility, timeliness, and accuracy (Wolstenholme et al 1993).

Information attributes, determined by the organisational goals, will provide additional information to the CN design. The most general way that information attributes will restrict the CN design is given by timeliness of data delivery. The time in which the data has to arrive to its destination must be considered and will restrict the network inputs (e.g. data rate). Having this information it will be easier to develop a CN model, which will closely match the IS/BP model, and a BP-IS-CN integrated model could be achieved.

4   THE IS/BP MODEL

This paper proposes a basic method to integrate IS data descriptions within a BP model. The method shall be called Information System/Business Process/Data Description (IS/BP/DD). This method will be aimed at bridging BP and CN simulation environments using SIMPROCESS and COMNET software packages. The IS/BP/DD method will provide a graphical and structured method for expressing knowledge about the behavioural aspects of an existing or proposed IS within a BP model in a simplistic way. A two-model level will depict the method. In the first level the BP process is identified. The BP model will be an ordinary BP model which will include the prevalent IS, if one exists, but will not offer details of the deeper behaviour of the IS process.

The second model level IS/BP, will provide detailed information about the information systems involved. For each process that involves the use of IS there will be an IS/BP level linked with it. How the BP and an IS/BP level will be formed will be explained.

First we shall detect the data that is used by the IS and that is implicit in the BP model. A BP model in SIMPROCESS is basically formed by using four building blocks: entities, resources, activities and connectors. Those blocks are the primary source of data that will feed the model and will represent the overall process. The entities that traverse a process and are related with IS are generally conceived to represent a document (e.g. issues, orders, certificates, etc.) and, generally, do not specify the information conveyed (e.g. the entity order may contain detailed information like products, client name, date of issue, etc.)

For the purposes of the method proposed, the entities that are defined in the BP level and are used on IS processes will be named Document Entities (DE). The data that a DE may convey will be decomposed, according with the IS/BP necessities for that specific process, into sub-entities each of which will be called an Information Entity (IE). The latter will be used to compose an IS/BP level of the process.

The design of the IS/BP model must follow the same structure as that of the BP model. The major concern of the IS/BP level is to describe graphically the composition, location, direction, size, and frequency of the IEs.

The location and direction of the IEs will be shown graphically in SIMPROCESS. Figure 2 is an example to show how with the aid of the connectors and icons the flow, location and direction of the IEs can be represented in a SIMPROCESS model.

Besides the IEs characteristics listed above, the transmission of the IE to a remote or local host performs three major transactions, a) to request data (query), b) to store data (storage), and c) to perform numeric or/and relational data operations (process). Those transactions must also been indicated on the IS/BP level.

Query, storage and process transactions may involve the use of more than one IE and may also involve more than one IE transmissions. Hence the decomposition of each transaction may be needed.

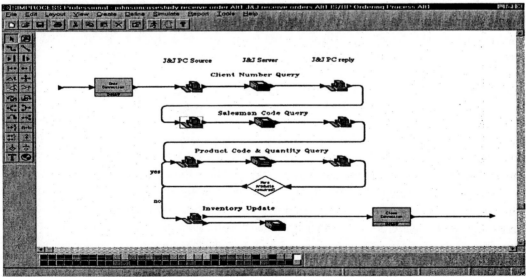

Figure 2: IS/BP level

SIMPROCESS has a file document attached to each icon, which in turn, represents an IE transmission. Composition, amount, frequency of data, and process involved must be described as shown in Figure 3

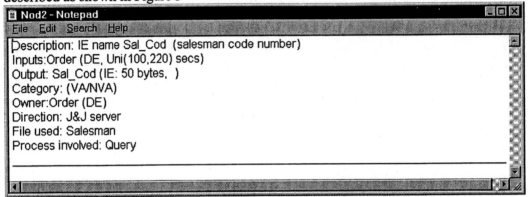

Figure 3: Description of composition, amount, and frequency of IEs in SIMPROCESS

In the Description field the name of the IE and a description of the entity must be recorded. The Input field describes the incoming entity and its arrival rate. If it is the first arrival point of the process, the name of the generating DE will be used. The field Output describes the name of the IE that will be output from an activity and the departure rate. The size, in bytes, of the IE will also be described. The category field is a field filled by default by SIMPROCESS and will not be used. The owner field will be used to describe the parent DE of the IE.

Three new fields will be added. Direction will identify the IE destination server. File used will describe the main file where the IE will perform its transaction (storage, process or query). Finally the Process field will describe the process involved in the transaction: storage, process or query.

5   A FRAMEWORK TO INTEGRATE IS/BP AND CN MODELS

A business process model is formed basically by building blocks, which will produce the source of data that will feed the BP model. The second source of data will be given by the IS/BP, which will produce the source of information from which the CN model will be fed. Entities and resources building blocks produce the data that will be used by the CN model, which in terms of the network will be transformed into traffic flow, message source, response source, and application source icons and their corresponding properties. Activities and connectors of the IS/BP model will be related with links and nodes of the network model.

In order to integrate COMNET III and the IS/BP levels a CN-IS/BP process table must be generated. The contents of the table will be described in Table1.

Process tables contain the necessary information to represent the traffic flow generated by the IEs on the business process. Query, storage and process transactions may involve the use of more than one IE. When the decomposition of a transaction is implied it will be indicated in the process table by typing (transaction) after the name of the transaction in the *description* field. The description of the IEs that will perform the transaction will be indicated in a "transaction table". In this table a new record is included at the end which indicates the size, direction, and description of the output transaction Table 2.

New IE transactions may be involved within the transaction table, hence a new decomposition may be involved and a *sub-transaction* table may be created from the previous transaction table. It might be a father-child relationship between the process, transaction, and *sub-transactions* tables.

With the previous information, COMNET III is able to re-create an application. Once the process and transaction tables are created it is necessary to relate them with the CN model.

Name of the Process											
Parent DE	DE Frequency	From	IE Frequency	IE or Transaction name	Description	Size (bytes)	To	Process Involved	Time (milliseconds)	Reply	Size(bytes)
Name of the DE from which the IE is decomposed	Frequency that the DE will transverse all the process	Node or Server where the IE will be transmitted through the network	Frequency that the IE will transverse IS/PDL level	*IE* name	IE Description	size of the IE	Node or Server where the IE will be received in the network	Query, Storage or Process	Time that takes the process to perform its job	Information that will be replied	Size of the information that will be replied
Name of the DE from which the IE is decomposed	Frequency that the IE will transverse all the process	Node or Server where the *transaction* is activated	Frequency that the *transaction* will activated	Name of the *transaction*	Transaction Description	size of all the IEs involved or the transaction	Node(s) or Server(s) where the transaction will perform its task	Type of the transaction: Query, Storage or Process	Time that takes to perform its job	Information that will be replied to the sender at the end of the transaction	Size of the information that will be replied at the end of the transaction

Table1 Process Description Table

Name of the transaction								
IE Frequency	IE name	Description	Size (bytes)	To	Process Involved	Time (milliseconds)	Reply	Size(bytes)
Frequency that the IE will transverse the transaction level	IE name	IE Description	size of the IE	Node or Server where the IE will be received in the network	Query, Storage or Process	Time that takes the process to perform its job	information that will be replied	Size of the information that will be replied
					type of the transaction	Time that takes the transaction to perform its job	description of the data to be replied on the end of the transaction	size of the data to be replied on the end of the transaction

Table2 Transaction Description Table

The Relationship between DEs, IEs and CN modelling parameters
DEs Route and location of data. The route that a DE has to take may diverge according to the different IEs of which the entity is composed, specifically, the IEs that will travel through the network.

Routing of DEs. The route of each of the IEs within a DE will directly affect the following CN parameters

- The link type and the parameters of the link type (bandwidth, propagation, etc.). When an IE has to travel through the network, it has to be carried by a link; hence it may affect many of the link parameters.
- The destination parameters (destination type, destination list) of the message and

source icons on the CN model will be related to each of the IEs that together form the DE.

DEs location. The location of the DE may be different to the location of the IEs that the DE contains. The location where an activity and its corresponding connectors on the BP model are placed and the different DEs, hence IEs that are contained on the activity will give the location of the application, message, and response sources on the CN model. The location of the IEs will be related with the location of the CN nodes.

DEs measure. Measuring entities on a CN model is by the use of packets, which are dimensioned in bytes or messages. Because the size of the message will be dependant on the network configuration, it is more appropriate to measure the entity in bytes, which is a standard dimension. In general the number of bytes that define a DE on the BP model will be directly related to the IEs bytes quantity. However, at the time of decomposition of the DEs into IEs, the amount of bytes in each IEs will not necessarily be the same, and the most important objective is to observe which of the IEs travel through the network and how many bytes are conveyed in each transaction. The latter will contribute to the network traffic.

Once the location of each of the sources is placed in the network model, the amount of bytes that each IE will convey has to be introduced. The number of bytes in an IE will be directly related to the message size calculation, and message size units of the message of the corresponding source in the COMNET III model.

DEs generation frequency. The frequency with which a DE is generated in the BP model, is the same for the IEs that form the DE. The frequency that a DE is generated on the BP model will be used in the first arrival, interarrival, and last arrival times of the source in the CN model. It will also direct the type of scheduling (i.e. iteration time, receive message, triggering event)

The information that COMNET III requires to create a CN model based on the BP model, is contained in the transaction tables. Following the graphical information given by the BP-IS/DDP and the transaction tables, it is feasible to create a COMNET III model, which will be linked with the SIMPROCESS BP model thereby achieving the goal of bridging SIMPROCESS and COMNET models.

6   SUMMARY AND CONCLUSIONS

This paper highlighted a need to bridge the BP and IT simulation environments. In order to accomplish this, IT was decomposed into two distinct areas, IS and CN. Following this decomposition, the relationship between BP and the decomposed areas IS and CN was studied. Since it was found that the relationship between BP and CN simulation environments could not be done directly, and that the BP and IS objectives and approaches are very similar, the idea of joining BP and IS into one simulation environment was proposed.

After following the IS/BP/DD method and framework, it can be concluded that the integration of BP and CN model environments may be complex, but can be achieved through the proper definition of the data flow in the IS included in the BP model.

The BP-IS/DDP method and methodology suggested in this paper are supported by the use of the SIMPROCESS and COMNET III software packages. Specifically, the IS/BP/DD method relies strongly on SIMPROCESS features. However, it is logical to assume that a general methodology will not strictly be limited by those software packages and can be proposed.

It is believed that further research on this phase may lead to the development of an automated or semi-automated mechanism to integrate BP and IS models, which will provide sufficient data to create a CN model. At the same time, similar techniques can be proposed to automate the integration of the information provided by the BP/IS level with the CN model.

References

Childe, S.J., Bennett, M (1994) Frameworks for understanding Business Process Re-engineering, International Journal of Operations & Production Management. Vol. 14, No 12, pp. 22-34.

Curtis B, Over, Kellner J. (1992) Process Modelling, Communications of the ACM /September 1992/vol35, No.9, pp. 10-15.

Davenport T. H. and Short, J.E. (1990) The New Industrial Engineering: Information Technology and Business Process Redesign, Sloan Management Review. 31,4, pp. 11-27.

Kettinger, W, Teng J and Guha S (1997) Business Process Change: A Study of Methodologies, Techniques, and Tools, MIS Quarterly/March. 21,1, pp. 55-80.

Law, M.A., McComas, M.G. (1996) Simulation of Communication Networks, Proceedings of the 1996 winter simulation Conference.pp. 73-77.

Ould, M.A., (1995) Business Processes: Modelling and Analysis for Re-engineering and Improvement, John Wiley & Sons, 1995.

Painter, M.K., Fernades, R., Padmanaban, N., Mayer, R.J. (1996) A Methodology for Integrating Business Process and Information Infrastructure Models. In Charnes, J.M., Morrice, D.J., Brunner, D.T. and Swain, J.J. (Eds.), Proceedings of the 1996 Winter Simulation Conference, San Diego, California, December, pp. 1305-1312.

Wolstenholme E., Henderson, S., and Gavine A. (1993) The evaluation of management information systems: A dynamic and holistic approach, Wiley, Chichester

CHAPTER 42

EMERGING TECHNOLOGIES: CAN THE INTERNET ADD VALUE FOR SMES?

Margi Levy* and Philip Powell**
Warwick Business School*, University of London**

Abstract

Emerging technologies, such as the Internet, are viewed as enabling firms to alter radically their competitive position. The Internet allows global trading and there are, potentially, few limits to growth. What is less clear is whether small and medium sized enterprises (SMEs) can take advantage of the opportunities. This paper presents four new pieces of evidence on SMEs' use of the Internet. The first is a recent DTI survey. The second is questionnaire research carried out in the West Midlands under the auspices of Warwick Business School. The third element is the European Small Enterprise IT Study. The final element is case studies of 43 West Midlands SMEs that analyses and models attitudes to information and communication technologies. In contrast to the surveys, the cases show that actual use of the Internet may be far less among growing businesses and the reasons for this are discussed. The paper demonstrates that those that do exploit the Internet mainly use it for research rather than trading. In order to give impetus to Internet use, the paper argues the Internet can only be of value to SMEs if they take a radical, collaborative approach to its implementation. It argues that the future may lie with the development of enterprise networks rather than individual competitive gain.

1   INTRODUCTION

Emerging technologies, particularly the Internet, are seen as enabling organisations to alter radically their competitive positioning. For instance, the Internet provides the opportunity to trade globally and, theoretically, the possibilities for businesses to grow and develop are endless. It is less clear whether small and medium sized enterprises (SMEs) can benefit. The paper presents evidence from three surveys on Internet use in SMEs. Case studies of 43 West Midlands SMEs' use of the Internet is then presented and attitudes to and, employment of, information and communication technologies (ICT) discussed. In contrast to the surveys the cases shows that use of the Internet may be lower than reported among growing businesses. It demonstrates that those that exploit the

Internet mainly use it for research rather than trading. The paper suggests that the Internet may offer SMEs the ability to form co-operative alliances to gain business advantage with benefits in the reduction of customer power, as SMEs are able to offer customers a better service, based round the skills of multiple SMEs. The paper looks at how SMEs may benefit from setting up such alliances.

2   GETTING VALUE FROM IS - OPPORTUNITIES FOR SMES

IS have long been used by organisations to automate transaction processes to improve efficiency and reduce costs. However, Venkatramen (1991) suggests that ICT have the capability to revolutionise business. In addition, Scott Morton (1991) shows that there is a need to integrate strategy, structure and systems with people and processes in order for value from ICT to be fully realised. However, Naylor and Williams 1994 suggest that SMEs use the simplest forms of ICT, although they may try to address sophisticated problems. Adoption of ICT in SMEs is generally reactive rather than proactive (Levy et al 1997). However, Yetton et al (1994) demonstrate that innovative adoption can change the basis on which business is transacted.

SMEs are cautious about the adoption of ICT (Hagmann and McCahon 1993). They seek a reasonable return on investment and the ICT contribution to success is ranked lower than other factors (Ryan and Hepworth). Indeed, ICT adoption is in response to a recognised problem, rather than as part of a strategy (Ryan and Hepworth, Levy et al 1997). SMEs are unlikely to do this unless the owner is a risk taker and has personal knowledge of ICT potential. Ryan and Hepworth find skills such as marketing and human resource management are thought by entrepreneurs as more important than technological competence. This paper considers the role of ICT in adding value to SMEs, in particular focusing on the emerging technology of the Internet.

3   SME USE OF THE INTERNET

The Internet is mooted as a major change mechanism in the 21st Century. Businesses are no longer fixed by geography as they can compete globally both for customers and suppliers through the Internet (Senn 1998). The Internet offers the opportunity to disseminate information and the ability to trade directly. While there are some concerns about the trading security, improved encryption and the ability to develop intranets and extranets mean the threat is mitigated. The next sections highlight findings from three recent surveys on Internet adoption in the UK and Europe.

3.1   DTI Survey on SMEs and the Internet
The DTI commissions an annual survey on ICT adoption in a number of major economies: France, Germany, Japan and the US. The survey considers adoption in 100 micro firms (fewer than ten employees), 200 SMEs (10-250 employees) and 200 large

firms Questionnaires and some interviews in the UK are used too. The interviews show that there may be lower Internet adoption in SMEs than indicated by the survey. As discussed later, this may be more valid and it questions the value of the Internet as a business facilitator.

In the UK 49% of firms (37% of SMEs) have Internet access. It is primarily used as an information source by 90% of these, with e-mail use at 65%. Only 47% use it for advertising and marketing, about 10% for sales and 26% for purchasing. Problems identified include security fears, speed of access, and difficulty of finding information due to volume. Only 8% of micro firms and 23% of SMEs have web sites providing a presence rather than a contributing to advertising and marketing. Indeed, Ryan and Hepworth point to the local nature of SME trading, arguing it is unlikely that they have the inclination or capacity to extend their markets geographically. However, 15% of SMEs report EDI use and 48% e-mail. This suggests that while the Internet is not used for trading, SMEs are using ICT for customer communication.

3.2   West Midlands Survey
The second survey is the West Midlands (WM) survey (PWC/Warwick University/Wolverhampton University 1997) which investigates the main Internet uses in 824 firms. These are promotion of products via a Web site, communication with customers/suppliers by e-mail, and research and information gathering. 25% of firms have a web site, with 20% using the Internet to collect information. 28% use it to communicate with customers and suppliers while 57% do not use it. There is variation between sectors; the construction industry using it least and the service sector most.

Of micro firms, only 13% use the Internet for promotion, 19% for communication and 12% for research, 74% do not use it. The situation is better in SMEs with 26% using it for promotion, 30% for communication and 22% for research. Large firms have much more exposure to the Internet: 43% use it for promotion, 41% for communication and 24% for research; only 36% do not use it.

3.3   European Small Enterprise IT Study
This study of 80 small firms across Europe used a telephone questionnaire. About half the firms use the Internet primarily for communication (66%) and research (47%). About 25% of small businesses use it for marketing yet only 10% for trading. However, the majority believe this use will grow, especially in the UK where the need to work more collaboratively is cited as a reason for greater investment in electronic commerce.

3.4   Conclusions from the Surveys
Table 1 summarises the survey findings. The major use of the Internet is to indicate a market presence with the most users having a Web page. A secondary use is information gathering, particularly competitor identification, although it is not clear that this extends as far as competitor analysis. The findings from the DTI survey and the European SE IT

survey are broadly similar, while the W. Midlands survey stands out as suggesting there is less adoption of Internet technologies. This may be reflected in the general approach to ICT among SMEs that are indicated in the surveys. However, it may also be due to the limited perceptions of investment payback.

	DTI	WM	SEIT
Advertising	47%		24%
Research	90%	20%	47%
Communication with customers	58% (50%)	28%	66%
On-line trading	11%		10%
Business-Business Trading	20%		15%
Web Site	37% (23%)	25%	
Internet Access	49% (40%)		56%
E-Mail	50% (24%)		

Table 1: Survey Results on Internet Usage

3.4.1   ICT Use in SMEs

The DTI survey shows 52% of micro firms do not see the value of ICT. Finance is the most popular use of PCs with 79% of firms using computerised accounting systems. Accounting, managing information and customer service are the main uses for 60% of small firms. In the UK, only 48% of micro firms have PCs with modems and only 15% of SMEs (no micro firms) use remote access. This is also reflected in the WM survey and the European SE IT study that find IT mainly used to reduce costs and for administrative activities.

The emphasis on cost reduction suggests a limited perspective in SMEs on using ICT to improve growth and competitiveness. Levy et al (1997) find many SMEs unable to grasp the value of management information to assist growth. Two areas, competitor analysis and financial analysis, stand out. For example, a heating engineer was convinced it had no direct competitors, purely based on the managing director's feelings. However, casual research indicated a large firm nearby could easily pose a threat. Again, few SMEs carry out analysis on customer profitability. This is relatively simple as there are financial analysis tools available, but the dominant driver for SME owners is the size of the order book, which is a proxy for profitability. Often, small customers are a drain on resources, but the SMEs do not appreciate this.

The DTI interviews highlight the importance of a champion for the introduction of ICT. Customer influence is important, particularly for the adoption of EDI, while a key inhibitor is an inability to quantify benefits. These findings are not tested in the other surveys but the importance of the owner as champion is cited by Blili and Raymond (1993), and Naylor and Williams (1994). Levy et al (1998) find customers important in EDI adoption, mainly due to collaborative relationships. The inability to quantify benefits is discussed in Ballantine et al (1998) who suggest that SMEs are driven to invest by necessity, and cost is the main consideration.

Internet access for SMEs in the DTI survey has grown from 27% in 1997 to 40%. What is unexplored is the form this access takes - whether it is an active business resource used regularly as part of business operations or whether it is a tool that sits on the managing director's desk. There is also a question over the size of the firms using the Internet; with 52% of smaller firms still staying they cannot see the value of ICT. Indeed, the survey highlights this and it is discussed later. The DTI survey reports research suggesting size is important, with only 16% of micro firms using the Internet, while use increases with size.

Leading-edge firms believe there is a need to be a leader in Internet adoption, but there is little evidence of short term returns. For example, one medium-sized firm has invested £2m in the development of a Web site including an on-line catalogue without knowing whether it will recoup this. In addition, the knock-on effects for their business that has different prices throughout Europe has not been calculated.

Generally, use of the Internet is lower in the cases discussed below reflecting a picture similar to the WM survey. There may be three reasons for this. First, the cases were undertaken over a three year period and Internet adoption is increasing. Yet, there is little indication of increasing adoption in more recent cases. Second, the case firms predominantly have 10-50 employees, reflecting their background as smaller SMEs participating in a Business Growth programme. Third, the nature of the region's industries may influence adoption.

Business Growth firm owners look to develop the skills to grow their businesses. They tend to be more innovative and higher risk takers, recognising the need for investment. The expectation is of a greater awareness of the value of ICT, but ICT investment is primarily based on improving efficiency. For example, job costing is a major issue for manufacturers, and one which makes wooden pallets has recently spent invested considerably to develop a system to support this. A photographic designer is in a similar position and the focus of their future ICT investment is job costing. This illustrates that ICT investment in SMEs is reactive. These findings echo Ryan and Hepworth in that ICT is fairly low on SMEs' priority lists. A few are beginning to use the Internet for research purposes, although this appears to be the domain of the MD and to reflect their awareness of ICT in general, rather than as part of strategy. For example, the MD of the pallet firm uses the Internet to identify competitors.

The next section investigates the detailed case research that suggests Internet adoption may be less than identified by the surveys.

4   GETTING VALUE FROM ICT: THE SME CASE

The paper uses an analytical framework developed by Levy et al (1998) to assess the impact of the Internet as an enabler for SMEs to add value. The framework has two dimensions: strategic focus for ICT adoption and customer dominance. The first reflects the two main purposes of ICT adoption: cost reduction and value adding. Cost reduction represents the traditional use of ICT by SMEs based upon their incremental and reactive adoption (Hashmi and Cuddy 1990, Blili and Raymond 1993). Value adding focuses on the adoption of ICT for competitiveness, which is identified as a possible success differentiator for SMEs (Yetton et al 1994).

The second dimension of customer dominance is recognised as a key issue for SMEs. On one hand, SMEs are dependent upon customers in two instances. First, when they are starting up and second if the SME becomes a first tier supplier to a major customer, the likelihood is that the SME will have few customers. On the other, as SMEs grow through market share, their customer base increases and individual customers have less power.

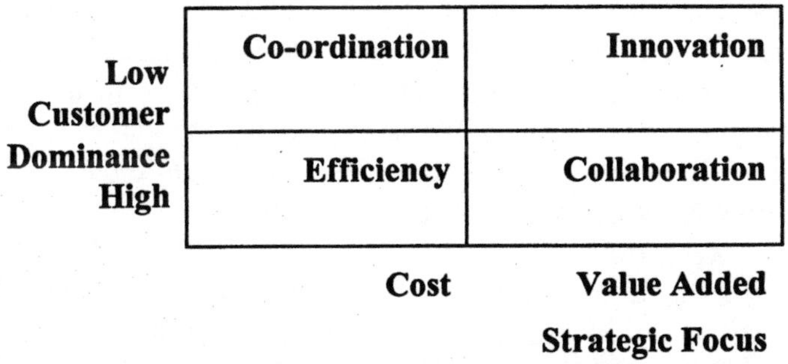

Low **Customer** **Dominance** **High**	**Co-ordination**	**Innovation**
	Efficiency	**Collaboration**

| | **Cost** | **Value Added** |

Strategic Focus

Figure 1: Framework of IS Approaches in SMEs (Levy et al 1998)

The model identifies four approaches to ICT exploitation by SMEs. The efficiency quadrant reflecting the position of many start up firms and those that effectively exploit simple systems to run the business efficiently (Naylor and Williams 1994). The co-ordination quadrant recognises the needs of growing firms to manage and increasing their customer base, often through the addition of a database. Internal networking of systems may begin here. Both these quadrants are cost focused and provide SMEs with the facility to manage more efficiently and effectively.

The use of ICT to add value to SMEs is seen in the other two quadrants. Collaboration starts to see the incorporation of emerging technologies with the introduction of EDI to manage relationships with major customers. While this is mainly driven by customer push, there are benefits in planning and managing production as well as developing more collaborative relationships. The innovation quadrant represents pro-active introduction of ICT by SME owners. They recognise the competitive market demands different ways of working and that ICT may provide the tools. The Internet is a possible ICT to exploit here.

5 BACKGROUND TO THE CASE RESEARCH

Case research has a long tradition in IS research as a method of providing rich, contextual data. This research uses cases undertaken in 1995-8 on 43 SMEs in the W. Midlands to assess the role of IS. Analysis of the case material is based on Levy et al's

(1997) work on the transferability of IS planning frameworks from large organisations to the SME sector. Each case was conducted over one week during which the MD, the senior management team and other employees took part in a number of semi-structured interviews each lasting 1-2 hours. Background and market material and the outcomes of the interviews were analysed and reported back to provoke further discussion. Figure 2 shows the adoption of ICT for the case organisations.

Most cases reflect incremental ICT adoption, but there is little evidence of innovative uses of technology. Pragmatism is the norm with a focus on operational improvement rather than value adding. This underpins the survey findings that the predominant investment in ICT is to support back office, or secondary value chain activities. Most firms have accounting and word processing and a number use spreadsheets to analyse internal costings. Garden Health Care's MD uses spreadsheets effectively to monitor budgets and costs. Customer databases are used by those with a large customer base. There is the beginning of networking internally, although the database management is not always good. For example, Warwick Training Brokerage allowed the database to be updated by all employees without any controls on accuracy.

On the value adding front EDI is used, but often operationally rather than exploiting its potential. This tends to be customer-driven as it is a prerequisite for an SME to be a preferred supplier to a major customer, particularly in motor manufacturing, a key regional industry. For example, Birmingham Clutches uses EDI to receive forecasts and orders from a major manufacturer. Similarly, MRP is now seen as a qualifier to be a first tier supplier, rather than providing strategic advantage. The Internet is used by a few firms for research, but only a handful have Web pages. Stratford Designs uses Internet technology to communicate with customers, mainly to download designs and have e-mail discussions. The Pallet Manufacturer's MD, makers of wooden pallets for the motor industry, uses the Internet from home do research on competitors, but the business does not have an Internet presence. Figure 3 shows the various ICT applied to the framework in Figure 2.

Investment in ICT in the case firms is driven by the owner or general manager. Their knowledge is critical. Unsurprisingly, the main focus is on operational systems with the drive to improve productivity and lower costs paramount. However there are a few SMEs that do see ICT playing a major role. For example, Radio Mast Surveyor's owner has invested heavily in Lotus Notes and LANs to link various branches. Indeed, the use of ICT has enabled him to grow faster as survey information is shared among staff. However, he has not invested in Internet technology as a means of doing business. While a cleaning company in Redditch has a highly developed network of PCs linked to a number of their outworkers' homes, the MD will not invest because he could not see the relevance to his business that was primarily carried out at a local level.

	word processing	Accounting	Customer Databases	Job Costing	EDI	MRP	e-mail	Performance Measurement	Project Management	Internet	CAD	LAN
Efficiency												
Garden Health Care	X	X										
Tree House Health	X	X										
Car Tubes Co.	X	X										
Recycling and Training	X											
Chemical Analysis Co.	X	X										
Bird Designs	X	X										
Landrover Repair Co.	X	X	X									
Family Solicitors	X	X										
Electrical Accreditation Institute	X	X										
Precision Tool Manufacturers	X	X										
Energy Waste Management Services	X	X										
Queensway PhotographicDesigners	X	X										
Model Car Importers	X	X	X									
Rugby Lenses	X	X										
Chemical Resin Co	X	X										
Henley Engineers	X	X										
Enamel Box	X	X										
Coventry Solicitors	X	X										
Box Co.	X	X										
Coventry Designs	X	X										
Heating Engineers	X	X										
Pallet Manufacturer	x	x										
Warwick Insurance	X	X										
Co-ordination												
University Arts Centre	X	X	X									
Regional Travel	X	X	X									
Warwick Training	X	X	X									
Seven Stars Printers	X	X		X								
Coventry Events Mgt	X	X	X									
Landfill Gas Extraction	X	X	X	X								
Coventry Training	X	X	X									
Henley Coaches	X	X	X									
Electric Tick	X	X	X									
Cable Manufacturers	X	X		X			X					
IT Charity	X	X	X		X		X					
Biottech IT	X	X	X									
Collaboration												
Birmingham Clutches	X	X			X	X		X				
Radio Mast Surveyors	X	X					X	X		X		X
Heath Springs	X	X			X	X		X				
Solihull Lighting	X	X			X	X						
Car Paint	X	X			X	X						
Stratford Designs	X	X								X	X	
Clutch Assemblers	X	X			X	X	X					
Giveaway Designs	X		X									X
Innovation												
Flower and Samios	X	X	X	X	X		X	X	X	X	X	X

Figure 2: ICT Use in SMEs Cases

	Co-ordination	Innovation
Low	Word processing Accounting Customer databases	Word processing Accounting Customer databases E-mail, Internet MRP EDI CIM LANs
High	Word processing Accounting	Word processing Accounting MRP EDI Performance Measurement
	Efficiency	Collaboration

Customer Dominance

Cost Focus   Value Added

Strategic Focus

Figure 3: Information Systems Used By SMEs (Levy et al 1998)

The need to demonstrate benefits from the Internet is a factor in non-adoption. There is also be a lack of awareness by SME owners of the capabilities of ICT in general. Yet, SMEs use communication technologies to work with major customers. The cases show a more gloomy picture than the surveys, but tend to confirm the proposition that the region lags behind others. There may be a need to intervene in the process to improve adoption. The next section discusses whether there are really opportunities from the Internet for SMEs and offers an approach that might bring collaborative benefits.

6   OUT OF TIME OUT OF PLACE: THE FUTURE OF SME BUSINESS ON THE INTERNET

While there is considerable rhetoric about the value of doing business on the Internet, it is less clear that it provides much value for businesses either in market share or profitability. Reynolds (1997) argues that having an Internet presence is not a source of sustainable competitive advantage as the technology can be easily copied. He suggests that there are two strategic uses. First , the Internet can be an information medium for new products and services. Second, it can be used to provide value-added services that cannot be easily provided otherwise. If this is a problem for large firms, SMEs will experience even more difficulty in gaining strategic advantage from the Internet using existing thinking. Thus, SMEs need to ponder their existing strengths and whether the

Internet can be used to improve or leverage them.

Castells (1997) argues that while the global economy is enabled through IT, organisational structures are changing to take account of the possibilities for trading. He describes the concept of the 'network enterprise' as a linkages between firms and groups of firms for specific projects. These linkages cease once the reason for them no longer exists. In essence, this is an extension of Mintzberg's concept of the networked organisation. In the 'network enterprise' project teams are extra-organisational.

In the project-based organisation, information becomes a key resource that needs to be available everyone. There is a need for an information strategy to identify core information requirements. In the 'network enterprise' information requirements are similar but the information is shared. This requires different forms of systems and the Internet can provide the mechanism for inter-organisational exchange. Networks currently exist along the supply chain with customers linked through a tiers of suppliers. The Internet changes the notion of first tier suppliers to include more than one SME so economies of scale can be utilised by a number of first tier suppliers concurrently. Figure 4 represents the current situation based upon current thinking about competitive advantage along the supply chain with pressure exerted back along the supply chain leaving SMEs with limited power in relation to customers.

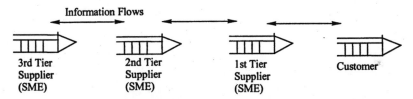

Figure 4: SME Information flows in the value chain

Figure 5 shows the outcomes from network enterprises where SMEs network to satisfy customer requirements. The networks are fluid and an SME may be in more than one network at any time. It is dependent upon information networks being strong so that SMEs can identify quickly potential project partners. The advantage for customers is that SMEs are looking at the opportunities from collaboration to develop products or provide services more effectively. The quality of product should be better as the network enterprise should consist of the best skills available to complete the project.

There are already a number of experiments in Europe to develop networks of SMEs. For example, Tavano and Guida (1998) suggest that a transport services industry network will enable a 'meta-organisation' with the best practices from each participant. They highlight three key areas for the success: organisational structures, inter-firm relationships and IS. Hof and Pallot (1998) recognise network enterprises require different tools and processes for success. They suggest this will occur at two levels, the formal - delivery of the product or service - and the 'maturation' layer that depends on collaborative relationships.

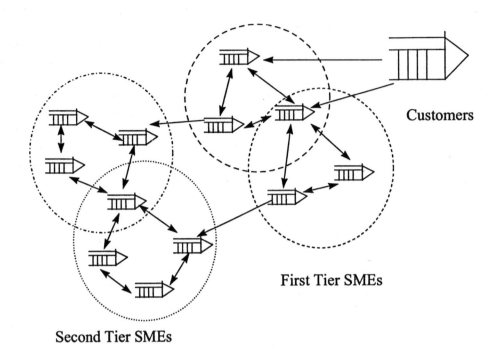

Figure 5: An Enterprise Network View of SMEs

Kanter (1994) argues that collaborative advantage can be gained by firms working together. This requires sharing information that is necessary for the collaboration to be effective, the organisations need to review work practices so that the arrangement can work, they need to be formally constituted and trust. She gives an example of network collaboration where participants are able to solve each other's business and infrastructure problems. Sharing information is central, and one way is through the development of information strategies that focus on possible areas of collaboration. SMEs can be encouraged to develop flexible systems that enable enterprise networks to work easily.

7   CONCLUSIONS

A number of surveys suggests growing Internet use among SMEs, although smaller SMEs are not adopting it. This is mainly due to a focus on cost reduction and improving productivity that can be done through more traditional ICT. The SME owner plays a critical part in decisions on ICT investment and needs to be convinced of benefits from the Internet.

When the Internet is used by SMEs it is not used for electronic commerce, either customer-to-business or business-to-business. A reason might be that EDI is already being used by many SMEs for customer-to-business trading. Business-to-business trading may be a way forward, but is currently hampered by limited investment in Internet by local businesses with which many SMEs trade.

There is discrepancy between the W. Midlands and the other areas in Europe in Internet investment. The region has Objective 2 status, recognising that needs inward investment to stem unemployment and boost growth. The government is currently supporting projects, including education and training, to boost Internet adoption. Many projects support the need for the radical approach put forward above to gain synergy from the strengths of SMEs, their niche markets and entrepreneurial flair in developing relationships. The Internet can bring added value to SMEs though this may not be possible through traditional business routes. The added value will come from SMEs working together to build on individual strengths.

References

Castells M (1997) An Introduction to the Information Age, City, 7, May 1997

Department of Trade and Industry (1998) Moving into the Information Age: International Benchmarking Study 1998.

Blili S. and Raymond L (1993) IT: Threats and Opportunities for SMEs, Int. J. of Information Management, 1993, 13, 439-448.

Dutta S and Evrard P (1998) European Small Enterprise Information Technology Study, INSEAD Working Paper 98/06/TM

Hagmann C. and McCahon. C (1993) Strategic Information Systems and Competitiveness, *Information and Management*, 1993, 25, 183-192.

Hashmi M S and Cuddy J (1990) Strategic Initiatives for Introducing CIM Technologies, in Faria L (Ed), Computer Integrated Manufacturing - Proceedings of 6th CIM-Europe Conference, Lisbon, 1990, Van Puymbroeck Springer Verlag.

Hof C and Pallot M (1998) Fast Reactive Enterprise, in Proceedings of Competing in the Information Society, Genova, Italy June 1998.

Kanter R. M. (1994) Collaborative Advantage: The Art of Alliances, Harvard Business Review, July -August 1994, 96-108.

Kanter R.M. (1995) Thriving locally in the global economy, Harvard Business Review, September 1995,152-160.

Levy M., Powell P., Merali Y., Galliers R.: Assessing IS Strategy Development Frameworks in SMEs, in Murphy C, Galliers R, O'Callaghan R and Loebekke C (Eds) Proceedings of 5th European Conference on Information Systems, Cork, June 1997

Levy M, Powell P and Yetton P (1998) SMEs and the Gains from IS: From Cost Reduction to Value Added in Proceedings of IFIP 8.2/8.6, Helsinki Finland, December 1998

Mintzberg H and Quinn J (1991) The Strategy Process: Concepts and Cases, 2nd. Ed. Prentice Hall.

Naylor J. and Williams J. (1994) The Successful Use of IT in SMEs on Merseyside,

European Journal of Information Systems, 1994, 3(1), 48-56.

Reynolds J. (1997) The Internet as a Strategic Resource, in Willcocks L Feeny D and Islei G (Eds), Managing IT as a Strategic Resource, McGraw Hill

Ryan J and Hepworth M, Building of an Information Society and Its Impact on SME Growth.

Scott Morton M. S. (Ed.): The Corporation of the 1990s, Oxford University Press 1991.

Senn J A (1998) Capitalizing on Electronic Commerce: The role of the Internet in Electronic Markets, Information Systems Management, Summer 1998, 15-24

Tavano R and Guida M (1998) European Transportation industry - virtual organisation? In Proceedings of Competing in the Information Society, Genova, Italy, June 1998

Venkatramen N, (1991) IT Induced Business Reconfiguration, in Scott Morton M. (Ed.) The Corporation of the 1990s, Oxford, University Press, New York.

West Midlands Business Survey (1997), Price Waterhouse, Warwick Business School, Wolverhampton Business School

Yetton P, Johnston K and Craig J.: Computer-Aided Architects: A Case Study of IT and Strategic Change, Sloan Management Review, Summer 1994.

CHAPTER 43

BUSINESS TO CONSUMER INTERNET COMMERCE: MAKING SLOW PROGRESS FOR THE NEXT GENERATION

Wendy L Currie
Brunel University

Abstract

This paper considers the link between Internet commerce and competitive advantage. It explores two key issues. First, the extent to which Internet commerce has created a power shift from the supplier to the customer. This thesis contends that customers will, over time, become more powerful and discriminating in their evaluation of products and services offered over the Internet. Second, we examine the topic of the new economics of Internet commerce. This is based on the premise that, as the Internet expands into core and peripheral business processes and functions, new performance indicators will be required to measure success and failure factors.

1. INTRODUCTION

In the last few years, the Internet and its possibilities for business and commerce have become inextricably linked with the concept of competitive advantage[3] (Glazer, 1991). Much of this analysis is upbeat and tends to equate the impact of Internet commerce with success stories rather than failure scenarios. For example, Attal (1997, p. 25), writing about the benefits of the Internet claims that, *The Internet and new technologies associated with it enable small businesses to compete and gain access to markets previously reserved for large global corporations'.* So a key advantage for the small and medium enterprise (SME) is that it will be able to use a Web site to appear as large as its main rivals. Traditional business variables used to measure performance in terms of size,

---

[3] The concept of competitive advantage has been widely discussed in the literature. In particular, see Porter, M. (1985) Competitive Advantage: creating and sustaining superior performance. Free Press, New York.

structure and geographical proximity to customers and suppliers will become less important in a virtual society. This is because an SME, like its larger rival, will be able to communicate much more effectively with its customers and suppliers in what has been described as *networked based businesses* (Coyne and Dye, 1998). As a consequence, other performance measures will replace traditional ones. These may include, customer relations, new product and service development, flexibility, managing intellectual property and knowledge assets (Christiaanse and Venkatraman, 1998).

In this paper, we focus on two key issues which link competitive advantage to Internet commerce. First we consider whether Internet commerce has created a power shift from supplier to customer. This thesis has been advanced by Hagel and Armstrong (1997) who claim that, *'Virtual communities have the power to re-order greatly the relationship between companies and their customers. Put simply, this is because they use networks like the Internet to enable customers to take control of their own value as potential purchasers of products and services'.* Hagel and Armstrong, 1997, p. 8). With the growth of business to consumer Internet commerce, this view contends that customers will, over time, become more powerful and discriminating in their evaluation of products and services offered over the Internet. Clearly, much depends on how the Internet develops and how businesses target new and existing customers. Notwithstanding these points, the notion that customer power will increase is an important one in the literature and therefore worthy of attention. Second, we examine the topic of the new economics of Internet commerce. This is often placed within the wider domain of the virtual society or the economics of networked-based businesses. The central argument which binds this work is based on the premise that, as the Internet expands into core and peripheral business processes and functions, new performance indicators will be required to measure success and failure factors. This is an important issue given that Internet commerce may realise cost savings in some parts of the business and increase costs in other areas. So an important question is likely to be: Who will benefit from the virtual or network based economy? So far, there appears to be few definitive answers to this question, albeit much speculation and hype.

2. A POWER SHIFT FROM SUPPLIER TO CUSTOMER?

In this section we explore the merits and criticisms concerning the thesis that Internet commerce will shift power relations from the supplier to the customer. In short, Hagel and Armstrong, (1997) suggest that up till now, suppliers have tended to use the advantages of information to give them additional bargaining power in their commercial transactions with their customers. Their argument is based on a simple logic which concedes that, *'If one party gains access to more information, that party tends to be able to extract more value from transactions than a party with access to less information'.* They continue by stressing that, *'In most markets today, vendors (suppliers) are armed with comparatively more information than their customers. They use this information to target the most attractive customers for their products or services and to engage in what economists call *price discrimination* - the practice of charging one customer one price and other customers another, depending on what the market will bear. Price discrimination is perfectly legal, to be sure, but it does illustrate one of the ways in which vendors tend to capture market surplus at their customers' expense'. These authors conclude that, *'Virtual communities are likely to turn these market dynamics upside down by creating 'reverse markets' in which power accrues to the customer'* (Hagel and Armstrong, 1997, p.17). The concept of reverse markets is an important one, although the evidence to support it currently remains thin on the ground. Notwithstanding this point, the authors give five defining elements of the virtual community business model as follows:-

Distinctive focus as to membership: Virtual communities are identified by a specific focus, to help potential members readily understand what kind of resources they are likely to find there and to help community organisers to meet members' needs. For example, the focus may be on a geographic area (say, Atlanta or Paris), a topical area (sports or foreign affairs), a vertical industry (law firms or plumbing supply manufacturers) or functional expertise (market research or purchasing management).

Capacity to integrate content and communication: Virtual communities provide a broad range of published content (including, where appropriate, advertisements and vendor information) consistent with the distinctive focus of the community, and they integrate this content with a rich environment for communication. Communication capability - through bulletin boards on which members can 'post' messages accessible to all, chat areas where real-time written 'conversations' are conducted, and e-mail - allows members to maximise the value of this content, enabling them to clarify their understanding of the content by communicating with its publisher and to evaluate the credibility of the content by communicating with each other.

Appreciation of member-generated content: In addition to published content, virtual communities provide environments for the generation and dissemination of member-generated content. This is perhaps the most empowering element of a virtual community. It gives members the capability to compare and aggregate their experiences, which in turn creates for them a fuller range of information and a perspective independent of vendors and advertisers on the resources that are important to the members.

Access to competing publishers and vendors: Virtual communities are organising agents for their members. As such, they will seek to aggregate the broadest range of high-quality resources possible, including competing publishers and vendors, and to maximise the information and product options available so that their members can make more informed, cost-effective decisions on what resources they need.

Commercial orientation: Virtual communities will increasingly be organised as commercial enterprises, with the objective of earning an attractive financial return by providing members with valuable resources and environments through which to enhance their own power. It is precisely this profit incentive that will shape the evolution of virtual communities as vehicles to augment the power of their members. Members will value this power and richly reward the community organisers that deliver it to them most effectively, abandoning those which compromise on this value proposition. It is in giving a net gain in value to their members that community organisers will realise a substantial net gain of their own. Of course, many of the early examples of virtual communities involve non-commercial (one might even say anti-commercial) initiatives, but our focus will be on the commercial potential of this new system for organising resources on the network.

Table 1: Five elements of the virtual community
(Source: Hagel and Armstrong, 1997, p. 8-9.)

Whilst it is apparent that consumers will be able to use the Internet to generate information about products and services, the extent to which they will compare and contrast the different offerings of competing businesses is the subject of much debate. For example, many customers of banks tend to stay with the same institution even though they may experience consistently poor service. They may take the view that competing banks offer equally poor service so there is little point in spending the time transferring from one bank to another. The impetus to thoroughly research the products and services offered by different banks is usually low, and customers tend to take a reactive rather than proactive approach. Even with the estimated growth of Internet users, it is doubtful that individuals will exercise their powers of choice about the products and services they purchase unless other factors prevail. In the case of the financial services sector, it is likely that banks will have to target their customers much more closely and entice them with new and improved products and services if they are to enhance their competitive advantage. To this end, banks will need to give their customers a more personalised service rather than treat them simply as an *account number*. In the past twenty years, it is certainly the case that the banking sector has become much more streamlined and routinised, with many existing customers complaining that, *'I don't even know my bank manager any more!'*. Such a view in the light of the large IT spend of banks, has done little to enhance their image. Whilst this trend towards customer anonymity has led many to criticise the banks for becoming *faceless institutions*, the extent to which Internet technology can reverse this situation is unclear. At the positive end of the spectrum, banks will need to target specific customers and offer them personalised or targeted banking services rather than continue with their blanket marketing and advertising approach. Whilst some banks are already doing this, it is likely that those financial services institutions which can develop a product and service differentiator (unmatched by their rivals) will be the ones which gain a competitive advantage.

Recent surveys point to the relative lack of progress in exploiting Internet commerce. For example, the management consultancy firm Ernst and Young (see Nua Internet Surveys, 1998) found that banks have no concrete conception of how to structure themselves on-line or generate profit from on-line transactions. They claim that by 2000, banks will be spending the same amount of money on Web applications to develop their on-line presence as they currently do on branch networks. Despite this, the report found that banks displayed an apparent ignorance of the Internet. Jonathan Charley, Banking Partner with Ernst and Young added that while most banks were willing to invest in on-line technologies, very few had any kind of strategy outlined for the future and even fewer had any idea of how to generate profit on the Internet. Similarly, a survey of the leading banks in over 26 countries found that 96 per cent did not expect to generate more revenue from on-line transactions. Only 34 per cent believed that the Internet would help them maintain existing customers (Nua Internet Surveys, 1998). These findings suggest one of two things. First, that banks are conservative and risk-averse institutions which are slow to jump on the bandwagon of Internet commerce. Second, that banks are doing their homework on the potential advantages and disadvantages of Internet commerce and have come to the conclusion that a cautious approach is the best policy. Notwithstanding the hype which surrounds Internet commerce, an important factor underpinning the *take-up* of Internet banking services is the number of people connected to the Web. Whilst estimates vary, one prediction is that a total of 320 million people worldwide will be on-line by 2002 (IDC, 1998b). We will explore some of these issues in the next section.

3. NEW ECONOMICS OF INTERNET COMMERCE

Another important thesis which has emerged in recent years concerns the shift in economic relations and Internet commerce in the wider global information society (GIS). Many writers contend that traditional theories of the economics of information will become obsolete. As more and more people communicate electronically using universal open standards, this expansion in connectivity will change peoples' behaviour and, in turn, alter the cost structures of companies. According to Evans and Wurster, 1997, p71) *This explosion in connectivity is the latest - and, for business strategists, the most important - wave in the information revolution. Over the past decade, managers have focused on adapting their operating processes to new information technologies. Dramatic as those operating changes have been, a more profound transformation of the business landscape lies ahead. Executives - and not just those in high-tech or information companies - will be forced to rethink the strategic fundamentals of their businesses. Over the next decade, the new economics of information will precipitate changes in the structure of entire industries and in the ways companies compete'.*

Much of the literature on the economics of information has explored dynamic changes in the traditional value chain (Porter, 1985). Internet commerce offers companies the opportunity to reduce operating costs by simply developing much closer links with their customers. The process of dis-intermediation is therefore one which has significant implications for the debate surrounding the economics of information. However, the process of deconstructing a vertically integrated value chain does not automatically transform the structure of existing industries and companies. On the contrary, many companies will need to develop a well thought-through business strategy before they place too much faith in the perception that Internet commerce is the panacea which will enhance their competitive position. At the present time, there are few detailed, longitudinal case studies on the new economics of the virtual or networked-based economy within specific business sectors. This is because Internet commerce is relatively new and many companies have yet to decide if they should invest in this area. Indeed, reliable business models on the economics of Internet commerce are thin on the ground. Some are too general to be useful for specific business sectors, and others measure only tangible assets and costs. Since many of the benefits and pitfalls of Internet commerce are thought to be intangible, it appears that companies should attempt to develop their own tailored cost and information management systems to enable them to develop a reliable picture of their overall performance.

As Internet commerce develops, each business sector will define its own dynamics, and economic transformation will vary in speed, intensity and scope. It is therefore unwise to make hard and fast predications about how these changes will affect specific business sectors as a whole. Evans and Wurster (1997) identify eight fundamental strategic implications of the changing economics of information:-

1.	Existing value chains will fragment into multiple businesses, each of which will have its own sources of competitive advantage
2.	Some new businesses will benefit from network economies of scale, which can give rise to monopolies
3.	As value chains fragment and reconfigure, new opportunities will arise for purely physical businesses
4.	When a company focuses on different activities, the value proposition underlying its brand identity will change
5.	New branding opportunities will emerge for third parties that neither produce nor deliver a primary service
6.	Bargaining power will shift as a result of a radical reduction in the ability to monopolise the control of information
7.	Customers' switching costs will drop, and companies will have to develop new ways of generating customer loyalty
8.	Incumbents could easily become victims of their obsolete physical infrastructure, and their own psychology

Table 2: Eight strategic implications of the changing economics of information.
(Source: Evans and Wurster, 1997, HBR, pp. 71-82)

It is well documented in the literature on Internet commerce that traditional markets and hierarchies governing companies will undergo much transformation. Terms such as globalisation, outsourcing, information and communication technologies (ICTs) and international economic markets and conditions are all said to play a part in re-shaping existing value chains of companies. Traditional business models tend to draw a distinction between company and supplier. The company is usually described as having a functional, product or matrix organisation structure where it negotiates with independent suppliers for the procurement of goods and services. This has now become a false dichotomy in advanced capitalist society as company structures and their economic relationships with suppliers have become much more complicated. Equally, concepts such as *vertical integration* - where all the materials and parts that make up a product are sourced and controlled by one organisation - is a business model which is fast becoming out of date. Traditionally, a company's assets have been measured simply in terms of raw materials, capital equipment and property. Yet in a virtual company, the value chain is likely to fragment into multiple businesses. There is a shift towards a horizontal supply-chain that is more flexibly integrated. Since a company's assets are not only tangible but also include intangible assets such as, brand value, intellectual property, human capital (people), virtual integration, information management, quality of service and customer relations, they need to be factored into performance measurement exercises. Otherwise, a company may end up with a distorted picture of its overall economic strengths and performance.

Since the structure and configuration of companies continues to undergo vast changes, acquiring a detailed understanding of the economics of information may be akin to trying to capture an image of a moving target. For example, companies wishing to focus on their core business competencies (Prahalad and Hamel, 1994) may choose to outsource all their non-core functions and operations. Whilst outsourcing is not new and has been a major activity in many industries for some time (e.g. automobiles, insurance, construction, etc) (Currie and Willcocks, 1997), it may change the economics of ownership and control within companies and, by so doing, inject greater complexity into existing cost structures. With the growth of Internet commerce, it is likely that outsourcing will increase as companies procure a range of goods and services, which are critical to their business, from a wide network of suppliers. Examples of this may be found in a variety of business sectors like financial services, retailing and publishing.

In the banking sector - which is often described as risk-averse, cautious and resistant of change - the development of Internet banking increasingly involves the creation of partnerships. Banks no longer provide all their products and services from in-house resources since they are becoming more dependent upon external partners, suppliers and agents. The major high street banks are fast becoming invisible as money becomes increasingly electronic. Some people have even posed the question: Are we moving towards a cashless society? The development of digital cash systems, which allow payment of bills through home computers and the introduction of smart cards that automatically debit charges from checking accounts are becoming more widespread in society. Direct payment systems and automatic teller machines (ATMs) have reduced the need for banks to dispense cash in large quantities. For customer convenience, ATMs are increasingly located away from banks, in supermarkets, railway stations, cinemas and other locations. The need for bank branches is disappearing as more complex transactions can be handled over the telephone, or on-line. This suggests that the entire economic structure of the financial services market is being transformed by Internet commerce.

Banks are being dis-intermediated at every stage in the supply chain. On-line brokerages, such as Charles Schwab and E*Trade are reporting huge levels of transactions at cut-price rates. On-line brokers of basic banking services, insurance and stock trading are likely to replace traditional agents rapidly, as the level of on-line trading is forecast to rise by a factor of four by 2000. By that time, almost every US bank plans to have an on-line service available on the web, with 42% offering advanced services such as on-line bill payments. Most notably, Citibank have stated their ambition to have 1 billion customers for it's banking services by the year 2010, from their current position of 60 million. They have made it clear that this can only be achieved through on-line growth (IMRG Ltd, 1998).

Whilst the evidence suggests that the percentage of on-line banking is currently small and is therefore unlikely to threaten the existing revenue streams of banks (see above), banks may increasingly come under threat as new entrants become serious competitors. These new businesses will take advantage of network economies of scale as banks face new competition from outside the traditional banking sector. This will be encouraged by low barriers to market entry. For example, the retailing sector in the UK has made inroads into the financial services with some supermarkets now offering their customers banking services. This is likely to continue. The management consultants Booz-allen & Hamilton claim that 'a transaction over the Internet costs one-tenth of what it does at the bank'. In addition, *'Independent researchers have estimated that finding a high rate certificate of deposit can take 25 minutes on the telephone, but only one minute using an electronic agent on the WWW'* (Edmondson, 1997, p. 76). Banks will therefore have to re-evaluate their existing products and services with a view to seeing whether they can offer them on the Internet to increase their profit margins.

With the increasing fragmentation of value chains, new opportunities will arise for purely physical businesses. People may procure goods and services electronically, yet their delivery will be via a traditional (road, rail, postal services) route. Books, computers and food, etc, are examples of this process. Since retailers will not have the need to position these goods in expensively decorated stores and shops, but use a warehouse instead, cost savings may be transferred to the customer. As Evans and Wurster (1997, p. 80) point out, *The new economics of information will create opportunities to rationalise the physical value chain, often leading to businesses whose physically based sources of competitive advantage will be more sustainable'.* Clearly, connectivity will be a major factor in stimulating changes to physical value chains. For in spite of the success of ventures such as electronic bookselling at Amazon.com, the vast majority of people continue to purchase their books from high street bookstores and even through mail order. So far, the advantages of electronic bookstores are, enhanced information about the products (reviews of books, customer bulletin boards), superior choice compared with traditional bookstores (Amazon.com has over 2.5m books listed), reduced inventory (no need for book store), ease of access (customer can order book at any time of day and night), superior search facilities (well designed Web site), and discounted goods. Cost savings therefore accrue to both company and customer.

Evans and Wurster (1997, p. 81) claim that, *'Because a brand reflects its company's value chain, deconstruction will require new brand strategies'.* They cite the example of banking where brand identity is tied up with the importance of branches and ATMs rather than being based upon products. As more banks develop their Internet sites, it is likely that brand identity will become increasingly related to product provision. These authors also stress that new branding opportunities will emerge for third parties that neither produce a product nor deliver a primary service. Information providers, e.g. a restaurant reviewer is one example. Another important element which will alter the economics of information is that bargaining power will shift as a result of radical reduction in the ability to monopolise the control of information. Given that the Internet has been labelled an unregulated 'wild west', where individual searches for information can generate many thousands of 'hits', an important service involves the selection, categorisation and sorting of information. New intermediaries may be well positioned to provide such services, and they may end up building up a considerable power base in their ability to monopolise the control of information.

The new economics of Internet commerce will be more pronounced in the virtual (digital) delivery rather than the physical delivery of goods and services. Whilst companies will need to identify key performance indicators which reflect changes in their markets, products, services, operations, logistics and customer profiles, etc, it is apparent that many old business models will no longer be relevant in an Internet commerce environment. In the next section, we consider a variety of goods and services which will become increasingly delivered to customers in a digital format.

4. CONCLUSION

The digital delivery of goods and services within a business to consumer context will have the most significant impact on informing debates on power shifts from suppliers to customers and the new economics of the virtual society. The examples given in this paper are just a few which illustrate the changes currently taking place in commercial sectors like news and business and information services. Yet the evidence across the spectrum of commercial sectors is variable. This suggests that business to consumer Internet commerce is currently surrounded by much hype, with only a few examples where competitive advantage is a possibility. Notions of a power shift to customers, labelled 'reverse markets' by Hagel and Armstrong (1997) are a long way off when we consider some of the current impediments to developing Internet commerce. First, there is a wide diversity between government attitudes as to whether Internet commerce should be governed by an international legal and regulatory framework. Whilst Europe is more bureaucratic in its approach, the US government prefers a policy of self-regulation, albeit recognising the problems with this approach (Financial Times, 1998). Second, there are many structural and commercial problems which impede progress towards seamless Internet commerce. At the present time, many companies are reluctant to make a large financial investment to develop an infrastructure to support Internet commerce when there remains too many unanswered questions about regulation, tax, data and consumer protection, intellectual property rights (IPRs), etc. Third, the psychological barriers which deter people from making purchases on the Internet include, lack of trust, no access to the Internet, inertia and also fears about protection and security. Taking these considerations as a whole, it would appear that, for business to consumer Internet commerce to thrive, much work is yet to be done. To this end, ideas about power shifts to the customer and reverse markets are a little presumptuous when placed in the context of wider governmental, organisational and individual concerns.

References

Attal, J (1997) 'Technology empowers small businesses'. Electronic Commerce in Practice, ICC, London.

Christiaanse, E., Venkatraman, N. (1998) 'Monitoring and influencing as key capabilities in electronic channels'. 6th European Conference on Information Systems, 4-6 June, Aix-en-Provence, pp. I,233-246. Euro-Arab Management School, Spain.

Coyne, K.P., Dye, R. (1998) 'The competitive dynamics of network-based businesses'. Harvard Business Review, January/February, pp. 99- 109.

Cronin, M. (ed) (1996) The Internet strategy handbook. Harvard Business School Press, Boston.

Currie, W., Willcocks, L. (1997) 'In search of value-added IT outsourcing'. Fast Track, Business Intelligence, London, Autumn.

Evans, P.B., Wurster, T.S. (1997) 'Strategy and the new economics of information'. Harvard Business Review. September/October, pp. 71-82.

Financial Times (1998) 'Regulators at odds', 8 October, p.20.

Hagel, J., Armstrong, A.G. (1997) Net gain: expanding markets through virtual communities. Harvard Business School Press, Boston.

Hamel, G., Prahalad, C. (1994) Competing for the future. Harvard Business Press, Boston.

Glazer, R. (1991) 'Marketing in an information intensive environment: strategic implications of knowledge as an asset'. Journal of Marketing, Vol. 15, No. 55, pp. 1-19.

Guthrie, R., Austin, L.D. (1996) 'Competitive implications of the Internet'. Information Systems Management, Summer, pp. 90-91.

Maddox, K. (1997) 'Information still killer app on the Internet'. Advertising Age, 6 October.

International Data Corporation (1998) 'The global market forecast for Internet usage and commerce'. http://www.idc.com/f/HNR/225.htm.

Nua Internet Surveys (1998) Banks are in the dark'. Nua Ltd, New York, US.

Porter, M. (1985) Competitive advantage. The Free Press, New York.

Prahalad, C., Hamel, G (1990) 'The core competence of the corporation', Harvard Business Review, 68, 3: pp. 79-91.

US Department of commerce (1998) The emerging digital economy, April. http://www.iitf.nist.gov/eleccomm/glo_comm.htm.

Verity, J.W. (1996) Invoice? What's an invoice? Business Week, June 10, pp. 110-112.

CHAPTER 44

BUILDING A BASE FOR ELECTRONIC COMMERCE: TOOLS FOR STORE GENERATION AND MARKETING

Colin Charlton, Jim Geary, Janet Little and Irene Neilson
Connect, The Foresight Centre, The University of Liverpool

Abstract

Electronic commerce is viewed as an important tool for economic regeneration. Successful exploitation of the power of the Internet however requires more than the creation of a WWW site. At a minimum, sites must fulfil essential business functions: - the promotion of product and service, the provision of data and information and the processing of business transactions. Further, these functions must be achieved in a fashion that adds value to a customer's interaction with the business. The critical issue now facing non-profit making centres for the promotion of electronic commerce is how to achieve such objectives within the constraints of available resources. This paper considers the role that computer based tools for automated on-line store generation, customisation, maintenance and marketing can play.

1   INTRODUCTION

Electronic commerce is viewed as an important tool for economic regeneration. In contrast to traditional methods of retailing, electronic marketing via the Internet offers extremely low start-up costs and relatively low running costs, together with unprecedented access to a global market. Furthermore, the geographic anonymity and physical neutrality of a web site creates, to some degree, an equality of opportunity in which small companies can compete with large ones, new enterprises with old-established ones, and geographically remote businesses with those situated at the traditional centres of commerce. These reasons make electronic commerce a particularly attractive prospect for small and medium sized enterprises (SMEs) and as a means for economic regeneration in disadvantaged regions (Bangemann, 1994).

2   THE PROMOTION OF ELECTRONIC COMMERCE

The effective and efficient promotion of the conditions in which electronic commerce can flourish within a region is generally recognised as involving both social and technical processes. Awareness has to be created in the local community of the possibilities raised by electronic commerce. The opportunity for businesses to translate increased awareness into action has then to be provided at low cost and low risk.

Economically deprived regions of the UK have been fortunate in the latter regard by the availability of European Funding for the creation of regional centres which specialise in the provision of advice and training in the skills required for electronic commerce. An example of such centres is Connect, the Internet Centre for Merseyside Businesses at the University of Liverpool, Merseyside (http://www.connect.org.uk/). Centres such as Connect have been able to offer free or heavily subsided courses on Internet related technologies to local businesses. They have also created large regional WWW sites that offer businesses the opportunity to sample the marketing potential of the WWW at zero or no cost. Grouping local businesses together in a common centre has been viewed as a way of achieving critical mass and visibility. Schemes such as the Quickstart programme in Merseyside have enabled businesses to establish a World Wide Web (WWW) presence with the minimum of investment. The Quickstart programme offers businesses a free 2-hour consultation session with a graphic designer during which time the client's corporate identity is reviewed and alternative designs for a WWW site explored. A functional on-line WWW site is established within 2 days of this initial consultation. If necessary, Connect acts as a mediator of all customer interactions with the site. Email queries from customers are automatically translated into faxes or printed as hard copy and sent to the business if the latter does not have their own email account. There is thus no need for a business to invest in the technology required for electronic commerce until the usefulness of the technology to the business has been empirically demonstrated. Nearly 2,000 businesses have had a WWW site created in this manner (Charlton, 1998).

3   FURTHER EVOLUTION

Regional advisory centres such as Connect may be seen as meeting many of the required conditions for the successful diffusion of an innovation, (in this case the Internet), to the business community (Rogers, 1983, Sarker, 1995; Charlton et al, 1998 a, b). Fear of the technology has been removed, awareness of possibilities offered by the technology has been generated and the opportunity to try out the technology at low cost has been provided.

Increasingly, however, successful exploitation of the power of the Internet requires more than the creation of a WWW presence. There is no longer any novelty value in a business having a WWW address. Nor do attractive graphics ensure return site visits. At a minimum, sites must fulfil essential business functions: - the promotion of product and service, the provision of data and information and the processing of business transactions. (Such sites are commonly referred to as stores). Further these functions must be achieved in a fashion that adds value to a customer's interaction with the business but at low cost (Ho, 1997). Thus, the critical issue now facing non-profit making centres for the promotion of Electronic Commerce is how to achieve such objectives within the constraints of available resources. The remainder of this paper considers the role computer automation might play in the generation and marketing of on-line stores.

4   ENABLING KEY BUSINESS FUNCTIONS AUTOMATICALLY

An on-line store, regardless of size, requires an effective means of advertising the product; a detailed catalogue of the product; an efficient order placement & processing system; an effective & secure means of purchasing products; a variety of methods (e.g. phone, fax, email) for communication about and confirmation of orders (Palmer, 1997). In addition, individual businesses may require certain specialised functions: - an accountant may wish an on-line diary in which to advertise financial advice seminars; a publisher may want a facility for the broadcasting of information about new books or a chat room for discussion of books. A system is thus required which not only effectively and efficiently automatically generates the *key generic operations* of an electronic store but also allows *customisation* of that functionality to meet the particular requirements of an individual business. Any store so generated must also be easy to maintain by the client if efficiency in production is to be maximised. Customisation and maintenance cannot therefore assume any specialist computing or programming skills.

Such a system can be generated through combining CGI technology with the use of Java applets. CGI technology can be used to generate the basic framework for an on-line store. An archive of Java applets will allow this functionality to be readily augmented. Customisation and maintenance of the store by the client or graphic designer may be realised through a WWW based interface without the assumption of any programming knowledge. The details and relative merits of such a system, as implemented at the Connect Internet Centre for Merseyside Businesses, are discussed below.

4.1   The process of on-line store generation

The details about the client's business that are required for generation of an on-line store are acquired by a graphic designer in consultation with the client or are abstracted from the client's WWW site if one already exists. The graphic designer then inputs these details into a database using a WWW based interface to the latter. All client details are held in the database. The database is initially populated with only a few examples of the product catalogue. Further development of the content of the catalogue is the responsibility of the client who is trained for this task by the graphic designer. Training generally takes less than one hour. The client is also provided with a printed manual of instructions. On-line context sensitive help is also available.

A functional store layout including a product catalogue and order processing system is then generated on the fly from this database using cgi-scripts. Each store is generated with its own individual checkout point. Customers can select items for purchasing from different sections of the store's catalogue or indeed from different stores. Items selected for purchasing are placed in a 'shopping basket' and paid for at each individual store checkout point. The selections made by a customer may be reviewed at any time and a running total of purchases obtained. Customer orders are automatically checked for completeness then faxed or sent by email to a business. Security of transactions is assured through use of Netscape's Secure Socket layer and by the encryption of all email interactions with a business. Customer details given during the ordering process such as shipping address, (though not credit card details), are stored for the duration of the browser session only. Although customer details could have been stored between WWW sessions through the use of cookie technology, this option was rejected. In our experience, customers are reluctant to accept cookies and actively avoid sites that employ the latter. Such fears have been noted by other researchers (CommerceNet, 1997). The ordering process we have implemented avoids the usability problems identified in empirical studies of ecommerce sites (c.f. Tilson et al, 1998).

As of November 1998, 16 stores have been generated by the system with a total of approximately 3,700 products. Examples of stores generated by this process may be viewed at http://www.merseyworld.com/mall/. Victoria House, which took less than an hour to construct, is the smallest store placed on-line using this system. LR Supermarket is the largest. The latter receives orders from around the world and has had thousands of pounds worth of orders since going on-line in this format in October 1998.

4.2   Customisation of a store

The client creates the look and feel of a particular business through individualisation of the store's graphics - the background texture, logo etc- and by the editing of the generic product catalogue. Editing of the content of an on-line catalogue is through a password protected WWW interface to the database that holds the client's details (Figure 1). On logging on to the system, the client is presented with a WWW page with drop down menus of options; text field entries for company descriptions etc. A frame-based layout is used. The editing options are displayed in the LHS frame; the options for a selected edit in the RHS frame. All changes are made to a test database accessed through a test server. Only when the client confirms the revised design is the latter mirrored to the database on the live server. Clients can therefore experiment with alternative designs of their store before becoming committed to a particular design. Extensive data validation checks are always performed on any of a client's submissions before the latter are accepted by the system.

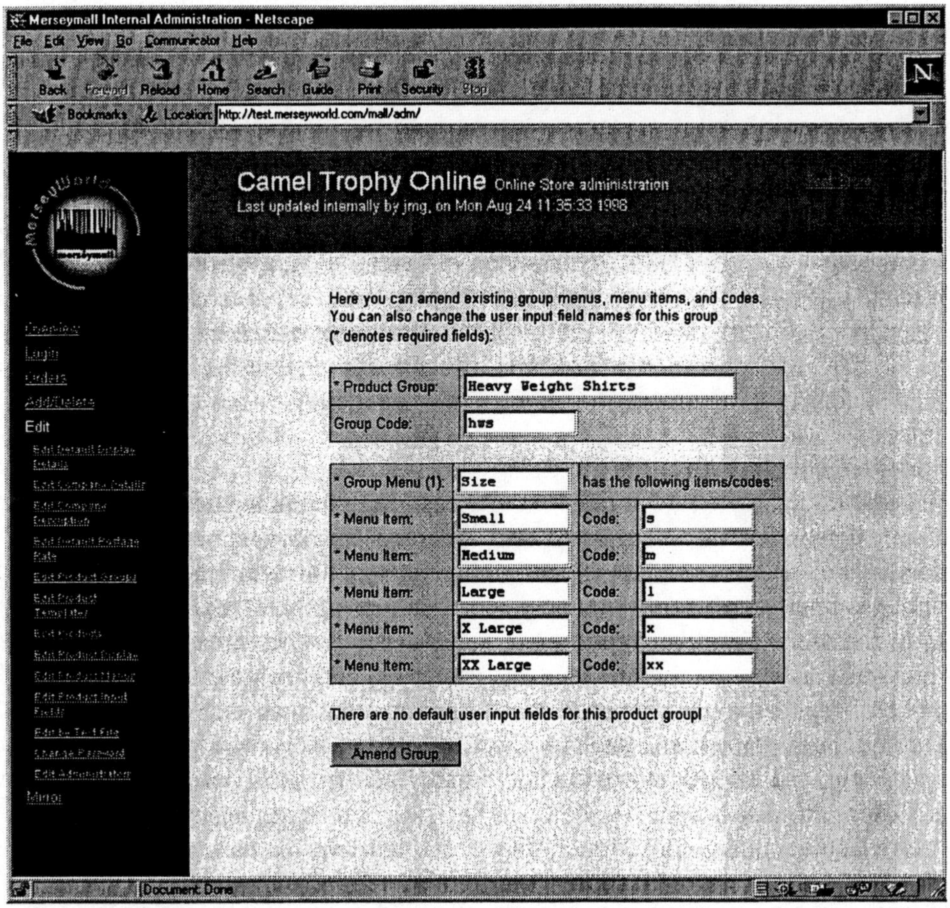

Figure 1: Web interface for customisation of the product catalogue for Camel Trophy

4.3   Organisation of the product catalogue

Figure 1 also illustrates some aspects of the organisation of items in the product catalogue. At the top level of the catalogue is the 'group'. In its simplest form, this defines the category into which products can be added. A group may have menus and input fields associated with it. In Figure 1 the group called 'Heavy Weight Shirts' has a menu called 'Size' with the menu items 'Small', 'Medium', 'Large' 'X Large' and ' XX Large'. It has no associated input fields. However, if the store offered a monogramming service then the group would also have an input field associated with it into which the customer would type the desired monogram.

Directly under the top level is the 'Template' (This editing option can be seen in the LH frame of Figure 1, below that for 'Edit Product Groups'). Templates are defined under specific groups and they dictate what information is needed to add a product to a group. All templates have a default set of fields, such as product name, product code, description, price etc. Extra fields can be added to a template if the business wishes to display more information about the product. Each template also inherits the menus, input fields etc of the group. These menus and input fields are also inherited when a new product is added to the group (unless the user selects the 'no inheritance' option).

For example, a furniture business may set up a group called 'Chairs'. Now, it may sell both standard and reclining chairs. For the standard chairs it may wish to simply display a description, but for the recliners the business may wish to display some of the options of the reclining feature i.e. hydraulic, pneumatic, or electrical. The business would thus set up two templates under the group 'Chairs'. One they would call 'Standard Chairs' and the other 'Recliners'. To the recliners the business would add the extra field 'Options'. Now when the business added a standard type of chair to the store they would use the 'Standard' template, and for recliners, the 'Recliners' template.

4.4   Augmented functionality: the Java Archive

Client desire for additional specialist functionality has been accommodated through the creation of an archive of Java applets (http://www.merseyworld.com/applets/). Each applet is documented and designed to be configurable by a non-programmer or graphic designer through simply editing the parameter specifications of its HTML <applet> tag.

Applets in the archive vary in type. Some serve a purely decorative or advertising function, providing a 'state of the art' feel to a store. Others, such as the Folding List applet have been designed to provide specialised interface functions such as navigational support. Finally, there are applets, such as the Chat applet, Newswire applet, Address Book and Datebook applet, which provide additional services. The Chat applet provides an on-line forum for discussion. To date, it has predominantly been used on sites concerned with Entertainment, http://lottery.merseyworld.com/, but has recognised value in other contexts such as education (McConnell, 1998) or real-time business communications (Poon and Strom, 1997). The Newswire applet broadcasts the latest news about a site or store and is of obvious value to on-line newspapers and other types of publishers, see http://www.merseyworld.com/. The Address applet provides customers with easy access to the contact details of members of a business or large organisation, see http://www.knowsley.gov.uk/email/address.html The Datebook applet facilitates the viewing of forthcoming events as calendar entries through a familiar desk-calendar style interface. It permits clickable links between event entries, allowing navigation between corresponding events. This applet is used extensively by Knowsley Council to inform the general public of council events. Community organisations and local businesses can themselves add events to the datebook through a WWW form interface to the applet.

New applets are designed in response to requests from clients for novel functionality. All applets are designed to be as small as possible to facilitate speed of loading and can be turned off by the user. All the applets are displayed within the browser page. This does not appear to present any usability problems despite suggestions in the literature that function serving applets should be displayed in a separate window from the browser

(Nielsen, 1998). An alternative HTML page is always available for customers accessing a site or store through a non Java enabled browser.

5   TOOLS FOR MARKETING OF THE ON-LINE STORE

Once created a WWW site or store has to be effectively promoted as an integral part of a business. Registration of a site or store with the major search engines on the WWW is an important, albeit first-step, in the effective marketing of the site or store. This first step is however difficult for a business to make on their own for several reasons. First there are thousands of search engines, directories, indexes on the WWW of varying quality and importance (http://www.webmaster.com/). A local business does not have the knowledge required to effectively select those services that would effectively promote his/her site or store. Secondly, even if a business had such knowledge the process of registering with several thousand or even just several hundred search tools would be exhausting. Search engines vary in the type of information they require about a site and few tools exist to facilitate this process. Automation is required to facilitate this aspect of site or store marketing. At Connect, a tool, Signpost, has been designed for this purpose.

Use of Signpost (http://signpost.merseyworld.com/) integrates human with computer intelligence. Human intelligence is used to keep track of developments in search engine technology and on the emergence of new, useful search engines such as Goggle. A database of such sites and their requirements is maintained. Signpost utilises this database. Signpost requires a client to submit only one set of details of about their site or store. Signpost then checks these details are against this comprehensive database of search resource data. Information relevant to a particular search engine is automatically filtered from the client's submission & packaged by Signpost into the exact format required by the search resource. Signpost then connects to the search resource, and the packaged submission is sent to the resource's submission CGI script. The search engine's CGI script accepts this data as though it came from its own submission form, processes it and sends back a response document. The response document from the search resource is checked by Signpost to determine the result of the submission, and the result is recorded. This process is repeated in turn for each search engine. Finally an email giving details of successful submissions and relevant omissions is sent by Signpost to the client. Any problems or delays in the submission of site or store details to a search engine are resolved by Signpost, sometimes aided by technical support staff. All the client has to do is submit their details of their site or store once and it is accurately relayed to all appropriate search facilities on the WWW.

This tool constitutes an advance over most other facilities for site or store registration on the WWW. The main type of alternative facility is simply a WWW page with links to the submission forms of the main search engines or directories. This user still has to repeatedly enter the details of the WWW site. Some semi-automated facilities exist which will handle multiple submissions to a variety of search engines. The client has to handle problems. The only comparable alternative to Signpost in the UK is Broadcast (http://www.broadcast.co.uk/).

5.1   QUALITY CONTROL & STATISTICS

Maintaining the currency of the site and obtaining feedback on customer usage patterns is also important in the effective marketing of a WWW site or store. At Connect, businesses are provided with a WWW interface to a suite of software (http://www.support.com/) which can be used to check the validity of links used in the site, the syntax of the underlying HTML code, the load that the use of graphics is placing on the site download time etc. The client acquires the skills necessary for such tasks through the Connect Centre's training programme.

Analog (http://www.statslab.cam.ac.uk/~sret1/analog/) software is used to automatically collect a variety of statistical information about site or store usage: - accesses, page requests, hosts served, linked sites, the search terms being used to discover the site or store etc. As the statistical display offered by Analog is not user friendly, an automated system has been set up within Connect to translate Analog output a more comprehensible display format. This system will automatically provide statistical feedback on a site or store performance by email to any business that requests the service. This information, provided it is judiciously interpreted (Hurwitz, 1997), can provide a business with useful feedback on the impact of particular promotional campaigns. The impact of an IT campaign on accesses to the Knowsley Borough Site, for example, was monitored in this way.

6   EVALUATION

Dynamic generation of HTML pages from a central database of client details using cgi-scripts is an efficient method of providing a service to the business community. It retains currency of information. Latest offers, daily news can readily be provided. Calculations can be performed on store interactions and records of transactions maintained. However, the back-end database to the system has to be running 24hrs per day. This can be tricky to achieve - full backups may mean making the database overnight for a hour or two a month. If the database goes down, then no alternative service can be offered. Service may be slow unless the database machine and/or net connection between database and Web server is fast and a heavy load is placed on the WWW server. Technical solutions can however be derived for several of these problems.

Users have experienced no significant difficulties with the Web based interfaces to the systems we have described. The systems are accessible through any browser and browsers are common on every computing platform. New businesses are readily trained to use the WWW store editing system in less than one hour. The main request from businesses is for greater customisation in the design of the WWW store. For example, the default specification for postage bases charge on geographic location, and order value.

This allows businesses to specify postage charges for UK, Europe, or World wide delivery in each of 3 order value bands. Occasionally a merchant will ask for something like a set postal charge for the UK, and a 'percentage of order' charge for Europe and the rest of the world. Obviously, to implement all and every possible variation of a business function is not feasible and a balance has to be made between ensuring a degree of flexibility in the system and efficiency of processing. In general terms, clients are pleased with the system.

7 CONCLUSION

This paper has demonstrated how CGI scripts and an archive of Java applets can be combined to create an automatic system for the generation, customisation and maintenance of WWW stores which nonetheless satisfies customer requirements for a high quality, functionally effective WWW presence. Tools to facilitate the effective marketing of WWW sites and stores are also described. Such systems are essential if businesses in economically deprived areas are to successfully use the Internet to advantage. Indeed, if the critical mass essential for true electronic commerce is to flourish, it may be argued that there is a *general* need for developers to focus their effort on site development software that is readily affordable, can be deployed universally and imparts control to the user (Lapp, 1997).

References

Charlton, C., "Building an Electronic World: putting 1,001 businesses on-line" HP DutchWorld 98, Hewlett-Packard Netherlands B.V, September 1998-12-15.
Charlton, CC, Gittings, C, Leng, P , Little J and Neilson, I "Diffusion of technological innovations: Bringing businesses onto the Internet, the case study of Connect" ,in "Information Systems and Technology Innovation and Diffusion", T J Larsen and G McGuire (Eds) Idea publishing group, USA, 1998a, 247-292.
Charlton, CC, Leng, P and Neilson, I "The Role of Intermediaries in Electronic Communication and Trading", Proceedings of International Workshop "The Future of Interactive Communication", Helsingborg, Sweden, June 1998b.
Commerce Net (1997) http://www.commerce.net/research/pw/bulletin/97_09_b.html.
Hurwitz, R (ed) "WWW Site Measurement : A Collective Interview", WWW Journal, Issue 3 1997.
Ho, J. "Evaluating the World Wide Web: A Global study of Commercial Sites", Journal of Computer Mediated Communication, 3(1), June 1997.
Hoffman, D. L., Novak, T. P., and Chatterjee, P. "Commercial scenarios for the Web: Opportunities and challenges" Journal of Computer-Mediated Communication, 1, (3) 1995. Available: WWW URL http://209.130.1.169/jcmc/vol1/issue3/hoffman.html.
Lapp, R.S (1997) Cost-Effective Internet Strategies, Handbook of Business Strategy, 11th July, 1997 http://www.i-2.com/economiesPressHobs07-97.html.

Mc Connell, D "Electronic discussion groups and distance learning", Proceedings of the Conference on Networked Life Long Learning, Sheffield, April 1998.

Nielsen, J , "Applet Usability: Stepping outside the page" The Alert Box, 15th October, 1997 http://www.useit.com/alertbox/9710b.html.

Palmer, JW "Retailing on the WWW: The use of Electronic Product Catalogs", Electronic Markets 7(3), 1997.

Poon, S. and Strom, J, "Small business use of the Internet - Some realities", Proceedings Internet Society Conference, Kuala Lumpur, 1997.

Rogers, E.M., Diffusion of Innovations, New York: Free Press, 1983.

Sarkar, M. B., Butler, B. and Steinfield, C. "Intermediaries and Cybermediaries: A Continuing Role for Mediating Players in the Electronic Marketplace", Journal of Computer-Mediated Communication 1(3), Dec 1995.

Tilson, T, Dong, J., Martin, S. and Kieke, E (1998) " Factors and principles affecting the usability of four ecommerce sites", Our Global Community Conference Proceedings, http://www.research.att.com/conf/hfweb/proceedings/tilson/index.html (IBM report).

The Bangemann Report (1994) Europe and the global information society: recommendations of the European Council. Brussels. European Commission. http://www.ipso.cec.be/infosoc/.

Acknowledgements

Connect has a staff of approximately 80 people all of whom contribute to the success of the centre. We would like, however, in particular to acknowledge the work of Paul Ward who designed the software for the presentation of statistical data about site performance and Simon Morris who designed many of the applets in the Java Archive.

CHAPTER 45

ORGANISATIONAL INNOVATIONS THROUGH INFORMATION SYSTEMS: SOME LESSONS FROM GEOGRAPHY

Feng Li and Howard Williams
University of Strathclyde

ABSTRACT

Despite the significant progress in research on information systems and organisations in recent years, a major shortcoming of most such work is the lack of geographical considerations. This is surprising given the inherent spatial nature of networked information systems. In this paper, we will highlight a series of valuable lessons that can be learnt from geographical research on the information economy. In particular, we argue that the emergence of the electronic space and the consequent co-existence of 'two spaces' (i.e. the electronic space and the physical space) represent a fundamental change in the environment for organisations, and this change has been, and will continue to be, a main source of organisational innovations. The empirical evidence from our case studies is used to illustrate some emerging tendencies. A number of themes for further research will also be highlighted.

1. INTRODUCTION

With the emergence of the information economy, rapid development and proliferation of information systems (IS) have enabled organisations to manage internal activities and processes and external relations in radically different ways. Since the 1980s most organisations have been experimenting with various organisational innovations in order to become more efficient and effective in the market (e.g. Applegate, 1994; Li, 1997). IS can not only be used by organisations to collect, store and manipulate information, but also to transmit information over long distance at the speed of light. This capacity of ICTs in redefining relations between people at physically separate places and in resolving the compromise between fixity of capital location and the geographical flexibility of its use has been a main source of organisational innovations - including how functions, tasks and people are distributed and managed between different locations and between the hierarchy and the market (Li, 1995a). In this process, activities can be transferred from the local to the global arena, so that geographical differentiation between places can be more fully exploited and markets in far away places can be more easily reached.

This is, however, not to say that distance will no longer matter in the networked information economy. On the contrary, as will be discussed later in the paper, geography has never been more important because ICTs allow organisations to exploit minute differences between physically separate places, for example, in terms of local labour market conditions, the nature of cultural facilities and of institutional structures. Utopian, futurologistic perspectives on the post-industrial society - that the constraints of space and time and the particularities of place diminish and disappear altogether and all information will be found in all places at all times (Godfrey, 1979; Toffler, 1981) - have increasingly been criticised and abandoned (Hepworth & Robins, 1988; Gillespie, 1991; Goddard, 1992). Nevertheless, the influence of such Utopian views remain clearly visible in organisation and management thinking, and progress in the geography of the information economy since the 1980s have been slow to be adopted in non-geographical research - including research on information systems and organisations.

In this paper, we would explore the relevance of geographical research on the information economy to research on information systems and organisations. In particular, we advocate the concept of 'two spaces' as a result of the emergence of the 'electronic space' which co-exists with the physical space and place of this world. The emergence of the electronic space is leading to a fundamental change in the agglomeration economy: whereas in the physical space what have been agglomerated are physical entities and people in specific places; but in the electronic space, what are increasingly being agglomerated are of 'experiences' linked together through electronic means. This change is increasingly being reflected in the new behaviours of organisations and individuals in the information economy. In this paper, the key features of the electronic space (and place), its relationship to the physical space and place, as well as the implications for organisations will be examined in detail. Some case studies and emerging business phenomenon over the last decade or so will be used to illustrate some new tendencies. In the last section, a number of new themes for further research will be highlighted.

2. LIVING IN 'TWO SPACES': LESSONS FROM GEOGRAPHY

Since the late 1980s, numerous studies have been carried out about the geography of the information economy (e.g. Hepworth, 1989; Goddard, 1992; Li, 1995a). One of the main conclusions is that to understand the new spatial dynamics of corporate activities in the information economy we need to shift our focus from the geography of space (or geographical separation) and place (or the unique characteristics of particular socio-cultural settings) to the geography of flows (Castells, 1985; Hepworth, 1989; Goddard, 1992). ICTs allow information capital to be accessed instantly from, or transmitted to, remote locations (Hepworth, 1989). So the locational patterns of the (networked) information capital cannot truly represent the geographical patterns of its use. To understand the new spatial dynamics of the information economy we need to look at the flows of information - not just where the information capital (e.g. computers and information resources stored in them) is located but also where it is used (Hepworth, 1989; Li, 1995a). Associated with this is a fundamental change in the agglomeration economy where the focus is increasingly being shifted from the agglomeration of physical entities and people to the agglomeration of 'experiences', with profound implications for organisational learning, work organisation and inter-firm relations.

Hepworth (1989) advanced the concept of 'communicability' to interpret the movement characteristics of networked information capital and its spatial dynamics. This concept highlighted the qualitative difference between the geographical mobility of information capital through computer networks from alternative conceptions of capital mobility (e.g. the physical relocation of firms or fixed capital investment), which signified the co-existence of two geography in the information economy - the geography of places or capital formation and the geography of flows or mobility. Several approaches have been developed to study the geography of flows in the information economy. Moss (1987) and others (e.g. Castells, 1985) advocated the study of the geographical patterns of the telecommunications infrastructure and the volume of data flows on the network. Hepworth (1989) examined the topology of computer networks used by multinational companies as representations of the physical layout of their equipment (computers, terminals, front-end processors, concentrators, etc.) and communications links over space. Recognising that analysing the topology of the corporate network does not take into account the nature and characteristics of information flows embedded in it, Li (1995a) advocated the study of the 'functional network' - the patterns of information flows embedded in the corporate network - rather than the technical configuration of the corporate network itself as did by Hepworth and others.

Since the 1970s, a great deal has been said about the 'death of distance' and the 'end of geography' but such views were often based on limited empirical evidence from particular aspects of certain sectors (e.g. global financial integration) (e.g. O'Brien, 1992); or futuristic predictions about the potential impacts of telecommunications (e.g. Martin, 1978; Godfrey, 1979; Toffler, 1981; Mandeville, 1983). The flaws with such views are evident, and Hepworth and Robins (1988) argued the view that advances in telecommunications will finally and irrevocably overcome the 'tyranny of distance' needs to be seen as part of a broader modernisation myth concerning the impact of technology on society. Such views are, 'at one and the same time, influential, wishful, misleading and irresponsible'. They are so because of the way technology and technological change are conceptualised outside of any social, economic, political and cultural contexts. On the basis of what changes technology might possibly effect, extrapolations are made about what will, necessarily and inevitably, occur (Gillespie, 1991). The reality is that even in the information economy, geography still matters, and the geography of the information economy is significantly different from the conventional geography of space and place of the industrial economy. ICTs redefine geography, not eliminating it! The physical space and place is still fundamentally important to us at all levels of society and the economy even in the information age.

Despite the significant progress made in geography on the information economy over the last ten years, such progress has been slow to spill into research on information systems and organisations. The neglect of space and place is surprising given the inherent geographical nature of information systems. In particular, with the rapid development and proliferation of ICTs (particularly the exponential growth of the global information infrastructure such as the Internet) and the firm establishment of the information economy, organisations increasingly have to operate in two spaces simultaneously - the physical space and the electronic space. These two spaces are not mutually exclusive and they sometimes overlap with each other in the organisation and execution of activities, but many rules governing these two spaces are fundamentally different. To survive in the information economy, organisations must not only exploit geographical differences and overcome geographical constraints in the physical world, but also increasingly they have to exploit opportunities and face threats in the new emerging electronic space. Given the strategic importance of information in the contemporary economy, it is perhaps actions about and in the electronic space that will separate winners from losers.

The emergence of the electronic space is not only relevant to large, multinational organisations operating from multiple locations, but increasingly it is also becoming relevant to smaller organisations selling or sourcing supplies from wider areas. Indeed, even for some small organisations serving primarily the local market, the electronic space can still be highly relevant. One example is that people often check the web pages of local PC stores to find out which one offers the most suitable product at the most competitive price. The point is, all organisations have to learn to live in 'two spaces' if they want to survive and thrive in the information economy.

The emergence of the electronic space, however, does not mean that the significance of the physical space has decreased. Many characteristics of the physical space will continue to affect the operation and development of organisations. As Harvey (1989) argued that with the support of advanced information systems, organisations are increasingly able to exploit minute geographical differences to good effect. Small differences in what the space contains in the way of labour supplies, resources, infrastructures and the like become of increased significance. An important paradox is that the less important the spatial barriers the greater the sensitivity of capital to the variations of place within space, and the greater the incentive for places to be differentiated in a way that is attractive to capital. This point will be picked up again later.

The co-existence of 'two spaces' represents a fundamental change in the environment in which organisations are embedded. Although the electronic space perhaps has emerged since the telephone and radio were invented, it has only become essential to organisations in the last ten years or so as the advanced information infrastructure becomes widely available and as the information economy becomes firmly established. In particular, different from the telephone (voice communications) which has improved the geographical flexibility of labour (other geographical flexibilities have mainly been derived from this), data communications increase the flexibility of both labour and information capital (Hepworth, 1989). So the level of flexibility to organisations in terms of 'who and what locate where' have increased dramatically. This is especially so given the growing significance of information in both capital and labour formation in the information economy.

With the emergence of the electronic space, the nature and characteristics of the 'place' has also been radically redefined. At one extreme, virtual places within the electronic space are increasingly being created - enabling people physically located in different places to meet in the same virtual place (e.g. a virtual discussion/ chat room). In essence space and place have converged into one. This is not to say that the physical place - 'the unique characteristics of particular socio-cultural settings' (Goddard, 1992, p274) - is no longer relevant to individuals and organisations. On the contrary, local characteristics will continue to affect the effectiveness of communications between people from different places even in the 'virtual place'. Indeed, even though in the electronic space, the 'friction of distance' based on the transportation model for certain information capital and products has been eroded, other frictions of distance derived from differences between places (e.g. local culture, language) will continue to work. A new model based on telecommunications and transportation is needed to understand the new dynamics of the space economy.

The implications of the 'two spaces' for organisations are extremely profound, and many lessons can be learnt from new theories on the geography of information economy that have been developed in the last ten years or so. Instead of living in the physical space and place and overcoming distance by transportation, organisations now have to deal with different combinations of physical and electronic spaces and places. These spaces and places can co-exist with one another and/or be flexibly integrated. The enormous geographical and organisational flexibility that can be derived from these combinations imply that organisations have to adapt the way they organise internal activities and external relations, the way they manage production, distribution and services, and the way they deals with suppliers and customers. Although decisions regarding 'who and what locate where' remain critical to many organisations (for some organisations this may no longer matter in significant ways), the number of options open to all organisations and individuals - the flexibilities and choices they have - have increased significantly. How to exploit innovatively these two spaces and manage the enormous complexity associated with this will be one of the most significant challenges to management over the next decade.

3. TWO SPACES: A BRIEF COMPARISON OF KEY CHARACTERISTICS

The emergence of the new electronic space is a fundamental aspect of the information economy. To a large extent this electronic space is embedded in - and often intertwines with - the physical space and place, but some distinctions between them are clear. People or organisations can exist in two spaces simultaneously or 'move' between them in sequence. New flexibility for both individuals and for organisations has mainly been derived from the emergence of this new electronic space, and in recent years many organisational innovations have been developed to exploit this flexibility.

Because the telecommunications infrastructure (hence the electronic space) has largely been created to improve communications between people in the same and/or different places, the similarities between these two spaces, both in their characteristics and in the rules governing their use, are relatively easy to understand. For example, the communication between two individuals through an electronic medium tends to be more effective if some conditions of the physical place in which face-to-face contacts normally take place can be recreated (Li & Gillespie, 1994). However, significant differences exist between the physical space and the electronic space.

The most profound difference between the two spaces is the speed of communications. In the physical space, the speed of communication depends on the mode of transportation, but in the electronic space, communications happen at the speed of light. It is the 'instanceness' of communications that separates the electronic space from the physical space. Many other differences between these two spaces are closely related to this feature.

Another significant difference between the two spaces is the content of communications. In the physical space the content of communication can be both informational and physical, and very often the information is embedded in physical items - be they books, reports, or human heads. However, at the current stage of scientific development, what can be communicated in the electronic space is information alone.

Despite the 'instanceness' of communications, the electronic space is far from frictionless - the geographical patterns of the telecommunications infrastructure and its bandwidth, the costs and various rules and regulations governing its use, to name but a few factors, all significantly affect its features and the way it is used. Even today, some information (e.g. human intelligence) cannot be effectively transmitted over the wire. In addition, to understand the implications of telecommunications for spatial relations and the true features of the electronic space, ICTs need to be conceptualised as integral to particular social formations, and in consequence, necessarily constituting and expressing the dominant social relations and values of those formations (Robins and Webster, 1988). As Harold Innis (1951) persuasively argued, all communications media, and the technologies that underpin them, contain an inherent 'bias'. The information infrastructure, which underpins the electronic space, cannot be separated from the social, political, economic, and cultural contexts in which the infrastructure is embedded.

In examining the geographical impacts of ICTs on large organisations and on the wider economy, Gillespie *et. al.* (1987) argued that the analogy of telecommunications as the 'electronic highway' of the information economy (Castells, 1985) is misleading, because unlike the transportation infrastructure, computer networks and telecommunication innovations cannot be divorced from the particular institutional structures in which they are embedded. Such innovations are integral to particular production, organisation, distribution and co-ordination structures and have no existence independent of these structures. The access to and ownership of a connection to a network does not necessarily imply that access is available to all possible facilities of the network or indeed that the existence of facilities is known or understood. An individual user may be restricted by hardware or other physical limitations, or human imposed control to a minor subset of the overall facilities available on the network (Tolmie, 1988). This is true not only at the global level (e.g. the Internet) but also at the organisational level. For example, the use of the corporate network in a multinational organisation (and various information resources embedded in the network) depends critically on not only the technological configuration of the network, but also more importantly, on a wide range of other factors such as the corporate hierarchy, the functional division, the technical and other competence of the users and so on. When studying the characteristics of the electronic space, the naive assumption that the 'friction of distance' can be transcended and that ubiquitous ICTs will bring about a decentralised society of electronic cottages must be abandoned (Goddard, 1994). Some of the main differences between the two spaces are outlined in Table 1.

	Physical Space	**Electronic Space**
Content	Physical and Informational	Informational
Medium	Transportation	Telecommunications
Speed of movement	Depends on the mode of transport	Light/ instant - infrastructure (bandwidth), costs, regulation etc. restrict speed
Distance	Major constraint	Doesn't matter (except cost in some cases)
Places	Separated	Local characteristics matter; Can converge with space; Virtual places
Time	Matters	Matters but events can suspend in time
Identity	Defined	Can be recreated independently of the identity in the physical space/ places

Table 1. A Comparison between the Physical Space and the Electronic Space:

The emergence of an electronic space has profound implications for organisations as well as individuals. The 'ICTs revolution' based on the convergence of telecommunications and computers can greatly improve the geographical mobility of not only information labour but also information capital and resources in the electronic space. So the geographical flexibility in the organisation of people, tasks and functions, internal processes and external relations can be significantly increased. To understand this process, however, one key question needs to be answered is the relationship between the physical space and the electronic space, in particular, how individuals 'move' between the two spaces and indeed, how individuals and organisations 'live' in two spaces simultaneously!

Space is primarily about geographical separation (i.e. distance) between places and between individuals in different places, and it needs to be overcome in the execution of certain tasks or the organisation of some processes. In the physical space, distance is overcome by transportation - by moving people or physical products between places or by spatial agglomeration of physical entities and people in particular places. In the electronic space distance is overcome by telecommunications, and agglomeration can happen through computer networking rather than by physically locating various entities together. As the information economy is firmly established, more and more information capital or resources can be transmitted across the telecommunications network, which means information capital located in physically separated places can be integrated in the electronic space; and to some extent the physical distance between information workers in different places can be more effectively overcome by advanced telecommunications than by telephone alone. In reality, the electronic space and the physical space complement each other and they mesh together flexibly as one in the organisation of certain business processes or the execution of some tasks. The result is vastly increased flexibility in the way activities or processes can be organised.

At one extreme, the electronic space can exist independently of the physical space, and the electronic space and the physical space can co-exist in parallel to each other. People and organisations can meet at various temporary or permanent electronic (virtual) places (e.g. virtual conference/ chat rooms) in the electronic space and the physical location of the participants are largely irrelevant. Nevertheless, there are limits to what functions the electronic place in electronic space can fulfil, and even in the electronic space and place, features of the physical place and space still matter significantly. For example, the communication in the electronic space and place is restricted to information alone, and anything involving physical products still needs to be supplemented by the physical space; and time zones still restrict the flexibility of the electronic space; and characteristics of the physical places (e.g. culture, language) significantly affect the communications between individuals in the electronic space in similar ways as in the physical space. Nevertheless, the options opened up to organisations and individuals are numerous and eventually this may fundamentally reshape the way internal activities and processes and external relations of organisations are managed and conducted and the way people work. In the next section, some case studies are used to illustrate some of the features discussed in this section and their implications for organisations are highlighted.

4. ORGANISATIONAL IMPLICATIONS: SOME CASE STUDIES

ICTs have allowed organisations new flexibility in the management of information capital, the location of facilities, functions and people, and the way they deal with suppliers and customers (Hepworth, 1989; Li, 1997, Li & Williams, 1997). However, this flexibility is a double-edged sword and as the level of flexibility increases so is the level of complexity in the organisation of internal activities and processes and external relations. ICTs can be used to overcome many conventional geographical constraints, and by doing so the environment in which all organisations operate has become increasingly more complex. Indeed, many constraints to organisations derived from the characteristics of the physical space and place are no longer as significant, and sometimes irrelevant, in the electronic space, so organisations are now able to do many things in ways impossible in the past. Even some basic rules governing organisational design and inter-organisational relations have been radically redefined with the emergence of the new electronic space (Li, 1997; Li & Williams, 1997).

Back in the 1950s and 1960s, the widespread adoption of telephones has significantly affected the corporate structure of the industrial economy - the physical separation of control from production and distribution, the concentration of decision making in core regions and the decentralisation of branch plants in peripheral regions and developing countries. Telephones allow management to control remotely located activities in peripheral regions effectively (e.g. Goddard, 1977). A parallel has often been draw between the telephone and transportation in their space and time adjustment effects on productive, distributive and managerial operations. Like transportation, the telephone played a critical role in providing for production and locational flexibility in firms and government, without which the mass production economy could not possibly have evolved as it has done.

A new wave of exploitation of the electronic space began since the 1980s as the 'ICTs revolution' and the information economy gather momentum, and computer networks were made the explicit technological focus of such studies (Hepworth, 1989). In particular, different from the telephone (voice communications), where locational flexibility has been derived from the improved geographical flexibility of labour, data communications increase the flexibility of both labour and information capital. Indeed, in this new electronic space underpinned by the convergence of computers and telecommunications, even the nature and functions of the telephone have been redefined. Apart from its conventional use, more and more new functions have been added to the telephone by using the number pad as an input device to control remotely located 'computers'. As our case studies will show, many leading organisations have successfully exploited the flexibility associated with the emergence of the electronic space and place; and a wide range of organisational innovations have been developed in recent years to exploit this dramatically improved flexibility. However, such organisational innovations have rarely been systematically conceptualised from a geographical perspective. Given the inherent spatial nature of computer networks a geographical approach to organisational innovations and information systems would be of great theoretical and practical relevance.

5.   CORPORATE RESTRUCTURING IN THE ELECTRONIC SPACE

With the emergence of the electronic space through the development of corporate networks, organisations are able to undertake radical corporate restructuring within the parameters of its existing geographical structure by reorganising information flows between different sites and functions. In other words, new organisational structures can be achieved through reorganisations in the electronic space without major relocations in the physical space. By doing so, the cost and time required to undertake corporate restructuring in response to internal and external changes can be significantly reduced.

One example was a large wood door and window manufacturer in the UK. The competitive advantage of the firm was based on being a low cost producer of customer-specified products in locally defined markets. Consequently, the firm was organised on a geographically based, multi-site structure in which each site was primarily a duplication of others. Each production site was relatively autonomous, designing and manufacturing non-standard products tailored to local requirements. However, the locally defined market collapsed over a period of three years, and the firm was forced to shift its focus to standard, mass-produced products (e.g. the DIY market) for the south-east England. The market re-orientation required the firm to restructure its branch plants, where sales and distribution were separated from production and then centralised and managed at the corporate level. The production activities were reorganised between different branch plants so the structure of production was transformed from previous geographical duplication (i.e. each branch plant is primarily a duplication of others) to geographical specialisation (i.e. each branch plant specialises in making a specific range of products). However, this corporate restructuring was mainly achieved not by relocating people and facilities, but by reorganising the information flows between different sites so the functional composition of different sites are redefined. A corporate network was developed to support the redefined information flows and the new corporate structure. By doing so, spatially separated activities are effectively re-integrated through the computer network. Similar changes have been found in a series of other large organisations in the manufacturing, retailing and financial services sector. This capacity of ICTs enables organisations to undertake corporate restructuring more easily and more frequently in response to changing internal and external conditions (Li, 1995a).

Process Integration via the Electronic space

Separating activities (or different parts of an activity) in an organisational process over space can significantly undermine process integration, which until recently has been a major compromise that most organisations have to live with (Li, 1997). However, with today's ICTs, this compromise can to a large extent be resolved for many activities, because spatially separated activities can be electronically re-integrated. By doing so, an organisation can gain enormous flexibility in locational choices and in the way various activities are organised and conducted.

In service sectors, such as the retail branches of banks and building societies, many back-office activities have conventionally been co-located with front-office activities in the same premise. However, in recent years, back-office activities (e.g., cheque clearing) are increasingly separated from front-office activities (e.g., serving customers), and then the former are centralised and relocated to spatially separated, functionally specialised administration centres. These spatially separated back-office and front-office activities are then re-integrate electronically. This, on the one hand, reduces the amount of administrative work in retail branches and leaves these branches more space and time to serve customers; and, on the other hand, centralising and specialising back-office activities from several retail branches (normally located in expensive population centres) and relocating them to specialised administration centres in low cost areas can lead to scale economy and reduction of office overheads. In some cases, this spatial separation has happened across regional and national boundaries. The situation in retailing is quite similar.

The implications for organisations are extremely profound as they can gain enormous locational flexibility in organising various activities. On the one hand, organisations can make radical changes in their organisational structure within their existing corporate geography - by reorganising the information flows linking different sites rather than by physically relocating facilities or workers (which has been discussed in the last section). On the other hand, organisations can disintegrate activities further and relocate them to different places in order to exploit geographical differentiation in cost factors while maintaining process integration.

Similar to separating the front- and back- office activities, key developments in ICTs also allowed the customer service functions to be carried out via the telephone in a back-office environment - the 'back-officing' of front-office activities. The introduction of new tele-mediated services has resulted in new forms of organisations in some sectors, as well as new ways of service delivery to customers at low costs. In most cases, this change involves the concentration of service supply from geographically dispersed locations in downtown areas (for instance, numerous retail outlets in population centres) to a few central locations in cheaper areas, often away from the downtown. The link with customers conventionally maintained via face-to-face contact is maintained by telecommunications over distance.

Until recently, front-office activities are seen as immobile, because they have to be located in physical proximity to their markets, and their effectiveness is based on face-to-face contacts with customers. For many front-office activities this remains the case today, but since the late 1980s, key developments in ICTs - particularly in advanced voice telephone systems and integrated information systems - have led to the relocation and concentration of some conventional front-office activities that required an interface with the customer - essentially separating the service provider and the customer over space and re-integrate them via telecommunications. The evolution of intelligent networks, the introduction of automatic call distribution systems together with the introduction of toll-free or local rate telephone numbers allowed certain sectors to provide services to their customers from one or a few central locations via the telephone, without undermining the effectiveness of the services. The telephone network is supplemented by a data network providing essential information to the operators. By doing so, many conventional front-office activities are essentially being pushed into a back-office environment. The organisation can gain a series of benefits ranging from lower overhead (office and labour), scale economies, higher efficiency and improved services (extended hours).

Such development has been extremely fast in recent years, as has been reflected in the rapid growth of 'call centres' in the field of tele-services (e.g., tele-banking, tele-insurance, and tele-reservation services). Direct Line, the extremely successful subsidiary of the Royal Bank of Scotland, became the largest motor insurance service firm in the UK only a few years after it was launched, and its household insurance and mortgage businesses have also been growing rapidly. Instead of setting up numerous high street retail outlets, the firm is organised as six service centres in the UK, which are linked together by a private corporate network. All business is conducted via the phone and supplemented by postal mails. The company has now successfully moved into the US market. Other insurance direct writers such as Churchill and The Insurance Service have also steadily increased their share of the motor insurance market in the UK.

Most banks in the UK launched telebanking services in recent years, such as the Midland Bank's First Direct, as well as the telebanking services by TSB and the Bank of Scotland. Telebanking not only allows banks to move away from traditional retail banking based on a large network of expensive retail branches in high streets (though such branches will still be useful), but also allows the service to be extended to 24 hours a day, 365 days a year. Some US and European banks are now entering the UK retail banking market this way.

Another example is found in the telesale operation of a major airline (BY). The majority of BY's customers have traditionally been based in the Southeast of England. As a result, around 90% of telesale staff were located at Heathrow. Since the late 1980s, BY rationalised its operations, with telesale centres being set up in Manchester, Belfast, Glasgow and Newcastle as well as Heathrow. The operation was monitored and controlled from a call management centre at Heathrow, and the new structure was underpinned by a number of innovations in its information systems. By developing an integrated private network, and by using British Telecom (BT)'s intelligent network service to route calls from customers to the most convenient call centre, the five central locations are integrated into one 'virtual office'. More importantly, staffs are increasingly moved from the expensive Heathrow to other cheaper locations. Currently, the interface between UK and the rest of the world is also being developed. For example, when US lines are busy, calls are automatically routed to the UK at no extra costs to clients. This innovation enabled the airline to reduce costs and improve the quality of its reservation services.

6. WORKING IN MULTIPLE PLACES

A series of other new business phenomenon can also be conceptualised by using the 'two spaces' concept. Examples include international projects involving geographically distributed team members and the so-called multi-organisational workers (people offering their special expertise to several clients via electronic means). One concept dealing with the geographically dispersed teams is team-telework (Li & Gillespie, 1994), which is primarily concerned with people in different locations participating in the same project via electronic means. Team-telework can take several organisational forms. At one extreme is the sequential participation by members on a common task with the support of ICTs. That is, when a job is assigned to a team, one team member can start working on it at a location or locations convenient for him/her. Then the work-in-progress is passed to other members of the team sequentially via telecommunications. Other members can either work on it immediately or wait until a time at a location convenient for him/her. The work is therefore passed around the team members over time and space – essentially different parts of the work is integrated in the electronic space.

At the other extreme, geographically dispersed team member can participate in the execution of the work task simultaneously in an electronic place - like teleconferencing but often the members are supported by multi-media communications incorporating voice, data, videos, pictures, graphics and shared whiteboard on which all members can see, comment and make changes in real time. By doing so, the need for physical co-presence of team workers is being replaced by a tele-mediated co-presence. Such a solution can significantly increase the geographical flexibility in the organisation and execution of work. In essence, the physical places where the members are located are linked together by the electronic space - or more precisely, the meeting takes place in a virtual, electronic place.

Between these two extreme scenarios, team-telework can take numerous organisational forms, supplemented by face-to-face contacts. The adoption of such practices will have a major impact on the nature of the workplace and on emerging forms of organisations. In all cases, the emergence of the electronic space and place enables individuals to be involved in different teams, working with geographically dispersed colleagues via electronic means. In particular, they can be present at multiple 'places' simultaneously or travel between 'places' in no time. Such flexibility is not possible in the physical space.

7. OTHER BUSINESS PHENOMENON

Many other business phenomena also call for the study of the 'two spaces'. One such new area is the practice of trade unions (Information Strategy, 1998). Until recently, most studies have shown that employees and trade unions are losing more power in the face of globalisation and the irresistible march of flexible working practices. However, a powerful new weapon has been discovered that by using the cyber space, trade unions can gain strength they have never gained in history. Through the so-called cyber picketing, a campaign was organised against Bridgestone, the Japanese tyre maker, in a dispute with Firestone, its subsidiary in the USA. The bombardment of the company's site on the web and of its e-mail addresses was one of a number of campaign techniques successfully used by the United Steel Workers of America prior to an agreement being reached in a dispute over pay and working conditions (Information Strategy, 1998). The campaign was co-ordinated in support of the American union by the International Federation of Chemical, Energy, Mine and General Workers Unions (Icem) from its headquarters in Brussels. Since then, Icem, with about 20 million members world-wide, has begun to realise what a potentially powerful weapon it has in the cyber space. Operations such as this would have been difficult to co-ordinate in the physical space: in essence the dispute has been fought between the employer and an international trade union in a virtual place (alongside the battle between the local trade union and the employer in a physical place)!

Another significant new development is the so-called 'electronic neighbourhoods' in various 'on-line communities', which have been developing extremely rapidly. In June 1998, the Internet company Geocities announced that two million members had signed up in its 40+ themed electronic neighbourhoods (increasing from 10,000 in October 1995!), and overall there are over six million people in various electronic virtual neighbourhoods (May, 1998). McKinsey Consultants, John Hagel and Arthur Armstrong, argued in their book, *Net Gain*, that such virtual communities have the power to greatly re-order the relationship between companies and their customers. Various companies are already responding by moving in these 'virtual places': in essence they are already living in 'two spaces'. These companies are buying the equivalent of 'electronic retailing space' in various on-line communities, and marketing efforts are increasingly differentiated in the plethora of distinct electronic neighbourhoods. The individuals in these neighbourhoods are also living in 'two spaces', and the two spaces can either be closely linked together (e.g. some friends in the physical space also meet in the virtual space) or largely independent of each other (e.g. one can even create an entirely new identity in the electronic space!). The fully business implications of such developments need to be systematically examined and closely monitored.

8. SUMMARY AND FUTURE RESEARCH

In this paper, we explored the relevance of progress in geography on the information economy to research on information systems and organisations. The 'ICTs revolution' does not mark the 'end of geography' or the 'death of distance'. On the contrary an extremely complex new geography is being created. We believe the emergence of the electronic space that co-exists with the physical space and place as a fundamental aspect of the information economy. The geographical flexibility deriving from the 'two spaces' for both information capital and labour has been, and will continue to be, a main source of organisational innovations.

Living in 'two spaces' poses a significant challenge to organisations large and small in the information economy because the level of flexibility and complexity in the way they can organise internal activities and processes and external relations have been increased dramatically. To manage the new flexibility and complexity, new mindsets, new strategies, new organisational structures and processes and inter-organisational relations, new management techniques and new ways of working are needed. To address such issues we believe the following questions need to be systematically examined.

The first question need to be answered is the nature and key characteristics of the electronic space and its relationship to the physical space and place, particularly from an organisational perspective. This is a challenging task given that the technological infrastructure and the institutional framework regulating its use are still evolving rapidly. Such developments thus need to be closely monitored and their implications for organisations and individuals systematically explored. Progress in geography on such issues may be particularly relevant, which has been developing rapidly.

The second question needs to be examined is how people and organisations 'move' between the two spaces sequentially, or 'live' in two spaces simultaneously. The emergence of the electronic space not only affect the relationship between people in different locations - even within the same building the use of e-mails has to some extent changed our behaviour. One way to explore such issues is perhaps to use the concept of the so-called 'virtual place', which can either be the venue for geographically dispersed workers to 'meet' or be the 'place' for shared information capital or resources. However, to fully understand the dynamic and flexible relationships between the physical and electronic spaces and places requires a systematic approach. Another important factor, time, may also need to be brought into the picture as its features in the organisation and execution of work are also being radically redefined.

Third, as the case studies have shown, the geographical flexibility for information capital and labour deriving from the new electronic space has been a main source of organisational innovations, and even some of the 'rules' of organisational design and basic assumptions about the nature of firms and market may have been redefined. It is therefore important for information systems and organisational research to conceptualise emerging business phenomenon from a geographical perspective. Findings from such research, along with research finding from existing approaches, can then be used to theoretically inform researchers and practitioners in forming business strategy, in undertaking corporate reforms and in developing new organisation and management theories for the information economy.

References

Applegate, L. M (1994) Managing in an Information Age: Transforming the Organisation for The 1990s. In Baskverville, R., Smithson, S., Ngwenyama, O., & DeGross, J. I. (eds.), *Transforming Organisations with Information Technology*. North-Holland, Amsterdam

Castells, M (1985) High technology, economic restructuring, and the urban-regional process in the united states, Castells, M (ed), *High technology, space and society*, Sage, London

Economist, The (1998) 'Telecoms: So the elephants danced', *The Economist*, August 1-7 1998: 20-22

Gillespie, A, J Goddard, M Hepworth and H Williams (1987) Information and communications technology and regional development: an information economy perspective, paper presented at *OECD ICCP seminar*, 7-9, 1987, Athens

Gillespie, A (1991) 'Advanced communications networks, territorial integration and local development' in Camagni, R (ed.) *Innovation Networks: Spatial Perspectives*, Behaven Press, London

Goddard, J (1977) Telecommunications and office location, *Regional studies*, 11

Goddard, J (1992) New technology and the geography of the UK information economy, Robins, K (ed.) *Understanding information business, technology and geography*, Belhaven, London

Godfrey, D (1979) 'All information in all places at all times' in Godfrey, D & Parkhill, D (eds.) *Gutenberg Two*, Porcepic Press, Toranto

Harvey, D (1989) *The condition of postmodernity*, Basil Blackwell, Oxford

Hepworth, M and K Robins (1988) Whose information society? a view from the periphery, *Media, culture and society*, 10

Hepworth, M (1989) *Geography of the information economy*, Belhaven, London

Information Strategy (1998) 'The cyber picket line', *Information Strategy* July/August 1998, Vol. 3 No. 6: 7

Innis, H. A. (1951) *The Bias of Communication*, University of Toranto Press, Toranto

Li, Feng and Andy Gillespie (1994) 'Team Telework: An Emergent Form of Work Organisation', in Baskerville, R *et al.* (eds), *Transforming Organisations with Information Technology*, North Holland/IFIP WG8.2, Amsterdam, 1994, 397-418.

Li, Feng (1995a) *The Geography of Business Information,* John Wiley, Chichester

Li, Feng (1995b) Structural Innovations through Information Systems: Some Emerging Tendnecies in Europe, *Journal of Management Systems* 7(3): 53-66

Li, F & Williams, H (1997) Collaboration through Inter-Firm Computer Networking. In Avison, D E (ed) *Key issues in information systems.* McGraw-Hill, Berkshire: 433-449

Li, Feng (1997) From 'compromise to harmony': Organisational re-design through information and communications technologies. *International Journal of Information*

Management, 17 (6): 451-464.

Li, Feng (1998) Team telework and the new geographical flexibility for information workers. Igbaria, M & M Tan (eds) *The Virtual Workplace*, Idea Group Publishing, Hershey

Mandeville, T (1983) The spatial effect of information technology, *Future*, February 1983

May, M (1998) The electronic neighbourhood, *Information Strategy* July/August 1998, Vol. 3 No. 6: 45

Moss, M (1987) Telecommunications, world cities and urban policy, *Urban studies*, 24: 435-546

Naisbitt, J (1984) *Megatrends*. Warner Books, New York

O'Brien, R (1992) *Global Financial Integration: The End of Geography*, The Royal Institute of International Affairs/Pinter Publishers, London

Robins, K and M Hepworth (1988) Electronic space: new technologies and the future of cities, *Future*, April

Toffler, A (1985) *The Adaptive Corporation,* Bantam Books, New York

CHAPTER 46

IT/IS IN RURAL SMES: A QUALITATIVE STUDY OF THE METAPHORS GENERATED BY FEMALES IN SMES IN A RURAL COUNTY IN ENGLAND

Lorraine Warren
University of Lincolnshire and Humberside

Abstract

An qualitative study from research in progress on female SME owners in rural areas is reported. Information technology and information systems (IT/IS) issues were discussed in a focus group-like setting. The data generated was explored by means of textual analysis to identify the nature of the metaphors generated by the women in relation to IT/IS. The purpose was to inform the information systems analysis and design community on user pereptions of IT/IS. Insight was also provided into the group's perceptions of the potential gains and losses afforded by the growing use of IT/IS in society, primarily in work-related situations, but also in the home. The metaphorical analysis revealed ambiguity and ambivalence to the potential benefits of IT/IS, particularly in relation to work/home conflict.

1. INTRODUCTION

This study was initiated through contact with an organisation for professional women in a rural county in England, referred to as the 'Link' in this paper. The Link were set up in collaboration with the Training and Enterprise Council (TEC) of the county town and has currently around seventy members. The purpose of the Link is to provide networking opportunities for women, who may experience professional isolation due to a range of factors, including geography, family commitment and exclusion from existing male-dominated networks. Although the group is aimed at all professional women, a large proportion of the members are sole traders, or work in small businesses, perhaps because it is here that the need for networking opportunities is most keenly felt.

A range of activities take place at regular intervals; for example, visits to local companies and large organisations are arranged, and speakers invited to discuss current issues, such as the Year 2000 problem. The Link also enables the dissemination of information from the TEC itself. The particular activity which led to this project was the establishment of a lunch group, which meets once every two months at the local university's School of Management. Although this group is open to all members of the Link, a fairly stable nucleus of regular attendees has established itself, most of whom fall into the sole trader/small business category referred to above. The purpose of meeting at the university is to be in contact with one of the largest providers of education and training in the region, and to engage with current thinking on a range of business issues. Each lunch is hosted by a member of the academic staff of the university (usually myself) who acts as facilitator for a group discussion of a particular topic of concern, chosen by the group itself. Past topics have included leadership, difficult employees, and employment law. The purpose of the discussions is to share perceptions, information and experiences on particular topics, with a view to learning from others in a relaxed and informal atmosphere. The discussion topic which forms the basis of this paper was loosely formulated as information technology and information systems (IT/IS).

This event provided an opportunity for research which could inform diverse areas about the group's perceptions of the role of IT/IS in their working lives. The primary focus chosen for this study relates to the use of metaphor, to increase understanding of the questions faced by those involved in information systems analysis and design. . The theoretical underpinnings of this study are discussed in section 2. As a secondary outcome, this study will also contribute to the literature on IT/IS in Small/Medium Enterprises (SMEs). Little research has been carried out in this area, though there are some interesting studies, notably those of Blili and Raymond (1993); Cragg and King (1993); DeLone (1981); Igbaria et al (1998); Jackson et al (1990); Kagan et al (1990); Lai (1994); Montazemi (1988); Naylor and Williams (1994); Raymond (1990); Raymond and Pare (1992) and Yap et al (1992).

With regard to methodology, the event presented a ready-made site for qualitative research, as the women seek to explore problematic issues through sharing and communication in a setting of their own choosing. This lent itself to the choice of textual analysis to identify and explore the nature of the metaphors generated by the participants in relation to IT/IS. Methodological issues are discussed in section 3. In section 4, issues emerging from the study are discussed.

2. THEORETICAL BACKGROUND

The ubiquitous nature of metaphor in constructing and making sense of social reality has long been recognised through the influential texts, *inter alia*, of Lakoff and Johnson (1980) and Ortony (Ed., 1993). This importance has long been recognised by organisational researchers, in large part due to the seminal work of Morgan (1986), who presents eight metaphors which can be used by researchers to diagnose and evaluate organisational life, using each metaphor as a lens to bring out different aspects of a situation. The acknowledgement and use of metaphor has also permeated other fields, such as systems thinking, where image generation is linked to creativity (see for example, Flood and Jackson, p.51), and also IT/IS, where in many cases, metaphor has been explored as part of determining user perceptions and requirements. Most notable in IT/IS are the works of Boland, 1989; Hirschheim and Newman, 1991; Kamm, 1995; Kendall and Kendall, 1993; Lanzara, 1983; Lupton, 1994; Madsen, 1989; Schon, 1979; Walsham, 1993.

Some of these researchers (Kendall and Kendall, 1993) have used a different approach to Morgan's, going straight to the language of the organisational members to identify metaphors in use, rather than presenting users with an 'alien' set of metaphors. This attempts to avoid the 'metaphorical trap' of Boland (1989), who recognises that metaphor is so pervasive, that we "cannot not use metaphors" and cautions against their being used in an instrumental way:

"The multi-vocal, ambiguous nature of language and the way metaphors evoke nested complexes of symbolic meanings which, in turn, evoke a reverberating set of others make it impossible to just pick one out and use it in any clear, precise way. Language is not a tool and is not something we can step outside of."

This study follows the second strand of metaphorical thinking, drawing upon the work of Kendall and Kendall, who suggest the use of focus groups as a useful method of exploring user generated metaphors, as during the course of the event, one participant builds on and adds to another's metaphor. They cite the work of Bormann (1975), who calls this process of building "chaining out". In their study, sixteen organisations were studied using focus groups (and interviews), in an attempt to match user-generated metaphors to IS design methodologies. Users were not prompted to talk about metaphor, rather, general questions were asked, the metaphors allowed to emerge. The metaphors were then classified according to a categorisation from Clancy (1989): *journey, war, game, organism, society, machine*. In addition to confirming the usage of these metaphors, a further three were added by Kendall and Kendall: *family, jungle* and *zoo*.

Although this study draws on the work of Kendall and Kendall, there is a significant difference, in that the concept of user-generation of metaphors was extended here. No pre-existing categorisation was used: the categories, as well as the metaphors were allowed to emerge from the discussion itself.

3. METHODOLOGICAL ISSUES

This event presented itself as a natural site for qualitative research, which I could legitimately join as a researcher/facilitator, In view of my history with the group. In terms of conventional qualitative research settings, the group could loosely be classified as a 'focus group' in that a number of participants were drawn together to informally discuss a topic for around an hour, in the presence of a facilitator. Such sessions are usually recorded by video or audio tape for further analysis (Morgan, 1988).

This group was composed of twelve participants: eight sole trader/businesswomen, two representatives from the TEC and two lecturers from the School of Management. Apart from my own role as Facilitator, no roles or distinctions were explicitly drawn between the participants in the group; most of them already knew the other participants. The session was audiotaped. The participants knew that this particular event was the focus of my own personal research and that I was interested in their views on IT/IS. No additional information was given by me at any stage, nor were further questions on my research posed by the group. Other than this distinction,, my role as Facilitator progressed as usual, as I posed some trigger questions to the group to initiate conversation. Although a lot of ground was covered in the conversation, few trigger questions were required to keep the conversation going. The discussion was punctuated with jokes and laughter, and no one person dominated. This was in part because most of the group had met on a number of occasions previously, and had perhaps gone through the 'Forming and Storming' stages, to 'Norming and Performing'. Examples of questions asked included "What does the term *Information Society* mean to you?", "Has anyone totally restructured their business around new technologies?" and "Who makes IT/IS decisions in your organisation"? The event lasted around eighty minutes in total, with some short interruptions concerned with lunch service. A transcript of the event was later prepared and analysed for IT/IS-related metaphors.

Focus groups have long been established with market research, but their use as a research technique is increasing in the social sciences. However, there is little in the literature to provide a rigorous framework for analysis and interpretation. Catterall and Maclaran (1997) identify two main approaches to analysis in the literature: firstly, the holistic, interpretive approach of "annotating-the-scripts" which involves reading the transcripts (and/or listening to the audiotapes) and writing interpretive thoughts about the data in the margins. The benefits of this approach are that "each transcript is considered as a whole rather than as a set of discrete responses....it allows the analysts to re-experience the group, body language and tone of the discussion"(p. 3). This is contrasted to a more quantitative approach, where the emphasis is on content analysis through the counting of words or text segments, with computers often used to assist the analysis. In this study, the first approach was chosen, in line with the theoretical aim of allowing metaphors and categories to emerge through the interpretation.

Searching for metaphors within the transcript was not straightforward; there were few usages of metaphors which stood out clearly. as, to give an example, *"you have to have a canary cover for it"*, where the ANIMAL metaphor is obvious. The deeply embedded nature of metaphor in language discriminates against a straightforward selection, categorisation and count. The notion of metaphor involves the recasting of one concept in terms of another, enabling us to conceptualise things in different ways, thereby generating a whole range of linguistic expressions, such as "he's taking the wrong path in applying for that job", or, "she's not got very far in life" and so on. Such expressions are so much part of our daily conversation that we hardly recognise them as being metaphorical, unlike a statement such as "this organisation is like a zoo!", which we would use to invoke consciously a whole range of entailments and associations, on the lines of Bormann's "chaining out". This ubiquitousness makes it difficult to separate out what is literal, or analogous, or metaphorical in language. Thus the selection and categorisation process is inevitably problematic as subjective choices are made. There was no evidence of "chaining out".

After going through the transcript eight times, I arrived at the selection, categorisation and count presented in Table 1, which is ordered according to the order of emergence in the transcript of the metaphorical theme in question. The count itself is only significant in giving some indication of the extent to which a particular metaphorical theme occurred in the transcript. As well as metaphorical themes, some literal themes which were explored at some length are also presented, with representative quotations, to illustrate the subtlety of the distinction being made. Clearly, there is overlap with the themes in Table 1 -- no clear and distinct separation is implied -- but little obvious metaphorical language emerged concerning these subjects. Note that the participants settled on the use of "technology" rather than IT/IS.

Metaphor: Technology is a(n):	F
FAST MOVING VEHICLE WHICH MAY LEAVE YOU BEHIND *"it's increasing at a rapid rate of knots, it's, the problem is actually trying to keep up with it, that's the difficulty"* *"[schools] will be one of the things that drives it"* *"they're being cut out of the loop if they don't follow the technology"*	4
GATEKEEPER *"it will actually start to marginalise certain sections of our society...they're going to be more and more pushed into certain areas of society"*	2
MONSTER/GIANT *"it's a nightmare...we've got a dinosaur of a system"* *"I can tell you lots of really horror stories"* *"so how do I get the information that's critical to my business...without having this barrage of this massive amount of information, and that for the small business is going to be quite a difficult thing to overcome"* *"What's round the corner...that's the unknown, that's quite scary"*	6
ANIMAL WHICH CAN BE TAMED/NEEDS TENDING *"harnessing the power of information does free us up"* *"you almost have to have a canary cover for it"* *"there aren't the resources ...to track all that [information] for me"*	5

COMMODITY	1
"[have to have someone] who is enthusiastic enough to sell it to the staff"	
TEMPTATION/ADDICTION	5
"you have to be very strict with yourself" *"he's had a ball"* *"it's knowing when to stop"*	
OMNIPRESENCE	6
"it's quite surprising how many different aspects of our life it touches" *"technology is creeping up on all our lives and we don't realise it yet"* *"we're all like hamsters in wheels"* *"You just become the voice in the background...these things can quite happily talk to one another"* *"each new change pushes out ripples"*	

Table 1: Frequency of metaphors identified (F = Frequency)

Literal themes:

BENEFITS OF AUTOMATION

"it's [technology benefited the insurance agency a great deal...now, instead of people spending hours calculating rates and doing all sorts of calculations, at the touch of a button, you can have the information when you need it"

"you can share that with so many people so quickly through the Internet"

WORK/HOME CONFLICT

"we can now work 24 hours a day....oh wonderful!"

"my husband is a consultant, and he works at home, and he's always in his office, which used to be our study, with all the machinery around him, and he's never off duty, he's always there"

NEGATIVE EFFECT ON SOCIAL INTERACTION

"thinking about televisions being antisocial...technology is even more so"

"you have to teach them [teenagers] how to speak to people, how to empathise with people, because they're used to interacting with machines"

TOO MUCH JARGON

"[have to have someone] who is enthusiastic to sell it to the staff in words they understand"

"my husband said...make sure he does this and this and this - more jargon, more gobbledegook"

DIFFICULTIES OF COSTING

"manually can be just as quick"

"there's the cost of training...you spend all that money and then 6 months down the line, they hand in their notice and you've got to start all over again...it can be counterproductive, but you still need the technology"

LEARNING CURVE

"if I look back 5 years ago and said I would be doing this in 5 years time I wouldn't have believed it"

"every organisation has to go through that learning curve"

4. EMERGENT ISSUES

Qualitative research is often criticised for revealing difference and fragmentation without providing any guidance for future improvement. My intention is to return to the women at a future date and to explain the process which was carried out and present the results. I would expect that this group of highly motivated and articulate women would be capable of working with my interpretation to develop and generate their own metaphors to initiate whatever shift in thinking (if any) they might desire on an individual basis, should they wish to do so, and so benefit from the exercise. Working with the metaphors should provide more fertile ground for exploration and discussion, than concentating on the literal.

Whilst it would be unwise to generalise from one study, in terms of informing a wider community, the extracts given above (both metaphorical and literal) indicate the degree of ambivalence and ambiguity which the participants had in relation to IT/IS. On the one hand, participants were proud of their learning capability and enjoyed the benefits both of automation and access to information. On the other hand, there were clear concerns about keeping up with innovations which could radically alter the face of business activity, the intrusion of the computer into home life, and the potential cost in terms of time, money and mental resources. Concerns were also expressed about the wider impact of technology on society.

This study suggests that those involved in the processes of IT/IS analysis and design should be aware of the mixed models which users may be using to view the technological world. The notion of the boundary between work and home life was of key significance to this group of users. The overall mood was perhaps best summarised by one of the participants who remarked almost at the end of the event:

> *"We accept that we've got to get on with it but that's about as good as it sounds, I don't see anybody jumping up and down"*

References

Blili, S. and Raymond, L. (1993) Information Technology: Threats and Opportunities for Small and Medium-Sized Enterprises, *International Journal of Information Management*, Vol. 13, December, pp. 439-448.

Boland, R. J. (1989) Metaphorical traps in developing information systems for human progress, in *Systems Development for Human Progress*, H. K. Klein and K. Kumar (eds.) pp. 277-290, North Holland: New York.

Bormann, E. G. (1975) *Discussion and Group Methods: Theory and Practice*, 2nd edition, Harper and Row: New York.

Catterall, M. and Maclaran, P. (1997) Focus Group Data and Qualitative Analysis Programs: Coding the Moving Picture as Well as the Snapshots, *Sociological Research Online*, Vol. 2, No. 1, http://www.socresonline.org.uk/socresonline/2/1/6.html

Clancy, J. J. (1989) *The Invisible Powers: The Language of Business*, Lexington Books: Massachusetts.

Cragg, P. B. and King, M. (1993) Small-Firm Computing: Motivators and Inhibitors, *MIS Quarterly*, Vol. 17, No. 2, pp. 47-59.

DeLone, W. H. (1981) Small Size and the Characteristics of Computer Use, *MIS Quarterly*, Vol. 5, No. 4, pp. 65-77.

Flood, R. L. and Jackson, M. C. (1991) *Creative Problem Solving: Total Systems Intervention,* John Wiley and Sons: Chichester.

Hirschheim, R. and Newman, M. (1991) Symbolism and Information Systems Development: Myth, Metaphor and Magic, *Information Systems Research*, Vol. 2, No. 1, pp. 29-62.

Igbaria, M., Zinatelli, N. and Cavaye, A. L. M. (1998) Analysis of Information Technology Success in Small Firms in New Zealand, *International Journal of Information Management*, Vol. 18, No. 2, pp. 103-119.

Jackson, W. M. and Palvia, P., (1990) The State of Computers in MIS in Small Businesses and Some Predictive Measures of Computer Use, *Journal of Computer Information Systems*, Vol. 31, No. 1, pp. 49-53.

Kagan, A., Lau, K. and Nussgart, K. R. (1990) Information System Usage Within Small Business Firms, *Entrepreneurship, Theory and Practice*, Spring, pp. 25-37.

Kamm, R. (1995) Information and the Mechanistic Metaphor: The Place of Information in Organizational Thought, *Systems Practice,* Vol. 8, No. 5, 1995, pp. 517-536.

Kendall, J. E. and Kendall, K. E. (1993) Metaphors and Methodologies, *MIS Quarterly*, Vol. 17, No. 2, pp. 149 - 171.

Lai, V. S. (1994) A Survey of Rural Small Business Computer Use: Success Factors and Decision Support, *Information and Management*, Vol. 26, pp. 297-304.

Lakoff, G. and Johnson, M. (1980) *Metaphors We Live By*, University of Chicago Press: Chicago.

Lanzara, G. F. (1983) The Design Process: Frames, Metaphors and Games, in *Systems Design For, With and By the Users*, U. Briefs, C. Ciborra and L. Schneider (eds.), pp. 29-40, North Holland: New York.

Lupton, D. (1993) Panic Computing: The Viral Metaphor and Computer Technology, *Cultural Studies*, Vol. 8, No. 3, pp. 557-568.

Madsen, K. H. (1989) Breakthrough by Breakdown: Metaphors and Structured Domains, in *Systems Development for Human Progress*, H. K. Klein and K. Kumar (eds.) pp. 277-290, North Holland: New York.

Montazemi, A. R. (1988) Factors affecting information satisfaction in the context of the small business environment, *MIS Quarterly*, Vol. 12, No. 2, pp. 239-256.

Morgan, D. L. (1988) *Focus Groups as Qualitative Research*, sage: California.

Morgan, G. (1986) *Images of Organization*, Sage: California.

Naylor, J. B. and Williams, J. (1994) The successful use of IT in SMEs on Merseyside, *European Journal of Information Systems*, Vol. 3, No. 1, pp. 48-56.

Ortony, A. (Ed.) (1993) *Metaphor and Thought*, 2nd edition, Cambridge University Press: New York.

Raymond, L. (1990) Organisational Context and IS Success, *Journal of Management Information*, Vol. 6, No. 4, pp. 5-20.

Raymond, L. and Pare, G. (1992) Measurement of Information Technology Sophistication in Small Manufacturing Businesses, *Information Resources Management Journal*, Vol. 5, No. 2, pp. 1-13.

Walsham, G. (1993) *Interpreting Information Systems in Organizations*, John Wiley and Sons: Chichester.

Yap, C. S., Soh, C. P. P. and Raman, K. S. (1992) Information Systems Success Factors in Small Business, *Omega*, Vol. 20, No. 5/6, pp. 597-609.

CHAPTER 47

WORKING MEMORY SPAN AS A USABILITY FACTOR IN A VIRTUAL COMMUNITY OF ELDERLY PEOPLE

J Jerrams-Smith**, D Heathcote* and L White**
**University of Portsmouth, *University of Bournemouth

Abstract

The present study examines the working memory capacity of elderly users of computers in relation to the design of a virtual community interface for such users. This research investigates whether age-related decrements in working memory span can account for poor performance in two common computing tasks associated with the use of a standard virtual community interface. Task 1 demonstrated that elderly subjects had significantly smaller working memory spans than younger subjects and that, compared to younger subjects, elderly subjects performed poorly in a multiple windows task which involved concurrent processing and storage. Task 2 examined the short term storage of icon labels in the presence of a concurrent processing load and established that icon span was considerably greater in the younger subjects than the elderly group. It was concluded that interfaces which load working memory (i.e. those that require concurrent processing and storage) are inappropriate for elderly users and suggestions for the design of interfaces for users with reduced WM capacity are offered.

1   INTRODUCTION

A Virtual Community (VC) consists of people who are not necessarily able to communicate in person, but who are linked electronically, either by an intranet or by the Internet. This report examines the effect that normal ageing has on the user's ability to utilise a VC and focuses on whether the decline in working memory (WM) capacity associated with old age (see Baddeley, 1986) can be partially compensated for by an appropriately designed interface.

Previous work by the authors for British Telecom on the *'Telecare Companion'* provided a prototype VC interface which aimed to be both attractive and easy to use (John, Jerrams-Smith, Heathcote & Boucouvalas, 1998). In addition, some related issues concerned with improved guidance for navigation through an intranet or the Internet are addressed in a concurrent project (Jerrams-Smith, Heathcote and Boucouvalas, 1996; Lamas, Jerrams-Smith and Gouveia, 1996).

1.1   Possible benefits of the virtual community

A virtual community may be of considerable value to elderly people who are housebound as a result of chronic illness. In addition, many elderly people live alone and receive few visitors, either because they have outlived many of their friends, or because their family live elsewhere. The VC provides a means of engaging in social interaction even when movement outside the home is difficult or impossible.

Because the design and development of VCs is still in its infancy, many important research issues remain to be investigated. As a starting point, an intranet version of the VC would provide a limited and more easily controlled environment for its users than allowing access to the Internet as a whole. An intranet is intended for a relatively small localised community and its use would enable participants to make rapid contact with medical staff so that health problems can be dealt with expeditiously, helping to avoid the development of more serious medical problems and thereby improving quality of life for seniors as well as reducing the burden on medical services (John et al., 1998). The VC would also enable seniors to contact other helpers about everyday problems concerning finance and housing and it would also encourage new contacts with other elderly people in the area. Extension of the VC to the Internet would enable home shopping and banking and, equally important, encourage contact with family and old friends in distant places and the pursuit of established and new hobbies and interests in collaboration with others of all ages across the world.

1.2   Some of the problems faced by the elderly in using computers

The most important aspect of developing an interface for such a VC is to ensure that it encourages elderly people to participate by supporting their needs in an effective way. Many seniors are likely to fear new technology with its unknown functions and incomprehensible jargon. They may also have physical problems related to sight, hearing, muscular strength, speed of reaction and motor control. In addition, although long-term memory may decline with age, additional problems for seniors are also likely to result from the gradual decline of some cognitive abilities produced by a diminution of the processing capacity of working memory (Baddeley, 1997).

1.3   What is working memory ?

The most influential model of working memory (WM) has been developed by Baddeley (e.g. Baddeley & Hitch, 1974; Baddeley, 1986; Baddeley, 1997). Working memory refers to the temporary storage and concurrent processing of information. Its three major components are the central executive (CE), the visuo-spatial sketchpad (VSSP) and the phonological loop (PL). The VSSP and PL are slave systems under the supervisory control of the CE and are used for the temporary storage of visuo-spatially coded and phonologically coded material respectively (see Heathcote, 1994). The CE is an attentional controller and is responsible for the execution of various control processes including updating the contents of WM, retrieval and rehearsal of information form long-term memory, recoding information (e.g. recoding from verbal to visual information) and the inhibition of irrelevant information. The CE also monitors goals and errors and is involved in planning, decision making, reasoning and comprehension (see Baddeley, 1997).

1.4   Working memory and the elderly

In normal ageing short-term storage per se remains relatively unimpaired (as measured by digit span, Craik, 1977). Similarly, the recency effect in free recall remains fairly normal in the elderly (Craik, 1968; Raymond 1971). In contrast, Broadbent and Gregory (1965) and Talland (1965) showed that tasks which require the manipulation of information are impaired during normal ageing, so that, for example, performance of the backward digit span procedure is impaired (Bromley, 1958). In addition, Broadbent and Heron (1962) provide evidence that the memory performance of the elderly is impaired by performance of a secondary non-memory task, such as visual search, although when required to undertake each task separately, elderly people perform normally.

Such results indicate that while normal ageing produces little impairment of short-term memory (STM) in tasks which need only passive storage, the processing capacity of the CE may be reduced with the result that the performance of the elderly in tasks which require both processing and concurrent storage may be poorer than that of younger subjects. In addition, Rabbitt (1981) suggests that although working memory processes are important for memory tasks, it is also centrally involved in non-memory tasks such as comprehension and visual search.

1.5   Implications of reduced WM capacity for the virtual community

Elderly people are unlikely to participate in the VC if they have difficulty using its interface. Reduced WM processing capacity is likely to be an important factor in the ability of the elderly to use computers and to carry out everyday information processing tasks. We are therefore currently investigating various aspects of the VC which are likely to be problematic for those with age-related reductions in WM capacity, in order to guide the development of a suitable interface for such users. As the foregoing discussion suggests, it is the processing component of WM which requires support from the VC interface; the addition of various forms of "extended working memory scratch pad" to the interface may not solve the problems of elderly users if their function is merely to provide a form of external storage.

2   TASK 1: THE MANIPULATION OF MULTIPLE WINDOWS

2.1   Rationale

Many interfaces make use of multiple windows which, although designed to support users in carrying out their tasks, are likely to present particular problems for elderly people since their utilisation may involve a relatively high working memory load. It appears likely that the manipulation of multiple windows involves central processing and concurrent storage. We therefore devised an experiment to investigate multiple windows task performance as a function of age and working memory span.

We hypothesise that the manipulation of multiple windows requires considerable information processing by the central executive of WM. The load on the CE may include: concurrent goal monitoring (to match graphical images and their associated text), planning and decision making (deciding where to place windows so that they are easy to find again), updating the contents of WM (move from one image/text pair to the next), recoding (forming a visual representation of the display from text), inhibition of irrelevant information (previous text/image pair), error monitoring (attending to responses in order to identify erroneous icon/text combinations). These control processes are in addition to the storage loads on the VSSP and PL inherent in this task.

Thus, performance of the multiple windows task may be sensitive to differences in the central processing capacity of users. Therefore we predict that, overall, the performance of seniors on this task will be poorer than that of the younger subjects. In order to determine whether such a difference reflects differences in working memory span between the old and young, two versions of the windows task were used: a structured version designed to minimise the WM load and an unstructured version in which the WM load is relatively high. The rationale of this procedure is that if the poorer performance of the seniors reflects their smaller WM capacity, the performance of the seniors should be particularly sensitive to the reduction in WM load afforded by the structured conditions (i.e. structuring the task should be of more benefit to the seniors than to the younger subjects). Thus, we would expect a two-way interaction between age group (young/senior) and the nature of the task (structured/unstructured). As an additional precaution, the WM span of each experimental subject was measured using a standard technique.

2.2   Method

There were 32 subjects aged 25-92 years. Half the subjects were aged 65 years or over and the remaining subjects were aged under 65 years. A lap-top computer was used to carry out the tests. Each subject was shown how windows could be moved and how the window shade worked. The subjects then took part in three introductory learning tasks to ensure that they understood the task to be performed. The multiple windows task consisted of dragging ten windows (each containing a single picture) to a new location on the screen and once all picture windows had been moved, dragging the associated text and placing it under its correct picture window. This meant that the subject had to find each window a second time.

For the few subjects who were physically unable to drag the windows and associated text, the experimenter followed the instructions of the subject. Time taken to drag the window (as opposed to "thinking time") was subsequently eliminated from the results. Responses were recorded by an automated logger which was running throughout the experiment and which recorded all mouse movements, mouse down, mouse up, key down, key up and their relative timings. Performance was measured in terms of the number of correct drags completed in the time allowed.

In addition, all the subjects were tested for Working Memory Span (WMS), which provides a measure of the concurrent storage and processing capacity of working memory. We selected the WMS test by Turner and Engle (1989).

2.3   Results

Younger subjects produced approximately 20% more drags than the seniors (see table 1). In order to test the statistical reliability of this difference an independent samples *t-test* was applied to the data. The test revealed a statistically significant difference between the seniors and the younger subjects ($t = 2.44$, $p = .021$, two-tailed). The effect size was calculated (i.e. (mean young − mean seniors)/ standard deviation) and found to be $d = 0.87$. This is a large effect size and compares favourably with those of other published studies (see Clark-Carter, 1997).

Young	Senior
18.06	15.25

Table 1: The mean number of correct drags as a function of age group

The seniors were generally unable or unwilling to utilise the assistance provided in the structured condition and, as a result, comparisons involving the structuring variable were not meaningful. However, measures of working memory span were obtained (using Turner & Engle's procedure). The overall mean working memory span was calculated and subjects were assigned to 'high' or 'low' working memory span groups on the basis of their scores relative to the mean. The results revealed that approximately 80% of the younger subjects had high working memory spans while, in contrast, 100% of the seniors were found to have low working memory spans. Thus the poorer performance of the seniors on the multiple windows task coincides with their poorer working memory span, lending some tentative support to the suggestion that performance in the windows task is partly related to working memory span.

3   TASK 2: ICON LABEL STORAGE WITH A CONCURRENT PROCESSING LOAD

3.1   Rationale

Many computing tasks involve working with folder icons while engaging in concurrent and related problem solving activity. The current experiment seeks to examine some of the fundamental elements of such tasks. The task requires subjects to solve problems while simultaneously recognising and remembering different folders which in a real computing task would contain information pertinent to the problem solution. As with Task 1, we hypothesise that this desktop task involves a load on the central executive of working memory which includes: concurrent processing (to solve the arithmetic problem while concurrently retaining the word list), updating the contents of WM (adding to the word list, holding the answers to sub-problems for the addition task), error monitoring (ensuring correct words are being remembered, checking correctness of addition). This will be in addition to the storage loads placed on the VSSP and PL by the task.

3.2   Method

There were 32 subjects aged 25-92 years (classified as: seniors $>= 65$ yrs and young < 65 yrs). A lap-top computer was used to carry out the tests. Each subject was shown a screen containing 5 folder icons. A simple sum without an answer then appeared on the screen and was also read to them by the experimenter (e.g. $(2 + 5) - 2 = ?$). Once the subject had given an answer a word appeared on screen under one of the folder icons and was read out loud by the computer and by the experimenter. After 3 seconds the word disappeared and another sum appeared. This was repeated four times, with the word appearing under a different folder each time. At the end of the 5 words, the subject was asked "Can you remember any of the 5 words?". The words recalled correctly by the subject were recorded. Two of the younger subjects and one of the seniors failed to take the test.

3.3   Results

The mean icon working memory spans for senior and young subjects were calculated and are displayed in table 2. Icon span was found to be over 100% greater in the younger subjects than the seniors. Indices of skew and kurtosis were computed and the corresponding z scores were found to be insignificant ($p > .05$ all) indicating no significant deviation from normality (note that the use of parametric statistical tests is acceptable even when there are moderate departures from the normal distribution but not when there are significant departures, Howell, 1997; Kirk, 1995). A comparison was made between the icon spans of the senior and young subjects which revealed that senior icon spans were significantly smaller than those of the younger participants ($t = 5.8, p < .001$). The effect size was found to be $d > 2.00$, indicating a very large magnitude of effect (see Clark-Carter, 1997).

Young	Senior
3.71	1.67

Table 2: Mean WM icon span as a function of age group.

An overall mean was calculated from the data (collapsed across age group). Subjects whose performance fell below the mean were classified as 'low' icon span and those whose performance was above the mean were classed as 'high' icon span. Of the seniors, only 25% fell in the high group while for the younger subjects 94% were found to have high icon span (see table 3).

	Young	Senior
High Icon Span	94%	25%
Low Icon Span	6%	75%

Table 3: WM icon span (high/low) as a function of age group

4   DISCUSSION: DESIGN AND DEVELOPMENT IMPLICATIONS FOR THE VIRTUAL COMMUNITY INTERFACE

Although the facility to use many windows which are simultaneously open is of great value to users in general, the results of Task 1 indicate that the use of multiple windows may cause particular problems for users who have reduced WMS (including, but not limited to, elderly people). Although these problems can be overcome by ensuring that interfaces intended for the elderly allow no, or very limited, use of multiple windows, care will be needed to ensure that alternative designs for such interfaces do not themselves add to the load on central working memory capacity.

In addition, the results of Task 2 suggest that current interfaces which use a standard desktop metaphor are likely to be too difficult for many elderly people to use successfully and therefore that the interface for an elderly Virtual Community should not be over elaborate and involve as little manipulation of information as possible. Interfaces designed for elderly people should aim to allow the user to perform the operations necessary to achieve their goal in the absence of concurrent activity. Such an interface should involve sequential rather than parallel task demands thus reducing the concurrent processing load.

References

Baddeley, A.D. (1986) Working memory. Oxford University Press, Oxford, UK.

Baddeley, A.D. (1997) Human memory: Theory and practice (rev. ed.). Psychology Press, East Sussex, UK.

Baddeley, A.D. & Hitch, G.J. (1974) Working memory. In Recent advances in learning and motivation vol. VIII *(G.Bower,* Ed) pp. 47-90. Academic Press, New York.

Broadbent, D.E & Gregory, M. (1965) 'Some confirmatory results for age difference in memory for simultaneous stimulation' British Journal of Psychology, vol 56, pp. 77-80.

Broadbent, D.E & Heron, A. (1962) 'Effects of a subsidiary task on performance involving immediate memory in younger and older men.' British Journal of Psychology, vol 53, pp. 189-198.

Bromley, (1958) 'Some effects of age on short-term learning and memory.' Journal of Gerontology, vol 13, pp. 398-406

Clark-Carter, D. (1997) Doing Quantitative Psychological Research. Psychology Press: East Sussex, UK.

Craik, F.I.M. (1968) 'Two components in free recall.' Journal of Verbal Learning and Verbal Behaviour, vol 7, pp. 996-1004.

Craik, F.I.M. (1977) 'Age differences in human memory.' In Handbook of the psychology of ageing. (J.E. Birren and K.W. Schiae, eds.) von Nostrand Reinhold: New York.

Heathcote, D. (1994) 'The role of visuo-spatial working memory in the mental addition of multi-digit addends.' Current Psychology of Cognition, vol 13, pp. 207-245.

Howell, D.C. (1997) Statistical methods for psychology (4th ed.). International Thomson Publishing, London, UK.

Jerrams-Smith, J., Heathcote, D. & Boucouvalas, A. (1996) 'Communications issues for users of networked multimedia/hypermedia systems.' Proceedings of the Third Communications Networks Symposium, Manchester Metropolitan University, UK.

John, D., Jerrams-Smith, J., Heathcote, D.,& Boucouvalas, A. (1998) 'The Telecare Companion.' Proceedings of the First International Symposium on Communication Systems. Sheffield Hallam University, UK.

Lamas, D.R., Jerrams-Smith, J. & Gouveia, F. (1996) 'Computer aided information navigation : project description.' In Proceedings of WebNet 96 : World Conference of the Web (H. Maurer, Ed) Association for the Advancement of Computing in Education, AACE, San Francisco, CA.

Kirk, R.E. (1995) Experimental design: Procedures for the behavioural sciences (3rd. ed.). Brooks/Cole, USA.

Rabbitt, P. (1981) 'Cognitive psychology needs models for changes in performance with old age.' In Attention and Performance vol X (JD Long and AD Baddeley, eds) Erlbaum: Hillsdale, NJ, USA.

Raymond, B.J. (1971) 'Free recall among the aged.' Psychological Reports, vol 29, pp. 1179-1182.

Talland, G. (1965) 'Three estimates of the word span and their stability over the adult years.' Quarterly Journal of Experimental Psychology, vol 17, pp. 301- 307.

Turner, M.L. & Engle, R.W. (1989) 'Is working memory capacity task dependent?' Journal of Memory and Language, vol 28, pp. 127-154.

CHAPTER 48

DEVELOPING OBJECT-ORIENTED MODELS WITHIN THE FRAMEWORK OF CLIENT-LED DESIGN

Minghong Guo, Zimin Wu and Frank Stowell
De Montfort University

Abstract

Client-Led Design (CLD) framework proposed by Stowell and West is based on the "interpretive" system thinking which attempts to overcome the difficulties of handling human-centred complex problems in conventional software engineering. In CLD, the activity model represents the description of some defined purposeful activity. This type of model is the result of inquiry processes facilitated by the Appreciative Inquiry Method in which user objectives may be explored and made explicit. However CLD in its original form did not include a 'hard' technical specification, which is essential for creating a computer-based information system. This paper reviews a possible solution attempted, the integration of OO modelling with the activity model in CLD, to reach the aim of transforming the problem description into a technical specification that is suitable for implementation.

1. INTRODUCTION

To meet the uncertainty and conflicting nature of an information system, Jacobson, et al. (1992) has pointed out that a modern IS development technique is expected to have the following properties:

- It must support the iterative development of a system over the entire life cycle.
- It should view each iteration as a change to an existing system.
- It must support the entire chain from changed requirement to the functioning system.

This proposition seems to correspond well with the 'soft' systems methodology that is characterised as cyclic learning, interpretive, flexible to change and so on. Many researchers suggested using a so-called 'soft' methodology to handle the problem description, so as to fully explore and accommodate the rich information in the problem area, and in the meantime, use a 'hard' methodology to concentrate on a specific point of view and transform it into a technical specification. But, crossing the gap between these two methodologies without compromising both of them has become a significant task that we must confront. (Lander *et al*, 1997)

2. THE FEASIBILITY OF A LINK BETWEEN 'SOFT' AND 'HARD' METHODS

Soft Systems Methodology, SSM, (Checkland, 1981) has the advantages of accommodating rich information of the problem situation, and is flexible to change. It encourages user's involvement and is useful in helping to understand, to handle the ill-defined problems. SSM does not produce a final answer, but accepts that the inquiry procedure is never-ending. 'Hard' system approaches, e.g. SSADM, allow the use of powerful techniques, but are not able to fully explore and describe the user's requirement where there should be many considerations to be taken into account.

The authors have asked "could a 'soft' and 'hard' methodology be linked to bring the great benefit of their complementary advantages?" Others have said, " Will it lead to a compromise of both?" The question many authors debate is if it is possible to reconcile their fundamental philosophical conflicts. After examining in some detail the philosophical antecedents of both 'hard' and 'soft' information system methodology, Probert (1996) concluded "both schools have epistemological roots in empirical foundationalism." Although the type of belief held in soft and hard methods in basic is different, one is "experiential belief derived from the subject's current conscious state", the other is " extrinsic beliefs about the external world". "Both could gain from a mutual cross-referencing, given the truth indicative nature of *bona fide* subjective judgements, and the ineliminably subjective nature of objective judgement." Lewis (1993) also argues that, in practice, there is an ineluctable core of subjectivity that is simply not recognised by practitioners in the labelled objective based data analysis. If we accept this argument, a link between 'soft' and 'hard' methodology seems therefore theoretically feasible.

3. THE STRATEGIES TO CROSS THE GAP

Based upon the above discussion, several attempts have been made to provide a link between 'soft' systems analysis and 'hard' systems development technique. There are two main strategies that have been explored (Mingers, 1995): grafting, that is to say, front-ending the Information System Development (ISD) with SSM and embedding, whereby the whole system is developed under the general ethos of SSM, with the hard design element incorporated within it.

Grafting, which is easier to realise, seems to be deficient. By transforming the concept in the SSM into the 'hard' technical design, much of the richness of the SSM analysis faces the danger of being lost. The advantage of the SSM, which is to recognise the different meanings and interpretation based on the different context, has been suppressed in the interest of developing a single hegemonic information system. The combination of the two methodologies is rather incomplete, and distinct, Without the cyclic feedback of SSM, the comparison between what is realised and what is intended, or what impact has been brought to the established system cannot be realised.

We can argue that embedding which is far more complicated than grafting is properly a better choice for ISD. Having a SSM based framework, we could introduce some technical element when appropriate without compromising the overall cyclic learning, interpretative environment. It is therefore the thinking process behind SSM that is important rather than SSM itself.

4. CLD - A POSSIBLE FRAMEWORK TO INTEGRATE SSM WITH 'HARD' SYSTEMS DEVELOPMENT TECHNIQUE

CLD, Client Led Design (Stowell & West, 1994), is a framework explicitly based upon the work of Vickers ("appreciative" system) and Checkland's SSM. The authors provide a meta-level framework attempted to accommodate both 'soft' problem appreciation and 'hard' technology for information system specification and development.

CLD shifts seamlessly from the 'soft' interpretive ideas into technical specifications. In CLD, the intention is that the user has been empowered to take control of the whole process of ISD that is free from technical implication or limitation. The approach emphasises the concepts of "appreciation" and "interpretivism". This "appreciative" approach is intended to encourage users to improve their understanding, capture a clear view, and finally embrace the rich information of the entire problem situation. The ISA (Information System Analyst), instead of being an objective observer, is responsible for the requirement analysis and technical provision, and has become a facilitator, or a teacher. He / she is involved in the information system and is responsible for helping the client to demystify the technology, to clarify and define their views, and to take control of the whole ISD process.

The CLD framework is represented as five phases: Appreciate, Define, Specify, Implement, and Re-evaluate. These five phases need not be followed sequentially. Each phase is iterative and has an impact upon the whole process. Each is intended to facilitate the user to express their ideas and reflect upon the relationship between the expression of the different phases. So the whole CLD framework becomes "an iterative cycle of events in which the clients define and agree to technology being implemented, updated, extended, and replaced in a time-scale appropriate to their need." (Stowell & West, 1994)

The CLD framework is still incomplete, since how to link the appreciative problem description to a technical specification has not been fully resolved. Suggestions have been made that the technical specification can be developed from an activity model. The problem is how and in what form we should extract the information from the activity model and redefine it into a technical specification suitable for implementation in order to get an ideal result. Object-orientation (OO), as a major direction in the software engineering might be a possible answer.

5. OO - A POSSIBLE CANDIDATE TO BE EXTRACTED FROM THE ACTIVITY MODEL IN CLD

Object-oriented development is considered as "a new way of thinking about software based on the abstraction that exist in the real world". (Rumbaugh, *et.al* 1991). This development technique has the advantages of abstraction, reusability, and modularity, which are essential for producing high quality software. The benefits we get from OO are reflected by its increasingly dominant position in software engineering.

Different from traditional functional decomposition, OO methods can model perceived reality more naturally. Thus assume that the perceived reality is a web of related objects, each having particular behaviour or activities. The selection of objects is one of the key points of the OO modelling. Eckert & Golder (1994), and Prins (1996) have argued that it is the depth and quality of problem situation understanding that underpins, first, the identification of candidate objects from the situation and, secondly, from these candidate objects, the selection of appropriate and meaningful objects. However, the traditional OO modelling technique gives little or no practical support to undertake the process of gaining a rich understanding of the problem situation. OOA (Coad & Yourdon, 1991) proposed that the analyst should observe first-hand experiences, listen actively to the domain expert's advice, reuse previous results, look for structures, things or events remembered and so on. But it does not offer any practical methodological tools to help us achieve this. OMT (Rumbaugh, *et.al*, 1991) tried to use noun phrases in a problem statement to elicit the candidate objects and also provided some rules to help the analyst to find the significant objects in the model. The followings are examples of the rules: a significant object is not redundant, irrelevant and vague; it should not be used as attribute, operation, or some implementation construct. Discovering the problem of the inconsistent system view between the analyst and the client, OOSE (Jacobson, et.al., 1992) is based on use-case-driven design. By organising the analysis and design around actual usage scenarios, it elicits objects according to three kinds of categories: entity object, interface object, and control object. From the above discussion, we could see that all of these modelling techniques have recognised the importance of the user requirements to the system. However, they just assume the requirements (the use case, scenario, or problem statement) as given, and do not propose any ways to facilitate the user's involvement to provide a complete and correct definition as the basis for further modelling. The Unified Modelling Language (UML), which is based upon the above modelling techniques, also has such problems.

These traditional modelling techniques still belong to the 'hard' school of thinking. They lack an appreciating activity to attain a deeper understanding of the real-world situation, hence inadequate requirement analyses. Consequently the potential of OO modelling cannot be fully realised. So here we review a proposal of using a 'soft' approach to help to identify and extract the object based on CLD. By applying investigative and learning cycle facilitated by the CLD framework, we could obtain an activity model that encapsulates the scenario of an individual or a group of clients of the whole system. The activity in the model is in no sense to be viewed as an algorithm, but as a system. It is a collection of interacting tasks, which between them achieve the desired results. On the other hand, "an object is characterised by a number of operations and a state which remembers the effect of these operations" (Jacobson, et al., 1992). The object itself is an abstraction of a group of related tasks to act in a particular role. And the interaction between the activities could be simulated by the interaction of the object. So by focusing on the activity or operation, we could see a similarity or a possible connection between the activity model and the object model.

(Liang et al.,1997;1998) have proposed a way to try to use the activity model (conceptual model) in CLD as a medium of appreciating and understanding a problem situation to build an object model. They suggested that by applying a series of questions such as "who does the activity?" (Actor); "who affects this activity?"(Owner); "who is affected by this activity"(Customer) to each activity in the activity model, the corresponding 'actor', 'owner' and 'customer' can be identified. Then, according to the notion of the client server contract described by (WirfsBrock et al.,1990), the 'actor' can be regarded as a 'server' object, 'customer' as a 'client' object and 'owner' as a 'support' object. For example, "A library member borrows, returns, and reserves one or more books. ", we could extract "librarian" and "library member" as the object that is responsible for the activities of borrowing, returning, and reserving, "books" as the object that is acted on by the activities. Further, by exploring the relationship among the actors, owners and customers, according to their responsibilities in a problem situation, we could specify the object structure. An association structure is defined, if an actor/owner/customer inherently depends on another actor/owner/customer. In the example above, then, the library member's activity is relevant to the books, so the "library member" object has an association structure with the "book" object. An inheritance structure is recognised, if some kind of activity is mentioned by multiple actors/owners/customers that could be specialised and generalised. "Librarian" and "Library member" are both people. So their common character as people could be extracted. An aggregation structure is attained, if one actor/owner/customer consist of another actor/owner/customer. An investigation of the link between activities could also help to specify the behaviour for an actor object.

6. CONCLUSION AND FUTURE WORK

The work by Liang et al. is an innovative way of OO modelling. It successfully captures the connection between the object and activity model. By integrating the OO technique into the CLD framework used to bring about the appreciation of the problem situation, the deficiency of the user requirement analysis is partially overcome. The users are encouraged to take part in and play a crucial role in the system development. The development process might be time-consuming since the users have to answer many of the aforementioned questions and the various tables that record this answering have to be processed. However, it indeed encourages users to think more deeply about the system and help them clarify their views. Eventually, the user requirement can be clearly defined. This approach corresponds with the goals of SSM. The work by Liang et al. provides a possible solution to the implantation of a technical specification in the CLD framework. However, this approach is still at an early stage and several issues require more research, e.g.:

- We need to consider how to avoid early reliance on sequential properties because they are subject to change. The issue is thus how to make the ordering of the activities within the activity model more compatible with the object technology
- We should also avoid the tendency towards a functional approach which is based on processes (action), otherwise it would defeat the purpose of the OO approach.

Moreover, the validation of OO models, the introduction of changes to the system, dealing with the conflicting user answers and the introduction of abstract objects which cannot be obtained from the user's answers are still missing parts. Further research is needed to complete and enrich the CLD framework by addressing these issues.

References

Checkland, P.B., Systems Thinking, System practice. Wiley, Chichester, 1981.

Coad, P. & Yourdon, E., Object-Oriented Analysis. 2nd ed. Prentice Hall, Englwood Cliffs, NJ, 1991.

Eckert, G. & Golder, P. "Improving object-oriented analysis". Information and software Technology, 36(2), pp 67-86,1994.

Jacobson, I., Christerson, M., Jonsson, P., & Övergaard, G., Object-Oriented Software Engineering, A use Case Driven Approach. Addison-Wesley, Harlow, 1992.

Lander, L., McRocbb, S. & Stowell, F.A., "Bridging the gap between IS Definition and IS Specification". In Stowell, F. et al. (eds), System For Sustainability. Plenum Press, New York, pp583-588, 1997.

Lewis, P.J., "Linking soft systems methodology with data-focused information system development". Journal of Information System, 3, pp169-186, 1993.

Liang, Y., West, D. & Stowell, F.A., " The possibility of linking SSM with object-oriented information system development". In Stowell, F. et al. (eds), System For Sustainability. Plenum Press, New York. pp 589-594, 1997.

Liang, Y.,West, D. & Stowell, F.A., "An approach to object identification, selection and specification in object-oriented analysis". Information Systems Journal, 8, pp163-180, 1998.

Mingers, J., "Using soft systems methodology in the design of information systems". In Stowell, F. (ed), Information systems Provision. McGraw-Hill, Maidenhead, pp18-50, 1995.

Prins, R., Developing Business Objects. McGrawHill, Maidenhead, 1996.

Probert, "The metaphysical foundation of soft and hard information systems methodologies". Paper presented at the UK Operational Research Society Conference, 1995.

Prins, R., Developing Business Objects. McGrawHill, Maidenhead, 1996.

Rumbaugh, J., Blaha, J., Premerlani, M., Eddy, F. & Lorensen, W., Object-Oriented Modelling and Design. Prentice Hall, Englewood Cliffs, NJ, 1991.

Stowell, F.A.& West, D., Client-Led Design. McGraw-Hill, Maidenhead, 1994.

WirfsBrock, R.J, Wilkerson,B. & Wiener, L., Designing Object-Oriented Software. Prentice Hall, Englewood Cliffs, NJ, 1990.

CHAPTER 49

HYPER-TMODELLER: A CASE TOOL FOR LIVING DEVELOPMENT PROCESSES

Nandish V Patel
Brunel University

Abstract

Information systems developers in business organisations have to establish systems requirements in organisationally dynamic or changing environments. In this paper, a living CASE tool called Hyper-Tmodeller is proposed to facilitate requirements gathering under organisationally dynamic conditions. The notion of tailorable information modelling is introduced, and is proposed as a suitable approach for modelling information requirements in dynamic development environments. Potential users of systems are treated as active designers and developers of systems using Hyper-Tmodeller in the tailorable information modelling approach discussed in this paper.

1. INTRODUCTION

Approaches to information systems development that separate systems specification from implementation, like the life cycle model in (Sommerville 1992), are unrealistic in changing organisations where requirements are likely to change. (Swartout and Balzer 1982) argue that systems development is the intertwining of specification and implementation in program code. The pace of organisational change makes the separation of systems specification and implementation largely unworkable, especially in large, complex projects. The spiral of change model for tailorable information systems, proposed by (Patel 1998) regards specification and implementation as one process, or that specification and implementation are non-distinct. This is a valid view of systems development and *usage*, as it is difficult to draw a clear-cut distinction, in temporal and task terms, between systems specification and implementation in informational systems terms.

In this paper Hyper Tailorable Modeller, abbreviated to Hyper-Tmodeller, is proposed as a living CASE tool for making the systems requirements process flexible by treating specification and implementation as a single process. Making the requirements process tailorable is a practical advancement of (Paul's 1993) arguments for research into a software development paradigm that is living and Hyper-Tmodeller arises from the work on developing tailorable information systems by (Patel, 1997). It is a practical computer tool for dynamic modelling of information requirements under changing organisational conditions. It is an appropriate tailoring tool to enable users to tailor the information systems requirements process.

The rationale for developing Hyper-Tmodeller is discussed in Section 2. Aspects of tailorable information modelling that require dynamic development processes are discussed in the following Section. In Section 4, the idea of potential users being information modellers or systems developers is considered. Section 5 details the proposed systems architecture for Hyper-Tmodeller, while Section 6 provides some technical details for its design. Some concluding remarks are offered in Section 7.

2. HYPER-TMODELLER: A LIVING CASE TOOL

The design of Hyper-Tmodeller is an explicit recognition of diversity and dynamism in the environment of information modelling. Hyper-Tmodeller is based on (Patel 1998) spiral of change model of tailorable information systems. The Spiral of Change model for systems development is the view that the organisational environments in which systems have to be developed and, importantly, used is changeable. The various modelling tools in Hyper-Tmodeller enable modelling of dynamic aspects of the work environment, such as changing business objectives, policies, and procedures. These are the kind of organisational changes that are likely to require re-defining systems requirements, and causes difficulties in methodological approaches as described by (Baskerville et al 1992).

The notion of tailorable information systems facilitating learning should be considered in addition to Trigg's other triggers for user-tailoring activity namely "diversity", "fluidity" and "ambiguity", quoted in (Kjær and Madsen 1995).

To integrate theoreticians' and practitioners' views, (Bellotti 1992), proposes that an appropriate design rationale be explored. So an interactive tool is required to enable users and developers to configure, and re-configure, information models until they are "satisfied". This basic information structure is determinable through tailorable modelling using Hyper-Tmodeller.

Tailorable modelling is conceived to be a process of abstraction from the relevant business domain: abstracting generic features that identify links among organisational tasks, employees and associated information requirements. The purpose of tailorable information models is to *re-present* business in a general form in tailorable information systems, one that can be continuously tailored by users for varying and changing information needs, and clarification or learning of business situations.

Tailorable modelling using Hyper-Tmodeller would require users (or systems analysts) to begin by graphically mapping organisational situations. Changes in tailorable information models to match changing organisations can be represented by generic structures which themselves can be tailored, in this way features of systems tailorability for tailorable information systems become designed into tailorable information models. Tailorable models are conceived to be direct maps of changing organisations for tailorable information systems designs, consequently, systems tailorability would be provided in actual tailorable information systems through tailorable information models.

Tailorable information models can be of individuals, groups, or business processes in organisations. The aim in Hyper-Tmodeller is to discover structural links between organisational tasks and associated information and the variations in information needs that occur in these units. These links are distinct from notions of data becoming information through processing. A structural link in a tailorable information model may be thought of as an organisational task, or other aspect of organisational work, which connects an organisational employee with necessary information to complete that task successfully, efficiently, and effectively. In this sense, tailorable information modelling is an attempt to re-establish the primacy of organisational task analysis which, as (Friedman and Cornford 1989) observe, was displaced by structured methodologies emphasising stages of systems development.

3. SOME CONCEPTUAL FOUNDATIONS OF THE PROTOTYPE HYPER-TMODELLER

This sub-section details the initial thinking supporting the concept of a dynamic computer tool, Hyper-Tmodeller, which is able to capture changing and tailorable information. Hyper-Tmodeller is proposed as a tailorable information systems analysis tool.

Business policies are actually programmed into traditional information systems, and when policies change, as they do quite frequently, traditional information systems are unable to cope with the changes. In Hyper-Tmodeller, such policies would be identified and made tailorable. Users' work environments are made complex by the fact that they have to communicate with colleagues. The development of systems tailorability has to consider this vital human aspect of information systems, which is termed *ontological exchanges* of information. Hyper-Tmodeller enables interactive modelling by allowing various potential users (various managers, work groups, other employees) to individually model their perspective of their work environment. These disparate models are amalgamated by Hyper-Tmodeller to provide an organisational view of the proposed tailorable information system.

The kind of modelling supported by Hyper-Tmodeller may be described as end-user modelling (see Section 4 below for details). The aim is to create models or representations of organisational variability and to use these to understand and design tailorable systems architectures. Hyper-Tmodeller allows modelling by the eventual users of proposed information systems.

Hyper-Tmodeller may be used in several ways. Potential users of information systems may do the actual modelling. Alternatively, the modelling may be done by systems analysts who make models of users in their organisational environment, where all things are dynamic or likely to change in the longer term, and give these models to users to validate. Users may validate systems analysts' models by adding, deleting, or changing them. Finally, both users and systems analysts could do the modelling together, either starting from scratch or working from an initial model provided by systems analysts or users.

In all case, a systems development dialogue is initiated between potential users of tailorable information systems and developers, but the difference being those potential users become active designers. The use of Hyper-Tmodeller results in visible tailorable information models that can be discussed. The use of visual reasoning and thinking in Hyper-Tmodeller means that graphical representations of dynamic information environments can be enabled which increase understanding.

The purpose of Hyper-Tmodeller is to inform the design and validation of systems tailorability in information systems, and to use these to understand and conceptualise tailorable information architectures. The aim is to enable user of information systems to make graphical and textual representations of the organisational structure of their business activity. The reason being that users may have better cognitive models and better understanding of their roles in changing organisations and a better understanding of the information they require to complete their organisational roles.

The use of Hyper-Tmodeller has several benefits for users and information systems developers. Its use enables users themselves to learn what they are required to do in organisations and what tailorable information they require. This type of tailoring tool is necessary because, as (Paul 1993) asserts, users cannot know at the outset of systems development what to specify for design purposes. The use of Hyper-Tmodeller by users also leads to an understanding of what information they would like to tailor in systems. Finally, it enables developers to understand better what is required from proposed systems and to cope with changing requirements.

Users learn about their own work environments while modelling, understanding relevant organisational processes and issues. In this sense, Hyper-Tmodeller provides a learning environment, and allows users to explore their working environment, through graphical interfaces. Modelling through the highly graphical interface of Hyper-Tmodeller enables users to externalise and objectify their work environment and gain a deeper understanding of their information needs and business practice in terms of systems development.

The use of Hyper-Tmodeller would result in drawings, graphs, text comments, and documentation, supplied by user-modellers to systems analysts to investigate further an application area. The result would be a visible and subsequently tailorable information model, which may be used to base discussions around and exchange ideas of required systems tailorability. In effect tailorable information modelling is a simulation of potential tailorable information systems as proposed by Gardner et al., 1996. The use of Hyper-Tmodeller may be regarded as a simulation of the information system to be developed.

4. END-USER MODELLING

The earlier discussion on engenders the view that potential users may be regarded as systems modellers. This type of systems modelling by users of information systems is here termed end-user modelling, and is discussed in this section.

The assertion by (Paul 1993) that business users cannot know what their present information requirements are or what they will be in the future. This requires tailorable information systems developers to aid users to learn of their organisational environment, but in particular to learn of their organisational roles and associated information required for completing those tasks. The purpose of Hyper-Tmodeller is to enable users to explore their information needs. The spiral of change model depicts that user's work environments are continuously changing, therefore there is a need to understand the use of tailorable information in systems. Modelling information systems on the basis of Hyper-Tmodeller does not assume that users know what they require in terms of information. Rather such modelling enables them to play with iconic representations of aspects of their work and its informational environment and so produce a picture of what is currently happening in the organisation both in terms of actual work and its associated information. Any change in the work itself or its environment may be easily re-modelled because of the dynamic feature of Hyper-Tmodeller. Such a medium needs to be flexible and so hypermedia technology is considered suitable because of its ability to form links dynamically.

The aim of this kind of end-user modelling is to improve communications between users and systems analysts, which is poor in systems development using the life cycle model. Users and systems analysts learn about changing organisational work and its environment by understanding organisational policies, processes, and procedures. This communication is facilitated by visual reasoning through the visual representations of the organisational information environment provided in Hyper-Tmodeller. The end-user models themselves may then be used as strategies for proceeding with systems development.

The use of Hyper-Tmodeller by users is not supposed to produce an *agreed* tailorable information system model. It is envisaged that its use by multiple users would actually produce disparate views or multiple (personally tailored) information systems, and that these views would be accommodated in tailorable system architecture of the kind proposed by (Stamoulis et al. 1996).

Some essential features of an information systems model derived with the use of Hyper-Tmodeller need to be stated. Such models are true in the sense that they resemble the form of tailorable information systems but not the content. The content aspects, like exact system specifications in systems development methodologies, would be deferred and be designed to be tailorable by users. In a sense, the designed tailorable information systems would have the same structure as the organisation, but no pre-specified, fixed procedures. Users in actual organisational situations using deferred system's designing would determine these.

The intention of end-user modelling is to achieve an active environment, where a change made to the tailorable information model in the tool would reflect in the operational information system.

Once a prototype of HyperTmodeller has been developed, it is envisaged that it will be evaluated by finding appropriate cases where it can be used in trials. A real case will be sought, where it can be used in parallel with current information modelling practice. This should provide comparison of the tool's usefulness.

5. HYPER-TMODELLER'S MODULES

In this subsection a tentative structure for Hyper-Tmodeller is detailed. This structure incorporates aspects of the case data, which led to the generalisation of systems tailorability through deferred system's designing. In determining a structure of the modules for Hyper-Tmodeller the kind of organisational change observed in the case organisations during systems development and usage has been considered, and the aim of thinking of Hyper-Tmodeller is to allow information systems to be modelled in such dynamic environments. A modular design for Hyper-Tmodeller was thought efficient to ensure its development, and each module functions to perform a separate aspect of tailorable information modelling. These modules are now briefly described.

There are four modules envisaged in Hyper-Tmodeller. These are Originator-Creator, Discoverer-Designer, Logographer, and Tailorable Information Systems Analyser modules. Together these modules permit potential users to represent their organisational work in informational terms and as they themselves perceive it. In this sense, Hyper-Tmodeller facilitates ontological systems design following (Winograd and Flores 1993).

Originator-Creator

The originator-creator module functions to create an initial tailorable information model. The creation is done through discovery and learning and is akin to drawing ideas onto blank electronic paper. The initial tailorable information model may be put together by systems analysts or users. If the initial model is provided by systems analysts than users may amend it, by adding or deleting or changing aspects, to reflect their perceptions of what they think is happening in their organisational tasks and the need for information. Alternatively, users could generate initial tailorable information models and systems analysts could use these to understand better users' needs.

Discoverer-Designer

The discover-designer module is where actual tailoring is done, so all the required tailoring tools (Ttools) are provided here. Once an initial tailorable information model has been created in the originator-creator module it is amended and refined in this discoverer-designer module. If a tailorable information model has been provided by systems analysts, users may add other observations to it or they may delete some aspects of it. Using various types of tailoring tools made available in the module can do this or they could create their own tools and link-types, as shown in the bullet points below. If an initial tailorable information model is provided, users could be asked their opinions or comments regarding it, which they could add in text boxes using the text tool. The amendments to a tailorable information model by systems analysts or users are done according to their perceptions of the organisational situation being modelled, which facilitates the notion of ontological systems design.

To enable modelling of changing organisations, Hyper-Tmodeller should contain appropriate functionality. Some features might be:

- appropriate icons of business activity;
- moving of icons (as in desktop interfaces);
- each tailoring activity connecting to a amalgamating program;
- talk-links (I talk to X for such and such reason);
- need-links (I need X or Y information from him or her);
- browse links (I browse through this or that document for information);
- information links (I need this or that information, now and then, regularly).

Diagrams allow modelling-users to view, modify, and create pictures of the organisational settings they work in. Visual thinking is a useful provision in Hyper-Tmodeller, because modelling-users would be able to see pictorially their tailorable information system. Visual images also enable sharing of ideas publicly to minimise misunderstanding.

Given the spiral of change model of tailorable information systems, Hyper-Tmodeller contains functionality to model organisational settings dynamically, thereby catering for organisational change during systems development and usage. Amongst Hyper-Tmodeller's features are appropriate icons for creating and tailoring information-links; for instance, "I-need" link-types for information that users need. Associated with this link-type is a "frequency-link" for stipulating the temporal occurrence of the need.

Another feature is the "talk" link-type. As tailorable information systems are considered to be quintessentially human processes or ontological exchanges, and because talk is an important communicative aspect of these human processes, the talk link-type is essential to modelling tailorable information systems. The human variable of the general spiral of change model is undoubtedly complex, and aspects like talk are features of that multifarious complexity. Talk and other living aspects, such as business meetings, have to be facilitated in any modelling of tailorable information systems.

The link-types in Hyper-Tmodeller are structural business links. At present four types of structural links are envisaged which modelling-users can use to create tailorable information models, covering business policies and issues. Four types of structural business links which recognise the need for tailorable information can be modelled in Hyper-Tmodeller.

Procedural links. As organisational procedures change the need for associated information is likely to change too. Modelling-users can use procedural links that model users' organisation procedures associated with their organisational tasks and responsibilities.

Process links. Various processes are involved in organisational work, and as these change the associated information is likely to change too. The processes involved in performing organisational tasks are modelled by using "process links".

Causal links. As one organisational event changes its effect on another means that the need for information changes. Causal links are used to model events that are causally related.

Policy links. Business Policies are actually programmed as fixed algorithms in traditional information systems. As organisational policies change, their associated information changes too. Policy links are used to model policy invoked to do particular organisational tasks.

Logographer

The logographer is the documentor module, documenting all the modelling actions in the Originator-Creator and Discoverer-Designer modules. The logographer also collects all the tailoring. Such as all the links, moves, all the text comments, and drawings done by modelling-users. Documentation in tailorable information systems development has to be dynamic as argued by (Gardner and Paul 1994). Given that there is organisational change any mechanism for creating systems documentation would have to be dynamic. This documentation is made available dynamically to systems analysts and users through hypertext and to technical systems designers and programmers to translate users' ideas of the tailorable information they want.

Tailorable Information Systems Analyser

The Tailorable Information Systems Analyser (TISA) module collects all designed material, configurations, junctures of tailoring, diagrams, and configures them into an amalgamated version which could be treated as a model of a tailorable systems architecture. It is possible to do the amalgamation around an object-oriented database structure to preserve the flexibility and required tailoring modelled.

The TISA amalgamation is a concurrent procedure, and available to modelling-users through tailorable windows. Alternatively, when many modelling-users are simultaneously using Hyper-Tmodeller, their individual views are made available to each other through shared windows or captured snap-shots in real-time of the modelling process. That way modelling-users can learn what other members of the organisation think they do in relation to each other, allowing modellers to base their tailorable information models around each others' perceptions of their organisational work.

6. SOME TECHNICAL DETAILS

Hyper-Tmodeller requires a platform capable of manipulating various communicative digital multimedia. This includes text, graphics, sound, and pictures or images. The software configuration should allow the creation, mixing and linking of text, creation of graphics and sound. The implemented Hyper-Tmodeller should be portable across most machines.

To facilitate the use of flexible text, graphics, sound and images hypermedia is suitable software for designing Hyper-Tmodeller. Hypermedia is itself a very flexible software medium. The main reason for considering Hypermedia is its ability to create connections dynamically among objects. To facilitate the capture of changing user requirements it is necessarily to enable dynamic linking of objects.

There are various hardware platforms that may be used to run Hyper-Tmodeller. Both micro-computer platforms such as Apple Macintosh and workstation platforms such SUN's SPARC-stations using X-windows and OPEN WINDOWS window manager. However, to make Hyper-Tmodeller accessible to a wider user group the micro-computer platform is preferable because of the prevalence of micro-computers. The arrival of new micro-processors from Intel, such as the MMX technology, capable of manipulating various media on micro-computers make the proposition of Hyper-Tmodeller more feasible.

To capture actual living aspects of business activity, it may be necessary to raise Hyper-Tmodeller to multimedia level. To store actual pictures of work processes certain additional hardware would be needed. A video digitiser, a video camera, a tape player and an audio digitizer would be needed to capture pictures and sound. In addition appropriate software to capture audio and video would be needed. Work is being done to design Hyper-Tmodeller. Object-oriented techniques have been examined to design how information would be organised and stored, and how it would be accessed and retrieved. Designs incorporating classes and objects in Hyper-Tmodeller have been identified.

7. CONCLUSIONS

The proposed HyperT-modeller is based on the idea that requirement gathering under dynamic conditions needs a dynamic information modelling approach. There is a need to understand information requirements in terms of tailorable information to allow for changing requirements. CASE tools for requirements gathering need to be flexible and the type of dynamic modelling of tailorable information envisaged in Hyper-Tmodeller is a recognition of the intertwining of changing information needs and systems development and usage.

Note: Two diagrams in Section 5 illustrating the use of HyperTmodeller have been removed because of page restrictions. They are available form the author.

References

Baskerville R., Travis J. and Truex D. (1992), Systems Without Method. In *IFIP Transactions on The Impact of Computer Supported Technologies on Information System Development*. (Kendall K., Lyytinen K. and DeGross J. Eds.), 241-270. North-

Holland, Amsterdam.

Friedman A. L. and Cornford D. S. (1989*), Computer Systems Development: History, Organisation and Implementation*. Wiley, Chichester.

Gardner L. A. and Paul R. J. (1994), A Fully Integrated Environment for Layered Development (FIELD) in Information Systems. *International Journal of Information Management*, 6. 437-484.

Gardner L. A., Taylor S.J.E. and Patel N.V. (1996), Active User Designs in Hypermedia for Better Simulation Model Specification. *Journal of Intelligent Systems* 6 (1) 5-24.

Kjaer A. and Madsen K.H. (1995), Participatory Analysis of Flexibility. *Communications of the ACM* 38 (5) (May) 53-60.

Mumford E. (1993) "The Participation of User in Systems Design: An Account of the Origin, Evolution, and Use of the ETHICS Method", In: Douglas S. and Namoka A., *Participatory Design, Principles and Practice*, Lawrence Erlbaum Associates, London. 257-270.

Patel N V. (1997) Tailorable Information Systems: Deferred System's Design for Changing Organisations. In: Manchester Metropolitan University, UK. Proceedings of the 7th Annual BIT Conference, BIT '97, Business Information Management - Alternative Futures, November 5/6 1997. (The Proceedings are only available in CD-ROM format).

Patel N V. (1998), The Spiral of Change Model for Coping with Changing and Ongoing Requirements. To appear in the Special Issue of *Requirements Engineering*.

Paul R. J. (1993), Why Users Cannot 'Get What They Want'. *ACM SIGOIS Bulletin* 14 (2), (December 1993). 8-12.

Sommerville I. (1992), *Software Engineering*, (Fourth Edition). Addison-Wesley, Wokingham.

Stamoulis D. S., Patel N. V. and Martakos D. I. (1996) A Systems Architecture Model and Implementation Platforms for Tailorable Information Systems. In *Proceedings of the Fourth European Conference on Information Systems*, (Coelho J. D., Jelassi T., König W., Kremar H., O'Callaghan R, and Sääksjärvi M, Eds.), Lisbon, Portugal, July 2-4. 313-322.

Swartout W. and Balzer R. (1982), On the Intertwining of Specification and Implementation. *Communications of the ACM*, 25 (7), July 1982. 438-440.

Winograd T. and Flores F. (1993), *Understanding Computers and Cognition*. Addison-Wesley, Reading, Massachusetts.

CHAPTER 50

THE CRITICAL APPROACH TO SOFTWARE DEVELOPMENT

Myrvin F Chester
University of Wolverhampton

Abstract

The modern philosophy of science (particularly that of Karl Popper) is used to cast light upon the theory and practice of software development. The paper discusses the critical approach to software development in which software deliverables (seen as the equivalent of scientific hypotheses) must be subjected to rational criticism as well as empirical testing, and can never be proved to be correct.

1. INTRODUCTION

A fruitful area in which to look for a philosophical basis for software development is the modern philosophy of science. This area of philosophy has revolutionised the way scientists think about their work, and it can be used to throw light upon the way software developers carry out theirs.

Although it deals with other philosophers as well, this paper is mainly concerned with the views of the philosopher Karl Popper as initially expounded in his work *Logic der Forschung* (Popper, 1934), which was translated into English as *The Logic of Scientific Discovery* in 1959. The essential argument of this teaching is that no scientific theory can be known to be true: there are no provably true theories. This paper argues that, following the same logic, no computer system and no software development deliverable can ever be proved to be correct. Therefore, no computer system can ever be expected to be perfect and can only ever be expected to be an approximation to the system that is required. Furthermore, even if a perfect computer system or deliverable can be produced, it can never be proved to be perfect.

A useful way of viewing any deliverable in the software development process is to see the deliverable as a hypothesis — the developer's theory — of what is actually required. Viewed in this way, Popper's ideas on the way that theories in science develop can, to a great extent, be applied to the way software deliverables are developed. The terms 'theory' and 'hypothesis' will be used interchangeably, and the term 'deliverable hypothesis' will often be used to convey the connection between a software deliverable and its hypothetical nature.

From this perspective, the paper develops a criticism of the way software is produced in the light of a critical or scientific approach to software development.

2. THE PROBLEM OF INDUCTION

The history of the philosophy of science has been greatly concerned with what, if anything, constitutes scientific proof. Science has purported to discover true theories about the world, and to be able to demonstrate that these theories are true. Traditionally, scientists have collected data about an area of the world and, from these data, developed theories about the general state of that area of investigation. It was argued that the quality and quantity of the collected data constituted proof that the generalised theories were true. Scientists were taking particular cases and, from these, producing generalised theories. This method of argument is known as induction.

At least since the days of Francis Bacon (1561-1626), induction was the main method of reasoning in science and the justification for its claim to derive true ideas about the world. Induction is 'in logic, [the] method of reasoning from a part to a whole, from particulars to generals, or from the individual to the universal' (Britannica CD 98). Induction is employed in science when evidence is collected and the assumption made that theories about the general world can be reasoned out from that evidence.

The philosopher David Hume (1711-1776) seems to be the first to have questioned such assumptions and pose what was later to be called *the problem of induction*. An example of this problem concerns the rising of the sun. No matter how often the sun has been observed regularly to rise and set, even a great number of such instances does not constitute *'a positive reason for the regularity, or the law, of the sun's rising and setting. Thus, induction can neither establish the law nor make it probable'* (Popper, 1983, p. 31). As Hume wrote, *'...there can be no **demonstrative** arguments to prove, **that those instances of which we have had no experience resemble those of which we have had experience.'*** (Hume, 1739, p. 91, original emphasis)

There are considerable implications of the problem of induction to the development of information systems; and this paper discusses several of these.

Many important philosophers since Hume have found themselves forced to accept the logic of his argument. This paper discusses the reactions of five these, Hume himself, Immanuel Kant (1724-1804), Bertrand Russell (1872-1970), Alfred Jules Ayer (1910-1989), and Karl Popper (1902-1994).

3. COPING WITH THE INDUCTION PROBLEM

Hume wrestled with the induction problem. Finding nothing wrong with the logic of his position, he wondered why everyone, including himself, seemed to act as if induction were a way of proving general theories from particular facts. He concluded that this trait was unavoidable because the human mind is, *'so constituted that when, having in our experience found A and B to be constantly conjoined, we meet with an A we expect it to be followed by a B; and when we meet with a B we presume it to have been preceded by an A.'* (J. Passmore in Magee, 1988, p. 148).

Our experience of the constant conjoining of A to B constitutes the particular facts of which we are aware. Our expectation that in the future B will be preceded by A, is our theory of what will happen. That theory seems to be proved by our previous experience. In Hume's view it is a psychological fact that humans have to accept that induction works, regardless of what logic might suggest to the contrary. Hume wrote that *'All inferences from experience, therefore, are effects of custom, not of reasoning.'* He believed that, *'Thus it is that custom, not reason, is the great guide of life. In short, the idea of cause and effect is neither a relation of ideas nor a matter of fact. Although it is not a perception and not rationally justified, it is crucial to human survival and a central aspect of human cognition'.* (Britannica CD 98 on Hume)

The work of Hume and Kant separated knowledge into that which can be proved by the intellect alone (Kant's 'analytic knowledge'), and that which depends upon the senses (empirical knowledge). Analytic propositions are true or false regardless of the state of the world; while the truth of empirical propositions depends upon their correspondence with the way the world really is. Analytic propositions are made in logic and mathematics, while empirical propositions are the stuff of scientific theories.

Kant's great work the *Critique of pure reason* (Kant, 1781) was written as his answer to Hume's problem. While admitting the logic of Hume's position, Kant insisted that induction was an *a priori* principle being known by the mind without it requiring logical proof.

Russell, again agreeing with Hume's basic position but disagreeing with Kant's solution, wrote that *'induction is an independent logical principle, incapable of being inferred either from experience or from other logical principles'* (Russell, 1912, p. 647). He reasoned that, if induction were not allowed, it would mean that all empirical science would be impossible. He refused to accept this conclusion because he thought that, if science were impossible, there would be *'no difference between sanity and insanity. The lunatic who believes he is a poached egg is to be condemned solely on the ground that he is in a minority'* (Russell, 1912, p. 646). Instead, he proposed that logic presents innumerable possibilities for a correct theory, and the point of experimentation is to select, by deduction, the bad theories from the good ones. So *'leaving to experience the task of deciding, where decision is possible, between the many worlds which logic offers for our choice'* (Russell, 1912, p. 148).

The Logical Positivists (a group of philosophers and scientists meeting in Vienna, also known as the Vienna Circle) made further proposals about empirical statements. They and their British representative Ayer (1936 and 1959) argued that many statements and questions purported to be concerned with the way the world really is. However, some statements (principally those from metaphysics and religion) were impossible to check with the real world, because they could not be verified with sense data, and were therefore meaningless or fictitious. Induction was seen by them as just such a problem. Ayer (1972, p. 67) stated that, *"Thus it appears that there is no possible way of solving the problem of induction, as it is ordinarily conceived. And this means that it is a fictitious problem, since all genuine problems are at least theoretically capable of being solved"*. Their position on scientific proof therefore remained, in Chalmer's (1982. p.11) words, *'that particular brand of inductivism'*.

Popper was published by the Vienna Circle but diverged from them in the way he viewed induction and scientific advance. He completely accepted Hume's logic about induction, and, as a result, he argued that science cannot offer a method of discovering true facts about the world. In his book *Realism and the Aim of Science* (Popper, 1983), Popper wrote that the main points of his solution to the problem of induction were as follows (Popper, 1983, pp. 33-34):

1. Acceptance of the view that theories are of supreme importance, both for practical and theoretical science.
2. Acceptance of Hume's argument against induction: any hope that we may possess positive reasons for believing in our theories is destroyed by that argument.
3. Acceptance of the principle of empiricism: scientific theories are rejected or adopted in the light of the results of experimental or observational tests.
4. Acceptance of critical rationalism: scientific theories are rejected or adopted (though only temporarily and tentatively) as being better or worse than other known theories in the light of the results of rational criticism.

He concludes that the problem of induction is meaningful and has no solution, and 'Thus the real situation is quite different from the one visualized by the naïve empiricist, or the believer in inductive logic. He thinks that we begin by collecting and arranging our experiences, and so ascend the ladder of science'. (Popper, 1968, p. 106)

In place of the principle of scientific induction, Popper offers the idea that science progresses by one theory being superseded by another theory. Each theory holds for a while ('though only temporarily and tentatively') until displaced by a yet better theory.

It is with the Popperian view of theory development and the way it can be applied to software development that this paper is mainly concerned.

4. SOFTWARE DELIVERABLES AS HYPOTHESES

The presentation of a software deliverable is tantamount to making the statement: "This deliverable contains a correct representation of the users' requirements for a particular part of the system and at a particular stage of the life cycle". Such a statement is either true or false — it is a hypothesis, a proposition, that will be accepted or rejected by the IS developers and their users. It is an empirical statement about the world in the same way that a scientific hypothesis is a statement about the world, and it must be treated in the same way in order to investigate its truth or falsehood. Therefore, following Popper, since no scientific hypothesis can be proved to be true, no IS deliverable can be proved to be a correct representation of the users' requirements. The best that can be done is that the deliverable is criticised and tested as thoroughly as possible.

So, for the purpose of this paper, a software deliverable is seen as the developer's hypothesis or theory of the deliverable that is really required. It is assumed that there is a correct, or perhaps a set of correct, deliverables that would fulfil the user's requirements or needs, and that each actual deliverable (such as the systems analysis report, the systems design, and each program) is the developer's hypothesis of what the correct deliverable ought to be. The present author has noted that: *'The aim of science is to get closer to the truth of nature's laws, and the aim of commercial information systems development is to produce systems which are as close as possible to the requirements of the user'* (Chester, 1998).

What then can be done about determining the truth or falsehood (the correctness) of a software deliverable hypothesis?

5. THE CRITICAL APPROACH TO SOFTWARE DEVELOPMENT

In the quotations from Popper (1983) above, it can be seen that his view is that no scientific hypothesis can ever be proved. No amount of evidence or calculation can demonstrate without doubt that a theory is correct. All theories and hypotheses are therefore temporary, and hold until shown to be incorrect or until superseded by better ones. A theory is disproved by failing a test that has been applied to it. In the case of scientific theories, Popper suggests that such a test need not only be empirical *'... in the light of the results of experimental or observational tests'*; it may also be one of criticism. In *'critical rationalism: scientific theories are rejected or adopted (though only temporarily and tentatively) as being better or worse than other known theories in the light of the results of rational criticism'*.

In science, this aspect of rational criticism is often glossed over in favour of empirical testing. However, Popper realised that scientists study theories not only as hypotheses to be tested but also in a logical way. Criticism is particularly important when looking at software development deliverables. The 'critical approach' to software development, which elsewhere the writer has referred to as the 'scientific approach' (Chester, 1998), combines these two aspects of testing. Testing by criticism as well as by experiment, together with the assumption that a deliverable can never be proved to be correct.

6. RELEVANCE TO THE PRACTICE OF SOFTWARE DEVELOPMENT

Systems deliverables are descriptions of the current or proposed system, or parts of that system, at various levels of detail. They follow logically from those that have already been accepted after criticism and testing. So, for instance, the systems design follows from the agreed analysis of the current paper-based system. Empirical testing of deliverables can present problems because many are produced in the form of documents, either written or diagrammatic. In these cases, often the only test available for such deliverables is that of being scrutinised carefully by qualified human beings. As has been mentioned, criticism of scientific theories is also a very important aspect of scientific development, and the criticism of systems deliverables by qualified personnel is an important factor in producing high quality information systems.

Not only is it true that human beings make mistakes which testing and criticism may discover, but there is also a philosophical reason for thorough testing and criticism. For no matter how careful developers are and no matter how faultless are thought their methodologies, there can never be absolute surety that the systems that are developed are correct. In a previous paper the present author has noted that, *'All that can be known is that the deliverables have passed the best tests that can be devised, and that they have been endorsed after the thorough criticism of qualified personnel. Therefore, any deliverable, no matter how it was developed, must be thoroughly tested and criticised. This principle is accepted wholeheartedly by software engineers, and supported by the modern philosophy of science'*. (Chester, 1998)

7. PROBABILITY OF FAILURE

The problem of induction also affects the *probability* that some deliverable hypothesis is correct. Popper (1983) writes that a regularly observed event *'can neither establish the law **nor make it probable'*** (emphasis added). This runs counter to the common idea that thorough testing of computer systems somehow reduces the probability of errors being present.

Popper and Hume believe that no amount of experience will affect the probability of the truth or falsity of a theory. For instance, the number of white swans encountered will not affect the probability of meeting one day with a non-white swan. This probability does not reduce as the number of white swans seen increases. The theory that all swans are white may have been tested by observation many times and not been found to fail — but that is all that can be claimed. Therefore, in software development, though deliverables are tested and criticised, this will not affect our knowledge about the likelihood of errors presenting in the future. There is, however, the Popperian concept of the degree of corroboration of a theory. As stated by Popper, this is: 'a concise report evaluating the state ... of the critical discussion of a theory, with respect to the way it solves its problems; its degree of testability; the severity of tests it has undergone; and the way it has stood up to these tests' (Popper, 1972, p. 18). Also: 'Instead of discussing the "probability" of a hypothesis we should try to assess what tests, what trials, it has withstood; that is, we should try to assess how far it has been able to show its fitness to survive by standing up to these tests' (Popper, 1934, p. 251).

Viewing the development of software in this way, all that can be said about the correctness of its deliverables is that they have a certain degree of corroboration with what is required. The more testing and criticism that the system has been subjected to, the happier developers and users can be to accept the system, but it will not reduce the probability of the system failing in the future.

8.   THE CRITICAL APPROACH AND SOFTWARE DEVELOPMENT PRACTICES

Adopting the critical or scientific approach to software development may well cast doubt upon some of the practices commonly found in IT departments and promoted by academics. The writer has covered much of this ground before in Chester and O'Brien (1995) and Chester (1998); the following is a résumé of three areas of concern.

Formal methods

Formal Methods perhaps causes the most anxiety for followers of the critical approach to software development. From its inception by writers such as Dijkstra (1975, 1989) formal methods has held out the hope that computer systems can be developed to be free from errors.

There are practical problems with such claims, including the concern that even if a program can be developed so as to be a perfect reflection of a specification written in a logic language (a calculus), there can be no certainty that the original specification was correct. However, this paper is concerned with the philosophical objections. In the view of the critical approach to software development, the finished deliverable, the program, can never be proved to be correct by logic alone. The development of a program cannot be viewed as an analytic problem provable without subjecting it to empirical testing. It cannot be proved to have been correctly produced from the specification, regardless of the method used to do so, nor to be correctly representing the requirements of the user.

Sometimes science stresses the importance of experimentation and ignores, or reduces the importance of, critical rationalism. Proponents of formal methods have been criticised for reducing the importance of empirical testing by claiming that the rationalism of their methods means that experimentation may not be required. For instance, Dijkstra (1975) writes: '*[W]e have ... "a calculus" for a formal discipline — a set of rules — such that, if applied successfully: (1) it will have derived a correct program; and (2) it will tell us that we have reached such a goal*'. There seems little necessity, therefore, to test a program that has been proved to be 'correct', and that has been generated by a calculus that has told us that the program is correct.

This view of the down-grading of testing by formal methods is not new, it has been taken by other writers such as Parnas (printed after the paper of Dijkstra, 1989), who states, in criticism of Dijkstra, that: '*There is no engineering profession in which testing and mathematical validation are viewed as alternatives. It is universally accepted that they are complementary and that both are required*'.

Popper would never allow that any empirical hypothesis can be claimed to be true because it had been produced by logic or mathematics. Even logic and mathematics have many examples of claims to correctness which have subsequently been found to be incorrect. To name a few: the claims of Frege to have derived arithmetic from logical principles was disproved by Russell; and Russell and Whitehead's similar claim was disproved by Gödel (see Bell, 1953). Also, the recent proof of Fermat's last theorem by Andrew Wiles had to be corrected because the first attempt was found to contain errors. The use of logic and mathematics by no means assures the correctness of any theorem, theory or hypothesis even for analytic propositions, still less for empirical ones.

Goguen (1990) can be quoted in support of the sceptical view of the critical approach to software development; he writes: *'[T]he modern world has developed a kind of arrogance which is damaging to the very projects that it seeks to sustain: [by] proposing methodologies to guarantee the absences of error'* (p.1). Also: *'[B]ugs are inevitable. If they don't occur in coding, they will appear in design, specification, requirements, or use; they may arise by misinterpretation of what the customer says, by inadequate modelling of the situation in which the program must run, by inadequate documentation or understanding of the tools being used, ... and in many other ways'* (ibid., p. 5).

The philosophical viewpoint of the critical approach to software development is that any deliverable hypotheses has to be empirically tested and critically evaluated and even then its correctness still remains doubtful.

Prototyping

Some prototyping techniques appear to resemble scientific enquiry closely. A first-cut prototype is generated, being a tentative hypothesis of what is required, and that is tested by a user and criticised so that it can be modified to produce another, better hypothesis. However, closer inspection reveals some doubts with respect to the critical or scientific approach.

Popper pointed out the importance of rational criticism in scientific work, and this paper has extended that to the development of software. It is important that those who are qualified to do so carry out this criticism; the person criticising a deliverable cannot be just anyone. The user who is involved in the prototyping process may not be qualified as a software tester and may not therefore be able to test a system thoroughly. Also, it is comparatively easy for an experienced IT developer to fool a user into thinking that the system is working properly when in fact it is not.

Analyst-programmers

The writer has explored the problems of the employment of analyst-programmers before (e.g. Chester, 1992; Chester and O'Brien, 1995). When two jobs are combined into one, as when the specification of a program is carried out by the same developer who is to write the program, there is a great danger that the positive effects of having two developers are lost.

In the case of software development, Chester and O'Brien (1995) pointed out that there is much fruitful interaction between the specifier and the programmer that allows criticism of each other's work. When one person is employed instead of two, the chance for this criticism is lost. It is rare to find a human being who is capable of being as critical of their own work as would be another qualified people. The statement of Aron (1983) that *'no amount of additional effort will help the builder [of a product] to see a remaining error'* once they are convinced it is correct, is true not just for program code, but for any deliverable. Also, Chester and O'Brien (1995) write that: *'If one person is employed to specify a program and also to carry out the design, code and testing of that same program, then there are great dangers that errors, gaps, redundancies, and obfuscations will not be discovered until it is far too late'.*

The critical approach to software development suggests that great care must be taken so that ways of working do not reduce the possibilities for the important function of the criticism of deliverable hypotheses by qualified personnel.

9. CONCLUSION

The modern philosophy of science can be usefully employed to cast light upon the way software is developed. In particular, the views of Karl Popper that no scientific theory can ever be proved can be extended to suggest that no software development deliverable can ever be proved to be a correct representation of the user's requirements.

Scientific theories are tested empirically and also criticised by other scientists. All deliverables are the developers' hypotheses of what is actually needed and must be tested empirically if possible, but also subjected to the criticism of qualified personnel other than the originating developer.

This critical approach to software development leads to a critique of the claims of some formal methods proponents about the correctness of the deliverables produced by such techniques. Also, the fact that criticism can only be effectively carried out by qualified people leads to the suspicion that some practices of prototyping are suspect because unqualified users are utilised to test and criticise the prototyped system. Furthermore, the employment of analyst-programmers can be questioned because the practice of using one member of staff where two were used before can reduce the possibilities of criticism of each other's work.

Philosophy can be used to criticise the way software developers work. A careful review of the views of the modern philosophers of science may allow computing professionals to obtain a deeper understanding of the practices they carry out to develop software.

References

Aron, J. D., *The program development process – the individual programmer.* Addison-Wesley, Reading, Massachusetts, 1983.

Ayer, A. J., *Language, truth and logic.* Gollancz, London, 1936.

Ayer, A. J., *Language, truth and logic (2ⁿᵈ Ed.).* Penguin, Harmondsworth, England, 1972.

Ayer, A. J. (ed.), *Logical positivism.* Free Press, Glencoe, 1959.

Bell, E. T., *Men of mathematics vol. 2.* Penguin Books, Harmondsworth, Middlesex, 1953.

Chalmers, A. F., *What is this thing called science (2ⁿᵈ Ed.).* Open University Press, Milton Keynes, 1982.

Chester, M. F., *Analyst-programmers and their effect upon software engineering practices,* (Dissertation for MSc in Information Technology). University of Nottingham, Nottingham, 1992.

Chester, M. F. and O'Brien, M., 'Analyst-programmers seen as harmful to software quality.' *Third BCS-ISM Conference on Information Systems Methodologies,* 1995, pp. 63-74.

Chester, M. F., 'The logic of scientific systems development.' *EASE-98,* Keele, 1998.

Dijkstra, E., 'Guarded commands, nondeterminacy and formal derivation of programs.' *CACM, vol.* 18, 1975, pp. 453-457.

Dijkstra, E., 'On the cruelty of really teaching computer science.' *CACM,* vol. 32, 12, 1989, pp. 1398-1404.

Goguen, J. A., *Four pieces on error, truth and reality.* Technical Monograph PRG-89, Oxford University Computing Laboratory, Oxford,1990.

Hume, D., *A treatise of human nature.* Dent, London, (1974), 1739.

Kant, I., *Critique of pure reason.* (Everyman edition, 1934), Dent, London,1781.

Magee, B., *The great philosophers.* Oxford University Press, Oxford, 1988.

Popper, K., *Logic der Forschung, translated into English as The Logic of Scientific Discovery, 3rd edition, 1968,* Hutchinson, London, 1934.

Popper, K., *Objective knowledge.* Oxford University Press, Oxford, 1972.

Popper, K., *Unended quest: an intellectual autobiography.* Collins, Glasgow, 1976.

Popper, K., *Realism and the aim of science.* Routledge, London,1983.

Russell, B., *A history of western philosophy.* Counterpoint edition 1984, Allen & Unwin, London, 1912.

CHAPTER 51

AN ARISTOTELIAN APPROACH TO THE METHODOLOGICAL RESEARCH: A METHOD FOR DATA MODELS CONSTRUCTION

Esperanza Marcos and Alfredo Marcos
University Rey Juan Carlos, University of Valladolid

Abstract

Software Engineering (SE) research differs in nature from empirical and formal sciences. It shows as well some special traits in relation to other technological disciplines. For this reason, traditional research methods are not always directly applicable to the research in the SE field. In this paper, we discuss the nature of the SE research and the complex net of relationships that it maintains with other branches of knowledge. We conclude that new research methods more adapted to the SE research are needed. Focusing on a specific aspect of this field, the database modelling, we propose a method for the object model construction.
'Generally, I start my courses on the Scientific Method saying to my students that the scientific method doesn't exist' (Popper, 1985).

1. INTRODUCTION

From the XVI century on, an important advance in scientific development took place. This advance also affected to the research methods. For this reason, new research methods, more appropriated to the scientific studies of the age (astronomy, medicine, mathematics and physics), were developed. Descartes (1970) disqualified the scholastic logic, and he developed new mathematical and *deductive* methods. Bacon (1975) wrote at length on *empirical* methods as a radical change from the scholastic methods. Among the empirical methods we can include *inductive* method and *hypothetical-deductive* method.

These three methods (deductive, inductive and hypothetical-deductive), with their different variants, constitute the methods of scientific research used now. The hypothetical-deductive is, perhaps, the most commonly used method because, besides its empirical character, it pay attention to creativity and deductive reasoning. However, from the XVI century until now, knowledge has experienced important advances and new disciplines, like SE, have been developed. In our opinion, engineering research differs in nature from traditional sciences. For this reason, in the same way that in the XVI century new research methods more appropriated to the science of the age arose, now, it is necessary to define other ones that are applicable to the concrete problems of the SE research.

In the section 2 we review some different classifications of disciplines. We analyse which of them are more appropriated for our methodological query. In the section 3 we propose a research method for a concrete problem of the SE: the data models construction, applying it to the MIMO metamodel definition. The study of a research method for a concrete and typical problem of the SE, will allow us justifying in a practical way the thesis defended in this paper. At the same time, it will allow us arguing in depth about the differences between traditional research (hypothetical-deductive method has been chosen for the discussion) and research in the SE field. Section 4 summarises the most relevant conclusions of the paper.

2   SOFTWARE ENGINEERING: WHAT KIND OF DISCIPLINE IS IT?

Maybe the most common classification of sciences is the following one: the *formal sciences* (logic and mathematics) that use deductive research methods, and the *empirical sciences* (for instance, biology, chemistry, etc. and, according to some authors, human and social sciences, as anthropology or history) that use empirical research methods (inductive and hypothetical-deductive).

Engineering is obviously connected with scientific disciplines, but it cannot be classify neither as formal nor as empirical sciences. *Empirical sciences*, in order to find some answer to many questions, focus on the study of the existent objects. In this way, through the hypothesis creation, observation and experiment, they can get answers to these questions. On the other hand, engineering *builds* new objects. In this sense, engineering doesn't look just for knowledge *on* certain objects, but it looks mainly for *knowing how to build* new objects.

It is also obvious that we cannot classify engineering as *formal sciences* although these ones are an essential base for engineering (specially for SE). Engineering, in contrast with formal science, needs to be consider as a productive discipline. Mathematics are generally considered (see Bung, 1985) as a very useful discipline for any other science and for technology, since it allows us formulating scientific and technological knowledge in a rigorous manner. Logic is usually employed as a formal language. Since Bertrand Russell (1977) posed the idea that mathematics is just logic both areas of knowledge have progressively approached.

Bunge (1976) proposes another classification that sorts the sciences in *pure* and *applied* sciences. According to Bunge, technologies are applied sciences. He considers, for example, the electric engineering as a physical technology, or the medicine as a biological technology. According to this classification, we don't know where the SE, as well as other engineering branches, should be classified. The reason is that SE, as well as the other engineering disciplines, is not a *mere* application of other sciences, and, in any event, SE is not a direct application of *just one* pure science.

This idea is upheld by Aracil (1986), who strongly criticise thinkers who don't consider engineering as sciences, but as mere applied sciences. However, Aracil distinguishes between science and engineering. According to this author, the main difference is that sciences study how things are, whereas the engineering focus on how things should be in order to build new objects. He states, *'the sciences are in charge of natural things, while the specific domain of the engineering is the artificial things'*.

The study of *how things should be* suggests an interesting relation between engineering and other areas of practical knowledge, like ethics or politics, because all of them are connected with human action and its "methodology". The "methodology" of ethics is, basically, the prudence, that takes into account the time and circumstances, as the urgency or the profitability, that traditional sciences don't consider.

Engineering research is, in fact, different from traditional scientific research, but we should not overemphasise their differences until the limit of forgetting their common traits: on the one hand, traditional science is not just knowledge, but also action; on the other hand, engineering produces nor just action and objects, but also knowledge. The traditional concept of science could be enlarged in order to include, besides empirical and formal sciences, those called by Aracil *engineering sciences*. Another possibility is to keep the distinction between science and engineering. We think that this is just a terminological question. It is a more important task to identify the common traits and the differences.

Besides the philosophers of science, there are other relevant authors in the SE area claiming for the need of defining an "engineering science". So, for instance, Blum (1996) distinguishes between science and technology and compare the task of scientists and engineers. Blum states: *'I reject the narrow definition of software engineering coming from the computer sciences; indeed, I intend to design a new computer science for software engineering...'*, and he continues defining the computer technology science as *'the study of transforming ideas into operations'*.

As we have already said, the SE could fit in Aracil's *engineering sciences* or in Blum's *computer technology sciences*. Independently of the term we use for the SE classification, we can affirm that it is not possible to consider the SE as a traditional science (either formal or empirical science). For this reason no traditional method of scientific research (see, for instance, Chalmers (1984), Fetzer (1993)), can be applied to the research in the SE field without adaptation. In addition, SE is not a simple applied science. In the last years, philosophers of science, has reasonably insisted that science is also action, not just knowledge; in a correlative way, we should insist that the engineering is also knowledge, and not just application. The difference between science and technology can be found in the ways that action and knowledge are developed in both of them but not in that, the first one just knows and the second one just applies.

There are different research topics related with the SE. The most classic could be the model, methodology, technique, metric, etc. definitions. However, some of them have an experimental character. It is important to outline that when we speak of the research in SE, we refer to the resolution of those problems whose nature is purely of engineering, such as the construction of new models or methods. In these cases, it is not possible to apply experimental methods, since the object of study doesn't still exist. According to Gallego (1987), the object of the empirical science *'resides outside us and it just exists in the external world'*. Therefore, their knowledge is, basically, an experimental nature knowledge and, in addition, such a experimentation should be based on the reality. As Fetzer (1993) states: *'The science needs more than 'empirical adaptation' to be successful'*, it needs knowing reality. This is not the case of the engineering whose knowledge has an important component of creativity that hinders the elaboration of a method for the problem resolution inside this environment. However, once the new object has been created (for example, a new data model), this become a real object. In this moment, it is already an existent object that will be susceptible of study by empirical methods.

SE contacts in some way with traditional science, and it is obviously related with other technological disciplines, as well as, in other aspects, it is close to the practical wisdom. So, SE could obtain methodological inspiration from all this fields, and conversely, no method imported from another discipline could be directly applies without adaptation. In this sense, we can get valuable suggestions exploring and applying to our case the Aristotelian classification of sciences (see Grene (1985)). Aristotle classifies sciences according to different dimensions (see table 1).

We find the Aristotelian classification of sciences a good guide to our research because it is *multidimensional* and *comprehensive*: on one hand, it sorts sciences by different criteria, and, on the other hand, the notion of science here is quite wide, it includes natural sciences as well as ethics, technique or theology.

In both senses (by its multidimensionality and by its comprehensiveness), the Aristotelian classification fits better with our purposes than other traditional divisions, like *formal versus empirical sciences, pure vs. applied science, science vs. technology*, or *human vs. natural sciences*.

SE produces abstract entities, like models. In the measure it produces such devices, and they must work inside a computational system, it should act as any other technological discipline. However, the abstract character of its typical outcomes approaches SE to formal sciences. SE also yields the know-how connected with model construction, and in this sense, as a knowledge on procedures, SE resembles other branches of practical wisdom, like ethics or politics.

Criteria	Sciences classification
According to its results	-Theoretic sciences: the main result is knowledge (mathematics, natural sciences...) -Practical sciences: the main result is an action (ethics, politics...) -Productive sciences: the main result is an object (techniques, as pottery or sculpture, fit here)
According to the kind of entities took as study objects	-Some sciences study substances (theology, natural sciences...) -Other ones study entities that are not substances (mathematics, ethics, politics...) -Finally, other sciences study what Aristotle calls "accidental substances" (techniques)
According to the type of necessity of its reasoning	-Absolute necessity: mathematics, theology -Hypothetical necessity: natural sciences, ethics, politics, techniques
According to the lasting time of its object	-Eternal: mathematics, theology -Non eternal: natural sciences, ethics, politics, techniques
According the tense of its premises	-Present tense: theology, mathematics -Future tense: natural sciences, ethics, politics, techniques
According the kind of acting causes	-Only formal and final causes: theology -Only Form and something alike to mater: mathematics -Formal, material, final and efficient cause: natural sciences, ethics, politics, techniques

Table 1: Classification of sciences according to Aristotle.
Summary and figure taken from Marcos (1996)

SE reasoning is typically hypothetical or conditional: "if we want to develop such or such computational tools, we should proceed this or that way". SE procedures and products are necessary only in the case we are looking for satisfying a given demand, so its reasoning goes hypothetically. This trait brings SE close to other technological disciplines and to other branches of practical wisdom. Formal sciences, on the contrary, has traditionally been the field of absolute necessity (this is not the place to discuss whether Aristotle were or not right in attributing hypothetical necessity to natural science).

The question on what kind of entities SE produces and studies is still for us an open one. Maybe the models of SE must be viewed as substances, or as abstract properties of a more basic substance, like information, or as accidental substances. However, the second options seems to us the more probable one. If this is the case, SE would be closer to formal sciences than to other technological disciplines, which products are always accidental substances (in Aristotelian terminology).

We cannot decide here on the lasting time of SE study objects, and we recognise that it is a complex question linked with the philosophy of formal science. SE models, as other abstract entities devised by the mathematicians, exhibits a double face: on the one hand they have been discovered at a given moment, but, on the other hand, they are outside the temporal course because its abstract character. Nevertheless, we can let aside this problem that perhaps lacks methodological implications. It is also an open problem the question of causality, but probably it should also be approached along the lines of general philosophy of formal sciences.

Regarding the tense of the premises, SE resembles more technology and practical wisdom than any other discipline. The reasoning in SE starts from premises in future tense dealing with future states of affairs that we want to produce, to avoid or to improve. SE, in contrast with natural and formal science, must take into account temporal and local circumstances, like the urgency, the economical resources, the current state of the hardware, the market demands, the commonly acknowledged values, like confidentiality, and so on... The importance of temporal and local circumstances in SE reasoning brings it close to practical wisdom.

Once we have discussed the nature of SE along the relevant dimensions of this classification, and the net of connections we can envisage from it, we are in a better position to apply and adapt a plurality of methodological guidelines to a particular research case.

In the following section, a research method for the resolution of a characteristic problem of the SE is proposed. This application to a concrete problem will allow arguing about each carried out step, understanding in which way they are different of a traditional research. For the comparison, the hypothetical-deductive method has been chosen since, besides being now the most extended method, it combines aspects of the empirical and deductive methods.

3 DEFINITION OF A METHOD FOR DATA MODEL CONSTRUCTION

Next, an overview of a SE research method, proposed in Marcos (1997), is presented. The method has a generic part (figure 1) and a specific part (figure 2). The first one is applicable to any research type. The second one is the method to resolve the specific problem and it will change depending on the concrete problem that we want to solve. In some cases, this part could be based on other existent methods as, for example, the experimental one. In this part, we will explain the method used for a real case: the construction of an object metamodel, called MIMO, for the database design.

MIMO was conceived as an object metamodel that should support the database design in the different development phases (analysis, design and construction). Whit this aim, MIMO should integrate the main existent object models: UML (analysis and design), ODMG and SQL3 (design and construction).

The generic method is a general method of work, figure 1, based on the steps to follow, according to Bunge (1976), in every scientific research. Although these steps are based on the hypothetical-deductive method, due to their generality, they are applicable, with certain modifications, to any research type and even to the resolution of any problem type that we try to solve. It consists of the following steps:

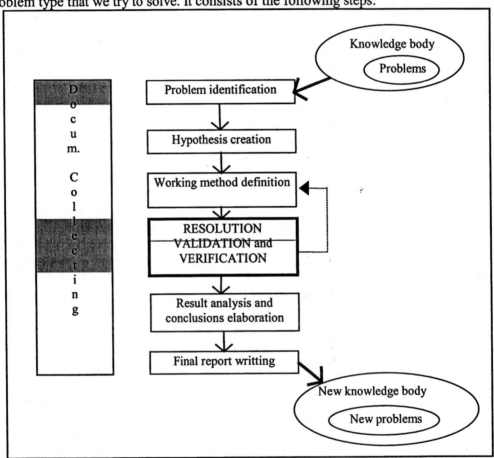

Figure 1: Generic research method

3.1   Problem identification
The first step consists on determining, among the problems without solving inside our knowledge field, which one we are going to solve. Whit this aim, firstly, those problems whose resolution can give place to a research work (according to Bunge, to a work of scientific research) are selected. Among the selected problems, we have to choose just one. It, as the professor A. Olivé explained in the II JIDBD[vii] (Madrid 1996), will have to be a novel topic (that is to say, a non-resolved problem) and with some practical interest. It should also be, in our opinion, a resoluble problem in a reasonable period with the

available means. In addition, we think that it is also important that the chosen topic arouse a special interest in the investigators involved in the work.

3.2 Hypothesis creation

Once defined the problem to be broached, we have to go on with the following step that consists on the work hypothesis definition. In the traditional methods of scientific research, the hypothesis is formulated in causal terms (if A happens then B happens). These hypotheses are fact conjectures that the scientific method will have to contrast and to verify. The following sentence could be an example of a casual hypothesis: "if the level of noise affects to the attention degree of an individual, a noise that super a certain threshold can diminish the efficiency of an individual realising a work". According with a scientific method (in this case an empirical method) "experiments", measuring levels of noise and attention, will have to be done in order to draw conclusions from the defined hypothesis.

However, it is easy to check that the hypothesis in a SE research, in general, does not fit with a cause-effect position. The reason is, as we have already said, the differences between the nature of the SE research and the nature of the traditional sciences research. If we formulated the hypothesis in causal terms, we would also change the aim and the character of our research. It is important to remember that the aim of our research is the construction of a new metamodel that, not existing yet, it is not susceptible of experimentation. Therefore, the hypothesis will be formulated as the description of the new object that we want to build (in our case, it will be the description of an object metamodel).

3.3 Working method definition

None of the studied methods proposes, as a phase of the method, the definition of the method to follow for the problem resolution, verification and validation. However, see figure 2, we consider that it is necessary since, against the opinion of Bunge (1976), we think that there are not an universal method of problem resolution, but each problem requires its own method. However, several authors disagree with Bunge. So, for example, Popper (1985) states: *'Generally, I start my courses on the Scientific Method saying to my students that the scientific method doesn't exist'*. In the same way, Chalmers (1992) defends the thesis that there is not an universal method. In fact, in our case, it is not possible to detail the method for the new model definition phase that constitutes, in fact, the problem resolution centre. The method will consist, fundamentally, of studying the existent models, reflecting about them and determining its advantages and limitations. Finally, a new model will be proposed and, this one will have to support the advantages of the studied models, overcoming, as much as possible, the found limitations in the previous studies. Getting a better proposal of model will depend, in a great extend, on the creativity and common sense applied to the new model construction. Kosso (1992) speaks of the similarity between the scientific reasoning and the general reasoning and he states: *'between science and common sense there are only some shades of differences'*.

In addition, there should be a feedback between the resolution validation and verification phase and the phase of the working method definition (indicated by a discontinuous line in figure 1), because, in our opinion, the working method is refined as you advance in the problem resolution. So, we can say that the definition of the working method does not conclude until the resolution, validation and verification phase has concluded.

3.4   Resolution, verification and validation

Figure 2 summarises the method to follow for the resolution, validation and verification of our concrete problem: definition of an object metamodel. We can observe that the proposed method is closer to some methods traditionally used in SE than to the methods of scientific research. The reason is that the character of the problem to solve is also nearer to the problems of the SE environment than to the problems that the scientific research tries to solve. Resolution, verification and validation phases are presented together since there is a feedback between them, in such a way that the complete resolution process includes also the verification and validation steps.

Scientific research methods and, particularly the one proposed by Bunge (1976), only point out the necessity to verify the posed hypothesis (or the proposed theory in the formal sciences). However, in our case, the ***verification stage*** has two different tasks: the *validation* task, that means checking that the model has been built according to the posed hypothesis, and the *verification* one, that means checking that it has been correctly built, that is to say it is a consistent model.

The resolution phase could correspond to the hypothesis creation in an empirical method or to the theory elaboration in a deductive method. In this way, verification of the empirical method would be equivalent to validation in our method, while the theory verification in a deductive method would be equal to the consistency proving in our method, that is to say, to the real verification task.

3.5   Result analysis and conclusions elaboration

In this phase, the posed hypothesis at the beginning of the research is contrasted with the achieved results. It should be checked in which manner the objectives have been fulfilled, as well as the degree in which the problem has been solved. In this phase, it is very important to define those aspects that has not been possible to solve, as well as the new arisen problems as a consequence of the research. These new problems will become starting points of new research works.

3.6   Final report writing

In this phase, a systematic report explaining the research we have carried out, has to be drawn up. It has to detail: the work hypothesis, the justification of the work, the used research method, the research process, the obtained conclusions and the studied bibliography. In addition, it will have to detail any other relevant question for the understanding and evaluation of the developed work, as well as for future investigator that want to continue the undertaken work. In this phase, it is convenient to stand out the importance of the "research ethics".

At the end of the research work, the initial knowledge body has been modified (generally, it will have been enlarged) and the starting problems has changed. Some of them will have been solved, others will have been modified (diminish or not) and, in addition, new problems, originated by the carried out research, will arise. This new knowledge body, with its new problems, will give rise to other research works.

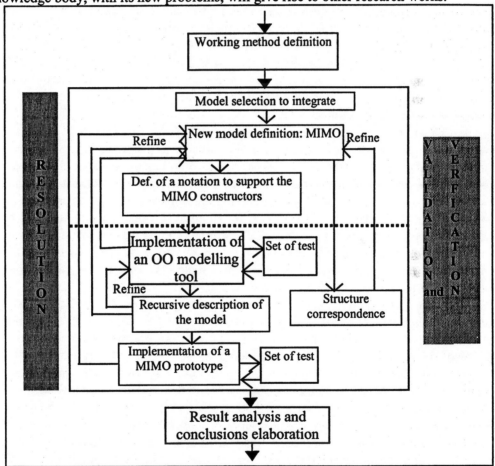

Figure 2: Working method for the concrete problem resolution

3.7   Documentation collecting
Documentation collecting generally appears as the first stage in every research work. However, in our opinion, it has to be acquired, and analysed, during the whole research

process. Nevertheless, there are two phases in which this task should be specially intense: during the problem identification because it is necessary to collect a lot of general documentation; during the resolution, verification and validation phase because it is necessary to consult the a more specific bibliography about the concrete problem. The documentation collecting task will be prolonged until the research process concluded, in order to be up to day about the related works.

4   CONCLUSIONS

The character of research in engineering, and in particular in SE, differs from traditional sciences (empirical and formal sciences). For this reason, traditional methods of scientific research (deductive, inductive, hypothetical-deductive and their variants) are not completely appropriate for the SE research. It is necessary to keep in mind that the aim of the engineering is the creation of new objects, while the experimental and formal sciences seems to study the existent objects. Formal sciences analyse, by contrast with empirical sciences, abstract objects.

In this paper we have argue about the special nature of SE and about the reasons because traditional research methods are not always appropriate for SE research. Following as a guide the Aristotelian classification of sciences we have envisaged the complex net of relationships SE maintains with other disciplines, not only with formal and empirical sciences, but also with other branches of technology as well as with practical wisdom. As an example, a method for the object model construction has been posed. This method was used in a real Ph.D. research work. It was defined for a specific case of research inside the SE environment, but it could be used, with not many modifications, in a great number of problems: methods construction, definition of another type of models (functional, dynamic...), etc.

Despite the terminological discussions, arguing whether it should be called *engineering sciences* or *techniques*, it is important that SE starts to investigate in a rigorous and proper manner. SE research have to be as rigorous as the research in traditional sciences in order to be considered as serious as the research in other knowledge branches. For this reason, it is indispensable to use rigorous research methods (traditionally called scientific methods), but adapted to this new area of knowledge.

Now, we are working in a generic method applicable to any research problem in the SE field whenever this problem was a typical problem of engineering. However, this method won't be valid for those problems that, still belonging to the SE environment, are not really engineering problems. So, for example, the data modelling (model construction) is an engineering topic, but the database query optimisation (a very close problem to the data modelling) cannot be considered as an engineering problem. Experimental methods fit better to this kind of problems. For this reason, the first necessary step should be the classification of the problems relative to the SE. This classification will allow deciding how many research methods are necessary in order to cover the most relevant SE problems.

Acknowledgements

We want to thank A. de Miguel and M. Piattini for their valuable comments on a previous version of this work. This paper is a part of a research program supported by the Government of Castilla y León which reference is VA 46/98.

References

Aracil, J. (1986). Máquinas, sistemas y modelos. Un ensayo sebre sistemática. TECNOS, S. A. Madrid,.

Bacon, F. (1975). Novum Organum Scienciarum. Translated by Larroyo. Porrúa, México.

Blum, (1996). Beyond Programming: To a New Era of Design. Oxford University Press.

Bunge, M. (1976). La Investigación Científica. Ariel, Barcelona.

Bunge, M. (1985). Epistemología. Ariel, Barcelona.

Chalmers, A. (1984). ¿Qué es esa cosa llamada ciencia?. Siglo XXI de España Editores, Madrid, 2ª edition.

Chalmers, A. (1992). La ciencia y como se elabora. Siglo XXI de España Editores, Madrid.

Descartes, R. (1970). Discurso del Método. Translated by García Morente. Espasa Calpe, Barcelona.

Fetzer, J.H. (1993). Philosophy of Science. Paragon House. United States.

Gallego, (1987). Ser Doctor. Cómo redactar una Tesis Doctoral. Fundación Universidad-Empresa. Monografías Profesionales:107. Madrid.

Grene, M. (1985) 'About the Division of Sciences'. In Gotthelf, A. (ed.). Aristotle on Nature and Living Things, Mathesis Publications and Bristol Classical Press, Pittsburgh.

Kosso, P. (1992). Reading the Book of Nature. An Introduction to the Philosophy of Science. Cambridge University Press.

Marcos, A. (1996). Aristóteles y otros animales. Una lectura filosófica de la Biología aristotélica. PPU, Barcelona.

Marcos E. (1997). MIMO: Propuesta de un Metamodelo de Objetos y su Aplicación al Diseño de Bases de Datos. Doctoral Thesis. Faculty de Informatique (U.P.M.). Madrid.

Popper K. (1985). Realismo y el objetivo de la ciencia. Tecnos, Madrid.

Russell B. (1977). Los Principios de la Matemática. Espasa Calpe, Madrid.

---

vii Round table on research taken place in the II working days about databases research and teaching. University Carlos III from Madrid, July of 1996.

CHAPTER 52

RAPID AND PARTICIPATORY IS ANALYSIS AND DESIGN: A MEANS TO DEFY THE 'ANATOMY OF CONFUSION'?

Simon Bell
Open University,

1. CONFUSION IN IS?

Those working in the field of information systems (IS) development are well aware that the field is confusing and complex. It is confusing in that the basic rules and properties of the field are in a constant state of flux. It is complex in that the field is young and is continuing to diversify and extend into new domains. The potent mixture of confusion and complexity extends across all areas of the field. At any time it appears that the developers of new technologies are confused (e.g. see Collins and Bicknell 1997), that the providers of IS 'solutions' are confused (e.g. the description of the London Ambulance information system Bicknell 1993), that the developers of information systems (no matter how well supported and financed) are confused (e.g. City of London Taurus project Drummond 1996) and that the final users of all technology based information systems are in a constant state of confusion, occasionally relieved by plateaus of peace (e.g. the brief period when the 286 chip was dominant and the rate of change in applications software seemed to slow down for a while). Technologists, IS developers, retailers and users seem to regularly share in the confusion of the field.

Checkland and Holwell ascribe this confusion largely to the accelerating pace of technology and the inability of theory to keep up. As soon as the practitioners have tested and documented some new case of IT development and the theorists are pondering upon the meaning and impact of such technology (e.g. the advent of ISDN lines and groupware and implications for distance working) then the technology moves on again and the process of theorising is groping to keep up.

The processes by which IS are planned and designed come under the category of analysis and design. Of course there are numerous IS design approaches:

- The highly structured and documentational (e.g. see the various texts which deal with Structured Systems Analysis and Design Methodology (SSADM) such as Ashworth and Goodland 1990).

- The people centred (for example the approaches advocated by Mumford 1995; Checkland and Holwell 1998).
- The approaches which are essentially machine-based such as Rapid Applications Development - RAD - (see the description in Jones and King 1998).

These three categories are not exhaustive but are indicative of the range of approaches. Structured, machine-based and human activity focused approaches all have their values and related problems and all require different skills and training in their practitioners. However, even with the range of approaches available to the organisation for planning the development of IS - there continues to be confusion and copious examples of IS failure.

Nowhere is the process of confusion more evident than in the experience of the developing countries and transitional economies in their relationship with IT/IS. Theorists and practitioners in industrialised countries have severe problems with IT and the development of IS. These problems are compounded when issues of poverty, poor infrastructure and lack of training and education are evident.

2. DEVELOPING COUNTRIES/ TRANSITIONAL ECONOMIES AND IS

IS projects and Developing Country/ Transitional Economy (DC/TE) status combine to make very complex projects. Anecdotally the failure rate of such projects is very high and the negative impacts such projects can have on organisations in these contexts can also be high. Researchers and consultants moving into the area of IT/IS projects in DC/TEs are in a particularly vulnerable position - especially if these researchers and consultants are not indigenous people and have the further difficulty of not having a wide ranging understanding of the local context. They can see themselves as being between two highly risk-prone realities of confusion and complexity - development projects and IT projects.

Thinking about projects in DCs in particular and drawing from the work of Biggs (Biggs 1989) it can be argued that IT/IS projects are following along a well-worn path of technological assistance. Biggs describes the experiences of research scientists working on agricultural research stations in developing countries in the 1980s. Although they were developing agricultural technologies for local farming communities they were often isolated and isolating in their practice. Often remote from the community which they are expected to serve, there is a detailed history of research based on agricultural research stations being misdirected and misapplied. Biggs argues that this was because scientists based their work on professional assumptions about problems rather than on problems actually faced by farmers. In ascertaining why many projects based on research–station technology are not successful with local farmers, Biggs addresses two issues:

- Firstly, the process of technology adoption and questions relating to the value of experts' work when divorced from local needs and aspirations.
- Secondly, the capability and willingness of farmers to make use of 'solutions' not tested and improved by themselves.

More recently, Chambers (Chambers 1997 / page 205) has emphasised this point concerning the 'expert' and has criticised the traditional development project as being essentially non-participatory and working off an expert-view rather than the equally (if not more so) important view of local stakeholders. The conclusion to this is the startling observation that expert opinion grounded in local need and undertaken with local consent and participation has a greater chance of being relevant and sustainable than approaches which are characterised by remote, aloof, technology-driven fixes. Yet the fix or "solution" model would appear to be the model driving most IT projects.

If the development project side of the issue is confusing and complex, the IT element might be seen as being worse. The litany of disasters relating to IT are numerous. Both private and public sectors are prone to massive IT project failure (£80 million in the case of Taurus) . It has become an issue beyond the computer press with main-line television programmes such as the UK BBC's "Money Programme" alluding to a "Computer Triangle" causing the failure. The "triangle" is an interesting phenomena. In this programme the problems of IT projects are related to:

- Experts. These are often more of a source of problems than an aid to problem solving.
- IT systems designed without reference to existing packages and tried and tested fixes.
- The ownership of the IT project - who is in charge?
- These three issues can be summarised as relating to:
- The appropriateness of the expert,
- `The appropriateness of the package and,
- The identification of the owner

Similar issues have been expressed by Collins (Collins and Bicknell 1997). The triangular model described above has a lot in common with the views of development project failure set out earlier in this section. Biggs identified the expert as remote from the problem context. Chambers notes the problem of inappropriate technological solutions and also the problem of ownership of projects in terms of participation and inclusion in decision making processes. Most recently Checkland has indicated that information systems projects are often driven by outdated theories of organisational processes (Checkland and Holwell 1998). The triangle would seem to have relevance to both IT and development project contexts. My concern as an academic and a practitioner is to address the difficulties in the domain of IS adoption in DC/ TEs and set out a process approach which might aid all those involved in avoiding the confusion.

3. RAPID INFORMATION SYSTEMS DEVELOPMENT (RISD) AS A HEURISTIC DEVISE IN IS PLANNING

An observation arising from preliminary research was that highly detailed and exhaustively documented approaches to IS (such as SSADM) were generally not applied (through lack of training or fear of the daunting 'manuals' which came with them maybe). Where such approaches are applied they are often applied badly and the only alternative appeared to be the imposition of technology without any form of planning at all. RISD/ Multiview arose as a suggestion for dealing with this confusion. The RISD/ Multiview idea is simple in form, being an adapted and simplified version of the Multiview approach originally devised by Avison and Wood-Harper (Avison and Wood-Harper 1990). Multiview, as originally devised is a five 'view' methodology for investigating and developing information systems.

This five-step approach advocated by Avison and Wood-Harper was further expanded in Bell and Wood-Harper (Bell and Wood-Harper 1998) to a sixth stage involving the development of hardware, software, training and implementation strategies. It is argued that the team involved in analysis and design is often best placed in the organisation to recommend on procurement and implementation strategy.   This view was further reinforced by research/ experience which indicated that those who produce the procurement list often pay scant attention to the results of analysis and design.

In essence Multiview in its RISD form is intended to allow the problem context in which an IS is being proposed to be viewed from a number of perspectives, from a number of epistemological stances, in a number of sensible ways. The reasoning behind this approach relates to the value of gaining a range of perspectives - this value can be gauged in terms of:

- Triangulation - perspectives will re-inforce or contradict each other reducing the potential for single view errors (e.g. taking one standpoint and then seeing all problems in terms of that standpoint).
- Confirmation - the process of RISD/ Multiview increases the likelihood that presenting problems will be confirmed as actual problems.
- Reflective practice - the action research requirement of the RISD/ Multiview approach requires the analysis team to change role in the context and reflect upon their practice

The major intended strength of the RISD/ Multiview approach is the manner in which the approach can be applied rapidly by non-specialists in a cyclic and learning/ reflective practitioner manner (a theme later developed in Bell 1996; Bell 1997). The central themes of RISD as developed from Multiview was that information systems could be planned rapidly (or existing plans rapidly reviewed) by means of a non-specialist team, ideally with assistance initially anyway by a person with familiarity with the approach, with the approach being used as a template of good practice and as a means to develop the successive stages of the IS in a systemic and systematic manner. Further, the approach can be seen as a cycle of IS thinking with the team, or elements of it, constantly reviewing the IS in place (the implemented IS) and the IS in plan (the potential evolution of the IS). This cyclic form of adoption is set out in Figure 1. The figure demonstrates RISD as a cycle with the review and planning of IS always beginning with an adapted Soft Systems Methodology analysis (SSM) and resulting in the planning of the procurement components of the system and implementation strategy. To reiterate, the cycle indicates that the approach is on-going and that the themes for RISD are participation, evolution and continuous learning.

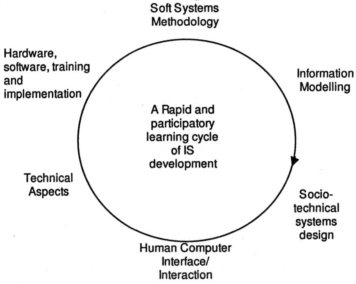

Figure 1: RISD/ Multiview as a Learning Cycle

4. AVOIDING CONFUSION?

One of the primary requirements of RISD is to provide a rapid and participatory approach to IS design which avoids the majority of the problems of IT and development projects set out in section 2 above and at the same time allows the planners of such systems to respond rapidly to changes in technology. Such systems will inevitably tend to be 'fairly quick and fairly clean' and, although far from perfect, are designed to provide sensible and useful information. Further, I argue that this approach, derived from work in participation in developing countries and transitional economies and eclectic methodology building in the UK has potential for use in many contexts in the industrialised countries where approaches to IS tend to exclude the majority of employees within organisations whilst appearing bureaucratic and over proceduralised.

In 1994 I was involved in the development of a Management Information System (MIS) in China (see Bell and Minghze 1995). This first phase of an MIS project was developed making use of both RISD/ Multiview analysis and design approach and the Logical Framework approach to project planning. The 1994 cycle of RISD/ Multiview activity undertaken in participation with Chinese colleagues produced a design which was to prove relevant and useful as well as practical. During Phase 1 I worked with Chinese colleagues both in China and the UK on the six stages of RISD, developing the plan of the system in four weeks and then assisting local staff in developing this as a software platform over the following six months. To some extent only time will tell how valuable the exercise has been but despite inevitable difficulties with implementing and developing the system in a rapid manner (e.g. the rate of change evident in the Chinese economy and the inevitable impacts which this had in terms of necessary modifications to project design), there were significant successes in terms of levels of training, competence in systems development and the ability to turn learning into new, evolutionary systems. Now in 1998 there is an opportunity for further development in the second phase of the project. This phase is also being planned in participation with local staff and is now based upon the learning cycle approach to analysis and design - building off the success and failures, strengths and weaknesses of the first phase (see Figure 2.). Phase 2 will begin with the new team reviewing the good and bad points of the first analysis and developing their new IS from the basis of this evaluation. RISD/ Multiview now contains explicit use of the Learning Organisation approach as developed by Senge (Senge, Ross et al. 1994) and this approach has now been adopted and adapted by the Chinese organisation in question (Linsheng 1998).

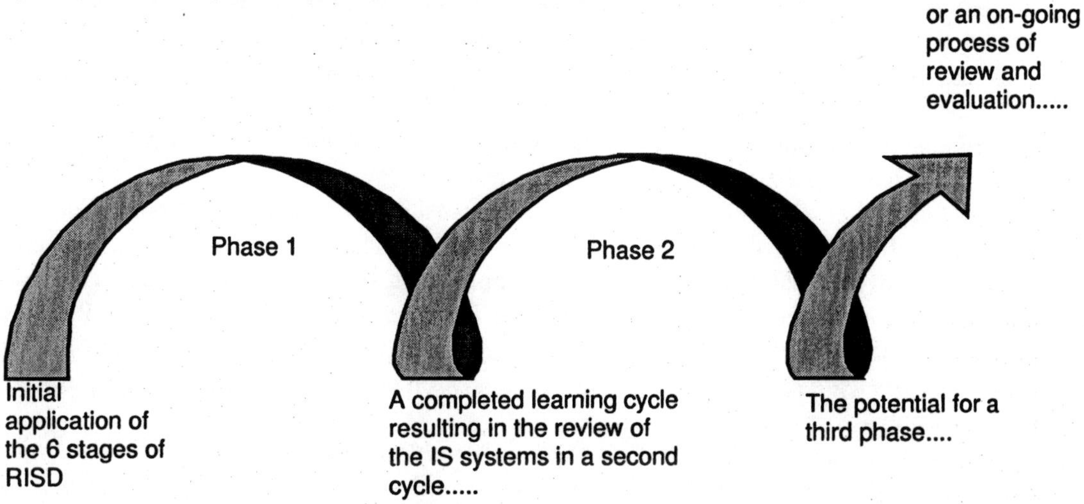

or an on-going process of review and evaluation.....

Phase 1

Phase 2

Initial application of the 6 stages of RISD

A completed learning cycle resulting in the review of the IS systems in a second cycle.....

The potential for a third phase....

Figure 2: Learning Cycles in the use of RISD

The Learning Organisation (LO) five elements (systems thinking, personal mastery, mental models, team working and shared vision) are applied by means of a reflective exercise during each of the six stages of RISD/ Multiview. It is the intention of the approach that LO, when applied with systems analysis, should provide the practitioner team with the prompts to question the information that is being gathered and reviewed. RISD/ Multiview is intended as a learning approach undertaken as an action research project. The inclusion of reflection on the five learning organisation disciplines should result in learning (both positive and negative) being retained by the team and taken forward for future analysis.

All analysis and design produces mixed results. As indicated in the section above in discussing phase 1 of the current project and in section 2 of this paper, all approaches to analysis and design are capable of producing spectacular negative as well as positive results and this is in part a limitation of the approach and in part is due to unforeseen problems and changed contexts in the organisation in question. In my own use of RISD/ Multiview I have recorded mixed results (e.g. see Bell 1996; Bell 1996). My claim would be that the use of RISD when applied rapidly is low cost, practical and results in the useful outcome of the organisation benefiting from significant learning as well as significant potential for IS development. At the very least, if confusion still results from the implementation of the IS project then, following RISD procedures, the sources of confusion should be more clearly understood.

5. CONCLUSIONS

In reflection a number of points arise:

First and most importantly - to avoid the confusion of the organisation - it is essential for the analysis and design process to be owned and employed by the organisation in question. Each analysis and design methodology which builds up levels of complexity and unnecessary technocracy in the development of information systems effectively robs the organisation in question of the capacity to develop its own information system and share in the learning which this analysis produces.

Secondly, the developing countries and transitional economies have been the recipients of many projects over the years which constitute impositions of remote technocrats over local needs. The recent experience of information systems design indicates that this phenomenon is developing into the relatively new area of IS. The primary intention of the RISD/ Multiview approach is to provide an approach which is useable by the wide range of new practitioners now emerging in the developing countries and transitional economies.

Thirdly and finally, one of the hall-marks of analysis and design to date has been the stunning inability of authors to explicitly describe failure and problems. For confusion to be avoided and complexity to be understood and simplified it is essential that lessons are learned and practitioners share their experiences of both the science and art of the analysis and design process.

References

Ashworth, C. and M. Goodland (1990). *SSADM: a practical approach*. London, McGraw-Hill.

Avison, D. E. and A. T. Wood-Harper (1990). *Multiview: an exploration in information systems development*. Maidenhead, McGraw-Hill.

Bell, S. (1996). *Learning with Information Systems: learning cycles in information systems development*. London, Routledge.

Bell, S. (1996). "Reflections on Learning in Information Systems Practice." *The Systemist* 17(2): 54-63.

Bell, S. (1997). "Not in Isolation: The necessity of systemic heuristic devices in all development practice." *Public Administration and Development* 17: 449-452.

Bell, S. and L. Minghze (1995). MIS and systems analysis applications in China: a case study of the Research Institute for Standards and Norms. *Global Information Technology and Socio-Economic Development*. M. Odedra-Straub. Nashua, Ivy League: 153 - 160.

Bell, S. and A. T. Wood-Harper (1998). *Rapid Information Systems Development: systems analysis and systems design in an imperfect world: Second Edition*. London, McGraw Hill.

Bicknell, D. (1993). Any takers for a stretcher case? *Computer Weekly*. London: 14.

Biggs, S. D. (1989). The Role of Management Information Systems in Agricultural Research Policy, Planning and Management in the Indian Council of Agricultural Research. New Delhi.

Chambers, R. (1997). *Whose Reality Counts? Putting the first last*. London, Intermediate Technology Publications.

Checkland, P. and S. Holwell (1998). *Information, Systems and Information Systems: Making sense of the field*. Chichester, Wiley.

Collins, T. and D. Bicknell (1997). *Crash: ten easy ways to avoid a computer disaster*. London, Simon and Schuster.

Cyranek, G. and S. Bhatnagar, Eds. (1992*). Technology Transfer for Development: the prospects and limits of information technology*. New Delhi, Tata McGraw-Hill.

Drummond, H. (1996). *Escalation in Decision Making: The tragedy of Taurus*. Oxford, Oxford University Press.

Jones, T. and S. King (1998). "Flexible Systems for Changing Organizations: Implementing RAD." *European Journal of information Systems* 7: 61-73.

Linsheng, H. (1998). Learning Organisation and Computer Supported Management. Beijing, China International Engineering Consulting Corporation.

Mumford, E. (1995). *Effective Requirements Analysis and Systems Design: the ETHICS method*. Basingstoke, Macmillan.

Senge, P., R. Ross, et al. (1994). The Fifth Discipline Fieldbook: Strategies and tools for building a learning organisation. London, Nicholas Brealey.

CHAPTER 53

APPLYING SOCIAL-TECHNICAL APPROACH FOR COTS SELECTION

Douglas Kunda and Laurence Brooks
University of York

Abstract

Selecting Commercial-Off-The-Shelf (COTS) software components to fit requirements is still a problem because of the "black box" nature of COTS components and the rapid changes in marketplace. This paper describes the problems of COTS software evaluation and reviews existing frameworks to support COTS software evaluation and selection. Although a number of initiatives have been proposed to deal with the COTS software evaluation problems, they do not adequately address the non-technical issues. The paper presents a method of applying social-technical approach for COTS software selection and recommends customer participation in the COTS software evaluation and use of a social-technical evaluation criteria.

Keywords: COTS software evaluation, social-technical evaluation criteria, customer participation

1   INTRODUCTION

COTS software component selection is a process of determining "fitness for use" of previously-developed components that are being applied in a new system context (Haines, 1997). Component selection is also a process for selecting components when a marketplace of competing products exists. Selection of a component can also extend to include qualification of the development process used to create and maintain it (for example, ensure that algorithms have been validated, and that rigorous code inspection has taken place).

There are three phases of COTS software selection: 1) criteria definition, 2) identification of candidate components and 3) evaluation. The criteria definition process essentially decomposes the requirements for the COTS software into a hierarchical criteria set and each branch in this hierarchy ends in an evaluation attribute (Kontio, 1996). The criteria include component functionality (what services are provided), other aspects of a component's interface (such as the use of standards) and quality aspects that are more difficult to isolate, such as component reliability, predictability, and usability. The identification of candidate components also known as alternative identification involves the search and screening for COTS candidate components that should be included for assessment in the evaluation phase. In the evaluation phase the properties of the candidate components are identified and assessed according to the evaluation criteria.

Software systems do not exist in isolation, they are used in social and organisational contexts. Experience, and many studies, show that the major cause of most software failures is people, rather than, technical issues (Curtis, Krasner and Iscoel, 1988, Le Quesne, 1988). Even with the availability of a wide range of advanced software development methodologies, techniques and tools, serious problems with software are still being faced. It is the people and culture of the organisation that determines how any system is used. For example, poor training may result in people not co-operating with the information system leading to failure and project abandonment (Avison, 1995).

Le Quesne (1988) showed that certain aspects of the design of information systems would make its likely success dependent on characteristics of the particular organisational environment. Friedman and Kahn Jr. (1994) give two examples of computer systems that passed technical muster, but posed ethical concerns or made little sense for the social context of their use.

Current approaches and proposed frameworks for COTS software selection do not adequately deal with these human, social and organisational issues. For example, the SEI Technology Delta framework does not deal with political and economic factors (Brown 1996). This paper presents a social-technical approach for COTS software selection, with the focus on the participation of customers in the COTS software evaluation.

2   PROBLEMS OF COTS EVALUATION AND SELECTION

Successful selection of COTS software to fit requirements is problematic because:

Lack of well defined process - Most organisations are under pressure to perform and therefore do not use a well-defined repeatable process (Kontio, 1996). The COTS selection process is implemented in an 'ad hoc' manner. This makes planning difficult, appropriate evaluation methods and tools are not used, lessons from previous cases are not learnt and the evaluation process efficiency reduced.

Evaluation criteria - There are problems associated with the definition of the evaluation criteria. Sometimes evaluators include immaterial and inappropriate attributes in the criteria, leading to incompatibilities (for example, confusing technology with product attributes). However, the more considerable problem is that evaluators tend to focus on technical capabilities at the expense of the non-technical or "soft" factors such as the human and business issues (Powell, 1997).

"Black box" nature of COTS components - Lack of access to the COTS internals makes it difficult to understand COTS components and therefore makes evaluation hard.

At times even the supporting documentation for these components is incomplete or wrong.

Rapid changes in market place - COTS evaluation is difficult because of rapid changes in COTS components in the market place. For example, a new release of the COTS component may have a feature that is not available in the component that is currently being evaluated.

3   CURRENT APPROACHES AND FRAMEWORKS

There are currently three strategies to COTS evaluation: progressive filtering, keystone identification and puzzle assembly (Oberndorf, 1997). Progressive filtering represents a strategy whereby a component is selected from a larger set of potential components. Starting with a candidate set of components, progressively more discriminating evaluation mechanisms are applied in order to eliminate less "fit" components. In keystone selection strategy, a keystone characteristic such as vendor or type of technology is selected first before selecting the COTS products. Often, interoperability with the keystone will become an overriding concern, effectively eliminating a large number of other products from consideration. The puzzle assembly model begins with the premise that a valid COTS solution will require fitting the various components of the system together as a puzzle. The puzzle assembly approach applies an evolutionary prototyping technique to build versions that are progressively closer to the final system.

A number of initiatives have been proposed to address the COTS component evaluation problems to ensure more effective use of COTS in software development. Boloix) (1995) and Brown (1996) have identified the following approaches as current practice (in various combinations), by software development organisations in evaluating new technologies:

- obtain objective technology data by documenting case studies in other organisations;
- gather subjective opinions and experiences with the technology by attending trade shows and by conducting interviews with, or sending questionnaires to, technology vendors and users;
- multiple-criteria evaluation approaches, which include subjective and objective evaluations, consider both user and system constraints equally;
- conduct focused experiments to mitigate high-risk aspects;
- demonstrate the technology's feasibility with a pilot project;
- compare the technology to existing practices by conducting a shadow project and examining the results of both approaches; and
- initiate demonstrator projects in the organisation to acquire phased exposure to the technology.

While there are several efforts focusing on component qualification, there is little agreement on which quality attributes or measures of a component are critical to its use in a component-based system. SEI's Technology Delta framework helps evaluate new software technology (Brown, 1996) while Procurement-Oriented Requirements Engineering (PORE) is a template based method to support requirements acquisition for COTS product selection (Maiden, 1998). Another technique Off-The-Shelf Option (OTSO) addresses the complexity of component selection and provides a decision framework that supports multi-variable component selection analysis (Kontio, 1996). Other approaches focus on assessing the software product, process and their impact on the organisation (Boloix, 1995). These evaluation approaches typically involve a combination of paper-based studies of the components, discussion with other users of these components and hands-on testing and prototyping.

However, what is missing in these approaches is the "soft" issues. An appropriate COTS software evaluation framework should be simple to use and address the political and economic factors that often separate a winning technology from other contenders (Carnegie, 1998). This paper proposes the participation of customers in the evaluation process because this is a major issue that brings a social dimension to the systems development. In addition, the method presented in this paper recommends selecting the underlying technology before selecting the COTS product.

4   SOCIAL-TECHNICAL APPROACH TO COTS EVALUATION: PRINCIPLES AND FRAMEWORK

The Social-Technical Approach to COTS Evaluation (STACE) framework is being developed by the authors of this paper to facilitate a simple, quick and inexpensive social-technical approach to COTS selection process. The STACE framework has been developed through literature survey and empirical studies documented elsewhere (Kunda, 1998).

4.1   Principles
Although STACE has greatly been influenced by the work of Kontio (1996) and Maiden (1998), it is based on a number of important principles:
1) Support for a *systematic approach* to COTS evaluation and selection. Most organisations select their COTS components in an ad-hoc manner. For example, there is a need to reuse lessons learnt from previous evaluation cases by maintaining a database of evaluation results. Appropriate techniques are recommended resulting in a quick and inexpensive method of evaluating COTS components.
2) Support for *evaluation of both COTS products and the underlying technology*. Most COTS evaluation frameworks emphasise either on COTS products evaluation or technology evaluation. This method proposes selecting the underlying technology before selecting the COTS products.
3) Use of *social-technical techniques* to improve the COTS software selection process. Research has shown that most software failures are due to people rather than technical issues. Furthermore research has shown that customer participation can

improve ownership (Ives, 1984) and success of the software system. Experience also shows that most COTS product selection is based on non-technical factors rather than just the technical factors. Therefore STACE recommends the use of a social-technical evaluation criteria and customer participation in the COTS selection process.

4.2 The STACE framework

The STACE method (see Figure 1) comprises four interrelated processes: 1) requirements elicitation; 2) social-technical criteria definition; 3) alternatives identification; and 4) evaluation or assessment.

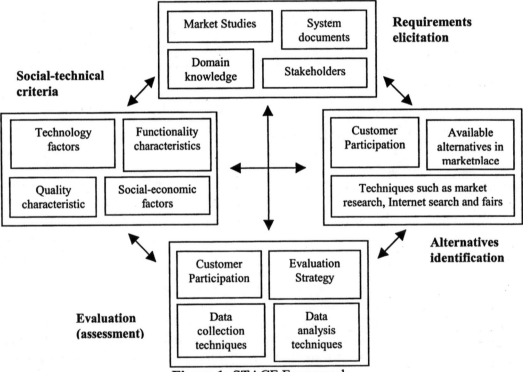

Figure 1: STACE Framework

In the requirements elicitation process, the high-level customer and systems requirements are discovered through consultation with stakeholders, from system documents, domain knowledge and market studies (Sommerville, 1996). In the social-technical criteria definition process essentially the high-level requirements from the requirements elicitation are decomposed into a hierarchical criteria set and each branch in this hierarchy ends in an evaluation attribute (Kontio, 1996). Alternative identification includes searching and screening for COTS products/ technology that will be assessed in the evaluation stage. This process is driven by guidelines and criteria defined in the criteria definition process. Evaluation process involves ranking of identified COTS alternatives against the social-technical evaluation criteria by examining capabilities, reading documentation and experimentation.

The following sections describe details of the social-technical criteria definition, identification of alternatives and evaluation process.

4.2.1 Social-technical criteria

The evaluation criteria are parameters against which the COTS product is evaluated and upon which selection decisions are made (IEEE, 1993). The criteria definition process derives these attributes (see Figure 1) from high level requirements, themselves derived from the requirements elicitation process. These should then be revised to incorporate feedback from alternatives identification and evaluation processes. Another possible source of information in defining the criteria is experience from past evaluation cases.

This process may include tailoring of the criteria based upon customer needs and priorities. For a system to be cost-effective it must be driven by essential requirements, not optional or the "nice to have" requirements. Using some existing standard checklist or template to define the criteria is highly recommended. The social-technical criteria include: 1) technology factors, 2) functionality characteristics, 3) product quality characteristics, and 4) social-economic factors.

Technology factors - A technology is a specification or framework that provides for integrating components. The COTS component underlying technology is the basis for the component's interoperability, portability, reusability, maintainability and adaptability. The COTS underlying technology is selected from high-level customer requirements. For example, the customers could specify that they prefer a system that is based on CORBA technology. However, an understanding and evaluation of the underlying assumptions about the technology must be elicited and analysed before commitment to a particular technology. A number of issues may be evaluated when considering selecting a particular technology. They include:

- *Functionality* - customer functional requirements that the technology should support for example support for distributed objects, platform support, real time processing.
- *Performance* - the quality measures that address how well a technology functions such as dependability, efficiency, resource utilisation, usability. For example the way the technology handles memory management issues can be assessed.
- *Framework and architecture style* - the type of infrastructure that provides the binding from disparate components such as object request broker mediated, message bus, database and blackboard (Haines, 1997).
- *Interface standard* - interfaces are the means by which components connect and interact. The degree to which a software component meets certain standards can greatly influence the interoperability and portability of a system (Haines, 1997).
- *Security* - the capability of a technology to manage, protect, and distribute sensitive information. For example Microsoft employs "Authenticode" based on cryptographic

public and private key technology using digital certificates and signatures on components (Microsoft, 1996).

- *Concepts of evolution and versioning* - the technique that the technology uses to handle problems of new version and migration. In a component world, versions of components can be prolific and therefore version management is an important issue (Szyperski, 1998).
- *Development environments* - the availability and maturity of development environments to support the technology (Szyperski, 1998).

Functionality characteristics - ISO/IEC 9126:1991(E) defines functionality as a set of attributes that bear on the existence of a set of functions and their specified properties. The functions are those that satisfy stated or implied needs. The functional requirements may be represented in the form of scenarios or use-cases and should include essential customer requirements and customer standards. The functionality characteristics help in the initial selection of alternatives. For example, a user may specify that they want a system that will enable them to conduct business on the internet.

Product quality characteristics - ISO/IEC 9126:1991(E) defines software quality characteristics as a set of attributes of software products by which its quality is described and evaluated. COTS component quality characteristics are behavioural properties that the product must have and should match the customer's non-functional requirements. The product quality characteristics do not necessary change from application to application. Examples include, maintainability, reliability, portability and performance (Kontio, 1996). However, this should be reviewed and adapted in accordance to customer requirements and priorities.

Socio-economic factors - these are non-technical factors that should be included in the evaluation and selection of COTS components such as costs, business issues, vendor performance and reliability. Costs include direct costs, such as the price of the COTS software products, and indirect costs, such as the cost of adapting to local needs as well as training costs. Organisational issues include people and process problems that must be overcome before successfully implementing the COTS based system, such as management support and internal organisational politics, staff skills and attitudes. Vendor performance and reliability includes vendor infrastructure and stability, period of vendor business, vendor reputation, references, customer base and track record. These are most frequently overlooked factors that bring in the social dimension in the evaluation criteria. A number of social-economic issues must be considered when selecting a product or technology (see table 1). They include:

- *Business issues* - the financial case for buying a particular product or technology. Business issues include cost of product/technology, licensing arrangements, additional cost of adapting and integrating the products, training and support costs, cost of maintenance or replacement with upgrades.
- *Customer capability* - examples of customer capability include customer experience with product/technology, customer expectations, internal organisational politics, and

customer/organisation policies or preferences.
- *Marketplace variables* examples of marketplace variables include product or technology reputation, maturity and stability of a product, product or technology restrictions, market trends and viability of products over long period.
- *Vendor capability variables* - the performance and capability of the vendor and examples include vendor profile, reputation, certification, stability, available training and support.

Major factors	Decomposition into sub-factors
1) Business issues	Cost of adapting and integrating; Licensing arrangements; Maintenance (upgrades) costs; Product costs; Support costs; Technology costs; Training costs.
2) Customer capability	Customer expectations; Customer experience; Organisational policies; Organisational politics.
3) Marketplace variables	Market trends (viability); Product/technology reputation (maturity, stability); Product/technology restrictions.
4) Vendor capability	Availability of training and support; Vendor certification; Vendor reputation; Vendor stability.

Table 1: Examples of social-economic (non-technical) factors

4.2.2 Search for alternatives
The search for candidate COTS components is conducted through market surveys; Internet search; product publications and sales promotions; and computer fairs and shows. The identified components are screened to reduce them to reasonable number so that they can be evaluated in details.

The next step in this identification process is to obtain information about the COTS products or obtain the COTS products or both. This information may consist of evaluations by independent evaluators, reports from vendors, a demonstration of the product capabilities by the vendor and information obtained directly from users.

The alternative identification depends on customer requirements, social-technical criteria and the initial screening (evaluation). However the adopted search techniques, customer participation and availability of products have an impact on the success of this process and the whole COTS selection process.

4.2.3 Evaluation (assessment)
The evaluation involves contacting vendor technical support for evaluation information, review of vendor documentation and product testing for quality and functionality. It includes evaluating COTS performance, interfaces and ease of integration, comparing short-term and long-term licensing costs against integration costs. The weighting and ranking scheme for measuring suitability for instance the use of a 1-to-5 scale is defined during this process. The reasons for selecting each component and the reasons for rejecting others should be recorded.

The evaluation criteria definition and identification of alternatives have a significant impact on the evaluation success (see Figure 1). The following factors also impact on the

evaluation process success:
1) **Evaluation strategy** - STACE proposes to employ the keystone identification strategy with the technology as the keystone issue. The separation of COTS underlying technology from COTS products during evaluation allows fair comparisons between products. The other advantage of separating products from technology is that useful literature is available on technology comparisons, since technology change is not as fast as product change.
2) **Data collection techniques** - there are a number of data collection techniques such as examining the products and vendor supplied documentation, viewing demonstration and interviewing demonstrators, executing test cases and applying the products in pilot projects. STACE proposes selecting appropriate techniques depending on resources and experience. In addition data collection may include interviewing actual users of the products, and examining sample outputs from projects that have used the products. Other techniques include cards sorting and laddering, outranking methods and feature analysis technique (Maiden, 1998).
3) **Data analysis techniques** - STACE recommends the use of the Analytic Hierarchy Process (AHP) to consolidate evaluation data in order to select the "best" components among alternatives. There are tools available to support the AHP techniques. AHP was developed by Saaty (Saaty, 1990) for multiple criteria decision making and has been successfully used in software selection (Kontio, 1996) (Zviran, 1993). The AHP technique is based on pair-wise comparison between alternatives. The result of this pair-wise comparison is converted to a normalised ranking by calculating the eigenvector from the comparison matrix's largest eigenvalue. The advantages of the AHP technique are (Kontio, 1996, Zviran, 1993):
- a systematic approach for consolidating information about alternatives using multiple-criteria;
- an objective weighing technique for setting the weighing scale for qualitative and quantitative data, and
- it allows for consistency checking.

4.2.4   Customer Participation
Customer participation refers to the behaviours and activities of the customers during information system development and customer involvement refers to the participation in the system development process by representatives of the target user group (Ives, 1984) (Eman, 1996). Participation may lead to increased user acceptance by developing realistic expectations about the systems capabilities, providing an arena for bargaining and conflict resolution about the selected product and leading to system ownership by users.

Customer participation may vary from direct, where all parties are affected by the system are involved, to indirect, where employee representatives serve on decision-making committees (Ives, 1984). Mumford (1995) proposes three types of participation:

consultative, representative and consensus. STACE recommends representative or consensus customer participation in the selection process of the COTS product and its underlying technology.

5 THE STACE PROCESS IN OPERATION

Figure 2 illustrates the main COTS evaluation process. The approach pre-supposes that essential customer requirements have been acquired, possibly in the form of high level scenarios and use cases. These requirements can be acquired using simple techniques such as brainstorming and interviews. It also assumes that the customers will be part of the evaluation team. It begins with the selection of the technology or standard on which the products will be based and proceeds to the selection of the COTS products.

Step 1: Select the underlying technology or other keystone issues. Select the underlying technology from high-level requirements for example Distributed Component Object Model (DCOM) from Microsoft Corporation. The requirements should be explored with customers in order to select the technology on which the COTS products will be based and the selected technology should handle the use-cases for the system. The selection process involves 1) defining the evaluation criteria, 2) search and screen for available alternatives, 3) revising the criteria and requirements based on available technologies, 4) assessing and selecting the "best" technology among alternatives (refer to *steps 2-5* on product selection). This can be augmented by reviewing component technology literature (eg. Szyperski, 1998).

Step 2: Define social-technical evaluation criteria for COTS products based on the selected technology. Derive the social-technical criteria from high-level customer requirements and the selected technology. A decision to use some existing checklist or template to define the criteria should be made at this stage. This should include defining a simple weighting or ranking scheme for measuring suitability such as a 1-to-5 scale. The criteria should include functionality issues, technology and interface issues, quality characteristics and non-technical issues (see section 4.2.1).

Step 3: Search and screen for available COTS products. Search the marketplace to identify candidate COTS components through market surveys and other techniques like Internet search. The search criteria at this stage should be limited to functionality issues. The identified components should then be screened to reduce them to reasonable number so that they can be evaluated in detail in the next phase. This can be effectively achieved by quick review of documentation on the identified COTS components.

Step 4: Revise requirements and social-technical criteria based on available COTS products. Examine the screened components whether they can handle the requirements or use-cases for the system. Revise the social-technical criteria and update the use-cases based on available components. The selection of the "best" among the packages available depends on the assessment of their compatibility with the requirements specification and the prioritisation of these requirements.

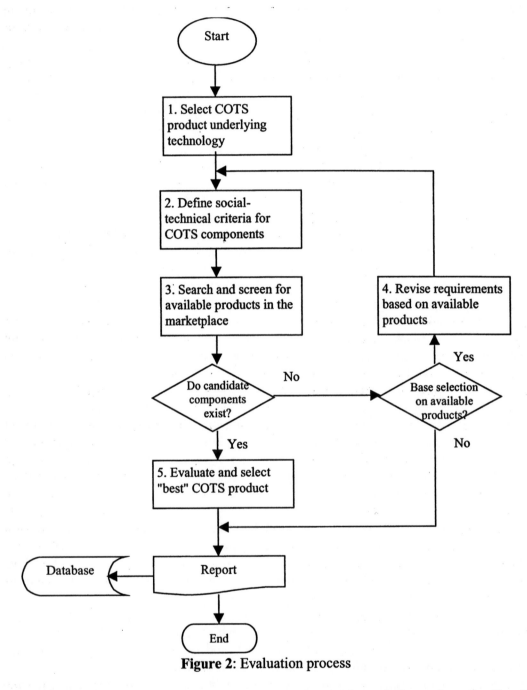

Figure 2: Evaluation process

Step 5: Evaluate the candidate components rigorously and then select the "best"

COTS product. It is important to thoroughly evaluate each product selected from the screening process in order to select the "best" product among alternatives. The evaluation may involve further review of product documentation, testing for quality and functionality and experimentation within operating environment. The evaluation should include ranking of the candidate products according to the evaluator's preferences. Record the reasons for selecting each component and the reasons for rejecting others. The data should be consolidated using AHP method with some support tool.

6   CONCLUSIONS AND FUTURE PLANS

COTS-based Software Development (CBSD) focuses on building large software systems by integrating previously-existing software components (Haines, 1997). CBSD success depends on successful evaluation and selection of COTS software components to fit customer requirements. The literature shows that successful selection of off-the-shelf systems to fit customer requirements remains problematic (Maiden, 1998). Existing frameworks for COTS evaluation such as the Delta and OTSO are inadequate because they do not incorporate the social-economic factors satisfactorily. In addition these frameworks are laborious and too complex to be adopted for general use.

The method presented in this paper provides a framework for social-technical approach for COTS selection. It allows the definition of social-technical criteria and the participation of customers during the evaluation process. The method further advocates the selection of underlying technology before evaluating and selecting COTS software components to ensure fair and more realistic comparisons.

The STACE framework has been developed through literature survey and empirical studies documented elsewhere (Kunda, 1998). Further work will include elaborating and validating the STACE framework through a number of case studies in the UK. It is expected that this future work will lead to adapting and testing the framework for developing countries. Developing countries have a number of problems that block the diffusion and efficient/effective exploitation of IT systems, such as lack of infrastructure, skilled human resources deficiency, economic constraints and application problems (Mohan, 1990) (W'O Okot-uma, 1992). CBSD can provide support for organisations in developing countries to reduce costs related to software systems development and procurements. In addition it is expected that the framework will be the basis for developing a guidebook for project and maintenance managers in developing countries regarding the process of evaluating and selecting COTS software components in CBSD.

References

Avison D. E and Fitzgerald G., *Information Systems Development: Methods, techniques and tools*, McGraw-Hill Book Company, London, 1995

Boloix Germinal and Robillard Pierre, *A Software System Evaluation Framework*, IEEE Computer Vol. 28 No. 12, pages 17-26, December 1995

Brown Alan W. and Wallnau Kurt C., *A Framework for Systematic Evaluation of Software Technologies*, IEEE Software, September 1996

Carnegie Mellon University, *CBS Activity Areas*, Carnegie Mellon SEI, Available WWW (online) <URL:http://www.sei.cmu.edu/cbs/overview.html>, 1998

Curtis Bill, Krasner Herb and Iscoe Neil, *A field study of the software design process for large systems*, Communication of the ACM, 31(11):1268-1286, November 1988

Emam Khaled El and Quintin Soizic and Madhavji Nazim H., *User participation in the Requirements Engineering Process: An Empirical Study in Requirements Engineering 1996*, Springer-Verlag London Limited, London, pages 4-26, 1996

Friedman Batya and Kahn, Jr. Peter H., *Educating Computer Scientists: Linking the social and technical*, Communication of the ACM, 37(1):65-70, January 1994

Haines Capt Gary, Carney David and Foreman John, *Component-Based Software Development/ COTS Integration*, Software Technology Review, Available WWW (online) <URL:http://www.sei.cmu.edu/str/descriptions/cbsd_body.html>, 1997

IEEE std 1209-1992, *IEEE Recommended Practice for the Evaluation and Selection of Case Tools*, IEEE, New York, 1993

ISO/IEC

Ives Blake and Olson Margrethe H., *User involvement and MIS success: A review of research*, Management Science, Vol.30, No.5, pages 586-603, May 1984

Kontio Jyrki, *A Case Study in Applying a Systematic Method for COTS Selection*, Proceedings of the 18th ICSE, IEEE Computer Society, 1996

Kunda Douglas, *Identifying current practices for COTS software − leading to best practices for developing countries* Qualifying Dissertation, Department of Computer Science, University of York, York, 1998.

Le Quesne P. N., *Individual and Organisational factors and the Design of IPSEs*, Computer Journal, 31(5):391-397, 1988

Maiden Neil A. and Ncube Cornelius, *Acquiring COTS Software Selection Requirements*, IEEE Software, pages 46-56, March/April 1998

Microsoft Corporation, *Microsoft Authenticode Technology*, Available WWW [online] <URL:http://www.microsoft.com/security/tech/misf8.htm>, 1996.

Mohan Lakshmi and Belardo Salvatore and Bjorn-Andersen Niels, *A contigency approach to managing information technology in developing countries: Benefiting from lessons learned in developed nations* chapter in Information Technology in Developing Countries, Bhatnagar S.C and Bjorn-Andersen N. (editors), Elsevier Science Publishers, North-Holland, pages 15-22, 1990

Mumford Enid, *Effective Systems Design and Requirements Analysis: The ETHICS Approach*, Macmillan Press Ltd, Hampshire, 1995

Oberndorf Patricia A. and Brownsword Lisa and Morris Ed, Workshop on COTS-Based Systems, Software Engineering Institute, Carnegie Mellon University, Special Report CMU/SEI-97-SR-019, November 1997

Powell Antony, Vickers Andrew, Lam Wing and Williams Eddie, *Evaluating Tools to*

Support Component Based Software Engineering, Proceeding of the 5th International Symposium on assessment of software tools, IEEE Computer Society, Los Alamitos, 1997

Saaty T L, *The Analytic Hierarchy Process*, McGraw-Hill, New York, 1990

Sommerville Ian, *Software Engineering*, Addison Wesley Longman Limited, Essex, 1996

Szyperski Clemens, *Component Software: Beyond Object-Oriented Programming*, Addison Wesley Longman Limited, Essex, 1998

W'O Okot-uma Rogers, *A perspective of contextual, operational and strategy: Problems of Infomediation in Developing Countries* a chapter in Social Implications of Computers in Developing Countries, Bhatnagar S C and Odedra Mayuri (editors), Tata McGraw-Hill Publishing Company Limited, New Delhi, pages 10-25, 1992

Zviran Moshe, *A comprehensive Methodology for Computer Family Selection*, Systems Software Journal, 22:17-26, 1993

CHAPTER 54

INFORMATION SYSTEMS EVALUATION: CURRENT THEMES

Ian Owens
University of Glamorgan

Abstract

A key issue facing any organization is whether they receive value from their investments. In view of the large amounts invested in the development of information systems the ability to evaluate these investments is growing increasingly important. Companies have traditionally found it very difficult to measure the costs and benefits of IS effectively. The issues of IS evaluation and the value of IS investments are consistently cited by Chief Information Officers and Chief Executive Officers as areas of major interest. The main aim of this review is to investigate research that has examined the issues surrounding IS evaluation and the value of IS to organizations. The issue of post-implementation evaluation receives special consideration. The paper is structured as follows: first, the current themes in IS evaluation literature are examined, and two frameworks that have been suggested for IS evaluation are described. The evidence of the current evaluation practices of UK companies is then considered. The paper concludes with a hypothesis suggested by the author that will form the basis of further research work.

1. INTRODUCTION

A key issue facing any organisation is whether they receive value from their investments. It has been estimated that the amount invested in information systems and other computing resources by businesses in the United States accounts for nearly 40% of capital investments each year (Salmela 1997).

A body of work emerged in the 1980s that seemed to suggest that investment in information technology (IT) and information systems (IS) could provide a business enterprise with a distinct competitive advantage over its rivals (see Porter and Millar, 1985; Parsons, 1983; McFarlan 1984).

A brief scan of the literature relating to this topic illustrates the enormous amount of work that has been done in this area since the 1980s. Many researchers have suggested that increased productivity and other advantages to investments in IT and IS are rather more difficult to measure than have previously been reported. This body of work has been described as 'IT productivity paradox' (Brynjolfsson, 1993). Loveman (1988) stated:

Despite years of impressive technological improvements and investments there is not yet any evidence that information technology is improving productivity or any other measure of business performance.

This implication that organisations that have invested in information systems and information technology have not yielded value from these investments in terms of increased business performance is reinforced by Salmela (1997) who stated:

Cross-sectional studies on the relationship between IS investments and organisational performance were not able to establish a uniform positive relationship between IS investments and organisation's economic performance.

Recent surveys have indicated that the issue of measuring benefits derived from investments in IS is an area of concern for senior managers in many large organization's (Whiting et al, 1996). Measuring benefits and IS effectiveness is consistently reported in the top 20 on the list of most important IS issues by the members of the Society for Information Management (SIM) (Dickson & Nechis, 1984; Niederman, Brancheau & Wetherbe, 1991; Watson, Kelly, Galliers & Brancheau, 1997). More recently Pervan (1998) found that 'Measuring IS effectiveness and productivity' was ranked in the top ten most critical issues by Australian Chief Executive Officers (CEOs) and Chief Information Officers (CIOs).

Productivity and effectiveness are only two measures of information systems utility. Other measures can include increased efficiency, product innovation, and cost reduction. Attempts to measure the utility of IS and the benefits deriving from IS have proven difficult to many researchers, perhaps as a result of the many measures one can apply to IS. Reading the literature on IS value and IS evaluation it is clear that the majority of recent work is aimed at discussing the evaluation of IS at the proposal or feasibility stage. Very little work has been done on the subject of post-implementation evaluation (with the exception of Ward and Peters). One IS manager of a multinational insurance company suggested a possible reason for this discrepancy in a recent communication with this researcher. The IS manager wrote:

There is a major difficulty... persuading the business community to invest time and energy to track the benefits post application implementation. No one has any problem with putting together a Cost Benefit case, the business is very keen on tracking costs but extremely reticent to track the benefits they themselves originally claimed.

This paper will examine the current IS evaluation literature, and look at two frameworks that have been suggested for IS evaluation, and examine evidence of the current evaluation practices of UK companies.

2. INFORMATION, INFORMATION SYSTEMS, INFORMATION TECHNOLOGY AND BUSINESS VALUE.

In much of the published research IS and IT are grouped together as a single entity, IT/IS. When examining the value of IS to organizations it is important to examine the relationship between information, information systems, information technology and business value. Business value is mediated through human activity systems that are supported by information systems, which are mediated through information technology. An IT strategy should be driven by the IS strategy that, in turn should embody the business strategy of the organization. Information that is up to date and relevant to business activities is the product which business users demand from information systems (Kumar 1990).

Information is increasingly seen as valuable organizational resources for companies. Glazer (1993) suggests that attempts to assess the value of IS may be over concentrating on the technology used to provide IS rather than the information itself. He states that studies that have measured a negative or minimal return on investments in IS may be measuring the wrong variables. He defines two classes of organization, the cost-driven organization and the information-intensive organization. The cost-driven organization is concerned with the recover of costs associated with investments in IS.

In contrast, the information-intensive organisation focus on the 'information value chain', rather than the recovery of costs. The information value chain consists of four distinct links:
1. Data is first collected and structured
2. Data is transformed through structuring into usable information
3. Information is analysed, interpreted and modelled, transformed into knowledge
4. Knowledge then forms the basis for decision-making. (Blattberg et al 1992).

Business value can be added at any point in the information, IT, IS chain, depending on how each entity is managed by the organisation. Hitt and Brynijolfsson (1996) have found that investments in IT have resulted in increased productivity and created substantial value for customers. However, they found that while increased investment in IT has added value to business activity, it has not substantially increasing firms' profitability.

3. MEASURING THE VALUE OF INFORMATION SYSTEMS.

How well a firm is able to convert spending on information resources such as investments in information systems may depend upon the type of work the firm is engaged in. Studies that show return on IT investment (Harris & Katz 1991) have concentrated on traditional information intensive industries, for example the insurance industry.

Studies that have found the opposite to be true have concentrated on manufacturing or information non-intensive industries (Lovemen, 1988; Olson & Weill 1989). Therefore, it is sensible to assume that information intensive industries are more likely to achieve measurably improved performance from investment in information resources.

Olson & Weill (1989) have found that firms differ in their ability to benefit from investment in information resources. He found four internal factors that may contribute to this:

- Top management commitment to IT and information investment;
- Organizations previous experience with IT and information systems;
- Organizations previous satisfaction with IT and information systems;
- The extent of political turbulence within the organization.

Owens et al (1996) found that within industries other, structural factors must also be considered when examining why some firms are more effective than others are in developing and using information systems effectively. These external factors include:

- The state of the market;
- The financial standing of the firm prior to the introduction of information systems;
- The size of the firm, and it's subsequent ability to benefit from economies of scale; and
- The nature of the industry, i.e. traditional information intensive industries; banking, insurance etc. versus traditional non-information intensive manufacturing industries.

One additional factor that has emerged from this investigation was the nature of the company's growth. In other words problems can arise when a company has grown through acquisition of an existing company, rather than through organic growth. This has led in a number of cases to the acquisition of information systems that are incompatible with the company's existing information infrastructure.

Glazer (1993) found that studies that focus on cost-driven organisations often conclude that the costs of IS development and provision are not justified. Studies that concentrate on information-intensive organisations have found the opposite to be true. Therefore, organisations that focus less on technology than on information itself have found a measurable return on investments in IS.

4.   FRAMEWORKS FOR MEASURING THE VALUE OF IS

A number of frameworks have been suggested in the literature for evaluating investments in information systems. The majority of the frameworks focus on the feasibility or justification stage of IS projects, rather than providing frameworks for ascertaining whether expected or anticipated benefits actually materialise. Exceptions to this include work done by Ward and Peters these frameworks are discussed later in this paper. The majority of the frameworks published have not been operationalised or implemented.

Indeed recent surveys of firms IS evaluation policies have found that the majority use traditional Cost Benefit evaluation techniques to evaluate IS investments (Willcocks and Lester 1991, Ballantine et al 1997). These findings are collaborated by Owens et al (1996), and are discussed in more detail later in this paper.

Guy Fitzgerald (1998) has recently described a framework that combines traditional investment appraisal techniques with other less traditional measures to form a multidimensional approach to IS evaluation at the feasibility stage.

Fitzgerald first differentiates between different types of IS projects, he defines two main types of project. Efficiency Projects: These are taken to be projects aimed at reducing the costs of performing a task, and Effectiveness Projects: These projects are those aimed not only at cost reduction, but rather at doing things differently to better achieve the desired result.

This approach calls for eight tasks and evaluations to be undertaken by organisations considering making an investment in an IS.

1. Identify costs.
2. Assess the contribution to the business strategy.
3. Analysis the expected benefits.
4. Identify 'second order effects'.
5. Evaluate the flexibility of the project.
6. Assess the practicality or implementability of the project.
7. Risk assessment.
8. Test the business idea.

The first four tasks may well form part of a traditional cost benefit analysis (Misham, 1988), while the remaining tasks are aimed at assessing the risk of the project and the potential value to the business. It would be an interesting exercise to operationalize this model and apply it to review actual IS projects. Indeed this model may be a suitable tool for performing a 'before and after' evaluation to determine the extent to which projected benefits to the business actually occur post IS implementation.

The life cycle approach suggested by Ward et al (1996) describes an approach that is process-based in focus, aimed at understanding what has to occur to ensure that expected benefits from IS investments actually materialise. This approach stresses the need to evaluate every stage of an IS project, from the proposal or justification stage, through the implementation and post-implementation phases. The authors term the overall process of evaluation and realisation of benefits as benefits management and define this as follows: *'The process of organising and managing such that potential benefits arising from the use of IT are actually realised.'*

The research team developed a process model of benefits management that had been tested with reviews of actual IS projects. The model formed the basis of the subsequent survey, and is comprised of five main tasks:

• Identification and structuring benefits

In this stage benefits are identified, and for each suitable business measures are developed. The benefits are structured so as to provide a better understanding of the linkages between technology effects, business changes and overall business effects.

- Planning benefits realization

A specific responsibility for the realization of each benefit is allocated within the organization, and a benefits realization plan is produced.

- Executing the benefits realization plan

The business changes identified in the benefits realization plan are carried out in accordance with the plan, alongside the implementation of the IT changes.

- Evaluating and reviewing results

A before and after review is conducted to see if the expected business benefits have materialized as a result of the implementation of the IS project.

- Potential for further benefits

As a result of the post implementation review of the project new, unexpected benefits may now appear achievable. As a result of this stage any further benefits can be identified and planned for.

Ward et al surveyed sixty organizations and found that very few has a comprehensive process for managing the delivery of benefits from IS/IT investments. Perhaps more surprising was the finding that only just over 50% of those surveyed had formal methodologies for:

- Systems development and/or
- Project management and/or
- Investment appraisal.

The researchers also found that as a result of the lack of any concerted effort to evaluate projects post-implementation very few of the survey groups learn from project successes or project failures. (Ward et al 1996)The researchers have subsequently further developed this research and produced a set of guidelines for effective benefits management. The issue of managing benefits from IS and IT investments has also been discussed by Peters (1996). He found that by continuing evaluation through the projects' lifecycle the project sponsors have a better understanding of how best to manage the project to produce the anticipated benefits.

5.   CURRENT EVALUATION STRATEGIES FOR IS INVESTMENTS.

An important area of research is that which has sought to determine whether organizations actually bother to evaluate IS investments, and if they do what strategies or methodologies they actually employ. Ballantine et al (1996) surveyed 96 UK companies sampled from the Times' Top 1000 companies' list. The survey was conducted in 1993, and sought to address the following issues:

- How widespread is the practice of IS/IT evaluation within organizations?
- Why are IS/IT investments not always evaluated at the feasibility stage?
- To what extent do problems arise with the evaluation process

- To what extent does evaluation depend on organizational factors, such as project cost and level of organizational turnover?
- Where does responsibility for evaluation exist (corporate or business unit level), and within that area, who is specifically responsible for evaluating investments?
- To what extent does consultation take place with internal stakeholders during the evaluation process, and which stakeholders could usefully have been consulted, but were not?
- To what extent do formal evaluation procedures exist?

It is interesting to note that the survey did not address the issue of post-implementation evaluation. One factor that emerged from the research is that out of the 97 companies surveyed, 10 did not evaluate projects routinely at the feasibility stage. If projects are not evaluated at this stage, how can it be possible to conduct any meaningful evaluation later? It also emerged that in the majority of cases the groups responsible for conducting the evaluation where drawn from the IT or IS department, the next largest evaluation grouping was the finance department, with user departments only being involved in a minority of project evaluations.

Perhaps more interesting was the finding that the majority of the companies surveyed employ cost/benefit and other investment appraisal techniques to evaluate IS investments at the feasibility stage in much the same way as they evaluate other capital investments (Ballantine et al, 1997). The most commonly used investment appraisal techniques used by the companies surveyed were:

1. Payback (68%).
2. Cost benefit analysis (66.7%).
3. Return on investment (ROI)/ Average Rate of Return (ARR) (48.1%).
4. Net present value (27.8%).
5. Return on management (13.0%).
6. Profitability Index (1.9%).

(Ballantine et al, 1997).

The survey also found factors other than those of a financial nature used to evaluate IS projects where basically the same as those considered when evaluating other capital projects. These factors include: Increased operational efficiency, improved quality of service, strategic importance, improved management information, increased productivity, improved quality of the product, and innovation. The researchers conclude that while most of the literature on IS and IT evaluation appears to suggest that these projects are somehow more difficult to evaluate than other investments, in real life any difference in evaluation techniques used are relatively minor. Moreover they suggest that '... the evaluation of IS/IT projects is not as rigorous as that for other capital projects' (Ballantine et al, 1997).

The findings presented by Ballantine et al have been collaborated in a study conducted in Australia by Wong and Behling (1997). They survey 68 large organizations to determine what cost benefit analysis techniques they used to evaluate IS projects. The researchers found that 81% of the survey respondents used conventional financial techniques to evaluate IS projects.

6. CONCLUSIONS.

The research presented here is meant to serve as an introduction to what is a varied subject that has attracted the attention of a wide variety of researchers in recent years. The evidence that companies tend to evaluate IS investments only at the feasibility stage and by employing conventional financial appraisal techniques may in part account for the findings that IS investments are failing to pay dividends for organizations.

It is hard to understand how the benefits of IS investments can be quantified if projects are not evaluated through their lifecycle, from the proposal and justification stage through to the implementation and post-implementation stages.

One hypothesis presented here is that only by conducting 'before and after' evaluation of the type suggested above can the benefits be tracked and lessons learnt. Projects that have proved to be failures or successes can feed information into the organizations knowledge base to help project sponsors make informed decisions about future IS investments. The researcher will test this hypothesis by evaluating one or two implemented mission-critical IS projects in a UK-based multinational engineering company. The results of this investigation will be published in due course.

References.

Ballantine, J A, Galliers, R D, Stray, S J. (1996) Information systems/technology evaluation practices: evidence from UK organizations. *Journal of Information Technology*, 11, pp. 129-141.

Ballantine J A, Stray SS (1997) A comparative analysis of the evaluation of information systems and other captal investments: empirical evidence. *Proceedings of ECIS '97*, pp. 809 – 822.

Blattberg R, Glazer R, Little J. The marketing information revolution. Harvard Business School Press, Cambridge MA, 1992.

Brynjolfsson, E. (1993) The productivity paradox of information technology. *Communications of the ACM*, 36(12), pp. 67-77.

Dickson, GW, Nechis, M. (1984) Key information systems issues for the 1980s. *MIS Quarterly*, 8, pp. 135-149.

Fitzgerald, G. (1998) Evaluating information systems projects: a multidimensional approach. *Journal of Information Technology*, 13, pp. 15-27.

Glazer R. (1997) Measuring the value of information: The information-intensive organisation. *IBM Systems Journal*, 32 (1), pp. 99-110.

Harris S.E., Katz J.L.(1991) Firm size and the information technology investment intensity of lifer insurers. *MIS Quarterly*, 15, pp. 333-352.

Hitt, L, Brynolfsson, E. (1996) Productivity, profit and consumer welfare: Three different measures of information technology's value. *MIS Quarterly*, June.

Kumar, K. (1990). "Post implementation evaluation of computer-based information systems: current practices." *CACM* 33(2), pp. 203 - 213.

Loveman G.(1988) An assessment of the productivity impact of information technologies, *Working Paper, Management in the 90s*. Sloan School of Management.

McFarlan, W.F.(1984) Information technology changes the way you compete. *Harvard Business Review*, May - June.

Misham, E J. Cost Benefit Analysis (4th Edition). Unwin Hyman. London 1988.

Neitherman, F, Branchaeu, J C, Weaterbe, J C (1991). Information systems management issues for the 1990s. *MIS Quaterly*, 15, pp. 475-499.

Olson M.H., Weill P.(1989) Managing investment in information technology: mini case examples and implications. *MIS Quarterly*, 13(1), pp. 3-17.

Owens, I, Wislon T.D., and Abell, A. Information and business performance: A study of information and services in high performing companies. Bowker-Saur 1996.

Parsons, G. L.(1983) Information technology: a new competitive weapon. *Sloan Management review*, 25(1), pp. 3-13, Fall 1983.

Pervan, G. (1998) How chief executive officers in large organisations view the management of their information systems. *Journal of Information Technology*, 13, pp. 95 – 109.

Peters, G. From strategy to implementation: identifying and managing benefits of IT investments. In *Information Systems: Evaluation and Management*. Edited by Leslie Willcocks. Chapman and Hall. 1996.

Porter, M., Millar, V.E. (1985) How information gives you competitive advantage. *Harvard Business Review*, 63(4), pp. 149-160.

Salmela H. (1997) From information systems quality to sustainable business quality. *Information and Software Technology*. Vol 39, no. 12, pp. 819 – 827.

Ward, J, Taylor, P, Bond, P.(1996) Evaluation and realization of IS/IT benefits: an empirical study of current practice. *European Journal of Information Systems*, 4, pp. 214-225.

Watson, R, Kelly, G G, Galliers, R D, Brancheau, J C.(1997) Key issues in information systems management: an international perspective. *Journal of Management Information Systems*, Spring, 13(4), pp. 91 – 115.

Whiting R, Davies J, and Knul M. Investment appraisal for IT systems in *Investing In Information Systems: Evaluation and Management*. Edited by Leslie Willcocks. Chapman and Hall. 1996.

Willcocks, L, Lester, S. (1993) How do organisations evaluate and control information systems investments? Recent UK survey evidence. *Journal of Information Systems*, 2, pp. 5-39.

Wong J W, Behling R. (1997) Using conventional methods to perform cost-benefit analysis (CBA) on proposed information systems (IS) projects: an Australian study. *Journal of Computer Information Systems*, Summer 1997, pp.30-36.

CHAPTER 55

SOFTWARE COST ESTIMATION RESEARCH: WHERE NEXT?

GA Bell, MA Cooper and JO Jenkins
City University, London & Middlesex University

Abstract

This paper proposes an interdisciplinary approach to developing a system dynamics model to explain software project cost. We have reviewed literature from the software engineering discipline, systems dynamics discipline and systems movement to find support for our claims. We have produced a conceptual model to explain how algorithmic cost models can be developed and applied to estimate the cost of future software projects. Additionally, we have derived a one-dimensional scheme based on Burrell and Morgan's work to clarify the theoretical assumptions that underpin cost models for software projects. Finally, we introduce the evolving approach we call "Costing as Learning" with its key characteristics

1 SOFTWARE COST ESTIMATION RESEARCH

We begin with the argument that researchers in cost estimation have pursued the goals of accuracy and consistency when constructing algorithmic cost models. Our investigations suggest that these goals have not always been achieved when estimating software projects. We argue that the new goal of cost estimation research should be to construct better explanatory models, which should lead to more accurate and consistent estimates.

We have examined several well-known cost models *e.g.* COCOMO (Boehm 1981). Additionally, we have reviewed independent empirical investigations by researchers not involved in the original development of the model. This survey was concerned with: the validation of cost models; cost model comparison using actual project data and cost model comparison using hypothetical project data. Our research indicates that the magnitude of the relative error (MRE), mean magnitude of the relative error ($\overline{MRE}$) and Predictor level (Pred(l)) are the best indicators of accuracy and consistency of cost models. Our findings indicate that the accuracy and consistency of the identified cost models is poor, and more significantly, there has been very little improvement in cost estimation research in the last decade (Bell forthcoming Ph.D. thesis).

We believe by achieving the goal of better explanatory models we will gain a more detailed representation of the development process. This could produce more accurate and consistent estimates within the cost explanation and cost projection modes. Furthermore, we contend that research in Software Process Improvement (SPI) frameworks, Software Process Models and Representational Measurement Theory contribute to our interdisciplinary approach to cost explanation (Bell and Jenkins 1998).

Lehman (1997) argues SPI frameworks play only a limited role in process improvement except at the lower levels of the maturity framework. In primitive processes, the introduction of a new methodology may have a significant local impact and yield a visible improvement in some aspects of the overall process. He contends that the introduction of new software engineering innovations produces local feed forward steps, but the global negative loops stabilise their impact. Hence, the view that the introduction of new software technology produces no significant improvement to the software development process, because of the dominant negative feedback loops. He also observes that a software product evolves to meet new requirements from the application domain. Information is essentially fed back from the user/customer to the developer who responds to the requests. Feedback can play an important role in determining the evolution of the software application. Moreover, Lehman views the software development process as a multi-loop feedback system. We hypothesise that within a global representation of the development process, dominant feedback loops which explain the software project cost can be found.

1.1   System Dynamics

System Dynamics is a form of system theory based on a servo-mechanistic perspective. We selected SD to develop a meta-explanatory cost model as it aims to explain the dynamical behaviour of a system through modelling its structure. The main goal of an SD model is to represent a stakeholder's view of a situation, which can be used to explore different assumptions through various scenarios. A review of the SD literature has identified several researchers who have applied it to software engineering discipline. Abdel-Hamid (1984) contributed the first SD model of software development management. The objective of his research was to enhance systemic understanding of the general process by which software development is managed. However, Bell (*ibid*) argues that the research methodology selected ensured the model was not owned by the participants. Hence, there are concerns with the findings of the investigations of different software project management policies.

The verification and validation of SD models can be viewed as a set of confidence tests which have to pass the stakeholder's level of satisfaction to ensure model ownership and meaningful outcomes to various strategies. In the 1980s there was a significant amount of research into verification and validation, because of implementation difficulties. These innovations enable the modeller to work more closely with the stakeholders and through facilitation capture their mental models. This has led to a new type of SD approach labelled Interactive SD practice (Lane 1998).

1.2   The Systems Movement

The Systems Movement is concerned with the concepts of systemic wholeness and systematic analysis. It encompasses various disciplines *e.g.* Management Science. Checkland (1981) identifies two fundamentally different ways of undertaking an inquiry in which systems ideas are applied. These have been labelled hard systems thinking (HST) and soft systems thinking (SST). Different HST methodologies have given rise to descriptions of processes consisting of well defined and ordered steps towards identifying the best solution given past performance measures. The problem is viewed as a given and the hard systems thinker generally attempts to produce the best solution, *i.e.* "the how", through the use of a mathematical technique.

SST emerged in an attempt to produce methodologies capable of tackling pluralistic situations which some HST methodologies found difficult. A pluralistic situation is reflected by a multiplicity of values, preferences and understanding of the situation. Systems ideas used in SST are applied differently from HST. Rather than view the world as containing systems to be identified and explored, the world is seen as being understood by using systems as mental constructs to help the stakeholder/ facilitator make sense of it. SSM (Checkland 1981) provides a general learning framework to capture the subjective views of stakeholders through the use of rich pictures which facilitate dialogue; to structure the problem situation; to identify discussion issues and propose solutions to create change. The main aim of the soft systems thinker is to identify the problem, *i.e.* "the whats", relevant to that social situation which requires solving or controlling.

Ackoff (1979) highlights the inappropriateness of traditional OR methodology through focusing on its practice of optimisation and pursuit of objectivity. He argues that to overcome these deficiencies there is a need to re-conceptualise OR, its methodology and the way it is practised. The forecast and prepare methodology and interactive planning methodology are two distinctive planning approaches, which are respectively associated with traditional and re-conceptualised OR.

1.3   Analysis of Algorithmic Cost Models

We analyse cost estimation into two modes namely, Cost Explanation and Cost Projection (see figure 1). There are two fundamental approaches to developing a cost model within the cost explanation mode. The traditional approach is to identify a major factor whose significance has not been fully analysed *e.g.* team size. A new cost model is developed using past data and compared with one or more existing models. We contend that this traditional approach to constructing an algorithmic cost model is linked to the Machine Age (Ackoff 1979). We call it the *ex post* analysis approach as researchers implicitly view costing as a complex problem, which is considered to be a given. Researchers have pursued the goals of accuracy and consistency when replicating the cost of completed software projects *i.e.* "the how", and as stated earlier, these goals have not been satisfactorily achieved.

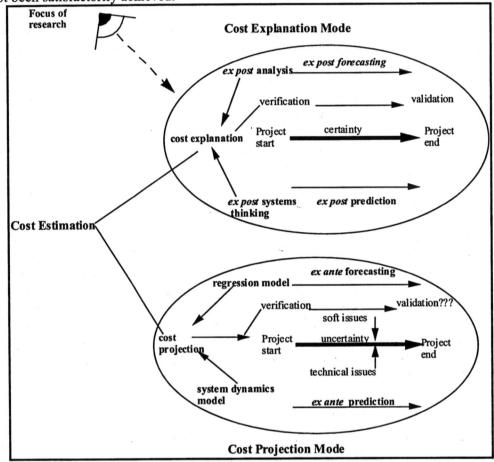

Figure 1: Conceptual model of the analysis of algorithmic cost models

The alternative approach is linked to the Systems Age (Ackoff 1979) and aims to improve the explanation of cost, which should lead to more accurate and consistent estimates in the two cost modes. Costing is viewed as a group of complex problems that are interrelated, dynamic and perhaps transient. These problems are framed using the systems thinking method; consequently, we label it the *ex post* systems thinking approach.

We contend that different types of practices are found in the *ex post* systems thinking approach. Moreover, we consider our research is linked to the Interactive SD practice, for we are attempting to explain the cost of the completed software application from the point of view of the project manager. The *ex post* systems thinking approach is linked with HST and the unit of analysis is the feedback loop. The goal of this approach is to explain the cost of a completed software project accurately, *i.e.* "the why" and "the how".

We contend that a cost model underpinned by the *ex post* analysis approach is linked to *ex post* forecasting. A cost model constructed through the *ex post* systems thinking approach is linked to *ex post* prediction. In the cost explanation mode, *ex post* forecasts and *ex post* predictions validate the accuracy of the cost model using completed project data sets.

The underpinning assumption of a forecast is that what has happened in the past will determine the future. We believe this assumption is less tenable the more time there is between the start and completion of a project, because of the greater likelihood of unforeseen events. When a problem emerges which may affect the project cost, the type of techniques, *e.g.* regression analysis, and models, *e.g.* COCOMO, cannot be represented until data has been collected. It is clear there is a need for regularly updating the model when data becomes available to allow new forecasts to be made. We believe *ex ante* forecasting attempts to produce the best solution, *i.e.* "the how", but does not provide an adequate explanation, *i.e.* "the why".

Ex ante prediction is based on the application of causal laws of change to current or past situations. This underpins the development of our explanatory cost model using the *ex post* systems thinking approach. Ackoff (1983) argues that the future depends on what will be done between now and then and much of what will be done is a matter of stakeholder choice. This implies that the future is subject to stakeholder creation. Our explanatory cost model will evolve in the cost projection mode at the beginning and during the development of the application in order to represent unforeseen cost. Therefore, we argue that in the cost projection mode verification of the explanatory cost model is extremely important to ensure model ownership and confidence in the *ex ante* predictions.

Weetman (1998) combines a set of methods to improve the Goal/Question/Metric (GQM) methodology (Basili and Rombach 1987) and we view it as an informal approach to software process improvement. She suggests that this soft approach could be labelled The Holon Methodology, after Checkland (1988). This follows part of Bell's (*ibid*) explanatory cost model that frames the software development process. Key aspects of SSM are applied within the framed system to capture the relevant problems which need to be measured. We believe that this approach can be used to capture the significant problems, *i.e.* "the whats", that have to be represented within our explanatory cost model. Essentially, we are advocating the use of a soft methodology within a hard methodology. It is clear that there is a need to continuously update the *ex ante* prediction when new data is available or new representations are needed. Our cost model attempts to explain accurately *both* "the why" and "the how" of the best solution and takes into account important stakeholder issues that emerge, *i.e.* "the whats". Our analysis suggests there are significant characteristic variations in developing cost models. This is reflected in the underpinning meta-theoretical assumptions related to philosophy of science and theory of society. Therefore, it is important to highlight the similarities and differences in these assumptions, which provides a basis for a different category of thought for developing a cost model.

2   METHODS AND METHODOLOGIES: HIGHLIGHTING THE DIFFERENT THEORETICAL ASSUMPTIONS

Burrell and Morgan (1979) developed a framework for exploring social theories and their relationships with different approaches to studying organisations. This framework highlights the underpinning assumptions about how people behave, how they communicate and make decisions, how knowledge about such processes can be gained and what form such knowledge can take. They contend that their framework can be used to investigate a wide variety of disciplines related to the social world. We outline the analysis of certain researchers in historical order, to justify the positioning of various methodologies/ practices on our one-dimensional scheme. This will assist in positioning algorithmic cost models within certain social theories.

2.1   The One Dimensional Analytical Scheme
The functionalist and the interpretive paradigms associated with sociology of regulation can be found at the top of our one-dimensional scheme (see figure 2). The conceptualisation of social science in terms of the four sets of assumptions related to ontology, epistemology, human nature and methodology are located at the bottom of the figure. The social theories that are associated with the functionalist and interpretive paradigms are positioned above the assumptions on the nature of social science. The arrows pointing upwards indicate the general meta-theoretical assumptions underpinning that category of thought. We have positioned the work of certain researchers for they either influence the positioning of the algorithmic cost models or contribute to our interdisciplinary approach to developing an explanatory cost model.

Checkland (1981) discusses the key characteristics of SSM, Systems Engineering, RAND Systems analysis and traditional OR, associating SSM with SST and the rest with HST. Most HST methodologies assume the problem, *i.e.* "the what", is given and the usual objective is to find the best solution, *i.e.* "the how". Moreover, the modeller must have some involvement in the situation to clarify various points that emerge, though the mathematical model is essentially viewed as black box. We contend that HST is underpinned by that intellectual framework which underwrites functionalist social science and the natural sciences, and contend that SST shares its intellectual framework with the interpretive paradigm. Checkland believes that SSM is linked with hermeneutics and phenomenology.

Ackoff's (1979) revolutionary re-conceptualisation of OR has guided the evolution of new SD practices and this has significantly influenced our work. The important features of traditional and re-conceptualised OR are reflected in the two distinctive planning approaches labelled Forecast and Prepare Methodology and Interactive Planning

Methodology (see figure 2).

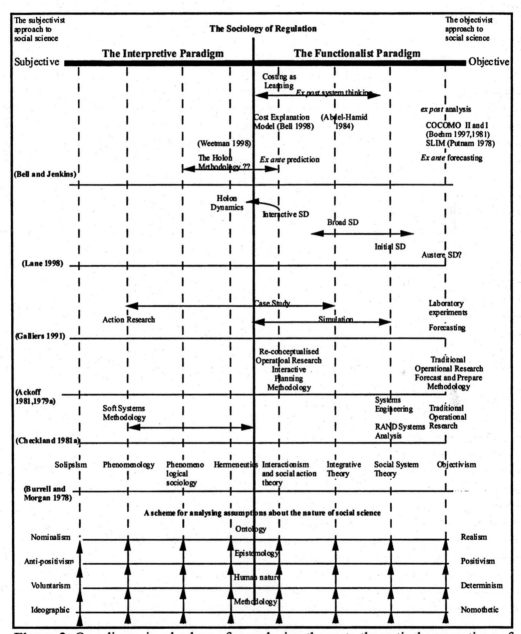

Figure 2: One-dimensional scheme for analysing the meta-theoretical assumptions of Cost Models

In a review of Information Systems, Galliers (1991) has categorised the most prominent research methods as Scientific (laboratory experiments, field experiments, surveys, case studies, theorem proof, forecasting, simulation) or Interpretivist (subjective/argumentative, reviews, action research, descriptive, futures research, role/ game playing). Galliers investigates their strengths and weaknesses which links them to the relevant social theory.

Lane (1998) explores the different social theories that are implicit in past, present and perhaps future SD practices. We will initially examine, in chronological order, relevant SD practices that focus on explanation, *i.e.* underpinned by the sociology of regulation, and then move to tailored uses of SD, which influence our research. Lane believes that the original practices which began with the development of SD and continued on for the next two decades can be grouped together and labelled Initial SD. He contends that Initial SD can be linked to social systems theory. Hence, this practice is a form of systems theory based on a positivist view of the social world, which takes a realist and deterministic stance. Lane claims that Burrell and Morgan's analytical scheme can guide future SD practices. He contends that approaches grounded in the interpretive paradigm should be called Holon SD practice. These models are nominalist representation instruments, which assist stakeholders to create their social situation through the construction of shared meaning. An ideographic methodology is applicable for the model building for it is viewed as a personal experience, which can be only understood in its full context. Holon SD is influenced by some of the work in Interactive SD practice, and this subjectivist stance is the one that Lane and Vennix are moving towards. Lane and Oliva (1994) attempt to synthesise SSM and SD in order to achieve this objective. This combination assists in identifying problems and providing desirable and feasible solutions, *i.e.* SST encompassing HST. Lane suggests that Holon SD practice can be associated with hermeneutics.

3   SOFTWARE COST MODELS: HIGHLIGHTING THE DIFFERENT THEORETICAL ASSUMPTIONS

COCOMO (Boehm 1981) and important derivatives are associated with the *ex post* analysis approach and can be found in the Cost Explanation Mode. These cost models are underpinned by the theory of reductionism and are closely linked to the machine age. Additionally, modellers isolate themselves from the situation to develop a cost model and compare it with existing models. We argue that cost models associated with *ex post* analysis are linked with objectivism.

Figure 2 indicates that the *ex post* analysis approach has similar meta-theoretical assumptions to those of traditional OR. Validation of the model is achieved through comparing the *ex post* forecasts with relevant past project data sets. We believe that the nature of these cost models concentrate on "the how" when replicating the cost of completed projects, for their explanation is limited, and their accuracy and consistency poor. Therefore, we contend that the new objective of cost estimation research is to provide a clearer explanation of past project cost, in other words, to concentrate on "the why" and "the how". Hence, we adopt the *ex post* systems thinking method and the selection of SD was made with this objective in mind. However, there are different SD practices which can be found within the *ex post* systems thinking approach.

Abdel-Hamid (1984) developed the first SD model in software engineering, though it was not developed specifically for project costing. The objective of his research was to enhance systemic understanding of the general process by which software development is managed. We believe Abdel-Hamid's research is linked to Broad SD practice, and therefore, is associated with integrative theory (See figure 2). The meta-theoretical assumptions can be found in the middle of the functionalist paradigm. Researchers from this category of thought are fundamentally systems theorists and then interactionists. We argue that the models are black boxes, with researchers searching for common structures that are independent of individual cognition, though they may discuss specific aspects of the model with experts.

We have discussed this model with an experienced project manager from a major UK organisation that produces software applications for the Ministry of Defence and he disagrees with many of the structures. Moreover, Bell and Glijnis (1997) have reviewed several high level software process models which show there are various approaches to producing large software products. Consequently, we are not confident that all six organisations that participated in Abdel-Hamid's research produce software in the exact same way. We conclude that the SD model derived from Abdel-Hamid's research is not owned by the participants, and contend that the findings of the investigation of different software project management policies have no stakeholder meaning.

The new role of the modeller, *i.e.* facilitator, together with various verification and validation innovations has led to a conceptual shift towards the more subjective view found within the functionalist paradigm. Our approach to developing a cost model is linked to the interactive planning methodology and the Interactive SD practices. We view costing as a set of interrelated complex problems, which are framed using the systems thinking method. We select frameworks, methodologies, methods and techniques from different disciplines to address specific issues and suggest that our interdisciplinary approach belongs to the Systems Age. Since SD models should reflect the subjective views of the stakeholder to ensure model ownership, the frame of reference of the modeller changes from teacher to facilitator to ensure understanding of the stakeholder's point of view. We consider our cost model as a top down approach, reflecting the outlook of an expert who has managed the relevant software project and collected the appropriate data. Comparisons between the collected data and the ex post predictions are undertaken using agreed validation techniques. Our approach is firmly linked to Interactionism and Social Theory.

In the Cost Explanation Mode most algorithmic cost models are validated against relevant past project data sets and evaluated with other existing models to increase confidence in their use. At this stage the algorithmic model can be applied in the cost projection mode. The cost models that are underpinned by *ex post* analysis are linked with *ex ante* forecasting; our cost model is underwritten by *ex post* systems thinking which is associated with *ex ante* prediction.

In the Cost Projection Mode the estimator examines the client's requirements which are translated to a size estimate. The estimator usually selects and calibrates a cost model associated with *ex post* forecasting, to produce an accurate cost estimate for the proposed software application. However, this approach produces "the how" and its explanation is limited. We contend that the *ex post* analysis approach is linked with objectivism. Our survey of costing hypothetical projects using cost models underpinned by the *ex post* analysis approach indicated a wide spread of estimates, which suggests "the how" is likely to be extremely inaccurate. Moreover, new project requirements may significantly change the preparations which will violate deterministic causal law; hence, it is inevitable the estimates will be inaccurate.

We argue that *ex ante* prediction is an alternative approach to estimating the cost of a new software application. The estimator selects the explanatory cost model to represent the software development process. However, the requirements for the proposed software application may mean that changes to the development process are needed. In addition, problems related to the process may have become manifest after completion of a similar past project. We believe our model, which was developed in the cost explanation mode, could be used as an artefact to empower the estimator to facilitate dialogue with relevant stakeholders. Moreover, the emergent approach developed by Weetman (1998) could assist in identifying the new issues or "the whats".

We believe that this informal approach is associated with Phenomenological Sociology (see figure 2). To represent "the whats" in our model we contend that we are using an SST approach within our HST approach. The updated cost model must pass relevant verification and validation tests to the level of satisfaction of the stakeholders to ensure ownership. The model attempts to explain the cost estimate through highlighting the means to complete the proposed software product, *i.e.* "the why" and "the how". We contend that our *ex ante* prediction approach is linked to interactionism and social action theory. Our *ex ante* prediction approach has the same meta-theoretical assumptions as the interactive planning methodology and the Interactive SD practice (see figure 2).

4   SUMMARY AND CONCLUSION

Our conceptual model of the analysis of algorithmic cost models (see figure 1) and one-dimensional analytical scheme (see figure 2) assist in guiding and justifying the development of new types of algorithmic cost models. The one-dimensional analytical scheme *"is a heuristic device rather than ... a set of rigid definitions"* (Burrell and Morgan 1979, p xii).

The *ex post* analysis approach is the orthodox way of developing a cost model for estimating large software projects which is linked with objectivism. This category of thought has a unique set of characteristics, which are reflected in the extreme meta-theoretical assumptions (see figure 2). We have outlined the general approach to developing a new regression model and contend that this type of methodology concentrates on "the how" when replicating the cost of a past project. Bell (*ibid*) contends that researchers, linked with objectivism, have pursued the goals of accuracy and consistency when constructing this type of model.

Our analytical scheme allows the wider application of criticisms across approaches, *e.g.* Ackoff's (1979) attack on traditional OR to the *ex post* analysis approach to developing a cost model, as they both belong to objectivism. Ackoff argues that Traditional OR is identified with the use of mathematical algorithms and models rather than the ability to formulate management problems and maintain the solutions in a changing environment. This led to problems in practice, specifically quantitative inbreeding which has led to a catatonic state being reached. After investigating archetypal cost models and their derivatives, we suggest that a catatonic situation is emerging within cost estimation, because the dominant approach to producing a cost model is linked with objectivism. This may be one of the contributing reasons for the lack of real improvement in cost estimation.

Ackoff (1979) also highlights an indeterminacy with the forecast and prepare methodology which seems applicable to the dominant software costing practice. The effectiveness of the approach depends on the accuracy of the forecast. Therefore, it is important to understand the conditions under which a precise forecast is possible in principal, but not in practice. Ackoff argues that there are two sets of conditions for a precise forecast. Firstly, when nothing changes, so issues and choice do not exist. The stakeholders within the situation of concern can change their behaviour provided it does not affect others. In addition, the behaviour of stakeholders outside the problem situation must not alter, or this would constitute a change in the environment. Clearly, the social world is not like this: *"what we do affects others, what they do affects us"*(Ackoff 1979, p100). Secondly, the behaviour of that which we are forecasting is assumed to obey a deterministic causal law. A precise forecast of the future is possible provided the situation of concern and its environment does not deviate from the past. The OR practitioner assumes the world is mechanical in nature, however, social situations usually involve choice and purpose. Consequently, issues will emerge necessitating changes to the original preparations which will violate the deterministic causal laws; hence, a precise forecast is not possible.

We are currently building a cost model with a project manager using SD. The model is being developed in the Cost Explanation Mode. We view costing as a group of interrelated, transient and dynamic complex problems, hence, the use of the *ex post* systems thinking approach. The construction of the explanatory cost model is grounded in Interactionism and Social Action Theory, as we explain the cost of the completed application from the manager's point of view through replicating the dynamic behaviour patterns of the collected data. We use the case study method since the research is exploratory. To achieve model ownership the cost model has to pass verification and validation tests to the satisfaction of the manager. This research tests the hypothesis that an interdisciplinary SD cost model will improve the accuracy of estimates in the cost explanation mode. Consequently, we are also undertaking a comparative study of the manager's cost explanation model and a costing tool. We expect the explanatory cost model to evolve when applied in the Cost Projection Mode, with new technical and soft issues (see figure 2). We propose the use of the Holon Methodology for process improvement, which aims to capture "the whats" as perceived by the software project manager. This approach is grounded in Phenomenological Sociology. The relevant issues are represented in the model to the satisfaction of the manager. Hence, our assertion that explanatory models offer more, for they emphasis "the why" and "the how". As explanatory cost models are used more frequently in practice, common dominant feedback loops may be discovered given certain criteria. Furthermore, the search for regularities in Interactionism and Social Action theory is an extreme form of subjective functionalism. This type of research may be underpinned by General Systems Theory (GST), though clarification and refinements are needed. Costing as Learning is our name for this evolving research, characterised in Table 3.

	Characteristic
1	A systemic view of the software development process
2	An interdisciplinary approach to producing a cost model
3	The use of methodologies which enable the capture and expression of the manager's mental model
4	The researcher's role as a facilitator
5	Emphasis on verification methods and validation techniques
6	The continuous use of the explanatory cost model during development of the software application.
7	Establishing similarities with other explanatory cost models on completion of the project..

Table 3: Key Characteristics of the Costing as Learning approach

To conclude, we contend our ongoing research and the key traits of the "Costing as Learning" approach offer an important direction for estimating the cost of large software projects.

References

Abdel-Hamid, T.K. (1984) "The Dynamics of Software Development Project Management: An Integrative System Dynamics Perspective", *PhD. Thesis,* Sloan School of Management, MIT, Cambridge, MA, USA.

Ackoff, R.L. (1983) "Beyond Prediction and Preparation", *Journal of Management Studies*, Vol. 20, pp 59-69

Ackoff, (1979) "The Future of Operational Research is Past", *Journal of Operational Research Society*, Vol. 30, pp 93-104.

Basili, V.R. and Rombach, H.D. (1987) "Tailoring the Software Process to Project Goals and Environments", *Proc. Ninth International Conference on Software Engineering*, Monterey, IEEE Computer Society Press, Los Alamitos, CA.

Bell, G.A. (forthcoming) "An Interdisciplinary Approach to Software Project Cost Explanation", *PhD. Thesis,* City University, London, UK

Bell, G.A. and Jenkins, J.O.(1998) "Methodologies and Methods Chosen to Explain Software Project Cost", *International System Dynamics Conference,* Quebec, Canada.

Bell, G.A. and Glijinis, G. (1997) *Software Process Improvement Approaches and the SPACE-UFO Methodology (Report D121C),* ESPRIT project 22292- SPACE-UFO.

Boehm, B.W. (1981) *Software Engineering Economics,* Prentice-Hall, Englewood Cliffs, New Jersey, USA.

Burrell, G., and Morgan, G. (1979) *Sociological Paradigms and Organisational Analysis*, Gower, Aldershot, UK.

Checkland, P.B. (1988) "The Case for Holon", *Systems Practice*, Vol. 1(3), pp 235-238.

Checkland, P.B. (1981) *Systems Thinking, Systems Practice*, John Wiley and Sons, Chichester, UK.

Galliers, R.D. (1991) "Choosing Appropriate Information Systems Research Approaches", In Nissen *et al* (Eds) (1991) *Information Systems Research: Contemporary Approaches and Emergent Traditions*, North-Holland, Amsterdam, Netherlands

Lane, D.C. (1998) "Social Theory and System Dynamics Practice", *European Journal of Operational Research*, Vol. 113(3), scheduled to appear.

Lane, D.C. and Oliva, R. (1994) "The Greater Whole: Towards a Synthesis of SD and SSM", *Proc. 1994 International Systems Dynamics Conference,* Stirling, Scotland.

Lehman, M.M. (1997) "Process Modelling: Where Next", *Proc. International Conference on Software Engineering 1997*, Boston, IEEE Computer Society Press, Los Alamitos, CA, USA.

Weetman, J. (1998) "Enhancing GQM Through SSM: A Case Study", *MSc. Report,* City University, Department of Computing, London, UK.

CHAPTER 56

UNDERSTANDING THE BUSINESS BENEFITS OF IT-ENABLED COMMUNICATIONS IN ORGANISATIONS: DEVELOPING A SUITABLE RESEARCH MODEL

Karin Breu and John Ward
Cranfield School of Management

Abstract

This review explores the current understanding of the factors that affect benefits achievement in IT-enabled communication (ITEC) environments in organisations. Two types of gaps were identified in the literature. First, ITEC research is predominantly based on experimental methodologies in laboratory settings. The transfer of such findings to real-world organisations must be approached with caution. Second, ITEC research focuses centrally on the individual and group level. The organisation as unit of analysis is little represented in existing research. As a result, the business benefits perspective is widely neglected. On introducing the central concepts in current thinking, its theoretical fragmentation is recognised and the controversial views of the effects of communication technologies on conventional communication environments are extrapolated. From the perspective of achieving measurable benefits from IT and IS investments, evidence from the relevant studies is converged into a conceptual model for guiding future research.

1   INTRODUCTION

Focus group workshops with senior level IT professionals held at the Cranfield School of Management revealed the need for understanding the business and organisational improvements to be derived from new, IT-enabled communication (ITEC) environments. The questions raised at the workshops were examined in the light of existing literature both theoretical and empirical. The review enabled a relevant, workable model to be developed for further research to improve our understanding of the effective management of ITECs in organisations.

2   COMMUNICATION IN ORGANISATIONS: A LITERATURE REVIEW

The field of organisational communications is scattered across a diversity of discipline (Banks and Riley, 1993). Against the voluminous amount of theory and research on communication in general, the domain of ITEC is a rapidly growing, yet, still emergent field of practical and theoretical interest. This reflects less the novelty of communication technologies for organisational applications but rather their pervasive adoption in recent years (e.g., Mantovani, 1996). Interested in understanding the effective management of ITEC, we examined the existing theory essentially from an organisational perspective.

2.1   Models of Communication

Traditionally, the communication process was modeled as information transfer, a two-dimensional exchange of information between the sender and the receiver of the communicated message (Argenti, 1998). Under this view, communication media are channels that transport information between the parties involved in the communication act. The capacity of communication channels for transferring information is independent of the specifics of the context in which they are employed. This model of communication has been outdated by the more recent view which suggests that communication is typified by a further, essential characteristic: next to the transfer of data, communication involves also the transfer of meaning (Mantovani, 1996). For media-based communication to occur effectively, the processing potential of communication media must involve more than the mere capability of transporting data. The medium is more than the carrier of the message, the medium itself becomes a message (e.g., McLuhan, 1964; Trevino et al., 1990; Garton and Wellman, 1995). Meaning is socially negotiated and culturally determined. The technological capacities of media for data processing are context-independent, yet, their potential for transferring meaning is created and shaped by the organisational environment in which they are employed. Media are also symbols of something and this is defined in the particular context of the organisation (Sitkin et al, 1992). Taking this view, it is crucial to acknowledge the meaning-generating implications of media in order to fully understand the dynamics of use and effectiveness in technology-mediated communications (Chesebro and Bertelsen, 1996).

2.2   Organisational Needs for Communication

Communications research is based on a number of propositions on the fundamentals of organisations' needs for communication. To operate effectively in ever-changing environments, organisations need to process information to reduce uncertainty and to resolve equivocality (Daft and Lengel, 1984; 1986). Communication underlies most organisational processes and has therefore been considered the essence of organising as organisational members interact internally and externally to co-ordinate activities, to disseminate information, and to make decisions (e.g., Weick, 1987).

2.3 The Concept of IT-Enabled Communications

ITEC media introduced to organisations not only novel forms of communicating but also new opportunities for organising activities. ITEC media have been defined to include electronic mail, voice mail, computer bulletin boards, computer conferencing, groupware, group-decision support systems, extra- and intranets, as well as other new forms of structured communications supported by technology (Steinfield, 1992). The contrasts in traditional and new communication environments emanate from the unprecedented capabilities that technology-supported communications offer (Malone and Rockart, 1991). The typifying characteristics of IT-based communication media have been developed around the categories of synchronicity, transmission speed, textual and graphical nature of the medium, its multiplicity of connections, and its storage and manipulation facilities (Garton and Wellman, 1995).

2.4 ITEC Research

The discussion of current thinking follows a recent classification of the field into the domains of the object- or technology-focused studies and the social actor- or people-focused studies (Nass and Mason, 1990). The technology-focused perspective is interested in identifying the *effects* of new communication technologies on organisations, groups, and individuals. The social actor approach, in contrast, seeks to understand ITEC use from the perspective of the individuals and their *choice* behaviour in ITEC environments.

2.4.1 Media Effect Studies

The dominant paradigm in communication technology research is represented by the rational perspective and exemplified by media effect studies (Lea, 1991). The rational view studies the characteristics of communication technologies that condition their use and impact on communication processes (e.g., Finholt and Sproull, 1990; Lucas 1998). Under this view, technology is a determinant of organisational change that propels the organisation to adjust its activities, processes, and designs to the operational and structural framework that the technology fabricates (Lea 1991). The effects of ITEC media on organisations have been observed in a number of directions. ITEC environments enhance the scope of communication, change conventional patterns of communication, enable novel forms of organisational structure and design, which result in new ways of working and managing.

New Scopes and Patterns of Communicating Within the technology-focused studies, electronic mail received the core part of attention (Garton and Wellman, 1995; Rudy, 1996). Electronic mail is asynchronous, fast, text-based, one-to-one, one-to- many, or many-to-many. Its effects have been described with regard to the changed scope and patterns of communication (Malone and Rockart, 1991; Adams et al., 1993; El-Shinnawy and Markus, 1997). Electronic mail increases the scope of communication in terms of the breadth and capacity of the communication network. In contrast to conventional communication networks, a dramatic increase occurs in the number of participants in the messaging system, the number of interconnections between them, and the volume of message traffic flowing through the network (El-Shinnawy and Markus, 1997). Electronic mail also alters patterns of communication in increasing the vertical and horizontal communication flow through the organisation (Adams et al., 1993). Asynchronous media such as electronic mail remove time zones and geographical barriers and distribute messages to a large number of individuals simultaneously and rapidly. This has been seen as a core advantage of asynchronous communication technology. From an organisational-level perspective, electronic mail is a device for improving effectiveness and productivity in expanding the range of information and expertise and facilitating its exchange across the organisation and its decision makers (Adams et al., 1993; Lucas, 1998).

Electronic Groups   The electronic group at work is a new social and organisational phenomenon that offers significant research opportunities to expand current understanding of organisational behaviour and design (Finholt and Sproull, 1990). Through ITEC, organisations gain the benefit from flexible work structures that enable them to assemble experience and expertise independent of their physical location, thus increasing the speed of information exchange and decision making (Finholt and Sproull, 1990). Management policies strongly influence electronic group activities and the ratio of positive and negative consequences for the organisation. New media usage left to discretion and self-policing may account for negative effects such as information overload or abuse. Researchers recommend to design guidelines for use from the technical and the social perspective of the technology (Finholt and Sproull, 1990). At the social level, norms and codes for use should be endorsed to encourage responsible and effective technology use.

Network and Virtual Designs   ITEC enable the emergence of new organisational designs which have been depicted as the 'breakdown of hierarchy' (Marlow and O'Connor, 1997). The interactive, multi-level capabilities of communication technologies compel change in conventional organisational designs toward the 'network' or the 'virtual' organisation (Li, 1997). Bradley and Nolan (1998) propose that ITEC-based organisations capture value in shifting from the traditional 'make and sell' paradigm to the new, IT and ITEC-enabled paradigm of 'sense and respond'. Interactive communication networks enable organisations to sense and respond to customers' needs in real time swiftly and effectively. The speed with which advances are currently being made in the business applications of information and communication technologies triggers unprecedented change in organisations, industries, business and society that those who study them are only beginning to understand (Bradley and Nolan, 1998).

2.4.2   Media Choice Studies

Media choice research concedes to users an element of choice in the employment of communication technologies (Fulk, et al., 1995). The social actor position argues that the effects-centred perspective objectified technology in treating it as independent of its users, and de-contextualised technology in ignoring the socio-cultural setting in which it is used (Poole and DeSanctis, 1990; Fulk et al., 1995). In the social-actor perspective, technology use is a social process by which individuals and their social environments shape the application of technologies and thus the resultant organisational effects. Whilst media choice researchers agree in their opposition to media effects thinking, they suggest diverse views of choice behaviour, offering two principally different types of explanations: rational and socio-cultural theories of media choice.

Rational Explanations of Media Choice   Rational theories of media choice see individuals' choice behaviour driven by rational determinants, and hence suggest that the effects of technological systems on individuals and organisations are universal. Two schools of thought, social presence and media richness theory represent this perspective.

Social presence theory developed its argument for choice by identifying variations in the degree to which communication media convey the communication partners' social presence in the communication act (e.g., Rice, 1993). The concept of 'social presence' suggests that the communication act is constituted both by the words that are exchanged during a conversation and a range of non-verbal cues such as the speakers' facial expression and body language. Text-based ITEC media such as electronic mail are low in social presence. Media based on audio and/or visual facilities such as video and tele conferencing systems or voice mail are rated comparably high in social presence. Purely text-based ITEC media are less appropriate for social, intuitive or emotional communication tasks like negotiating and more adequate for less socio-emotional tasks like information exchange (e.g., Sproull and Kiesler, 1986). Effective communication is the result of matching the media capacity for conveying social presence with the socio-emotional characteristics of the communication task.

Media richness theory, originally proposed by Daft and Lengel (1984; 1986), views media choice as a rational process in which individuals match the objective characteristics of the communication medium with the content of the message. Communicative contents vary in their levels of complexity and equivocality. Similarly, communication media vary in their capability of processing message complexity. High levels of message complexity are termed 'richness' and low levels of complexity are termed 'leanness' (Daft and Lengel, 1984; 1986). The media richness perspective arrays communication media along a hierarchy of richness that denotes the media' capability for conveying message complexity and equivocality. The order in terms of richness starts from face-to-face as the highest, through to telephone, electronic mail, personal written text (letter, memo), formal written text (document, bulletin), and formal numeric text (computerised data) as the lowest. Rich messages require rich media, that is, the media that are capable of communicating complexity, equivocality, and ambiguity and that enable interactive communication for the participants to negotiate, discuss and clarify the meaning of the communicated message. Media low in richness are appropriate for resolving unequivocal issues and for processing standard, objective data that largely defy inconsistent interpretations. Communication effectiveness is dependent on individuals' rational choice of the medium that most closely matches the richness of the medium with the equivocality of the message (Daft and Lengel, 1984; 1986; Daft et al., 1987).

The media richness proposition of effectiveness has been defied in studies of managerial communication (Trevino et al., 1987; Finholt and Sproull, 1990; Alexander et al., 1991). These studies found managers insensitive to the correlation between media selection and effectiveness in showing an overwhelming bias toward the use of face-to-face communication irrespective of the richness of the communication task. Managers prefer generally rich media because they encourage interpersonal relationships, which are critical to the effective performance of management tasks.

Socio-Cultural Explanations of Media Choice   The socio-cultural perspective focuses on the power of the social and cultural environment in influencing media choice behaviour. The socio-cultural approach to media choice draws on three major streams of thought: structuration, symbolic interaction, and social influence theory (Fulk et al., 1995).

Building on Giddens's (1984), adaptive structuration theory in the context of technology use describes the process by which users manipulate the technologies to accomplish work, and the ways in which such action draws on, reproduces, or sometimes changes the social context within which they operate (Poole and DeSanctis, 1990; Weick, 1990; Yates and Orlikowski, 1992; Banks and Riley, 1993; Fulk et al., 1995; Orlikowski et al., 1995). It is individuals' interpretation of their work activities, the organisation, and the available technology that influences the ways in which they structure the technologies. The existing institutional framework of the organisation sets the conditions for technology use. In using the technology, individuals accommodate and adjust its capabilities to the practices, procedures and the social context of the organisation. The effects of communication technologies are the result of the social interactions that exist between its users and their structural context (e.g., Poole and DeSanctis, 1990; 1992). From a structuration view, technology use is a two-way process, the technological and the social context are both condition and consequence of each other: effectiveness is seen to depend on the negotiation and the purposeful management of technology use through codifying practices (Orlikowski et al., 1995; Mantovani, 1996).

The social-interactionist perspective argues that media choice is, in part, also informed by the symbolic meaning of communication media in a given context (McLuhan, 1964; Feldman and March 1981; Trevino et al., 1990; Chesebro and Bertelsen, 1996; Mantovani, 1996;). This was later acknowledged by the original proponents of media richness theory, in expanding their proposition for the symbolic-interactionist perspective (Trevino et al. 1990). In this revised view, they suggest that media choice is determined by an interplay of three factors: the complexity of the message (information richness model), contextual demands (time pressure, geographic distance) and the symbolic meaning of the medium. Others added to this view in suggesting that media choice is also determined by cultural and social norms and rules for use, as well as the availability of the medium for both the sender and the receiver of the message (Feldman and March, 1981; Sitkin et al., 1992).

The symbolic perspective also offers views of effectiveness in ITEC use. Communication technologies are "general-purpose media" (Orlikowski et al., 1995) or open-ended technologies (Weick, 1990) that allow a number of plausible interpretations of their purpose and use. Openness to interpretation offers the benefit of flexibility but also the potential of inappropriate use if the technology is not adequately adjusted to the organisation-specific norms for communication (Orlikowski et al., 1995). Therefore, the contextualisation of technology is crucial to effective use. This is not an implementation issue only but a continuous process in which technology is adapted to the context of use and in which technology, in turn, shapes and changes the very context in which it is used.

The social influence model of media choice acknowledges the propositions of media richness theory, yet claims that rational categories insufficiently explain choice (Fulk et al., 1990; Schmitz and Fulk, 1991). Social influence theory argues that the properties of media are subjective. Individuals' perceptions and use of media are, in part, dependent on individuals' personal attitude toward technology and on peer group use. The perception of media' properties and the decisions of application vary across contexts.

Media Choice in ITEC Environments   Media richness theory was further invalidated by empirical research into media choice behaviour in ITEC environments. ITEC media have been classified as low in richness, or social presence, and therefore as inappropriate for complex, non-routine communications (Trevino et al., 1990; Yates and Orlikowski, 1992; Rice, 1993; Markus, 1994).

Exploring the applicability of the media richness view to choice among *new* communication media, El-Shinnawy and Markus (1997) contested empirically the validity of media richness theory in ITEC contexts. Empirical support for media richness theory had only been established in the context of choice from traditional media or in situations where individuals choose between traditional and new media. Their study found that individuals choose media for their communication mode and documentation capabilities such as saving, filing, retrieving, documenting and manipulating messages. The communication roles of message sender and receiver that are excluded in media richness thinking were found to exert additional influences on media choice. A new typology of media richness based upon the characteristics of ITEC environments still needs to be developed. To be valid in the context of ITEC media, a theory of choice must be able to accommodate these other explanatory possibilities (El-Shinnawy and Markus, 1997).

This result is supported by the findings from another study that investigated electronic mail users in an organisation with the objective of discovering the criteria on which choices from available alternatives for communication were made (Lea, 1991).

Efficiency considerations in terms of media-task matching were not identified as rationales for use. Instead, users differentiated media in terms of verbal versus written communication modes, spontaneous versus planned communication, inconsequential versus important, emotionally poor versus emotionally rich, and requiring technology versus not requiring technology (Lea, 1991).

Rice et al. (1994) studied media richness theory by the example of a desktop video conferencing system that was implemented in an organisation to support communication between R&D departments in dispersed locations. The development of norms about how to use the system occurred through social processes that are viewed as the result of the interaction of individual assessments of the new technology and critical mass effects over time. Again, media richness theory was unsupported.

Steinfield (1992) suggests a research focus on the social context in which ITEC media are embedded. In contrast to rational choice models, a "wide range of empirical evidence suggests that factors besides task analysability and the resulting ambiguity influence the choice of a medium in any given situation" (Steinfield, 1992: 352). This includes time and distance constraints, social and organisational norms, symbolic meaning of the communication medium, and users' media experiences. Contrary to the expectations of the rational choice model, Steinfield's (1992) work demonstrates that IT-enabled communications are employed for non-routine communication tasks, and that social and contextual factors are very influential in media selection processes. In Steinfield's (1992) view, critical mass theory (Markus, 1990) and the social influence model (Fulk et al., 1990; Schmitz and Fulk, 1991) present more adequate approaches that shift the perspective beyond the match of physical attributes of media and communication tasks and examine the social dynamics of media choice processes.

Whilst rational and socio-cultural propositions compete in their views of media choice, integrative approaches suggest that only the assimilation of the two paradigms will improve the current, insufficient understanding of media choice (Sitkin et al., 1992; Bozeman, 1993; Webster and Trevino, 1995). These studies found that the explanatory power of the two competing approaches depended largely on the type of medium and on its newness within an organisation. In conventional communication environments, individuals' choice behaviour is underpinned by rational influences (Fulk and Boyd, 1991). Conventional media for communication are in use over long periods of time so that organisational members widely agree on their purpose and use. Whilst socio-cultural explanations of media choice are less relevant for understanding usage of traditional media, they largely influence choice in ITEC environments (Fulk and Boyd, 1991; Sitkin et al., 1992; Webster and Trevino, 1995). The introduction of ITEC media attracts a diversity of interpretations of the purpose and their use by the user community. Over time, those interpretations tend to converge so that choice will increasingly match with the objective characteristics of the medium and the communication task (Yates and Orlikowski, 1992; Markus, 1994). Further research is required that adopts a dynamic view of media choice and recognises the importance of rational and social influences on choice over time (Webster and Trevino, 1995).

2.4.3   Managing Effectiveness in ITEC Environments

Organisational-level effectiveness views have been developed around the notions of critical mass effects in the ITEC adoption and implementation stage, the exploitation of 'windows of opportunity', continuous training and development, and the negotiation of guidelines for use.

ITEC Adoption: Critical Mass Effects   Views of effectiveness in ITEC environments have been linked to the adoption and assimilation process of newly introduced communication technologies. Critical mass theory seeks to explain how universal and effective use of a new communication technology develops within an organisational community. Markus (1990), drawing on Oliver et al.'s (1985) theory of critical mass, argues that the diffusion process of ITEC is different from that of any other technological innovation because communication is a social process. The generation of benefits from interactive media is contingent on the use of the technology at the group or the business community level, so that the benefits of newly implemented communication systems will emerge as soon as a 'critical mass' of individuals begins to adopt the system (Markus, 1990; Lucas, 1998).

Exploiting "Windows of Opportunity"   Critical mass views can be related to Tyre and Orlikowski's (1994) concept of "windows of opportunity" that depicts the temporal pattern of technological adaptation in organisations. Their study found that the decisions and directions taken in the implementation stage are crucial determinants of the way in which technology will be used over time. This view is supported by Weick's (1990) proposition that "beginnings are of special importance" in determining the views that users adopt of new technologies and of the problems that subsequently arise. If the initial opportunity at the implementation stage is not exploited, ineffective use becomes routinised, which then can be changed only through purposeful intervention. The findings from their research were remarkably consistent across organisational and technological settings and this suggests that effectiveness gains are generically linked to understanding and exploiting the implementation process and, later, to seizing opportunities for intervention to change routine patterns of use.

Continuous Training and Development   Research into the role of training in the implementation of new communication technology found that it was offered typically at the implementation stage only, that it focused simply on the mechanics of the ITEC system's operation instead on its use and its integration into the working practices they are intended to support (e.g., Bullen and Bennett, 1990). Continuous support of users through training is critical to effective system's use (e.g., Adams et al., 1993). Studying electronic and voice mail, Adams et al. (1993: 13) concluded that although "much of the trade and practitioner literature tends to tout their advantages, benefits are contingent on implementation factors, such as training and the overall utility of the system".

Negotiating Guidelines of Use   The more open the communication system is designed in terms of time, place, sources and recipients, the more chaos can emerge in the flow of the information and its use (Mantovani 1994). Inefficiencies can be reduced in providing users of newly adopted ITEC with protocols that help them to develop effective patterns of use (Finholt and Sproull, 1990; Adams et al., 1993; Mantovani 1994). Yet, for guidelines to be effective, they must be negotiated by the system users (Orlikowski et al., 1995). Guidelines for use should be designed to differentiate ITEC from other media that are available for communication in the organisation and, also, to balance restrictions of usage against the danger of reducing their value.

3   CONCEPTUAL CONCLUSIONS

Traditional communication media are increasingly supplemented and replaced by ITEC systems. In the literature, there is general agreement over the proposition that new technologies for communication offer exciting opportunities and release unprecedented potential for changing and innovating organisational designs, processes, and operating practices. The current understanding of ITEC environments in organisations can be summarised as follows:

- Classic media richness theory, the most influential position on effective media use, fails to explain media choice and communication practices in ITEC environments.
- Other than in conventional communication environments where users base media choice on objective, rational factors, choice in newly implemented ITEC environments results from socio-cultural determinants.
- Effectiveness gains are contingent on the successful ITEC assimilation which requires changes in patterns, behaviours, and practices of communication and business operation.
- Based upon knowledge of the adoption and assimilation processes of IT and IS, it is assumed that there is a transition process at the intersection of conventional and ITEC environments for communication.

Individual Media Choice Behaviour Empirical research has demonstrated that individuals' choice in ITEC environments tends to be informed by socio-cultural determinants of how these technologies might most adequately and thus effectively be used. Selecting ITEC media for reasons such a peer group practices, personal preferences, or cultural routines, propels benefits delivery into a matter of chance. Organisations that seek to exploit the full potential of communication technologies need to develop behaviours in individuals that base media choice on rational, objective criteria, and this presupposes the identification of the benefit-critical factors of ITEC use through further research. The current structure and level of understanding points the way forward. The challenge for future research is to identify the generic enabling changes that organisations, groups and individuals need to perform in order to release high-level benefits from ITEC environments.

The Transition to ITEC Environments Current understanding of organisational practices of ITEC use fails to resolve the question of how to incorporate communication technologies effectively into business processes and, thus, how to turn technological potential into real business value. Effectiveness gains appear to be critically linked to the organisational, group and individual transition and adaptation process of developing conventional communication practices in ways that release the purported benefit potential of ITEC. Present understanding of the dynamics of transition in the context of ITEC insufficiently explains the specifics of this process in terms of its content, structure and contextual particulars.

4   A FRAMEWORK FOR FUTURE ITEC RESEARCH

This section presents the conceptual framework that builds on two pillars: the business benefits perspective in IT and IS investments (Ward et al., 1996) and concepts of ITEC effectiveness. Media richness theory as the most prominent view of effective media usage argues that choice is crucially linked to effectiveness. Developed from research in conventional communication environments, recent studies demonstrate that media richness theory inadequately explains choice in ITEC environments (Lea, 1991; Steinfield 1992; El-Shinnawy and Markus, 1997). The rational choice argument of the media-task matching view has been contested in ITEC environments, where choice was found to be informed by socio-cultural factors (Fulk and Boyd, 1991; Webster and Trevino, 1995).

Scholars have pointed out the difficulties of anticipating the impact of newly applied technologies (e.g., Bell, 1973; Orlikowski and Hofman, 1997). They argue that in the instance of the adoption of new technologies, organisations lack ways of recognising that its most important effects may be not to let people do old things more efficiently but, instead, to do new things that were not possible or feasible with old technology. Taking the view that the outcomes of the application of novel technology are, in general, uncertain, it can be assumed that benefits delivery is a process that is little understood in the context of ITEC. Research still needs to explore what effective management for business benefits entails in ITEC.

If choice in ITEC environments is a socio-cultural phenomenon (Fulk and Boyd, 1991), business benefits delivery is contingent on whether users make appropriate choice decisions or not. Benefits management in Ward et al.'s (1996) concept is contingent on rational choice behaviour. Benefits management in ITEC environments may involve the management of choice behaviour, which requires a shift from subjective, socio-cultural determinants of choice to objective, rational behaviours of choice. The proposition is exhibited in figure 1. It is supported by a number of studies that suggest that the influences of media use change over time (Rice et al., 1994; Webster and Trevino, 1995). The introduction of novel ITEC media attracts a diversity of interpretations of purpose and use by the user community. Those interpretations tend to converge over time so that choice will increasingly match with the objective characteristics of the medium (Yates and Orlikowski, 1992; Markus, 1994). In absence of codified and socially shared views of their meaning and purpose, newly introduced communication technologies tend to be used by individuals' orientation by peers' patterns of usage (Sitkin et al., 1992). As a result, practices of use tend to create ways of working that bear the potential of both yielding effectiveness as well as ineffectiveness. Over time, a pattern of use of a new communication medium emerges, and, as a result, rational influences of choice come increasingly into prominence driving the rationales for choice from the social to the rational paradigm. To date, this particular transition process has not been explored. Further research is required that adopts a dynamic view of media choice and recognises the importance of rational and social influences on choice over time (Webster and Trevino, 1995).

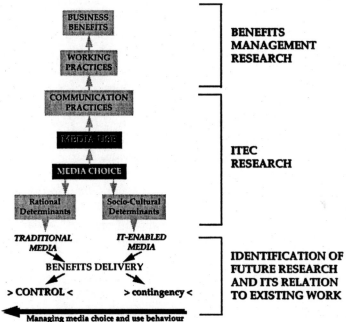

Figure 1: 'Conceptualising Benefits Management in ITEC Environments'
Source: Compiled by the authors.

Such work must seek to understand the dynamics involved in shifting choice from socio-cultural to rational factors in order to enable organisations to utilise ITEC effectively. The fundamental research question needs to address whether effective ITEC use is contingent on a change management process. This includes the question whether the transition from ITEC media choice based on socio-cultural determinants to choice based on rational determinants is crucial for benefits delivery. Future research into the underpinning factors of socio-cultural determinants of choice, the content and structure of the transition process, and the determinants of effectiveness of rational ITEC use is prerequisite for understanding business benefits delivery in ITEC environments.

Taking a business benefits perspective, we are essentially interested in how ITEC can improve those working practices that are strongly supported by communication activities. In our view, it is crucial to understand how people need to change communication behaviours and working practices in order for ITEC to be used effectively. Media choice theory has studied communication behaviour and drawn the implications of choice to individual, group, and organisational effectiveness.

The research project which has started in September 1998 will study the implementation of a range of ITECs in five different organisational contexts.

References

Adams, D A; Todd, P A and Nelson, R R (1993) 'A comparative evaluation of the impact of electronic and voice mail on organizational communication' *Information & Management* vol 24 pp 9-21.

Alexander, E R et al. (1991) 'The effect of individual differences on managerial media choice' *Management Communication Quarterly* vol 5 no 2 pp 155-173.

Argenti, P A (1998) [1994] *Corporate Communication*. Burr Ridge, IL: Irwin. Banks, S P and Riley, P (1993) 'Structuration theory as an ontology for communication research' *Communication Yearbook* vol 16 pp 167-196.

Bell, D (1973) *The Coming of Post-Industrial Society*. New York: Basic Books.

Bozeman, D P (1993) 'Toward a limited rationality perspective of managerial media selection in organizations' *Academy of Management Best Paper Proceedings* pp 278-282.

Bradley, S B and Nolan, R L (1998) 'Capturing value in the network era' In Bradley, S B and Nolan, R L (eds) *Sense and Respond*. Boston, MA: Harvard Press, pp 3-29.

Bullen, C V and Bennett, J L (1990) 'Groupware in practice: An interpretation of work experience' *Proceedings of the Conference on Computer Supported Cooperative Work* Los Angeles, CA, October.

Chesebro, J W and Bertelsen, D A (1996) *Analyzing Media: Communication Technologies as Symbolic and Cognitive Systems*. New York: Guilford Press.

Daft, R L and Lengel, R H (1986) 'Organizational information requirements, media richness and structural design' *Management Science* vol 32 no 5 pp 554-571.

Daft, R L et al. (1987) 'Message equivocality, media selection, and manager performance: Implications for information systems' *MIS Quarterly* vol 1 no 1 pp 355-366.

El-Shinnawy, M and Markus, M L (1997) 'The poverty of media richness theory: explaining people's choice of electronic mail vs. voice mail' *International Journal of Human-Computer Studies* vol 46 pp 443-467.

Feldman, M S and March, J G (1981) 'Information in organizations as signal and symbol' *Administrative Science Quarterly* vol 26 pp 171-186.

Finholt, T and Sproull, L S (1990) 'Electronic groups at work' *Organization Science* vol 1 no 1 pp 41-64.

Fulk, J et al. (1990) 'A social influence model of technology use' In Fulk, J and

Steinfield, C (Eds) *Organizations and Communication Technology*. Newbury Park: Sage pp 117-139.

Fulk, J and Boyd, B (1991) 'Emerging theories of communication in organizations' *Journal of Management* vol 17 no 2 pp 407-446.

Fulk, J et al. (1995) 'Cognitive elements in the social construction of communication technology' *Management Communication Quarterly* vol 8 no 3 pp 259-288.

Garton, L and Wellman, B (1995) 'Social impacts of electronic mail in organizations: A review of the research literature' *Communication Yearbook* vol 18 pp 434-453.

Giddens, A (1984) *The Constitution of Society: Outline of the Theory of Structure*. Berkeley, CA: University of California Press.

Lea, M (1991) 'Rationalist assumptions in cross-media comparisons of computer-mediated communication' *Behaviour and Information Technology* vol 10 no 2 pp 153-172.

Li, F (1997) 'From compromise to harmony: Organisational re-design through information and communication technologies' *International Journal of Information Management* vol 17 no 6 pp 451-464.

Lucas, W (1998) 'The effects of e-mail on the organization' *European Management Journal* vol 16 no 1 pp 18-30.

Malone, T W and Rockart, J F (1991) 'Computers, networks and the corporation' *Scientific American* vol 265 no 3 pp 92-99.

Mantovani, G (1996) *New Communication Environments: From Everyday to Virtual*. London: Taylor & Francis.

Markus, M L (1990) 'Toward a "critical mass" theory of interactive media' In Fulk, J and Steinfield, C (Eds) (1990) *Organizations and Communication Technology*. Newbury Park: Sage Publications pp 194-218.

Markus, M L (1994) 'Electronic mail as the medium of managerial choice' *Organization Science* vol 5 no 4 pp 502-527.

Marlow, E and Wilson, P O'Connor (1997) *The Breakdown of Hierarchy: Communicating in the Evolving Workplace*. Boston: Butterworth-Heinemann.

McLuhan, M (1964) *Understanding Media: The Extension of Man*. Cambridge: MIT.

Nass, C and Mason, L (1990) 'On the study of technology and task: A variable-based approach' In Fulk, J and Steinfield, C (Eds) *Organizations and Communication Technology*. Newbury Park: Sage Publications.

Oliver, P et al. (1985) 'A theory of critical mass I. Interdependence, group heterogeneity, and the production of collective action' *American Journal of Sociology* vol 91 no 3 pp 522-556.

Orlikowski, W and Hofman, J (1997) 'An improvisational model for change management: The case of groupware technologies' *Sloan Management Review* Winter pp 11-21.

Orlikowski, W et al. (1995) 'Shaping electronic communication: the metastructuring of technology in the context of use' *Organization Science* vol 6 no 4 pp 423-444.

Poole, M S and DeSanctis, G (1990) 'Understanding the use of group decision support systems: The theory of adaptive structuration' In Fulk, J and Steinfield, C (Eds) (1990)
Organizations and Communication Technology. Newbury Park: Sage pp 173-193.

Rice, R E (1993) 'Using social presence theory to compare traditional and new organizational media' *Human-Communication-Research* vol 19 no 4 pp 451-484.

Rice, R E et al. (1994) 'Individual, structural and social influences on use of a new communication medium' *Academy of Management Best Papers Proceedings* pp 285-289.

Rudy, I A (1996) 'A critical review of research on electronic mail' *European Journal of Information Systems* vol 4 pp 198-213.

Schmitz, J and Fulk, J (1991) 'Organizational colleagues, media richness, and electronic mail: A test of the social influence model of technology use' *Communication Research* vol 18 no 4 pp 487-523.

Sitkin, S B et al. (1992) 'A dual-capacity model of communication media choice in organizations' *Human Communication Research* vol 18 no 4 pp 563-598.

Sproull, L and Kiesler, S (1986) 'Reducing social context clues: Electronic mail in organizational communication' *Management Science* vol 32 no 11 pp 1492-1512.

Steinfield, C (1992) 'Computer-mediated communications in organizational settings: Emerging conceptual frameworks and directions for research' *Management Communication Quarterly* vol 5 no 3 pp 348-365.

Trevino, L K et al (1990) 'Understanding managers' media choices: A symbolic interactionist perspective' In Fulk, Janet & Steinfield, Charles (Eds) *Organizations and Communication Technology*. Newbury Park: Sage.

Trevino, L K et al. (1987) 'Media symbolism, media richness, and media choice in organizations: A symbolic interactionist perspective' *Communication Research* vol 14 pp 553-574.

Tyre, M J and Orlikowski, W(1994) 'Windows of opportunity: Temporal patterns of technological adaptation in organizations' *Organization Science* vol 5 no 1 pp 98-118.

Ward, J et al. (1996) 'Evaluation and realisation of IS/IT benefits: An empirical study of current practice' European Journal of Information Systems vol 4 pp 214-225.

Webster, J and Trevino, L K (1995) 'Rational and social theories as complementary explanations of communication media choices: Two policy-capturing studies' *Academy of Management Journal* vol 38 no 6 pp 1544-1572.

Weick, K (1987) 'Theorizing about organizational communication' In Jablin, F M et al. (Eds.) *Handbook of Organizational Communication* pp 97-122. Newbury Park: Sage.

Weick, K (1990) 'Technology as equivoque' in Goodman, P S et al. *Technology and Organizations*. San Francisco, CA: Jossey-Bass pp 1-44.

Yates, J and Orlikowski, W (1992) 'Genres of organizational communication: A structurational approach to studying communication and media' *Academy of Management Review* vol 17 no 2 pp 299-326.

CHAPTER 57

SOCIAL CONSTRUCTION OF AN INTERPRETIVE STUDY OF INFORMATION SYSTEMS - REFLECTIONS ON A CASE STUDY

Gamila M Shoib
University of Cambridge

Abstract

This paper presents work in progress on a study of the use of information systems for decision making in the subsidiary of a multinational FMCG company in Egypt. It serves as a contribution to the sparse repertoire of reflexive studies on IS. The research focuses on the social construction of Information Systems-informed decision making processes in this organisation. It is grounded in an interpretive social constructionist stance. A discovery-oriented case study method is employed. 98 interviews conducted with 45 individuals, participant observation over a period of 9 months and two questionnaires constitute the core of the data collected. This is supplemented by a wealth of documents and electronic data gathered on site and 3 months "tele-researching". The paper is a reflexive account of the evolution of the study's constituting elements during its various stages.

1. INTRODUCTION

This paper traces the work in progress on a study of IS use in a multinational company in Egypt. Starting with the theoretical birth of the study, the paper describes the work in terms of its focus, methodological grounding and its research method. The study's initial configuration was a qualitative, multi-case study based on interviews. It focused on the decision making model underlying IS implementation in an Egyptian context. Since then it has evolved into an ethnographic in-depth case study using a mix of qualitative and quantitative data collection methods, namely semi-structured as well as structured interviews, participant observation and document analysis. The paper contributes to the sparse IS literature of reflexive studies. In so doing, the paper shows by example how the contents of the structure of a research study are socially constructed (see Figure 1). The structural elements of the study are also socially constructed yet the treatment of their construction is considered beyond the scope of this paper. The contents of these elements are socially constructed by (the available knowledge of and researcher choices about) epistemology, ontology, interplay between theory and field data, and reflexivity.

Since its beginning in October 1996, the study has changed names and focus several times. At first it underwent several iterations between thought and theory followed by several iterations between practice and theory. This evolving quality of the study is one of its main characteristics which stems from its interpretive nature and a desire to maintain a considerable degree of openness to the field data and a willingness to modify initial assumptions and theories (Walsham 1995). Reflexivity is an essential part of social science research and has many advocates (Giddens 1984, Walsham 1995). As humans attempting to study other humans, thus changing their and our subjectivity, we need to reflect on the research act as a whole, namely ourselves, the subject of our inquiry, our relationship to our *explanandum* as well as the whole research process. Reflecting on the study has and still does constitute an integral part of it.

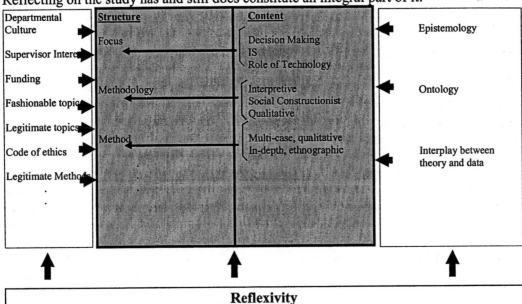

Figure 1: Structure and Elements of a Research Study

2. INITIAL REARCH FOCUS

The research topic can broadly be divided into three general areas of interest: decision making (DM), Information Systems (IS) use, and Egypt as a case of an emerging "non-Western" market. A review of the decision-making literature shows a bias towards Western interpretations (Miller et al. 1996, Shoib 1997). As an Egyptian researcher this sparked my interest in the "cultural boundedness" of decision-making. As a computer scientist by background, I was further intrigued by the assumption of a rational decision-making model underlying IT development and implementation (Salzman and Rosenthal 1994) and how this assumption interacts with a non-Western environment. The plan at that point (June 1997) was to cover the various literatures depicted, namely decision making, IS development and use supplemented by the literature on the Egyptian context (society, religion, culture etc.) and various theoretical frameworks that have been used to tackle the research questions.

Social Constructionism (Berger and Luckmann 1966) as a fundamental and basic view of the human condition, which involves the individual, group and societal level, lent itself as a most powerful "tool" for grasping this under-researched cultural and societal context. In addition, the decision making literature showed a lack of sensitivity to any other epistemology other than positivism (Miller et al 1996). As a "pioneering" study, the choice of an exploratory study that focuses on understanding from the "natives' point of view" seemed the most suited. Qualitative research therefore suggested itself as the appropriate methodological direction (Denzin and Lincoln 1994). A cross sectional collective case study (Orlikowski and Baroudi 1991, Stake 1994) was selected as the method of choice to be represented in the final PhD dissertation, using a mix of realist, confessional and impressionist writing (Van Maanen 1988). The case study has been found to be the most suitable form for the research of areas where theory is still young and in its formative stages (Walsham 1993). The increase in the use of the case study as a method for the study of IS in organisations is a further indicator of the suitability of this method for IS research (Walsham 1995b).

Building on Barley (1986) and Walsham (1993), the study initially proposed to use a "framework" of analysis where scripts would be analysed along three dimensions which constitute Giddens' (1984) modalities (see Figure 2). It consisted of selected theoretical frameworks that have been used for making sense of IS, namely Pettigrew (1987), Kling and Scacchi (1982), Kling (1987), Giddens (1984), Walsham (1993), and Barley (1986). Framework selection criteria were: interpretive epistemology, focus on context, and suitability for the study of processes and allowance for the incorporation of IS. It was envisaged that this "framework" would be used to investigate two levels: business processes and system processes, i.e. scripts within and without the computer system. Analysing scripts of the two levels (organisational & IS) along the same dimensions would provide insight into the role of IS as well as otherwise obscured characteristics of either organisational process or IS use.

A further investigation of the IS literature took the study more towards the role of technology (IS) in terms of user/developer perceptions of it (Orlikowski 1992) and the effect this relationship has on the use of technology for decision making purposes in an organisation. A focus on user perceptions in terms of assumptions, expectations and knowledge (or more generally user interpretations) transformed the study's social constructionist stance from an underlying philosophical stance to a focus and an "operationalisable" approach. Orlikowski's (1992) review of the literature on the role of technology shows a technological, social and soft determinism divide congruent with an epistemological/ontological divide between objective, subjective and combined views of reality. In so doing, she points to a shortage in studies of the third "school".

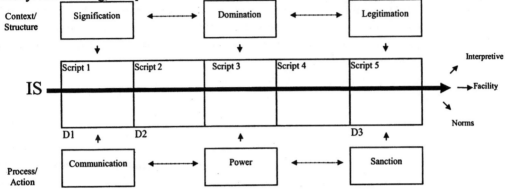

Figure 2: Initial Proposed Framework; Shoib (1997)

From the repertoire of concepts dealing with assumptions/expectation Orlikowski and Gash's (1994) notion of *technological frames* was chosen to study user interpretations (use mode) and system designer interpretations (design mode) of the role of technology. Investigating a set of *frame domains* derived from the empirical setting across user groupings, the interpretations of the user and designers are reconstructed and compared yielding an insightful analysis of the IS use. There again the openness to the empirical setting and focus on perspectives was the attraction for selection.

In addition to the gap in the literature on Technology as Trigger to Change and the lack of social constructionist studies of IS, I believed that such a basic approach which focuses on interpretations in terms of assumptions, expectations and knowledge would provide an invaluable insight into the under-researched context of Egypt. The approach is also flexible enough to be feasible in any organisational context. The exploratory nature of this study also suggested a focus on "the basics". In addition, the social constructionist nature of the approach together with the *in situ* nature of technological frames creates a very context-sensitive approach, which captures cultural aspects (organisational as well as national). The design mode/use mode "divide" and the congruence of the two realms, is a rich ground for the investigation of embedded "western" concepts of decision making and their interaction with the (potentially) "different" cultural and social context. Finally, the study could constitute a rich starting point for a further study of organisational subcultures within companies in emerging markets.

Sensitizing concepts (Blumer 1954, Olaisen 1990), as defined by van den Hoonaard (1997), offered themselves as an intermediate approach between rigid constructs on the one hand and grounded theory on the other (Glaser and Strauss1967). A review of decision making concepts (Shoib 1997) emerging from the three major choice paradigms of 1) rationality/ bounded rationality 2) power 3) politics and 4) garbage cans, together with theories on the use of and role of IS were reinterpreted into sensitising concepts. These sensitizing concepts, described above, represented the broad areas or topics for the interview questions and served as the guiding constructs for the semi-structured interviews that were conducted as well as the everyday perception and analysis of observations. The use of concepts, reinterpreted as sensitizing devices, also allowed for an epistemological reconciliation with the predominantly functionalist literature on decision making (Miller et al. 1996) and thus furnished the study with a body of knowledge that may have otherwise not been beneficial.

3. RESEARCH METHOD

Guided by topics and social constructionism as the chosen research's epistemology, I proceeded to choose the research method. As Figure 3 depicts, the overall (interpretive) premise of the work is that social theory is presupposed to be of value for understanding the human condition. Interpretive social theory does not aim to find universal laws or the one objective truth (Burrell and Morgan 1979, Walsham 1993). Furthermore, the study's level of focus is the organisation, not the individual. The social constructionist assumption does indeed transcend the boundaries of the individual, i.e. the organisational and the societal boundaries, yet the individual and the society are dealt with here as a context or supplement to the organisational focus. The chosen research method is the case study.

Interviews appeared the most suitable form of data collection given the study's interpretive and qualitative nature (Myers 1997) and chosen case study method (Walsham 1995b). Semi-structured interviews were deemed the best choice from the repertoire of interviewing methods. They also presented a good balance between theory and openness to field data and fit well with the use of sensitizing concepts. They were thus chosen in order to: 1) reduce the risk of imposing theoretical concepts on the empirical environment, 2) contain the flow of the interview, and 3) reduce the complexity in managing the field data collected.

4. SYNOPSIS OF FIELDWORK

The fieldwork to date may be broken down into several phases. In January 1997 I returned to Egypt for the "Access Negotiation". The actual fieldwork started in December 1997. The first three months I perceive as the "Gaze unto reality". The six months after that were spent "Digging Deeper" into the focus, guided by the initial theory and field insights. In the following paragraphs, the different phases of the fieldwork will be described.

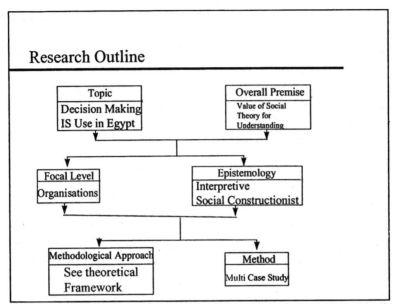

Figure 3: Initial Research Outline (adapted from Walsham 1993); Shoib (1997)

RESEARCH ACCESS

In January 1997, I gained access to seven conglomerates in the manufacturing segment of Egyptian industry. Gaining this access was part of my strategy to do an exploratory multi-case study. In the summer of 1997, I gained in-depth access to the subsidiary of a multinational (US-based) corporation in Egypt. Faced with the choice between a multi-case study and a single in-depth ethnographic study, I decided to choose the latter. My level of information and people access in the multinational company was extremely good given that I had previously worked for the organisation. My level of access with the other seven conglomerates stopped at the chairman level and was superficial, at best. I was also faced with a total lack of available public knowledge on any of the companies and the risk of only very basic non-computer-based IS. In addition, my correspondence with the companies, since gaining access, also suggested a shallow disposition to be researched and a lack of genuine interest on the conglomerate's part. Research is unfortunately not a widespread phenomenon in Egypt and it seldom transcends the boundaries of university campuses into the "real world" (Ali 1995). In addition, an ethnographic study was even more in line with the epistemological grounding of the study, namely social constructionism (Walsham 1995b).

GAZE UNTO REALITY (December 1997 – February 1998)

During the Gaze unto reality phase I moved to Cairo, Egypt and was given a role as a systems analyst in the target organisation. I was expected to do the same job as any other analyst but was given the freedom to select the project(s) that I wanted to focus on. This role allowed me total access to the organisation and rapport with colleagues and interviewees who perceived me as a member of the organisation. After 3 months of involvement in various projects, 15 unstructured interviews and extensive daily participant observations, I spent two weeks away from the field. During that time I analysed the data I had gathered so far with a view to select an attractive empirical focus that matched my initial research results with the business opportunities. The focus that I finally chose in a way suggested itself and had a life of its own. I was involved in a SAP migration project, in distributor systems support and in sales systems support. SAP was undergoing some resistance and its future was undetermined, which made it unfeasible in terms of research time frame. The second area was too focused on distributor systems which were in essence autonomous business partners of the company. Focusing on them would have moved me away from the company and lost me my most valued asset, namely incredibly good access. In addition to these retrospective reasons, the third area of my involvement, sales automation support seemed to have occupied the majority of my time in those three months. It was also the area about which I found myself most knowledgeable due to my exposure. Consequently I was able to find many ideas that linked up with my initial research interests and had concrete business benefits for the company.

DIGGING DEEPER (March 1998 - July 1998)

The decision was thus made to focus on the Sales automation and reporting system in the next stage. My business task was to come up with what was termed "current best approach" (abbreviated CBA) for using the laptops and all the tools or software that was provided on them. The objective of the task was to standardise the reporting system and bring the sales force to the same competent level of computer usage. This project also gave me an opportunity to interview the entire sales organisation in depth as well as conduct practical sessions with them during which they showed me how and what they used their laptops for. The interviews were semi-structured and the so-called practical sessions were totally unstructured. They provided me with an opportunity to probe further into areas that were raised during the interviews. In addition to the sales force and their middle and top management I interviewed the computer support team in the computer department and their middle and top management. This included former as well as current (where applicable) individuals who were involved in the sales automation project that took place in 1996. As a sales systems analyst myself, I was involved in the roll out of the second generation of computers which was meant to provide the force with more computational power and capabilities.

TELERESEARCHING (August 1998 -)

Armed with a company laptop, an internal email address, access to CompuServe, access to the company's and sales department's Intranet, I am still able to be virtually part of the organisation despite my physical displacement. This stage of the project evolved during the "Digging Deeper". This development was triggered by a number of pragmatic considerations: 1) I wanted to have exactly the same laptop and software that my interviewees had in order to be able to better understand their language and relate to their problems and working conditions. 2) The company's desire to benefit from my data analysis until the completion of the study 3) A desire on my part to extend my access to data and to my explanandum for as long as possible 4) A desire on my part to benefit from the opportunity of having an advanced personal laptop that would contain all my data and give me independence from our unreliable departmental computing facilities.

5. FOCUS REVISITED

I had thus far been interested in the "East meet West" scenario of the Egyptian context meeting the rational decision-maker underlying IS design. My interview questions were, however, general enough to encompass various foci yet specific enough to make the research guided. This was very much in line with the exploratory nature of the research method. At this stage the initial data analysis suggests an additional area of interest: knowledge engineering and management. The sales force had not been "properly" trained when their operation was first computerised in 1996. They were then, and to a large extent still are, computer illiterate. Many of them are still incapable of operating their laptops beyond entering customer orders and looking at one shipment report. I have reason to believe that this is largely due to the fact that they were given an initial shock of computer knowledge and then left to their own devices to make sense of this new "monster". In addition, the computer department was severely under-staffed at the time of the computerisation of the Sales force in 1996. "Trial and error" was basically the main learning mechanism compounded with a strong culture of friendship and helpfulness that I believe to be typical of the company's Sales force and Egyptians in general. On the other hand, they do not appear to have done anything to improve their status quo which perpetuated the non-ideal working conditions for two whole years. This situation, I believe, made it difficult for me to see or to get into any specific observations about the assumptions of the rational decision-maker and the Egyptian users, mainly because the users were at a severe disadvantage. However, having said that, I believe that an investigation in the congruence of design and use modes, as suggested by Orlikowski (1992), which is based on user perceptions of technology and its developers and vice versa, appears to be an essential starting point. I do not, however, wish to impose any rigid focus on my data and intend to keep my senses open to what the field data has to say.

6. RESEARCH METHOD REVISITED

With the decision to focus on one case study as opposed to multiple cases, I moved away from a broad research perspective to a deeper one. In the former, the challenge is more on managing the quantity of the data and in the latter it is more a matter of quality. After 9 months in the field, I strongly believe that my decision to do one in-depth case study compounded with my role in the organisation, has enriched my study in terms of data quality, verification opportunities and access to what would normally be inaccessible realms of human interactions. With the role within the organisation came a change to the case study method and semi-structured interviewing as the core data collection method. Participant observation lent itself as a supplementary and enriching source for more data. Opportunities for unstructured interviews constituted an integral part of the CBA. As a (virtual) member of the organisation I am part of the company email system and was/am copied on all internal company and departmental material circulated to employees at large. In addition to this wealth of data, my personal interactions with colleagues-turned-friends during coffee and lunch breaks provided another source of information, which under the usual case study interviewing circumstances would be inaccessible to researchers.

The CBA also provided an opportunity to actively change the research environment. That gave the research method a new unplanned direction, namely towards action research (Schoen 1983, Cancian and Armstead 1993, Denzin and Lincoln 1994, Reason 1994). It is my intention before the CBA implementation to ask the sales force to fill in a questionnaire pertaining to their experience so far and my conclusions about the set up. After a few months of adaptation to the new system, namely the CBA, I will be asking them to fill in another questionnaire to collect information about the change that I have introduced and the new situation. This data will be useful both for the research as a continuation to the story post my intervention as well as serving as the follow-up phase to closing the implementation of the CBA.

7. FURTHER RESEARCH

A return to the literature on Actor Network theory (e.g. Walsham 1997) and Knowledge Management (e.g. Schendel 1996, Spender and Grant 1996, Spender 1996, Tsoukas 1996, Szulanski 1996, Zuboff 1988, Nonaka et al. 1995) seems appropriate prior to the start of the data analysis. In addition, a review of the literature on the role of the researcher (e.g. Van Maanen (1979, 1988), Nandhakumar and Jones (1997)) is planned as preparation for the theme of reflexivity in the dissertation. This, together with the repertoire of previous literature reviews, will serve as the theoretical foundation for the dissertation. Themes identified through use of the sensitizing concepts will guide the analysis and the further evolution of the study. I anticipate that once the data analysis is completed the focus may be a different one from where I believe the study to be currently heading. Having said that I do not wish to impose such a judgement on the process. I would, once again, like to remain open to the data and the sensitizing concepts to guide my path. Pragmatically speaking, though, and for the purpose of completing my PhD I will have to make use of the literatures I have reviewed and therefore would not expect that the focus would change radically. But it will certainly evolve. And that is how I believe it should be. Every study is constrained by pragmatic considerations of time, space, material and human effort.

8. CONCLUSION

The paper represents a series of reflections on the constituting parts of my study of IS use, namely the study's focus, methodology and method. These elements are an integral part of any scientific endeavour. They socially construct new research efforts as well as frame our perceptions of existing literature. We all have to pragmatically conform to these imposed structures which have come to constitute our knowledge of what research is and what it should be. In the evolution of the contents of its structures, a study is socially constructed by the existing literature on its subject areas, legitimate methodologies and methods within its epistemology and ontology, and pragmatic considerations of field access and time frame. Reflexivity is, however, believed by the author to be the trigger for the evolution of a study, especially one that is guided by an openness to field data and interviewee subjectivity. It has certainly enriched my experience of the literature, my organisation and myself in these past years. The study thus also represents a retrospective and introspective account of how an openness to field data leads the researcher to different terrains, and how the interplay between theory and practice moulds a study into its final shape and form. Few IS researchers, even of an interpretive epistemology, ever attempt such accounts. This is very unfortunate given the important role that reflexivity plays in the research effort, especially one of interpretive epistemology. Reflexive accounts enrich the knowledge transferred between researchers and should provide us with more control over the social construction of our field and profession.

References

Ali, A. J. (1995). "Cultural Discontinuity and Arab Management Thought". *International Studies of Management and Organizations*, Vol. 25, No. 3: 7-30.

Barley, S.R. (1986). "Technology as an Occasion for Structuring: Evidence from Observations of CT scanners and the Social Order of Radiology Departments". *Administrative Science Quarterly*, Vol. 31: 78-108.

Berger, Peter and Luckmann, Thomas. (1966). *The Social Construction of Reality: A Treatise in the Sociology of Knowledge*. London: Penguin Books. (1991 reprint).

Bijker, and Law, J. (eds.) (1992). *Shaping Technology/Building Society: Studies in Sociotechnical Change*. Cambridge, Mass: The MIT Press. (Original 1987, Third Printing)

Bijker, W.E., Hughes, T.P. and Pinch, T. (eds.) (1990). *The Social Construction of Technological Systems: New Directions in the Sociology and History of Technology*. Cambridge, Mass: The MIT Press. (Original 1987, Third Printing)

Blumer, H. (1954). "What is Wrong with Social Theory?" *American Sociological Review*, Vol 19: 3-10.

Bostrom, R.P. and Heinen, J.S. (1977). "MIS Problems and Failures: A Socio-Technical Perspective, Part I-The Causes". *MIS Quarterly*, Vol 1, No 3: 17-32.

Burrell, G. and Morgan, G. (1979). *Sociological Paradigms and Organisational Analysis*. London: Heinemann.

Cancian, F. M. and Armstead, C. (1993). "Bibliography on Participatory Research". *Collaborative Inquiry,* Vol 9.

Denzin, N. K. and Lincoln, Y. S. (1994). *Handbook of Qualitative Research*. Thousand Oaks: Sage Publications.

Denzin, N.K. and Lincoln, Y.S. (1994). "Introduction: Entering the Field of Qualitative Research". In Denzin, N. K. and Lincoln, Y. S. . *Handbook of Qualitative Research*. Thousand Oaks: Sage Publications.

Giddens, A. (1984). *The Constitution of Society*. Cambridge: Polity Press.

Giddens, A. (1993). *New Rules of Sociological Method: A positive Critique of Interpretative sociologies*. 2nd Ed. . Cambridge: Polity Press.

Glaser, B. And Strauss, A.L. (1967) . *The Discovery of Grounded Theory: Strategies for Qualitative Research*. Chicago: Aldine.

Gupa, E.G. and Lincoln, Y.S. (1994). "Competing Paradigms in Qualitative Research". In Denzin, N. K. and Lincoln, Y. S. . *Handbook of Qualitative Research*. Thousand Oaks: Sage Publications.

Hamilton, D. (1994). "Traditions, Preferences, and Postures in Applied Qualitative Research". In Denzin, N. K. and Lincoln, Y. S. . *Handbook of Qualitative Research*. Thousand Oaks: Sage Publications.

Huberman, A.M. and Miles, M.B. (1994). "Data Management and Analysis Methods". In Denzin, N. K. and Lincoln, Y. S. . *Handbook of Qualitative Research*. Thousand Oaks: Sage Publications.

Kling, R. (1987). "Defining the Boundaries of Computing Across Complex Organisations". In Boland, R. and Hirschheim, R. (eds.). *Critical Issues in Information Systems Research*. New York: Wiley.

Kling, R. (1996). "Computerization at Work". In Dunlop,C. and Kling, R. (eds.). *Computerization and Controversy*. 2nd Edition. London: Academic Press.

Kling,R. and Scacchi, (1982) "The Web of Computing: Computer Technology as Social Organization". *Advances in Computers*, Vol 21: 1-90.

Miller, S.J. , Hickson, D.J. and Wilson, D.C. (1996). "Decision Making in Organizations". In Clegg, S.R., Hardy, C. and Nord, W.R. . *Handbook of Organizational Studies*. London: Sage.

Miles, M.B. and Huberman, A.M. (1984). *Qualitative Data Analysis: A Sourcebook of New Methods*. Newbury Park, CA: Sage.

Nandhakumar, J. and Jones, M. (1997). "Too close for comfort? Distance and Engagement in Interpretive Information Systems Research". *Information Systems Journal*, Vol 7: 109-131.

Nonaka, I. And Takeuchi, H. (1995). *The Knowledge-Creating Company*. New York: Oxford University Press.

Olaisen, J. (1990). *Pluralism or Positivistic Trivialism: Toward Criteria for a Clarified*

Subjectivity in Information Science. Research report 1990/2. Sandvika: HandelshΦyskolen BI Norwegian School of Management.

Orlikowski, W.J. (1992). "The Duality of Technology: Rethinking the Concept of Technology in Organizations". *Organization Science*, Vol 3, No 3: 398-427.

Orlikowski, W.J. and Baroudi, J.J. (1991). "Studying Information Technology in Organizations: Research Approaches and Assumptions". *Information Systems Research*, Vol 2 No.1: 1-28.

Orlikowski, W.J. and Robey, D. (1991). "Information Technology and the Structuring of Organizations". *Information Systems Research*, Vol 2 No. 2 :143-169.

Pettigrew, A.M. (1987). "Context and Action in the Transformation of the Firm". *Journal of Management Studies*, Vol 24, No. 6: 649-670.

Reason, P. (1994). "Three Approaches to Participative Inquiry". In Denzin, N. K. and Lincoln, Y. S. . *Handbook of Qualitative Research*. Thousand Oaks: Sage Publications.

Salzman, H. and Rosenthal, S. R. (1994). *Software by Design: Shaping Technology and the Workplace.* New York: Oxford University Press.

Schendel, D. (1996). "Knowledge and the Firm". *Strategic Management Journal*, Vol 17, Winter Special Issue: 1-4.

Schoen, D. A. (1983). *The Reflective Practitioner: How Professionals Think in Action.* New York: Basic Books.

Shoib, G.M. (1997). *The Use of Information Systems for Decision Making in Egyptian Organisations.* Unpublished First Year Report. The Judge Institute of Management Studies, University of Cambridge.

Spender, J. C. (1996). "Making Knowledge the Basis of a Dynamic Theory of the Firm". *Strategic Management Journal*, Vol 17, Winter Special Issue: 45-62.

Spender, J. C. And Grant, R. M. (1996). "Knowledge and the Firm: Overview". *Strategic Management Journal*, Vol 17, Winter Special Issue: 5-9.

Stake, R.E. (1994). "Case Studies". In Denzin, N. K. and Lincoln, Y. S. . *Handbook of Qualitative Research*. Thousand Oaks: Sage Publications.

Szulanski, G. (1996). "Exploring Internal Stickiness: Impediments to the Transfer of Best Practice Within the Firm". *Strategic Management Journal*, Vol 17, Winter Special Issue: 27-43.

Tsoukas, H. (1996). "The Firm as a Distributed Knowledge System: A Constructionist Approach". *Strategic Management Journal*, Vol 17, Winter Special Issue: 11-25.

Van den Hoonaard, W.C. (1997). *Working with Sensitizing Concepts: Analytical Field Research.* Qualitative Research Methods Series 41. Thousand Oaks: Sage Publications.

Van Maanen, J. (1979). "The Fact of Fiction in Organizational Ethnography". Administrative Quarterly, Vol 24, No 4: 539-550.

Van Maanen, J. (1988). *Tales of the Field: On Writing Ethnography.* Chicago: University of Chicago Press.

Walsham,G. (1993). *Interpreting Information Systems in Organizations.* Chichester: John Wiley and Sons.

Walsham, G. (1995a). "The Emergence of Interpretivism in IS Research". *Information Systems Research*, Vol 6, No 4, December : 376 - 394.

Walsham, G. (1995b). "Interpretive Case Studies in IS Research: Nature and Method". *European Journal of Information Systems*, Vol. 4: 74-81.

Walsham, G. (1997). "Actor-Network Theory and IS Research: Current Status and Future Prospects". In Lee, A.S. , Liebenau, J. And DeGross, J. I.(eds.). *Information Systems and Qualitative Research.* London: Chapman Hall.

Zuboff, S. (1988). *In the Age of the Smart Machine.* New York: Basic Books.

CHAPTER 58

STRUCTURATION THEORY AND CONVERSATION MODELLING: A POSSIBLE INTERPRETIVIST APPROACH TO BRIDGING THE GAP IN INFORMATION SYSTEM DESIGN

Donna Champion
De Montfort University

Abstract

This paper is a review of the reasons for adopting an Interpretivist perspective and describes an approach to modelling the requirements for Information Systems (IS) from the perspective of the people using the IS. Building on the work of Giddens (1984) and Winograd and Flores (1986), Harris and Taylor (1998) suggest a means of modelling conversations within an Interpretivist framework. It is suggested that it may be possible to apply these ideas to defining client's requirements for IS, providing a more detailed link between an 'appreciative analysis' and a formal definition whilst maintaining forwards and backwards traceability.

1. INTRODUCTION

This paper describes the initial stages of research carried out as part of an EPSRC funded project within the "Systems Engineering for Business Process Change" (SEBPC) programme. The aim of the project is to develop a unified mechanism for IS definition. The initial research will be to investigate potential means of modelling clients' natural language descriptions of their Information System (IS) requirements that can provide a detailed link to the full technical specifications required for the development of the IS. The paper initially reviews the reasons for adopting an Interpretative perspective and critically evaluates some current Interpretative approaches. The fundamental aim in adopting an Interpretative approach to the research is to develop an appreciation of the problem situation from the perspective of the people involved. Crucially this "appreciation" needs to be represented in ways that are open, understandable and useful to everyone participating in the development of the IS. A means of modelling IS requirements is developed which applies the conversation modelling of Winograd and Flores (1986) and the co-ordination mapping of Harris and Taylor (1998).

A Definition of an Information System

For the purpose of this research an 'information system' (IS) is considered as being concerned with human communication involved in purposeful activity. The presence of computers, or other technical devices is not considered to be essential, although it is likely that some form of Information Technology will play a part in the communication system. The definition adopted here is that proposed by Stowell and West (1994, p. 22), i.e. an information system is considered to be:

> "...the notional whole through which the provision, manipulation and use of appropriate data to enable decision making to take place is managed".

2. AN INTERPRETIVIST APPROACH TO ELICITING IS REQUIREMENTS

Many authors have argued that conventional structured methods of IS design have failed to meet with expectations and are limited in their ability to deal with complex social issues in organizational settings (Galliers, 1987; Lyytinen, 1988). One of the reasons cited for this failure, is the emphasis on technological considerations inherent in structured design methods. For example, Hirschheim et al (1995) describe data modelling approaches as having the belief that it is possible to represent pure, factual reality, i.e. these methods are underpinned by a rationalistic approach to the world. Winograd and Flores (1986) argue that this approach views meaning as being built up systematically from smaller elements, each discrete element also having its own significance. They believe that such a stance fails to take into account that interpretation is fundamental to understanding. Gadamer (1975) suggests that any individual interacting in the world, does so from a position of pre-understanding, or prejudice, which includes assumptions implicit in the language used in a situation. Language in turn is learned through active interpretation. Gadamer argues that:

> 'The very idea of a situation means we are not standing outside it and hence we are unable to have any objective knowledge of it. We are always within the situation and to throw light on it is a task that is never entirely completed'. (Gadamer, 1975, p. 268).

To facilitate the recognition of this view, many authors have argued for an Interpretivist approach to research (Checkland, 1981; Winograd and Flores, 1986; Stowell, 1991; Lewis, 1993). The belief inherent in this philosophical stance is one of meaning being socially constructed and research from this perspective aims to explore the many meanings created by the people within a situation. Soft Systems Methodology

(SSM), developed by Checkland and others (Checkland, 1981; Checkland and Scholes, 1990) is a well documented example of such an approach. The fundamental aim of SSM is to recognise different viewpoints and through accommodation retain this diversity in any changes that occur as a result of any investigation into a problem domain.

Criticisms of Interpretative Methodologies

Flood and Jackson (1991) regard SSM as being too idealistic, and argue that it is first necessary to change the political structures within a situation; they see SSM as failing to recognise issues of conflict and coercion, including "false consciousness", where people do not even realise that things are not on the agenda. They acknowledge SSM accepts each view as being equally valid, but feel that the methodology favours the managerial agenda in a situation, as it leaves closure of the debate to the prevailing power structures and so does not alter the distributions of influence. Checkland and Scholes (1990) counter this in their description of a more developed version of SSM, mode 2, arguing it is possible to undertake a political analysis by asking questions about how such managerial influences are expressed in the situation under investigation. Flood and Jackson's work is influenced by the philosophy of Habermas (1984) and they, as with other approaches subscribing to the ideas of Habermas, argue for taking an emancipatory approach. This philosophical stance is based in the belief that it is in the interests of the people involved within a situation, to be freed from any distortion in communications due to the effects of coercion and influence, Flood and Jackson themselves admit this is possibly "assuming a superior position over other orders of life" (Flood and Jackson, 1991, p. 242).

An approach within an Interpretivist philosophy stems from the view that building an 'appreciation' of a situation engenders accommodation and that it is essential to endeavour to be aware of who is absent from discussion and to work ceaselessly to try to acknowledge the whole problem (Vickers, 1984). Vickers (1970) suggests that there is a tendency to view human activity and decision-making in terms of achieving goals. He argues that a more appropriate view of organizations is that of relationship-maintaining systems as this engenders the view that life is experiencing relationships rather than merely attaining objectives. These views have influenced the work of Stowell and West (1994) in the development of Client-Led Design (CLD), they suggest an interpretative framework to enable clients to manage the design of an IS from description through to the technical specification. One of the main problems with this type of approach to IS design is that the very plethora of information produced renders it difficult to reduce a client's description of IS requirements to the formal definition required for a technical specification. In software development and IS design, the emphasis is moving towards Object Oriented Design (OOD) methods as these approaches facilitate rapid development, reusability and an ease of maintenance. There is on going research being carried out in this field which is attempting to link an interpretative, client-led analysis of the problem domain directly with OOD specifications for IS.

3. LINKING INTERPRETIVIST APPROACHES TO OO DESIGN

Liang, West and Stowell (1998) made an attempt to undertake Object Oriented Design (OOD) by first understanding the problem domain through a process of rich analysis. Liang et al, argue that in current OOD the focus is on the vocabulary of the problem statement, and as different participants will have different understandings of each word and interpret statements in different ways, this will result in a limited appreciation of the problem situation. Coad and Yourdon (1991) adopt Object Oriented Analysis (OOA) based on the structures in a domain, though they do not explain how to achieve an understanding of such structures, or how any designs are validated. Liang et al (1998) suggest an Interpretative approach beginning with an initial investigation of the problem domain achieved via iterations of the learning cycle. The aim being to appreciate the various views and opinions of the people involved by focusing on the purposeful activities within the situation. They then suggest that the activities identified by the clients can be used to specify objects and their behaviour. This approach seems promising, though it still has difficulties specifying the attributes of objects, due to the lack of information concerning the data acted upon by the activities. More research is needed to develop this approach.

There may be some value in investigating some other kinds of model to represent the ideas of clients which can emphasise different perspectives and so enable other characteristics of the situation to be made explicit. Lander et al (1998) argue that an Interpretivist approach aims to maintain the correspondence between the clients IS definition and the technology which enables it. They suggest a model is needed that makes explicit how real-world technical specifications are derived from conceptual ideas, enabling forwards and backwards traceability. Flores and Ludlow (1980) and Winograd and Flores (1986) suggested a different perspective, that of viewing language as taking action within a situation and regarding an organisation as a network of interrelated communicative acts.

4. VIEWING 'LANGUAGE AS ACTION'.

The foundations of this approach are in the theory of Speech Acts developed by Searle (1969). Searle characterises utterances into different types of speech act and classifies them according to their propositional content (subject matter) and illocutionary force, (i.e. the way the speech act is uttered e.g. a request, or an order). Searle argues that within a speech act various degrees of commitment are involved; when making promises, or acknowledging a state of affairs, an agreement is reached between the speaker and listener. According to Winograd and Flores (1986), this concept of commitment is a vital dimension of language as it is this aspect that characterises human discourse. They treat utterances not as statements of fact about an objective world, but as actions within a space of commitments. Winograd and Flores (1986) regard a network of speech acts as constituting "conversations for action", and plot these in a diagram that represents the possible states of the conversation, but one that does not show the mental states of a speaker and listener. They feel this perspective helps make explicit issues which tend to remain unnoticed, in particular this approach reveals the obscuring of responsibility that occurs in treating a computer as an autonomous agent.

Suchman (1994) criticised this approach for lacking a framework for the process of tackling any conflict. Suchman subscribes to Habermas' ideas concerning control and emancipation (1984) and suggests taking a more emancipatory approach. Dietz and Widdeshoven, (1991) criticised the original Theory of Speech Acts by Searle (1969), as they feel he fails to explain the co-ordination of action between socially acting people, and also suggest taking an emancipatory approach. Hirschheim et al (1995) criticise conversation modelling for being over complicated and suggest this has prevented the technique from being used and tested in the field, and so reduced its recognition.

It is the belief of this author that any approach adopting the ideas of Habermas (1984) concerning emancipation of people within problem situations is inappropriate, as inherent within this perspective is a belief that an outside intervention is required to release people from their constricted circumstances. This in turn assumes that individuals within a situation are helpless and want to be emancipated, and also that those intervening are in a position to improve the situation. Working within an Interpretivist philosophy and researching into IS design, means it is essential to be certain that the underpinning theory represents an adequate explanation of organizations as being relationship-maintaining systems (Vickers, 1970) and any techniques used, provide a means of modelling that maintains the correspondence between clients' IS descriptions obtained from iterations of the learning cycle and the technology which enables it (Lander et al, 1998). Harris and Taylor (1998) argue that conversation modelling can be approached from an Interpretivist perspective. They feel the ideas of "organizational structuration" presented by Giddens (1984) explain the social co-ordination of action within an organization, and suggest deriving conversation models similar to those described by Winograd and Flores (1986) within this framework to produce co-ordination maps.

Co-ordination Modelling

Giddens' theory of structuration (1984) regards social structure as the pattern of interaction created by social practices situated in time. He argues that structures are continually re-enacted through interaction and over time a pattern emerges. Structuration Theory has been used by other researchers such as Orlikowsky and Robey, (1991), to describe how the social and technological factors interplay to create and constrain organizational structures and processes. Harris and Taylor (1998) argue that if one regards an organizational structure "as a pattern of dyadic interactions of agents in roles", it is possible to map the conversations for action that occur and it is these conversations that co-ordinate the purposes of the organization. In their paper, Harris and Taylor (1998) produce an example of a co-ordination map of a process that they suggest represents the roles and relationships in a more precise way than has previously been achieved. Recognising the limitations of co-ordination maps, Harris and Taylor admit that because of the level of detail produced by this method, it is not feasible to map all of the layers of all interacts, and so choices have to be made as to what is reasonable and useful to map in this way. They believe that the real strength of this approach is that the model represents the philosophical view "of organizations being socially constructed through language" and so is consistent with an Interpretative ontological stance. These ideas are to be investigated within the present research project.

5. PRESENT RESEARCH

The aim of the SEBPC project is to find a way to provide a bridge between the clients natural language descriptions of IS requirements and the formal definitions used in technical specifications. The view taken in this paper is that a 'soft systems' approach to problem definition and understanding, frees people from traditional modes of thinking and allows new, creative ways of working to be developed; primarily as it recognises the diversity of opinion existing within a situation. Gaining a deep understanding of the domain in question is considered fundamental to this research. Building on the work of Vickers (1970), Checkland (1981) and Stowell and West (1994) the study aims to explore ways of enabling a collaborative learning environment and of representing a rich appreciation of the situation under consideration. It is suggested here that conversation models in the form of co-ordination maps may be a useful tool for articulating the clients' descriptions of the IS design derived during iterations of the learning cycle. It is hoped this approach will

- be directly traceable to the collaborative learning process undertaken by the people who are going to use the IS, providing the forwards and backwards traceability necessary for client validation of any technical specification.
- be a much more detailed representation than that produced by other methods from which it may be feasible to generate the finite definitions needed for technical specifications in a manner that is accessible to everyone with the situation.
- be able to provide a means of modelling any proposal for the real world IS, or chosen parts of it which may highlight any limitations and constraints within a proposed design.

It is hoped to report to conference on some of the initial work and on the framework for inquiry designed to conduct the investigation in a spirit of learning, as is consistent with an Interpretative stance.

References

Coad, P. and Yourdon, E., (1991), *Object Oriented Analysis* 2nd. Ed. Prentice Hall, Englewood Cliffs, NJ.

Checkland, P.B., (1981) *Systems Thinking, Systems Practice* John Wiley, Chichester.

Checkland, P.B. and Scholes, J., (1990) *Soft Systems Methodology in Action* John Wiley, Chichester.

Dietz, J.L.G. and Widdeshoven, G.A.M., (1991), "Speech Acts or Communicative Action?" in: Bannon, L. et al, (Eds.) *Proceedings of the Second European Conference on Computer Supported Cooperative Work* Kluwer, Dordrecht pp. 235-248.

EPSRC Funded Research Project, "Developing a Unified Mechanism to Information System Design". Funded in the second round of the programme for: *Systems Engineering for Business Process Design.* Web Page: http://www.cms.dmu.ac.uk/STRL/projects/project.10.html

Flores, F. and Ludlow, J., (1980) "Doing and Speaking in the Office" in Fick, G. and Sprague, R. (Eds.), *D.S.S. Issues and Challenges* Pergamon Press, London.

Flood, R.L. and Jackson, M.C., (1991) *Creative Problem Solving: Total Systems Intervention* John Wiley, London.

Gadamer, H., (1975) *Truth and Method* (Translated and Edited by G.Barden and J.Cumming) Seabury Press, New York.

Galliers, R., (1987) *Information Analysis: Selected Readings* Addison Wesley, Reading.

Giddens, A., (1984) *The Constitution of Society: Outline of the Theory of Structuration* Polity Press, Cambridge.

Habermas, J., (1984) *The Theory of Communicative Action 1. Reason and the Rationalization of Society,* Beacon Press.

Harris, G.B. and Taylor, S., (1998) "Organizational Structuration: Interaction and Interrelation." Presented at 14th. EGOS Colloquium, Maastricht, The Netherlands, July 1998. Download at: http//www.workframe.com?WFI_CORP/OrgStrctHTML.htm

Hirschheim, R., Klein, H.K. and Lyytinen, K., (1995) *Information Systems Development and Data Modelling: Conceptual and Philosophical Foundations* Cambridge University Press, Cambridge.

Lander, R., McRobb, S. and Stowell, F.A., (1998) "Can Interpretivism Enable Participatory Design?" Unpublished Paper, De Montfort University, Milton Keynes.

Lewis, P., (1993) "Linking Soft Systems Methodology with Data-Focused Information Systems Development." *Journal of Information Systems* 3 (3), pp.169-186.

Liang, Y., West, D. and Stowell, F.A., (1998) "An Interpretivist Approach to IS Definition using Object Modelling." *Information Systems Journal* 8, pp.163-180.

Lyytinen, K., (1988) "Stakeholders, information system failures and soft systems methodology: an assessment." *Journal of Applied Systems Analysis* 15, pp.61-81.

Orlikowski, W.J. and Robey, D., (1991) "Information Technology and the Structuring of Organizations." *Information Systems Research* 2, pp.143-169.

Searle, J.R., (1969) *Speech Acts: An Essay in the Philosophy of Language* Cambridge University Press, Cambridge.

Stowell, F.A., (1991) "Towards Client-Led Development of Information Systems", *Journal of Information Systems,* 1, pp.173-189.

Stowell, F.A. and West, D., (1994) *Client-Led Design: A Systematic Approach to Information System Definition* McGraw-Hill, London.

Suchman, L., (1994) 'Do Categories have Politics? The Language Action Perspective Reconsidered', *Computer Supported Cooperative Work* 2 (3) pp.177-190.

Vickers, G., (1970) *Freedom in a Rocking Boat* Allen Lane, London.

Vickers, G., (1984) *The Vickers Papers* Harper and Row, London.

Winograd, T. and Flores, F., (1986) Understanding Computers and Cognition: A New Foundation for Design Addison Wesley, Reading.

CHAPTER 59

APPLYING STRUCTURATION THEORY WITHIN INFORMATION SYSTEMS RESEARCH

Zahid I Hussain and Donal J Flynn
Department of Computation, UMIST

Abstract.

We are currently conducting case study research in an NHS hospital. Our main research goal is to apply structuration theory to explain some of the factors which shape the process involved in obtaining requirements for an information system. We explain the hospital context, elements of the theory, and reflect on theory advantages and disadvantages as well as the insight provided into actions involving power and sanctions within the hospital.

1   INTRODUCTION

This research highlights the use of structuration theory (Giddens 1979, 1984) to explain some aspects of the process of requirements development for a clinic information system (IS) in an NHS hospital. This is a complex organisational situation with a large number of factors that shape the requirements process. We are interested in developing and testing theory to understand the social aspects of this process, and our primary research objective is to apply structuration theory (ST) to explain the factors which shape the structure and process involved in obtaining the requirements. We chose this theory as several researchers, for example Walsham (1993) suggest that it has good potential to explain social behaviour. We anticipate that an increasing demand in the new millennium will be a request from users of all types to focus more on the social (rather than the technological) nature both of the requirements development process as well as that of the eventual system. To satisfy this demand, it will be necessary to generate proposals for newer methods for the development of requirements that will better satisfy the needs of users of such systems. Our second research objective is to refine relevant theory through practical experience of its applicability. Similar benefits are given by Macintosh and Scapens (1990) and Orlikowski (1992) who used principles of ST in analysis of IS projects.

The paper is structured as follows: organisational context, research method, application of ST to the hospital, holistic application, reflections and criticisms of ST, reflections on our research method and conclusions.

2   ORGANISATIONAL CONTEXT

2.1   The hospital

Our research concerns a large NHS hospital in Yorkshire. Such an organisation is complex and has evolved over many years through continual reforms and changes, and many stakeholders, such as Government, unions, doctors, nurses and local authorities have attempted to shape its structure, with some of these changes being politically motivated. Today, to a large extent, it may be seen as a set of subcultures, each with its own interests. But local subcultures or hospital cultures are informal and are very complex to investigate. One has to learn about each speciality and department in order to make sense of their subcultures.

There has been an increasing attempt to develop NHS guidelines to help create common structure across the hospital. Organisation-wide standards and codes exist on managing and co-ordinating clinical and administrative matters and much emphasis has been placed on efficiency and effectiveness. Recent reforms have resulted in publications of hospital performance tables that show departmental efficiency across the organisation; this hospital like most hospitals tends to reach between 80-95% of the nationally defined target. However, it is becoming difficult for hospitals to improve, due to limited funding, insensitivity of hierarchically-organised management and the top-down flow of commands. IT is seen as a tool for automating the existing manual and/or inefficient parts of the organisation. It seems to have begun a new revolution in the NHS with IT often perceived as a vehicle for major improvements by most middle management and the younger generation of workers.

2.2   Requirements process

We studied a project that involves the merge of seven geographically and procedurally separate day clinics into one clinic in a single location. This involves the integration of different subcultures and value systems, aiming to create a single clinic culture.

IS development is only one part of this integration process, concerned with the need to support administrative aspects of the new clinical procedures, and we focused on the requirements process, carried out by five teams: operational team (drafting clinic operational policy and functions), documentation team (drafting new forms and documents), administration team (deciding on the new administration system), IT team (designing and implementing the clinic IS), and strategic group (supervising the other teams). The main stakeholders were primarily non-IT staff and were drawn from future system users.

IS requirements were influenced by four factors: (1) system requirements from two other hospitals who were already using an IS to accomplish similar functions: these had been implemented and their use was discussed with relevant people in the hospitals; (2) previous functional requirements, originating from clinical change envisaged two years before the project start date, when the actual purpose and role of the new clinic had been discussed; (3) feedback from prospective IS users, where frequent users were interviewed by the project manager; (4) project team discussions, where a large proportion of functional and personal requirements came from the project teams, which met fortnightly to investigate new ideas and clinical workings.

The main functions of these teams were to: (1) brainstorm ideas on the clinic/system, (2) discuss and evaluate ideas, (3) debate the most important issues, (4) assign further investigation tasks to team members to test the viability of particular options, (5) make decisions and add them to the overall team outcome. Teams discussed a wide set of aspects of the new clinic, including functional, ethical, human resource and technological issues and they designed the logical and physical aspects of the clinic. Hence the system requirements generated by these teams were determined by those who would also use the system.

Toward the end of the project the teams merged and reconciled differences. The requirements from the teams coupled with user requirements replaced large parts of the requirements from the two other hospitals. Furthermore, the user requirements were evaluated against the requirements from the five teams to determine the degree of bias and distortion within them.

3   RESEARCH METHOD

The most suitable research method for applying ST was the case study approach, as, due to theory complexity we had to have a good understanding of the research organisation. Regular visits to the hospital over a nine-month period were made to gather data and learn common organisational myths, tales, stories and rumours. A number of other research approaches supplemented the basic method, for example, un/structured interviews, non/participant observation, seminars and discussions and secondary literature research. The researcher has to be open minded about selecting from possible types of approaches, bearing in mind the required insight into the project context, process and its likely content.

3.1   Application of Structuration Theory to the Hospital

3.1.1   Introduction
Structuration theory provides a framework for understanding social situations in terms of

social structure and human interaction. It is concerned with: (1) the influence on human interaction of institutional (structural) aspects of social life such as rules, procedures and power structures, (2) the production and reproduction of these structural aspects through human interaction. The term "duality of structure" refers to a central concept of the theory, expressing the notion that structure not only influences interaction, through the medium of modality, but is also produced or reproduced by interaction. A representation of ST, based on Giddens (1984), is shown in figure 1.

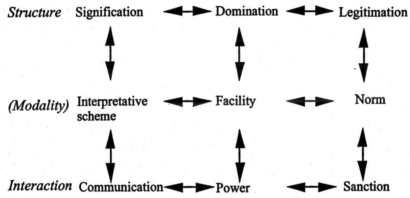

Figure 1: Dimensions of the relationship between action and structure in ST

Figure 1 shows social structure and human interaction subdivided into three dimensions and linked by three modalities. When humans interact for communication purposes they draw on interpretative schemes such as stocks of knowledge to make sense of their own and others' actions; in so doing they produce and reproduce structures of signification. For example, in the hospital, such signification structures include sets of standard terms and their meanings for use within the new clinic. Human agents utilise power in interaction and draw upon facilities, such as their abilities to allocate resources, to re/produce structures of domination such as management hierarchies and procedures for mobilising resources. Domination is a capability that creates command over material factors.

Humans also sanction (justify) their behaviour by drawing upon norms such as standards of personal morality to re/produce legitimation structures that, for example guide clinic procedures.

3.1.2 Structure dimension

Structure is made up of a continuous sequence of actions, is continuously re/produced by the actors involved and is based on their beliefs and actions. Structure changes as actors' beliefs or values change and only exists as memory traces unassociated with any type of physical existence.

A number of *signification structures,* for example standard codes were created for the clinic, such as operational codes for daily running and co-ordination, defining the breakdown of functions and patient flow, and document codes for the creation of new integrated documents for all specialities. Many codes are based on NHS guidelines: for example administrative codes defining quality levels for individual tasks and IT codes, based on the NHS IM+T strategy, which sets quality standards for the IS and for its hardware and software components.

Through their job roles in the *domination* structure of the management hierarchy, key stakeholders (unit manager, IT executive, project executive, and planning executive) control clinic resources such as finance, IT and medical equipment and thus influence the project. Their ideas became codes of practice in the clinic operational strategy and thereby part of new domination structures. However, there were also informal leaders who motivated, dominated and repressed others; their influence depended on competence in political skills, their value to others and their links with the NHS executive.

Legitimation structures are made up of policies, strategies, methodologies and objectives that serve as legitimation frameworks to justify and underpin structure decisions. Many legitimation structures were devised by project teams during discussions, although certain policies were constantly referred to relevant NHS guidelines such as IM+T to ensure that they "fitted in" to this framework. At other times, NHS guidelines were discussed and customised to suit the project.

3.1.3   Interaction dimension

The *communication* aspect of interaction involves generating ideas about the change process and the requirements for the new clinic. Ideas are brainstormed in teams and team leaders assign tasks to members to investigate before the next meeting. Those individuals who often have their ideas accepted are those with good knowledge of signification structures relevant either to the hospital or to clinic procedures.

Power is often utilised by individuals in interaction using their formal job status within a domination structure, which they seek at least to maintain and possibly extend; they also use their personal and political skills. They monitor others to keep a close watch on those who could hinder their aims. If an individual attempts to challenge their ideas, they are dealt with through their dominant personality.

Individuals often claimed that their ideas were *sanctioned* by various legitimation structures such as NHS, hospital or clinic rules. Although the degree to which their ideas conformed to actual rules was questionable, they constantly attempted to sanction their behaviour in this manner. These "successful" individuals demonstrated considerable knowledge of relevant rules and guidelines. These were useful as they prevented individuals from losing their direction and introducing totally unacceptable ideas. However, other important sanctioning activities drew on existing stakeholder values as well as management and worker expectations concerning fulfilment of stakeholder requirements. Individuals were extra cautious about conforming to these sanctions. Those who were not sure either did not contribute in the teams or enquired further.

3.1.4   Modality dimension

Modality is a bridge between action and structure and actors draw on modalities, such as stocks of knowledge and skills to allocate resources, using these together with appropriate action to produce and reproduce structure. Modality is more tangible than structure and helps to give meaning to the actions of individuals.

Modalities are often used to explain and communicate meaning in interaction and may provide standard vocabulary from a stock of knowledge. For example, when discussing the IS, jargon was used, as stakeholders were told that the IS would look like Microsoft Access and would conform to the Windows standard. They came to believe that the IS would not be difficult to use and would not be a dramatically new system. Therefore, they used their stock of knowledge about Access and Windows to conceptualise the new system.

Various types of knowledge within an *interpretative scheme* are used to assist in communication. Stakeholder experience of the NHS, clinic procedure and systems analysis was important, and team members were selected on the basis that they possessed relevant knowledge. Stakeholders also draw upon their skills for judging and choosing a particular outcome within discussion.

The ability to control resources, for example staff and equipment, is a *facility* for achieving domination. Workers who build their stocks of knowledge, for example will be seen as acting to learn more about the IS, which they may then use to gain greater power and domination over those who are novices. In addition, motivation skills help others to achieve a particular goal and negotiation skills help to reconcile differences towards a particular target. Finally, advice can also be used as a facility that helps to make effective decisions and create a suitable structure.

Norms at the hospital were made up of organisational and personal values. Actors drew on norms by expressing their commitment and by agreeing or disagreeing with others. For example, during a team meeting some individuals suggested that perhaps some consultants might benefit from using an auto-type typing package for patient notes instead of transcribing them to their secretaries. This idea was challenged solely because it did not seem to conform to the hospital image and there were questions about consultants' credibility.

3.2   A holistic application of ST

Although consultants (clinic medical managers) agreed to clinic integration there were issues that they wanted to keep under their own control. Amongst these issues were the documents produced for doctors, patients and relevant bodies. A majority of consultants wanted to retain the existing styles of documents despite the introduction of the IS, which would allow them to customise documents and produce patient data faster and more accurately. Their justification for this requirement was that they wanted customised layout, speciality-specific language, specific logos and treatment of patient data for reports. We believe that the consultants wanted to manage their own documentation because they wanted to portray a particular image of their speciality and to manipulate patient data before reporting to management and other bodies. They also wanted to safeguard their specialist clinic from a complete integration with other specialities.

Representatives from the specialities represented these interests during team meetings where they highlighted the benefits of allowing their speciality to customise their own output. In terms of ST they wanted to sanction the autonomy of their speciality. They also used communication aspects of the interaction dimension as they communicated the needs of their speciality to the teams in which they participated. From the modality dimension they used the interpretative scheme by using their knowledge and experience to convince others and they used their negotiation skills to achieve a consensus of team members.

They eventually succeeded in including these requirements in the final requirements, so they involved the signification and legitimation elements of the structure dimension. As the proposed version of the IS did not include these requirements the IT team decided to delay until this facility was included. This did appear in a later version and the IS contract was signed for implementation from December 1998 as opposed to September 1998, although system training had begun from September 1998.

We believe that a key factor in shaping this episode, typical of the requirements process as a whole, was the need for decisions concerning requirements to be *sanctioned by user agreement*. This was chiefly due to the need to integrate the independent day clinics whilst recognising their autonomous specialities, based on two types of consideration: (1) practical, as only the day clinic staff possessed the knowledge of their clinic procedures, and (2) political, as the consultants within the day clinics were so powerful that many of their wishes had to be met. This differs from other types of requirements process where the key shaping factors may be, for example the sanctioning of requirements on the basis of the transfer of an existing domination structure into the requirements, or by reference to legitimation structures. Legitimation structures such as NHS guidelines were used in the clinic project but these were relatively high-level and did not significantly influence the nature of the process.

It was interesting that the power dimension of interaction of the few dominant consultants was deployed in a "hidden" or proxy manner. Although the speciality representatives did not show any dominance in their approach to the teams, the domination of the consultants was apparent to all. In fact, the representatives avoided showing that they were representing the interests of their consultant. This suited them as this would affect their credibility in the clinic as full time workers, as the consultants only visited the specialities a few hours a week. Keeping a good face was very important to them.

In this example, the demand by the consultants was against the organisational legitimation structures concerning the IS and could be regarded as disruption. However, their action may be seen as using their power to establish their norm of clinic autonomy as legitimation aspects of the new structure dimension.

3.3   Reflections and Criticisms of ST

ST was applied after observing stakeholder actions. We did not ask direct questions concerning ST elements as we thought that actors would have difficulties in giving an account of how, for example their actions became structures. However we did ask hypothetical questions in interviews to prompt the stakeholders to provide an account of their experience that we could translate into ST terms. Brooks (1997) applied structural notions of ST through longitudinal studies at a manufacturing organisation to focus on its implementation of new technology.

We found the ST emphasis on power was useful in identifying how a few key stakeholders were highly influential in steering this project due to their dominant hierarchical status. The different ways in which stakeholders sanctioned their behaviour, especially using their dominant status, was also revealing. Communication interaction to re/produce structure was, naturally, highly relevant to this research situation.

We would not go as far as Macintosh and Scapens (1990), who criticise ST for being too eclectic and for relying on disciplines that are ontologically inconsistent and epistemologically incompatible. But understanding ST was difficult as it is based on multidisciplinary foundations. Researchers require a substantial lead time to reach an adequate understanding of ST.

To apply ST to an organisation a researcher needs to develop a good holistic understanding, as the theory looks at the actors involved and their mental reasoning within their organisational context, needing to take into account many factors. The researcher needs to spend enough time in the organisation, getting to know its actors and their personalities. We agree with Macintosh and Scapens (1990) that ST can be best applied using a case study approach.

It is difficult to distinguish between modality and structure. Modalities are a bridge between action and structure and serve as reference point for actors to create appropriate structure. For example, a set of operational rules can be seen as structures if they determine how actors behave. They can also be seen as modality if they act as knowledge or reference for taking actions. If they are seen as modality, it is questionable as to how this modality was created.

A difficulty in interpreting observations in terms of ST concerns the multi-faceted nature of its elements, as a signification structure, for example, may also act as a domination as well as a legitimation structure. It is difficult for the researcher to decide, for example, whether an actor's motives behind an action that produces structure emphasises one or more of these structure dimensions.

We observed that actors spent a significant amount of time monitoring their own actions, and the actions of others, for several reasons: to safeguard their interests, to make sure that their own action conforms to the actions of others, to compare their own and decisions of others and to reflect upon success and failure of certain actions taken by others. This type of action is not emphasised in ST (although the concept of "discursive consciousness" appears relevant) but we intend to investigate it further as it may provide important clues as to the meanings that actors construct from structure and from the actions of others.

We found that it takes a long time to apply ST to even a very short set of interactions, to produce a narrative in ST terms that makes sense to we, the researchers and that reflects our view of what is happening in the research situation. In addition, such ST narratives are lengthy, as ST elements are interdependent, and we are conscious that the impatient reader may lose patience and find the richness of the account rather indigestible.

ST is a very high-level theory and leaves many gaps in its explanations. Kawalek (1997), in a discussion of an IS strategy case study, concludes that ST is valuable in its emphasis on social issues, but warns that the way in which it is used often neglects wider societal influences. Monteiro and Hanseth (1995) state that a limitation of ST is its abstract nature and that it does not, for example, identify how power interests are inscribed into information systems.

3.4   Reflections on our Research Method
We perceive our position as researchers in this project as non-participatory and non-neutral. The researcher who carried out the field work (ZH) attended meetings as an observer and did not take an active part in the development process. According to the research philosophy categories of Orlikowski and Baroudi (1991), we adopt a stance that is not positivist or critical, but interpretivist, characterised by attempting to "get inside" the research situation with an emphasis on the importance of subjective meanings.

4   CONCLUSIONS

We find that ST is a useful tool for analysing this research situation, mainly as it draws attention to the exercise of power and sanction which we find are important in shaping the requirements process. One of its attractions is that it can provide a holistic account of the process. The ST concept of duality of structure, whereby structure influences action which produces structure, appears to be a relevant, if high-level, model of the process. We have reported our main reflections on ST and it is our view that ST, which we locate some way towards the end of the anti-positivist spectrum of research methods (Galliers 1997), is very applicable to information systems research. One reason for this, as shown by the holistic ST application discussed above, is the way in which ST can point to hidden agendas of actors; another, not discussed here, is ST's emphasis on unintended consequences of actions. Both these features make ST a potentially powerful tool in describing the richness of complex social situations.

Future research is currently underway in another NHS hospital where we intend to apply ST with an emphasis on constructing narratives of different episodes, as we believe this method of presentation heightens the theory's explanatory capabilities. We are considering whether to discuss such narratives with development process participants to see if they find this a suitable method for understanding accounts of the process.

Our research is part of the drive to explore the potential of theory such as ST or actor-network theory (Underwood 1998) as the basis for new approaches to IS development that recognise the importance of social issues.

References

Brooks L (1997) Structuration theory and new technology: analysing organizationally situated computer-aided design (CAD), *Information Systems Journal* **7**, 133-151.

Galliers R (1997) Reflections on information systems research: twelve points of debate. In Mingers J and Stowell F (eds) *Information systems: an emerging discipline?* McGraw-Hill, London, 141-154.

Giddens A (1979) *Central Problems in Social Theory*, Macmillan, London.

Giddens A (1984) *The Constitution of society: outline of the theory of structuration*, Polity Press, Cambridge.

Kawalek J P (1997) Operationalising Giddens in information systems strategy, *Proceedings of 5th European Conference on Information Systems (ECIS'97)*, Cork, Ireland, 19-21 June 1997, 721-736.

Macintosh N B and Scapens R W (1990) Structuration theory in management accounting, *Accounting, Organizations and Society* **15**(5), 455-477.

Monteiro E and Hanseth O (1995) Social shaping of information infrastructure: on being specific about the technology. In Orlikowski W J, Walsham G, Jones M R and DeGross J I (eds), *Information technology and changes in organizational work*, Chapman and Hall, London.

Orlikowski W J (1992) The duality of technology: rethinking concepts of technology of organizations, *Organization Science* **3**(3), 398-427.

Orlikowski W J and Baroudi J J (1991) Studying information technology in organizations: research approaches and assumptions, *Information Systems Research* **2**(1), 1-28.

Underwood J (1998) Not another methodology: what ANT tells us about systems development, *Proceedings of 6th International Conference on Information Systems Methodologies*, Jayaratna N (ed), 3-4 September 1998, University of Salford, Salford, UK.

Walsham G (1993), *Interpreting Information Systems in Organizations*, Wiley, Chichester, UK.

CHAPTER 60

DIRECTIONS FOR INFORMATION SYSTEMS RESEARCH ON THE INTEGRATED ELECTRONIC PATIENT RECORD

Christine Urquhart* and Rosemary Currell**
*University of Wales Aberystwyth, **University of Wales Swansea

Abstract

Discusses philosophical perspectives which may help consideration of appropriate research methodologies for investigations on the electronic health record, one of the commitments of the 1998 Information Strategy published by the UK Department of Health. Perceived problems concern confidentiality of the data items and professional accountability. Foucault's ideas on discourse provide a different perspective to the purposes of patient records, and the construction and interpretation of the knowledge associated with the record. Foucault's perceptions on power and knowledge can be applied to the problem of confidentiality for the record. Implementation may be difficult and the problem, as a dialectical perspective, reminds us, will be to deal with change adequately.

1   INTRODUCTION

One of the commitments of the recent information strategy for the NHS (Department of Health, NHS Executive 1998) is to provide lifelong electronic health records for every person in the country. As the strategy acknowledges, this requires debate about the structure, content and use of the electronic health records among health professionals, managers and the patients and carers. This paper reviews some of the pertinent research issues, examining philosophical and research perspectives for this type of information system.

2 ELECTRONIC HEALTH RECORDS - HISTORY AND POLICY DEVELOPMENT

If integration of patient care information is so important, the question that might be asked is why progress has been so slow? Weed (1968) indicated possible links between patient care, the record and education thirty years ago. Within the UK at least, different health and social care professional groups have maintained separate record keeping systems, integration has been slow and the links between continuing education and clinical audit (involving record review), a matter of debate (Hopkins 1996). Recent concerns have focused on the confidentiality and security of the patient record on an NHS-wide network (Anderson 1996).

The definition of the electronic patient record and the electronic health record requires some clarification as the terms are used interchangeably. For the purposes of this paper the definitions in the information strategy document (Department of Health, NHS Executive 1998) will be used. The electronic patient record (EPR) describes the record of the periodic care provided by one institution, whereas the electronic health record (EHR) describes the concept of a longitudinal health record of a patient's health and healthcare. At present the manual equivalent to this is the Lloyd George envelope held by a patient's GP (currently maintained for legal reasons, as GPs are required contractually to retain paper records under the Terms of Service). The UK EPR programme currently has five EPR and (ICWS, Integrated Clinical Workstation) sites and the International Medical Informatics Association has working groups (e.g. IMIA WG13).

For a new generation integrated record or EHR, Rigby et al. (1998) suggest that the research agenda should acknowledge that the extended primary health care team is a major organisational redesign in health care, although it is disguised as incremental change. Mapping the structure and content of the record should consider clinical user processes. Atkinson & Peel (1998) also stress that an electronic patient record system will involve major organisational and technological changes but prefer to view the process of implementing such changes as growth, a maturation process involving around four stages. The emphasis is more on an 'evolutionary' process, defined by the authors as a process of slow process of adaptive fit to the environment. Views on evolutionary processes vary, but to think that there is, or can be, a set goal, is possibly misleading. Most palaeontologists now believe, for example, that birds and 'flight' developed from small ground dwelling dinosaurs whose feathers originally served other purposes.

2.1 Electronic health records - perceived policy issues
The concerns of the strategy document (Department of Health, NHS Executive 1998) surround unauthorised access to electronic records and the protection of patient privacy, data quality, implementing common clinical terms, and sharing of information between health and social care professionals. Health professionals need to ensure that patients are informed of intentions to share information. Protocols should ensure that access to

personal identifiable information is only on a 'need to know' basis. As recommended in the Caldicott Committee report (1997), the solutions being investigated cover the 'people' issues as well as the technology, as the lack of staff awareness of the privacy implications may be the major problem (France 1997). A key recommendation of the Caldicott report (1997) is, however, the need for agreement on the effective use of privacy enhancing technologies, communication standards and access controls. Avgerou & Cornford (1998: 89) note that there is generally little methodological guidance for integrating analysis with systems integrity and security. A security model proposed for control of access to the record (or parts of it) to authorised health professionals allows patients to control access to certain data items (Griew et al. 1996). Despite the attractions of greater accountability, and more transparent clinical governance, there are social and legal implications of this 'virtual' record which may be viewed out of the context of the care in which it was constructed.

3   INFORMATION SYSTEMS RESEARCH PERSPECTIVES ON THE ELECTRONIC HEALTH RECORD

For the policy maker and the manager the research questions concern the required content of the record, authorisation and validity of the content, and the relationship of the electronic health record to other clinical, managerial and external information systems. For the clinician the questions concern the place of the electronic health record within clinical processes and professional practice. For the patient, there is the possibility of more control, e.g. in the patient-held record, as has been tried in midwifery/obstetrics (Elbourne et al. 1987) and child health (Lakhani et al. 1984) with more research necessary to determine what information patients should hold (or record) about their care, and in what format.

The following sections consider how different philosophical perspectives might clarify those research questions, to ensure that the questions being asked are set in a way that are sensitive to the problem, and that the problems are defined as clearly as possible.

3.1   Construction of the problem - the sociological perspective

Medical practice throughout the twentieth century in the Western world might be viewed as becoming more scientific and 'rational', requiring precise description of clinical observations. Progress in medicine (as a scientific discipline) might now be hampered by the lack of standardised terminology and unreliable procedures for recording data (Berg 1997: 21). From this viewpoint, Berg (1997) argues that the record serves medical research, and the practising clinician is a cog in the wheel of medical research. A variation of scientific medical practice presumes that clinicians practise scientific methods in their medical work. For the problem-oriented record Weed (1968) proposed that all data, action plans and progress notes of all personnel involved should be organised around the problems of the patient, so that the doctor would be able to organise the problems of each patient in a way that promoted scientific action.

The consensus view, therefore, was that the poor quality of the record hindered scientific medical practice, with some placing more stress on the medical research per se and others placing more stress on the doctor as a rational medical scientist. The rationale for the electronic record is often based on the poor state of current paper-based medical records (Berg 1998) and, unsurprisingly, the information strategy document (Department of Health, NHS Executive 1998) comments '*The sight of hard pressed NHS professionals rummaging about in buff folders or hand writing referrals and test requests will be consigned to history as soon as possible*'. Before consigning the buff folders to history the sociologist might query just how doctors generate and use the information in these buff folders. Are they used for the rational scientific paradigm of examination, differential diagnosis, diagnosis, treatment and evaluation of treatment, or are there other purposes of use? The question is perhaps not how the record is expected to be read, but how it is actually read.

3.2   Applying Foucault's ideas of discourse to the electronic health record

In a critical discussion of Foucault's theory of discourse, Freundlieb (1994) suggests that the beauty of many new theories is their very vagueness - and Foucault's theory on discourse and discursive formations is included in this group. That said, Foucault's contribution as a philosopher is acknowledged as providing insights into the social use of language. Foucault's ideas concern the question of determining why a particular 'statement' appeared, rather than another, the conditions of the statement's existence and correlation with other statements. While it might be argued by linguists that Foucault's approach to discourse analysis lacks the rigour of more formal text analysis, Foucault's appeal to information systems researchers probably lies in the way ideas about knowledge, and its construction are related to discourse and social communication.

Merely asking the question why this statement, rather than another, provides some insights into the use of the medical record. Linguists might similarly approach the question by considering the communicative purpose of a particular unit of text. The purpose of notes on a record can be considered according to the purpose (what is this for), the form (why this presentation), the content (why these words) and the intended recipient of the communication.

The rationalist view might be that the record represents a record of actions taken, and evaluations of observations, in the way that a laboratory notebook might record the chemical substances used, the procedures followed, observations on the course of the experiment and analysis to determine outcomes. The record may contain such information but detailed studies of the way clinicians actually work question whether the rationalist experimental paradigm is practised. Strauss et al. (1985) describe medical work as the management of the patient's trajectory, and clinicians do not appear to accept the examination results as given facts but rather see these as things to be constructed and reconstructed to keep the patient's trajectory 'on track' (Berg 1998). If clinicians operated in a purely scientific mode of clinical reasoning, the medical record should support clinical problem solving in an expert system sense. However, in a review of studies of the development of expertise in medicine, Schmidt et al. (1990) conclude that expertise is not related to the development of better clinical problem solving skills. Instead, the content specificity of problem solving performance suggests that experienced clinicians rely on 'illness scripts' which are based on actual or 'prototypical' patients and contain clinically relevant information about a disease as it might manifest itself and proceed. Tanenbaum (1994) observed senior clinicians asking juniors to tell ' *the patient's story'*.

One view of the medical record is that it has a communicative purpose to the doctor of an 'aide - memoire' to help explain to themselves why certain actions might be taken, just as one word at the beginning of the line of a song reminds one how the rest of the line goes. The reason why records may appear incomplete, with personal abbreviations, cryptic notes, may be that for the doctor, this is all that is necessary, at the time, to explain what to do next with the patient's trajectory. The explaining also has an element of professional justification for actions taken. Berg (1998) discusses an example which illustrates how a seemingly brief entry 'works' for the insider who understands who made the entry, and would therefore be aware that other data had been collected, and that this entry simply validates what has been done already, selecting the important items only. In cases where diagnosis is uncertain (e.g. ulcerative colitis or Crohn's disease) Wilkinson & Solomonides (1998) note that clinicians requesting a histopathology report often submitted what they refer to as a 'clue' in the History box of the pathology request form. The conclusion may be 'consistent with Crohn's' but confirming presuppositions may preclude possibilities that the findings are consistent with other conditions. The problems Wilkinson and Solomonides (1998) have in examining a set of records covering 50 years of specialist hospital treatment of bowel diseases such as Crohn's and ulcerative colitis reflect the problems of the archaeology of knowledge, in Foucault's terms. Distinguishing between fact and ambiguity in the records is often extremely difficult, though in contrast the pathology reports (arguably more representative of a purely scientific rational approach) have a more structured format and stylized vocabulary.

The Foucauldian perspective calls for examination of how the statement correlates with other statements and what other statements are excluded. Berg (1998) suggests that the items on a medical record can only be understood within the context of their use, or, as Van der Lei (1991) stressed, data should only be used for the purpose for which they were collected. In contrast, the information strategy document (Department of Health, NHS Executive 1998) envisages that potential uses of the electronic health record include '*analysing anonymised and aggregated subsets of EHR data for epidemiological research, needs assessment and service planning and in support of clinical governance'* (section 2.21) while maintaining '*It is essential to create and maintain accurate, complete, relevant, up-to-date and accessible EPRs.'* (section 2.27).

When observing clinicians actually reading paper-based records, Nygren and

Henriksson (1992) found that some clinicians were guided by clues regarding layout, and format, and reading patterns include triggering of a memory picture. Several clinicians pointed out that they found it useful to be aware of what was not included in the record. In many respects the clinician appears to be using temporal clues in the way expected of event-based personal information retrieval (Bovey 1996). The structure (rhetorical organisation) of a part of the medical record itself, and the physical organisation of the paper-based medical records help navigation.

Nurses and midwives have often kept records which are separate from the medical record. Recent work on nursing informatics, use of nursing terms and nursing records in the UK has been conducted by the Nomina Group (1998). In the USA the National Council for Nursing Research expert panel on nursing informatics co-ordinates and directs such work. Other studies (e.g. Hale et al. 1997) have investigated whether the data obtained from the records is actually an accurate reflection of the nursing care given to patients - a 'taken for granted' assumption of much of the thinking behind the electronic health record. For computer based patient records, a review indicated variable levels of accuracy (Hogan et al. 1997).

Social workers and those working in mental health services may have a very different viewpoint of the purpose of the record and its desirable format (e.g. long versus short). There is more of an emphasis on the psychosocial aspects and this may complement other clinical data (Benbassat 1996). There may be far more emphasis on narrative and the record may be viewed as a '*transformative medium*' in which therapeutic encounters co-construct client narratives (Brown et al. 1996). Doctors may value brevity and vital clues, other professionals may value the whole story.

There are many areas of health and social care where communication is necessary but lacking. In recent reports on child health services (UK Parliament. Select Committee on Health 1997) (Welsh Office 1997) there is a call for urgent action to deal with the fragmentation of service provision between health, education and social services, a problem as around 9% of children are limited in some way by a longstanding illness, such as asthma (OPCS 1995). The prevalence of some chronic disabling conditions has increased as case fatality falls and the expectation of life of affected individuals increases. Increasingly, information stored on the child's health record will need to be shared among health, education and social services. While there remains some doubt whether one electronic medical record can suit all clinical disciplines (Hayes 1998) one wonders about the scale of the problem of sharing information with non-clinical professions such as teachers and social workers.

3.3 Applying Foucault: some research questions
Some of cited studies in the previous section could be said to be in sympathy with a Foucauldian perspective in that their concerns included:
- purpose and intent of the record - why this rather than another
- conditions of existence of statements and the discourse community.

It is relatively easy to see that this perspective provides some insights into how the record is actually being used, and how it is valued. The problem might be in relating this to the technology drive of an information strategy which is concerned with improving the cost-effective use of information technology within the health service.

For the present information strategy, there are two main approaches being considered: messaging (data-push) and browsing (data-pull) (Department of Health, NHS Executive 1998: 2.75 and 2.78). The data push approach requires nationally agreed standards for the structure of clinical communications (2.84) and the content, organisation, language and terms used will have to mean the same thing to recipient and sender. From a Foucauldian perspective the questions to be asked may concern what should be included, what should be excluded and how such messages will be used with other 'statements'. The problems of format and the value of the format (long versus short) as a prompt and indication of the credibility of the recipient may remain an issue even for the data pull approach which could offer more tailored ways of satisfying different professional needs. The idea that a discourse community may validate 'truth statements' in different ways (Ollson 1998), and that such communities' interpretations will change over time provides a reminder that future users and usages need some consideration in the concern to improve present clinical communications.

4   IMPLEMENTING A RECORD SYSTEM: POWER AND DIALECTICS

One of the functions possible with a computer based patient record system is the support of care pathways, or protocols. These represent agreed routes for care for particular conditions in particular groups of patients, based on consensus agreement and frequently on the best research evidence available. To some extent these are formalized, and transparent representations of what happens (or might happen) in the normal process of care, or the *'articulation'* of clinical work which as Strauss et al. (1985: 151) describe as *'managing and shaping a trajectory involve calculating and carrying out numerous lines of work, which, viewed closely, are constituted of clusters of tasks... articulation work must be done to assure that the staff's collective efforts add up to more than discrete and conflicting bits of accomplished work'.*

The computer based record system could then be seen as a decision support system. The evidence on clinical decision support systems is optimistic, though somewhat equivocal on the effect on patient outcomes (Johnston et al. 1994). The problem may be one of perspective: looking at the decision support tool in isolation may be counter-productive and Berg (1997: 175) argues that the recursive nature of tool plus practice, that interlocking of the decision support tool and practice means that research should look at the process of design and change. To some extent Atkinson & Peel (1998) acknowledge the problem of the changes required for the electronic record, but the solution is seen as one of *'education and positive experience of using the EPR.....the effectiveness of, and clinician's performance against, clinical pathways or protocols, potentially become exposable. This provides a considerable opportunity for organisational learning and development.'* Argyris & Schon (1996) point out some of the difficulties in ensuring that such 'organisational learning' actually takes place, as well honed theories of action, or behavioural practices often ensure that conflicts are not addressed in a constructive manner. Atkinson & Peel (1998) imply that the slow gradual approach will help to persuade the electronic patient record users of the benefits. Their methodology is based largely on soft systems methodology, emphasising the human/machine activity system (Atkinson 1997).

The electronic record potentially makes audit easier, provided that such data is recorded securely. Perceptions of power and responsibility may be altered, particularly as the concept of the integrated record means that some information at least may be shared among different professionals and possibly also with the patient. Patient-held records may be desirable for episodes of care in which several professionals are involved, at different sites, over a period of time. Over a longer time period, views on confidentiality, attitudes towards rights and responsibility for record keeping may alter on both the part of the patient and the professional. Keeping a secret briefly is relatively easy, having a duty of care to keep the secret for all time is difficult, and the problems associated with accidental leakage of information all the greater. Who is watching whom - or should the question be who is watching for whom?

Foucault's image of the panopticon is frequently cited when discussing the increasing possibility of surveillance with IT and information systems. The term 'governmentality' (Kamm 1998) covers the wider introduction of practices and knowledge that make social problems tractable or comprehensible. Foucault's insights remind us that power may operate in ways that are not apparent to us, and that there is nothing simple about power, as it is a complex network of power, truth and subject (McGowen 1994). Such insights may not make the problem of patient access to records, or authorised professional access to data subsets, more tractable but they indicate that the issue may be more complicated than password controls and user authentication. Foucault's question concerning what permits this to be said, rather than something else, helps us to identify some of the unwritten rules and values behind practice which is superficially rational.

4.1 Researching the effects of power and rules

For empirical research, some investigation of the policies underlying practice might be revealed through policy capture analysis (Rossi and Anderson 1982) or through the use of vignettes used in a factorial manner (e.g. Tait and Chibnall 1997). For example, sets of hypothetical situations are varied systematically across factors identified as possibly relevant. Analysis (e.g. through logistic regression) can yield relationships between the factors and identify the factors which do influence judgment and choice, and which rules, formal and informal, are actually followed in practice (e.g. Schall 1983). Surveys (e.g. Shrier et al. 1998) suggest that knowledge about confidentiality is poor, and in these circumstances it is important to understand through careful analysis of judgment policies and informal rules how decisions are made (or not).

Contradictions are possible, if not probable in information systems development. If dialectics is a way of understanding the world which focuses on the concepts of change, interconnection, and contradiction, then dialectics may serve as a reminder of the limits of information systems (Robinson 1998). For the electronic health record which is designed to be used by different health and social care professionals, and also (partly) by patients, agreement is required on the Clinical Terms, but it is a problem in classification and thesauri construction that the meaning of terms can change over time, and that the abstractions created from real world phenomena will vary from person to person. Atkinson and Peel (1998) view the process of patient record system becoming progressively more united and unified. It is perhaps an anodyne view of rationalist hopes - postmodernists might doubt the basis on which this view is constructed.

5   CONCLUSION

This overview of some of the challenges facing development of the electronic health record as an information system has indicated how the problems can be considered from various philosophical perspectives. These perspectives may help in posing questions, and from these questions appropriate research methods can be considered.

References

Anderson, R.J. (1996) 'Patient confidentiality - at risk from NHS-wide networking.' In Richards, B. & de Glanville, H. (eds.), Current Perspectives in Healthcare Computing 1996, Harrogate, March 1996. Weybridge: BJHC Ltd, pp. 687-692.

Argyris, C. and Schon, D.A. (1996) Organisational learning II: theory, method, and practice. Wokingham: Addison-Wesley.

Atkinson, C.J. (1997) 'Soft information systems and technologies methodology, SISTeM©: a case study on developing the electronic patient record', Requirements Engineering, Vol. 2, pp. 1-22.

Atkinson, C.J. and Peel, V.J. (1998) 'Transforming a hospital through growing, not building, an electronic patient record system.' Methods of Information in Medicine, Vol. 37, pp. 285-293.

Avgerou, C. and Cornford, T. (1998) Developing information systems 2nd edition. : Macmillan, Basingstoke, UK.

Benbassat, J. (1996) 'The social worker's record of the hospitalized patient: a physician's perspective.' Israel J. Psychiatry Related. Sciences, Vol. 334, pp. 246-252.

Berg, Marc. (1997) Rationalizing medical work: decision support techniques and medical practices. MIT Press, Cambridge, MA, USA.

Berg, M. (1998) 'Medical work and the computer-based patient record: a sociological perspective', Methods of Information in Medicine, Vol. 37, pp. 294-301.

Bovey, J.D. (1996) 'Event-based personal retrieval', Journal of Information Science, Vol.

22, No.5, pp. 357-366.

Brown, B., Nolan, P., Crawford, P. and Lewis, A. (1996) 'Interaction, language and the 'narrative turn' in psychotherapy and psychiatry', Social Science and Medicine, Vol. 43, No. 11, pp. 1569-1578.

Caldicott Committee. (1997) Report on the view of patient-identifiable information. Report of the Committee chaired by Dame Fiona Caldicott. Department of Health, London, UK.

Department of Health, NHS Executive (1998) Information for Health: an information strategy for the modern NHS 1998-2005. Stationery Office, London (also available [Online] at http://www.imt4nhs.exec.nhs.uk/strategy/full/contents.htm, checked 1 October 1998).

Elbourne, D. et al. (1987) 'The Newbury Maternity Care Study: a randomized controlled trial to assess a policy of women holding their own obstetric records', Brit. J. Obstetrics and Gynaecology, Vol. 94, No. 7, pp. 612-619.

France, E. (1998) 'Data privacy in medicine: a perspective offered by the Data Protection Registrar', Brit. J. Healthcare Computing & Information Management, Vol. 14, No.2, pp. 20-22.

Freundlieb, D. (1994) 'Foucault's theory of discourse and human agency', In Jones, C & Porter, R (eds) Reassessing Foucault: power, medicine and the body. Routledge, London, pp.152-180.

Griew, A.R. (1996) 'Gaining consensus for and implementing the principles of internal data security for the electronic patient record in the NHS', In Richards, B & de Glanville, H. (eds), Current perspectives in healthcare computing conference 1996, Harrogate, March 1996. BJHC Ltd.,Weybridge, UK, pp. 425-431.

Hale, C.A., Thomas, L.H., Bond, S. and Todd, C. (1997) 'The nursing record as a research tool to identify nursing interventions', Journal of Clinical Nursing, Vol. 6, No. 3, pp. 207-214.

Hayes, G.M., (1998) 'Can one electronic medical record suit all clinical disciplines?' In Richards, B & Wood, H. (eds.). Current perspectives in healthcare computing conference 1998, Harrogate March 1998. BJHC Ltd, Weybridge, UK, pp.241-248.

Hogan, W.R. and Wagner, M.M. (1997) 'Accuracy of data in computer-based patient records', J. J. Amer. Medical Informatics Association, Vol.4, No. 5, pp. 342-355.

Hopkins, A. (1996) 'Clinical audit: time for reappraisal', Journal of the Royal College of Physicians of London, Vol. 30, pp. 415-425.

Johnston, M.E., Langton, K.B., Haynes, R.B. and Mathieu, A. (1994) 'Effects of computer-based clinical decision support systems on clinician performance and patient outcome', Annals of Internal Medicine, Vol. 120, pp. 135-142.

Kamm, R. (1998) 'Information systems and the use of Foucault: the implications of critical philosophy', In PAIS II: Second symposium and workshop on Philosophical aspects of information systems: methodology, theory, practice and critique, University of the West of England, Bristol, July 1998.

Lakhani, A.D., Avery, A., Gordon, A. and Tait, N. (1984) 'Evaluation of a home based health record booklet', Archives of Disease in Childhood, Vol. 59, No. 11, pp. 1076-1081.

McGowen, R. (1994) 'Power and humanity, or Foucault among the historians', In Jones, C & Porter, R (eds.) Reassessing Foucault: power, medicine and the body. Routledge, London, pp. 91-112.

NOMINA Group. (1998) Report on the Nursing Informatics Research Project. NHS Centre for Coding and Classification, Loughborough, UK.

Nygren, E. and Henriksson, P. (1992) 'Reading the medical record. I. Analysis of physicians' ways of reading the medical record', Computer Methods and Programs in Biomedicine, Vol. 39, pp. 1-12.

Olsson, M. (1998) 'Discourse: a new theoretical framework for examining information behaviour in its social context', In Information Seeking in Context: Proceedings of the 2nd international conference ISIC 2, Sheffield, August 1998. Taylor Graham, London.

OPCS (Office of Population Census and Surveys). (1995) The health of our children, Decennial supplement. OPCS DS no 11.

Rigby, Michael et al. (1998) 'New generation integrated record keeping as an essential requirement of a primary health care led service', Brit. Medical J., Vol. 317, No. 7158, pp. 579-582.

Rossi, P.H. and Anderson, A.B, (1982) 'The factorial survey approach: an introduction', In Rossi, .H & Nock, S.L. (eds.) Measuring social judgments. Sage, Beverley Hills, USA, pp.15-67.

Schall, M.S. (1983) 'A communication rules approach to organisational culture', Administrative Science Quarterly, Vol. 28, pp. 557-577.

Schmidt, H.G., Norman, G.R. and Boshuizen, H.P.A. (1990) 'A cognitive perspective on medical expertise: theory and implications', Academic Medicine Vol. 65, pp. 611-621.

Shrier, L. et al. (1999) 'Knowledge of and attitudes toward patient confidentiality within three family medicine teaching units', Academic Medicine. Vol. 73, No. 6, pp. 710-712.

Tait, R.C. and Chibnall, J.T. (1997) 'Physician judgements of chronic pain patients', Social Science and Medicine Vol. 45, pp. 1199-1205.

Tanenbaum, S.J. (1994) 'Knowing and acting in medical practice: the epistemological politics of outcomes research', J. Health Politics, Policy and Law, Vol. 19, No. 1, pp. 27-44.

Weed, L.L. (1968) 'Medical records that guide and teach', New England J. Medicine, Vol. 278, pp. 593-600, 652-657.

Welsh Office (1997) Health of children in Wales. Welsh Office NHS Wales, Cardiff, UK.

CHAPTER 61

THE IMPACT OF THE HOSPITAL INFORMATION SUPPORT SYSTEMS INITIATIVE ON THE OPERATION & PERFORMANCE OF ACUTE HOSPITALS

NF Doherty, M King and CG Marples
The Business School, Loughborough University

Abstract

Over the past fifteen years failures and mis-applications of information technology within the NHS have frequently made the headlines. This study seeks to investigate whether some of the lessons from early IT failures have now been learnt by investigating the impact of the hospital information support systems (HISS) initiative. Senior IT executives from twelve acute hospitals took part in semi-structured, in-depth interviews. The primary conclusion to be drawn from this study is that the deployment of information systems is now well underway within the acute sector although the level of integration is lagging behind. It is demonstrated that these systems are now perceived to be delivering real organisational benefits, especially in the managerial and administrative domains. Furthermore, it is shown that IS implementation is having an impact on the working practices and culture of these organisations.

1   INTRODUCTION

The NHS is a huge and complex organisation, whose operations and strategic focus could be greatly enhanced by the focused application of IT, to support improvements in productivity, management effectiveness, and the quality of care delivered to the patient. The recognised importance of IT within the NHS stems from the 1980s, with the publication of the inaugural national strategy for IT (DHSS, 1986). Since then there has been a headlong drive for improvements in the quantity and quality of information, resulting in millions of pounds being invested in IT (Keen, 1994). In 1991, however, a National Audit Office report (NAO, 1991) concluded that: '*The management of computer systems [within the NHS] was often weak, with many failures to follow good practice, resulting in poor value for money'*. Furthermore, high profile system failures such as those within the London Ambulance Service (LAS, 1993) and the Wessex Regional Health Authority (CofPA 1993) have propelled the NHS's IT strategy to the top of the political agenda. More recently, this appraisal of the situation has been supported by Clegg *et al* (1997) who conclude: *'The health sector is still seen as performing rather poorly in the field of IT'*.

The primary aim of this paper is, therefore, to investigate whether the problems reported throughout the 1990s continue to affect current implementations of HISS; one of the NHS's newer and more ambitious attempts to harness the power of IT to deliver major improvements to organisational performance. The following section of this paper introduces a summary of the content and objectives of the HISS initiative, and the methods by which an interview schedule was developed, validated and ultimately executed are discussed in section three. The research results are presented in a series of tables that are discussed in the fourth section. Finally the importance of the findings is then assessed in the concluding section.

2 THE HOSPITAL INFORMATION SUPPORT SYSTEMS (HISS) INITIATIVE

One of the most visible manifestations of the NHS's commitment to the focused application of IT to improve its operational performance has been the Hospital Information Support Systems (HISS) initiative, launched in December 1988 by the NHS Executive. The objective was to investigate how comprehensive and integrated computer systems could provide the better information that was required by all major acute hospitals in the United Kingdom, for the costing and pricing of services, to facilitate the clinical audit, improve the monitoring of outcomes and the quality of patient services, and to help hospital managers organise their services more effectively (NAO, 1996). A hospital information support system is based upon the patient administration system (PAS), which stores the patient's demographic details and a summarised medical history, in addition to holding details of waiting lists, appointments and hospital attendance. This central system can then be linked to a variety of departmental modules which typically include: theatres, pathology, pharmacy, nursing, accident & emergency, maternity and order communication / results reporting systems. The exact composition of a HISS will be dependent upon the range of services offered by a particular acute hospital; for example, not all acute hospitals offer accident and emergency or maternity services.

The HISS initiative has now been active for ten years. It has encouraged all acute hospitals to implement highly integrated information systems by funding pilot projects within targeted hospitals from which the lessons learned can then be disseminated throughout the NHS. The degree of success experienced by hospitals in adopting HISS technology has been far from perfect. For example, a recent National Audit office report (1996), having reviewed the performance of six trusts, concluded that: *'the projects investigated have encountered problems along the way, and have been slow to deliver benefits'*. Whilst the results of the NAO study are of interest there is also a need for more up-to-date research to review whether this position has changed. A research project was therefore initiated to investigate the impact of the HISS initiative on the operation and performance of acute hospitals that addressed the following three explicit research objectives:

- To assess current levels of progress in the deployment and integration of Hospital Information Support Systems.
- To identify the organisational benefits realised through the introduction of HISS
- To explore the impact of HISS on the structure and function of acute hospitals.

From a healthcare perspective this research is important as it builds upon, and updates, the material from the NAO report (1996) by using a wider sample, a broader scope and more rigorous research methods. Furthermore, it was envisaged that the exploration of these objectives, might provide some insights into the NHS's patchy record on IT implementation. From an IS perspective this research is also important as it addresses two issues whose critical significance have been acknowledged in the literature, namely: integration (Venkatraman, 1991; Segars & Grover, 1996) and the organisational impact of IT (Clegg et al, 1997; Doherty & King, 1998). These issues have attracted little attention in sector-specific studies, which can provide greater clarity in their conclusions. By concentrating on one specific sector (the NHS) and one specific type of system (HISS) many confounding factors are removed and variations in the impact of systems can be studied more precisely.

3 RESEARCH METHOD

This section describes the design, validation, targeting and execution of the research instrument, before reviewing the analysis strategy that was used to investigate the research objectives in more detail.

3.1 Design and Validation of the Interviews

In selecting an appropriate research instrument it was necessary to remember that the research was primarily exploratory, providing new insights into the organisational impacts of highly integrated information systems within the NHS. Consequently, in-depth personal interviews were considered to be the most appropriate data collection method. A series of questions was devised and incorporated into a semi-structured interview guide, which provided a framework for explicitly addressing the stated research objectives, whilst also ensuring that all interviewees were given every opportunity to raise issues, and highlight concerns that they perceived to be of significance. Having developed a draft structured interview it was validated by pre-testing on three senior IT executives from the NHS. This exercise centred upon identifying any problems with the focus, clarity and suitability of the questions. The pre-tests resulted in a number of important enhancements being made to the interview, both in terms of wording and content, before it was ultimately used.

3.2   Targeting and Execution of the Interviews

The individual best placed to provide information on group or organisational attitudes and behaviour within information systems research projects is typically the Chief Information Officer (CIO). The equivalent of the CIO in British hospitals is the Information Management and Technology (IM&T) Director, who holds overall responsibility for the strategic direction, and ultimately the success, of the acquisition and implementation of systems. Thus, IM&T Directors were targeted for participation in the interviews. In some NHS Hospitals the post of IM&T Director does not exist, and consequently one or more IM&T managers will report to another Director on the Hospital's board; typically the Finance Director. In these instances, either an IM&T Manager or the Finance Director was targeted. Ultimately, senior IT executives from a total of twelve acute hospitals agreed to participate in this research project.

3.3   Analysis Strategy

Having conducted and tape-recorded the interviews, the results were immediately written up in a standard format. From these transcriptions the text was reduced, to make it more meaningful, using the process of 'in-vivo' coding; in this method, the codes originate from the respondents themselves (Strauss & Corbin, 1990). The coded transcripts were then analysed using both within-case analysis and cross-case analysis (Miles and Huberman, 1994). The following section of the paper presents the results of a variable-oriented approach to cross-case analysis (Ragin, 1987), as the aim of the research was to explore the fundamental nature of the organisational impacts, rather than to compare and contrast different approaches.

4   RESEARCH FINDINGS

To make the discussion more meaningful the research findings below are related to the three specific research objectives proposed earlier.

4.1   Progress in the Development & Operation of HISS

One of the major objectives of this piece of research was to assess current levels of progress in the deployment and integration of hospital information support systems. This issue was primarily addressed by asking interviewees to comment on the status of each of the major components of HISS. The results of this exercise are presented in table 1.

The results clearly indicate that certain of the modular components of HISS are further ahead in terms of their operational status than others. For example, the 'patient administration', 'financial' and the 'personnel / payroll' modules are fully operational in all twelve of the trusts visited. This is not perhaps surprising, as the 'patient administration system' (PAS) is almost a pre-requisite for an integrated hospital information system, whilst the financial and personnel / payroll systems are fairly simple systems which can deliver significant productivity benefits and therefore have now been in existence for many years. At the other end of the scale the level of uptake of the 'casemix' and the 'order communications / results reporting (OC & RR)' modules is much lower. This is probably because these are two of the most complex components of a fully integrated HISS. Indeed, a number of trusts reported that they had been obliged to abandon their original attempts at these modules and were now working on replacements, or alternatively had only succeeded in implementing part of the system. This latter situation was most prevalent in the case of the 'order communications / results reporting' module where many trusts reported success in the development of an automated results reporting service, but far less success in the direct capture of orders at the point at which the need for a test, procedure or service is identified.

Module	Fully Operational	Partly Operational	Under Developm't	Part of Plan	Not being considered
P. A. S.	12	-	-	-	-
Financial systems	12	-	-	-	-
Personnel / payroll	12	-	-	-	-
Pathology	10	2	-	-	-
Radiology	10			1	1
Nursing	6	1	-	1	4
Theatres	6	2	4	-	-
Maternity	5	1	1	3	2
Casemix	3	4	3	1	1
O. C. & R. R.	2	6	1	3	

Table 1: Progress in the Acquisition of HISS

In addition to commenting on the state of progress with regard to the specific applications identified in table 1, interviewees were also invited to identify any other HISS applications that they has developed or were developing. The most commonly quoted additional application (10 out of 12 interviewees) was the 'accident and emergency' (A & E) module which is responsible for monitoring the admission and treatment of all patients arriving at a trust's A & E Department. Other modules which were frequently mentioned were the 'pharmacy' module and the 'professions allied to medicine system' (PAMS), which supports the activities of physio-, occupational and speech therapists. Many respondents noted that their pharmacy systems were currently little more than stock control applications because of the US origin of many of the healthcare packages. As one respondent went on to explain: *'the pharmacy system is currently being re-written as it can't cope with the ward-based approach to the dispensing of drugs as opposed to the US model where drugs are administered to individual patients in their private rooms'* (**trust 8**). Indeed, this highlights a wider problem facing acute hospitals when implementing hospital information support systems: the match between the deliverables supported by the available packages and the hospital's requirements is often inadequate, necessitating major re-writes to the package or changes to the hospital's working practices, or sometimes both.

When asked about the overall level of progress, in percentage terms, with regard to the deployment of HISS, the answers were mixed. At the lower end of the scale, two hospitals had only achieved 25% of their overall HISS plan, whilst at the other end of the spectrum two hospitals reported progress levels of over 80%; the average progress for the twelve trusts was a little under 60%. The interviewees were also asked to consider the degree of integration that had been achieved with regard to HISS. The PAS module generally forms the hub of a HISS implementation, and is of necessity well integrated with such other modules as have been deployed. The links between the 'pathology' and 'results reporting' modules were also common, which is perhaps understandable, as the pathology module is where test results are initially generated. More generally, however the reported levels of integration were not as high as might be expected, with comments such as: *'underway, but not complete'* (**trust 5**); *'access to information rather than transference of data'* (**trust 3**) or *'many links are one way, so there is still much to accomplish'* (**trust 9**).

The above discussion begins to provide an indication of the sheer scale and complexity of HISS. For example, the number of component modules at each trust surveyed is twelve or more, and they cover almost every aspect of an acute hospital's operational activities. A further indication of the scale of HISS is the significant numbers of personnel already actively using HISS, typically 500 or more at each trust. As one IM&T Manager (**trust 2**) noted: *'every member of staff, with the exception of the ancillary trades, is now a registered, and in most cases active, user of HISS'*. The complexity of HISS is evidenced by highly interconnected nature of a HISS implementation, and once more by its requirement to support such a wide variety of operational processes. It is highly likely that it is the sheer scale and complexity of the HISS project, both important risk factors (Willcocks & Margetts, 1994), that are at least partly to blame for the poor performance of HISS to date (NAO, 1996).

4.2   Benefits Realised through the Introduction of HISS

Having confirmed that the deployment of HISS is now well underway, it was also important to explore the impact that this was having on the performance of trusts. This issue was explored by asking the interviewees to assess the contribution of HISS to the trust's performance, in eight key areas, using a 5 point Likert scale. Interviewees were also asked to identify specific examples of tangible benefits that HISS had delivered. The results of the Likert analysis, which are presented in table 2, indicate that the most obvious benefit of the introduction of HISS has been in the creation of an information-oriented culture. Although this benefit is probably the least tangible in terms of the trust's overall performance, it has important, positive implications for the completion of the HISS project and for the introduction of future technological initiatives. On the other-hand a number of interviewees noted that the creation of the information-orientated culture brought with it the problems of *'the management of expectations'* (**trusts 1, 2, 3, 6 & 9**) where resources were inadequate to cope the demand for IT. It is also interesting to note that whilst the delivery of managerial and administrative benefits score relatively highly, perceptions of the ability of HISS to deliver clinical benefits is less positive; *'the impact has been seen greatly on the administrative side, but has yet to be fully seen on the clinical side'* (**trust 2**). A possible explanation of this was presented by one of the interviewees who suggested that: *'Despite the length of time spent on HISS, very few clinical benefits have been realised as yet. The focus is now moving away from the administrative side of the trust's operations to the clinical side. The strong administrative focus has in part been due to the central NHS's executive requirements and also to the clinician's perception that HISS is an administrative system'* (**trust 10**).

Perceived Benefits	Score
The implementation of HISS has led to a more information-orientated culture	**4.2**
The implementation of HISS has led to significant improvements in the efficiency of clerical and administrative procedures.	**3.8**
The implementation of HISS has facilitated the generation of high quality management information.	**3.8**
The introduction of HISS has resulted in improvements to the accuracy and quality of information provided to patients	**3.5**
The implementation of HISS has resulted in significant improvements in the quality of management decision-making	**3.2**
The implementation of HISS has improved the quality and frequency of communication between staff throughout the trust	**3.0**
The introduction of HISS has resulted in improvements to the quality of patient care	**3.0**
The implementation of HISS has led to significant improvements in the efficiency of clinical procedures	**2.7**

Table 2: The Benefits Realised Through the Introduction of HISS

When specific examples, were sought, of how HISS had contributed to the performance of acute trusts, a variety of examples were proposed. The following all reflect the ability of HISS to deliver managerial / administrative benefits:

- *'The theatre module has helped to re-allocate cancelled or postponed operations, greatly improving the overall theatre through-put rate'* (**trust 9**).

- '*The introduction of HISS has greatly reduced the level of clerical effort on the wards and within medical records*' (**trust 8**).
- '*From a commercial point of view, HISS has been absolutely vital allowing the trust to manage its income stream far more effectively*' (**trust 7**).
- '*Information from HISS has enabled the number of cancelled and postponed appointments (20,000+ per annum) to be greatly reduced*' (**trust 1**)
- '*The operations of the A & E department have been transformed by the new system; it is now far quicker to get patients registered, assessed and treated, resulting in a far better throughput of patients*', (**trust 6**).

Although the above examples were all considered to be administrative / managerial in orientation, it is interesting to note how many of them also have implications for patient care. For example, improvements to throughput in A & E departments, operating theatres and outpatient departments must have consequences for clinical effectiveness and ultimately patient care. Whilst the number of specific examples of clinical benefits was far fewer, the following notable examples were presented:

- '*The availability of an efficient and reliable mechanism for the ordering of tests and reporting of results is allowing clinical staff to concentrate more on their primary responsibilities*' (**trust 7**).
- '*The introduction of the electronic link between the order communications and pathology modules has greatly reduced the number of repeat tests due to lost results. This has greatly reduced the number of repeat investigations, which has a very positive impact on the performance of clinical staff and the care of patients*' (**trust 4**).

Although the impact of HISS has been most obvious on the managerial and administrative side, there is a high level of expectation that benefits will be realised, in the near future, on the clinical side, especially when the 'order communications and results reporting' modules become fully operational. As one interviewee noted: '*the big impact of HISS is still to come. Clinicians will ultimately spend less time pushing paper, and more time caring for patients*' (**trust 5**). An additional potential clinical benefit of HISS was noted by another interviewee who commented: '*The richness and quality of the data collected on patient care will ultimately impact on areas such as clinical audit, but this hasn't happened as yet*' (**trust 10**).

4.3   The Impact of HISS on the Structure & Function of Acute Hospitals

It has been recognised that the introduction of sophisticated information systems is likely to precipitate significant organisational change. (Hornby *et al*, 1992; Doherty & King, 1998). To investigate whether the introduction of HISS had major organisational implications for acute trusts, interviewees were asked about its impact on the organisation's structure and culture as well as its working practices. Each of these three potential impacts is considered in the following discussion:

- **Working Practices & HISS:** One IM & T Director (**trust 2**) summarised the consensus view when commenting: '*HISS is greatly changing the ways in which* *personnel undertake their responsibilities'*. An IM & T Manager (**trust 10**) noted: '*We certainly use IT as an explicit catalyst for organisational change, especially the design of working practices'*. Unfortunately, in many instances it was suggested that these changes were not planned and had occurred inadvertently; *'although HISS has undoubtedly precipitated changes to working practices, this was not a deliberate strategy'* (**trust 9**). Some of the more interesting examples of changes to working practices include: the rationalisation of pathology (**trust 12**); consultants managing their own waiting lists (**trust 1**); and the introduction of electronic communications with G.P.s (**trust 4**).

- **Organisational Culture & HISS:** There is some evidence that the introduction of HISS has induced cultural change within acute trusts through the empowering of users (**trusts 1, 3, 8 & 11**) and by facilitating staff flexibility (**trust 1**) but it is probably in the area of co-operation between different teams and departments that the greatest cultural impacts have been noted. For example as one IM & T Manager (**trust 10**) noted: *'There's a lot more talking between disciplines and a lot more sharing of information'*. This is an interesting example of how the introduction of HISS is having a cultural impact, which may in the longer term also precipitate structural changes if the erosion of departmental boundaries continues and becomes formalised.

- **Organisational Structure & HISS:** In the area of structural changes precipitated through the introduction of HISS, there was little direct evidence of major impacts. Many interviewees noted that their trusts had undergone radical structural change but most of these had been precipitated by alternative factors, such as trust mergers or central NHS initiatives. The one clear example of HISS impacting upon organisational structure was where: *'the responsibility for admitting patients has been delegated to the ward clerk and the central admissions department has now been closed'* (**trust 1**).

The importance of IT-induced organisational change was well summarised by one interviewee who commented: 'Progress is two-thirds in terms of the deployment and integration of systems, but only half-way if you take into account the changes to culture and working practices that are needed to make the systems fully effective' (**trust 11**).

In summary, there is evidence to suggest that HISS implementation is already having an impact on working practices and culture, and to a lesser extent on structure.

5   CONCLUSIONS

As information technology plays an increasingly dominant role within organisations of all shapes and sizes, it is important to understand how it is affecting the operation and performance of specific types of organisation. This study, which focuses upon the impact of information systems within acute hospitals, is significant, because it presents a sector-specific view of the role and importance of IT. The research has demonstrated that hospital information support systems are very large-scale and highly complex systems, which have a very significant organisational impact. It is primarily these characteristics which make their development and implementation such a high risk undertaking and probably account for the problems highlighted in this and previous research. However, it is also shown that the implementation of these systems is now well under way, and they are perceived to be delivering real organisational benefits, especially in the managerial and administrative domains, and that systems are beginning to have a positive impact on the working lives of employees, both individually and collectively.

This study has also highlighted the following key lessons:

- More effort is needed to realise the benefits of clinically orientated systems, such as 'order communications and results reporting' and 'casemix'.
- Fully integrated information systems have a significant impact on working practices and the structure and culture of organisations.
- The organisational re-design aspects of IT projects need to be explicitly considered if the benefits of technology are to be fully realised.

Whilst this exploratory study has provided many interesting insights and has helped to establish a research agenda in this area, there is now a need for more structured, survey-based research to explore the impact of HISS on the performance and operations of acute hospitals throughout the UK, so that these conclusions can be validated more generally.

References

Clegg, C., Axtell, C., Damadoran, L., Farbey, B., Hull, R., Lloyd-Jones, R., Nicholls, J. Sell, R. & Tomlinson, C. (1997). Information Technology: a study of performance and the role of human and organisational factors, *Ergonomics*, 40(9), 851-871.

CofPA. (1993). *Wessex Regional Health Authority Information Systems Plan*. London: HMSO.

Denzin, N. K. (1989). *Interpretive Biography (Qualitative Research Methods Series Volume 17)*, Newbury Park, CA: Sage

DHSS (1986). *A National Strategic Framework for Information Management in the Hospital and Community Health Services*. London: DHSS.

Doherty, N. F. & King, M. (1998). The consideration of organizational issues during the systems development process: an empirical analysis, *Behaviour & Information Technology,* 17(1), 41-51.

Hornby, C., Clegg, C., Robson, J., McClaren, C., Richardson, S. & O'Brien, P. (1992) "Human & Organisational Issues in Information Systems Development", *Behaviour & Information Technology*, Vol. 11 No. 3, pp. 160-174.

Keen, J. (1994). *Information Management in Health Services*, Buckingham: The Open University Press.

L.A.S. (1993). *Report of the Inquiry into the London Ambulance Service*. London: London Ambulance Service.

Miles, M. B., and Huberman, A. M. (1994). *Qualitative Data Analysis*, Thousand Oaks,

California: Sage Publications

N.A.O. (1991). *Managing Computer Projects in the National Health Service.* London: HMSO.

N.A.O. (1996). *The NHS Executive: The Hospital Information Support Systems Initiative.* London: HMSO.

Ragin, C. C. (1987). *The comparative method: moving beyond qualitative and quantitative strategies,* Berkeley: University of California Press.

Segars, A. & Grover, V. (1996) Designing Company-wide Information Systems: Risk Factors and Coping Strategies, *Long Range Planning,* 29 (3), pp 381-392.

Strauss, A. & Corbin, J. (1990). *Basics of qualitative research: grounded theory procedures and techniques.* Newbury Park, CA: Sage Publications

Willcocks L. &. Margetts.H. (1994). Risk Assessment and Information Systems, *European Journal of Information Systems,* 3 (2), 127-138.

Venkatraman, N, (1991) 'IT-induced Business Re-configuration', in *The Corporation of the 1990s,* Scott-Morton M. (*ed*), Oxford University Press.

CHAPTER 62

SPECIALIST ENVIRONMENTS FOR DATABASE DESIGN: ISSUES IN MEDICAL RESEARCH

Hugh Preston and Jeffrey Jones*
University of Wales, *International Blood Group Reference
Laboratory

Abstract

Fields of specialised scientific research are characterised by their singular and complex use of computers as operational tools. Each effort in database design must be original and unique. This paper examines issues of information system design with a focus on the applicability of chosen techniques in a specialised environment. The context is the Molecular Genetics Department of the International Blood Group Reference Laboratory. The paper indicates how the design of the Rhesus Information Tracking System was able to meet the current needs. Rapid Application Development (RAD) prototyping forms the basis of the investigation linked to interview, questionnaire and observation techniques in order to establish requirements for interoperability. A number of generic issues are highlighted by the research.

1   INTRODUCTION

The issues within database design and development inevitably include those beyond the immediate boundaries of individual databases. Integrity of data, connectivity of information systems and security are amongst these. Central control leads to standardisation which supports the application of the latest versions of system development methodologies on a large scale. For example, medical and associated administrative information systems in the UK have been developed primarily through the Structured Systems Analysis and Design Method (SSADM) together with the associated project management methodology, PRojects IN Controlled Environments (PRINCE) (Avison & Fitzgerald, 1995). There has been significant research into the resulting information systems which have a broad range of uses. (Marcel, 1996 and Bourn & Davies, 1996).

Within the health sector, however, there is also information that is of a specialised nature and some associated areas of scientific research are characterised by the unique nature of the information that emerges. Although a variety of generic software may be able to work with DBMS schemas to describe the data, each effort in database development must incorporate the original and unique characteristics of the system's context. If a commonly understood methodology is to be used it should encompass an overview of a systems approach rather than prescribe a particular technique. As such, it will be more of a view than a methodology. A contingent method geared towards incorporating the needs of users incrementally through prototyping would appear to be appropriate (Beynon-Davies et al. 1997 and Beynon-Davies, 1998). There is some evidence that standardised methodologies are of only limited value anyway (Fitzgerald, 1997 and Wynekoop & Russo, 1997). In any event, there has always been a wide range of methodologies (Avgerou & Cornford, 1993 and Fitzgerald, 1996). Recent thinking in database design includes more flexible approaches such as the Rapid Application Development (RAD) method.

This paper looks at the design of a database for handling files related to work within a highly specialised scientific environment. The investigation and development took place within the Molecular Genetics Department of the International Blood Group Reference Laboratory. The study looks at information needs identified within this organisation and it will indicate how the design of the Rhesus Information Tracking System (RITS) was able to meet current needs. RAD prototyping forms the basis of the investigation linked to interview, questionnaire and observation techniques in order to establish requirements for interoperability. In order to focus on needs investigation, the associated development devices of Specialists With Advanced Tools (SWAT) and Computer Aided Software Engineering (CASE) are not explored in the context of this study. In particular, the place of this specialist database within the much broader information strategy of the National Blood Service will be examined.

2   THE RESEARCH PROJECT

The National Blood Authority (NBA), established in April 1994, is charged with the responsibility of the re-organisation of the fourteen independent Regional Centres of the Blood Transfusion Service in England, the Bio-Products Laboratory (BPL) and the International Blood Group Reference Laboratory (IBGRL), into one co-ordinated service - the National Blood Service (NBS). Cost reduction and service enhancement can only be achieved with accurate, reliable and timely information available to the NBA, the purchaser, the patient and to the blood donor.

The Molecular Genetics Department (MGD) of the International Blood Group Reference Laboratory (IBGRL) performs both reference and research functions from internal and external sources. On a functional basis IBGRL may be divided into three main areas: Reference, Research and Development and Pure Research. There is a high degree of collaboration between these sections from which highly specialised services may be called upon when required. It was recognised that the current MGD information system relating to these functions was inefficient, consisting of a combination of indexed paper records and fragmented spreadsheet files. A system study would be limited by a need to utilise the organisational network system. The MGD provides two main services:

- *Haemolytic Disease of the Newborn (HDN) reference service*
- *Biochemical research*

Information system problems were identified in a number of areas within these main services:

- *User support* - the MGD HDN Reference Service performs a supportive role. The information system currently in use does not fulfil user needs since data are fragmented and essential demographic; statistical and financial information is either not available or not easily provided.
- *Specialist requirements* - small numbers of intricate and highly involved technical investigations are performed and commercial software cannot satisfy the needs of this relatively small niche of the service. As a consequence, the development of an in-house bespoke database was investigated to meet the more esoteric needs of the MGD.
- *Multi-user access* - the recently completed NBA Corporate Strategy review is likely to lead to far-reaching changes in the physical distribution, organisation and management practices of the NBS. Currently, there is little infrastructure to support electronic interfaces between various centres, their user hospitals, each other and the head office at Watford. However, with connection to the National Health Service (NHS) X.400 messaging service, electronic mail (e-mail) communications between the NBS and its customers would become possible. The NBS, where possible, will use common, proven technologies and adopt NHS IT standards (NHSE Information Management Group, 1995).
- *Connectivity and interoperability* - these are of key importance, both between the MGD and the core systems at each of the transfusion centres, and with the Enterprise Information System (EIS) and Finance systems. Within a transfusion centre, services will be made available across Ethernet LANs where they exist and a variety of Netware, UNIX and propriety protocols will be supported.

2.1   Study objectives
- To establish an effective approach to developing a specialist database with an established database management system (DBMS)
- To implement this development to meet the needs of the MGD, using Visual FoxPro 3

3   RAPID APPLICATION DEVELOPMENT (RAD) PROTOTYPING

As described earlier, RAD is a relatively recent philosophy in software development which requires an holistic approach (Beynon-Davies et al. 1997). Instead of the usual development cycle of analysis, design, sign-off, coding, testing and finally implementation, the task or project is approached in a totally different way. The user is involved as an integral part of the development team, not just a bystander and eventual evaluator. The development team itself becomes less technical and more business-driven introducing a multi-disciplinary quality to the process. The system should adopt an evolutionary role with live, working programs presented to the user quickly and regularly. Modular development brings shorter development cycles. This means using advanced flexible tools. For RAD to be effective, object-oriented programming offers lots of advantages. Its aim to break programs down into objects, results in units that are sufficiently general purpose that they can be reused in other programs. The programs created are easier to understand, easier to debug, and generally easier to maintain. The reusability of the program parts means time will be saved in future projects. The creation of classes and the application of the characteristics of inheritance, encapsulation and polymorphism serve the needs of a RAD approach well (Scholtz, 1994). The understanding of the systems users is also enhanced (Mentzas, 1997). The key elements of large-scale RAD are:

- *Joint application development* (JAD) where users and systems professionals work together to analyse and design the system.
- *Specialists with advanced tools* (SWAT) teams composed of three or four skilled and motivated systems professionals using computer aided software engineering (CASE). These increase productivity and work quality as well as minimising development time.
- *Prototyping* - users are shown what they will receive and can react to it. The CASE tools facilitate prototyping by enabling SWAT team members to create screen designs, models and so on while interacting with users.

Within MGD, the scope for applying each of these elements is limited by the small size of the department. JAD, however, is less constrained since information requirements are the core elements of any system and the specialist nature of the information determines that some sort of incremental approach is advantageous. The specialists and the tools that they use must offer the advantages of their larger scale equivalents, but may be identified from individuals and software tools that already exist or are easily acquired. This was the case at MGD where one individual had responsibility for system development, working with others within the department. The software was Visual FoxPro 3 with its object-oriented development environment which provides RAD support on a scale well beyond that of the software's origins as a basic database management system.

4   INVESTIGATION

The use of RAD prototyping was seen as highly appropriate in terms of system development, but this needed to be complemented by an investigative method that would identify characteristics of the organisation that should be embodied in the database. Survey methodology was used to establish existing levels of service/research activities and the information requirements for the RITS system. Data were collected by the following means:

Interview: The reference manager and four laboratory staff were interviewed to obtain a broad view of information needs. This process was extended using RAD so that staff views could be incorporated in parallel with system development.

Questionnaire: This was self-administered to the above staff to obtain specific data requirements. The questionnaire was structured to identify a number of key points. These include the objectives of the MGD, reference service provision and research functions, specific information needs and methods of information storage, retrieval and dissemination. In addition, staff were asked to design sample printout formats that would be required for output.

Observation: Systematic activity and statistical sampling were performed to identify the volume of data the system would be expected to handle.

Guidelines: Technical and standard NBA specifications were provided by the NBA IT department.

4.1 Summary of survey results

The results of the investigation indicated a range of technical, functional and system management issues. An examination of these highlights the specialist nature of the information but also identifies issues of integrity, connectivity and security that a broader based system would have. Brittain and MacDougall's claim that, *'the NHS has more stand-alone information systems that do not interact with one another than perhaps any other organisation, certainly in the UK'* provides a view of a wider issue influencing system development (Brittain & MacDougall, 1995, p. 127).

4.1.1   Technical requirements

The survey revealed that specimen samples and results must be faithfully linked to patient information and an audit of the accuracy of this record and subsequent changes must be available. There must be facilities to add and update test and patient information. The system must provide the facility to exchange data with other information systems within the service using SQL. Access rights must be capable of configuration at any level. In addition, the system must provide management information about the day-to-day running of the laboratories. The system should provide the facility to review all, or a selected part, of the patient information over a defined period of time. The system should interface with the NBA core system using a common coding system. In view of expected use of MGD's service, the system must be capable of handling 200 samples per year with a potential increase to 1000.

In terms of performance, screen based queries should achieve a response within five seconds and feedback from the system during data entry should be immediate. 24 hour operation should be possible and system support and maintenance should not unreasonably interfere with normal operation.

Issues of connectivity should be addressed through conformance to the POSIX standard (ISO 9945-1:1990) and network communication should be possible using TCP/IP. The National Health Service (NHS) standard of X400/88 should be complied with and other NHS standards should be applicable where appropriate. ASCII flat file data export should be possible.

4.1.2   Functional requirements

In order to meet the needs of the reference and research functions of MGD, referred to earlier, the system requires the following features. It must be possible to allocate a unique identifier to each sample and it must be possible to identify the source of the request, the patient and the type of sample. Identity and contact details for the referring doctor/scientist should be recorded and the destination of the sample reports should be apparent. Urgency of tests should also be available.

In addition to full details of the patient names, sex and date of birth; a unique patient number used by the referring source, together with NBS's reference number and the NBS centre where any previous tests had been carried out should be recorded. Changes to patient details and links to results recorded for relatives of the patient should be easy to incorporate. Full details of samples with clinical information, coded and free-text, should be possible. Suitability of samples for testing and condition of samples also needs recording. Details of repeat tests and batch failures as well as scanned images should be available. The system output should be available in various specified types, eg. e-mail, fax, letter, tables etc. Multiple addresses for transmission and a record of transmissions should be available.

4.1.3   System management requirements

Facilities for the management of system performance and or tuning of performance should be built in at user access level. File and system information should be readily available, together with effective backup and recovery facilities that don't affect the system performance or availability. Verification of backed up data should be available. Unique user identifiers and establishment of an audit trail of system use should be built in. The trail should record log-on and log-off, use of facilities and data manipulation. The trail should be capable of management by the system manager. Basic accounting facilities relating to system costs should be available.

5   SIGNIFICANCE OF FINDINGS

Objective - To establish an effective approach to developing a specialist database with an established database management system (DBMS)

The initial survey provides MGD with a view of system requirements that does not immediately point to commercial software that has not been subject to substantial in-house bespoke design. RAD offers the opportunity for this to take place through the use of CASE tools and through prototyping that enables incremental development.

Furthermore RAD methods were implemented in view of the limited time scale of the RITS project (Martin, 1991). As discussed earlier, RAD does not apply to any kind of unique software, but rather is an information system oriented set of practices that consists of a combination of JAD sessions, prototyping and CASE tools together. JAD produces savings by shortening the elapsed time required to gather a system's requirements, both in terms of the validity of the requirements and by reducing the number of costly, downstream requirement changes (Wood & Silver, 1995). Its success depends on effective leadership of the JAD sessions; on participation by key end-user and developers and on achieving synergy during JAD sessions (Beynon-Davies et al. 1997).

Prototyping as an evolutionary tool (figure.1) is a lifecycle model in which the system concept is developed through the project. The user is demonstrated the part of the system of interest and the prototype is developed based on the feedback received. This is especially useful when requirements are changing rapidly and produces steady, visible signs of progress. The main drawback of this kind of prototyping is that it's impossible to know at the outset of the project how long it will take to create an acceptable product. This is mitigated by the fact that customers can see steady signs of progress and they therefore tend to be less uncomfortable about project development.

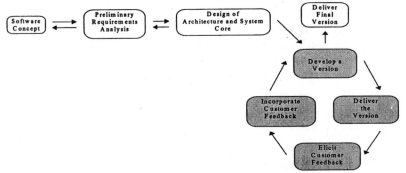

Figure 1: Evolutionary delivery model. Optimum obtained from variability in control through staged delivery and flexibility by evolutionary prototyping.

Objective - To implement this development to meet the needs of the MGD, using Visual FoxPro 3

The requirements identified in the survey have been met by the RITS system either wholly or partly in the following ways.

User support - the RITS system provides an integrated and structured purpose designed database. This is within the framework of a powerful DBMS that facilitates RAD through support of techniques such as prototyping. All related data are now available in a variety of requested formats and easily accessible via an intuitive menu system. Demographic, statistical and financial information is now available via screen display and hard copy printout.

Specialist requirements - the nature of the work and the provision of service offered by MGD emphasises specialised information needs. Commercial off-the-shelf software packages are currently not available to provide the facilities that the department require to offer an efficient and high quality service. The cost of commercial bespoke software application development was deemed to be too high for such a relatively small application in a small market niche. The chosen option was to develop an in-house bespoke application with low risk, low cost and high facilities. Accordingly the application was relatively cheap to produce and maintain, facilities can be specifically developed for user needs and not adapted from existing software and the response time for an update or problem can be rapid. However, technical support and maintenance services could not be guaranteed at all times. This is not a problem with the hardware since cover is provided by a separate service contract. Additional large scale facilities may only be provided by commercial software development. However should large scale development be required in the future the data file structures are of standard format and can simply be ported across to the new application.

Comparison of user system requirements with current RITS system functionality highlights shortcomings in only a few specific areas:

Technical mandatory requirements (compliance in 19 out of 24 requirements)

Non-compliance in the main areas of data exchange, core system connectivity and communication standards. Since the core system and communication hardware have not as yet been installed these facilities will have to be added at a later date. A facility for archiving data will also be developed.

Technical desirable requirements (compliance in 5 out of 14 requirements)

An interface using a common coding system will be developed after the installation of the appropriate hardware. Training facilities and context sensitive help will also be developed. Facilities are currently not available for system tuning or manipulation of auditing functions.

Functional mandatory requirements (compliance in 28 out of 29 requirements)

E-mail facilities will be developed on the availability of relevant hardware.

Functional desirable requirements (compliance in 0 out of 2 requirements)

Remote requesting should be available after the installation of the relevant hardware.

The main areas of non-conformance are in data exchange and communications. These relate to the remaining problem areas identified at the beginning of the study, those of multi-user access, connectivity and interoperability. The availability of these facilities are determined by the installation of supporting software and hardware.

5.1   Future developments of the RITS system

The primary issue for the RITS lay in its non-compliance with criteria for connectivity and inter-operability. This is almost inevitable in a small scale system developed in-house, but can be resolved incrementally through the adoption of standards that larger scale systems meet. This will require the assimilation of NHS Data Standards. The Data Standards Open Systems Interconnection (OSI) methods are concerned with defining the necessary standards to allow computer systems to exchange information. For information to be shared across the NHS, the development of nationally agreed Data Standards is essential. The NHS Data Dictionary will contain all the Data Standards for the whole of the NHS. In addition, the NHS has adopted a number of coding systems such as the International Classification of Diseases (ICD), Healthcare Resource Groups (HRGs) and Read Codes (computerised coding for clinical information). The objective for networking on an NHS-wide basis, is the provision of any-to-any connectivity nationwide (NHSE Information Management Group, 1995). Therefore, consideration of all these standards must be made in any future developments, especially concerning connection to the NHS Wide Area Network.

In an effort to standardise the information systems throughout the NBS, national 'core' and specialist services IT systems will be installed coupled with a telecommunications infrastructure which will enable the various TCs to communicate with user hospitals, each other and the head office. The NHS X400 messaging service will allow electronic mail (e-mail) communications between the NBS and its customers. NHS IT standards (NHSE Information Management Group, 1995) should be adopted wherever possible.

6   CONCLUDING COMMENTS

The study on which this paper is based was aimed to produce tangible results in the form of an information system to meet the requirements of a limited user group within a small-scale environment. Consequently, it looked at technical and functional issues that would shape the eventual form of the system. From the study it became evident, however, that the issue of integrity and, in particular, the issues of connectivity and security would be core to the system's success. Given the scale of the department, it was clear that a one-off successful system was unlikely. The RAD philosophy for system prototyping, allied to several survey techniques, offered a feasible solution. The availability of CASE tools within database software reduced the need for a small organisation to acquire the tools of the larger organisation but they had to be operated with the knowledge that a local view will eventually need to incorporate elements of the larger environment. The issues of connectivity that have been identified are the results of this. Consequently, future versions of the system will need to be prototyped to establish the extent to which they meet user requirements in the face of the 'big issues' encountered in the local development of databases. These same issues highlight questions that specialist institutes in most fields of medical research need to address.

References

Avgerou, C., & Cornford, T. (1993) 'A review of the methodologies movement,' Journal of Information Technology, Vol. 5, pp. 277-286.

Avison, D., & Fitzgerald, B. (1995) Information Systems Development. McGraw-Hill, London, UK.

Beynon-Davies, P. (1998) 'Rapid Application Development: an empirical assessment,' Proceedings of the Third United Kingdom Academy of Information Systems (UKAIS) Conference, University of Lincoln, McGraw-Hill, Maidenhead, UK, pp.127-40.

Beynon-Davies, P., Tudhope, D., & Mackay, H. (1997) 'Integrating rapid application development and participatory design,' Proceedings of the Second United Kingdom Academy of Information Systems (UKAIS) Conference, University of Southampton, McGraw-Hill, Maidenhead, UK, pp. 317-33.

Bourn, M., & Davies, C. (1996) 'A Prodigious Information Systems Failure.' Topics in Health Information Management, Vol. 17, pp. 34-44.

Brittain, J.M., & MacDougall, J. (1995) 'Information as a resource in the National Health Service.' International Journal of Information Management, Vol. 15, pp.127-133.

Fitzgerald, B. (1996) 'Formalized systems development methodologies: a critical perspective.' Information Systems Journal, 6, pp.3-24.

Fitzgerald, B. (1997) 'The nature of usage of systems development methodologies in practice: a field study.' Proceedings of the Second United Kingdom Academy of Information Systems (UKAIS) Conference, University of Southampton, 2-4 April 1997 (Key Issues in Information Systems), McGraw-Hill, Maidenhead, UK, pp. 331-344.

Marcel, B. (1996) 'New barcodes - portable data files.' British Journal of Healthcare Computing & Information Management, Vol. 13 No. 2, pp. 48-49.

Martin, J. (1991) Rapid Application Development. Macmillan, New York, USA.

Mentzas, G.N. (1997) 'Re-engineering banking with object-oriented models: towards customer information systems.' International Journal of Information Management, Vol. 17, pp. 179-197.

NHSE Information Management Group, (1995) IT standards handbook: NHS Version 2, NHSE, London, UK.

Scholtz (1994) 'Object-oriented programming: the promise and the reality.' Software Practitioner Vol. 1, pp. 4-7.

Wood, J, & Silver D. (1995) Joint Application Development, 2nd Ed. John Wiley & Sons, New York, USA.

Wynekoop, J.L., & Russo, N.L. (1997) 'Studying system development methodologies: an examination of research methods.' Information Systems Journal, Vol. 7, pp. 47-65.

CHAPTER 63

DATA WAREHOUSING, DATA MINING, AND KNOWLEDGE DISCOVERY

Michael Lloyd-Williams and Janet Collins
University of Wales Institute Cardiff

Abstract

The use of computer-based collections of data to support business decision-making activities has been commonplace since the early 1970s. More recently, the digital revolution has seen such data collections increase both in size and complexity to the extent that they are often referred to nowadays as data warehouses. Such data collections frequently conceal implicit patterns of information that cannot be readily detected by conventional analysis techniques, but which may often be usefully analysed using a knowledge discovery/data mining approach. This paper discusses the concepts of data warehousing, data mining and knowledge discovery. Details of a series of empirical studies are presented which serve to highlight the factors perceived as influencing the success or otherwise of the projects concerned, to illustrate the generic difficulties that may be encountered during the knowledge discovery, and to examine how these difficulties may be overcome.

1   INTRODUCTION

The use of computer-based collections of data to support business decision-making activities has been commonplace since the early 1970s (Sprague & Watson, 1996). More recently, the digital revolution has seen such collections of data grow in size, and the complexity of the data therein increase (Lloyd-Williams, 1998). According to Watson & Haley (1998), such data collections are nowadays often referred to as *data warehouses* - a term coined by Inmon (1992) in the late 1980s. However, advances in technology have often resulted in our ability to meaningfully analyse and understand the data we gather lagging far behind our ability to capture and store this data (Fayyad et al, 1996). Indeed, according to Fayyad & Uthurasamy (1996), a question commonly arising nowadays as a result of this state of affairs is, having gathered such quantities of data, what do we actually do with it?

It is often the case that large collections of data, however well structured, conceal implicit patterns of information that cannot be readily detected by conventional analysis techniques (Lloyd-Williams et al, 1995). Such data may often be usefully analysed using a set of techniques referred to as *knowledge discovery* or *data mining*. These techniques essentially seek to build a better understanding of data, and in building characterisations of data that can be used as a basis for further analysis (Limb & Meggs, 1995), extract *value* from *volume* (Scarfe & Shortland, 1995).

2 DATA WAREHOUSING, DATA MINING, AND KNOWLEDGE DISCOVERY

Although the precise definition of a data warehouse is debatable, it is generally agreed that it consists of a collection of historical data consolidated from a number of sources within the organisation, and is intended to support business decision making (Sen & Jacob, 1998). Gardner (1998) suggests that data warehousing should be viewed as a process rather than a product, the emphasis being on maintaining the level of flexibility required in order to meet the evolving needs of the enterprise. Watson & Haley (1998) describe the related concept of the *data mart*, which they describe as a smaller data repository representing a specific subject area. Although Watson & Haley (1998) discuss data mart in terms of being an alternative to a data warehouse, Sigal (1998) promotes the view that data marts (if required at all) should be extracted *from* a data warehouse, and not be viewed as a viable alternative.

Despite this apparent lack of consensus within the field of data warehousing, one point that is generally accepted is that the reason for capturing and storing such large amounts of data is due to the belief that there is valuable information implicitly coded within it (Fayyad & Uthurasamy, 1996). An important issue therefore is how is this hidden information (if it exists at all) to be revealed? Traditional methods of knowledge generation often rely largely upon manual analysis and interpretation (Fayyad et al, 1996). However, as data collections continue to grow in size and complexity, there is a corresponding growing need for more sophisticated techniques of analysis (Fayyad et al, 1996). One such innovative approach to the knowledge discovery process is known as *data mining*.

Data mining is essentially the computer-assisted process of information analysis (Limb & Meggs, 1995), and can be performed using either a top-down or a bottom-up approach. Bottom-up data mining analyses raw data in an attempt to discover hidden trends and groups, whereas the aim of top-down data mining is to test a specific hypothesis (Hedberg, 1995). Data mining may be performed using a variety of techniques, including intelligent agents, powerful database queries, and multi-dimensional analysis tools (Watterson, 1995). Multi-dimensional analysis tools include the use of neural networks, such as described in the studies presented in this paper.

The data mining approach expedites the initial stages of information analysis, thereby quickly providing initial feedback that may be further and more thoroughly investigated if appropriate. The results obtained are not (unless otherwise specified) influenced by preconceptions of the semantics of the data undergoing analysis. Patterns and trends may therefore be revealed that may otherwise remain undetected, and/or not considered. However, it should be clearly stated at this juncture that this paper advocates the use of data mining techniques *in conjunction* with traditional approaches to information analysis, and not as a direct replacement.

2.1   The Knowledge Discovery Process

According to Adriaans & Zantinge (1996), there has been some confusion over the exact meanings of the terms *data mining* and *knowledge discovery*. Indeed, some authors use the terms synonymously and interchangeably. This paper adopts the philosophy of those - including Adriaans & Zantinge (1996) and Fayyad et al (1996) - who view data mining as being a key activity within the more elaborate process known as *knowledge discovery*. Therefore from this point on, the use of the term *data mining* within this paper is used to represent a specific activity within the knowledge discovery process, *viz*: the analysis of data by means of data mining software.

In its simplest form, knowledge discovery involves the capture of data and its manipulation to reflect the purpose of an investigation, the subjecting of this data to data mining software, and the interpretation of any results obtained. These results may in turn be subsequently used to direct the capture of further data which may also be fed into the knowledge discovery process, thereby completing the *virtual circle* of Berry & Linoff (1997). The studies presented in this paper were all performed using the approach proposed by Fayyad et al (1996) which asserts that the process of knowledge discovery comprises four basic stages; *selection*, *pre-processing*, *data mining*, and *interpretation*.

Selection involves creating the target data set. Large datasets which are not particularly complex may generally be subjected in their entirety to the analysis process. Indeed, the larger the amount of available data, the greater the likelihood that an identifiable trend or pattern may be identified. It is a common misconception to assume that a complete dataset may be submitted to data mining software, which in turn will resolve any problems and make sense of any inconsistencies that may be present. This is not in fact the case, and is partly due to the possibility that the data may well represent a number of different aspects of the domain which are not directly related. Subjecting such data to automated analysis may result in the identification of patterns or trends which may be found to be statistically significant. However, these patterns are likely to be trivial or meaningless within the context of the main purpose of the investigation.

Pre-Processing involves preparing a dataset for analysis by the data mining software to be used. The pre-processing activities may result in the generation of a number of (potentially overlapping) subsets of the original target dataset, rather than a single dataset. The manipulation of data during the pre-processing stage is sometimes referred to as *cleaning* (Hedberg, 1995). Pre-processing may also involve activities such as resolving undesirable data characteristics including missing data, irrelevant fields, non-variant fields, skewed fields, and outlying data points. All these characteristics have the potential to adversely impact upon any results obtained, sometimes in an extremely subtle manner. Such characteristics should therefore be either resolved (or at a minimum, recognised and documented) prior to any further activities.

Data Mining involves subjecting the cleaned data to analysis by data mining software in an attempt to identify trends or patterns, or to test hypotheses. Techniques commonly used include neural networks, data visualisation, genetic algorithms, and decision trees. It is strongly recommended that any results obtained via data mining are validated using traditional statistical techniques at this stage.

Interpretation involves the analysis of the results produced and will be driven primarily by input from experts in the domain under investigation. Results obtained may well instigate returning to previous stages to carry out additional activities in order to provide further information if necessary. Therefore, although the knowledge discovery process may be viewed as comprising distinct stages, it is in practice, highly iterative in nature.

3 EMPIRICAL STUDIES

This section present details of three studies of the application of the knowledge discovery approach to the analysis of information. In each case, the focus of the study is on data mining and knowledge discovery activities rather than data warehousing, although the data analysed could be viewed as being extracted from a series of data marts. The information analysed during these studies was extracted from the World Health Organisation's *Health for All Database, the Babies at Risk of Intrapartum Asphyxia* database, and a series of databases containing infertility information.

The studies were carried out primarily using a neural network technique known as a *Kohonen Self Organising Map (SOM)*. The SOM is able to organise data collections in terms of the natural relationships that exist within the data (Dayhoff, 1990). Indeed, the approach has been widely and successfully used in multivariate data analysis, and is often seen as the best choice of analysis tool from an interpretational point of view (Murtagh & Hernández-Pajares, 1995).

3.1 The Health for All Database

The World Health Organisation's (WHO) *Health for All (HFA)* Database was created to make health-related data collected by the WHO available to outside users. The Database contains statistical indicators for the WHO HFA targets relating to Health-for-All in Europe by the year 2000. Data relating to a range of conditions (including life expectancy; probability of dying before five years of age; infant mortality; and post-neonatal) was extracted for 39 European countries. Three subsets of data were extracted and analysed by SOM software in order to identify possible groupings. Finally, standard statistical techniques were used to evaluate the validity of the groupings. This investigation therefore made use of the bottom-up data mining approach described previously.

Preliminary work resulted in two distinct groups or clusters of countries in each year being apparent (Lloyd-Williams et al, 1996). It was observed that all countries in the first of the groups were from Central and Eastern Europe or from the former Soviet Republics, while all countries in the second group were from Northern (i.e., the Nordic countries), Western, or Southern Europe. A two-sample t-test was used to validate the groupings identified. The results obtained confirmed that the identified groups were significantly different or separated from each other.

In addition to the geographical division, the classification also appeared to reflect differences in wealth. A t-test was performed, and the result indicated a significant difference between the two groups in terms of GNP per capita. The observation that the classification appeared to reflect two different GNP groups suggested that GNP could be inter-related with the health indicators. In order to further explore this possibility, the coefficient of correlation was calculated between GNP and all seven HFA indicators used in the initial analysis. Results obtained indicated that GNP is strongly and positively correlated with life expectancy, and strongly but negatively correlated with the SDR for diseases of the circulatory system. Overall, the available data indicated that death rates for malignant neoplasms tended to rise with increasing affluence, while death rates for other diseases tended to fall.

Further work was then performed in order to obtain a finer classification. This work resulted in the identification of six groups, which were essentially sub-divisions of the two groups produced by the preliminary work (Lloyd-Williams & Williams, 1996). Characteristics of the groups ranged from the lowest life expectancy, coupled with the highest probability of dying before five and infant mortality rate (Group 1), to the highest mean life expectancy, coupled with the lowest probability of dying before five, and infant mortality rate (Group 6). Over time, mean life expectancy increased, while the probability of dying before five and infant mortality rate both decreased for all groups. Detailed summary statistics of each group may be found elsewhere (Williams, 1995). Group membership of all six groups remained relatively stable over the period under consideration. In order to validate the groupings a generalised t-test was used. Results obtained confirmed that the identified groups were significantly different or separated from each other. The classifications obtained can therefore be said to be valid based upon available data.

The success of the application of the data mining approach to the analysis of the HFA database may be attributed to a number of factors as follows. Careful initial selection of and associated pre-processing ensured that that the target dataset was largely complete, containing only highly relevant data appropriate to the investigation. No non-variant or skewed fields were included. Similarly, no fields in the available data contained outlying data points.

3.2   The Babies at Risk of Intrapartum Asphyxia Database

The Babies at Risk of Intrapartum Asphyxia database was analysed in conjunction with staff at the Sheffield Children's Hospital, UK. This database contains data collected from a wider study on the relationship between intrapartum asphyxia and neonatal encephalopathy (NE). Neonatal encephalopathy is a condition characterised by impairment of consciousness, abnormalities of muscle tone and of feeding. The database contains detailed obstetric data, including cardiotocogram (CTG) traces taken during labour. Both the foetal heart rate (FHR) and the uterine contractions are represented on the trace produced. Also present on the database are pre-labour assessments of maternal and antenatal risk factors that might influence the outcome of the labour. Factors relating to the quality of intrapartum obstetric care are also recorded.

In order to construct the database, the paper CTG traces were manually analysed by dividing each trace into 30 minute epochs, and then examining each epoch for abnormal FHR patterns. A severity score was then applied to each abnormality detected. Each of the patients represented on the database is therefore associated with a number of epochs, the average being 14 (the minimum being one, and the maximum being 40, indicating periods of labour of 30 minutes and 20 hours respectively). Each epoch in turn is further described using a number of parameters presenting various aspects of the associated FHR. All activities relating to data capture, analysis, and initial database construction were carried out by medical staff involved in the wider study on the relationship between intrapartum asphyxia and neonatal encephalopathy.

Due to the purpose of the main study, much of the data represented on the database is encoded, rather than being specifically represented. For instance, the baseline FHR in beats per minute (bpm) recorded on the database varies from 100-109 at the lowest level, to >180 at its highest. The baseline FHR is recorded on a scale of -2 (representing 100-109 bpm) to +3 (representing >180 bpm). These figures represent whether or not the baseline FHR is slower or faster than would be expected. The bradycardia parameter is used to indicate a slow FHR (< 100 bpm). In the absence of bradycardia, this parameter is set to zero (normal). A period of greater than three minutes with recovery is represented by a value of +3, and a value of +4 if there is no recovery. This use of a zero value to indicate a normal reading is employed in a large proportion of the parameters of the database.

The SOM software employed to analyse the dataset expects the data therein to be presented on an interval or ordinal scale. That is, that the range of parameter values stand in some relationship to each other. The software also expects values that lie adjacent to each other within a parameter range to be similar to each other. However, some parameters on the database occupy a nominal scale where parameter values do not relate at all to each other. For instance, the uterine contractions parameter is represented as zero (normal), +3 (over-contracting), or +1 (the recording of the contraction on the trace is technically poor). This parameter was therefore considered to be inappropriate for use in its existing form, and removed from the target dataset.

Initial work was not without its difficulties due to the nature of the data involved. At one stage of processing, 52% of the available dataset presented parameters that were all set to zero (indicating a normal response), apart from the baseline FHR. This extremely high level of non-variant data resulted in no discernible patterns being present at the early stage of work.

After performing further selection and pre-processing activities (including the removal of the majority of non-variant data), some success was achieved. Two distinct groups were identified within the database, and their existence statistically validated using a two-sample t-test. Further work involved the training of a neural network employing the radial basis function (RBF) approach to recognise the two groups, and to differentiate between members of these groups. During this period, an overall probability of correct recognition of 85% was achieved, providing further evidence that the groups identified did exist within the database.

Further work resulted in a refinement of the original two groups being achieved. The resulting four groups were again found to be statistically different from each other, each exhibiting specific combinations of FHR patterns. The use of the RBF software again resulted in successful identification of the groups, with 100% of records within the first group, 97% of records within the second group, and 99% of records within the third and fourth groups being correctly identified.

However, although the identification of statistically valid groups may indicate that this data mining exercise was successful, it should be noted that the data used to obtain these groups represented only a proportion of that available. The high proportion of non-variant data present precluded much of the database from being used in the analysis process. Further limiting factors in this case included the use of a nominal scale to represent certain parameters. The fact that the data provided had already undergone pre-coding by a subject expert also placed clear restrictions on the ability to perform any subsequent meaningful data manipulation, as the original data values were in many instances unknown, and the subject expert who had performed the coding, unavailable.

3.3 Infertility Databases

Despite recent improvements in infertility diagnosis and the increase in sophistication and variety of treatment techniques, there still appears to be great difficulty in successfully predicting how a particular patient will respond to a specific treatment. Although many types of data can be collected which in theory are relevant to the likelihood of successful treatment, in reality the complexity of the interactions between these parameters appear to be beyond the current capabilities of conventional methods of analysis. The primary aim of this investigation was therefore to investigate the use of the data mining approach in assisting in predicting whether a specific patient would be successfully treated using a particular treatment pathway. Against this background, three databases holding data relating to three different aspects of infertility diagnosis and treatment were provided for analysis using the data mining approach.

The first of these databases contained details of patients who had undergone ovulation induction with gonadotrophins. This database was analysed in conjunction with staff at the Jessop Hospital, Sheffield, UK. Ovulation induction with gonadotrophins is one of the first treatment options available to infertility specialists, and is aimed at patients who are not ovulating normally. For each of the patients represented, the ovulation induction database holds a variety of information relating to both patient characteristics and treatment outcome, i.e. whether the patient became pregnant or not. The main objective of this study was to attempt to identify the combination of patient characteristics that appeared to indicate a successful (or otherwise) treatment outcome. Such information would be of benefit to both patient and clinician in providing an indication as to whether a particular treatment pathway is likely to be successful, prior to embarking upon that pathway.

A second database containing details of patients who had undergone stimulated cycles of In Vitro Fertilisation (IVF) treatment was analysed in conjunction with staff at St. Michael's Hospital, Bristol, UK. IVF involves fertilisation of the female eggs outside of the body, and subsequently transferring the resulting embryos to the female's womb. Each of the patients represented by the IVF database had had three fertilised eggs implanted (perceived as being the optimal number required to achieve one successful pregnancy whilst avoiding multiple pregnancies). For each patient represented on the database, there were therefore four possible outcomes (0-3 pregnancies). The main aim of this study was to identify the characteristics of patients who are most likely to achieve a single successful pregnancy, the clinicians wishing to avoid the potential for multiple (and hence potentially complicated) pregnancies.

A third database containing details of patients who had undergone natural cycle IVF treatment was also analysed in conjunction with staff at St. Michael's Hospital, Bristol. Data held for each patient includes the diagnostic category (endometriosis, tubal damage, or unexplained infertility). The aim of this study was slightly different from the previous two described in attempting to determine whether any specific combination of parameter values could be associated with the diagnostic category of the patient.

The data mining approach failed to provide the information that was specifically required in all three of the cases described. During the initial stages of investigation, all three datasets provided appeared to be highly suitable for analysis using the knowledge discovery approach. Despite the fact that some parameters represented data values using a nominal scale, the original databases exhibited little missing data, few irrelevant fields, no non-variant fields, few skewed fields, and few outlying data points. Any limited undesirable characteristics that were originally present were subsequently removed during the selection and pre-processing activities.

The main problem encountered during this investigation appears to be fundamental in that the patterns representing the information required appeared not to be present within the available datasets. It was therefore concluded that the data mining approach was unable to assist in the analysis of the data provided. This appeared to be primarily due to the fact that the range of factors that fully determine a couple's ability to conceive is not known. It is therefore reasonable to assume that in this case, the pattern (or a recognisable proportion of that pattern) formed by these factors was not present in the data provided.

4   CONCLUSIONS

This paper has provided an introduction to the concepts of data warehousing, data mining, and knowledge discovery. It should be evident from the studies described that the potential for the success of a knowledge discovery exercise is determined to a large extent prior to the actual data mining activity, i.e. during the activities performed leading up to the production of the cleaned data. Extreme care should therefore be taken during selection and pre-processing activities in order to ensure that the target dataset contains relevant and usable data. This point was evidenced by the analysis of the Babies at Risk of Intrapartum Asphyxia database, where coding activities performed as a result of a wider study precluded much of the data from analysis by data mining. Given that the likelihood of success of a data mining project is highly dependent upon the quality and format of the data made available, the amount of time and effort required to prepare suitable data will be a very useful investment, even if at times the required effort might appear excessive when measured against the time available for the project as a whole. This point was emphasised by the success of the analysis of the HFA database (the extracted dataset being largely complete and devoid of undesirable data characteristics), and the subsequent successful analysis of the UK Health Service Indicators database described by Lake (1997), the target dataset again being carefully constructed, and exhibiting a lack of undesirable data characteristics.

It is also apparent from the studies described (and in particular, the analysis of the infertility databases), that if the data provided does not contain useful information within the context of the focus of the investigation, then data mining cannot generate such information any more than traditional analysis techniques can. However, it may well be the case that the data mining approach allows this conclusion to be reached more quickly than might ordinarily be the case.

Finally, it should be stated once more that this paper advocates the use of data mining as an approach that can be used to expedite the initial stages of information analysis in order that the results obtained may be more thoroughly investigated. It should be used in conjunction with traditional approaches, and not be viewed as a direct replacement.

References

Adriaans, P. & Zantinge, D. (1996) *Data Mining*. Harlow: Addison-Wesley. .
Berry, M.J.A. & Linoff, G. (1997) *Data Mining Techniques*. New York: Wiley.
Dayhoff, J.E. (1990). *Neural Networks Architecture: An Introduction*. New York: Van Nostrand Reinhol.

Fayyad, U., Piatetsky-Shapiro, G. & Smyth, P. (1996) "The KDD Process for Extracting Useful Knowledge from Volumes of Data" *CACM*, 39(11), 27-34.

Fayyad, U. & Uthurasamy, R. (1996) "Data Mining and Knowledge Discovery in Databases" *CACM*, 39(11), 24-26.

Gardner, S.R. (1998) "Building the Data Warehouse" *CACM*, 41(9), 52-60.

Hedberg, S.R. (1995) "The Data Gold Rush" *Byte*, 20(10), 83-88.

Inmon, W. (1992) *Building the Data Warehouse*. New York: Wiley.

Lake, S. *"Artificial Neural Network Classification of UK Hospitals Using Selected Health Service Indicators"*, Thesis, University of Sheffield, Sheffield, UK, 1997.

Limb, P.R., & Meggs, G.J. (1995) "Data Mining -Tools and Techniques" *British Telecom Technology Journal*, 12(4), 32-41.

Lloyd-Williams, M. (1998) "Case Studies in the Data Mining Approach to Health Information Analysis", *IEE/BCS Colloquium on Knowledge Discovery and Data Mining*. IEE, London, *IEE Digest 98/434.*

Lloyd-Williams, M., Jenkins, J., Howden-Leach, H., Mathur, M., Morris, C & Cooke, I. (1995) "Knowledge Discovery in an Infertility Database Using Artificial Neural Networks", *IEE Colloquium on Knowledge Discovery in Databases*. IEE, London, IEE Digest 95/021(B).

Lloyd-Williams, M. & Williams, S. (1996) "A Neural Network Approach to Analysing Healthcare Information", *Topics in Health Information Management*, 17(2), 26-33.

Lloyd-Williams, M., Williams, S, Bath, P. & Morris, C. (1996) "Knowledge Discovery in the WHO *Health for All* Database", In: Richards, B. & de Glanville, H. (eds) *Current Perspectives in Healthcare Computing. Proceedings of HC96*, pp. 551-556. Weybridge: BJHC.

Murtagh, F. & Hernández-Pajares, M. (1995) "The Kohonen Self-Organizing Map Method: An Assessment" *Journal of Classification* 12, 165-190.

Scarfe, R. & Shortland, R.J. (1995) "Data Mining Applications in BT" *IEE Colloquium on Knowledge Discovery in Databases*. IEE Digest 1995/021(B).

Sen, A. & Jacob, V.S. (1998) "Industrial Strength Data Warehousing" *CACM*, 41(9), 29-31.

Sigal, M. (1998) "A Common Sense Development Strategy" *CACM*, 41(9), 42-43.

Sprague, R. & Watson, H. (1996) *Decision Support for Management*. Upper Saddle River: Prentice Hall.

Watson, H.J. & Haley, B.J. (1998) "Managerial Considerations" *CACM*, 41(9), 32-37.

Watterson, K. (1995) "A Data Miner's Tools" *Byte* 20(10), 91-96. 4.

Williams, T.S. (1995) "*Knowledge Discovery in the WHO Health for All Database: Developing A Taxonomy of Mortality Patterns for European Countries*" MSc Thesis, University of Sheffield, Sheffield, England.

CHAPTER 64

CHALLENGES FOR USING MULTIPLE AGENT INFORMATION SYSTEMS ON THE WWW

M Devlin, TM Scott and MD Mulvenna
University of Ulster

Abstract

Due to the increase in WWW (World Wide Web) documents and services, the user community is becoming increasingly frustrated at poor response times, ambiguous search methods and the sheer density of information that complicates their information retrieval goals. Software agent technology is emerging as a solution to these problems. Agents can communicate information across multiple platforms enabling users to delegate tasks such as information retrieval without supervision. Primarily for agents to have effective utility in the WWW environment they must be able to communicate with other agents of different origin making the web a multi-agent information system. This paper introduces the concepts of multi-agent information systems and agent communication. It defines some of the fundamental problems that the WWW presents for agents and outlines the areas that pose a challenge to those who wish to deploy them. Barriers to communication are identified including variations in characteristics, language and ontology. The paper then discusses the broader aspects of agent communication difficulties that are posed by web architecture, goal specification problems and the nature of web pages themselves. Finally, recommendations are made including a proposed formalisation of agent theory to lessen user workloads.

1   INTRODUCTION

As the number of WWW documents and services increase in volume, users are faced with unsatisfactory response times, incomplete information (e.g., broken or erroneous links) and ambiguous search and retrieval methods. Consequently, users are often resigned to a tedious manual search through pages of short, ambiguous descriptions of page content in order to find what they want. The resulting user community often abandons their planned search goals and is becoming increasingly frustrated with the lack of perspicacity of a supposedly transparent information provision and exchange service.

Software agent technology is emerging as a solution to these problems. Through the use of this technology, it should be possible to make the Web virtually transparent to users (Etzioni et al 1995) and service providers. This will enable users to delegate tasks such as information retrieval and extraction, without supervision, to a group of appropriately 'skilled' agents. Ideally, agents should have the potential to traverse the web, using initiative to negotiate and communicate with peer agents, irrespective of language, platform, ontology, goal and task differences in order to fulfil user information objectives.

Primarily, for agents to have effective utility in the web environment, they must be able to communicate with other agents that are of different origin, making the web a multi-agent environment. However, there are several hurdles that must be overcome. This paper introduces the concepts of multi-agent information systems and agent communication. It defines some of the fundamental communication problems faced by agents on the WWW and the challenges that are still to be met by those who wish to deploy them in this environment. This paper explores research issues in agent technology that are being investigated in order to establish inter-agent communication and identify standards and protocols for the facilitation of optimum information gathering to lessen user workloads.

1.1 Software Agent Systems

As the term 'agent' has been applied in general terms and the exact nature of what constitutes agency has not been clearly defined, there are differing views as to the properties and capabilities agents possess, e.g., "An *Intelligent* agent is anything that can be viewed as perceiving its environment through sensors and acting upon that environment through effectors" (Russell & Norvig 1995) This definition embodies the agent with intelligent capability via the fact that it can sense its environment, however it could be argued that the tasks that it performs are merely those of any computer program. A simple task like creating a file, if one does not already exist, could be performed by any program and deemed as a sensing task and therefore not necessarily intelligent. Some definitions concentrate on a different property of agency, e.g., "*Autonomous* agents are computational systems that inhabit some complex environment, sense and act autonomously in this environment and by doing so realise a set of goals or tasks for which they are designed" (Maes 1995).

An autonomous agent must be able to make decisions and use its own initiative, but surely this is also a quality of intelligence? An agent that requires no intervention from a user could be deemed both intelligent and autonomous. Some definitions embody an agent with more human-like abilities e.g., "A *learning* agent uses machine learning techniques to 'learn' as they react and/or interact with external environments and users. It tries to improve its performance and learn it user's preferences and interests better to assist them." (Murugesan, 1998) It could learn:

- by observing and imitating the user,
- from (corrective) feedback from the user,
- by following explicit instructions from the user; and/or
- by asking other agents for advice" (Murugesan 1998)

As agent technology is in its infancy, not all agents possess the abilities listed above.

1.2   Agent Characteristics

As definitions of agency are diverse, it is useful to identify the nature of agents in terms of their *desirable* characteristics. These include *inter alia*:

Autonomy. An agent should be able to take the initiative and have a large degree of control over its own actions in the environment.

Goal-oriented behaviour. An agent should accept high-level requests that indicate what a human wants and is responsible for deciding how and where to satisfy requests.

Collaborative ability. An agent should not blindly obey commands but should have the ability to modify requests, ask clarification questions, or even refuse to satisfy certain requests.

Flexibility. An agent's actions are not scripted; it is able to dynamically choose which actions to invoke and in what sequence in response to the state of its external environment.

Self-starting ability. Unlike standard programs that are directly invoked by the user, an agent can sense changes to its environment and decide when to act.

Temporal continuity. An agent is a continuously running process, not a 'one-shot' computation that maps a single output and then terminated.

Character. The agent is able to engage in complex communication with other agents, including people, in order to obtain information or enlist their help in accomplishing its goals.

Adaptability. The agent automatically customises itself to the preference of its user based on previous experience. The agent also automatically adapts to changes in its environment (Etzioni et al, 1995).

In general, software agents interact with the user, system resources and other agents in order to achieve information goals. They encapsulate data along with processes or methods that act on that data. They communicate via messages much like client/server technology but go one step further in that they have beliefs, commitments and goals i.e. they apply reasoning capabilities to the data in order to achieve the goals they have been set by the user. Agents may be simple or complex and either work alone or in conjunction with other agents. A typical task that an agent may perform is to search a database that has been classifed in particular areas specified by the user. When the agent finds a match, an email is sent to the user giving the relevant information. One such agent is AdHound that searches a database of classified advertisements and emails the relevant adverts to the user when it finds a match (Murugesan, 1998).

1.3   Multi-Agent Systems

Multi-agent systems is the term given to agent systems that make use of, or consist of, several individual agents working in unison in order to achieve goals. This can refer either to a 'community' of agents who share the same domain and have no contact with agents outside that domain or to an environment such as the WWW in which multiple agents are deployed, each with differing goals and of different origin, with the ability to communicate with other agent entities in order to achieve their separate goals (e.g., retrieve information, purchase products, contract an information service etc.). Both types of Multi-agent systems can have agents with the ability to solve problems, collaborate and negotiate with other agents.

1.4   Agent Communication

In order for agents to have effective utility in an environment such as the WWW, they have to be able to communicate with other agents that are of similar or different origin from them. Ideally, a user should be able to send an agent out onto the WWW to look for information. This agent should be able to roam over the web communicating with other agents in order to locate that information and to obtain it on the user's behalf.

There are several different forms of communication that an agent ca undertake. They can communicate knowledge about themselves and the environment in which they reside, to other agents, pose and answer queries about their state and the environment in which they reside, request and command other agents to do something on their behalf, advertise and enter into contracts and acknowledge communications from other agents (Etzioni et al 1995).

The *communication language* of an agent can vary (LISP, Java etc.) and an *ontology* is the term given to the structures that describe how concepts are defined and associated internally by an agent and within that agent's domain. It provides a logical basis for an agent to interpret the concepts and structures it encounters within its domain and it determines how it views the world outside that domain.

Each of the communicating tasks (request, command, acknowledge etc.) has problems associated with it but even the simplest of these, that of posing and replying to queries, can be difficult if agents do not communicate in the same language, or if they use different terms to describe their knowledge of the world.

1.5   A Partial Solution to Differing World Views

Many agents at present use Agent Communication Language (ACL) to communicate. ACL has been described as the product of an agent-based software engineering mandate designed to attack the problems of incompatibilities between agent descriptions, resulting in "a universal communication language, one in which inconsistencies and arbitrary notational variations are eliminated" (Genesereth et al 1996). It has three main components, its vocabulary, an 'inner' language called KIF (Knowledge Interchange Format) and an 'outer' language called KQML (Knowledge Query & Manipulation

Language). ACL allows the designers of agents to 'encapsulate' the language the agent is written in inside ACL. This then helps other agents that use ACL to then interpret another agent's messages via the common language.

If agent designers standardise the adoption of ACL, it may help to solve some of the problem of differences in term usage. If a community of agents uses the same language to communicate and has the same ontology then there should be little difficulty in their effectively solving problems and achieving their goals within their domain. Outside such a community however there remains the problem of agents that do not use ACL.

1.6   Dealing with Ontological Variations

Agents that do not use a common language such as ACL will not be able to communicate outside their own domain. The attraction of the WWW as a multi-agent environment stems from the idea of multiple agents communicating and collaborating in order to retrieve information and services not available to them within their domains. Therefore the adoption of differing languages restricts the potential of multi-agent communication on the WWW. If agents do use a common language, there is still no guarantee that they will be able to understand each other. They may not have the same internal representation of knowledge i.e. ontology. On the WWW it is conceivable that agents can have many different ontologies and not all ontological descriptions may be available in the ACL dictionary. Differences in ontological descriptions between agents of alternative origin impose two problems for agent designers:

- How does an agent know how another agent's concepts are used and how they are connected to each other?
- How does an agent find relationships between their respective concept structures in order to make interpretation possible?

In order to communicate effectively an agent's ontology must not only be explicitly defined, but also to an agreed standard that enables open communication with agents that originate from sources outside their domain. Declarations must be sufficient to enable agents that encounter it to determine its origin, how it communicates and perhaps to provide an outline of its primary domain concerns upon initial contact. According to Petrie, (Petrie 1996) "The use of a publicly explicit ontology that allows term usage to be reasoned about for collaboration makes for stronger agenthood." If there is no facility for interpretation of ontology, then communication is at best difficult, at worst, impossible. As yet, there is no universally accepted ontology or an agent that can interpret all known ontologies.

1.7   Agent Modelling

According to criticisms of the Foundation for Intelligent Physical Agents (FIPA) proposal (FIPA, 1998), "It is not feasible to expect that all agents that might use a universal ACL will comply with a single agent model and there is not yet a consensus on a common model for a rational agent and it may take some time, experimentation and experience for one to emerge..." (Mayfield et al 1997). As this is the case, using the common language (ACL) in an object-oriented fashion to encapsulate the language that the agent is written may prove deficient for deciphering messages or interpretation.

All agents will have to have their ontology available publicly and they will have to retrieve ontological descriptions that match their own concepts. Not withstanding this, they may still have incompatibilities as regards relationships etc. within their own domain and that of another agent because they will not all have a standard model, an agreed basic set of properties that are common to all. They may therefore never be able to communicate fully.

2   TOWARDS AN ONTOLOGY MODEL

The specification for an Ontology service in FIPA 98 is based upon an agent community with agents that share the same ontologies. An ontology agent operates the ontology service. The ontology agent's role in the community is to provide services such as the discovery of public ontologies, to translate expressions between different ontologies and/or different content languages and to facilitate the identification of a shared ontology for communication between two agents (FIPA 1998). Each agent can request the services of the ontology agent by using a communicative interface to help them modify, translate and download ontologies that are from outside their own community or to redefine their own ontologies. This standard does seem to provide some answer to the ontology problem, however it still does not provide a solution to the problem of agreement on a basic agent model or even an ontology model and an ontology agent may further complicate the communication scenario, searching for concepts while an agent waits in the information space for a reply.

2.1   Structural Complexity
It would take an agent of great sophistication in terms of processing ability to interpret all ontologies and languages and to be able to translate them into an understandable form for themselves and other agents no matter what their learning capability and knowledge of the world. Ontological differences and agreement over what constitutes a 'suitable' ontology will be difficult to regulate if there are no formal standards or a protocol for creating agent ontologies, or if there is not an agreement as to type or models of agents that are acceptable.

The very nature and power of agents is undermined by having to consult an ontology repository or an ontology agent. Intelligence, learning capability and indeed autonomy within a mobile agent should be possible without this restriction which will take up valuable time and resources. This would lead to rather cumbersome agents. What really should be defined is a generic model for an agent that uses a common language and conforms to certain criteria and properties that are common to all agents. Agent system structures need to be simplified and formalised so agents can be autonomous, robust and efficient entities that use minimal resources and do not rely on other agents merely to function.

2.2   Goal Specification

In an environment that is static it is possible for an agent to build a correct model of the current state of its external world and when given a goal, it can call a suitable planning algorithm to create a plan of action in order to achieve that goal. However in an environment such as the WWW that is dynamic and heterogeneous and therefore difficult to measure, goal specification is a complex task for agent designers. The nature of such an environment means that agents have to be able to deal with uncertainty because they encounter incomplete and incorrect information:

- *Incompleteness.* This arises because the world is inaccessible. The agent may not be able to find something unless it asks.
- *Incorrectness.* This arises because the world does not necessarily match the agent's model of it (Russell & Norvig 1995).

In view of these anomalies in information, the goals that agents must be set can only be specified partially. Ideally an agent should be able to recognise a problem by reasoning about its surroundings and adapting its plans accordingly. In order to specify partial goals and change plans an agent must initially have a target, a main task that needs to be accomplished.

2.3   Defining the Main Objective

It makes sense that the primary tasks of individual agents have to be defined before they are sent into the information space. Yet, even if agents have the ability to learn about their environment, they may have several goals and ultimately one has to take precedence over the others. Defining the main objectives of an agent in the World Wide Web environment is complex because the environment is not static. It is difficult to define any objective that will not change over time. An agent must be able to adapt its plans in pursuit of its main objective or recognise that its main objective is unachievable. The ability to recognise when a task is unachievable can be simplified as a search. The agent searches for a target piece of information, finds it is not there and reverts to another action specified by the user. It is however more optimal for an agent to be able to recognise the best solution to a problem and in order to accomplish this the agent must have an awareness of all possible outcomes. The WWW is not easy to measure and therefore all possible outcomes are hard to predict.

2.3.1   Limiting Awareness

Agent designers need to determine how it can be assured that an agent has a true 'understanding' of its main objective. Simple agents will perhaps have only one goal and if they cannot achieve it, they terminate, but even this raises the question of how long an agent must wait before it 'realises' that its goal is infeasible. More complex and indeed more intelligent agents should be able to partially fulfil their goals by adapting their plans in cases where their main objective is unattainable. Instilling enough intelligence in an agent to enable it to make such decisions on behalf of the user is complex. An agent should be aware of its environment in order to make such decisions but the WWW is so vast that narrowing the agent's awareness to what is relevant to its particular goals is a task that requires focus.

2.3.2   Rules of Engagement

As agents have different goals, the question of equity needs to be resolved. We can auction information and bid for contracts etc. but if something goes wrong we need to determine which agents are most valuable and whose goals take priority. Transactions need to be regulated and monitored if equitable conduct is to be assured on the WWW. In defining a set of 'rules for engagement' we need to be able to prevent incomplete transactions, reneging and the likelihood of factions or monopolies. Agents must be traceable. An effective form of communication and collaboration must be supported by a set of rules (protocol) that ensures trust. These rules should be of sufficient weight so that assurances can be made that no one benefits form someone else's loss outside the bounds of normal business competition. Co-operation needs to be based upon a set of priorities that determine how long agents can engage, where they can go and who they can talk to. Effective communication relies upon a strict description of priority and a restrictive set of behaviours that limit agent interaction, perhaps selfishly to gaining their main objective. Herein lies a challenge. If agents encounter each other by chance they are likely to have very different goals. Communication needs to take place in a reciprocal fashion that accomplishes 'both' of the agents' goals. If both sets of goals are not accomplished or communication is not mutually beneficial, agents revert to being scavenger-like programs. There needs to be international agreement as to the legality of agent transactions on the Web.

2.3.3   Web Architecture

The nature of the Web (WWW) itself is not fully conducive to multi-agent systems at present. Existing protocols, languages and information structures require adaptation for the effective deployment of multi-agent technology.

2.3.4   Client Server Architecture

Petrie argues that the very qualification for 'agenthood' is that "An agent is an agent to the degree that it collaborates with other agents using volunteered messages" (Petrie 1996)

The nature of client/server protocols (such as HTTP) does not permit the initiation of messages. The client/server relationship only admits one reply to one request, which is the simplest relationship between two agents. This goes against Petrie's requirement of agenthood, that agents should volunteer information and initiate messages. In order to communicate, collaborate and solve problems, agents require a shared message protocol. Agents should be able to reason about the changing states in their environment and exchange multiple messages. This requires peer-to-peer communication between the agents and browser clients and at present this does not exist fully.

2.3.5   The Semi-Structured Nature of the Web

There is a recognised need to improve the readability of web pages. Web information is not currently present in the correct and unambiguous context that would complement the powerful searching capabilities that multi-agent systems can provide. This is because HTML, currently the pre-dominant mark-up language for the WWW, contains minimal constructs to describe content. There is no foolproof method of effectively determining their content apart from viewing each page individually. It is necessary to overcome the limitations of HTML structures that are used to describe WWW data if agents are to gather information that is pertinent to the user. At present natural language processing technology makes use of robots that use a variety of methods to gather limited semantic information about pages but these approaches lack a consistent structure. Even limiting a web agent's understanding to one topic like Computer Science web pages still proves surprisingly difficult to implement (Spector et al 1997). In order to perform problem solving of a sufficient standard, agent software needs to provide a structured communication mechanism that allows a co-ordination of activities and a thorough analysis of findings in order to produce the optimum solution to a user's request for information (Werkman 1995). Multi-agent systems need to be able to effectively filter unclassified information contained on the Web. Adoption of structures such as the World Wide Web Consortium's XML (eXtensible Markup Language) would help to make web pages more conducive to agent search and interpretation.

2.3.6   Security

According to Oren Etzioni, in order to create a Web that operates via multiple agents "It is likely that all effective communication and collaboration will rely on shared encodings of large amounts of common sense information about computers, networks, useful services and human activities. But the communication algorithms should allow one agent to convey new vocabulary (or the capabilities of a third agent) to another" (Etzioni et al 1995).

Variations in goals and business competition may limit the amount or type of information an agent may wish to reveal about itself to other agents and users may not want their details revealed to agents that search for information on their behaviour. Several polls indicate privacy is the number one concern that people have with the WWW today (Lawton 1998) When information extraction capabilities vary between agents that are allowed to roam freely in the common space, there is always potential for information abuse. Creators of multi-agent systems wishing to effect collaboration must ensure that it is not at the expense of the user. There is therefore a need to determine a standard for agent communication and collaboration that ensures the rights of users are protected and that information obtained is not misused.

3   RECOMMENDATIONS AND FURTHER WORK

Agents have the potential to lighten the workload of users and prove invaluable in managing information tasks. For the WWW to become a multi-agent system or an entity that makes use of multi-agent technology, current agent and WWW structures need to change. Recommendations include:

- The formalisation of agents or the concepts of agency so as to minimise structural diversity and complexity of agent entities.
- The adoption of new technologies and standards such as XML to make the web more conducive to agent interpretation.
- The standardisation of an agent language such as ACL.
- The development of protocols that facilitate peer to peer communication on a wide scale.
- An international agreement on behaviour on the WWW that ensures transaction integrity and security.

Future research will investigate the practicalities of multi-agent systems for information retrieval and communication in the WWW environment. This will include the development of agent software that mines the WWW to find, assess and re-present information.

4   CONCLUSION

Agent technology has the potential to eliminate many information retrieval problems that users are facing due to the increased popularity of the WWW. This paper has highlighted some of the main research challenges associated with deploying multiple agents that need to be resolved before this can happen. It has shown that communication between agents is restricted by the fact that 'agency' is not a definitive term and that languages such as ACL constructed to deal with the differences between agents are only a partial solution, as such languages are not adopted as standard. The semi-structured nature of the WWW and the fact that it continues to grow makes it imperative that new technologies are found to decrease user workloads. Deploying agents on the WWW raises many wider issues such as transaction security and equitable behaviour that need to be addressed by all users and service providers. It is perhaps too idealistic to expect agents to solve all information retrieval problems as agent technology is in its infancy. However, this is exactly the time that teething troubles should be identified so that the technology can move on without having to retrace its steps. WWW development and agent technologies go hand in hand and neither can function optimally in the future unless standards and formal models are created, implemented and enforced.

References

Abolfazi, Ali. Intelligent Software Agents as Tools for Managing Ethical Issues. IEMC96 in *Managing Virtual Organisations* (pp1-5) 1996.

Etzioni, Oren, Weld, Daniel, S. Intelligent Agents on the Internet: Fact, Fiction and Forecast. *IEEE Expert* Vol. 10, No.4, pp44-49, August 1995.

FIPA 98 Specification (part 12) Ontology Service ISO Template Version 3.0 1997-02-07 (to be published Oct. 1998).

Franklin, Stan & Graesser, Art. Is it an Agent, or just a Program? A Taxonomy for Autonomous Agents in *Proceedings of the Third International Workshop on Agent Theories, Architectures and Languages. Intelligent Agents III* pp21-35, *Springer-Verlag 1997*

Genesereth, Michael R & Ketchpel, Steven P. Software Agents in *Communications of the ACM*, pp48-53, July 1994

Lawton, G. The Internet's Challenge to Privacy, *Computer Magazine*. June 1998

Maes Pattie. Artificial Life Meets Entertainment Lifelike Autonomous Agents in *Communications of the ACM* Vol.38, No.11, pp108-114. 1995

Mayfield, James, Labrou, Yannis & Finin Tim. Comments on the Specification for FIPA'97 Agent Communication Language. *UMBC AgentWeb. 1997*

Mayfield, James, Labrou, Yannis & Finin Tim. Desiderata for Agent Communication Languages in *Spring Symposium on Information Gathering from Heterogeneous Distributed Environments*. AAAI 95

Murugesan San. Intelligent Agents on the Internet and Web, Potentials, Progress and Prospects. ICMAS '98 tutorial

Petrie, Charles J. Agent Based Engineering in *IEEE Expert,* Vol.11, No.6, Dec. 1996

Russell S & Norvig P. Artificial Intelligence: A Modern Approach, Prentice Hall 1995

Shoham Yoav. Agent Oriented Programming in *Artificial Intelligence* Vol.60 (1993) pp51-92

Spector, Luke, Rager, D, Hendler, J. Ontology-based Web Agents. *Proceedings of the First International Conference on Autonomous Agents.* 1997

Werkman, K.J., Negotiation Amongst Intelligent Agents During Information Retrieval From The Web@ http://www.cs.umbc.edu/~cikm/iia/submitted/viewing/werkman. html. CIKM95 Workshop on Intelligent Agents.

CHAPTER 65

USE OF XML IN A DISTRIBUTED REGIONAL INFORMATION SERVICE

Robert J Gautier and Tomos Llewelyn
University of Wales

Abstract

The Llwybr Project aims to prepare the people and businesses of Wales to take advantage of the Information Society. It has identified the need for a number of web-based Regional Information Services. We have built a prototype distributed Regional A to Z system, with very loose coupling between storage of data and its presentation to users. XML is used to represent data as part of an internal client-server protocol. The motivation for this architecture arises from the following requirements: to allow complete freedom for information providers to define and manage their own data, to permit service providers to define the way in which information is presented, and to enable a collection of such services to be integrated into a consistent whole.

1 INTRODUCTION

The main objective of the Llwybr-Pathway project is to prepare the people and businesses of Rural Wales to take advantage of the Information Society. Six separate areas of work (strands) have been identified in achieving this objective, one of which is aimed at providing Information Services for the region.

The authors work for the Llwybr Technical Support Centre, which is operated by the Computer Science Department at the University of Wales, Aberystwyth, and exists to provide advice, additional technical resources and technical "inspiration" to the rest of the project. The work described here arises from a request that we develop a proposed strategy for the provision of a Regional A-Z of Services.

Such a system would allow data from throughout the region covered by the project to be accessed by anyone, regardless of their location, in a consistent manner. In other words, a user need only be familiar with their local A-Z system but be able to access data from anywhere in the region.

During discussions it emerged that the individual partners in the project had differing requirements, and also wished to protect their own corporate image. A flexible solution was needed which would accommodate each partner's needs.

2   THE REGIONAL A-Z OF SERVICES

An A-Z of services has been identified by local authorities as one of the key information systems that they want to provide. Since people regularly travel across county borders, it is also a key requirement that users are able to access data from the entire region.

Flexibility is an important requirement because of the differing requirements that the partners have, and their existing investment in IT systems. The system must as platform independent as possible. Presentation of the data to the user must be controllable by each individual partner in order to conform to their bilingual policy (English and Welsh), and to promote their individual corporate identity. Some partners also use touch-screen kiosks which require a customised presentation of web pages.

A large monolithic central server was rejected in favour a distributed system where each partner would retain control of their own data, while sharing it with all other partners. This also makes the system more extensible, since new partners can simply implement their own compliant system.

3   SOLUTION STRATEGY/ARCHITECTURE

Our chosen solution introduces an extra level into the usual 3-tier approach (Orfali 1997, p47) to providing web content dynamically from a database. The purpose of this extra level is to separate the presentation (layout etc.) issues from the act of obtaining data from a database. By providing a standard interface through which web servers talk to back-end database servers, a distributed system can be created in which all participants can access all databases in the same way.

3.1   The System Interfaces
- **User Client.** This is simply a web browser, although it may in some cases be customised for a particular machine type (e.g. a touch-screen kiosk). In general, the lowest common denominator principle will be used when deciding which features of HTML may be used, but this will be a policy decision for the maintainers of presentation servers.
- **Presentation Server.** As its name suggests, the presentation server is responsible for formatting data before it is presented to the user. It also acts as an intermediary for queries made by the user. Although this tier is clearly identified in our architecture, and exists as a separate layer in our current implementation, we expect that its role will eventually be performed by a component closer to the user client than to the web server (i.e. a style sheet mechanism such as XSL).

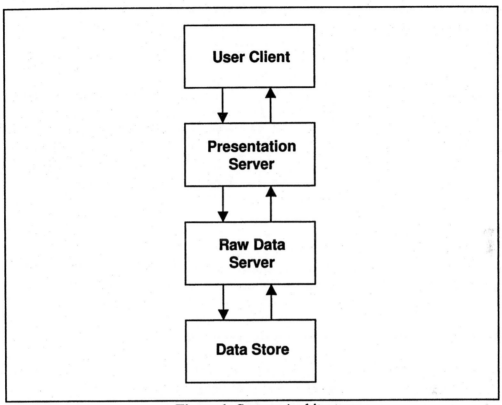

Figure 1: System Architecture

- **Raw Data Server.** The aim of this component is to provide a standard interface to the backend database, and its interface will be accessible via the Internet.
- **Data Store.** This is the backend database. The aim of the architecture is that any backend "database" may be used, from a simple flat text file to a large commercial database server. Within this architecture, the only client of the data store is the raw data server, and it has read-only access; updating and maintaining this store is (currently) beyond the scope of our architecture.

3.2 The System Interfaces

- **Data Store to Raw Data Layer.** This interface will be entirely implementation dependent since the architecture does not place any requirement on the technology used in the data store. In practice, it is likely that an SQL server of some kind will be used since these come in a variety of shapes and sizes, and one can usually be found to suit any occasion.
- **Raw Data Server to Presentation Server.** It is this level that permits regional integration. The interface presented by Raw Data Servers needs to be sufficiently consistent if interoperation is to be achieved. HTTP was chosen as the

communications protocol for this interface, firstly because this means that the server can be run as part of a web server, and also because we want to make it easy eventually to subsume the presentation server role into the user client. Requests take the form of HTTP POST or GET transactions, in which TQL queries are sent in URL-encoded form, and XML documents are returned.

- **Presentation Server to User Client.** The technology used to create HTML from the XML documents returned from the Raw Data server is an implementation choice. All that is required beyond a run of the mill web server is some means of including active content. Possibilities include Active Server Pages from Microsoft, PHP (a free server side scripting language), SSI (server side includes) or CGI. Naturally, any Presentation server will have to include some kind of XML parser, and must be able to POST queries to raw data servers.

3.3   Why XML and HTTP?

In introducing an extra layer into the system, we gave ourselves the job of defining a new interface, and one which was of critical importance to the long term success of the project. We felt that the world neither needed, nor would want, a completely new protocol and data representation, and in any case, a small evolutionary step would be more acceptable than a relatively large one. For this last reason, some potentially attractive alternatives were rejected *for the presentation-raw data interface;* these include Z39.50 and LDAP. The protocol everyone was familiar with (and which their firewalls were configured for) was HTTP. We were left with the need for a data representation which would be portable and easily processed. XML seemed an obvious choice.

A further attraction of XML was that we can expect browser support for it to grow, suggesting that we might eventually be able to perform all formatting in the browser. A secondary motivation was to encourage the Llwybr project to take note of XML: with tools such as Microsoft's IE, and Netscape Communicator planning to support XML, it may soon begin to be used on the World Wide Web, and may even prove to be the successor to HTML. XML is designed to be easy to parse, and for our application, because all the output from the Raw Data server is machine generated, to conform to a single DTD, a relatively simple parser would suffice.

3.4   The RESULTSET Document Type

The DTD we use is very simple —perhaps too simple. The principle document type used is called a *resultset* which borrows from database terminology. Query results are normally returned as tables, so resultsets contain one or more rows, which in turn contain one or more columns. A resultset element takes as attributes the standard fieldnames of the columns which are contained within the document, and a (TQL) operator. The columns in each row are assumed to be in the order given by the resultset attributes

This encoding is quite compact, because it encodes the names of the data items only once. However, this means that the meaning of sub-elements is context dependent; the item value in a particular <col> element depends on the position of that <col> element within a <row>, and the necessary information is encoded in the value of an attribute of the enclosing <resultset> element.

We could have used a different element type for each item type, e.g.

```
<resultset>
<row><name>Bob Gautier</name><email>rjg@aber.ac.uk</email></row>
</resultset>
```

But then the addition of new item types would have changed the DTD for the resultset. On the other hand, the introduction of structure into item values themselves would have been straightforward. Given that one has to modify the DTD to permit the use of an <email> element, one could easily permit (indeed, require) the following:

```
<email><user>rjg</user><domain>aber.ac.uk</domain></email>
```

We could also have put the item name into the <col> elements:

```
<row><col item="svc.title">Refuse Collection</col></row>
```

This was considered too verbose.

Compared to our chosen representation, either of the above alternatives are more amenable to processing with things like XSL. But it's not too hard to write processors for it in Java, or in any other language that has an XML parser (e.g. PHP, Tcl, Perl, C). Using such a language, implementing a transformation from our <resultset> structure to one of the above alternatives would be quite straightforward.

3.5   TQL

When making queries, it was found that SQL did not allow the kinds of queries frequently encountered by the system to be expressed succinctly. One such query type we have called the *partition query*. This is basically the request "give me all the *n*-character left sub-strings from field *x*", which is very useful when producing alphabetical indexes. The SQL for performing this kind of query looks something like:

```
SELECT DISTINCT
(SELECT LEFT(Service 1) FROM AtoZ
ORDER BY Service);
```

The equivalent TQL for this is:

```
partition svc.title 1
```

This effectively says "partition the Service Title field on the first character" or in plain English "give me the unique first letters of all the service titles". This is obviously rather more compact than the SQL above: less obviously, it has substituted a *logical* field name (svc.title) for a database field name (Service), and more importantly, it has isolated the client from syntactic details of the *particular* SQL dialect used by the underlying database. The logical schema used by TQL forms a part of the standard interface between presentation servers and raw data servers.

The syntax of TQL is much simpler than that of SQL, for a number of reasons. These include the fact that we wanted to be able to type TQL easily, and to keep the implementation of the parser as simple as possible so as not to place a burden on implementers of simple backend servers.

A TQL query is a sequence of lines, terminated by a line containing just a dot ".". Within a query, TQL statements are of the form

```
keyword parameters
```

This was chosen to be similar to the syntax of commands in Tcl, which in turn was inspired by Unix shells. As well as making TQL easy to type, it meant that we could implement (or at least prototype) TQL in Tcl, and could write TQL *clients* in Tcl too.

3.5.1   Partition:

The primary use of this keyword is to ask for an alphabetical list of first letters from the Service Title field. But it can be used on any field, and return any number of first characters from that field. It also returns the number of occurrences of each instance it finds in the count attribute of a row. e.g.

```
partition cont.name 3
```

would return the first 3 letters of all the Contact Names.

3.5.2   Select:

This is the equivalent of a WHERE clause in SQL. i.e. it allows you to specify which rows to select from the database.The form of the statement is "select <fieldName> <operator> '<value>'". Where <fieldName> is one of the standard field names, <operator> is either 'begins' or '=' and '<value>' is a value enclosed in single quotes. e.g.

```
select svc.title begins 'A'
```

Would select all the Service Titles beginning with A. A query can have multiple selects which will be concatenated with an AND. e.g.

```
select svc.title begins 'A'
select svc.dept = 'Environmental Services'
```

would return records where the Service Title begins with A and the Service Department is Environmental Services. The list of operators may be extended in future versions to cope with other types of query.

3.5.3   Require:

This is the equivalent of a SELECT clause in SQL. It allows you to specify which fields you want included in the result set. A query can have any number of require lines, each of which can list any number of fields, although the fields will be returned in the result set in the order which they are asked for. e.g.

```
require svc.title svc.desc
```

For debugging and testing, one can interact with a TQL server simply by connecting to it with telnet:

```
chwith:~rjg$ telnet localhost 4675
Trying 127.0.0.1...
Connected to localhost.
Escape character is '^]'
```

```
partition svc.title 1
.
<resultset>
<row><col> ... </col></row>
</resultset>
Connection closed by foreign host.
chwith:~rjg$
```

This is an example of the kind of XML which would be returned by a query:
```
<resultset cols="svc.title" op="begins">
<row count="48"> <col>A</col> </row>
<row count="26"> <col>B</col> </row>
<row count="99"> <col>C</col> </row>
.
.
.
<row count="37"> <col>W</col> </row>
<row count="12"> <col>Y</col> </row>
</resultset>
```

The `cols` attribute of the `resultset` element lists the (logical) field names of the elements of subsequent rows; each `row` element contains a number of `col` elements, one per field mentioned in the `resultset` header. For a partition query only (there are other kinds), a row may have a `count` attribute which indicates how many records would be selected by a further query selecting records matching this row. The `op` attribute of the `resultset` specifies the operator to be used in constructing the next navigational step; for example, to select all (48) records with titles beginning with A, one would take the logical field name, the operator, and the data value from the first row: `svc.title begins "A"`.

4   IMPLEMENTATION

We were originally asked to propose a solution strategy, but we wanted to check that our architecture would work, and to be forced to work out all the details. Therefore, we volunteered to build a prototype. To ensure that the prototype wasn't just a "toy", we chose a real client: Ceredigion County Council.

Our prototype was also intended as a model, on which other implementations could be based, perhaps by refining our original code. The design of our prototype therefore had to emphasise clarity and portability over performance.

Most of the databases to be used with the A-Z system will be relatively small, (of the order of a few thousand records), but we wanted to show that our architecture could be used with a real database system. We also wanted to show that we could use free software, and produce free software too.

These are the tools/packages we used:
- Java JDK (Sun Microsystems)
- Ælfred XML Parser (using SAX)

- MySQL
- TWZ JDBC driver for MySQL
- Apache Web Server

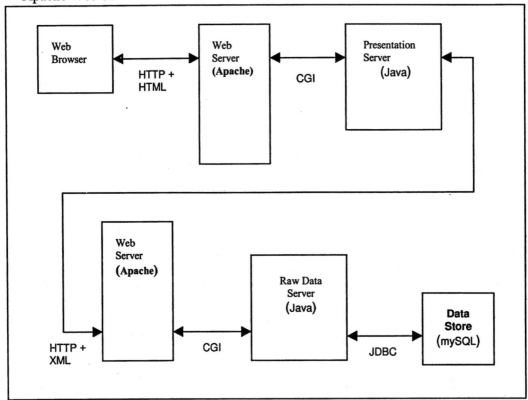

Figure 2: Implementation Details

5   RESULTS SO FAR

In order to have some data to work with, we transferred the data used by Powys'
prototype from the original Access database to our own mySQL database; this was a
simple export-import operation.

We then reproduced the original look-and-feel of the Powys prototype, using our
technology; this involved reimplementing the Active Server Page layouts in Java. The
lesson learnt here was that it is tedious to produce detailed HTML from a programming
language, but Java's object oriented structure makes it easy to construct a "house style"
class, from which "stylesheets" for particular pages are easily defined. As a result,
although the "house style" class is long and tedious, the classes that present individual
queries are very compact.

In order to demonstrate multiple presentation styles, and because our "client" was

Ceredigion, we then produced a set of presentation components which would apply a style similar to that of Ceredigion's main Website. We were fortunate here in having chosen counties with very different styles: Powys' is essentially monolingual, whilst Ceredigion's presents all information bilingually, with both languages on every page. Nevertheless, we were able to demonstrate the presentation of data originally provided by Powys, in Ceredigion's house style.

Finally, we have produced a proposed Llwybr "house style" presentation. Although our architecture has to permit information providers to impose their own presentation on data, partners also recognise the need for a default "regional" style. There are two uses for this: firstly, it will be provided as a part of the Regional A-Z software package as a "get you started" component, intended to be customised, and secondly, it would be used as the presentation service for a central regional "front end" to the integrated A-Z service. This third style takes yet another approach to bilingual presentation; only one language at a time is presented, but the user can change language at any point.

6   FUTURE WORK

6.1   Regional Server
We devised our architecture in response to a need to build an integrated *regional* service, whilst avoiding a need for a (single) regional server. There are a number of ways in which the regional service could now be provided, such as:
1.   Establish the single regional server (see *figure 3*)
2.   Merge datasets at the client (browser) end.
3.   Merge at the raw data server level
     This is our preferred approach: the regional raw data server is a piece of software which stands between the presentation servers and the raw data servers containing the actual data. This regional server accepts queries and replicates them to other raw data servers, and then merges the results and sends the merged result set back to its original client.

6.2   Proxy Servers; Providing Merged Data
The raw data server works by forwarding queries and merging, when implemented with its own cache, becomes a very useful system component.
When run within an organisation's Intranet (i.e. with relatively fast links to its clients) it can act as a proxy server; improving performance for A-Z users and reducing load on Internet links.

A "regional" server can also be used to merge the data provided by a number of local raw data servers, to present a collection of separately administered (and differently structured) datasets as a unit. For example, a county dataset might be comprised of data from different county departments, plus information from local voluntary groups, the chamber of commerce, and so on. These datasets might reside on separate machines, being merged into the one by an "Internet facing" merging server.

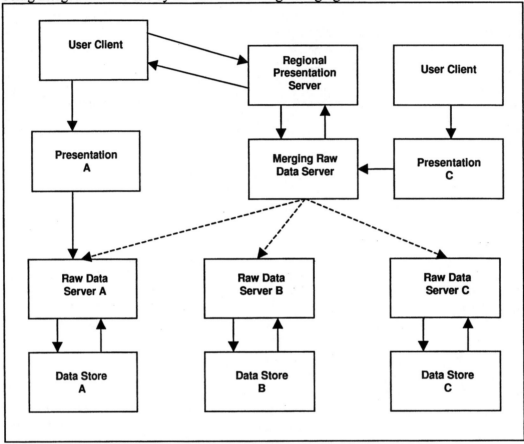

Figure 3: Possibilities for the Regional Server

6.3   Data Entry

Data entry and all the mechanics of data updating were excluded from the scope of our architecture, partly because authorisation and quality control requirements were very diverse, and partly because the need for a *single*, integrated update mechanism was far weaker than the need for a single, integrated presentation and query mechanism.

We have expected data maintenance to be solved as a part of the "data store" component, using whatever tools come to hand for the particular database system being used. For Ceredigion, for example, we are providing some Access forms which will use ODBC to interact with the mySQL database engine.

7 CONCLUSION

Although there is clearly a lot more work to do, we have demonstrated that our architecture can be implemented. Incidentally, we have shown that XML is usable, and that freely available software components are adequate for this kind of job.

Although our original task was to devise a strategy for presentation of Council Service data, our approach is applicable to other datasets, where multiple data providers want to merge their contributions to a whole whilst maintaining their right to set their own policy for maintenance of their own data, and for presentation of the whole. Even within Llwybr, we have another potential application in a Regional "What's On?" service.

8 ACKNOWLEDGEMENTS

The authors acknowledge the support and assistance of the Llwybr Regional Services Group, and in particular Simon Annetts and Janet Knill of Powys County Council Corporate IT Unit and William Howells and Geraint Lewis of Ceredigion County Council Libraries Department. We also thank John Woodbury for his help in proving that XML was usable.

Online Resources

<http://tsc.llwybr.org.uk/> This is our website where you can find a demonstration of the prototype
<http://www.ceredigion.gov.uk/>
<http://www.powys.gov.uk/> Some examples of County Council Websites.
<http://www.mysql.com/> Home of the MySQL database server.
<http://www.microstar.com/XML/SAX/sax.html> Information on the Simple API for XML.
<http://www.microstar.com/XML/Aelfred/aelfred.html> Information about the Ælfred XML parser.
<http://www.w3.org/Style/XSL/> Details of XSL (eXtensible Style Language).
<http://www.php.net/> Home of the PHP scripting language.
<http://www.javasoft.com/> Home of Java.
<http://www.sco.com/Technology/tcl/Tcl.html/> Useful collection of Tcl resources.

References

Light, Richard (1997), *Presenting XML*, Sams.net Publishing, ISBN 1-57521-334-6
Orfali, Robert and Harkey, Dan (1997), *Client/Server Programming with Java and Corba*, (1st Ed) John Wiley and Sons, Inc, ISBN 0-471-16351-1 (A much expanded second edition is now available.)

CHAPTER 66

INTERNET TECHNOLOGY IN DISTANCE –NOT DISTANT– LEARNING

A Pouloudi, LP Baldwin, C Angelopoulos and RM O'Keefe
Brunel University

Abstract

Higher Education, in the UK and elsewhere, is undergoing major change. Those involved in teaching at university level are being asked to respond to, among other factors, an increasing numbers of students and a demand for more open access to education. These, seen against the backdrop of a changing economic and social environment, mean that distance learning is gaining in popularity. Web technology, increasingly becoming more sophisticated, has the potential to play a vital role in distance learning. This paper examines the role of effective courseware in distance learning education, and calls for those designing such material to consider this within a broader learning environment. Five key elements that comprise the learning environment, and which contribute to the effectiveness of courseware delivery, are presented. We then argue that this view may be limiting in the traditional, objectivist, teacher-centred approach to learning and teaching still seen in much of the teaching and assessment practices at university level. With the current shift towards a more learner-centred view of teaching and learning, a brief overview of alternative models of learning, and how these may be supported by Web technology, are presented. This is followed by a discussion of distance learning and the central role of information technology in what has been termed 'the learning society'.

1   INTRODUCTION

The principles of distance learning date back to the eighteenth century, when Pitman started a teaching programme called correspondence education (Lockmiller 1996). The concept of distance learning has since remained based on these same principles (Rowntree 1992):

- Learning alone or in small groups.
- Learning at the learner's pace and in their own time and place.
- Less frequent help from a teacher.

- Active learning rather than passive.
- Learners taking responsibility of their own learning.
- Learning from other people besides teachers.

However, the means of delivery of distance learning material has changed, particularly as Internet technology has become more sophisticated and increasingly used. This paper considers the change of technology within the broader context of teaching and learning in the British higher education environment.

On-line (Web) education offers a new domain for delivering education at a distance, according to Mason and Kaye (1989). In their analysis of the existing domains and the new emerging domain that they describe as on-line education, they make a brief comparison of the traditional face-to-face education (classroom environment) the other distance learning mediums –packaged printed material, audiographics, video– and on-line media. On-line education has its basis in the mediated nature of distance learning education in order to broaden its reach in place and time –time/place independence– and furthermore it is highly interactive. It can also accommodate a unique many-to-many type of communication, enabling learners to communicate with their peers, that is, fellow students, through Internet on-line services. It is also able to host one-to-one interaction (tutor) and one to many (classroom/broadcast).

The rapid pace of technological change mirrors the rapid pace of change in higher education today. This can be witnessed in increasing student numbers, more open access to education, lack of resources and changing economic and social conditions in general. As a result of the increasing competition in the workplace and the economic constraints, higher education institutions and their staff also have become increasingly accountable to government in terms of their performance and use of resources (Ramsden 1992). In their effort to cope with this changing environment, those involved in teaching in higher education necessarily need to focus their attention on the delivery of courseware. This paper examines how this may be reflected in distance learning education but also makes the case for preparing courseware within a broader learning environment. The next section presents five key elements of the learning environment that contribute to the effectiveness in the delivery of courseware. The third section argues that this framework may be limiting if it only reflects a traditional tutor-centred model of learning and presents alternative models of learning that Web technology can support in a distance learning context. This leads us to a more general discussion of distance learning in 'the learning society' (Dearing Report 1997) and the need to consider the role of information technology in this broader context.

2   A CONTINGENCY FRAMEWORK FOR DELIVERY EFFECTIVENESS

The effectiveness in the delivery of courseware is contingent on a number of elements that form the learning environment. Thus, the student, the tutor, the subject matter, the institution and the technology are seen as important elements that ultimately influence the delivery effectiveness of distance learning material. These elements have been separated out in the following paragraphs for analytical purposes but, we will argue, are closely interrelated.

2.1   Learning environment: the student

One of the main differences for a student attending a distance learning course is that the student 'attends' courses without necessarily being present at the same time or place with the course tutor or peers. Consequently, it is often assumed that distance learning equals little interaction amongst participants (student-tutor or student-student interaction). However, the Web, through its asynchronous (Email, Newsgroups) and synchronous (IRC, Web-conferencing, chat rooms) communication mechanisms, is capable of enabling a supporting environment, one where the students form a virtual community. Forming such a virtual learning environment is crucial, and course developers need to ensure that the appropriate time and resources enable the formation of self-help groups (Wade and Smith 1994). Students can be supported by both peers and by tutors, both of which contribute to their engagement in effective learning (Rowntree 1992).

In a distance learning environment it is also important for students to have access to adequate technical support, as this is critical for the smooth delivery of distance learning courses, and on-line help must be provided (Bates 1996). In a distance learning course there are many approaches of how support can be given to participants. The support provided by the tutors, the institution and the technology are further discussed below.

2.2   Learning environment: the tutor

The main role of the course tutor is the delivery of course material in a way that will be best received by students. In order to make this more effective, distance learning tutors need to take a closer look at learners; learner profiles may help tutors to select individuals for a course (Calder 1994). The purpose of the profiling activity is two-fold. On the one hand it will help the learners to realise whether or not they have the abilities or/and interests required to attend the on-line course. On the other hand it will enable the teachers to better understand the needs, strengths and weaknesses of the potential learners of the programme. An important factor for achieving success in distance learning has been the degree to which teachers and support staff are able, by providing structured activities that utilise technology well, to encourage students to undertake responsibility for their own learning (Reid 1996). This entails understanding the needs of the students. This is particularly difficult in distance learning settings, where teachers do not have face to face contact and thus cannot respond effectively to possible misunderstanding on the part of the participants (Evans 1994). Another important type of support that the tutor is expected to provide distance learning students with is mentoring (the equivalent of the personal tutor system that most of the contemporary academic institutions have established). In this the tutor acts as a wise counsellor who takes a neutral position (Wade and Smith 1994).

2.3 Learning environment: the subject matter

It is also important to consider whether the Web is suitable for the delivery of a particular course. One would expect that not all scientific areas could be taught at a distance. This generally applies to courses that have an extensive demand for work on laboratory settings and workshops (e.g., medical studies).

2.4 Learning environment: the institution

Distance learning also relies on institutional support. Usually this includes technical support covering network, modem, hardware and software problems. However it is in a sense also offering academic support, having to provide some on-campus services through the Web, including the library, career advisory, funding, registry and others. It is essential that library provision is carefully considered, planned and implemented (Arfield 1994) and that appropriate technical support is provided so that students are not shut out of the "classroom" (Hiltz 1995). Ideally, support systems and services for a distance learner must mirror those provided for on-campus learners (IDE, 1998). It is important to note that the Web presence and delivery of distance learning materials will be influenced by institutional culture. For example, American universities tend to place a different emphasis on the use of advanced technology to deliver their materials than British universities (see Noble 1997). Similarly, information technology courses are more likely to make extensive use of sophisticated technology than others.

2.5 Learning environment: the technology

A key element of the learning environment is the way in which it is delivered. The main advantages and disadvantages of Web use in the delivery of distance learning courses are summarised in table 1.

The use of Internet technology in distance learning often reflects a conscious attempt to replicate the classroom experiences using this 'new' medium. Thus, the lecture, the office hours of tutoring, the blackboard, group discussions and collaborative assignments have all their electronic form through the Web. For these to be successful, particular attention needs to be drawn to issues of human computer interaction, enabling students to understand the way in which the system functions and consequently to be able to participate easily.

Similar to other content and delivery concerns, the interface design should reflect the profile of the users, both students and tutors. System developers together with the instructor should decide what will be expected for potential users to know about the medium and also what restrictions apply by the corresponding hardware such as the server (IBM Corporation 1997). Also, the technology needs to support learning requirements (Muehlbauer, 1998). A well structured web site can help both learners and instructors in completing their tasks.

Advantages
Asynchronous Learning A more flexible way of participating; students can tailor their study pattern to own abilities, opportunities and requirements (Charlett and Skinn 1996).
Synchronous Learning People can get involved into an educational effort at the same time but not necessarily in the same place (Charlett and Skinn 1996). It is possible to simulate the classroom environment on-line (Ownston 1997).
Active Learning – Interactivity Learning should be active in order to be effective (Bates 1991). On-line learning is not only active; it is interactive (Mason and Kaye 1989) as ideas, opinions and the necessary feedback from the instructor can be openly and easily exchanged between the interested parties.
Resource Availability, Access Students have access to a variety of resources. The Web is capable of providing this availability in an orderly presentation (Windley 1994). Access to libraries, governmental databases and academic repositories becomes easier, potentially eliminating the academic isolation associated with learning at a distance (Kubala 1998).
Anonymity in participation Several psychological, cultural and in general personal background characteristics prevent many participants from getting the attention of the class even when they feel that they have something important to contribute. The Web can offer anonymity either by requiring nicknames or by not presenting at all the identity of the participant during on-line discussions and message exchanges.
Advanced communication among learners The learners have to navigate their way through information, solve problems by co-operating with their colleagues and finally present the results of their work to the teacher. The Web through its email, newsgroups and conferencing capabilities can support these activities (Lin 1995).
Democratic, free nature The Web tends to diminish differences in social status. Furthermore intercultural activities are supported; for example writing in a second language is easier than speaking (Mason 1994).
Familiarity to Student's Learning Mode The new generation tend to be more visual learners than previous generations because their world is rich in visual stimuli (Ownston 1997). So using the Web in education is considered quite natural by students.
Ease of Learning the Media It is quite easy for participants to learn the basics about the Web.

Disadvantages
Bandwidth Problems The most commonly reported problem in on-line course delivery is that of bandwidth (Hiltz 1997). The current networking infrastructure does not permit fast retrieval of the requested files, especially if the requested pages are using advanced features of the Web such as Java applets, video etc. Such delays lead to frustration and greatly affect the effectiveness of the

Disadvantages
medium and educational process (e.g., The Concourse Project 1998).
Increasing Cost
The ever increasing demands in hardware and software in order to adopt new standards and the need to accommodate expensive expertise to maintain and support the corresponding infrastructure, considerably increase the costs. An effective strategy for minimising the impact of these costs is to concentrate Web development efforts and resources into the courses that accumulate the greatest enrolment (Ownston 1997).
Isolation
The feeling of isolation is often strong, coupled with a lack of motivation due to the physical absence of a tutor and other students. Extensive use of the asynchronous nature of the medium also contributes. Students also expect constant feedback, as a means to assess their performance against other students (Charlett and Skinn 1996). There is therefore a need to ensure a high level of interaction early on (Pinto 1995).
Management Difficulties
The dynamic nature of the information provided through the Web is an advantage. When it comes to managing these links, especially in "rich" linkage of web pages, it is a time consuming, boring yet important activity. The instructor must be sure that the links offered through the web pages of the course are up to date. There is also a problem for learners who may previously have been used to printed rather than on-line documentation and do not use the new medium effectively (Windley 1994).

Table 1: Advantages and disadvantages of using web technology in distance learning

There is no single medium of distance learning course delivery that is able to improve learning in a significant way on its own. Nor is it realistic to expect that the Web, used as a tool, will help students to develop new skills (Ownston 1997). So far, this paper has looked at the delivery of course material, thus focusing on the way in which the learning environment and its elements affects teaching effectiveness. This focus is limiting as it reflects a view of teaching and learning as one of disseminating knowledge (Ramsden 1992). In this view, knowledge exists as something apart from the people who have it. Teachers are seen as the experts whose main task is to organise and present this knowledge well. This model of teaching relies on the ability of students to understand and absorb the knowledge and procedures presented to them. The purpose of the next section is to shift the attention from teaching and delivery to learners and learning. This is in response to more recent models of learning suggested in educational research, which place greater attention on the role of the learner in the learning process.

3 CONSIDERING AN EDUCATIONAL PERSPECTIVE: MODELS OF LEARNING

As in a distance learning environment students tend to be isolated, they are expected to take a more 'active' attitude towards their learning, that is assume responsibility for it. However, this is actually translated in assuming responsibility for the time they spend studying rather than a more substantial change in the way knowledge is experienced and learning achieved. These assumptions represent a model of learning that has been predominant in higher education, but one that is increasingly criticised in the educational literature.

In the information systems literature, Leidner and Javernpaa (1995) contrast this *objectivist* model of learning with other approaches on how learners learn and argue similarly that "the effectiveness of IT in contributing to learning will be a function of how well the technology supports a particular model of learning and the appropriateness of the model to a particular situation". Thus, they classify different models of learning according to assumptions about the learning process, the realism of the context, knowledge and who is in control of the learning experience (Figure 1). Based on Leidner and Javernpaa's work, the following paragraphs briefly introduce these different models of learning and then discuss whether the Internet can support or accommodate the educational practice that is based on each model.

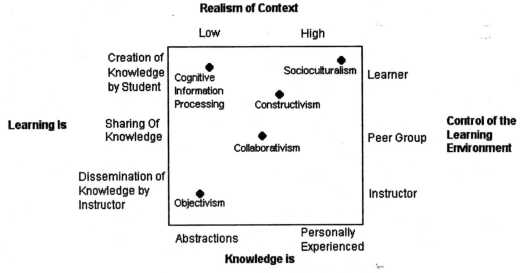

Figure 1: The Dimensions of the Learning Theories
(Source: Leidner & Javernpaa, 1995, p. 271)

The Objectivist Model of Learning: It is the traditional model of learning, widely used in the typical classroom environment and face to face mode of education. The tenet of the model is that there is an objective reality and that the goal of learning is to understand this reality (Jonassen, 1993). The main idea that this model is built on is that of passive learning. Knowledge is 'passed' from the teacher to the students with the latter being the mere recipient of the transmitted material. In order to maximise effectiveness, presentation of the course material is very important. The model is highly dependent upon the capabilities and "quality" of the teachers not only as far as their understanding of the topic is concerned but also on their communication skills.

The Web can easily support this model. A simple web page providing the material presented in class and perhaps some additional related links may be adequate for this. Also the complete set of notes can be provided either to be viewed on-line or for download. Although the capabilities of the medium would not be fully exploited in this way, it can be used as an effective delivery and presentation mechanism within this model.

The Constructivist Model of Learning: Constructivism challenges the idea that there is only one external reality but is based on the premise that each individual has a unique understanding of the world. The goal of this model is not to accurately transfer the content from the instructor to the learner (Dodge, 1996). According to this model the mind is not a tool for reproducing the external, objective reality, but rather the mind creates its own, unique conception of events (Jonassen, 1993).

The Internet, with its open access and effective linking mechanisms, can accommodate this model of learning as well. The advanced communication capabilities it provides also help its users to share their experiences, opinions and findings before creating their own understanding of the subject matter.

The Cooperative Model of Learning: Here, as in Constructivism, the learners are responsible for finding their way to knowledge. However, this is no longer the effort of an isolated individual. The whole process of assimilating and obtaining the educational content is carried out by teams of people who, by contributing their own understandings, lead the whole group to new, shared knowledge. Participation is the most critical characteristic of this model. The advantage is that learners tend to generate higher level reasoning strategies, a greater diversity of ideas and procedures, more critical thinking and more creative responses when they are actively learning in groups than when they are learning individually or competitively (Schlechter, 1990).

Again, in this case the Internet has quite a lot of applications that can be used to facilitate distance educational endeavours based on this model through means of both asynchronous and synchronous communication.

The Cognitive Information Processing Model of Learning: According to this model, learning involves processing instructional input to develop, test and refine mental models in long-term memory until they are effective and reliable enough in problem solving situations (Shuell, 1986). This model does not explicitly state how the learner gains knowledge, but claims that the educational climate can provide students with the necessary stimuli and opportunities to enable them to process information. The frequency and intensity with which a student cognitively processes instructional input controls the pace of learning.

The Web supports this model by enabling learners to set their own learning pace. The medium allows the storage of information but is also capable of presenting it in a way that suits the needs of learners. Furthermore it offers them access to other resources of knowledge, in order to clarify issues that they do not understand well.

The Sociocultural Model of Learning: The Sociocultural model is both an extension and a reaction to some of the assumptions of Constructivism. Its advocates (Iran-Nejad, et al, 1990; O'Loughlin, 1992) argue that both Constructivism and Collaborativism force the minority into adopting the understanding derived by the majority. So this model suggests that learners form their own, unbiased version of understanding that fits their cultural and social background.

The Web can accommodate such a model of learning in a way that protects the personal rights of the learners as it can provide mechanisms for the preservation of anonymity, thus 'hiding' what their national, cultural or social beliefs are. This waives some of the restrictions that learners often face in accessing resources in a way that corresponds to their thinking and life style. Thus, internet technology can provide support for a variety of learning models. At the same time, following an actor-network theory approach (Callon, 1986; Latour, 1987) we would argue that the development and use of internet technology also encapsulates the view of learning that distance learning participants adopt. As a result of the interdependence between the use of technology in distance learning and the underlying assumption about the purpose of courseware delivery and the way in which learning is achieved, it is important for tutors and institutions engaged in distance learning to be conscious of the learning theories they adopt.

4   DISCUSSION AND CONCLUSIONS

In contemporary Britain the objectivist model of learning is still prominent (Ramsden, 1992), particularly in science-based disciplines. However, educational research increasingly favours learning models that are student-focused rather than teacher-led. These models also advocate the use of the term 'learner' rather than student, thus emphasising the active, and indeed interactive, nature of learning. In order to strengthen the learning process and its outcomes at a national level, the Dearing Report (1997) actively advocates this view of learning. At the same time, student numbers increase whilst the available funding fails to meet the needs of educational institutions. Teachers and institutions are therefore faced with the challenge of changing and improving their understanding and support of the learning process in this environment. This challenge also pertains distance learning education as designers and distance learning tutors need to spend more time in supporting, inspiring and encouraging a more active involvement of their learners. The Internet can support this activity as long as it is not used in ways that contradict this student-centred learning model.

Overall, what makes a course successful is the combination of the content, learning environment and approach, the student's willingness and capabilities, the instructor's commitment, the resources and service availability, and finally the medium or combination of media that are used. The use of information technology has in turn important repercussions for educational institutions as well. For example, distance learning courses increase the visibility and student access to the institution and can therefore be used as a powerful penetration mechanisms to international educational 'markets'. But this also entails a number of risks that institutions need to take into account.

First, it is important to understand that the design of distance learning material for Internet access is unlikely to be easier or less costly that the design of more traditional classroom-based courses. Second, there is a danger for distance learning to be used as a pretext for the 'commercialisation' of courses and consequently education. There is some evidence of such perceptions in the United States, as the increasing adoption of distance learning programmes is interpreted as a tendency for educational institutions to run their programmes with less experienced, lower paid teachers, since the system will now hold the content, thus increasing their profit margins. Another possible danger in distance learning education would result from a compromise in the quality of course material for the sake of easier course set up. This could happen in cases where, by moving most of the content on-line, the instructor becomes just a secondary, 'third party' member of the educational practice.

To sum up, this paper has presented learning in a broader context, that is, one that is not limited to the learners and teachers but one that also considers other key elements of the learning environment. Technology is closely related to each of these elements. In a distance learning context in particular, it provides unique opportunities to reach out to distant learners, but concerns about the technology with regard to efficient learning tend to focus on the low level concerns of the delivery of courseware. Internet technology in distance learning plays its part but, we have argued, cannot be separated from more fundamental concerns related to the learning experience. It should, therefore, be seen as part of the complex interaction between those stakeholders that comprise this learning society. Distance learning is therefore not distant and distancing, but part of the wider world of education in general, or, as Schon (1987) calls education, the "soft, slimy swamp of real-life problems" (page 3) that all of us in education have to deal with.

References

Arfield J., "Flexible Learning and the Library". In Wade, Hodgkinson, Smith & Arfield (eds), *Flexible Learning in Higher Education*, Kogan Page, London, 1994.

Bates, A. W., "Interactivity as a Criterion for Media selection in Distance Education", *Never Too Far*, 16, 1991, 5-9.

Bates, A. W., "The Impact of Technological Change on Open and Distance Learning". http://bates.cstudies.ubc.ca/brisbane.html, 1996.

Calder J., *Programme Evaluation and Quality: A Comprehensive Guide to Setting up an Evaluation System*, Kogan Page, London, 1994.

Callon, M., "Some elements of a sociology of translation: domestication of the scallops and the fishermen of St Brieuc Bay" In Law, J. (ed.), *Power, Action and Belief: A New Sociology of Knowledge?* Routledge & Kegan Paul, London, 1986, pp 196-233.

Charlett, J. A. and Skinn, A., "Enhancing the Delivery of Partial Distance Learning by the Use of Collaborative Arrangements through Franchising". http://www.bre.polyu.edu.hk/careis/rp/cibBeijing96/papers/140_149/146/ p146.htm, 1996

Concourse Project. http://concourse.herts.ac.uk/concors3.htm, 1998.

Davies, G. K., "Higher Education's Big Problems: Can Technology Help Solve Them?". Keynote address at the semi-annual meeting of the Educom National Learning Infrastructure Initiative, Keystone, CO. June, 1995.

Dearing Report, *Higher Education in the Learning Society*, The National Committee of Inquiry into Higher Education, 1997.

Dodge, B., "Distance Learning on the World Wide Web". http://edweb.sdsu.edu/people/bdodge/CTPTG-Bib.html, 1996.

Evans, T., *Understanding Learners in Open and Distance Education*, Kogan Page, London, 1994.

Hiltz R., *The Virtual Classroom - Learning without limits via Computer Networks*, Ablex Publishing Corporation, Norwood USA, 1995.

Hiltz, R., "Impacts of college-level courses via Asynchronous Learning Networks: Some Preliminary Results". http://eies.njit.edu/~hiltz/workingpapers/philly/philly.htm, 1997

IBM Corporation, 'IBM Web Guidelines - The Complete Set'. http://www.ibm.com/ibm/hci/guidelines/web/print.html, 1997.

IDE, "IDE - Guiding Principles and Practices for the Design and Development of Effective Distance Education", http://www.cde.psu.edu/DE/ide/GP&P/GP&P.html, 1998.

Iran-Nejad, A, McKeachie, W, Berliner, D.C., "The Multisource Nature of Learning: An Introduction". *Review of Educational Research*, 60 (4), 1990, pp 509-515.

Jonassen, D.H, "Thinking Technology", *Educational Technology*, Jan 1993, pp 35-37.

Kubala, T., "Addressing Student Needs: Teaching on the Internet". http://www.THEJOURNAL.COM/98/mar/398feat4.html, 1998

Latour, B., *Science in Action : How to Follow Scientists and Engineers Through Society*. Open University Press, Milton Keynes, 1987.

Leidner, E. D., Javernpaa, S. L., "The Use of IT to Enhance Management School Education: A Theoretical View". *MIS Quarterly* 19, (3), pp 265-291.

Lin, N., http://www.sims.berkeley.edu/impact/Winter95/HTML/dist/ nancydist2.html, 1995.

Lockmiller, A. D. (1996), "Correspondence Education," included in Microsoft(R) Encarta(R) 96 Encyclopedia (c) 1993-1995 Microsoft Corporation. Funk & Wagnalls Corporation. http://webster.commnet.edu/roger/history.htm, 1996.

Mason, R. and Kaye, A., *Mindweave, Communication, Computers and Distance Education*, Pergamon Press, 1989.

Mason, R., *Using Communications Media in Open and Flexible Learning*, Kogan Page, London, 1994.

Muehlbauer, J., "The Navigation and Usability Guide".

http://webreview.com/wr/pub/98/05/15/thing/index.htmlz, 1998.

Noble, F. D., "Digital Diploma Mills: The Automation of Higher Education". http://www.journet.com/twu/deplomamills.html, 1997.

O'Loughlin, M., "Rethinking Science Education: Beyond Piagetian Constructivism Toward a Sociocultural Model of Teaching and Learning". *Journal of Research in Science Teaching* 29 (8), 1992, pp 791-820.

Ownston, D. R., "The World Wide Web: A Technology to Enhance Teaching and Learning?". *Educational Researcher*, 26 (2), 1997, pp. 27-33.

Pinto, M., "Impressions of ILS 609 and Distance Learning – Distance Learning Essay # 3". http://www.sims.berkeley.edu/impact/ Winter95/HTML/dist/marthadist3.html, 1995

Ramsden, P., *Learning to Teach in Higher Education*, Routledge, 1992.

Reid, A. K., "Impact of Technology on Learning Effectiveness". http://www.lucent.com/cedl/impact.html, 1996.

Rowntree,D., *Exploring open and Distance Learning*, Kogan Page, London, 1992.

Schlechter, T.M, "The Relative Instructional Efficiency of Small Group Computer-Based Training". *Journal of Educational Computing Research* (6), 3, 1990, pp 329-341.

Schon, D.A., *Educating the Reflective Practitioner*, Jossey-Bass, San Francisco, 1987.

Shuell, T.J., "Cognitive Conceptions of Learning". *Review of Educational Research*, Winter 1986, pp 411-436.

Wade, W. and Smith, A., "Off-site Support for Flexible Learners: Learning in No Man's Land". In Wade, W., et al (eds), *Flexible Learning in Higher Education*, Kogan Page Limited, London, 1994.

Windley, J. Philip, "Using WWW to Augment Classroom Instruction", http://lal.cs.byu.edu/people/windley/using.www.to.teach.html, 1994.

CHAPTER 67

EDUCATIONAL SYSTEMS AND SOCIAL CONTEXT

Julika Matravers
Leeds University

Abstract

Research in the area of computer-based education has led to the development of educational systems that provide tutoring to students on an individual basis. However, social interaction is increasingly viewed as an important contributor towards learning, and it has been recognised that classroom teaching could gain from computer-supported collaborative activities if the benefits of collaborative learning were better understood and recognised by teachers and system developers. This paper, therefore, is concerned with the potential of teaching theories that recognise learning as a social activity as a basis for both the improvement of the development of educational systems and a more successful integration of conventional systems into teachers' current teaching practices. For this purpose this paper first offers an overview of the teaching strategies that have served as a basis for the development of educational systems and how these theories have been implemented in existing systems. The paper continues with a discussion of the limitations of these systems. Social theory is then introduced as an alternative to the individual learning theories that have served as a basis for the systems described. Finally the paper demonstrates how a better recognition of social theory may lead to both a more successful utilisation of existing educational systems and the development of more successful systems in the future.

1   INTRODUCTION

A significant amount of research is carried out in order to develop educational systems that support successful learning, and different pedagogical theories have been favoured as a basis for the implementation of these systems. Still, the existing systems largely fail to be as successful as they promise.

It is apparent that the systems developed are purely based on teaching theories that treat learning as an individual process. No consideration is shown for the social context in which learning generally takes place and which may play an important role in the success of the learning process. This paper argues that a greater consideration for the theory that learning is a social activity, and therefore has to be viewed within the context in which it takes place, is urgently required. Such consideration can then promote both a better understanding of how existing educational systems may be more successfully integrated into the overall learning process and an improved basis for the development of educational systems.

For this purpose this paper first investigates the learning theories that have been used as a basis for the development of educational systems. It then continues with an investigation of the different kinds of educational systems that have resulted from the research based on these different theories and sets out the ways in which these systems have failed in offering successful learning. The paper then presents the theoretical basis for the more recent belief that learning has to be viewed within the social context in which it is taking place. It continues to offer some guidance on how a better recognition of this theory may remedy the weaknesses of systems that have been based on individual learning theories. Finally, the paper explores the capabilities of the theory of learning in context to improve future system development.

2   COMPUTERS FOR INDIVIDUAL EDUCATION - A LOOK AT LEARNING THEORIES

A significant amount of research has been carried out in order to use the computer as a teaching tool. Within the pedagogical theories that have had an impact on the development of educational systems a distinction can be made between the behaviourist, the cognitive and the constructivist approach.

2.1   The behaviourist approach
The idea of taking advantage of computer technology to serve as a 'teaching machine' emerged in the 1950s with the development of the first computer-based learning systems which were based on the theory within the behaviourist school of psychology (Elsom-Cook 1991). It was Thorndike in particular who, with his 'Law of Effects', had a significant influence on the development of early educational systems. His 'Law of Effects' suggests that in any given situation an organism has a number of possible responses, and the response depends on the strengths of the link between the situation and the response. The more 'satisfying' the state of affairs following the response the stronger the link (Sewell 1990). Although Thorndike based his theory on experiments which he had carried out with animals he believed that it could also be applied to human learning. Accordingly he argued that practice, repetition and reward form the basis for the acquisitions of skills. This idea was adopted as a basis for computer-based drill and practice programs, especially in the field of mathematics (Sewell 1990).

Thorndike's theory was extended beyond the field of mathematics by Skinner. Skinner views teaching as the shaping of behaviour without any recognition for internal processes and divides learning into 3 stages: the stimulus or situation the learner is encountering, the behaviour that is invoked and the reinforcement which follows the behaviour. It is therefore the task of the teacher, and accordingly of the computer-based system, to present the stimulus, observe and analyse the learner's external behaviour, and reward desired behaviour with the objective to maximise the probability of obtaining correct replies (behaviour) from the learner. The particular advantages in using these so-called drill and practice systems to support this kind of learning were seen in the ability of the computer to offer individual tutoring in the sense that the learner could advance through the material to be learned at his own pace.

2.2   The cognitive approach

The idea of modelling cognitive processes in order to understand and support learning became a major research approach in the 1950s and 60s and can be viewed as a rival approach to the behaviourist theory. Psychologists had the aspiration to study mental processes that are dedicated to the processing of information in the brain. Mathematical models were used to try and explain human abilities, and humans were viewed as active processors of information. The field of artificial intelligence emerged.

The field of intelligent tutoring systems, in particular, uses ideas from the field of artificial intelligence in order to create teaching environments that provide individualised tutoring (Kaplan and Rock 1995). Intelligent tutoring systems adapt the teaching process to the learner by exploring and understanding the learner's special needs, and by responding to these as a human teacher does. In order to provide this adaptability to the learner an intelligent tutoring system has to be capable of performing diagnosis of the learner's actions in order to infer the learner's cognitive states, such as his level of knowledge or proficiency. This process of diagnosis is supported through the use of the student model which records these cognitive states of the learner and is constantly updated by (the intelligence of) the system (Winkels 1992).

2.3   The constructivist approach

Jean Piaget is well known for his investigations into the way knowledge is structured and how the acquisition of knowledge requires the existing knowledge structures to change in order to accommodate new knowledge. He argued further that children's perception of their experiences are themselves modified in order to fit into these structures. Children are viewed as active learners within the world around them. Through interaction with this world they develop and refine their understanding of the world (Jones 1995). It was Seymour Papert who built on these ideas when he developed LOGO as a prototype of a system that provides children with a 'mathematical world' in which mathematical concepts are simplified. It is argued that in this way the learner can relate these concepts to, or fit them into, his existing knowledge following Piaget's theory (Papert 1980).

3   EXISTING EDUCATIONAL SYSTEMS - A CRITIQUE

The previous section has given an overview of the theories that have had, and continue to have, an influence on the development of educational software. However, although the use of computers for learning is generally encouraged and technology has advanced dramatically, the systems that have been developed have not become as successful as one might have hoped for. This section revisits the different kinds of existing applications and determines the main areas and causes for the lack of their success.

3.1   Drill and practice applications

Based on the behaviourist theory drill and practice systems aim at obtaining correct behaviour from the student within a tutoring interaction. However, drill and practice programs cannot cope with the kind of individualization sought by many teachers. A main criticism has been that these applications are not able to diagnose the behaviour of the learner in order to provide feedback or remediation of errors, even though it has recently been argued that learning can be improved if the learner can explore the reasons for making an error (Siemer and Angelides 1998). Also, experience has shown that in mathematics, for example, less competent children did not manage to catch up through the use of drill and practice applications as originally hoped, and a major criticism was that children failed to learn the underlying mathematical concepts.

3.2   Intelligent tutoring systems

Research in the field of intelligent tutoring systems has always had a strong focus on the development of student models in order to offer a tutoring process that adopts to the individual student. Intelligent tutoring systems are developed based on the assumption that within a problem solving context learners' thinking processes can be modelled, traced and corrected using computers (Derry and Lajoie 1993).

However, it is argued that research on complete and precise student models has not shown much progress and serious doubts exist whether such progress will ever be achieved (Bierman et al 1992). Furthermore, the diagnostic processes implemented have remained very domain specific. The systems developed, for example, largely fall into procedural domains such as geometry and programming. Also, it has been argued that the student models that have been developed do not provide a guarantee for good remediation. It is still unclear what information needs (or can) be formalized in order to provide a basis for remediation (Siemer and Angelides 1998). Another major criticism is the fact that student modelling has remained an exclusively cognitive analysis. However, effective tutoring also needs to account for issues such as the student's motivation and preference for a particular teaching strategy (Lepper et al 1993).

3.3   The constructivist approach: LOGO

Finally, there are the ideas of Piaget which have influenced the development of educational systems with Papert's LOGO environment as the classical example. Papert believed that LOGO would provide the learner with an environment that provides opportunities for personal expression and freedom that would revolutionize the classroom. However, LOGO has never become nearly as successful at it had been hoped for and where it was used the observations that were made were not greatly encouraging (McFarlane 1997). It was noticed that programming in LOGO does not necessarily lead to better problem solving skills and that the acquisition of cognitive skills was greater when the LOGO activities were carefully structured by the teacher (Jones 1995). However, the system does not obviously allow for such teacher involvement, and LOGO has been criticized for its strong reliance on the constructivist approach which appears to put so much faith into autonomous learning that the social context in which learning takes place is neglected (Crook 1994).

4   LOOKING AT LEARNING IN SOCIAL CONTEXT

The previous sections have shown that the systems that have been developed for learning, although based on some theory of learning, have not proved to be overly successful in supporting satisfactory learning. The major concerns that were identified were the inability to provide remediation and feedback for drill and practice applications, the lack of complete student models in intelligent tutoring systems, and the failure of constructivist systems, such as LOGO, to acquire the success that was originally hoped for and to offer the guidance that pupils appear to require. Furthermore, no suggestions have been made on how these systems, as they stand, can be integrated into existing teaching structures and practices in the classroom.

Conventional classroom teaching and learning tends to be carried out based on the assumption that learning is an individual process (Brown 1990). This view of learning has become dominant despite the fact that almost all other human activity, particularly all learning activities outside school, involve social contact. Even though there is evidence that people learn communally, ever since the first years of computer-based instruction teaching with computers has always been directed towards individualized learning. The social context in which learning may take place has largely been ignored within the development of educational software (Crook 1994).

This section argues that a greater consideration for social interaction within learning is required to develop more successful educational systems and to make current systems more successful. The theories of learning discussed above, although they represent different schools of thought, are commonly based on the assumption that the individual can be kept separate from the social context, and they all treat learning as an activity of the individual. This section, therefore, gives an introduction to the theory of learning in context. The paper then continues to illustrate how the application of the idea of learning in context may support both the resolving of the problems associated with existing computer-based learning applications and the development of more successful learning applications in the future.

4.1 The theory of learning in social context

A well known supporter of the theory that learning has to be viewed within its social context is the Russian psychologist Vygotsky (Wood 1988). Vygotsky argues that cognitive development is socially located and that the ability to learn through instruction is an intelligent activity in itself. In this sense the teacher who helps a learner through an exercise encourages the development of knowledge and ability and thereby contributes towards better learning. Therefore, a person's ability to learn is unveiled and supported in interactions with more knowledgeable others (Doise and Mugney 1984).

The belief that cognitive abilities result not from a simple interaction between the learner and the physical environment, but that such interaction is mediated by others coincides with a popular theory in the field of social psychology. According to social psychologists any approach that is limited to studying the individual's interactions with objects needs to be extended into a study of more complex situations in which several individuals are linked in terms of their interactions with or through an object (Doise and Mugney 1984). A better recognition and consideration of these learning theories may, therefore, help to understand and improve the use of educational systems.

The previous section has given an introduction into the ideas of learning in context. Although these ideas have remained general they call for specific areas and ways in which existing educational systems may be improved or better integrated into classroom teaching. This section offers some insight into the possibilities of how educational software may be better utilised and their future development improved through a better recognition of the theory of learning in social context.

4.2 Making the best of the present: Towards better system use

Although the overview of current systems given above sounds bleak, this section argues that there are numerous opportunities for overcoming their weaknesses by applying the ideas of learning in social context. The acceptance of, and provision for, the use of educational systems by groups of pupils rather than by individuals in isolation can present an opportunity to overcome the weaknesses of existing applications. This section presents these opportunities and illustrates how they can be used.

The criticism that drill and practice programs do not provide feedback and that intelligent tutoring systems generally fail to offer appropriate remediation due to problems of diagnosis may be rectified by having more than one student working on the same exercise. It is claimed that the collaboration of learners within a learning process reveals learners' different learning approaches (Lesgold et al 1992). When two people bring different viewpoints to a task, they may achieve greater insights from trying to reconcile the two positions or at least to understand how they could both be valid. A pupil can benefit from this kind of consultation with a companion since the companion can foster the development of knowledge through the so-called social-cognitive conflict.

In the collaborative learner-pair situation a cognitive conflict occurs when one learner's explanation or response does not match completely with the knowledge of the other student, who is then confronted with conflicting solutions. This situation occurs when one of the learners has solved a problem incorrectly. In their experiment, Mugny and Doise (1978) demonstrated that two students with different cognitive strategies progress more than students with the same cognitive strategy. This situation also occurs when one student approaches a problem in an incorrect way and hence requires remediation (Chan and Baskin 1990). A human learning companion can, therefore, support the provision of feedback and remedial tutoring within the use of drill and practice applications and intelligent tutoring systems by offering his approach to problem solving. If a learner makes an error within a task a companion learner may come in and offer his understanding, i.e. his viewpoint, of the same task. (Reusser 1993, Lesgold et al 1992). In this way collaborative learning may also compensate for some of the weaknesses of student modelling. A learning companion is often able to recognize the problems of his fellow learner, and even if the learning companion is unable to diagnose, i.e. explain the exact cause of, an error of his colleague, he may at least be able to offer an explanation when an error occurs. Also, for intelligent tutoring systems the student model which is being formed by the system lacks the advantages of a student model which may be formed by a human companion. A human companion may have the advantage of including information such as experience-based background knowledge about the learner.

Finally, the use of constructivist systems like LOGO appears to benefit from social interaction between learners and between the teacher and the learner. Experience has shown that working with LOGO has significant effects on children's social interactions, and that LOGO can lead to particular social benefits when used in groups (Jones 1995). In fact, it has been argued that the lack of success with LOGO may be due to its neglect for interpersonal support for learning (Crook 1994). Also, the integration of the human supervisor may solve the problem of lack of guidance in LOGO.

4.3   Making the best of the future: Towards better systems
It is obvious that a new, more socially grounded, understanding of learning does not only demand a better understanding and use of the systems that are currently used in schools. It also demands a revision of educational software development. However, the details and technicalities this requires from the developers must be manifold and their exact determination goes beyond the scope of this paper. Still, the implementation of a system that allows for learning in social context calls for opportunities for collaboration within the learning process (Crook 1994). This section offers some direction towards a revised basis for the development of educational systems.

There are a number of systems which seem to make some effort towards the implementation of such a more socially grounded theory. An example is the Bubble Dialogue system (McMahon and O'Neill 1992) which offers an environment in which pupils are supposed to associate themselves with a character within a particular scenario. These scenarios can be of different kinds and the characters can be taken over by either a learner or a teacher. Bubble Dialogue offers a step towards a better recognition of learning in context by offering an instructional environment for 'social formation' of the participants. Similarly a move away from the development of educational systems that attempt to offer individualized learning in which the human teacher is attempted to be replaced towards educational systems that try to integrate the teacher into the learning process may make educational systems more successful. Without the presence of the human tutor the quality and efficiency that educational systems can attain will be weakened. The human tutor may offer the instructional support that is required by the learner as proposed by Vygotsky. He may offer guidance according to the needs of the learner, support the teaching process in situations where the system comes to a hold or where the student does not feel that the system provides an appropriate service (Chan and Baskin 1990). Educational software has to be developed in such a way that it provides for the integration of the human supervisor (Reinhardt 1995, Elsom-Cook 1991).

Although this section has shown that there are opportunities for systems to account for some ideas of social theory by providing for collaborative learning, there remains plenty of scope for a proper formalization of the requirements for systems that allow for learning in context. Still, a better awareness and understanding of social learning theory is what is offered here as a first step towards better learning systems.

5 CONCLUSION

A number of different pedagogical theories have served as a basis for the development of educational systems. However, despite the extensive research that has gone into these applications they have failed to provide the success they promised. A reason for this lack of success can be found in the nature of the pedagogical theories that have been guiding their development. The theories used commonly view teaching as an individual process. However, the recognition of the context in which learning takes place has recently been recognised as crucial in order to make learning more successful.

This paper has shown that greater consideration for the social dynamics going on within groups of learners and the application of social theory can make the use of the computer for learning more successful in two major ways:

- It offers an opportunity to overcome weaknesses of existing computer applications, such as student modelling, remediation and lack of guidance. At the same time, the idea of collaborative learning an help to take better advantage of existing computer applications through an improved understanding of learning within groups .
- It offers a revised basis for the future development of educational software so that it fits into the social context in which it is used, i.e. so that it supports collaborative learning.

The issues discussed in this paper offer ground for further research to realise, and take advantage of, the idea of learning in context. However, they may also trigger further research in related areas. The encouragement of student collaboration may, for example, have further positive effects on the overall teaching process. Greater motivation, for example, has been associated with working in groups (Kaplan and Rock 1995). This issue may be worth exploring further in order to maximise the benefits. A further area to be explored is the idea of using content-free computer applications, e.g. word-processors and databases, to implement the idea of learning in social context. Finally, in order to realise the full potential of computer-supported learning in social context we need to be concerned with the training of teachers so that they can incorporate existing and future applications into their teaching practices and gain maximum benefits from their use.

References

Bierman D.J., Kamsteeg P.A. and Sandberg J.A.C. (1992) 'Student Models, Scratch-Pads, and Simulation', in Costa E. (ed) New Directions for Intelligent Tutoring Systems. NATO ASI Series, Vol. 91, Springer-Verlag, Berlin, Heidelberg.

Brown J.S. (1990), 'Toward a New Epistemology for Learning', in Frasson C. and Gauthier G. (eds) Intelligent Tutoring Systems. Ablex Publishing Corporation, Norwood, New Jersey.

Chan T.-W. and Baskin A.B. (1990) 'Learning Companion Systems', in Frasson C. and Gauthier G. (eds) Intelligent Tutoring Systems. Ablex Publishing Corporation, Norwood, New Jersey.

Crook, C. (1994) Computers and Collaborative Experience of Learning - A psychological perspective. Routledge, London.

Derry S.J. and Lajoie P.L, (1993) 'A Middle Camp for (Un)Intelligent Instructional Computing: An Introduction', in Lajoie, P. and Derry, S.J. (eds) Computers and Cognitive Tools. Lawrence Erlbaum Associates, Hillsdale, NJ.

Doise W. and Mugny, G. (1984) The Social Development of the Intellect. Pergamon Press, Oxford.

Doise W., Mugny G., Perret-Clermont A. (1975) 'Social action and the development of cognitive operations', in European Journal of Social Psychology, Vol 5, No.3.

Elsom-Cook M.T. (1991) 'Dialogue and Teaching Styles', in Goodyear P. (ed) Teaching Knowledge and Intelligent Tutoring. Ablex Publishing Corporation, Norwood, New Jersey.

Jones, A. (1995) 'Constructivist Theories of Learning and IT', in Heap, N., Thomas, R., Einon, G., Mason R. and Mackay, H. (eds) Information Technology and Society. Sage Publications, London.

Kaplan R. and Rock D. (1995) 'New Directions for Intelligent Tutoring', AI Expert, Vol, No 2.

Kaye, A. (1995) 'Computer Supported Collaborative Learning', in Heap, N., Thomas, R., Einon, G., Mason R. and Mackay, H. (eds) Information Technology and Society. Sage Publications, London.

Lepper M.R. and Chabay R.W. (1988) 'Socializing the Intelligent Tutor: Bringing Empathy to Computer Tutors', in Mandl H. and Lesgold A. (eds) Learning Issues fir Intelligent Tutoring Systems. Springer-Verlag, New York..

Lesgold A., Katz S., Greenberg L., Hughes E. and Eggan G. (1992) 'Extensions of intelligent tutoring paradigms to support collaborative learning', in Dijkstra S., Krammer H.P.M., van Merrienboer J.J.G. (eds) Instructional Models in Computer-based Learning Environments. Springer-Verlag, Berlin, Heidelberg.

McFarlane, A. (1997) 'Where are we and how did we get here', in McFarlane, A. (ed) Information Technology and Authentic Learning - Realising the Potential of Computers in the Primary Classroom. Routledge, London.

McMahon, H. and O'Neill, B. (1992) 'Computer-mediated zones of engagement of learning', in Designing Environments for Constructivist Learning. Springer Verlag.

Papert, S. (1980) Mindstorms: Children, Computers and Powerful Ideas. Harvester Press, Brighton.

Reinhardt A. (1995) 'New Ways to Learn', Byte, Vol. 20, No 3.

Reusser, K. (1993) 'Tutoring Systems and Pedagogical Theory: Representational Tools for Understanding, Planning, and Reflection in Problem Solving', in Lajoie, P. and Derry, S.J. (eds) Computers and Cognitive Tools. Lawrence Erlbaum Associates, Hillsdale, NJ.

Sewell, D.F. (1990) New Tools for New Minds - A Cognitive Perspective on the Use of Computers with Young Children. Harvester Wheatsheaf, Hemel Hempstead.

Siemer, J. and Angelides, M.C. (1998) 'Towards an Intelligent Tutoring Systems Architecture that supports Remedial Tutoring', AI Review, Vol. 12, No. 6.

Winkels R. (1992) Explorations in Intelligent Tutoring and Help, Frontiers in Artificial Intelligence and Applications Series. Amsterdam, IOS Press.

Wood, D. (1988) How Children Think and Learn - The Social Context of Cognitive Development. Blackwell, Oxford.

CHAPTER 68

THE MADNESS IN THE METHOD: A CRITIQUE OF OUR PEDAGOGY IN THE INFORMATION SYSTEMS FIELD

Brian Hopkins
Anglia Polytechnic University

Abstract

The paper starts from the assertion that in spite of considerable advances in computer hardware and in software development techniques over the years the levels of sophistication and of quality unquestionably achieved in those areas is sadly lacking in the finished products, namely the information systems (IS) delivered to the clients. It argues that one of the core reasons for this mismatch lies in the education and training of putative practitioners in the IS field where the emphasis is placed on techniques, methods and tools rather than on people as individuals, as groups and especially as full partners in the development process. The research draws on the experiences of the author as a practitioner, teacher and researcher, using discourse analysis techniques to draw out lessons and insights into our collective mindsets. It concludes with proposals for amendments to our curricula and pedagogy which, it is argued, can help to bring about more favourable reactions to our systems from our clients.

1. INTRODUCTION

The period since the 1970s in the UK has witnessed a succession of attempts within the IS/computing field, on the part of both practitioners and of academics to develop a set of tools and techniques which can be shown in practice to constitute a template for the analysis, design and implementation of IS which are likely to be "successful" - using the broadest possible interpretation of that elusive term.

Our search for that "holy grail" has been assiduous and has been sustained by the faith that its discovery is a real possibility, **if only we can discover the key to this particular puzzle**. In other words we do not truly consider the possibility that the search is in fact a futile exercise. So, the process continues with each novel approach being heralded (by its authors and supporters) as the long-awaited breakthrough.

Sadly, we do not appear to be any closer to finding our prize. The results of surveys and reviews published in the computing press and by consultants regularly record a disturbing level of dis-satisfaction on the part of the claimed beneficiaries of our information systems.

Paradoxically the same people (ostensibly) who complain in the surveys continue to insert advertisements in that same computing press seeking to recruit staff whose required background and experience seem to be dominated by technical prowess and proven facility in the use of specified methods, tools and techniques.

Also as a "logical" consequence of these demands the university sector accords similar priorities in its IS/computing courses arguing that (particularly in the post-1992 institutions) they have a responsibility to provide courses which prepare their graduates for careers in computing.

So, the vicious circle is complete; supposed beneficiaries are less than satisfied with the products of the universities (both people and the systems that they produce); nevertheless these same organisations demand more of the same - but "better"!; the universities, for a complex mix of reasons (which are investigated below) continue to try to meet those demands. The result is that little changes in our practice.

Yet, there **are** alternative, or at least complementary, visions and practices on offer. Over several years authors like Mumford (1979), Walsham (1993) and Introna (1997) in IS, J.C.Jones (1992) and Lawson (1990) in architecture, in the UK; Schon (1983) - in general professional practice - Greenbaum (1991) and Suchman (1987), Hirschheim and Klein (1989) and Winograd and Flores (1988) in IS, in the USA; Kyng, Ehn (1988) and others in Scandinavia have consistently argued the case for a more participative, creative, free-flowing and democratic approach to design in general (and in some cases for IS in particular). At the heart of their arguments lies an essentially pragmatic case built around a recognition that any proposals for change in these fields must, of necessity, carry economic justification. The cases have their foundations firmly set in action research and in practical experimentation where the ideas have been required to stand the tests of client satisfaction.

This brings us neatly around to the opening assertion in this paper, that the IS community too regularly fails this test. So we appear to be confronted by a paradox in which the IS practititioners persist with methods which too often generate unsatisfactory output systems even though there are tried and tested alternative approaches in their own and allied domains. The explanation is inevitably (at best) multi-faceted and hence to propose, even tentatively, any reasons or causes is to invite criticism - perhaps even dismissive scorn - and to provide an easy target for the advocates of the *status quo*.

Since the education of putative IS/computing practitioners must comprise one of the facets of the problem then a critique of our pedagogy is surely overdue. This paper considers and analyses the attitudes and mindsets of the university community in IS/computing as demonstrated through their publications, writings and documentation both external and internal. The technique employed is discourse analysis (DA) using especially the work of Potter and Wetherell (1994). This approach reviews analytically the words and phrases used, the pattern of contexts in which they are used and seeks to draw conclusions concerning the intention and impact of those words and phrases.

The paper first considers the extent of the focus within our curricula of tools, techniques and methods, ofering an explanation for their widespread inclusion. It continues with an assessment of the implications of this method-focused approach for the insights, perceptions and eventual practices of our graduates. There follows a set of proposals for a differently orientated curriculum together with projections of its likely outcomes.

2. THE PRIMACY OF METHOD

It is instructive to trace the paths by which the dominance of method in our pedagogy has been achieved, providing instances in support of this assertion as we develop the arguments.

As well as having philosophical roots in the Enlightenment tradition our teaching approaches in IS/computing owe much to the technical, engineering worldview based on unitary goals, unambiguous "rules" and testable outcomes which are encapsulated within the programming disciplines. The brief history of IS/computing has seen the elevation of programming and programmers to an elevated position in the professional hierarchy and in popular perceptions (not an irrelevance when one considers that this group includes many employers). So, the sets of skills which are indisputably relevant in this one - admittedly crucial - area of the discipline have become a form of benchmark for the more extended field which is IS in practice.

If we read through university prospectuses (which we can assume are intended to convey the flavour and image of the programes to the prospective student) for IS/computing we encounter repeated pointers supporting this stance; for example, phrases such as,

> *knowledge of formal techniques; use of mathematical ideas to develop concepts with useful applications; software systems need to be properly designed in much the same way that engineering structures need careful design; produce leading practitioners of computer software systems; learn methods for designing and implementing computer applications". (Hopkins, 1998)*

Although it can be argued that some of the above refer to courses in computer science and, say, software engineering where the rigorous rule-driven methods are essential, it is important to note that the same words and phrases also appear in the prospectuses for the more "business-orientated" IS/computing programmes. So, as well as reading about, for example, *human and managerial issues as well as technical ones; full understanding of the business context; understanding of the business context in which information systems are used; new breed of manager, combines business skills with expertise in IT; organisational politics; management of change and conflict (Hopkins,1998)*

we also come across (often on the same pages as the above) phrases like

up-to-date techniques and tools; the fundamentals of computing; a variety of architectures ... databases, client-server networks; techniques for implementing effective systems; industry standard methodologies; design and construction of quality software" (Hopkins, 1998)

This is a persistent, paradoxical pattern throughout the prospectuses reviewed. It indicates a reluctance to dispense with the traditional methods and thinking which are a legacy of the formative influences on our still-young profession. In addition within our university programmes we find amongst both student and staff groups fervent advocates of that same methods-rooted outlook. The latter are often from a programming background and see their methods as a legitimate transfer from that area into the wider area of systems analysis. The former welcome a set of rules and procedures which are clearly-defined and which they can "learn" and reproduce when required. Both groups are reassured by the conviction that through use of this methods-based approach there is a good chance that they will create an effective system.

Indeed, it is not only in the university prospectuses that we come across words and phrases transmitting these messages. It is instructive to note (at the level of a foundation topic within one of the business-orientated courses) that the learning objectives for a module entitled "Systems Development" make reference to the following expected emergent knowledge, understanding and abilities:

* *Review different approaches to systems development*
    * *Understand the need for engineering principles to be applied to the construction of software systems*
        * *Demonstrate an understanding of the skills required to investigate, analyse and design an information system and also some of the techniques used in systems development*
* *Account for and illustrate techniques for project control*
* *Describe and use in a basic fashion CASE tools for the aid of systems specification and design (Hopkins, 1998)*

This is followed by a module summary - which is used by the students to gain insights into the nature of the modules and to make choices - which states:

This module aims at giving the student a general overview of the approach to and methodologies used in systems analysis and design. In addition the

> *student will use a variety of techniques common to many methodologies (Hopkins, 1998)*

The vocabulary used conveys the impression upon the reader, that is, the undergraduate (and prospective practitioner), that this "enginering" process is founded on "technique" and "tools", the mastery of which is the key to success in this enterprise. It cannot escape our attention that **there is no reference made to any human intervention or participation**.

It has been interesting to observe, in the same study of our university prospectuses, that other disciplines (who are arguably in the same broad area of "design") adopt a somewhat freer, more flexible and more creative approach; for instance, in architecture, we read about

> *focus(ing) on ... the aesthetic and functional aspects of buildings ... distinguishing architecture from mere building; develop(ing) understanding of the design process to give the ability to evaluate the quality of ... buildings and townscapes; giving students an awareness of the many factors which influence how we use and relate to buildings; the ability ... to collaborate through the design process becomes very important; embraces disciplines from the physical and social sciences to the arts and humanities; students (being) encouraged to explore contemporary challenges in urban development (Hopkins, 1998)*

Here we find a much more extensive and inclusive view of what their purpose is, who is also involved in the process as well as how they should go about it. The words and phrases bring about a strong impression of a holistic process at the heart of the learning experience (and, by implication, at the centre of the practice of the discipline). It stands in contrast to the more limited, exclusive, rules-driven process implied in the IS/computing publicity.

The investigation reveals many more instances of this comparative narrowness on the part of IS/computing when set alongside other, arguably related, disciplines but there is insufficient space to develop this further. However, at this point it is probably useful to consider the role of the professional bodies in upholding the "methods" approach and to review briefly some of the thoughts of writers in the field who hold views at odds with the received wisdom.

The British Computer Society (BCS) is the professional body in the UK which represents the largest number of professional practitioners and also has the greatest influence on the shape and content of IS/computing curricula through its accreditation of courses in higher education institutions and through its own examinations. Therefore it should be instructive to apply DA to its public documents, especially those relating to the syllabus for its own examinations.

Before examining that it is probably also useful to reflect briefly on the mission, role and influence of professional bodies generally so that we can try to place the BCS stance in context. In spite of the reputation of the source, it is probably not too difficult to have some sympathy with George Bernard Shaw when he stated, in *The Doctor's Dilemma* that

> *"all professions are conspiracies against the laity" (Shaw, 1906)*

However, there are other sources, within the academic community, who have also had insightful commentaries on the professions in general. For instance in his book *The Sociology of the Professions* (1995) Keith M. Macdonald provides us with an analysis of the root motivations, the historical development and the processes of maintenance of position associated with a variety of professions as seen through his eyes and those of other observers. In the book he quotes Wilson (1933) who saw the professions as elements which

> *inherit, preserve and pass on a tradition ... they engender modes of life, habits of thought and standards of judgement which render them centres of resistance to crude forces which threaten steady and peaceful evolution" (Carr-Saunders and Wilson, 1933)*

It is apposite to note that, in the early 1970s - at a time when we in IS/computing were welcoming the "structured" approach to development of our systems - our colleagues in the social sciences were becoming increasingly critical of the functionalist orthodoxy upon which such thinking and practise was based. Here again, Macdonald quotes from several sources (Friedson, 1970; Murphy, 1984 and Larson, 1977) when he refers to a "professional project". This project investigated the assertions that professional independence stemmed from the power of the state; that its privileged position is gained initially through the influence of an elite group; that the cognitive and normative features of professions which are used to define them are typically prone to change but at the same time are used to draw boundaries of the professional domain and hence to determine membership; that establishment of a profession confers on its members a social prestige/status which in turn allows the profession to define social reality in the area in which its members operate and that the exclusivity derived from the above features enables members to claim a universal validity for their public pronouncements (in some cases, well beyond their particular domain).

Within the scope and aims of that project we can detect certain clearly-defined areas of investigation which are apposite to the themes of this paper. In the case of the BCS, we have a body which is striving to achieve the full status of a professional body in IS/computing and in doing so is defining "the cognitive and normative features" (see below) which it insists should be at the core of our professional practice. It is argued in this paper that, along with other parties - not least the academic community in IS/computing - the Society is attempting "to define social reality in the area in which its members operate". Therefore the BCS can be portrayed as a significant player in the process of defining the preferred approaches to be taken, in practice and through education and training, in the development of organisational IS.

A review of the syllabus content for the BCS confirms this analysis. It is a persistent feature of the public documents that they give prominence to the required knowledge and allied techniques but reduce the social and human to peripheral items (at best). For instance, the very sub-title which the Society has adopted is surely revealing of its ethos. "The Society of Information Systems Engineering" tells the reader a great deal about the underpinning worldview of the Society and hence its thinking and recommended practices. Although the sub-title undoubtedly owes much to the Society's links with the Institute of Electrical Engineers body, it is those very links which are themselves so revealing.

When we explore in more detail the BCS Examination Syllabus, (BCS,1997) we find both broad and detailed indications of the technique-orientated approaches described above; for example, in the introductory sections we read that

> *their knowledge should enable them to discuss technical matters with others who have specialised in different areas of computers from their own and to learn from such discussions (BCS, 1997)*

and that

> *it should also enable them to explain to a layman in simple language the problems, dangers, and difficulties inherent in the implementation of any computer system (BCS, 1997)*

The two quotations above, particularly the second, betray attitudes which are patronising, exclusive and misguided. It is especially noteworthy in the second quote that it is for the IS/computing specialist/professional to explain to the layman the "dangers and difficulties" involved in introducing computer systems. It seems likely that, after up to forty years of experiencing the impact of such systems, many of the "laymen" are only too well aware of these dangers and difficulties and, indeed, would be able to offer cogent advice in return, if only they were asked!

This set of attitudes is perhaps best summed up in another phrase from the introductory sections where it is stated that the syllabus concentrates on

> *... fundamental aspects which appear to have a lasting significance" (BCS, 1997)*

Here we witness a certain confidence - although the word "appear" provides an escape route - regarding the timelessness of the fundamentals of our discipline. This stands in contrast to a widely-held current view of the social world as a volatile and unpredictable brew of ingredients whose behaviour we do not fully understand and hence cannot foretell.

The combination and intertwined mutual influences of our major professional body and our university IS/computing departments are recognised (and they would claim as much themselves) as having significant formative impacts on the outlooks, attitudes and approaches taken by entrants to the community of practitioners of our discipline. When we add to this pairing the selection criteria used by their prospective employers when recruiting our graduates - a casual scrutiny of the job advertisements in the IS/computing press in any week is surely a celebration of the triumph of method - then we are confronted by a most powerful alliance appealing to the psychological and material aspirations of the intending practitioner.

Schon (1983) poses an apposite summative question on this matter:

> *How comes it that in the second half of the twentieth century we find in our universities, embedded not only in men's minds but in the institutions themselves, a dominant view of professional knowledge as the application of scientific theory and techniques to the instrumental problems of practice? (Schon, 1983)*

This core question is equally applicable in UK universities, would occasion similar embarassment or annoyance when posed here and still awaits a considered response. The persistent refusal to engage with the issue ensures the maintenance of the graduate attitudes described below and, as a consequence, the perpetuation of client dissatisfaction with their IS provision.

3. THE LEGACY OF METHOD

The worldviews of our graduates on entrance to the practitioner world are thus imbued with the positivist outlooks encouraged by the university curriculum which they have recently successfully completed, the mindsets of the teachers who were engaged in the delivery of the course (and, in many cases, in its design, structure and content) and the presence in the background (at least) of the BCS.

Clearly, the issue is far from being decided. The arguments continue between the advocates of the different pedagogies, but the *status quo* as represented by the instrumentalist, rationalist stance seems to be the dominant one, both in our courses (and their teachers) and in our professional institution. Attempts to alter these outlooks, or at least to challenge them intellectually and practically, often meet resistance or, on occasion, apathy and a refusal to engage with the issue (Hopkins, 1997).

The long-standing, almost endemic nature of this debate (and the fact that it is widespread throughout a range of intellectual and academic fields) has been described by Schon:

> *Even when practitioners, educators and researchers question the model of technical rationality, they are party to institutions that perpetuate it. (Schon, 1983)*

He has also pointed to the implications for design outcomes stemming from this stance.

> *From the perspective of Technical Rationality, professional practice is a process of problem solving. Problems of choice or decision are solved through the selection, from available means, of the one best suited to the established ends. But with this emphasis on problem solving, we ignore problem setting. (Schon, 1983))*

He expands on this important distinction in the following way:

> *Technical Rationality depends on agreement about ends. When ends are fixed and clear, then the decision to act can present itself as an instrumental problem. But when ends are confused and conflicting, there is as yet no 'problem' to solve. A conflict of ends cannot be resolved by the use of techniques derived from applied research. It is rather through the **non-technical** process of framing the problematic situation that we may organise and clarify both the ends to be achieved and the possible means of achieving them (Schon, 1983; emphasis added)*

Schon is making generalised points about the thinking and practices of professionals across the spectrum of such groups. He is drawing our attention to elemental dichotomies in thinking and practice which characterise and distinguish the professions from their predecessor groupings in, say, craft guilds, and indeed from some current philosophical trends within their midst, viz.

> *They are coming to recognise that although problem setting is a necessary condition for problem solving it is not itself a technical problem. (Schon, 1983)*

Observation, reading and listening all may be used , in their different ways, to inform ourselves of the legacy which our over-emphasis on method and technique has provided in both the thinking and the practice of IS/computing professionals. We have created, with the active connivance of the employers, a cadre of professionals who perceive the organisational information provision problems which confront them in terms of the selection of appropriate means to be employed , as opposed to the collaborative definition of ends and purposes matched to the requirements of their clients. We have encouraged a class of practitioners whose technical expertise is, in general, unquestionable but who see that achievement as a sufficient goal in itself; who take that stance further and argue forcefully, when clients complain about their information systems, that the fault lies with the clients themselves who do not properly understand the techniques and the technology and hence cannot effectively engage with them.

Further illuminating insights into the legacy in IS/computing of our emphasis on method and technique are provided by Introna (1997) who ,observes that:

A general uneasiness seems to prevail in many areas of the discipline. (Introna,1997)

He traces the growth of this unease through periods which he describes as the *"data processing era"* and the *"management information system era"*. He describes the traditional view of data being converted into "information" and the realisation/expectation that "managers" could use this as an important ingredient in their decision-making. He then states that:

This appears to be logical and fairly simple, but somehow things did not quite work that way; the enormous success of the data processing era has not been duplicated in the management information era. (Introna, 1997)

So, we can trace the formation of our present day legacy of method and technique from its philosophical roots in our Enlightenment traditions, through the ascendance of science and engineering, both conceptually and in practice, and match these developmental steps with the growth of IS/computing. In its early years (the 1960s and 1970s) our discipline achieved considerable deserved praise because of the efficiency and effectiveness with which we transferred the then existing largely manual data processing systems to computer-based equivalents. It was a period of rapid learning (through practical experimentation often involving mistakes) and of a "craft" approach to the work. In the second of those decades we witnessed the gradual acceptance of the validity of method and technique as the centrepiece of our project. This position may have been questioned since; it has never been reversed.

An approach which served us and our clients well in that "transaction processing" era has increasingly looked out of place in the "information provision" age for the very reasons that Schon has identified. It is ideal in circumstances where there is agreement about goals; it can be positively unhelpful in a situation where such agreement is not only absent but seems unlikely ever to appear.

Finally, Introna argues that:

the core of the problem is a lack of understanding of the assumptions that currently inform our concepts of the manager, information, management and power. (Introna, 1997)

The tools and techniques of that earlier period have become at least questionable as the driving force of our efforts to develop delivery systems which meet with the approval of managers. This is not to argue that we should dispense with them wholesale. It is to argue that they represent only a sub-set of the full range of approaches which we need to employ if we are to create genuinely supportive information systems in organisations.

4. BEYOND METHOD? TOWARDS A COMPLEMENTARY APPROACH

Although there is considerable criticism levelled at what is seen as an obsession with method it is also acknowledged that these approaches have been successful in aiding the development of computer-based IS **of a certain type**, namely those described as transaction processing.

Therefore it would be counter-productive if we were to argue that our university curricula in IS/computing should exclude consideration of technique and method. We should, surely, however be moving towards a course design stance where a method-based pedagogy is complemented by one which accords human and socio-organisational aspects at least equal weight.

At a deeper level than that we should also be injecting into our curricula more of the "artistry" referred to by Schon (1983), arguing as he does by implication, that the development of these skills and facilities is likely to prove much more fruitful for our graduates and their employers when together they confront the complex information provision problems characteristic of modern organisations.

Walsham (1993) states that " ... *the IS analyst, for example, has a role as an enactor of meaning and a moral agent in addition to that as a systems expert.*" and quotes Dunlop and Kling who assert that:

> *The dominant paradigms in academic computer science do not help technical professionals comprehend the social complexities of computerisation, since they focus on computability rather than usability ... Paradigms that focus on the nature of social interaction provide much better insights for designing computer systems in support of group work than does the computability paradigm. (Dunlop and Kling, 1991)*

So, arguably, we have a responsibility within our university IS/computing courses to engender and encourage that spirit of social sensitivity and awareness, to embed it along with the techniques and methods at the heart of our pedagogy. As Walsham concludes in his book:

> *... a positive future role for computer-based information systems in organisations and human society requires that large numbers of individuals do not accept the existing status quo without question, but instead strive to achieve full personal responsibility for their actions. The way to move in this direction may be to tread across a series of small stepping-stones rather than to leap great distances, but **the time to start is always now**. (Walsham, 1993; emphasis added)*

References

British Computer Society, (1997) *Examination Syllabus,* Swindon, UK.

Carr-Saunders, A.M. and Wilson, P.A., (1933) *The Professions*, The Clarendon Press, Oxford, UK.

Dunlop, C. and Kling, R., (eds), (1991) *Computerisation and Controversy*, Academic

Press, Boston, USA.

Ehn, P., (1988) *Work Oriented Design of Computer Artefacts*, Arbetlivscentrum, Stockholm, Sweden.

Friedson, E., (1970) *The Profession of Medecine*, Dodd, Mead and Co., New York, USA.

Greenbaum, J. and Kyng, M., (1991) *Design at Work:cooperative design of computer systems*, Lawrence Erlbaum Associates, New Jersey, USA.

Hirschheim, R. and Klein, H.K., (1989) "Four Paradigms of Information Systems development", Communications of the ACM, Vol. 32, No. 10, pp.1199-1216.

Hopkins, J.B., (1998) Unpublished papers from an ongoing doctoral project, Open University, UK.

Hopkins, J.B., (1997) *Twenty Five Years before the Class: a personal reflection on changing times in UK higher education*, unpublished paper from an ongoing doctoral project, Open University, UK.

Introna, L.D., (1997) *Management, Information and Power*, Macmillan, London, UK.

Jones, J.M., (1992) *Design Methods*, Van Nostrand Reinhold, New York, USA.

Larson, M.S., (1977) *The Rise of Professionalism: a Sociological Analysis*, University of California Press, London, UK.

Lawson, B., (1990) *How Designers Think: the design process demystified*, Butterworth Architecture, UK.

Macdonald, K.M., (1995) *The Sociology of the Professions*, Sage Publications, London, UK.

Mumford, E. and Weir, M., (1979) *Computer Systems in work Design: The ETHICS Method*, Wiley, New York, USA.

Murphy, R., (1984) 'The structure of closure: a critique and development of the theories of Weber, Collins and Parkin', British Journal of Sociology, Vol. 35, No.3, pp.547-567

Schon, D.A., (1983) *The Reflective Practitioner: How Professionals Think in Action*, Basic Books, USA.

Suchman, L.A., (1987) *Plans and Situated Actions: the problem of human-machine communication*, Cambridge University Press, Cambridge, UK.

Walsham, G., (1993) *Interpreting Information in Organisations*, John Wiley, Chichester, UK.

Winograd, T. and Flores, F., (1988) *Understanding Computers and Cognition:a New Foundation for Design*, Ablex Corporation, Norwood, N.J., USA.

CHAPTER 69

INFORMATION SYSTEMS WORK: PROFESSIONALISM AND PROFESSIONALISATION IN THE UK

Paul Beynon-Davies
University of Glamorgan

Abstract

In this paper we discuss the concept of professionalism and the process of professionalisation in the context of work in the information systems industry. Our intention is to examine some of the taken-for-granted assumptions about the professionalisation of information systems work, and provide a critique of this world-view. Our analysis is based on an examination of UK organisations and experience.

1   INTRODUCTION

On the 29th of October 1992 an information system (IS) of the UK National Health Service made the front story on the BBC's Nine-O-Clock news. It was claimed that a new computerised command and control system established at the headquarters of the London Ambulance Service (LAS) failed, and that as a direct result of this failure the lives of twenty people were lost (Beynon-Davies, 1995). A month or so later the British Computer Society (BCS) president and Vice President claimed that the breakdown in the LAS system could have been avoided if computer people were trained to professional standards. President Roger Johnson (Computer Weekly, 1992d) stated that:

> *The public are entitled to expect that the same professional disciplines apply in IT [Information Technology] as in other professions such as medicine and law.*

On the micro level, the clear implication of statements such as these is that the developers of the LAS system are seen as having acted in an unprofessional manner. This is echoed in a recent paper by Oz (1994) which characterises a large US IS failure in terms of professional mis-conduct. On the macro level, such statements reflect the idea that information systems failure is clearly identifiable with professionalism in information systems work. However, such statements also embody a whole range of assumptions underlying a particularly powerful perspective on modern-day information systems work. The assumptions centre around the idea of professionalism and professionalisation in information systems work.

In this paper we aim:

1. to make explicit some of these taken-for-granted assumptions, particularly by examining developments in the UK.

2. to provide a critique of this world-view by placing the debate in the context of a body of literature on the sociology of professionals.

2   WHAT IS A PROFESSION?

The ubiquity of modern information systems has caused a debate within the community involved in their development, management and deployment about the status of their work. In the UK, bodies like the British Computer Society (BCS) and the Institute of Electronic Engineers (IEE) have attempted to cast information systems work as a profession in much the same guise as lawyers, accountants, architects and the medical profession (Beynon-Davies, 1993).

Many occupational groups have sought professional status. However, there is little agreement about what constitutes a profession. Elliot (1972) discusses how the term *profession* is widely and imprecisely applied to a variety of occupations. The adjective *professional* is even more overworked, extending to cover the opposite of amateur and the opposite of poor work, two concepts which need not be synonymous.

Four models of professionalism seem significant in the sociological literature: trait models, functionalist models, power models, interpretivist models:

1. Trait Models. Trait models of professionalism present a list of attributes which are said to represent some common core of professional occupations. In this model the process of professionalisation is portrayed as a determinate sequence of events. An occupation is seen as passing through predictable stages of organisational change, the end-state of which is professionalism.

2. Functionalist Models. In functionalist models no attempt is made to provide an exhaustive list of attributes or traits. Instead the components of the model are made up of elements that have a functional relevance for society as a whole or to the professional-client relationship. In very general terms, the functionalist model proposes that professional groups contribute to the 'health' of society in providing expert services in crtical areas of human life.

3. Power Models. More recently, researchers have become interested in the process of professionalisation as power-play between occupational groups in their attempts to establish jurisdiction over expert work. The work of Abbot (1988) is representative of this approach.

4. Interpretivist Models. These models treat the concept of profession as a folk-concept

and the process of professionalism as a process of interpretation by human actors. Workers like Friedson (1983) have called for research on how people invoke the notion of professionalism and how they construct their notions of professionalism. The key question for this approach is how do certain occupational groups formulate their development in terms of professionalism.

2.1   A Trait Model

For the purpose of our initial analysis it is useful adopt one of these models and apply it to the area of information systems work. In the first half of this paper we utilise a trait model to highlight some of the key features of the professionalism debate in this area. In the second half of this paper we shall use elements of both power and interpretivist approaches to discuss some of the contemporary dynamics of professionalism in relation to IS work.

A trait model is constructed by collecting together some common features from occupational groups with a readily agreed professional status, e.g., law and medicine - this constitutes a preliminary trait model of a professional group. A feature analysis of such occupations leads to the development of the following 'ideal-type' (Jackson, 1970). A profession might be defined as a group of persons with:

1) an accredited corpus of specialist knowledge and skills
2) one or more formal bodies involved in organising the profession. In particular, the formal body will be involved in:
    a)   maintaining a code of conduct/practice and monitoring adherence to the code(s).
    b)   ensuring that only suitably 'qualified' persons enter the profession.
3) Some form of recognition of the professional status of members

2.2   An accredited corpus of specialist knowledge and skills

Classic trait analyses of professionalism maintain that to be a profession some agreement has to have been reached in the occupational group regarding the content of theoretical knowledge and practical expertise demanded of members of the profession.

A profession normally sees itself as having an essential underpinning of abstract principles which have been organised into some theory. Alongside the set of basic principles are various practical techniques for the recurrent application of at least certain of the fundamental principles. In this respect, Simon (1972) sees professions as denigrating knowledge that is 'intuitive, informal or cookbooky'. Murray (1991) describes the dominant ideology of professions as being one of technical rationality.

Abbot (1988) identifies three aspects of professional work which serves to define abstract knowledge: diagnosis, treatment and inference. These three aspects are seen as resources for asserting a profession's jurisdictional claims: claims to classify a problem, to reason about it, and to take action on it. A profession's formal knowledge system, embodied as a series of abstractions, serves as a means of legitimating professional practice in these areas. Abstract knowledge is also used as a means of generating new diagnoses, treatments and inference methods that can extend or support jurisdictional claims.

Derber et al (1990) cast professionals in the role of a new class which relies mainly on claims to knowledge rather than labour or capital as the basis for their quest for wealth and power. Such knowledge is credentialised, i.e., usually certified by some higher education institution. In this light, Jackson (1970) sees a definite link between the rise of the universities and the established professions such as law and medicine, particularly in the US. Abbot (1988), claims that in Europe (particularly in countries like France), the state has been more overt as a credentialising agency than educational institutions.

2.3   One or more formal bodies involved in organising the profession

Established professions such as medicine have long-standing bodies such as the British Medical Association (BMA) which organise professional activities for doctors within the UK. Such bodies maintain a code of conduct defining the limits of professional practice. The BMA also accredits recognised medical schools and ensures that only suitably qualified persons enter the medical profession.

Most professions build an ideology based around notions of professional behaviour. This usually includes aspects such as:

1. an orientation to the community interest
2. an internalised code of ethics
3. rewards based primarily in symbolic work achievement

In terms of professional ethics, Johnson (1985) suggests that professional codes of ethics address four types of obligations:

1. obligations to society
2. obligations to an employer
3. obligations to clients
4. obligations to colleagues and professional organisations

2.4   Some form of recognition of the professional status of members

Recognition is usually a critical aspect of professionalisation. Such recognition can take two forms: state recognition and public recognition. In the UK, Bott et al (1991) discusses state recognition as being embodied in the assignment of a royal charter to a collective body. This charter defines the extents of its authority and requires it to undertake certain duties and responsibilities.

A profession also needs public recognition, particularly from its potential customers or clients. Only with such recognition does the status of a profession act as a useful lever in the marketplace for occupational groups.

3   INFORMATION SYSTEMS WORK AS A PROFESSION

In this section we shall discuss whether information systems work in the UK constitutes a profession at the present time in terms of the trait model developed above.

3.1   Corpus of Knowledge and Skills

Oz (1994) maintains that while some people debate the label 'computer professional', particularly because of the variety of occupations encompassed by this broad term, software developers usually consider themselves professionals. In fact, he states that the responsibilities of the software developer may be more comprehensive, and hence require them to be more careful about their conduct, than other more traditional professions.

Using Abbot's (see section 2.2) compartmentalisation of professional knowledge:

1. Diagnosis in IS work probably refers to the claim made by IS professionals that they are the appropriate occupational group concerned with identifying information problems in organisations.
2. Treatment constitutes claims to being able to construct suitable technological solutions for such problems.
3. Inference denotes knowledge of the appropriate techniques and technology for matching information problems to information solutions.

However, perhaps resulting from the variety of occupations, there is little agreement concerning the corpus of knowledge and skills constituting information systems work. In the UK, a number of standards have been developed for IS work in the public sector, the most notable being the systems development methodology, SSADM (Skidmore et al, 1992), and the project management methodology, PRINCE (Bentley, 1992). The National Computing Centre runs certification programmes in systems analysis and project management centred around these approaches. Hence, in many ways, these approaches may be seen as attempts to systematise/rationalise the skills required of the IS practitioner. However, it is still not true to say that an information systems specialist has an agreed body of transferable knowledge and skills which he/she can take with him/her when moving between positions.

There is also a big question about whether purely technical knowledge is sufficient. For instance, Friedman and Kahn (1994) have discussed the importance of including material on social and ethical issues within standard computer science curricula. Also, institutions like the British Computer Society have become interested in broadening the skills expected of information systems engineers. The idea of a hybrid manager - a manager who combines information systems and business skills - has been much discussed (Palmer, 1990).

There is a related debate ongoing about training for skill or educating for knowledge in the IS area. Universities have traditionally seen themselves in the UK as imparting knowledge of IS technology, development and management. More recently, both private and public training organisations within the UK have emphasised the need for acquiring core skills or competencies in IS work. The rise of product-oriented training has been a particularly prominent example of skills-training in recent years. Many software producers now offer manufacturer-certified qualifications. Microsoft's MS Certified

Professional scheme is one notable example. Also resonant of this trend is the recent introduction of the National Vocational Qualification (NVQ) scheme. This scheme allows practitioners to be accredited 'on-the-job' with various levels of achievement in core competencies (Computing, 1995).

3.2   Formal Body
A number of bodies are competing to represent work within commercial computing in the UK. The main practical problem in turning information systems work into a profession is the fact that only a small proportion of persons involved in IS engineering activities appear to belong to bodies like the BCS. Informal estimates put it at something of the order of 20% of the IS engineering population (McMullen, 1996).

The BCS lays down a code of conduct and a code of practice. The code of conduct is concerned with questions of ethics; standards of behaviour. A member breaching these principles is said to be guilty of professional misconduct. The code of practice lays down, in very general terms, the way in which members shall approach the development of information systems. However, as Oz (1994) argues, although much of such a professional code of ethics is devoted to Johnson's set of obligations (section 2.2), in practice many contradictions and tensions exist between, for instance, obligations to clients, obligations to employers and indeed obligations to fellow colleagues in a software development project.

The BCS has a number of routes to membership: a person can apply for membership after a certain number of years experience in the field, a person can pass the BCS part 1 and part 2 examinations, or a person can pass a degree in computing at an accredited university. However, provision of formal routes of entry into a professional body must be cast against the perception that such membership has by potential entrants into the occupational group. A survey conducted by the IEE, for instance, found that the large majority of computer systems professionals are not members of any professional body and also beleive that the current institutional activities of such bodies are irrelevant to their needs (Elmore, 1996).

3.3   Recognition
The British Computer Society attained chartered status in 1984, and has therefore achieved an aspect of state recognition.

However, there is some debate about perhaps the more critical public recognition of bodies such as the BCS. For instance, during the highly public IS failure at the London ambulance service the BCS position does not seem to have been reported in the general press. Most of the statements made by the BCS were reported solely in the computing press (Beynon-Davies, 1994). In contrast, if a medical failure had occurred, it would have probably been unthinkable not to report the BMA's position.

The main arguments for professional status are that in a time of increasing disquiet over the quality of information systems, a body such as the BCS can guarantee persons able to build quality systems. This can quite clearly be seen as an attempt to promulgate an ideology of public service in information systems work. It is clearly one manifestation of the attempt to link issues of accountability with good practice in systems development (Nissenbaum, 1994).

3.4   Semi-Professions

Using a trait model, the key conclusion to be drawn is that IS work constitutes at most a semi-profession at the present time. Etzioni (1969) defines a semi-profession as being an occupational group in which 'their training is shorter, their status is less legitimated, their right to privileged communication less well established, there is less of a body of specialist knowledge, and they have less autonomy from supervision or societal control than *the* professions'. Teachers, nurses and social workers are given as three prime examples of the concept of a semi-profession.

4   THE PROCESS OF PROFESSIONALISATION

Many practitioners would probably agree that IS work constitutes at most a semi-profession at the present time. As evidence of this, frequent statements are made portraying the relative youth of computer-related work as compared to, for instance, work in medicine or the law. For instance, Gotterbarn (1996) states that, 'computing is at a stage in its development that engineering was at in the United States eighty years ago'.

Therefore, in this section, we examine the prospects for professional status in information systems work over the next decade. We conduct this analysis in terms of a number of positive and negative influences on the process of professionalisation.

In traditional accounts of professionalisation, the overall objective of most occupational groups aspiring to professional status is to claim a monopoly over occupational activities. This monopoly is normally justified in terms of ensuring quality of work and accountability. The monopoly is normally achieved by the professional body enforcing certain barriers to entry. Only those persons credentialised with professional knowledge and expertise are allowed entry into the profession.

However, Johnson provides a critique of the trait and functionalist models of professionalism. He maintains that a profession is neither an ideal-type nor an entity which functionally contributes to the well-being of society. A profession is not an occupation, it is a means of controlling an occupational grouping. Here, Johnson clearly presents an analysis of professions in terms of power relations in society. Professionalism is seen as a process of yielding power resources, such as the application of knowledge and skills, to further the interests of a given occupational grouping.

4.1   Professional Dynamics

Abbot's (1988) systems theory of professions provides a way of understanding the dynamics of professionalisation. He suggests that members of occupational groups formulate ideas of important tasks and of the expert knowledge needed to address these tasks. Each occupational group then competes with other groups in the same or similar domains of work for jurisdiction, or the legitimation of their view of both tasks and the expert work necessary to undertake them. Competition between occupational groups in one domain constitutes a system which achieves a temporary balance through what Abbot calls 'negotiated settlements', or temporary agreements on who does what in what territory. These temporary settlements are always subject to disturbance from factors both internal and external to the system of professions, resulting in jockeying for position until a new temporary settlement is reached. Typical disturbances result from technological change, organisational change, and the actions of legal or regulatory bodies.

Bradley (1995) provides an interesting analysis of information professions in US hospitals in terms of Abbot's framework. She illustrates how the disturbance of new external standards for hospital information management in the US are forcing groups like hospital librarians, information systems workers, and medical administrators to compete for jurisdiction of information management problems. A similar situation is described in Murray (1991) where competition is occurring between computing and accountancy professions over the lucrative market of business information systems.

4.2   Rapid Change

Murray's (1991) discussion of jurisdictional disputes between the 'profession' of the IS specialist and that of accountancy is founded in the recognition that these occupational groups hold ambiguous organisational and class positions; they each believe in the objectivity of their own techniques and practices and how these may be mobilised in the pursuit of occupational interests. Also, there is considerable overlap between the two specialisms as each struggles to expropriate the other's techniques and control of organisational resources. For example, the big five accountancy firms in the UK have moved into the lucrative management and IT consultancy business.

One could argue that there is a necessary dialectic between the rapid technological changes in the computer industry and changes in the division of labour associated with the IS sector. Such rapid change may act as a brake on the attempt to professionalise information systems work.

Abbot (1988), for instance, makes play of the way in which the commodification of knowledge can affect the ability of particular professional groups to maintain their position. He discusses how the very early computer coders who dominated the IS industry just after the second world war were effectively replaced by the introduction of compilers. Data entry clerks, and more latterly computer operators are two other occupational groups that have been subject to the process of commodification of knowledge.

It could be argued that this commodification of knowledge has continued within the industry up until the present day. It is evident, for instance, in the changes in the division of labour in IS work that has occurred as the technology has 'downsized' from large, centralised mainframes to distributed networks of personal computers.

Such technological and organisational changes have the potential to undermine the professional position of the IS specialist. On the one hand, a large amount of the corpus of knowledge and skills becomes diffused throughout the 'user' population. On the other hand the body of knowledge becomes either broadened in processes of hybridisation (section 3.1) or specialised in processes of market segmentation. This makes the maintenance of a unified and formalised career structure for information systems people an extremely difficult task.

4.3   Professional Development

As a practical step towards the goal of professional status, a formal scheme for professional development has been constructed by the BCS. This professional development scheme has also been adopted by many large organisations such as BP, British Gas, BT and ICI. The scheme is built on an industry structure model which defines some 40 roles in computing management, systems development, technical support, auditing and training. Each role can have a number of experience levels. At each experience level there is a description of the type of work done, the experience and skills expected and the training needed to prepare a person for the next level. A European Informatics Skills structure based upon this model is being positioned to support the mobility and transfer of IT skills in the single European market (Him, 1993). In this light, the BCS helped found the Council of European Informatics Societies (CEPIS), through which it gains access to the European Commission.

The main practical problem, at the time of writing, is that relatively few companies nationally are involved in the BCS professional development scheme. This makes it difficult for the body to enforce the PDS as an established career structure for information systems personnel.

4.4   Information Systems Work as Engineering

The BCS calls itself the Society of Information Systems Engineers. It is therefore not surprising to find that members of the BCS now have a route to chartered engineering status. The BCS became a chartered engineering institution in May 1990.

It is no accident that professionalism and chartered engineering status are married in the minds of a body such as the BCS. In many practitioner's minds the concept of engineering is equated with the application of scientific principles to the construction of artefacts such as buildings and bridges. For instance, Wright (1989) defines engineering as, 'the profession in which a knowledge of the mathematical and natural sciences gained by study, experience, and practice is applied with judgement to develop ways to utilise, economically, the material and forces of nature for the benefit of mankind.'

This straightforward characterisation of engineering as the application of science is one which has influenced much of the movement attempting to place information systems work on an engineering footing. This is clearly evident in the creation of the 'Hacker' as a negative role model for computing specialists. For instance, the DSDM Consortium (1994) characterise their atempt to develop a standardised methodology for Rapid Application Development (RAD) as a 'No Hackers Here' approach.

Shapiro argues that this equating of engineering with applied science is based on a naive understanding of the nature and history of engineering, and will ultimately serve to hinder rather than accelerate the professional development of software technologists. It is perhaps therefore not suprising to find that many in traditional engineering disciplines such as civil and structural engineering have long cast doubt over the purely scientific nature of the discipline. Petrowski (1985), for instance, provides the following definition of structural engineering: 'Structural engineering is the science and art of designing and making, with economy and elegance, buildings, bridges, frameworks, and other similar structures so that they can safely resist the forces to which they may be subjected.'

The important part of this definition is that structural engineering is seen to be as much art as science. Elegance of design is given equal footing with economy of design. The principles of aesthetics are at least as important as the principles of mechanics.

However, perhaps the most important reason that information systems work has been portrayed as engineering is that it is inherently bound up with the attempt to place the information systems specialist on a professional footing. What is interesting is that although information systems work has used engineering as a professional status symbol, there may be problems embodied in the professionalisation of engineering disciplines. For instance, Larson (1977) has cast doubt on the position of engineering as a profession. She makes a useful contrast with medicine. Unlike medicine:

1. engineering is not, and never has been a homogeneous area.
2. the physical nature of the engineer's product immediately involves the possibility that the buyer can be a different person from the consumer.
3. the engineer's marketplace is subordinated, ie, the services of an engineer are more likely to be mediated by organised clienteles than in a profession such as medicine which provides intangible services.

All of these characteristics make it difficult for engineers to maximise their effectiveness as a professional. The engineer is usually dependent on knowledgeable and powerful clients. The nature of an engineer's product implies that the public can obtain more direct evidence of a professionals capacity. This also makes it easier for the state to intervene and regulate an engineer's authority.

5   CONCLUSION

An analysis of established professions gives us the following key features as defining an ideal-type of profession: an agreed corpus of knowledge and skills; a collective body; public and state recognition.

Assessing Information systems work against each of these features leads us to conclude that at present it is at most a semi-profession. IS work has many of the trappings of a profession such as formal bodies and some degree of recognition. However, the formal bodies presently suffer from low membership and diffuse practitioner perception. Also, although bodies such as the BCS have achieved a degree of state recognition the recognition on the part of the general public is still problematic.

Information systems work as an occupation is clearly seeking full professional status. In Abbot's terms it is attempting to increase its occupational jurisdiction by various means. For instance, statements made by many in the aspiring professional bodies emphasise some of the classic elements of professional ideology. However, a number of positive and negative forces are likely to influence the process of professionalisation in this occupational area over the next decade.

On the positive side, collective bodies are attempting to strengthen their institutional position in the marketplace. The PDS and CENG initiatives in the BCS are clear examples of this. There is also clear evidence that IS people are achieving a certain degree of success in terms of increasing their jurisdiction over areas previously occupied by other professional groups. The area of information management is one notable example; the area of Business Process Re-engineering is probably another.

On the negative side, rapidly changing technology has meant a shifting base of knowledge and skills in the IS industry. The division of labour within the industry is less than clear cut, being subject to hybridisation on the one hand and specialisation on the other. Information systems engineering is also subject to the classic low power position of engineers compared to other occupational groups.

References

Abbot A. (1988). The System of Professions: an essay on the division of expert labour. The University of Chicago Press, London.

Bentley C. (1992). Introducing PRINCE: The Structured Project Management Method. NCC Blackwell, Oxford.

Beynon-Davies P. (1993). Information Systems Development: an introduction to information systems engineering. Second Edition. MacMillan.

Beynon-Davies, P. (1995). Information Systems Failure: the case of the London Ambulance Service Computer Aided Desptach Project. European Journal of Information Systems.

Bott F., Coleman A., Eaton J., Rowland D. (1991). Professional Issues in Software Engineering. Pitman, London.

Bradley J. (1995). Changing Dynamics of Information Management in Hospitals in the United States. Proc. of International Symposium on Health Information Management Research. Sheffield.

Computer Weekly. (1992). BCS President blames training for 999 failure. 19th Nov. 1992.

Computing (1995). Join the NV Queue. 25th May.

DSDM Consortium (1994). Dynamic Systems Development Methodology Overview. Ashford. Kent.

Earl M.J. (1989). Management Strategies for Information Technology. Oxford University Press, Oxford.

Elliot P. The Sociology of the Professions. Macmillan, London. 1972.

Elmore F. (1996). The Computer Systems Professionals Initiative. Professional Awareness in Software Engineering Conference. London.

Etzioni A. The Semi-Professions and their organisation: teachers, nurses and social workers. Free Press, New York. 1969.

Friedman B. and Kahn P. (1994). Educating Computer Scientists: Linking the Social and the Technical. Comm. of the ACM. 37(1). January. 65-70.

Friedson E. (1983). The Theory of the Professions: state of the art. In Dingwall R. and Lewis P (Eds). The Sociology of the Professions: Lawyers, Doctors and Others. Macmillan, London.

Gotterbarn D. (1996). Software Engineering: a new professionalism. Professional Awareness in Software Engineering Conference. London.

Him D. (1993). Professional Development Initiatives. Computer Bulletin. 5(2). April. pp 24-25.

Jackson J.A. (Ed.). (1970). Professions and Professionalisation. Cambridge University Press, Cambridge.

Johnson D. (1985). Computer Ethics. Prentice-Hall. Englewood-Cliff, NJ.

Johnson T.J. (1982). Professions and Power. Macmillan, London.

Larson M.S. (1977). The Rise of Professionalism: A Sociological Analysis. Univ. of California Press. Berkeley, Calif.

McMullen G. (1996). BCS and Professionalism. Professional Awareness in Software Engineering Conference. London.

Murray F. (1991). Technical Rationality and the IS Specialist: Power, discourse and identity. Critical Perspectives on Accounting. 2 (59-81). 1991.

Nissenbaum H. (1994). Computing and Accountability. CACM. 37(1). 73 - 80.

Oz E. (1994). When Professional Standards are Lax: the Confirm failure and its lessons. CACM. 37(10). 29-36.

Palmer C. (1990). Hybrids - A Growing Initiative. The Computer Bulletin. 2(6). August.

Petrowski H. (1985). To Engineer is Human: The role of failure in successful design. Macmillan, London.

Shapiro S. (1996) Getting Real: escaping the mythology that plagues software technology. Professional Awareness in Software Engineering Conference. London.

Simon H. The Sciences of the Artificial. MIT Press, Cambridge, Mass.

Skidmore S., Farmer R., Mills G. SSADM Version 4 Models and Methods. NCC Blackwell, Manchester. 1992.

Wright P. (1989). Introduction to Engineering. John Wiley, New York.

CHAPTER 70

BEYOND THE 'PRODUCTIVITY PARADOX': TEACHING THE NEXT GENERATION

Dave Chaffey and Simon Hickie
University of Derby

Abstract

The 'productivity paradox' suggests there is no clear correlation between the investment in information systems and the financial success of an organisation. Furthermore, the experience of many organisations when introducing new information systems (IS) is that it is extremely difficult to deliver a system which meets the needs of the business and is delivered on time and within budget. As a result of these problems with IS implementations there is a widely held perception that IS are "a necessary evil" which are difficult to manage effectively. Given these problems, and this perception of IS, there is a need within IS education to address these difficulties by acknowledging that these problems exist and then to identify approaches which can be taken by managers to reduce the risk of these problems occurring. This paper describes a learning approach which is based on identifying problems that exist in the use and management of IS and then recommending suitable methods of avoiding these problems. The approach is applied to different aspects of studying IS which are part of a typical degree course in business information systems or a more general business or management degree. A framework is suggested of the key problems that may occur in information management, IS development and information systems strategy definition. It is shown how different learning techniques based on solving these problems can be introduced that provide relevant training in how students can confront these problems in industry. With such applied training and knowledge, it should be possible to maintain the increase in the proportion of IS development projects which complete successfully and confine the productivity paradox to the 20th century.

1   INTRODUCTION

Writing in the Economist of June 16th 1990, John Browning stated that *Information Technology is no longer a business resource; it has become the business environment.* Through the 1990s and into the millenium the truth of this statement has been supported by the ever increasing expenditure on the information technology (IT) which is used to build information systems (IS) – in 1998, the Financial Times reported that annual expenditure would soon top $2000 billion worldwide.

Despite the increasing expenditure on IS, surveys show that the potential of IS are often not delivered, due to problems in the management, analysis, design or implementation of systems. Additionally, industry often complains of a shortage of the right type of skills to solve these problems.

The forthcoming millenium offers a suitable time to reflect on the effectiveness of current information systems teaching practice and suggest appropriate improvements. This paper sets out one approach of how IS education can be delivered to fulfill the requirements of industry.

A recent survey completed by NOP on behalf of Microsoft, in association with the CSSA and ITITO,ITNTO between September and December 1997 suggests two basic problems of managing IS which can be partly attributed to IS teaching at all levels:

1. There is a widely held perception that there is an information systems skills shortage (73% of managers in the IS industry believed there to be an IT skills shortage).

2. There is a mismatch between the skills taught and those required by industry.

The main cause of the skills shortage is the ever increasing demand for IT skills which is evidenced by the year on year growth in adverts for technical staff (for example in the SSP/Computer Weekly Quarterly Survey of Appointments Data and Trends, 130,000 jobs were available in the first half of 1998. This is 20,000 more than advertised in the whole of 1992 and 1993 together). This demand for skills does not, however seem to be satisfied from the supply of newly trained potential employees emerging from the educational system.

It is not the intention for this paper to explore the reasons for the skills shortage or the perceptions about IS in detail, rather it is to explore ways in which teaching and learning strategies can be modified to increase relevance to the workplace and accommodate the perceptions of participants which is in keeping with their pre-conceptions.

The modification to existing methods of teaching which is suggested, is to start from a more realistic portrayal of the problems that will be faced in the work environment. Perhaps, the most natural approach for an information systems lecturer to use is a positive "benefits based approach". In this, the well rehearsed benefits of information systems are explained as a method of reducing costs while giving improved capabilities and communications within a company (e.g. Senn(1995). Information systems development is then explained as the series of stages form analysis through design and implementation which need to be followed to deliver these benefits.

This paper describes a pragmatic alternative to the benefits based approach which starts from the premise that information systems often fail to deliver on their promise, suggesting that we need to understand the reason they have failed in order to use them more effectively in the future. In this approach, information systems courses will naturally continue to consider the positive benefits information systems can bring, but will also note the frequency with which these benefits are not delivered. This then leads to a study of the problems and a review of how the problems could be avoided, or their risk minimised.

This approach will show that the problem of IS management is not solely a technical problem, but will also involve issues in managing the human resources of an organisation. By demonstrating that information systems management requires knowledge of managing organisational change and human resources, this may also have the benefit of broadening the appeal of the study of the subject.

1.1   Structure
We start by briefly considering the productivity paradox and its relevance to teaching and then look at approaches to teaching three different aspects of information systems:
1. Information management and information technology.
2. The systems development lifecycle.
3. Information systems strategy.

These three different aspects of information systems are broadly equivalent to introductory material through to more advanced study on the second and third years of a degree course. The scope of this paper is focused on the teaching of undergraduate and postgraduate business information systems courses in schools of business, management and computing. It is not the intention to consider the teaching provision of software development skills, rather we will focus on the skills necessary to use and manage information systems effectively.

A general framework will be then developed which gives examples of problems and recommended solutions across the different aspects of study. Within each of these areas we will look at the details of the problems and the approach which can be adopted.

2   THE PRODUCTIVITY PARADOX

Studies in the 1980s and 1990s summarised by Strassman(1990,1977) suggest that there is little or no correlation between a company's investment in information systems and its business performance measured in terms of profitability or stock returns. A study of 468 major North American and European firms showed a random relationship between IT spending per employee and return on equity. This relationship is often referred to as the *productivity paradox*. Brynjolfsson and Hitt(1996) argue that the paradox may exist for a number of reasons including:
- mismanagement of projects

- mismeasurement
- lags occurring between the initial investment and payback

Note that Brynjolfsson and Hitt(1996) dispute the findings of Strassman and have completed their own surveys taking these factors into account and they conclude that expenditure on computer capital and IS staff do contribute significantly to total company output. However, their view is probably a minority one and there is much anecdotal and survey evidence of new systems failing to deliver.

It has also been argued by Malhotra(1997) that the increasing awareness of the productivity paradox amongst senior managers and management consultants has been responsible for the increasing interest in promoting knowledge management and organisational learning as described by Davis and Borkin(1994) and Sveiby(1997). Knowledge management places the emphasis on applying information technology to support sharing of knowledge between staff. It is suggested that in the past the focus has been too centred on technical solutions which undervalue the skills and contributions of staff. When developing organisational learning and metrics programmes (Davenport,1994) IS can be used to support business improvement in a way which is likely to give rise to improved performance performance.

2.1   Failure of project management?

In addition to the problem of systems failing to deliver the anticipated benefits, it has also proved very difficult to successfully complete the development of many information systems. Hammer and Champy, who originally invoked large scale redesign of processes using IS as a "change lever" (Hammer and Champy, 1993) now record that over 80% of business process reengineering projects fail, often due to mismanagement of the change process involved with introducing new IS. A recent extensive study reported by Bicknell(1998), has confirmed the parlous state of systems development projects. The US consultancy group Standish has analysed 23,000 projects completed in 1997 and 1998 of a range of sizes and found that:

- 28% failed to complete
- 46% were "challenged" by cost and/or time overruns
- 26% completed within the constraints of cost/time and delivering the anticipated benefits.

This clearly indicates a serious problem which is supported by other studies in the UK and Europe. On a more positive note it can be pointed out that this was an improvement on when the survey was completed in 1996 when failures ran at 40%. This indicates that the situation can be improved when projects are managed competently

3   WHAT DOES THIS IMPLY FOR TEACHING?

Given the productivity paradox and the failure rate recorded for IS development projects, an alternative to a benefits based approach to conducting teaching may be more appropriate to equip students and managers with the skills needed to successfully introduce information systems into their organisations. The approach we have adopted starts by briefly reviewing the benefits provided by information systems, but then noting some of the problems referred to above and demonstrating that the best method of avoiding the problems is to identify them in advance, understand the reasons why they occur and then take preventative action to reduce the likelihood of them happening. This is of course similar to the approach used in risk management during software development and this idea can be developed in more advanced courses in systems analysis and design.

To help emphasise the problem solving approach, a framework is presented to students which identifies the most significant problems and then reviews the solutions required to overcome these problems (Table 1). This framework can be introduced in introductory modules on information management and then revisited in more advanced courses on systems analysis and information systems management. Some learning outcomes of modules can also be related to the skills needed to manage the problems of information systems management.

To reinforce the idea of the problem-based approach students are asked to list the five worst problems they have faced in using information systems and managing information. The common problems are identified by pooling answers and then study turns to identifying what actions are necessary to reduce the likelihood of these problems occurring. This type of exercise can be used to identify the type of problems and solutions listed in Table 1. Of course, this exercise works particularly well with mature students who have direct experience of the problems of using and managing information systems. However, the majority of students have been exposed to using PCs and productivity applications and are familiar with the problems of information loss and poor information quality.

The suggested approach cannot be considered as radical, indeed many will incorporate aspects of such an approach into their teaching. What we are suggesting is a significant change in the emphasis of information systems teaching. The emphasis is placed on the difficulties that will occur in the development and use of information systems if they are not managed adequately.

4   APPLYING THE PROBLEM SOLVING APPROACH

In this section we review some examples of how the problem solving approach can be applied to different topics of IS management.

	Introduction to information systems	Systems Analysis and Design (Year 2)	IS strategy and management (Year 3)
Level of study	Introduction to information systems	Systems Analysis and Design (Year 2)	IS strategy and management (Year 3)
Main problem	1. Poor information quality. 2. Loss or failure of appropriate information in systems. 3. Selecting the appropriate computer, software and network. 4. Insufficient practical skills	1. Project overruns 2. User's requirements not met 3. Poor design 4. Failure of implementation of IS	1. Choosing the best structure for management of IS 2. Determining investment levels in an organisation. How to select new technology? 3. Approaches to strategy formulation of systems 4. Managing end-user development of systems
Sub-problems	1. Refer to different aspects of information quality such as: 1. Timeliness 2. Content 3. Form (presentation)(less important). (Is it delivered rapidly? Is it up-to-date?) (Is it accurate? Is it relevant?). 2. Information loss through deliberate or accidental loss, purchasing policy leading to incompatibility and higher price. Network or performance problems. 3. Computers that are over specified for the tasks the users needs to perform. Inadequate resources. "Requirements creep". Theft or destruction problems.	Poor estimation of number of tasks (tasks missing). Poor estimation of length of tasks. Features missing. Problems in ease of use. Data redundancy and database performance problems. Difficulties in updating systems. Problems in ease of use once system live. Errors during testing and company adopt ...	What balance between centralisation and decentralisation of information systems? Should these technologies be adopted: intranet, extranet, data warehouses, business intelligence software, enterprise resource planning. Should companies outsource different IS functions?. The productivity paradox. What is the value of IS strategy and business strategy. Relation to business process produced. Unnecessary development of systems. Poor quality of systems. Difficulty of maintaining systems. Top-down or bottom-up approaches. Unsatisfactory quality of service from IS infrastructure.
Solutions	Communication and infrastructure. Backup and restore. Access guidelines which diminish problems not solely referred to while maintaining flexibility of systems. Establishing procurement guidelines of business software e.g. – project management; spreadsheets and databases, planning, monitoring and management. Risk management techniques. Disaster recovery on choice of groupware, workflow and management systems. Validation, data audits, business continuity planning. Analysis of information flows and information effectiveness in an organisation.	Training in use. Detailed study of capturing requirements, design and then normalisation, defining them. Skills in capturing requirements, design and then normalisation from test to live system. Study of diagrammatically through IFD, DFD, process charts and ERD. Benefits design. HCI design. Database design and merits of different approaches from test to live system. Study of object-oriented details of testing techniques. Introduction to Use of standard methodologies (e.g. SS/ADM), or prototyping to avoid "re-inventing the wheel" with (e.g. RAD and DSDM) and object-oriented. Review of alternative acquisition methods from "off-the-shelf" to bespoke. Finding information on the Internet.	Study of merits of different location centralisation from test to live. Study of decentralisation? Review of early adopters and Griffiths (1996) "wait and see" approach to new) IS help-desk. Knowledge of service quality of measurement techniques (metrics) used to assess business and system performance. Evaluation of merits of evaluating cost/benefit and strategy return on investment. Analysis of advantages and disadvantages of outsourcing. Impact versus alignment of IS strategy and business strategy. How to select new technology? Methods for evaluating of classic evaluation at strategy initiation. Models described by Robson (1997) and Ward. Measuring quality of service levels. Application Review and evaluation at initiation. Providing training, guidelines and support. Difficulty of redesign process. Approaches to strategy formulation of systems.

Table 1: A framework relating problems encountered in information systems management to possible solutions

4.1   Introductory topics in information systems

Problems 1 through 4 in Table 1 are key topics in introductory modules on information technology or information management. In these modules, the change in emphasis in teaching is articulated by explaining that in the study of "information technology" the stress is often placed by vendors of systems (and even teachers) on the *technology* rather than the *information.* To the business user or manager, however, it is the quality of *information* that is vital to the company and the service it delivers to its customers. It follows that the content of the course should not concentrate on technology to the detriment of issues of information management.

Similarly, initial emphasis should be placed on the applications and functions of the *software* since this is what will deliver the business benefits. Hardware can then be specified as appropriate to use the software effectively. This is different from the natural inclination to concentrate on the features of the hardware and then specify the software.

A minimum technology coverage is, of course, necessary to provide the student with the skills to communicate with suppliers of systems and appreciate the advantages and disadvantages of different technical solutions. For example, the benefits and disadvantages of optical and magnetic storage could be evaluated. It is suggested, therefore, that it is useful to review the balance between coverage of technical and practical issues in existing programmes. The balance should be set according to the main target audience on the course – whether training general business managers or IS professionals who will require a higher technical content.

4.2   Topics in building IS/systems analysis and design

When studying the acquisition and development of IS we place the emphasis on the need for effective project management to prevent problems occurring. We start by considering famous examples of project failures (Collins and Bicknell, 1977 provide many UK based examples) and surveys of overall project success rates. We then go on to consider how risk management techniques can be applied to IS development projects.

4.2.1   Risk management

Risk assessment is used at the start of a project to determine the level of risk and develop plans for reducing this risk. Risk assessment for software projects has been described in detail by Boehm(1991). For students, risk management can be simplified to include the following stages:

- Identify risks including their probabilities and impacts.
- Identify possible solutions to these risks.
- Implement the solutions targeting the highest impact, most likely risks.

It is apparent that such an approach can be also applied when conducting feasibility assessments to anticipate problems with the introduction of new systems. Risk assessment can and should be used to consider the type of problems that occur throughout the systems development lifecycle. Risk assessment can also be applied to strategic decisions involving the development of a strategy to manage existing information assets within a company. For example, in an information systems strategy module we will ask delegates or students to list likely problems in outsourcing different IS functions and then ask them to identify solutions or counter-measures that can be put in place in a contract or service level agreement to reduce the likelihood of these problems occurring.

A useful framework of risks for students to consider is provided by Ward and Griffiths(1997) who identify project size, complexity, novelty, requirements stability and people issues as key risk factors.

4.2.2   Assessments using group problem solving for systems analysis

A problem solving approach can be used to provide experiential learning related to a real-world problem solving environment such as a team of consultants working with a customer to develop the requirements specification for a new system. The students are given the task of acting as consultants to a company. They must understand the needs of the customer and summarise them as a requirements specification. In a case study, students are asked to define a decision support system for a car manufacturer or estate agency who are wanting to evaluate the performance of their branch network across a country. The lecturer plays the role of the customer through answering questions from the perspective of several different people in the organisation such as the sales manager, a representative of branch staff and the IS manager. The analysis exercise can be conducted by the students asking questions face-to-face in a tutorial session or we have also used computer based conferencing where the students work in teams. Collaborative learning is a useful technique for assessment since it helps in developing a range of vocational team working skills – improving social interaction, problem solving and decision making (Alavi, 1994).

4.3   IS strategy topics

Some of the key strategic problems which need to be addressed by directors and IS managers are summarised in Part 4 of Table 1. An example of these is the way in IS services are structured within an organisation. This can include exercises on the merits of centralisation and decentralisation or outsourcing. Case studies provide a valuable tool to give the students an appreciation of the strategic decision making required to decide on the optimum arrangement. Such case studies, which often need to be fictitious examples developed to highlight the issues can be used for both coursework and examination assessments.

A further problem which is faced by managers in industry is the rate of introduction of new hardware and software which may mean that old systems may become obsolete. The frequency of use of the term 'legacy system' bears testimony to this. In a strategy module, techniques for dealing with change form a useful problem based subject for discussion. It is explained to the students that there are two main strategic alternatives for a company adopting new technology. The first is to be an early adopter who always tries to be the first to make use of new technologies to gain a competitive advantage. The second is to use a more conservative "wait and see" approach and not use new software until its use has been successfully demonstrated by other companies in your sector.

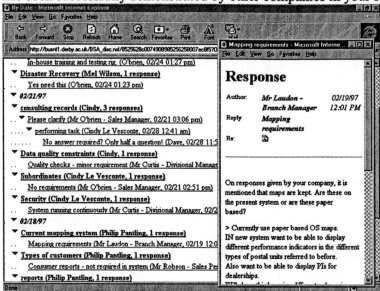

Figure 1: Computer conferencing of requirements capture using Lotus Notes

To illustrate the difficulties in deciding to adopt new technologies, we use debating exercises where teams of students argue for or against propositions such as: *"Despite the hype, the Network PC will remain a rarely used computing platform due to its inherent disadvantages"* and *"Data warehouses do not confer any additional benefits over existing decision support systems and executive information systems that have been used previously"*. These debates are valuable since the students must research the Internet and trade papers to understand the technology in question, assess its advantages and disadvantages and then argue for the position they have adopted. This process mirrors that which would be required by any business manager deciding on a new system. Such an assessment is also popular with students since it has a clear business application and its possesses a different format from many other assessments.

As a conclusion to the strategy module, future technologies or management trends are considered such as those highlighted in the final chapter of Chaffey et.al.(1999) which could solve some of the information systems management problems highlighted throughout the course. Such approaches may include:

- the use of enterprise resource planning (ERP) systems to integrate the information needs across and organisation and reduce the difficulties of dealing with multiple suppliers.

- adoption of object-oriented techniques which promote re-use and can potentially reduce project durations while improving software reliability
- purchase of off-the-shelf rather than bespoke development of packages which will enable sharing of the cost of ownership with other companies
- the introduction of data warehouses to manage and analyse information from across an organisation
- the use of intranets, groupware and workflow systems to assist in information sharing and collaboration within an organisation (Chaffey, 1998) and their relationship to organisational learning and knowledge management

When considering these approaches the students will become aware of the common features which many of these solutions share.

5 SUMMARY

The main elements of the approach we have adopted to learning, presented here as a series of guidelines for discussion ,which we hope will support us into the millenium are:
1. Acknowledge that from the outset that significant problems exist in the use and management of IS, which if solved can lead to clear business benefits when deploying information systems.
2. Structure teaching in modules around the problems that exist in each area of information systems management and base the learning outcomes around the solutions to these problems.
3. One approach to structuring the study of these problems is:
- information management problems (quality and loss of information)
- project management and systems analysis, design and implementation problems that arise when developing new information systems
- information systems management strategy problems such as dealing with change and how to structure information system services in a company.
4. Solutions should acknowledge the following:
- the role of the IS function to protect and yet make accessible the information resources of an organisation
- the importance of managing human issues, particularly when new systems are introduced
- the need to integrate technologies such as data warehousing and enterprise resource planning across an organisation
- the caution that should be adopted when evaluating and procuring new systems or using new management approaches which will require a significant investment in IS
- the requirement for building flexible systems which can be adapted to the dynamic business environment in which new management approaches will be required.

5. "Hands-on skills" in using productivity applications will be augmented by skills in using business applications such as decision support software, groupware and workflow software and accounting systems.
6. Assessment should be based around practical decision making exercises often centred on case studies and group work which test how the student can respond to the problems they may face when using or managing information systems in the "real-world".

References

Alavi, M. 1994. Computer-Mediated Collaborative Learning: An Empirical Evaluation. *MIS Quarterly,* 18, 2, 159–174.

Browning, J. (1990) Special report on Information Technology. June 17th 1990

Bicknell, D. (1998) Clark Kents hold keys to project success. *Computer Weekly* 9th July,

Brynjolfsson E and Hitt L. (1996) Paradox lost? Firm-level evidence on the returns to information systems spending. *Management Science.* 42/4

Boehm, B. (1991) Software Risk Management: Principles and Practices, *IEEE Software,* Vol. 8, No. 1, January 1991, pp. 32-41.

Chaffey, D. (1998) Groupware, workflow and intranets – Reengineering the enterprise with collaborative software. Digital Press.

Chaffey, D., Bocij, P., Greasley, A. and Hickie, S. (1999) Business Information Systems: Technology, development and management. FT Management, London.

Collins, T. and Bicknell, D. 1997. *Crash.* Simon and Schuster.

Davis, S., Borkin, J. (1994) The coming of knowledge-based business. Harvard Business Review. Sep-Oct 94 (72/5):

Davenport, T.H. (1993) Process Innovation:Re-engineering work through Information Technology. Harvard Business School Press, Boston.

Hammer, M. and Champy, J. (1993) Re-engineering the corporation: A manifesto for business revolution. Harper Collins, New York.

Inmon, W.H. (1996) *Building the Data Warehouse.* Wiley.

Malhotra, M. 1998. Deciphering the Knowledge Management Hype *The Journal for Quality & Participation* (July/August)

Robson, W. (1996) Managing Management and Information Systems. Pitman Publishing.

Senn J., (1995) *Information technology in business principles, practices, and opportunities,* Prentice-Hall International, Englewood Cliffs, N.J.

Strassman, P. (1990) *The business value of the computer* Information Economics Press. New Canaan, Conn

Strassman, P. (1997) *The Squandered Computer.* Information Economics Press. New Canaan, Conn.

Ward, J. and Griffiths, P.M. (1996) *Strategic Planning for Information Systems.* Wiley.

Karl Erik Sveiby, K.E. (1997) The New Organizational Wealth: Managing and Measuring Knowledge-Based Assets. Berrett-Koehler

CHAPTER 71

WHAT ARE THEY GOING TO DO NOW?

Martyn Clark and Tony Jenkins
University of Leeds

Abstract

This paper is concerned with the attitudes of newly enrolled IS undergraduates at the University of Leeds. In separate exercises the students were asked about the job market for IS professionals and the types of learning objectives which were most important to their personal agenda. The results show that the students questioned have a good understanding of levels of pay and remuneration in the job market but have little real understanding of the work undertaken by IS professionals. Misunderstanding the nature of IS work, the students expect to become programmers and, consequently, identify the development of programming skills as the most important learning objectives. The development of personal skills is also important but, programming apart, the students do not consider the learning objectives of the course important. These findings are consistent with the theory that as access to Higher Education is widened and as they encounter increasing financial pressures, students are adopting a strategic approach to studying: an approach which focuses on getting the highest mark possible and is not concerned with interest and understanding.

1. INTRODUCTION

As the numbers entering higher education have increased in recent years more attention has focused on issues of learning and teaching. When the intake was restricted to the five or six per cent of each cohort who excelled at A level and assessment in HE was based on similar types of examination, students could, generally, be relied upon to be sufficiently motivated and able to succeed irrespective of the quality of teaching they experienced. As participation levels expand beyond thirty per cent, however, this is no longer the case and in computing, broadly defined, issues such as the teaching of programming (Jenkins, 1998), students repeating courses (Sheard & Hagan, 1998) and the role of projects (Boyle & Clark, 1998) have concerned HE teachers.

Also receiving attention is the question of why students choose to enter HE and why they opt for particular degree courses. Of particular concern is the rise of the strategic student who has little interest in the course beyond attaining a sufficiently high grade.

This approach to studying is associated with becoming so concerned about gaining marks that understanding and interest suffer and much time is devoted to questions of how and what to study, often to the neglect of studying itself (Tait, 1996). Further, students adopting a strategic approach are likely to optimise time and effort by identifying aspects of their course which offer little or no reward in terms of their final degree classification and scaling their input accordingly. There is evidence that students studying a variety of degree subjects in a variety of institutions take a strategic approach student (Kneale, 1996).

This has particular implications for those teaching Information Systems because computing courses in general and the, arguably, more vocational IS courses in particular, can be viewed as an entry route into a lucrative career in the IT industry. It seems likely that a growing number of IS undergraduates will be concerned not with achieving understanding but with attaining their desired grade. It is also possible that students will enrol for IS courses having undertaken little research about the nature of the course and the work expected of them.

It is, of course, understandable that undergraduates have become more conscious of the job market and potential financial rewards. With the severe financial hardship that is now associated with studying in higher education this is surely inevitable. There seems currently little reason to hope that this situation will improve; indeed, with the recent introduction of fees it seems set to become an even more important factor. Most students leave the Information Systems degree course at Leeds with debts (in the form of overdrafts and loans) in excess of £4000. It is natural that future financial gain is a strong motivational factor in all students, if not the strongest factor.

This sad state of affairs is borne out by out experience at Leeds. In the 1997/98 session students in a class in an introductory module in information systems (in fact the module described in Boyle and Jenkins 1996) were asked to list the factors that they would consider when selecting a future job either within or without the IT industry. Over 80% of these students listed reasons directly linked to financial gain - by far the most popular specific factor was "initial salary" which was closely followed by "prospects for promotion and increase in salary". When this exercise was debriefed with the class they agreed that the anticipated high salaries and rapid growth in salaries was a very significant factor in their choice of degree subject. Very few would admit to being interested in "information systems" for its own sake.

2. THE 1998/99 INTAKE - KNOWLEDGE OF THE IT INDUSTRY

With this in mind we set out to assess how much the new 1998/99 IS intake actually knew about these rewards and the skills that can attract them. This assessment was undertaken with a group of 61 students, all of whom were studying for a degree in Information Systems or in Information Systems combined with another subject. During a professional development lecture early in the academic year they were asked to complete a short questionnaire which consisted of just two questions. This was undertaken as a classroom activity with questionnaires issued and returned within a period of approximately twenty minutes. Students were asked to work individually and assured that there were no 'correct' answers to the questions.

The first question described five roles in the IT industry as follows:

1. A systems analyst responsible for the analysis surrounding a new computer-based system in the banking industry.
2. A computer operator responsible for taking and storing backups of a computer system for a large airline.
3. A C++ programmer responsible for the development of code for a large travel agent's computer systems.
4. A management consultant who advises organisations at board level on future trends in the IT industry.
5. An IT manager who is responsible for all aspects of IT within a large engineering firm.

The roles were chosen to match a selection of those from the latest Computer Weekly survey of salaries in IT and students were asked to state what they thought the average salary of each person would be. We would then compare their opinions with the "true" figures given by the Computer Weekly survey. The results are interesting, and can be summarised as follows (all salaries are quoted in thousands):

Role	Comp Wkly	Av. By Class	Min	Max
Operator	19.7	22.6	10	45
Programmer	22.2	29.6	15	60
Consultant	73.3	45.5	14	160
IT Manager	50.1	46.5	15	100

Table 1: Estimates of Salaries

The most striking thing about the average figures is their overall accuracy. The students are least accurate with the Management Consultant role, but this is readily explained as it is the role with which we would expect them to be the least familiar. With the exception of this role, the students tend to overestimate for the more "junior" roles - this may represent their expectations or aspirations!

The ranges quoted are interesting. They show a remarkable range of opinions and show that some students are clearly completely out of touch with industry salaries at both extremes. On the whole, though, the variations in answers were slight, and there was clearly a consensus around the average figures. As we might expect, the greatest variations were surrounding the two more senior roles that would be the most remote from the students' experience.

One particular response worthy of comment was one that was so close to the salaries quoted in Computer Weekly that we might expect that the student had read the very article. This student went on to describe in some detail the additional benefits that would be available. The Consultant would, for example, also have a car and other benefits provided. Clearly this student was approaching his studies with all the correct priorities!

The second question posed asked the students to list the five skills that were currently most in demand by the industry. Our initial plan with this question was to collate the responses and compare them to the job vacancy survey also published by Computer Weekly. This survey presents an analysis of the recruitment advertisements appearing in Computer Weekly to derive an ordered listing of the current skills demanded by the industry. In the event, however, very few students answered the question in this way, and listed instead more general areas.

This was surprising. The most likely explanation, given by a small subset of the class in a later tutorial, was that they were unable to think of five specific skills - this group had not heard of Oracle, Novell, CICS, DB2 or indeed most of the top twenty skills in the survey.

This setback aside, the results were still interesting. 59 of the students produced sensible answers, and the following points were apparent:

- The students are convinced that the most important skill is programming. 47 of the 59 mentioned programming in general, 5 mentioned C++ specifically, 3 mentioned COBOL (although only two could spell it), and 3 more Java (significantly, though, two of these last appear to have been seated next to each other).

- The next most important skills are centred around database application and administration, with 22 students mentioning these. The only database system to get a specific mention was Oracle, mentioned by 1. Surprisingly, only one of these 22 mentioned SQL.

- 7 students mentioned the Millennium Problem, and one EMU. This is surprising given the coverage currently given to both these in the popular media, let alone the computing press specifically.

- The only other technical areas to gain more than one mention were web design with 5 mentions, and networking with 7.

- A striking 14 students (almost a quarter of our sample) said that the only skills in demand where what we would term "key skills" such as communication, the ability to work in a team, and so forth.

The answers to this question have shown us how little the students seem to know about the specific skills currently required by the industry. It is interesting to compare this knowledge with their rather more detailed and accurate knowledge of the salaries being paid in the industry.

The concentration on programming is interesting. A "show of hands" survey with the same group of students later indicated that over half of them expected to work in the IT industry as "programmers". Our experience with past graduates suggests that this expectation is very wrong, and that most will enter a role more closely resembling that of a systems analyst.

These are first year students, and the survey was carried out during their second week at Leeds. We would expect that they will gain more knowledge of the skills used in IT during the remainder of their course here but it is interesting to see that they have already taken an interest (and seemingly a greater interest) in the salaries that will be on offer.

3. THE 1998/99 INTAKE – SKILLS EXPECTATIONS

The response from the skills-related question in the questionnaire was disappointing. We set out, therefore, to explore the students' true depth of knowledge about the skills currently required by the IT industry. A second short questionnaire, similar to the first, was devised with more explicit instructions and a request to list the "five specific platforms, operating systems, packages or languages that are currently most in demand in the industry". The students were asked to list five skills in order – we would then compare their responses with the survey published by Computer Weekly. The survey was carried out in the fifth week of the students' first term. As before, we emphasised that there were no "correct" answers since measuring demand for skills is not a precise science.

Questionnaires were received from 56 students. The responses were collated and a total score was calculated with 5 marks being allocated to a first ranking, 1 to a last, and so on. The top five skills from the list were:

	Total Score	Students Listing
C++	209	53
Unix	109	36
NT	90	27
Java	69	27
Access	34	11

Table 2: Skill Rankings

For comparison, the top skills listed by Computer Weekly are, in order, NT, C++, Unix, Oracle, and Visual Basic. Computer Weekly ranks Java 11th and Access 23rd. The students ranked Oracle 8th and Visual Basic 10th.

It is remarkable how well informed the students appear to be. They are convinced that C++ is the most important skill – most of the students listing C++ placed it either first or second in their list, and 95% of them included it somewhere. A significant 64% included Unix, but its average score was lower (3 as opposed to 4 for C++). The presence of Java in the list is not surprising given students' level of interest in the Internet and related matters. It may well be, indeed, that their current views will match the reality they will find when they graduate in two and a half years' time.

An interesting observation from the questionnaires was that a significant proportion (18 of 56) of the students were unable to list five current skills. Others listed rather unexpected skills – dBase, Prolog, Fortran, SPSS, Paradox, WordPerfect and Pascal were all mentioned. This indicates that while many students are very well informed, there remains a significant number who are not. The failure to include COBOL is again surprising given the interest in the so-called Millennium bug. Only 6 students mentioned it to give a total score of just 15. COBOL remains 8th in the Computer Weekly list.

The influence of the students' course at the time cannot be discounted in the analysis of their responses. They were learning C++ programming on a Unix platform, and SQL and database skills with Access running under NT. It is possible that they were simply listing the only skills they were aware of. They were not, however, being taught Java in any part of their course.

4.   THE 1998/99 INTAKE - EXPECTATIONS

These findings support those of a second exercise in which the same students took part. During an introductory lecture nearly eighty single honours undergraduates newly enrolled on School of Computer Studies (SCS) degree programs were given a list of things they might like to learn as part of their studies. They were asked to rank them according to their personal aims, 1 being the most important and 20 being least desirable. Like the exercises reported above, this activity was undertaken as part of a classroom session with papers being handed out, completed and returned within approximately fifteen minutes. Again, much emphasis was placed upon the fact that no correct answers exist for this exercise.

In advance of the session a list of seventeen items was prepared. These fell into three groups, objectives taken directly from the School's modules (identified in Table 3 by the key SCS), key personal skills (PS) and a number of mainly PC and internet oriented skills not included specifically in modules taught by SCS (PC). In order to reflect accurately students' real learning intentions a fourth group of items (18-20) was nominated by students themselves during the lecture (ST). Table 3 shows the items in the order they were presented to the students.

1	Introduction to virtual reality work environments and their realisation	SCS
2	Advanced business spreadsheet applications using MS Excel	PCI
3	Ability to prioritise tasks	PS
4	Implementation of object orientation in C++	SCS
5	Object linking and embedding in MS Word	PCI
6	Understand different geometric modelling techniques	SCS
7	Determine the requirements, capabilities and performance of distributed multi-media systems	SCS
8	Windows NT Workstation file management	PCI
9	Social confidence	PS
10	Use CASE for systems modelling and implementation including automatic code generation	SCS
11	Java applet programming and evaluation	PCI
12	Self management	PS
13	Independence	PS
14	Internet resource locating and capture skills	PCI
15	Negotiating skills	PS
16	Use widely-applicable quantitative modelling techniques to support strategic decision making	SCS
17	Decisiveness	PS
18	C++ programming	ST
19	WWW design	ST
20	Game programming	ST

Table 3: Learning Objectives to be Ranked

The theory that students act strategically appears to be borne out by objectives nominated by the students. They are highly specific skills which are currently in demand and well remunerated. As Fig. 1 shows, however, they were not uniformly popular. The rejection of games programming is overwhelming - the only objective to be ranked twentieth by more than six students. Similarly, although there was some interest in web design, responses were not unequivocally in favour. There is, however, some reason to be sceptical about this outcome. They were suggested during the lecture and it may be that the students perceived some reaction from members of staff during this process and that their rankings include an element of providing the information that they thought we wished to hear.

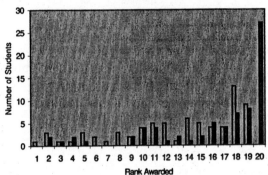

Fig. 1: Ranking of Games Programming and Web Design

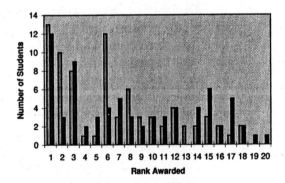

Fig. 2 C++ Programming

Rankings of objectives relating to C++ reinforce the findings stated above. *C++ programming* was nominated by the students as a key learning objective and, as Fig. 2 shows, the rankings show a considerable degree of consensus. Similarly, one third of those present rated in their top three the genuine module objective *implementation of object orientation in C++.*

The popularity of the C++ module objective is particularly significant when considered against the ranking of the other genuine module objectives. As Table 3 shows conclusively, C++ (question 4) is the sole genuine module objective rated highly by the students. Even *introduction to virtual reality work environments and their realisation*, (question 1) something we would expect to be very popular indeed, proves a poor second (a finding which reinforces the rejection of web design as a learning objective). The unpopularity of item 10, use of CASE tools, hurts deeply as this it is taken from the objectives of a new module unveiled for the first time in the session 1998/99 and targeted particularly at IS students.

Question	Number of Students Ranking		
	1	2	3
1	6	2	2
4	9	11	7
6	0	2	5
7	1	1	3
10	2	0	0
16	3	1	1

Table 4: Students' Ranking of Module Objectives

Fig. 3 Ranking of Personal Skills

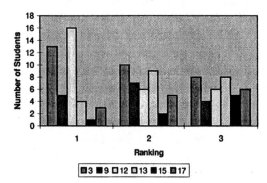

Fig. 4 Question 11: Java programming

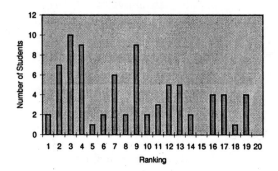

It is interesting that the students see themselves becoming C++ programmers and either dismiss, or are unaware, of the potential for the development and adoption of CASE technologies to release organisations from the need to hire programmers in large numbers.

The personal skill learning objectives were much more popular with the students. Fig. 3 shows the number of students placing these objectives first, second and third. Over half of the students placed the ability to prioritise tasks among their top three learning objectives and an equally striking 40% included self-management. These results truly are surprising and conflict with our experience of trying to interest students in the development of personal skills. Again it is interesting to speculate whether there is an element here of the students telling us want they think we want to hear, or whether the changes in the student population are such that repeated messages from employers about their requirements of graduate recruits are beginning to hit home.

Of the other objectives, i.e. PC and internet aspects, Java programming stands out as the most popular. As Fig. 4 shows, 35% of students included this among their top four learning objectives and this tends to support the idea that on arrival at university IS undergraduates see themselves becoming programmers. Java is not, however, a top priority and this supports the findings above that the internet is not a major concern of students at this point in their studies.

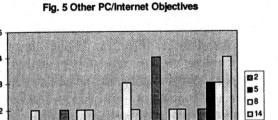

Fig. 5 Other PC/Internet Objectives

The students were not much interested in the other PC/internet objectives. As Fig. 5 shows the most popular of these was Windows NT Workstation skills but it is surprising that this was not weighted more highly given its prominence in job advertisements, and the fact that the most recent Computer Weekly survey (published in September 1998) reports that this is the currently most demanded skill in the industry. Again internet related objectives fare badly, showing that the students are at least consistent. The low ranking of Microsoft Office skills by IS and computing undergraduates is gratifying.

5. CONCLUSIONS

It is clear, then, that IS undergraduates arrive at university with a good understanding of the job market for IS graduates and the remuneration they can expect on completion of their course. They are much less clear, however, about the nature of the work they are likely to do as graduates believing strongly that this will mainly be programming. They see both Java and C++ as desirable skills though, surprisingly, Java and other internet related skills are not top priorities. Their awareness of pay related issues supports the suggestion of students taking a strategic approach to their studies as does their preparedness to admit that remuneration is the key issue in selecting a future employment. This is entirely understandable given the levels of debt incurred by students during their studies and is not undermined by the finding that they know little of what people actually working in IS jobs do.

It will be interesting, however, to see if these attitudes are maintained when this cohort come to select topics for their final year projects. Experience suggests that most final year students will go to some lengths to avoid a project requiring programming skills, preferring, instead, to become involved in some sort of mainly discursive internet related topic. Indeed, changes in the attitudes of these student towards the internet may be one of the key effects of being at university.

It is difficult to explain why students rated so highly the development of personal skills. It is most tempting to explain this as 'telling us what we want to hear' but the students had been with us for a very short time when the exercises related here were undertaken and it is questionable whether this time period was sufficient for them to form a view of the answers we would prefer. It is nevertheless true that the development of these skills is crucial to their chances of securing the lucrative employment which is so important to them and it is possible that the students have focused on personal skills as a way of furthering their job prospects.

The students' apparent lack of interest in the module objectives is the clearest evidence of a strategic approach to learning. Not only are they prepared to rate highly the programming skills which they consider important to their job prospects but the students are unashamed to give a low priority to course objectives. For newly recruited undergraduates to do this should concern IS teachers profoundly. It is clear that new approaches will be needed to stimulate interest and enable students to develop real understanding.

References

Boyle R. D. & Jenkins T (1996) "Generating Motivation in New Students of IT" Presented at the 4th International Conference on the Teaching of Computing, Dublin City University, Dublin, August 1996. Also available as University of Leeds School of Computer Studies Research Report 96.19, 1996

Boyle R. D. & Clark M.A.C. (1998) "Non-technical Issues in Undergraduate CS Project Work or What Are We (All) Here For?" in Holcombe M., Stratton A., Fincher S. & Griffiths G. (eds) *Projects in the Computing Curriculum*, London, Springer

Jenkins T. (1988) "A Participative Approach to Teaching Programming." Proceedings of the 3rd Annual Conference on Integrating Technology into Computer Science Education, New York, ACM, pp 125-129

Kneale P. (1996) "Staff and student perspectives of student motivation following modularisation, a tension in academia" University of Leeds, School of Geography, 1996

Sheard J. & Hagan D. (1998) "Our Failing Students: A Study of A Repeat Group." Proceedings of the 3rd Annual Conference on Integrating Technology into Computer Science Education, New York, ACM, pp 223-227

Tait H (1996) "Software to Help Students PASS.", Axis 3(3): pp 2-8.

LIST OF AUTHORS